Podcasting Bible

Podcasting Bible

Steve Mack and Mitch Ratcliffe

Wiley Publishing, Inc.

Podcasting Bible

Published by
Wiley Publishing, Inc.
10475 Crosspoint Boulevard
Indianapolis, IN 46256
www.wiley.com

Copyright © 2007 by Wiley Publishing, Inc., Indianapolis, Indiana

Published simultaneously in Canada

ISBN: 978-0-470-04352-3

Manufactured in the United States of America

10 9 8 7 6 5 4 3 2 1

About the Authors

Steve Mack has spent more than a decade at the forefront of the digital media industry. He is a principal at LUX Media (www.luxmedia.com), a firm specializing in interactive media design, live event and a/v production, encoding, hardware and software implementation, and training. Through its 501 division, LUX also offers hosting and consulting services targeted at progressive non-profit organizations.

Previously at RealNetworks for five years (http://www.real.com) as executive producer and media lab manager, Steve worked with high-profile customers and partners to create cutting-edge programming and presentations. Steve has produced some of the largest and most prestigious Internet broadcasts, including U2 live from Notre Dame (Yahoo Internet Magazine's "Top of the Net for 2001"), the ACLU 2004 Members Conference, President Clinton's inaugural address, and the first public live Internet broadcast of a Seattle Mariners game in 1995.

He has authored a number of books, including *Streaming Media Bible* (Wiley, 2002) and *Hands on Guide to Webcasting* (Focal Press, 2005). He also writes for numerous publications.

Before his current career in interactive media, Steve was a professional musician who traveled the world and released five albums' worth of material with critically acclaimed Irish rock group That Petrol Emotion. During this time he built, owned, and operated Bang Bang Studios in London, a commercial 24-track recording studio where he produced and engineered hundreds of releases. He is still active in the music industry as a producer/engineer and performer.

Mitch Ratcliffe is co-founder of several startups and an accomplished Internet executive. His most recent company, BuzzLogic, where he invented a technology for analyzing influence and value in social networks, recently launched its first product. His consulting business, Internet/Media Strategies Inc., has worked with America Online, EarthWeb, Audible, Time Warner, ZD Net, Comdex, and SoftBank, among others.

Mitch led the development of the ON24 Financial iNetwork, the first streaming news organization, from 1999 to 2001. He also developed and managed the ZDY2K Web site, a source of Year 2000 information and commentary on the ZD Net supersite. His Audible program, Adventures In Technology, was one of the first downloadable spoken word series about the evolution of media in the Internet era.

Mitch has served in numerous editorial positions with the likes of Digital Media and MacWEEK. He is the co-author of three books published by Random House, and his work has appeared in *Forbes, Fortune, PCWEEK, PCWorld, In-Formation, National Review,* and *Feed,* among others. He is a widely quoted commentator on digital technology and the networked economy.

He represents SoftBank on the board of Electric Classifieds and Match.com. He is a member of the board of advisors for several early-stage companies, including commercial wiki developer Socialtext and music training developer iVideoTunes.

Credits

Acquisitions Editor
Kim Spilker

Project Editor
Martin V. Minner

Technical Editor
Travis Petershagen

Copy Editor
Gwenette Gaddis Goshert

Editorial Manager
Robyn Siesky

Business Manager
Amy Knies

Vice President and Executive Group Publisher
Richard Swadley

Vice President and Publisher
Barry Pruett

Project Coordinator
Kristie Rees

Graphics and Production Specialists
Carrie A. Foster
Denny Hager
Stephanie D. Jumper
Alicia B. South

Quality Control Technician
John Greenough

Proofreading
Sossity R. Smith

Indexing
Infodex Indexing Services Inc.

Cover Design
Michael Trent

Cover Illustration
Joyce Haughey

Wiley Bicentennial Logo
Richard J. Pacifico

Preface

Podcasting is a relatively new field, and it's still undergoing many changes. What started off as a cool way to combine a bunch of existing technologies into a nifty way to distribute audio files has turned into a worldwide craze that now encompasses video, images, and other data types, and is used in education, government, and major corporations. It's safe to assume that the next few years are going to see even more changes in the field.

Currently, there are more podcasting business startups than you can reliably count, with more appearing each day. Each one has its own particular twist on how it is going to serve the podcasting community. Not all of them will be successful; this is just the business reality in any growing field.

The same goes for podcasters. Each day brings tens if not hundreds of new podcasts into existence. While we're incredibly excited about the level playing field that podcasting brings, we're old enough to know that this excitement level can't last, and that many folks are going to realize that maintaining and updating a podcast requires time, effort, and most of all, passion.

We sincerely hope that if you're passionate about something and want to share your passions with the world, this book helps you do so. We've tried to keep the information in this book as evergreen as possible. We try not to recommend any particular vendors, because their pricing models and service records may have changed by the time you read this. We do, however, try to go into detail about the business of podcasting, the basics of digital media production, and the options available to you as a podcaster. This information is much less likely to go out of date.

After reading this book, you should know how to calculate the investment in time and money that building a podcasting business requires. You should know how to produce a good sounding audio podcast, and a good-looking video podcast. To this end, we've included many worksheets and step-by-step examples for you to follow.

If you want to find out more or learn more about a particular aspect of podcasting, plenty of reference books on the market will serve you well. This book, however, should give you a firm theoretical foundation for everything you need to know about podcasting.

Because the world of podcasting is changing and growing so rapidly, we can't hope to be completely up to date. However, the process of creating a podcast and building a business remain the same, and the basic rule still applies: Create a good-quality program, and your audience will find you. We can't tell you what to make your program about, but we hope we can help you produce it to a high standard and grow it into a viable business.

Mac versus PC

The "pod" in podcasting obviously refers the ubiquitous Apple iPod, but podcasting is by no means limited to the Mac platform. Currently, an unusually high percentage of podcasters are on the Mac platform when compared to the general public, but this is bound to change. Of course, if you talk to the people at Apple, they'll tell you that everyone will be on a Mac someday!

We've tried to remain as agnostic as possible, including screen shots from both platforms. We both work on both platforms. We've tried to avoid using keyboard shortcuts because of the difference between the platforms (Option+click versus Ctrl+click). We hope that this won't interfere with your enjoyment of the book.

How to Get the Most out of This Book

The sections and chapters of this book are organized so that the neophyte can take it from the beginning, step-by-step. However, each chapter should also stand on its own, so if you really want to learn about one thing in particular, skip straight to that chapter and find what you need.

Icons: What Do They Mean?

Throughout the book, you'll see icons that point out certain details in the text. While they are relatively self-explanatory, here is what each indicates:

 Tips provide extra information about certain topics, or provide special workarounds or alternatives to a listed procedure.

 Notes are for background or supplementary information that may not be crucial to the understanding of the concept, but they're interesting nonetheless.

 Caution icons generally mean you should be paying attention. This icon points out crucial steps or possible pitfalls.

 Cross-Ref icons point out where you can find additional information about a topic elsewhere in the book.

How This Book Is Organized

This book is organized roughly in the order in which a podcast production takes place. While everyone's production chain is slightly different and there may be some overlap between sections, for the most part the sections should make sense.

Part I: Podcasting: Where It Came from and Where It's Going

Part I sets the scene for the rest of the book. It talks about the early days of podcasting and how existing technologies were combined to create the current phenomenon. It also includes an introductory chapter that shows you how to explore the world of podcasts that's already out there.

Part II: Podcast Production

Part II talks about how to record audio and video for a podcast. It covers all the tools you need, the basics of audio and video production, and the techniques that the pros use to get the best quality.

Part III: Encoding

You'll soon find out that the raw audio and video files you create using the knowledge you gain in Part II are too large to distribute on the Internet. Part III talks about the theory behind encoding and the various tools used to reduce the file sizes of podcast files.

Part IV: Distribution—Making Your Podcast Available to Your Audience

Part IV discusses distribution of your podcast. One of the great things about podcasting is that it doesn't really require any specialized equipment or software to distribute. However, as your podcast grows, you need to be aware of the potential costs that may arise and what your options are.

Part V: The Business of Podcasting

Of course, the end goal is to quit the day job and be paid to talk about what you're most passionate about. That's why you're starting your podcast, right? To do this, you have to build a business, and you have to understand the principles underlying building a successful podcasting business.

Part VI: Case Studies

The final section of the book includes a few case studies. These are three different real-life examples of how podcasting is being used today.

Appendix and Glossary

Appendix A offers some helpful podcasting resources. We also provide a glossary of terms.

Getting in Touch with the Authors

Before you write, check the book's accompanying Web site for tips, tricks, FAQs, and other useful tidbits at www.podcastingbible.com.

You can also reach the authors via e-mail. Mitch can be reached at godsdog@ratcliffe.com, and Steve can be reached at smack@podcastingbible.com.

Have Fun

Remember: Successful podcasts are ones that are based on passion. The daily care and feeding of a podcast can require lots of time and effort. Make sure you're creating a podcast that you look forward to doing, not a responsibility that adds more stress to your already busy life.

Acknowledgments

What a long, strange trip it has been. After the last two books, Steve promised himself he'd never write another book during the summer. But then his fiancée completed her degree, their cabin in Montana sold, and his consulting business took off like never before. Oh well. There goes another summer.

The same goes for Mitch. What seemed like a good idea in the beginning of 2006 took on a completely different look when his latest business venture, BuzzLogic, was ready to launch and proceeded to take up all his time. There went his summer.

Our names are the only ones on the cover, but this book certainly could not have been written without help and input from many people. Mitch has been active in the podcasting community for years. Steve was a relatively recent convert, but jumped in feet first and has been trying to tread water ever since.

We'd like to thank all of the fine people at Wiley who have helped us get this book finished: Michael Roney, the original acquisitions editor, Kim Spilker, who took over the reins, and Marty Minner, our esteemed editor. Gwenette Gaddis Goshert patiently corrected our grammar. Travis Petershagen, our technical editor, has been an endless source of inspiration and organization.

We didn't do this alone. Michael Lehman helped out, contributing to Chapters 15 and 16, and contributed the Microsoft case study. Erin Weible contributed the Ontario Science Centre case study. Andrew Fry helped with Chapters 20 and 22. Thank you all; you're all knights in shining armor as far as we're concerned.

Steve Mack and Mitch Ratcliffe

Contents at a Glance

Contents

Contents

Contents

Contents

Part IV: Distribution—Making Your Podcast Available to Your Audience — 309

Quick Start

Getting Started with Podcasting

This chapter provides a brief overview of the podcasting process, the tools you need, and how to use them. This chapter is light on explanation: Its purpose is to give you a whirlwind tour to get you excited to learn more about each step, so that when you start podcasting for real, you create first-class programming.

Part of this chapter involves signing up for a podcast hosting account, which brings up an interesting point. When you actually launch your podcast, you're going to want to stick with the name of your podcast and the URL of the site that's hosting it. If you go through all the steps in this chapter, you'll end up with a podcast that is live and on the Web. If you're not quire ready for prime time, we'll try to point out the steps you may want to skip until you're truly ready.

So with that brief introduction and a few words of caution, let's do it.

The Podcasting Process

Creating a podcast is just like creating any other kind of broadcast programming. There's a process to it, which can be divided into four phases:

- **Planning:** Before you hit the record button, it's a good idea to know what you're going to talk about.
- **Production:** After you've sketched out your podcast, perhaps even going as far as writing a script, it's time to record and edit.
- **Encoding:** The Internet is incapable of delivering raw audio and video files efficiently. Encoding converts your programming into a format that can be distributed more easily.
- **Distribution:** After your podcast is encoded, it is placed on a server so your audience can download it. It's also a good idea to get your podcast listed in a number of different podcast directories to make it easier for people to find.

After you've worked your way through all four phases of the podcasting process, the planning should begin for your next podcast. The process is cyclical and ongoing. If your podcast gains an audience, they're going to want updated content on a regular basis. More importantly, if you neglect your podcast for a while, you may lose the audience that you painstakingly built up.

Ideally, though, you're starting a podcast because you think it's going to be fun, and you have a topic that you're dying to unleash on the unsuspecting public. Passion is what drives the best podcasts, so be sure you're getting into something you're going to want to stick with.

Before You Start

This chapter assumes that you're reasonably familiar with your computer and can perform simple tasks like downloading and installing software from the Internet, opening and saving files, and finding files on your hard drive. In fact, the whole book assumes a certain level of computer proficiency. What we don't assume, however, is that you are familiar with podcasting. This chapter therefore starts by showing you how to find, subscribe to, and listen to a podcast. Then, after you've listened to a podcast, we'll show you how to record, edit, encode, and distribute your podcast.

These tasks can be accomplished in many different ways, and may different tools exist that you can use. For the purposes of this chapter, we're going to use the simplest, most common, and best of all, free tools. They may not be the tools you end up using to produce your podcast, but they'll give you a taste of what it's like. This makes you a better consumer if and when you decide to spend some money to buy better tools.

To begin with, we're going to find and subscribe to a podcast. Because podcasting was developed by and for iPod owners, we're going to use iTunes to do this, the free music jukebox software from

Apple. Podcasting is by no means limited to the iPod anymore, but podcasters still tend to be Mac users. A number of other software packages are available for you to find and subscribe to podcasts, but iTunes dominates the market at this point.

Of course, if you want to listen to your podcast on your portable media player, we assume that like millions of other people you've broken down and bought an iPod. In that case, the podcast is synched up to your iPod automatically. If you use a different portable media player, you're going to have to fend for yourself in this chapter. There are probably software packages that do the same thing as iTunes and automatically sync your portable media player to your jukebox software, but for the purposes of simplicity we're going to demonstrate the most popular solution.

When we start recording and editing, we're going to use a program called Audacity. Audacity is a free, open-source audio-editing platform that is available for both the Mac and Windows platform (and Linux, incidentally). Additionally, we'll use the LAME MP3 encoder, which is also free. Both can be downloaded from the Audacity site:

```
http://audacity.sourceforge.net
```

Of course, because you're going to be making a recording of your voice, you're going to need a microphone. Some multimedia computers come with cheap plastic microphones; laptops often have them built in. Later in the book when we discuss how to create high-quality podcasts, we'll be trying to convince you to spend some money on a good-quality microphone. For the time being, use whatever you've got.

That's really all you need for now. Let's begin by finding and subscribing to a podcast.

Finding and Subscribing to Your First Podcast

Finding and subscribing to a podcast is a snap. We're going to use iTunes, because it's the most common application. If you don't have it, you can get it for free at the Apple site.

1. Start off by opening iTunes.

2. Click Podcasts in the left column. If you've never clicked this before, you get a pop-up message telling you what a podcast is. Click the Go to Podcast Directory button.

   If you've looked at this section of iTunes before, you see either a list of your podcasts (in which case you should skip to the next section!) or a blank screen. To search for podcasts on iTunes, click the Podcast Directory link at the bottom of iTunes.

3. iTunes contacts the iTunes music store and automatically drops you into the podcasts section. You see links to new podcasts, the top ten podcasts of the day, and a whole lot more. There are lots of podcasts competing for your attention.

4. If you want to search, scroll down, and on the left side you find a search field you can type in. You also find a list of categories if you'd prefer to browse through the available podcasts. If something grabs your attention, go ahead and click it. If you want to search, type your search term(s) and click the small magnifying glass.

5. If you click a category, you are taken to a page with podcasts in that category. Searching gives you a list of results that match your search terms. Find something that looks interesting, and click it.

6. When you click a particular podcast, the top of the interface displays a graphic or logo for the show, a description, reviews, and even other podcasts that people who like this podcast subscribe to. The bottom half of the iTunes interface displays a list of available episodes. If you're ready to take the plunge, click the Subscribe button by the podcast graphic.

7. When you click the Subscribe button, iTunes may pop up a window asking for confirmation that you really want to subscribe. Click OK.

8. As soon as you click OK, iTunes begins downloading the most recent episode of the podcast. This takes a few minutes, depending on how long the podcast is and the bit rate that was used to encode it.

9. When the download process is complete, click play to listen to your podcast. With any luck you've made an interesting choice, and you're hooked on your first podcast. Wasn't that easy?

10. If you really like the podcast, you may want to see if there are any other episodes available. Click the small arrow to the left of the podcast title to see if any other episodes are available. You may also want to consider changing your subscription settings so that this is done automatically. Click the Settings button in the lower right.

11. The Settings dialog box lets you set how often iTunes checks for new episodes, whether to download just the latest episode or all of them and how many to keep. Unfortunately, you can't set settings for individual podcasts. Settings on this page are applied to all your podcasts. Choose your settings, and click OK.

12. That's it. You've now subscribed to your first podcast. Every time a new episode is available, iTunes downloads it automatically. To unsubscribe from a podcast, highlight the podcast and click the Unsubscribe button at the bottom of iTunes. Enjoy!

Recording Your First Podcast

Now that you've listened to a podcast or two, you're probably dying to get started with your own podcast. You've probably listened to a few other podcasts that are covering similar territory, and you think you can do it much better, right? Fine. This is where the rubber meets the road. It's time to find out if it's as easy as you think it is.

As mentioned previously, we're going to use Audacity to record your program:

1. Download and install Audacity if you haven't done so already. It's available for both Mac and PC, and it's free, so you have no excuse not to. If you'd like to try following along using different software, go right ahead. Audio-editing platforms aren't all that different.

2. Plug your microphone into your soundcard. Make sure you're plugging it in to the right input. If you're using a laptop, you may have a built-in microphone. You'll find out later that using this microphone doesn't provide the best quality, but for now it will do.

3. Open Audacity. The user interface is relatively straightforward, as indicated in Figure QS.1. The interface has four toolbars and a display window where recorded audio is displayed.

   ■ The Control toolbar has controls just like a VCR or tape recorder, as well as cursor tools you can choose from.

   ■ The Meter toolbar indicates what your recording and playback levels are.

FIGURE QS.1

Audacity is divided into the Control toolbar, the Meter toolbar, the Mixer toolbar, and the Edit toolbar.

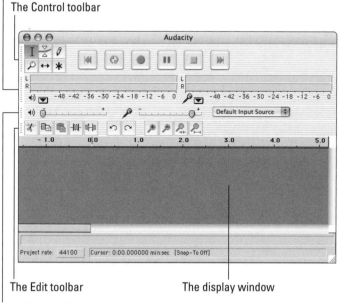

The Meter toolbar

The Control toolbar

The Edit toolbar   The display window

The Mixer toolbar

■ The Mixer toolbar allows you to adjust the playback and recording levels.

■ The Edit toolbar offers a number of simple editing commands such as cut, copy, and paste.

■ The display window displays a graphical representation of your audio file so you can highlight sections you want to work on.

4. The first thing you have to do is check your recording level. To see what your recording level is, you have to put the record meter into monitoring mode. Click the arrow next to the small microphone icon, and select Monitor Input, as shown in Figure QS.2.

NOTE   You can also turn the meter on and off by simply clicking it.

FIGURE QS.2

Monitoring the input level in Audacity

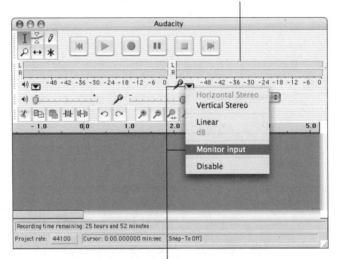

When the input level is being monitored, you see the level displayed on the input meter here.

If you don't see input levels, click the small arrow next to the microphone icon and select Monitor Input.

5. If you're still not seeing any level, you may need to check your Audacity Preferences to make sure Audacity is configured to use your preferred audio device. Choose Preferences from the Audacity menu to open the Preferences window, shown in Figure QS.3. Click the Audio I/O tab if it's not already selected, and choose your audio device from the Recording Device drop-down menu. Click OK.

6. By now, you should be seeing some level on your input meters. Adjust the level of your microphone by sliding the microphone mixer control until your input level is peaking in the -12 to -6dB range, as shown in Figure QS.4.

7. You're ready to start recording. Before you do, you should have a good idea of what you're going to talk about. You can edit out pauses and mental lapses, but it sounds much more natural if you plan what you're going to talk about. You may want to take a minute here to gather your thoughts and perhaps write them down. You don't need a complete script, but having at least a list of things you want to cover is very helpful.

FIGURE QS.3

Choosing your input device in the Audacity Preferences window

Click the Audio I/O tab.

Choose your device from the Recording Device drop-down menu.

FIGURE QS.4

Setting your input level

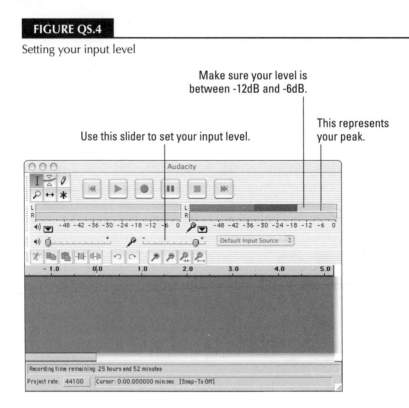

Make sure your level is
between -12dB and -6dB.

Use this slider to set your input level.

This represents
your peak.

8. When you're ready to begin, click the red record button on the Control toolbar. It usually takes Audacity a moment to start recording, so wait until you see an audio track appear and a cursor moving across the screen, as shown in Figure QS.5. It's a good idea to begin each recording with a countdown, to give Audacity a chance to get started and to give yourself a chance to relax. It doesn't have to be fancy. Something as simple as "Three... two... one..." will do just fine.

9. You're off! Talk as little or as long as you want. Podcasts are anywhere from a minute long to an hour or longer, though most are between five and twenty minutes long. If you make a mistake, don't worry. You can edit it out in a moment. The thing to remember is to pause before you start talking again, so you have a good place to edit. Just take a breath, and begin the sentence over again.

When you've had your say, stop the recording by clicking the yellow stop button. Save your project by selecting Save Project from the File menu, as shown in Figure QS.6.

FIGURE QS.5

Recording in Audacity

Click the record button to begin.

You should see a track
appear and the wave form
being drawn on screen as you talk.

FIGURE QS.6

Always save your project the second you stop recording.

Congratulations! You've recorded what just may be your first podcast. Piece of cake, right? In the next section, we'll edit the recording to make sure the beginning and end of your podcast are clean. If you made a few mistakes during the recording, you can fix those too. Don't worry; this is how it's done. Very few people in the world can cut a perfect "take." The ones who can are very well paid professional broadcasters. With a little practice (and a little editing), you'll get there yourself.

Editing and Encoding Your Podcast

After you've recorded your podcast and saved the project, it's time to listen to it and see what it sounds like. While you're listening, you may want to edit a bit, taking out "ums" and "ahs" or removing sections that just aren't very interesting. You can edit as you're listening, or listen to the entire podcast, make notes, and then go back and perform your edits.

Simple edits, where you're cutting out objectionable material, couldn't be simpler. Highlight what you want to get rid of, and hit the Delete key. Let's go back to the start of our file and start the editing process:

1. Open Audacity and your podcast project, if it isn't open already.

2. To go back to the beginning of your podcast, click the purple rewind button on the Control toolbar, as shown in Figure QS.7.

3. This podcast started with a countdown. You can see in the wave form where the speaker said "Three... two... one." Then there's a small silent gap before the podcast begins. Obviously, you want to get rid of this. To do so, put the cursor in the wave form window before the countdown, press and hold the mouse button, and drag across the wave form to highlight the portion of the audio that you want to delete.

4. To delete, you can either click the Delete key or click the cut icon in the Edit toolbar. Go ahead and delete; you can always click the undo icon to undo the change. The highlighted section disappears, and the wave form is redrawn to show the newly edited file. Isn't digital editing wonderful?

5. It is absolutely critical that you listen to the edit to make sure you didn't cut out something important. Click the play button, and listen to the edit. As long as it sounds okay, you can move on.

TIP The spacebar also serves as a play button in Audacity. If you have a section highlighted, pressing the spacebar plays back the highlighted section. This is a great way to make sure you're editing out the right stuff. Highlight the section you plan on editing, and hit the space bar to make sure nothing important is included there.

If you're just clipping off a countdown at the beginning of your podcast, chances are good that the edit will sound just fine, provided you left a nice quiet gap between the countdown and the start of the podcast. You really have to be careful when you're editing things out of the middle of your podcast. Sometimes taking out an "um" can make the result sound strange. Be sure to test all your edits.

FIGURE QS.7

Editing in Audacity

Click the Cut icon or use the
Delete key to delete sections.

Click and drag across
sections you want to delete.

Click the rewind button to return
to the beginning of the file.

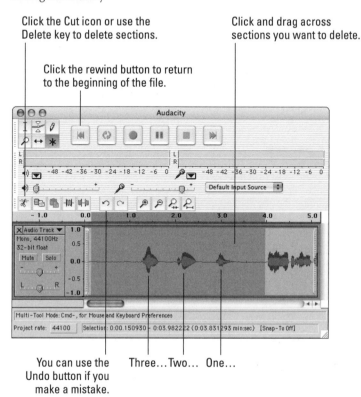

You can use the
Undo button if you
make a mistake.

Three...Two... One...

6. Work your way through the entire podcast, and clean it up as much as you think is necessary. Editing is fun and addictive, and you'll get better at it the more you do.

7. When you're finished editing, save the project again. It's important to do this so you don't have to recreate all your edits again.

8. Now it's time to encode the podcast to the MP3 format. This is the format most podcasts are in, because it plays back on virtually any portable media player. But before we do, make sure you've downloaded and installed the LAME encoding library. A link to the LAME download is available on the Audacity Web site, or if you'd like to go there directly the URLs are:

```
http://audacity.sourceforge.net
http://spaghetticode.org/lame/ (Mac)
http://audacity.sourceforge.net/help/faq?s=install&item=lame-
mp3 (Windows)
```

The LAME libraries don't have to be installed. They have to be downloaded and placed in a directory so that Audacity can access them. Be sure to remember where you place the LAME library, because you're going to have to find it in the next step.

 TIP   If you're only going to use the LAME library with Audacity, put the files in a LAME directory inside your Audacity folder.

9. Choose Preferences from the Audacity menu. This opens the Preferences window, shown in Figure QS.8. Click the File Formats tab, and then click the Find Library button to help Audacity find the LAME library. Audacity pops up a window asking if you want to find the LAME library. Click Yes.

FIGURE QS.8

Helping Audacity find the LAME library

Click the File Formats tab.

Click the Find Library
button to tell Audacity
where the LAME library is.

10. A Finder window opens. Browse to where you placed the LAME library, and click the Open button, shown in Figure QS.9. In our case, we put the LAME library in the Audacity folder (and we suggest you do the same). The Finder window closes, and Audacity displays what version MP3 library you downloaded in the MP3 Export Setup section of the Preferences window. Click OK to close the Preferences Window.

FIGURE QS.9

Finding the LAME library using Finder

NOTE If you're having trouble finding the LAME library, you can use Spotlight (on OSX) or Find (on Windows XP) to help find it.

11. Now that you've got the LAME MP3 library installed, encoding your file is a snap. Choose Export to MP3 from the File menu. Type a name for your podcast, and click Save, as shown in Figure QS.10.

12. Audacity pops up a window where you can edit the ID3 tags, which are displayed in iTunes and iPods, as well as in most other portable media players, as shown in Figure QS.11. It's important to fill these out. Fill them out, and click OK.

NOTE The LAME library included with Audacity doesn't include "Podcast" as a genre as of Fall 2006. You're going to want to change the genre to "Podcast" in another ID3 tag editing application (such as iTunes).

13. Audacity exports the file to MP3 format, giving you a progress indication, as shown in Figure QS.120. Depending on the length of your podcast and the speed of your machine, this can take anywhere from a few seconds to ten minutes or more.

FIGURE QS.10

Exporting to MP3 format

FIGURE QS.11

Entering ID3 tag information

14. When the export process is finished, test your file. It should sound pretty much exactly like the original in Audacity. If you missed any editing errors, you have to go back into Audacity and redo the edit. If it sounds good, you're ready for the next step: putting your podcast online.

FIGURE QS.12

Audacity exporting to MP3 format

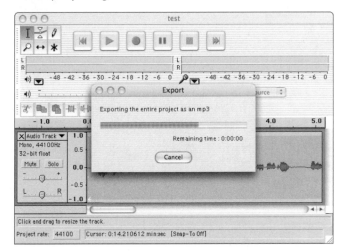

Putting Your Podcast Online

We're at the final phase in the podcasting process: distribution. It's time to put your podcast file up on a server so people can download it. If you want people to find your podcast, list it in a number of podcasting directories, such as the iTunes podcasting directory.

You can put your podcast online in a number of ways, and many of these are discussed in Part IV of this book, which deals exclusively with distribution. For now, to keep things easy, we're going to use an all-in-one service. A number of podcast hosting services offer free introductory service. For this example, we're going to use PodOmatic.

CROSS-REF For a list of other podcast hosting companies, please see Appendix A, "Podcasting Resources."

PodOmatic is a browser-based podcast hosting solution. In fact, they have a crazy system that actually allows you to record a podcast through a browser interface. In our case, because we've gone through all the trouble to record a podcast on our machine, we'll skip their tool and upload our podcast. First, you have to set up an account.

1. Open a browser, and go to www.podomatic.com. The PodOmatic home page features the most active podcasts and members of the PodOmatic community, as shown in Figure QS.13. With any luck, you'll be there soon. Click the Create a Podcast tab at the top right of the page.

2. The first thing PodOmatic asks for is your name, a URL for your podcast, and an e-mail address, as shown in Figure QS.14. Fill in the information, and click Continue. (Please read the terms of service before you click Continue.)

FIGURE QS.13

The PodOmatic home page

FIGURE QS.14

Choosing your URL on PodOmatic

3. Next it's time to choose a template for your podcast home page, as shown in Figure QS.15. You can choose from several, and you can customize your template later. Pick a template, and click Continue.

FIGURE QS.15

Choosing a template for your podcast home page

CAUTION This is where it gets serious. If you click the Post Episode button in the next step, you're live. You should know that when your authors went through this process to test the service, more than 200 people visited the site in less than 12 hours. The demand is out there, folks. We're serious. So if you're not ready for the world knocking at your door, you may not want to continue just yet.

4. Now it's time to post your first episode. Enter a title for this episode. You can also enter tags and comments if you want. Tags are used to help categorize your podcast. You can also upload an image, as shown in Figure QS.16. To upload the podcast that you just recorded, click the Post Episode button at the bottom of the page.

5. When you click the Import button, a small interface appears that lets you browse to find your podcast episode. Find your MP3 file, and then click the Post Episode button. You see a blue progress bar as your MP3 file is being uploaded. When the upload is finished, PodOmatic takes you to a page where you can e-mail friends from your Gmail, Yahoo, or Hotmail account and provides you with text so that you can copy and paste the URL for your podcast into any e-mail client, as shown in Figure QS.17.

If you don't want to use PodOmatic's e-mail blast feature, be sure to click the "Skip this Step" link.

6. Next, PodOmatic provides links for you to add your podcast to a number of popular podcast directories, as shown in Figure QS.18. We'd advise that you get listed in all of them. We won't go through the process for this now, but getting listed in the iTunes directory is detailed later in this section, starting with Step 12.

7. Finally, PodOmatic provides a page with a number of other things you may want to do, as shown in Figure QS.19, such as setting up the profile that is displayed on your podcast page.

FIGURE QS.16

Enter info for your podcast episode, and upload your MP3 file.

Enter information about your podcast.

You'll see the progress of your file being uploaded.

Browse to find your podcast.

Click the Post Episode button.

Click the Import button to upload your podcast.

FIGURE QS.17

PodOmatic lets you do some advertising to friends.

FIGURE QS.18

PodOmatic provides links to popular podcast directories.

FIGURE QS.19

PodOmatic helps you get the word out.

8. If you're like most folks, you can't wait to see your page and give your episode a listen, right? Click My Podcast Page at the top left of the page. This opens another browser with your podcast home page, as shown in Figure QS.20.

9. Note how the information you entered when you were posting the podcast is displayed on your home page. Visitors to your site can either click the play button to play the podcast in a pop-up embedded player, as shown in Figure QS.21, or subscribe to your podcast using one of the many subscription options.

TIP PodOmatic also offers an embedded podcast player that you can embed in your MySpace page (if you have one), your pre-existing blog, or any other Web page.

10. Be sure to subscribe to your own podcast so you can check to see that your podcast host is updating properly. Scroll down the page, and click the Subscribe via iTunes option. iTunes launches and adds your podcast to the list of podcast subscriptions.

You'll see iTunes pop open to the podcasts section, and your episode should automatically download. The various fields on your PodOmatic site are used in the iTunes fields. You can use the editing capabilities of PodOmatic to change these fields if you like.

FIGURE QS.20

Your very own home page on PodOmatic

The default title.

The episode name and comments.

[Screenshot of Steve's podcast page]

You can play the podcast from the Web page by clicking the Play button.

Scroll down to find numerous RSS subscription options for your listeners.

11. If you want to modify your podcast page, go back to the browser window with the main PodOmatic site and click Manage My Podcast link at the top right. You can edit your tagline and description, upload images, add to your profile, and do lots of other stuff to spruce up your podcast page, as shown in Figure QS.22. If you scroll down, you'll see statistics for your podcast and figures for how much storage and bandwidth you're using.

Okay, you've successfully uploaded your podcast, and created a home for it. The next thing you should do is publish your podcast in a number of podcast directories, in particular the iTunes podcast directory. Submitting your podcast to the iTunes directory is easy.

TIP Publishing a feed on iTunes is another one of those things you may not want to do if you're not quite ready for prime time.

FIGURE QS.21

PodOmatic's pop-up podcast player

12. Open iTunes, click Podcasts, and then click Podcasts directory at the bottom of your iTunes podcast library. This opens the iTunes music store and drops you into the Podcasts section. Click Submit a podcast in the left column.

13. This starts the submission process. The first step is to type in your RSS URL. You can find the URL of your RSS feed at the top of the My Podcast page on PodOmatic. Type it into iTunes, and click Continue.

14. Next, you must sign in to publish a listing in iTunes. You can sign in with an Apple ID, use an AOL screen name, or create a new account. Pick your poison, and carry on.

15. After you've signed in or created your new account, iTunes asks you to assign a category and sub-category to your podcast The categories leave a bit to be desired, but hey, iTunes is the biggest podcast directory, so find something that's close enough and go with it. Click Submit when you're finished.

16. That's all there is to it! The good folks at iTunes will take a look at your podcast and make sure that it's a valid podcast, and you'll be listed in a week or so.

FIGURE QS.22

PodOmatic's Manage My Podcast page

Congratulations. You've recorded, edited, and encoded a podcast. Then you opened a podcasting hosting account and put your file up live. You're on the way to being listed in iTunes. Your podcasting career has just begun!

Summary

This has been a whirlwind tour of the world of podcasting from the creator's perspective. You have lots more to learn, but wasn't this more fun than a barrel of monkeys? We hope it's whetted your appetite for more — more recording, more editing, more promoting your little podcasts, more information about the business of podcasting. This chapter covered these topics:

- The four basic steps to the podcasting process are planning, production, encoding, and distribution.

- You can find and subscribe to podcasts using iTunes.

- Plan your podcast before you press the record button.

- You can edit out your mistakes, provided you've left yourself a nice space on either side that you can edit around.

- Podcasts must be encoded before they can be distributed.

- MP3 is the most common podcast format.

- A number of free podcast hosting services can help you get out onto the World Wide Web with your little podcast.

- To get your podcast listed in iTunes, just click the Submit a Podcast link in the podcasts section of the iTunes music store and follow the prompts.

Part I

Podcasting: Where It Came From and Where It's Going

Chapter 1

Stars Being Born
Every Day

You've bought this book, or maybe you're reading this first page to get an idea about podcasting. Either way, you've heard about the explosion in listenership for podcasts, the self-produced programs made possible by ubiquitous cheap computing power that has replaced expensive studio production equipment. You'll find everything you need to know about the creative and technical challenges—because there are still many ahead of you—that you'll face as you begin the adventure of producing audio programs for your friends, family, company, or a global audience.

What Is Podcasting?

Just two years ago, at this writing, the idea of a "podcast" made its first appearance on the scene. Already as many as 10,000 people are podcasting and as many as 15 million listeners are downloading and listening to audio programming through Real Simple Syndication (RSS) channels. Early podcasters are earning a living from their work, while others have launched service businesses that deliver audio production for commercial clients. But for most, the vast majority, podcasting is about one-to-few communication facilitated by IP-based networks and simple tools (see Figure 1.1).

FIGURE 1.1

The tools of the podcaster's trade

The basics you need to do a podcast: A microphone and recording device, which could be an old tape player, a solid-state recorder, or your personal computer, editing software, and a place to host the resulting program. This sounds like a lot of pieces, but compared to the complexity of producing and distributing a radio or television program a decade ago, podcasting is self-produced media realized. In a nutshell, a podcast is, according to Wikipedia, a "direct download...file, but the subscription feed of automatically delivered new content is what distinguishes a podcast from a simple download or real-time streaming." This is a description of many different services that pre-date the introduction of podcasting; a more accurate definition, in our opinion, is this:

"A podcast is a series of audio (or video) programs delivered through a static URL containing an RSS feed that automatically updates a list of programs on the listener's computer so that people may download new programs using a desktop application. Programs can be delivered to the listener automatically or when they choose to download them."

Already there are variations on this definition, because podcasts can be delivered directly to handheld devices without the intervention of a desktop computer or software. Likewise, podcasts have changed radically as video has been added to the mix. Originally, podcasts were simply MP3 files, a widely used audio format. Today, podcasts include MP4 and other video file formats, as well as other audio formats such as Windows Media, Ogg Vorbis, and Audible that support subscription-based and advertising-based podcast business models.

If you remember something called "push" technology from the late 1990s, podcasting may sound familiar. Companies like PointCast Inc. distributed client software that periodically polled network servers, downloading massive amounts of topical content, including audio and video programming, dumping older content from the user's hard drive to make room for the new material. Pointcast's audience could browse the new content without any network latency, which was the rule in those dial-up times. It was the first attempt at non-streaming rich media delivery, but "push" was doomed to fail by its business model, which front-loaded costs for everyone — producers paid for distribution, and Pointcast incurred massive bandwidth and technology development expenses that killed the company before it could convert its audience into advertising revenues. The audience got everything for free, although Pointcast had plans to offer subscription-based programs before it collapsed well in advance of the rest of the Internet bubble's bursting.

However, push technology and podcasting are significantly different. Podcasting is built on open-source foundations. Instead of concentrating the distribution channel in the hands of a few companies like Pointcast, podcasting protocols allow any developer to add the ability to query a server to retrieve content to its application or Web service, and most importantly, podcasting allows anyone to place a program into distribution without having to go through an intermediary host that aggregates many channels of information. Pointcast is unneeded in many podcasting scenarios, because the podcaster can communicate directly with the listener. At its founding, podcasting was designed to subvert the economic equations of existing media, thwarting not just the role of the aggregator but also the advertiser.

CROSS-REF See Chapter 2, "Podcasting's Meteoric Trajectory," for a more complete history of the development of podcasting.

But much about podcasting remains controversial because of those initial assumptions about the revenue models, or lack thereof.

Discussion of podcasting is difficult, because it is so young. The people who helped launch the industry are very particular about what is a podcast and what isn't. Moreover, they are vocal about it. We'll cover these controversies throughout this book, but they can be summarized by saying that the technology is frequently mistaken for a genre. That is, people talk about podcasts like the form is a kind of poem or book, turning definitions of what a podcast should be into a kind of religious argument. Podcasts, according to programmer Dave Winer, one of the people credited with inventing the technology, should be free — in fact, according to Winer, podcasts were engineered specifically to defy advertisers' efforts to include promotional content in podcasted programs.

"If you're not using MP3, you're probably trying to make podcasting into a replay of previous media," Winer wrote on November 12, 2005, the day after an advertising tracking service was introduced by Audible Inc. "By design, podcasting took a poison pill at the very beginning of its life that made it impossible for the corporate types to subvert it without fundamentally changing what it is. That's why I was sure that Audible wasn't doing podcasting. Basically MP3 can't be rigged up to serve the purpose of advertisers, and that's why I love MP3. And only MP3 provides the portability and compatibility that users depend on. Any other method will force them to jump through hoops that they will resist. If so, then podcasting isn't for the advertisers."

Winer's initial choices about podcasting's technology reflect that he served the poison pill. Yet, by the time he wrote this, podcasts were being delivered in many different file formats, including Quicktime files that played on Video iPods from Apple Computers Inc. The cat was out of the bag, and new uses must and will be found for podcasting or users will route around the rigid boundaries.

In fact, if podcasting is going to remain relevant—and we think it will—the technology will be extremely pliant, supporting many file formats and many more business models. Had the inventors of the personal computer decided what kind of projects it could be used for, the PC would have been designed for failure. In fact, one of the fathers of the PC, Alan Kay, says today that the problem holding back the personal computer today is reliance on the narrow range of ideas he helped think up in the 1970s.

Why Podcasting Is Different

The unique thing about podcasting is the flexibility it enables for both producers and the audience. Both producers and audiences enjoy immensely more freedom today than they did in the broadcast schedule. Creative people, whether voice talent, writers, or ordinary people with a passion—about almost anything, from their hobby to the history of their family or a project at work—can find an audience. Even small audiences are eminently reasonable in podcasting, because the costs of producing and delivering programs are so low that any niche interest can be served. We saw the same phenomenon in publishing with the advent of computer desktop publishing, when a flowering of small magazines suddenly appeared to serve incredibly focused markets and newsletters sprouted in every industry and at every company.

Listeners, too, are freed in an important way: The schedule they listen on is in their hands, not controlled by the broadcaster who delivers the shows. Podcasts allow the complete reordering of the listening day, providing users who download programs the ability to start and stop a program at will, to listen at their leisure to programs at any time of the day or night. The result of this bidirectional freedom is a media environment where programming is offered by producers and selected and listened to by people on a fluid schedule and under a far broader range of business models than were possible before. Add to this easy-to-distribute environment the element of portability—a podcast can be loaded onto a variety of portable devices, from MP3 players to wireless telephone handsets—and the location of the listener has been radically transformed. No longer does listening to a program on the Web mean having to be tethered to your computer. Just export the show to your iPod and go.

Thousands, if not millions, of different messages can be delivered through a podcast. What blogs are to the newspapers, podcasts are for radio, deconstructing the strict order of the mass-media marketplace. Where radio and audio production have been rarified professions in the mass media era, the relentless march of Moore's Law has brought the tools and distribution networks that made those mass media expensive to experiment with and compete in to a generation known as podcasters. This book is your guide to producing programs and forging new channels of communication between your coworkers or family that are as easy to use as e-mail.

Voices make the podcast. For the past 85 years, since commercial radio first appeared, audiences have become accustomed to a narrow range of voices that are "professional," usually deeper than the ordinary speaker and paced like a race or a seduction, but decidedly not like everyone normally speaks. Podcasts break that monopoly. In less than a decade, commercial radio has descended into crisis as audiences flee to the Internet, in the form of streaming and downloadable programming, not to mention the allure of paid commercial-free radio broadcast from satellites in space. Podcasts burst on the scene in late 2004, claiming thousands of listeners in the first few months and millions within a year. Depending on which research firm you believe, between 30 million to 50 million people will be podcast listeners by the end of the decade. The monopoly that was radio is broken, dismantled, kaput.

A Podcast for Every Listener

Podcasting began with voices, just like radio. The first podcasters were also the medium's creators, hacking together technologies to make the programs they recorded available, and they will be remembered for their contributions — people like Frank Conrad, the Pittsburgh-based radio operator who first turned his ham radio transmitter into a foundation for popular entertainment. Conrad's audience grew through the auspices of a store that sold radios and advertised on his "station." Eventually, the station became KDKA in 1920, the first licensed commercial radio operation in the United States.

In podcasting, the voices began with Dave Winer, whose Morning Coffee Notes were among the first to be delivered via RSS. On his first program, from August 12, 2004, Winer related his ideas about blogging and journalism, beginning with a story of hellish travels:

"Good afternoon, everybody. This is your friend, Dave, calling in... checking in from New York, where it's hot and humid. You can tell that, you can hear the sound of the air conditioner in the background, probably. Had a very eventful trip across the country yesterday...."

Winer's podcasts allowed him to evangelize the technology itself. As one of the creators of RSS, he was interested in finding other uses for the XML (Extensible Markup Language) syndication format that let bloggers offer subscription services of their text feeds. Podcasting became its own best marketing in Winer's hands, as well as those of former MTV VJ Adam Curry, who introduced his Daily Source Code program on August 13, 2004.

Unfortunately, the early episodes of Daily Source Code are no longer available on the Web, but the show combined Curry's patter with his favorite independent music and "mash-ups" of popular music that he made himself. Curry's promotion of other podcasters was critical to the evolution of the medium, because he became one of the most reliable sources, in the early days, of new podcasts.

Fairly soon, several podcast indices offered links to new podcasts, which gave rise to what can only be called "surprising" new programs. Out of those lists, early "stars" rose. Dave Slusher, who'd done some radio in school and performed computer programming services in South Carolina for a living, was among the first to grab a loyal audience.

Slusher riffs in his program, *Evil Genius Chronicles*, about his day, the news, culture, technology, and coding over a music track. The effect he was aiming for was similar to National Public Radio's *This*

American Life, but what he created was uniquely Dave Slusher. What did it do for Slusher? His *Evil Genius Chronicles* podcast became a source of revenue from sponsors and the sale of a small collection of Evil Genius t-shirts, as well as advertising revenue from his blog, which saw more traffic. The show also made people aware of his coding skills, bringing him consulting work and, basically, making his effort to earn a living more flexible than he dreamed it could be.

The podcast is, for most people, another piece in a complex puzzle that makes an economic life possible. But it won't always be so.

Dawn Miceli and Drew Domkus, a married couple living on a shuttered dairy farm in Wisconsin, launched a funny, truthful show about marriage — their marriage and everyone else's — that combined banter and sex, sometimes recorded for The Dawn and Drew Show (see Figure 1.2). Dawn and Drew became some of the first to "go pro" as podcasters, earning their living on podcasting after a year "on the air." Their show is sponsored, and they won a slot on Sirius Satellite Radio. The couple has become something like celebrities, but not quite so full of bull as most of what passes for celebrity, because it is not manufactured but *captured* in sound.

The Longer Tail

Podcasting's history is evaporating as quickly as storage limits for hosting accounts fill up. We can't tell you what Adam Curry said, because there's no copy of the file accessible through any links exposed by Google and other search engines. Podcasters are often forced to purge their archives to keep their costs low, yet all these older programs make up the "long tail," the vast catalog of content that can serve the incredibly diverse interests of listeners for many years, but only if the programs remain available. What made the long tail interesting in the first place was the notion that at a site like iTunes or Amazon, which make available titles that couldn't be stocked in a retail store on CD or on shelves, was the fact that almost every title would sell in a year.

The problem podcasting has is a shortage of storage, which organizations like The Internet Archive (http://www.archive.org/) and Our Media (http://www.ourmedia.org/) are seeking to ameliorate by providing free storage to content that can be freely reused.

Welcome to Ourmedia.org   Requires Internet Archive Account
- Publish and store video, audio and other media that you created!
- Share and discover independent media. Connect to a global community!
- Learn how to create citizens media. Free storage & bandwidth forever!
- Do NOT post other artists' copyrighted works without permission. Ourmedia is about showcasing your creativity! Register now!

now in alpha

OurMedia's message: Share and share alike

However, podcasters have to know to go to these sites and upload their programs, and if they want to protect the content, they are left on their own. In the former case, society loses out, and in the latter, audiences and producers lose. As podcasting matures, a full range of business and sharing models will be needed to preserve the creative efforts of so many people.

FIGURE 1.2

Dawn and Drew: honest sex and marriage

That's not to say that Dawn and Drew are a success because they make money. Rather, they would probably be doing this show anyway, because the stories, the bickering, the funny criticisms and witticisms seem to flow out of these two. They exemplify the kind of honest passion that can be captured by a microphone and find an audience.

Anyone can build a business on this technology, but it still takes talent and a kind of excitement that makes producing a show thrilling every time the mic goes live. Another couple, Rob and Dana Greenlee, created *WebTalk Radio* long before podcasting came along, migrating to the new distribution technology when it swept away streaming as the preferred way to get audio over the Internet. Dana Greenlee says the problem is that after years, you start to think about producing as "time to make doughnuts, oh well." Indeed, *Wired Magazine* wrote about "podfading," the tendency for programs to disappear as producers lose interest. Keeping the excitement in a podcast is critical, whether you're going to deliver it to the world or to a small group.

But the Greenlees have enjoyed many rewards for their efforts, including executive jobs won by Rob and Dana's becoming the first podcaster for CBS Television, where she produced shows about the Fall 2005 television shows offered by CBS. Their podcasts were far less expensive than the radio program they'd previously produced, since they no longer had to pay for airtime on local stations, and their audience was dramatically expanded both geographically and in size by the move to downloadable audio.

Performers have shown the way to success, as well. Robby Gervais, star of the BBC's *The Office,* launched his podcast with friends Steve Merchant and (the astonishingly funny) Karl Pilkington (see Figure 1.3). The first "season," when it was hosted by the Guardian Unlimited, a London-based online newspaper site, achieved a huge audience, as many as 250,000 per episode, more than most cable channels can expect.

The show is funny and is clearly a performance, for no one can be quite as dense as Karl Pilkington pretends to be. Gervais, an accomplished actor and comedian, took his experience in radio to podcasting, building a show on quick transitions between conversational segments, very like radio. For these guys, who have worked together in media for years, the performance is natural. They've practiced their enthusiasm as their work and their natural humor shines through.

FIGURE 1.3

Karl Pilkington: genius stupidity as performance art

The precise moment that Ricky told Karl that, in a vacuum, a feather and a hammer fall at the same speed.

Gervais broke new ground when he partnered with Audible Inc. to offer the first subscription podcast, *The Ricky Gervais Show*, charging $6.95 for six shows, which is now in its third "season." The podcast also reinforces his relationship with fans and is just part of the total Gervais package.

Journalists, too, have made the transition to podcasting. Since the podcasting world began in and amidst technology, it was natural that some of the most successful podcasts would be about technology. This Week in Technology, or TWiT, hosted by Leo LaPorte, a radio and television host for many years, is a well-sponsored program that provides technology news and reviews, often in front of a live audience at retail locations and conferences, a kind of *Tonight Show* that makes obsolescence fun (finding new stuff to buy is entertainment). LaPorte manages to turn almost everything he does into a podcast, offering a variety of specialized programs, such as Inside the Net, that serve parts of his audience.

A news background trains the mind to make use of so many parts of every recording and experience, because news is made on a strict budget — now more than ever.

The last area where podcasting has just started to take hold is in business, where a budget is appreciated too. As a medium, podcasts enjoy a special quality of taking little time to produce. Podcasts are a natural for marketing and engaging customers in discussion about a company's products and services. With less than two years behind it, podcasting hasn't provided the business world enough examples of success to make it a major movement, but like the Web, television, and radio before, it will happen.

Corporate podcasts might be marketing vehicles, and companies certainly will find a way to sponsor audio delivered via RSS and download. Advertisers have begun making noise about the millions, even billions, they want to put behind new programs. Think, though, about how simple it is today to start your relationship with customers. From a local nursery that prints the URL for its podcast about gardening on its sales receipts to chains that distribute fliers at retail outlets advertising a contest that, like American Idol, brings the voice of the customer to the world through a podcast, the possibilities for programming are endless.

Summary

Podcasts speak; this book can't be heard. We give you the gospel in these pages, even as the podcast revolution continues at breakneck pace. Making podcasts, learning the tools you'll need to use, and understanding the distribution options and their implications for your budget are all that stand between you and those possibilities.

■ Podcasting builds on a broad range of media and Internet developments, including failed notions, such as "push technology," and the foundations of the Web and blogging, including hyperlinks, RSS, and news aggregator applications.

■ The basic tools for producing your podcast are a microphone and recording device, typically one's computer, and the software for editing a raw recording into a finished show. On the distribution side, you need to set up or purchase space on a Web server.

■ Developer Dave Winer made and distributed the first podcast on August 12, 2004, though many programs known as podcasts today predate his *Morning Coffee Notes* podcast. The key innovation was the combination of RSS and sound files delivered as enclosures.

■ Adam Curry and a number of other people contributed to the development of the first podcast receiver application, known as a "podcatcher." Curry's *Daily Source Code* podcast was the primary popularizer of the medium during its first year.

■ Podcasts are fun and personal, studied and slapstick. You don't need to copy anyone to be an original, but the pioneers in the format have paved the way at considerable expense. There is a lot to learn from them.

■ The first paid-circulation podcast was The Ricky Gervais Show, which featured Gervais, the star of the BBC's *The Office* sitcom, his *Office* co-creator, Steven Merchant, and Karl Pilkington, who acts inexplicably stupid (it's a wonder he's survived in this Darwinian world).

■ In this book for would-be podcasting pros we emphasize how to make money with podcasts in spite of the medium's original design, which attempted to prevent advertising and money-making. There's no reason you have to try to make money with your podcast — and if you just want to have fun you'll learn everything you need to know here — but, if you do want to make money, this is the book for you.

In the next chapter, we walk through the technologies and development of podcasting, an already riotous history that includes bickering, counterclaims to inventions, and stealth attempts to rewrite the story. On that foundation, you learn what these developments can lead to, including new markets for your creative work and the applications for podcasting in corporate and marketing settings.

Chapter 2

Podcasting's Meteoric Trajectory

Podcasting has a meteoric history because it has gained rapid adoption by producers and audiences, but also because it has enjoyed its share of interpersonal fireworks.

Be aware that there are self-righteous monsters in this field. Like some technical fields, podcasting is full of zealous believers who combine technical innovation with fixed opinions about how their tools should be used, so talking about the history of this medium is much more than light, around-the-water-cooler talk for many. Be warned that this can be a contentious subject.

In this chapter, we introduce you to the personalities who have shaped podcasting's first couple of years, focusing on their unique contributions, the beliefs they built into the technology and definitions of podcasting, and how progress has already changed the medium. For some early podcasters, who define the medium as involving only MP3 files, podcasting has already been betrayed by the introduction of other formats, advertising systems, and fee-based podcasting. These pioneers react as though color television diminished the glory that had been black-and-white TV in the 1950s.

From the foundations, we move on to the current crop of podcasting vendor offerings that have already begun to expand the applications of downloadable audio and look ahead at where podcasting is headed as individual producers and media companies alike experiment with new formats and business models.

IN THIS CHAPTER

A short history of podcasting

From curiosity to phenomenon

Today, tomorrow, and beyond

Digital Audio Grows Out

Podcasting emerged unexpectedly from the intersection of several technology developments. Since the commercial Internet exploded on the scene in the mid-1990s, audio has played an increasingly important role in the lives of users, who streamed and downloaded music, sports events, and audio books, among other things. But the channels for delivery remained relatively expensive or had gatekeepers who controlled access to their audiences.

RealNetworks, neé Progressive Networks, founded by former Microsoft executive Rob Glaser, pioneered the delivery of streaming audio. Despite competition from Microsoft, by decade's end RealNetworks had about a million subscribers to its premium streaming audio and video services, which included baseball games, bikini competitions, and music. Streaming, however, was useful only for connected computers — the disconnected laptop or any other digital device was likewise cut off from RealNetworks' streaming service.

Microsoft was the first to develop a system for delivering copies of audio and video files for playback on portable PCs, Sync N Go, largely because it hoped to make its portable operating system, Windows CE, the default platform for mobile media. It did not produce a hit, that is any show with millions of listeners, but a bunch of shows with tens of thousands or, even, hundreds of thousands of listeners, so Microsoft eventually shut it down. RealNetworks, in the meantime, focused on its server business, hoping to sell streaming capabilities to media companies. In both cases, the technology was thinking too big. Podcasting cracked the mold because it was satisfied with small audiences.

In 1995, Don Katz, then an author and columnist for *Esquire*, decided that the audiobook, then available mostly on audiotapes, was ripe for a transition to digital delivery. He and a few friends founded Audible Words, now known as Audible Inc., to develop this business. Unfortunately, no portable audio devices existed, so in addition to concocting a business based on delivering audiobooks, they also invented the first mobile digital audio player capable of synching with a server on the Internet. That device is in the Smithsonian today. By 1998, other portable digital audio player vendors, notably the Rio PMP300, made by Diamond Multimedia, had come into the market, and Audible began licensing its file format and playback technology, which tracked playback location, to those companies.

As the Web grew, media makers became increasingly enamored of the idea of delivering rich media — everything from audio and video to user-controlled animation. Network throughput in those pre-broadband days (hard to believe it was only a decade ago) was too slow to support delivering these media types in real-time. Images and audio would stop or stutter unbearably whenever they fell behind the viewer, which was all the time. The solution seemed to be to schedule downloads of programs and text content overnight, when the network was less busy and, more importantly, the computer user was asleep. Audible had led the way with this approach, scheduling the downloads of audiobooks and programs at night. Ideally, these downloads could be played back at the audience's leisure in applications that captured the data and presented it for playback. Folks called this "push" technology, because the producer of the content pushed the data to the client application arbitrarily. Push media failed for two reasons:

- The data storage requirements for the PC were vast, taking dozens or hundreds of megabytes on the hard disc to keep everything the subscriber *might* want to see.

- Push companies controlled the channel, preventing much new creative work from appearing on people's screens.

- Nothing new was on and push filled people's hard drives with programming and lots of text they never got around to viewing.

Because people could get the same stuff from the television or a news Web site, the economic model for push failed under the massive cost of delivering data that, for the most part, went unused.

Meanwhile, Steve Jobs had returned to Apple Computer in 1996. After beginning the turnaround of the company with the first of a new generation of Macintosh, he turned his attention to digital music. In 2000, he hired Tony Fadell, an engineer who had built several handheld computers at General Magic and Phillips, and asked Jonathan Ivie, a designer, to take a shot at building a market-redefining portable audio player. Thus, the iPod was born, and the first component of the transformation of streaming into podcasting was in place. Apple introduced the iPod, followed by the iTunes Music Store, with a proprietary file format that required music providers have a business relationship with Apple to gain access to its iPod customers. Although the iPod would play MP3 files ripped from an audio CD, the focus of Apple's effort was on its secure format. Apple also licensed Audible's format and signed an exclusive agreement with the company to provide its audiobook catalog through iTunes.

That was the commercial side of the world as we settled into the 21st century. A home-brewed technology movement was also afoot, growing from the open source ethos of Linux and the GNU software development community. It was here that Dave Winer, the developer who brought form to the blog, made his pivotal contribution to the emergence of podcasting.

It came from planet RSS

Winer had taken a key piece of Netscape technology, the Resource Description Framework (RDF) that built on the eXtensible Markup Language for describing data, and made it work as a remote procedure call on Internet Protocol networks, known as XML-RPC. RDF was a standardized approach to describing the parts of a Web page. Winer christened his invention Really Simple Syndication, or RSS. By linking it to remote procedure calls, Winer made subscribing to Web sites possible, so that readers could receive the contents of those pages as a "feed" that could be processed by an RSS-aware application called a news reader.

Compared to push applications, RSS was brilliantly open. Anyone with a Web page could put a subscription service out for all comers to grab and use. Download costs were far lower, because only the data people wanted was added to subscriptions. From this foundation, the blogging phenomenon, which Winer also led, took flight. But audio was still outside the blogging mainstream.

By 2003, lots of folks were experimenting with the idea of blogging with audio. Webcasting, the streaming of audio files, was giving way to the idea of downloadable files that could be played back on portable devices, not just PCs. Apple's iTunes store was actually selling songs. Several audio download services, still closed in various ways, had appeared, including I2Go's MyAudio2Go.com. Fermentation was bound to produce something new. One of the authors, Mitch Ratcliffe, posted a downloadable audio file of a parrot joke on his blog in September of 2003 (signifying nothing other than, if he was doing it, it wasn't obscure anymore). Eric Rice, co-founder of

Audioblog.com, had launched a downloadable version of his webcast about the television show *Buffy the Vampire Slayer,* and at *Webtalk Radio,* a tech talk show, Rob and Dana Greenlee were approaching a million downloads a month through their Windows Media Player placement on MSN. Stuff was going on when Dave Winer started the transition to podcasting.

CROSS-REF   RSS is discussed in Chapter 16, *RSS (Really Simple Syndication).* Be attentive to the flavors of RSS emerging, as Apple's iTunes has introduced a set of custom tags you need to know when promoting your podcast.

Ease of use, though, hadn't made its way to audio distribution. Tristan Louis, a media and Web site developer, had suggested the idea of using RSS to deliver audio files as early as 2000, but the blog of record for the nascent movement, Harold Gilchrist's *Audioblogger,* was still reporting the use of downloads through links in early 2004 — lots was going on, but the catalyst hadn't appeared yet.

The last yard, via USB

For several years, Dave Winer and Adam Curry, a former MTV VJ who had spent the 1990s building a digital technology consulting company (he was the idea guy rather than an engineer, though he can code), had been exchanging audio files by sending links to one another. Winer began to play with placing the audio in an enclosure in an RSS feed, distributing the Grateful Dead's *U.S. Blues* on Inauguration Day in January 2001. In September 2003, Winer created an RSS feed for journalist Christopher Lydon, who had put together a series of interviews with leading technologists and politicians. Another step in the path to podcasting was taken. In June 2004, Stephen Downes, a Canadian developer, began offering audio via RSS from his blog, making it the first regular source of RSS-based personally produced audio.

Winer's wiring up of audio RSS would make automatic download of programs as simple as blogging, but it took several more years, until early 2004, before he and Curry helped make the last connection that resulted in podcasting's birth.

The step in the functional chain missing from the stone soup of podcasting was the ability to synchronize an RSS download to a portable device automatically. Non-RSS synchronization was a part of several commercial applications, including iTunes, Audible, and Windows Media Player, an expected feature for most people with iPods and other portable audio players. People expected audio from the Internet to flow over the USB cable they plugged in to their portable audio player. RSS didn't have that last connection.

Amphetadesk, an RSS newsreader developed by Pete Prodoehl, had integrated audio support after the Lydon interviews were released. This made desktop playback easy, but getting the file to an application that delivered it to a portable MP3 player required a series of steps, too much management effort.

Adam Curry and Kevin Marks, an engineer with weblog search engine Technorati, collaborated or at least talked about how to create a script based on a script. Marks had developed an AppleScript, which became RSStoiPod, that automated the transfer of an audio file downloaded by Winer's blogging software, Radio Userland, to Apple's iTunes. It was the last stretch of data pipeline from the server to the portable device. In short order, two more programmers, August Trometer and Ray Slakinski, integrated that synchronization functionality into an audio-centric RSS client that they called iPodder (which has evolved to become Juice, the Windows podcatcher we describe in Chapter 3).

Podcasting had been borne, so it was time for some throes of agony to supplement the relatively painless birth.

What podcasting is not

Tiresome though the blogosphere could be when comparing itself to "mainstream media," with a literal voice some early podcasters went shrilly to work policing the limits of podcasting. People who had been doing audio downloads before were labeled "not podcasters," either because they didn't share a foggily described aesthetic with early podcasters or because of their continued use of other channels to distribute audio. A cottage industry sprang up to support gatherings that, like the Council of Nicea did the orthodoxy of the early Catholic Church, laid out the doctrines that made podcasting unique.

Some of the definitional details were correct, but these arguments quickly became personal and uselessly circular.

- Steve Rubel, whose Micro Persuasion weblog is quite influential, said of a New York Newsday program on August 11, 2005: "In my view, downloadable audio itself is not a podcast, as Newsday and the WB Network think it is judging by this page [a link to the page displaying the audio link]. You gotta have an RSS feed to distribute it and they don't." The definition of a podcast had been right, and it turned out that Newsday had a podcast feed.

- When Audible announced a podcasting service, Dave Winer wrote: "By design, podcasting took a poison pill at the very beginning of its life that made it impossible for the corporate types to subvert it without fundamentally changing what it is. That's why I was sure that Audible wasn't doing podcasting." The poison pill Winer refers to is his decision to thwart commercial insertion through the use of the MP3 file format, which is widely available but as inflexible as any other format available, as it is controlled by the Frauenhofer Society, a German engineering group that licenses MP3 to software and hardware developers. Any changes to MP3 to facilitate advertising insertion and tracking will result in new revenues for the Frauenhofer Society. The file format is a temporary feature of podcasting, as many others are already in use, but if Winer's definition of a podcast — only those feeds delivering MP3 files — had been enforced, it would be like television makers had decided that when the switch from black-and-white to color happened, the new colorful picture would not have been television but something new.

- When KYOU, a flagging San Francisco Bay Area radio station, started broadcasting podcasts instead of its ordinary fare, blogger-media critic Jeff Jarvis wrote: "This is still a big company handing over its time and using the second-person plural: YOURadio. We'll know we've arrived when the people take over the station for real and change the name to OURadio." Jarvis praised the development, but the branding rubbed him the wrong way. He quotes approvingly this comment by MasterMaq, another blogger: "KYOURadio is not a podcast radio station — they simply play content submitted by listeners." Apparently something happened to the audio transmitted over KYOU that made the podcasts aired into not-podcasts in some mysteriously metaphysical way. These hair-splitting distinctions armed many critics.

- Dave Slusher, commenting on the contending definitions of podcasting, provided an excellent summary of the technical features of a podcast, then this maxim, which suggests limits on podcasting that emphasize amateurism: "In summation: podcasting is based on 'asynchronous bundles of passion, automatically delivered to your device of choice while you sleep.'" The "bundles of passion" is apt, but for many it means that one can't make money at this, even if it takes all your time and people love what you do. Slusher takes advertising today, but many people argue that "podcasting" has already been subverted by efforts to route around Dave Winer's poison pill.

The debate has never ended, which is a fine thing, because podcasting is constantly evolving. The point, though, is that podcasting is not defined by limits; rather it represents a wide range of possibilities. Anything could be a podcast, from a recorded conversation over lunch to a grandmother's memory of her grandparents preserved for her family in digital audio and offered only to family members via RSS feeds. If Gutenberg had defined what could be in a book, it would have slowed things down dramatically. Instead, the printing press replaced scriptoria filled with monks within 70 years of its introduction because it was used to produce all sorts of books, not just Bibles. The second bestseller to come from the press was an accounting primer, by the way.

Transition State: From Curiosity to Phenomenon

Adam Curry's main role in podcasting was the popularization of the medium. His *Daily Source Code* podcast, a part-music, part-The-Man-Evangelizing-the-Medium, became something of a phenomenon in late 2004 and early 2005. Curry became podcasting's first star. He campaigned for ordinary people to "take back the media," something that later contributed to skepticism about his motives.

But first, the medium needed a name. Blogger Ben Hammersley, grabbing a portion of the name of the leading digital audio player, the iPod, had used the term "podcasting" in an article in The Guardian newspaper to describe Christopher Lydon's interview series in January 2004. It was on Curry's *ipodder-dev* mailing list, though, that the word was applied and it stuck, when Dannie Gregoire suggested it in September of that year. Variations on the theme appeared. Blogger Doc Searls described podcasting as Personal Optional Digital casting in an effort to describe the listener's essential role in choosing what flows to the device. "Pod" and "casting" were merged.

With a catchy handle, Curry put his MTV experience to work. His program combined mash-ups, remixed music, and an ample dose of promotion of the podcasts he enjoyed. Podcasters sent Curry their shows in hopes of hearing them recast on *Daily Source Code* and subscribed to hear it. Curry was funny and cool, the audience feeling gratified when they heard themselves or peers. It was a perfect storm of subscription-driven programming. And the thing about it was that much of the programming Curry featured was very good. A huge reservoir of talent was waiting to be heard.

Connections were important in another way that was helped along by Curry, who introduced iPodder.org, a directory of podcasts organized by theme. It was supplemented by many other directories, notably Podcast.net, PodcastAlley, and ultimately, iTunes, the Apple entry into the community. Podcasts, as with anything on the Net, had to be discoverable to lend to the success of the small producer. Contrary to the mass media that survive on blanketing the world with ads for their programming, the podcaster lives and dies on being found through directories and searches.

As the number of podcasters and listeners rose and the number of Google hits for "podcasting" climbed from the hundreds to the millions, the medium became a ripe target for commercial interests. Adam Curry was the first to capitalize on the momentum, launching a company, PodShow, that promised to promote podcasts and, in order to help podcasters earn a living, placed ads in programs. At the same time, Apple Computer came a-courtin' and signed Curry to help promote the integration of podcasting into iTunes. At launch, podcasting on iTunes was headlined by Curry, who appeared dressed in some kind of '60s hipster-cum-metrosexual getup that looked like it had been stolen from a '70s Blacksploitation movie. Finally, Curry did a deal to produce a "podshow" of podcasts for broadcast on Sirius Satellite Radio, which continues to this day. He was the showman who would toss gas on the fires of podcasting.

It was about the time Curry began to gain fame for his podcasting entrepreneuring that he had a falling out with Dave Winer, who in various blog postings claimed to be the real father of podcasting. For about a year, the two of them barely talked, according to reports, while Winer bickered with Curry in his blog and Curry, it appeared, mostly ignored him.

The boiling pot that was the Curry-Winer or Winer-Curry feud, depending on the partisans whom you were reading at the time, erupted again in December 2005, when the fact that someone using an Internet Protocol address (the network address of a computer connected to the Internet) that Curry owned had been editing the Wikipedia entry on the history of podcasting to remove contributions of others than Curry. In fact, Curry or someone working for him had repeatedly removed references to a number of contributors to the evolution of podcasting. Curry pretty much completed the immolation of his populist credentials when PodShow, his production company, introduced a contract for podcasters that was interpreted by many to require producers who worked with the company to assign all rights to their podcast to PodShow. Moreover, the producer reportedly had to agree to make all *future* productions they might do to PodShow on the same terms. As entertainment and publishing contracts go, it was straight out of the studio system of the 1930s and 1940s, when film stars were, albeit, pampered slaves, but slaves nonetheless. PodShow has been working to clarify and repair its contract terms.

These fireworks were peripheral to what was really happening to podcasting. Combining easy distribution with inexpensive production technology had suddenly put anyone with a good idea and a little marketing savvy on the map, able to be found by audiences. Advertisers quickly followed, though at first the approach to support of podcasts looked more like the National Public Radio model, where sponsors turned over a fee to the podcaster without regard to how many people might listen. Ad networks have only begun to form around podcasting at this writing, still largely on the sponsorship model, but as with the Net and television and radio before it, economically rewarding podcasting will eventually move from sponsor models to become a thoroughly measured medium.

That's not to say that podcasting is or ever will be all about the Benjamins. Rather, when someone wants to make a living on his talent, through podcasting audio or video, it will look more like the media we know today—the Web and television. Stars will come and go, making huge impressions on the public consciousness, as Jerry Seinfeld or Yahoo! did in other television and Web portals, while lots of moderate successes will change the basic landscape of choice available to the public. At the same time, a subculture of "free" podcasts offered by individuals and groups who just want to be heard will complete an alternative universe of audio and video that is available at no cost, though it may be sponsored *a la* NPR.

Media becomes democratized when anyone can take her shot at any kind of audience she seeks, regardless of how she bends or breaks the form and economic models. The what-it's-not factions, regardless of their special tweak of the definition of podcasting, are actually doing more harm than good when they place limits on the uses of a medium. Podcasting exploded onto the scene, morphing past all limits. We're not talking revolution, which does have its doctrines, but rebellion, the struggle of individuals to overcome the definitions laid upon them by the world. And, yes, some of them will become rich doing so.

Today, Tomorrow, and Beyond

Podcasting is the foundation for a new media landscape, where independently produced content coexists with "professional" programs created and distributed by big media companies. Apple is selling as many as 34 million iPods a year, based on current quarterly sales figures. ABC, NBC, CBS, Fox, and innumerable other production companies are offering shows for download.

Making the most of the opportunity to communicate is what you, the prospective podcaster, need to keep in mind as you contemplate where this market is going. A narrow definition of podcasting could prevent you from seeing how to apply these tools to the needs of your family, your company, or a vast international audience.

Podcasting isn't about making "shows" as though, like some 1930s Mickey Rooney/Judy Garland film, you've found out your dad has a chest full of costumes and Judy's barn is the perfect place to put on a fundraiser to save the pastor's ailing racehorse. It can be about establishing regular communication with your customers. If you're a dentist or a physician, think about printing a podcast feed address on your appointment cards and delivering a weekly minute-long recording about teenager's teeth or preventing the flu. A small business—even a large one—can use podcasts to promote new products and services or to offer tips on getting the most from something the company sells to improve post-sale satisfaction among customers. Workgroups within a company or across many companies can keep in constant contact by recording conference calls and making them available as podcasts for team reviews or just to let folks who miss a meeting catch up. Professors and school teachers can upload audio or video of their lectures for students to review and, if the lectures are great, maybe build a global "class" of thousands of students who subscribe in order to get a leg up on their own studies.

And podcasting can be all about the show. If you're already producing radio or television programming, the millions of new podcast-ready listeners buying iPods and other portable digital audio players each month are already looking for new ways to control their listening. Broadcasters who refuse to accommodate the audience's desire to listen on their own schedule risk losing their listeners and the advertising dollars that came with them. Likewise, if you've just dreamed of making a radio or television program, the podcasting market is still so wide open that you can have your shot at winning the first thousand audience members who, if they love your work, will help bring the next 20,000 subscribers. Plenty of local television programs succeed on audience numbers of those sizes, but podcasting doesn't limit you to the people within the reach of your radio or television signal. Podcast foundations could support media empires in the future, although there will be lots of work involved.

Summary

Podcasting's origins reach back to the beginning of the Net and further, making this medium a great evolutionary step forward based on the dramatic decrease in production costs and distribution. That's better than a revolution, because we can take steps based on existing business models and creative examples to build podcasts and podcast-based businesses. A little familiarity goes a long way when the market is wide open to innovators.

- The precursors of podcasting include Microsoft's Sync N Go service and Audible.com's downloadable audiobook technology. These were the pioneers of portable playback of audio.

- Push technology got part of the way to podcasting, but did not give the listener the freedom to carry a portable device and filled hard drives at a time when storage was at a premium compared to today.

- The evolution wasn't always a calm one. As fish turned their fins into limbs, they probably beat up the slow pokes stuck in the water too, and podcasting has come with lots of bluster and credit-grabbing that could discredit it if there weren't so much positive activity going on. Evolution sucks for the losers.

- The foundations of podcasting were laid on RSS, or Really Simple Syndication, a highly egalitarian approach to information distribution created in large part by Dave Winer.

- Working from that auspicious beginning, a number of people made the first suggestions for podcast-like functionality as early as 2001, but it took the integration of synchronization to portable players by Kevin Marks, Adam Curry, August Trometer, and Ray Slakinski, among others, to catalyze the end-to-end phenomenon we know as podcasting.

- Curry, the former MTV VJ, was critically important to the popularization of podcasting, as were several podcast portals, or indices, that allowed people to sample and subscribe to hundreds, then thousands of programs. By the time this book was conceived, podcasting had become a self-sustaining medium, attracting amateur and professional producers, as well as media companies.

In the next chapter, we walk you through the entire desktop listening and podcast discovery process.

Chapter 3

Exploring the World of Podcasting

In this chapter, we show you how to find, subscribe, and listen to thousands of podcasts available on the Net. The steps for getting audio files onto your portable audio player, such as an iPod, or burning a CD and listening on a desktop computer are few and easy to understand. We also introduce you to the client software used to subscribe to and download podcasts, including the wide variety available for the Windows, Macintosh, and Linux operating systems.

A variety of podcast portals offer lists of podcasts; we walk you through some of the better neighborhoods in podcastland, explaining the basic mechanics that make podcasting work. Finally, as part of that technical introduction, we explain the technical origins and personal conflicts that color the podcast landscape. After this chapter, if you just want to listen, you're ready to go. But we bet a big bag of fish that, after you've tried listening, you're going to want to start to speak with a podcast of your own.

The Basics of Listening

Listening is easy. Managing your subscriptions is easy. Keeping up with everything you can download with such ease is harder. That's because the listener is in control. Unlike broadcast media, where every listening choice is a zero-sum game, where choosing one program means you can't listen to the others, podcasting gives you the power to stack up a full schedule of listening and more.

First, you need to get an application commonly referred to as a "podcatcher," news reader, or aggregator. All these applications do the same thing; they visit a list of servers to check for newly posted files. Remember the comparison to push technology in Chapter 1? A push client was locked to a particular server.

If you had multiple push services, it meant running several different applications. With podcast and RSS, your subscriptions are handled by one application. Later in this chapter, we introduce you to the choices in podcatchers; here, we focus on what a podcatcher does.

As shown in Figure 3.1, a podcatcher running on your computer maintains a list of subscriptions in the form of uniform resource identifiers (URIs, also called URLs) that tell the application the name of each server and where subscription files are stored on a regular schedule that you specify. Each subscription is referred to as a "feed," which is the Web address of a file that describes the catalog of shows stored in a particular directory on a server. You may have feeds for several different programs on the server, each with a unique URL for the XML file for each show.

FIGURE 3.1

The podcatching process

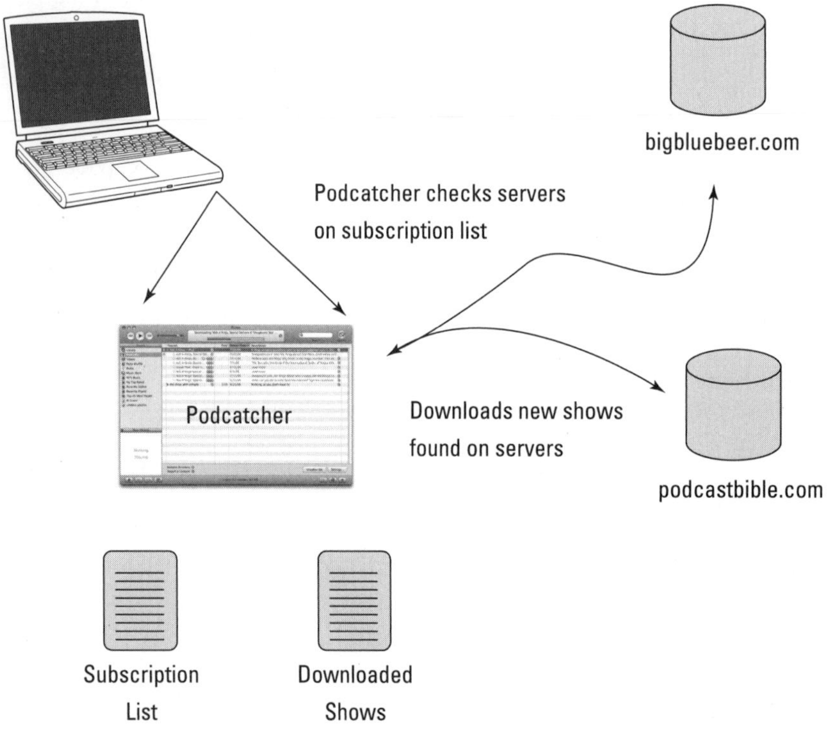

For example, let's say you've subscribed to a podcast called Big Blue's Beer Show, which is stored on a server named www.bigblueBeer.com in a file called "podxml.xml." The full address of the file is http://www.bigbluebeer.com/site/feeds/podxml.com, and you've set your podcatcher to visit the site every day at 6:00 AM to check for new shows listed in that XML file. When the application finds a new show listed in the podxml.xml, the full audio file is downloaded to your PC and stored in a directory where you can open it and listen, or the podcatcher application can identify new audio or video files and move it to your computer or portable audio player. The podcatcher then moves to the next subscription on the list, in this case, a PodcastBible.com podcast, and checks that server for a new show. At the end of the update process, your podcatcher has a list of programs that are downloaded and ready for listening.

Of course, you can have your podcatcher visit many servers, collecting programs all day long, but remember that audio files take lots of space on the hard drive. An hour of MP3 audio is typically about 30 MB in size. Like a digital video recorder for your television, podcatchers require some tending, with frequent weeding to keep space available for new programs.

Choosing Your Podcatcher

The podcatcher emerged as a standalone application for managing podcast subscriptions, but the functionality is now built into many of the applications you may use for e-mail, RSS feed reading, and your browser. In some cases, sites that aggregate podcast feeds also provide synchronization with your local audio application or allow listening in an online player, so you never need to download the podcasts or any software to your local hard drive.

Most important to your convenience is the ability to associate your podcatching with other kinds of audio management tools you have. If, for example, you have Windows and rely on Windows Media Player to listen to CDs, store MP3s, and synchronize your mobile audio device, you want a podcatcher that can hand files to Windows Media Player, identifying them as podcasts so that you can find and listen to them in your library. Macintosh users and many Windows-using iPod owners, on the other hand, want their podcatchers to deliver programs to the iTunes software they use for music, video, and MP3s, because it makes synchronizing to the iPod a snap.

With so many to choose from, the best way to start is to try a couple for yourself and see which one you like. We suggest visiting CNET's Download.com (http://www.download.com/) or Podcast Alley's Top 20 Rated pages (http://www.podcastalley.com/forum/links .php?func=toprated) to see what other folks are ranking among the best of the current crop. These are some of our favorites:

- **Juice:** A free (though donations are welcomed) open-source podcatcher for Windows, Macintosh, and Linux operating systems. Created on the foundation of the original pod-catch software, Juice evolved nicely to provide a simple, straightforward experience with links to interesting services for sharing and rating podcasts, which keeps you tapped into what's new in the podosphere. Download it at juicereceiver.sourceforge.net.

- **Nimiq:** Another free podcatcher, Nimiq has the added attraction that it also handles BitTorrent downloads, the most popular way to share files, especially music and video, between peers on the Net. It includes support for the emerging OPML browser features that allow you and others to share your playlists to improve community search. Download at http://www.nimiq.nl/

- **NetNewsWire:** A robust Macintosh RSS reader, NetNewsWire can handle podcast subscriptions, handing them to iTunes and adding custom category descriptions so that they are easy to find on your iPod. Although it isn't free at $29.95, it serves so many useful purposes for Mac users that we think it's highly worthwhile. Download a trial version at `http://www.newsgator.com/NGOLProduct.aspx?ProdID=NetNewsWire`.

- **Newsgator:** From the same company that makes NetNewsWire, Newsgator is the most advanced Windows RSS product available, integrating blog and news subscriptions, podcasts, and much more into Microsoft's Outlook productivity application and a hosted version on the Web that can be integrated into the Yahoo Messenger instant messager client. The cost is $29.95. Download a trial at `http://www.newsgator.com/`.

- **FeedDemon:** Newsgator has been accumulating a variety of podcatcher applications, including another widely used favorite, FeedDemon 2.0, which features custom organization of text feeds and podcasts, with direct download to a docked iPod. The software is $29.95. A free trial is available at `http://www.newsgator.com/NGOLProduct.aspx?ProdId=FeedDemon`.

- **iTunes:** Apple's music application, which comes on all Macs and in the box with any iPod for the PC, also is an outstanding podcatcher. It's free to download at `http://www.apple.com/itunes/download/`.

In a nutshell, look for a client that supports adding podcasts to the rest of your listening rather than having to create another catalog of audio on your computer. All the applications listed in this section meet that expectation and more. So let's look at how to install these applications.

Downloading and Installing a Windows Podcatcher

Let's download and install a podcatcher application now. If you're using a Windows PC, we suggest starting with Juice, one of the original and most robust podcatchers (formerly known as iPodder), which you can download from CNET's `download.com` or `juicereceiver.sourceforge.net`. In our example, we're installing Juice 2.2, and it is reflected in the filename referred to in these steps:

1. Follow the links to download the file. (You may be referred to a mirror site; choose one near where you are located to get the file quickly.) When your browser asks you where to save the file, choose the Desktop, as shown in Figure 3.2. A file called Juice22Setup.exe — the numbers in the name change as new versions are released — is stored on your desktop.

2. Close your browser, and find the Juice22Setup.exe file on the desktop. Make sure other applications are closed before beginning the installation. Double-click the file icon to open the installer application, and click the Next button in the dialog box that opens. You may read the License Agreement, which is a GNU General Public License that allows you to modify the software and that requires you provide the same rights to anyone to whom you may choose to distribute the software in the future. We'll assume you're okay with these conditions, so click the I Agree button, as shown in Figure 3.3.

FIGURE 3.2

When downloading the Juice installer, save the file to your desktop.

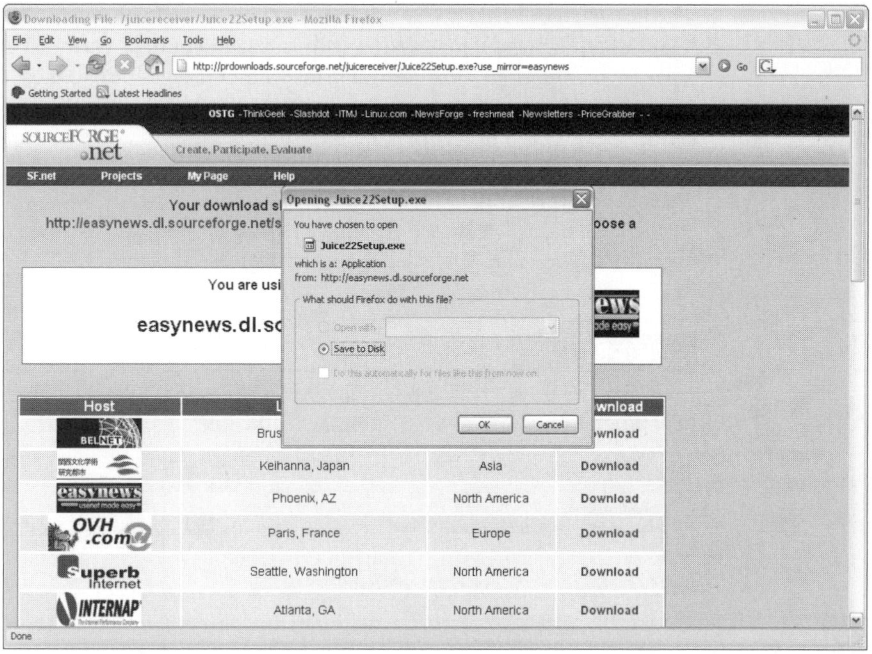

FIGURE 3.3

The Juice installer GNU GPL license

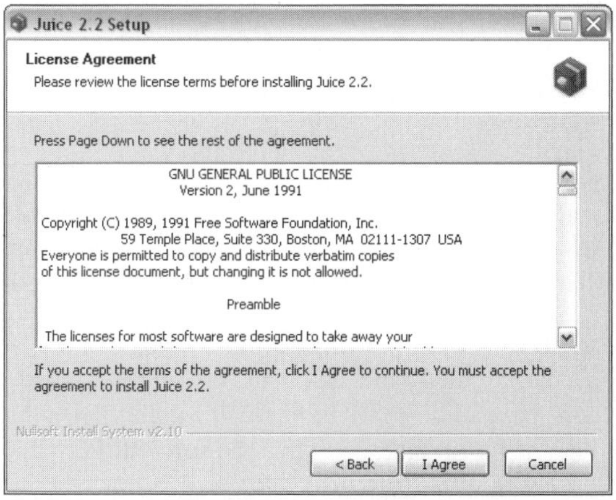

3. The next dialog box asks where you want to store the file, suggesting C:\Program Files\Juice, which we recommend you accept. Click the Next button.

4. The installer now asks if you want to install all the components of the application and whether you would like to have a desktop shortcut to Juice, which is checked by default. If you want to crowd your desktop with icons, accept this. The other option presented, however, is important, because you want your podcatcher to do most of its work without asking you when it can go do its business. We suggest that you check the "Add to Startup Group" box, shown in Figure 3.4, which makes Windows open the application every time you launch your PC. Doing this should not open any security holes on your PC, but it ensures that, when you want your podcasts, they'll already be downloaded. If you don't enable Juice to load at launch, you have to wait for podcasts to download whenever you open the application. Now click the Install button.

FIGURE 3.4

Checking the "Add to Startup Group" box ensures that Juice launches and checks for new programs whenever your computer is on.

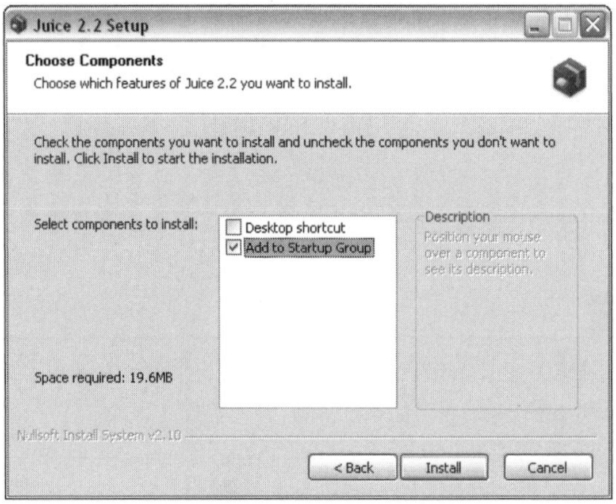

> **CAUTION** If you travel frequently or have a computer at work or elsewhere that you shouldn't be using for personal reasons, it's a good idea not to check the "Add to Startup Group" box so that Juice does not go to work downloading dozens of megabytes worth of podcasts when you log in to a wireless hotspot or while your boss is waiting for an important e-mail message from you.

5. Juice installs, listing the files it is modifying. The last dialog box tells you that the application has been installed successfully and asks whether you want to see the Readme file (we don't need no stinkin' manuals when we have a Wiley Bible close at hand!) and launch the application. Click the Finish button to open the application.

6. When Juice opens, the first thing it asks is if you would like to review a list of file types that it is not currently set to handle. The "Yes" radio button is selected by default; click OK.

7. The window that opens is the File Type Preferences pane of the Juice application, shown in Figure 3.5. You see a list of file types, indicated by file extension names or HTML tags, which are automatically handled by Juice whenever you click them in your browser. For each box you check, Juice becomes the default application to handle that file type when it is found by any other application, such as your browser. This means that if you've selected .rss in this pane and then you click an RSS feed on someone's site, Juice opens and adds the subscription automatically. The problem is if you click a text RSS feed, Juice subscribes to it. So we suggest that you leave this file type unchecked, so that your text RSS aggregator can handle those. The other options provided refer to podcast feeds, or feeds that are likely to contain video or audio, and are much less likely to conflict with other RSS readers. You can subscribe manually to feeds that include podcast files—Juice ignores all the text postings and downloads only the audio files. After making your choices, click the Save button.

FIGURE 3.5

When you first launch Juice, it asks you to review the file types it should open and play automatically. Selecting *.rss* makes all RSS feeds run through Juice, which extracts audio files for playback.

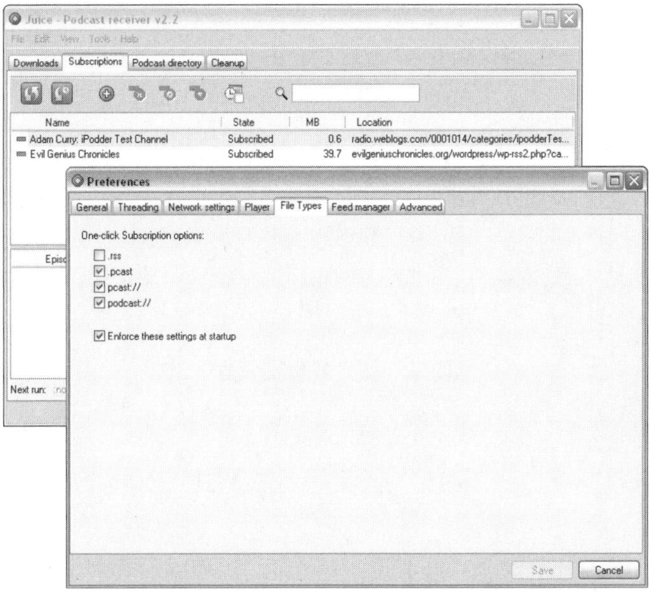

8. Finally, the File Type Preferences includes a check box to "enforce these settings at startup." You want to check this box so that Juice overrides other applications that may think it is their job to deal with these file types. After checking this box, click the Save button. The Juice application is installed. When you quit the application, it asks if you want to keep it running in the background. Again, with the same caveats about when you may want to disable background downloading, we suggest you leave the application running by checking the Yes radio button. Check the "Don't ask me again" box to avoid this dialog box in the future.

Now let's configure Juice to handle the various formats and tags in which you may find podcasts when surfing the Web, as well as how to store podcasts according to your preferences. Consider, for example, how you might listen to a series of short program, say of two to five minutes in length, compared to longer shows. Saving several short programs and listening to them in a single sitting makes sense for some listeners, but if your podcatcher is configured to toss programs after 14 or 21 days, you may not have more than one stored at any time. On the other hand, if you fall behind on listening to a longer show, perhaps a daily one-hour program from National Public Radio, having the podcatcher dump older programs so that you can get caught up is a good plan.

Setting Juice to regularly check subscriptions is what makes the podcatcher work when you are away. Click the Scheduler button (it looks like a clock and calendar) to open the Scheduler, shown in Figure 3.6. Juice can visit servers up to three times a day, at times you specify, or on a regular interval of between 12 hours and every 30 minutes. It's probably best to have the podcatcher working at night, when you aren't using the computer. Like e-mail, podcasts can take up your whole day if you don't limit how often new ones show up on your system. However, if you know your favorite podcasters are updating their shows at certain times of the day, setting the podcatcher to check shortly after those times can keep you up-to-the-moment.

FIGURE 3.6

Juice can be set to check podcast subscriptions several times a day at specific times or on a regular basis.

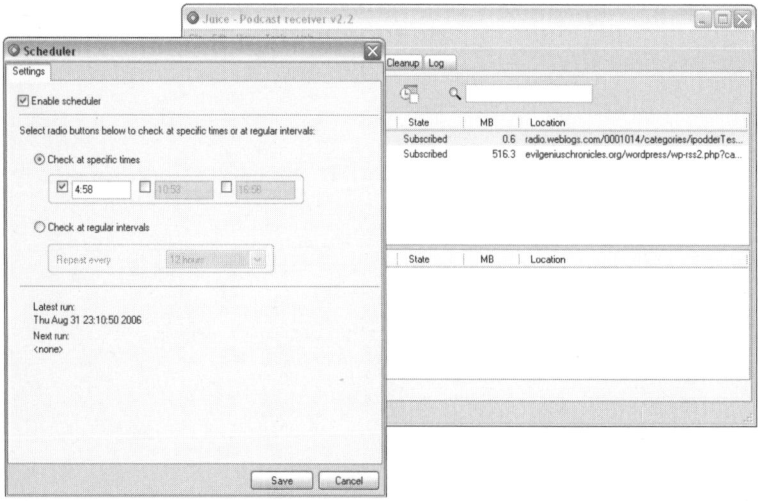

Next, select the General pane in the Preferences panel, shown in Figure 3.7, which covers the general behavior of the application. Juice should be left running in the background so it can continue to check for new podcasts when you aren't using it. The other important preference is the fifth box from the top, "Catchup skips older episodes permanently," which skips ahead of programs in your downloaded shows list without erasing them so you can hear the most recent podcast. You'll need to go back to play skipped shows manually, as Juice will ignore them in the future.

We don't suggest selecting the box for "Play downloads right after they're downloaded," because the podcatcher then counts them as played when looking for most recent *unplayed* programs. Click the Save button. You can tell Juice how long to hold onto files on a per-subscription basis, which we cover later.

Finally, select what media player you want to use when listening to a podcast. In Figure 3.8, we've moved to the Player pane of the Juice Preferences, where the media players available are listed by the application. We've selected Windows Media Player, but you can choose your favorite and Juice hands files automatically to it for playback or synchronization with a portable player.

FIGURE 3.7

The General preferences in Juice let you keep the application running so it can continue looking for new podcasts on a regular schedule.

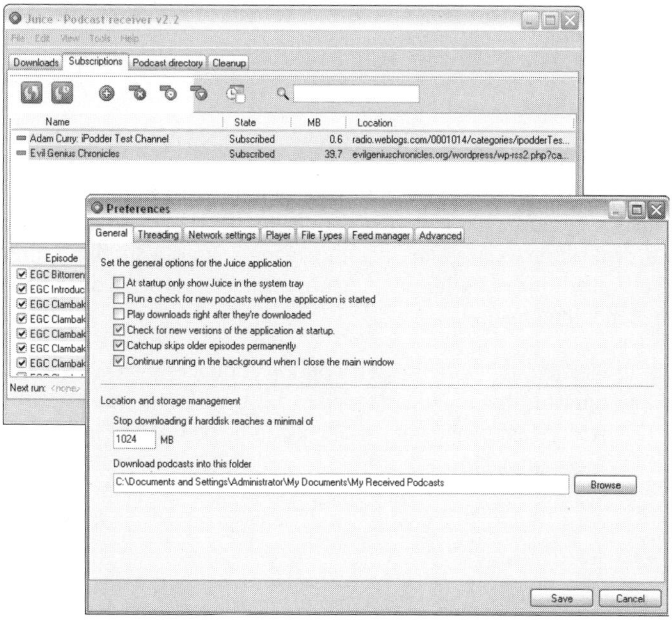

The Player pane in Juice Preferences, where a media player is associated with the podcatcher

Two player-specific options are displayed here, as well.

When passing files to iTunes, Juice can label the file as a custom genre, which iTunes uses to sort programs. By default, it hands files to iTunes as a "Podcast," but you could use something else, such as "News" if you use more than one podcatcher to segregate different types of programs. For example, you could use Juice to download news programs, passing them to iTunes with that genre label and find a folder on your iPod called "News," while a different podcatcher downloaded your music podcasts and loaded them in a different genre.

With Winamp, a Windows media application, the option is "Play button enqueues selected track." "Enqueues" isn't actually a word, but it means that the file is added to a list of files to play according to a last-in-last-played basis. If other files are playing or are queued to be played, the latest file goes to the end of the line.

Downloading and Installing a Macintosh Podcatcher

Before we get into using the Juice application, let's cover how to download and install a podcatcher on Mac OS X. If you have OS X, you already have Apple's podcatcher, which is built into iTunes. If for some reason iTunes isn't on your Mac, here are the steps to get and install it:

1. Open your browser, and type http://www.apple.com/itunes/ into the address field. This takes you to the Apple iTunes and iPod home page. Apple changes the design of this page frequently, but you usually see the iTunes software prominently displayed. Click the Download button in the iTunes promotion. If you can't find the iTunes download link in the main body of the page, look for the Download button in the blue bar at the top of the page below the tabs, which takes you to the iTunes download page.

2. On the iTunes download page, you can choose which version of the software you want. The Mac version is the default choice, because, we presume, you are using a Macintosh for this process. You don't need to give your e-mail address; just click the Download iTunes — Free button.

3. As the file begins to download, your browser proceeds to an Apple-hosted page that encourages you to spend lots of money in the future. Ignore this for now. If you are running Safari, Apple's browser, a dialog box opens warning you that the file contains an application. Click the Continue button. The file finishes downloading, decompresses, and appears in a volume on your desktop called iTunes with the current version number of the application. It contains two files: the installer, which is called iTunes.mpkg, and "Before You Install iTunes.app."

4. iTunes.mpkg is a Mac-specific UNIX installer file represented by an icon of a box with a cube flying out. Double-click this icon, brazenly ignoring the read-before-you-install file, which explains that if you want to use iTunes to listen to audio files, it is compatible with Mac OS X versions later than 10.2.8, and if you want to watch video files, you must be running Mac OS X 10.4.2 or later.

5. The iTunes installer opens, offering a dialog box explaining that it must check the software before it can be installed on your Mac. You must let this run, so click Continue. It takes a moment to complete the review of the operating system and hardware before displaying the welcome message. Again, click Continue.

6. iTunes is a carefully protected application. Apple has threatened to pull out of countries, such as France, that have demanded the security features of the iTunes application be revealed. Unlike Juice, the Windows application we installed in the previous section, the license for iTunes, which is part of the About iTunes dialog box, is restrictive and can include notices about how Apple or recording companies may prosecute people who use it to pirate copyrighted material.

7. After you click the Continue button, which you do twice to get through the About iTunes dialog boxes, if you do not scroll through the full body of the license text, you are presented with a dialog box that insists you agree to the terms of the license. By clicking Agree, you continue the installation. Clicking Disagree closes the installer.

8. The next dialog box presents you a choice, or lack thereof, about where to install iTunes. Because the application must reside on the startup volume of the computer, the installer selects your boot disc by default — represented by a big green arrow — and you cannot change it. This dialog box exists solely to keep you oriented to where the software is installed. Click Continue.

9. An Installation Type window opens, offering the ability to select the Easy Install, which puts all the components of the application on the hard drive, or a Customize option that allows you to select which features you want to use. Components you may need are highlighted. This choice is really only necessary if you have not previously installed an iPod driver for some versions of OS X or if you have an iTunes-compatible mobile phone. For almost everyone, except those who have purchased one of the early and poorly received Motorola handsets that play music, the button to choose is Easy Install. Click Install. Depending upon which version of OS X you are using, a dialog box may ask if it is okay to restart the computer after installation; if so, click Continue Installation.

10. The application installs, and that's it. iTunes can be set as your default media player for podcasts, even if you use other applications to gather subscriptions. For example, in the popular news aggregator, NetNewsWire (`http://www.newsgator.com/NGOLProduct.aspx?ProdID=NetNewsWire`), preferences allow you to set the application to hand files directly to iTunes for playback. If you need to restart, the installer tells you it's necessary, and you click Restart. Otherwise, you can close the installer and get started with finding your first podcast.

Subscribing to Your First Podcast in Juice

A number of podcast indices list popular podcasts, and most podcatchers come with a list of shows, but let's imagine that those don't exist and look at how to find a podcast on a site you're visiting. Some of the best programs you can find are ones you stumble across when reading, whether it's discovering the *Nature* podcast published by the eponymous British journal of science or a quirky individual podcast like Dave Slusher's *Evil Genius Chronicles*.

Finding the feed for a podcast when visiting a Web site can be difficult, because there is no standard way of announcing that a feed is available. Some sites deliver podcasts as part of their regular blog feed while others have dedicated podcast feeds. These services may be represented by an orange "RSS" tag, the closest thing to a standard user interface for subscribing to RSS feeds, but others may have a button or text link that says "podcast" or "Subscribe." As you can see in Figure 3.9, the Evil Genius Chronicles site has several different ways of subscribing, as well as links to individual shows in the text of Dave Slusher's blog. It demonstrates in how many different locations you may find a feed or links to individual shows.

Podcast feeds are often displayed in several places on a site, and sometimes it's hard to distinguish those feeds from regular RSS and links to individual programs.

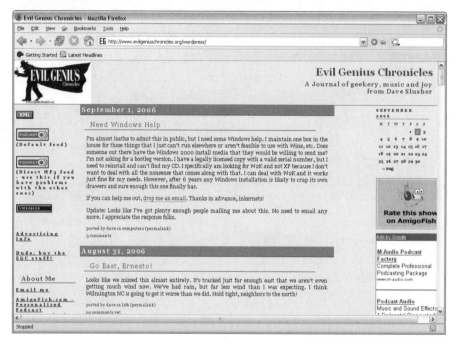

Slusher's RSS feed, which is linked to the orange XML button at the upper left of the page, includes his podcasts and written blog postings. If you want only his programs, that link is beneath the XML button, indicated by the Podcast button. But wait, there's another Podcast button immediately below that, which provides an additional feed in case the others fail. That's overkill, but in a technological world one must expect to experience some failures. You need only subscribe to one of those feeds. If you subscribe to more, your podcatcher downloads multiple copies of each show.

As explained previously, your podcatcher can be configured to add subscriptions automatically, but not all feeds should be handled this way, because text and audio RSS files may need to be passed to different applications. We subscribe manually to his feed following these steps:

1. Right-click the orange XML button to open the pop-up menu for your browser to copy the URI of the podcast feed. If you are using Firefox, select the Copy Link Location command in the pop-up menu as shown in Figure 3.10; if you are using Internet Explorer, select the Copy Shortcut command.

FIGURE 3.10

Copy the location of the RSS feed.

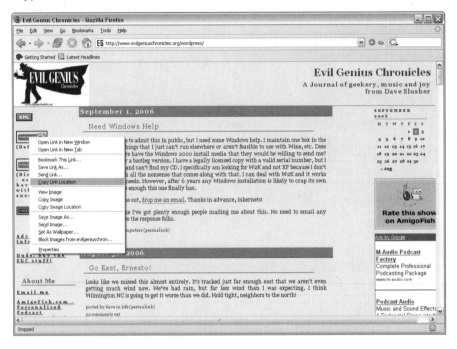

2. Now open Juice and click the Add new feed button, the green circle with a white plus sign in the center. A dialog box titled *Add a Feed* opens, as shown in Figure 3.11. Paste the URI you just copied into the URL field in the General tab of the dialog box. You don't need to add a title; Juice picks up the name of the show from the feed and fills in the Title field.

FIGURE 3.11

Subscribe to a podcast in Juice; just paste the feed address into the URL field.

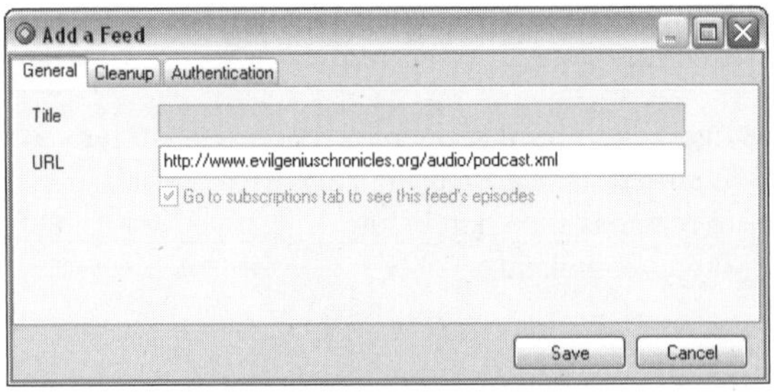

3. Don't close the Add a Feed dialog box. Click the Cleanup tab, where you can configure Juice to delete shows that are older than a number of days you choose. For purposes of this explanation, we're checking the box here to enable deleting of episodes older than 14 days, as shown in Figure 3.12. This prevents your podcatcher from filling your hard drive with podcasts, not to mention that it puts pressure on you to listen to shows before they are tossed out. Some shows may be worth saving longer. Click the Save button.

FIGURE 3.12

Check the cleanup preferences for each podcast. Some you'll want to keep longer than others.

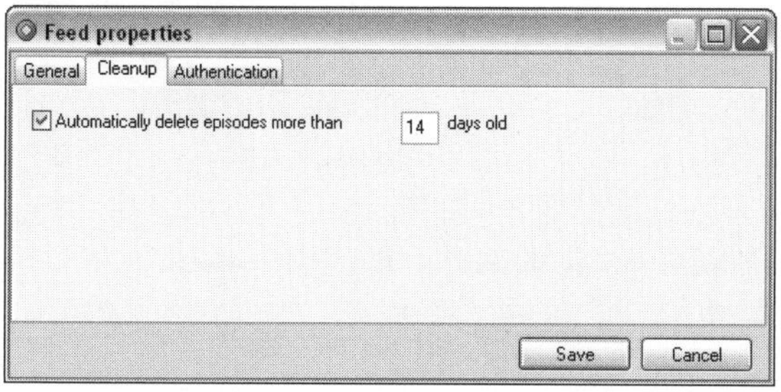

4. Juice immediately checks the RSS feed for programs that are available; it doesn't begin downloading old shows. Click the name of the feed in the main window of Juice to see a list of shows that can be downloaded. Congratulations, you've subscribed to your first podcast.

5. Don't be satisfied with titles alone when you are deciding what to listen to for the first time. Podcasters usually include show notes that describe the guests, the topics discussed, and any music that may be included. This is passed along as part of the RSS feed, in metadata that can be viewed by clicking the title in Juice, as shown in Figure 3.13.

6. When you find what you want, click the green arrow beside title or click the tile and select the "Play episode in..." option. Juice passes the file, in this case to Windows Media Player, and it begins to play.

To get more information about a particular show, click the title and select Show Notes to see what the producer has to say about who's on or what music is playing.

Subscribing to Your First Podcast in iTunes

iTunes' interface is basically the same in Macintosh and Windows, though here we're going to walk through the subscription process in the Mac version. Again, let's assume that you've got an RSS reader that typically handles your RSS subscriptions, so we've copied the URL of the XML file used by CNET's *Buzz Out Loud* podcast RSS feed. Now, open iTunes and click the Advanced menu, where the second option is Subscribe to Podcast.

1. Select the Subscribe to Podcast... option in the Advanced menu, which opens a dialog box where you paste the URL of the podcast RSS feed of the program. When you click OK in this dialog box, iTunes queries the server and retrieves a list of available shows. It downloads only the last podcast immediately, leaving the rest for your review and, if you like, downloading. iTunes also continues to check the server on a regular schedule for new shows, downloading new programs as they are released.

2. iTunes doesn't display lots of information about each show, so you can Ctrl+click (with a one-button mouse) or right-click (with a three-button mouse) the title and select Show Description to read show notes, which include guest lists, topics discussed, and songs played on the program.

3. If you select Get Info, you get a much more complete view of the metadata for the pod-cast and individual shows, including the show logo, encoding format, bit rate, sample rate, and so forth. Click the Info pane in the Get Info dialog box to see the show notes.

4. To play a podcast, double-click the title in the iTunes library.

Portable and CD Playback

Podcasting wouldn't be what it is without the iPod and other portable devices that let people replace their radios with self-scheduled programming. One of the reasons Apple's iTunes has succeeded to the degree it has is its early integration of podcast subscriptions and the fact that it is not only the default music library for any iPod user, but also the only step between subscription and portability needed. With other portable players, there's a bit of jury-rigging to connect the podcatcher to the device, though you also get more flexibility, as well, because you can mix and match different features.

The forgotten option for many, however, is burning a CD so that you retain a permanent copy of programs that play in many legacy audio systems, notably the dashboard CD players of so many vehicles. All the major media players handle this conveniently. Windows Media Player and iTunes, for example, make it easy to build a playlist by selecting podcasts. Just burn and go.

Where to Find Podcasts

You'll run across podcasts all over the Web on blogs and sites you already visit, but seeing shows organized by category or using social tags, which listeners use to collaboratively categorize podcasts and identify popular programming, can help you find your way to intriguing new podcasts. A number of sites collect all or most of the podcasts on the Net. Here's a selection of some we find especially useful:

- **iTunes:** Despite many criticisms, iTunes has mastered the integration of podcasting—audio and video podcasting—with commercial services. http://www.apple.com/itunes/

- **Podcast.net:** A kind of Yahoo! directory of podcasts, Podcast.net uses tagging to identify topics along with categorization of the programming. The site provides an online player, so it keeps you within its borders rather than making you subscribe using your own podcatcher. http://www.podcast.net/

- **Odeo:** Besides being a broad index of everything podcast, Odeo is a self-serve podcast production system that lets people produce their own podcasts. We like the listener-authored reviews and use of social tags, which help expose interesting programming. Odeo has an embedded online podcast player, but it doesn't provide easy access to subscription URLs. Rather, it keeps people within the Odeo world. http://www.odeo.com/

- **Yahoo! Podcasts:** Hey, it's commercial, from Yahoo!, but it's comprehensive and there are real people doing some discovery of new and interesting stuff, as a magazine editor does when he tells you what he likes. Subscription links are available from the site. http://podcasts.yahoo.com/

- **Podcast Alley:** Created by Chris McIntyre and no one else, the site is largely the work of podcasters who want to get more attention for their shows, but it also does a fine job of tracking what's popular and what's changed recently by genre or a specific title. Subscription links are provided so that they can be pasted directly into an aggregator. http://www.podcastalley.com/

- **Podcasting News:** Another wide-ranging directory, though it takes some effort to get through all the listings under each category. But you get direct links to browse recent shows or to subscribe. Lots of good listener ratings. `http://www.podcastingnews.com/`

- **NPR Podcast Directory:** While the programming choices are limited, this is a great guide to the public radio podcasts from all over the United States. From individual segments from Morning Edition and other NPR shows in a daily best-of collection to local issues shows, this is where to look. `http://www.npr.org/podcasts`

- **Melodeo:** A recent entrant in the business, Melodeo is a combination of podcast directory and social network. It combines commercial and "amateur" podcasts with discussion by members, rankings, and a nifty interface that delivers most of its information through pop-ups within the page that let you navigate to forums where people are talking. The system also bundles and delivers podcasts to some mobile phones as streams (you need a very generous data plan to make this affordable). `http://www.melodeo.com/`

- **Audible Wordcast:** Another relatively new player, Wordcast blends the fee and free subscriptions offered by Audible and others into a single resource where you can find amateur and "professional" podcasts from the New York Times, Ricky Gervais, and many others. `http://wordcast.audible.com/`

Searching Podcasts

In stark contrast to text documents, which are easily searched — Google just looks for words in documents, after all — podcasts are difficult to search because they must be transcribed by man or machine first and then searched. The science of transcription is young and, based on our experience with companies claiming to search audio and video, partially an act of smoke and mirrors. Most of the search tools we've reviewed look only in metadata — the text associated with a podcast — rather than searching the content of programs. In many cases, people who are as inexact or error-prone as machines are involved at some point, and almost always there is a very spotty result. As computational power increases, this will improve. These are the major players:

- **PodScope:** This site searches both audio and video on the Web, mostly podcasts. Our results showed very poor results, where, for example, a search for Microsoft Vista (without quotes) yielded only three results while a search for "Vista" returned dozens of results, many referring to Microsoft. Some unique neologisms from podcasts, such as "Ninternship" from the popular *Ask A Ninja* podcast, were not found at all. `http://www.podscope.com/`

- **PodZinger:** A much more complete index, PodZinger is offered by BBN Technologies, a commercial provider with a long history. It purports to search almost 300,000 podcasts at this writing and returns much more complete results for common words, like Microsoft Vista and Vista — more than 1,000 each — while failing to find unique words, such as Ninternship. `http://www.podzinger.com/`

- **Pod Razor:** The service is obviously using metadata describing shows rather than transcribing the shows themselves before searching. `http://www.podrazor.com/`

- **AOL Search Podcast Beta:** This has all the hallmarks of beta software, but the results are impressive, if sparse, because they return results from within the body of shows. Keep your eye on this one. `http://podcast.search.aol.com/`

- **Digital Podcast:** An interesting effort in podcast search, we found the results poor, but the excerpts of programs displayed were more comprehensive than many other search providers delivered, even if there were lots of extraneous characters in the results indicating imperfect machine translation. `http://www.digitalpodcast.com/`

Summary

Now you're listening to podcasts and ready to get into production. You're getting into the really fun part of podcasting — podcatching! This chapter covered the following topics:

- Podcasting is really a mechanism for capturing the address of an XML file describing available programs, scheduling times to check for new shows, and downloading those files to your computer or through your computer to a portable device.

- Podcatchers are a type of application initially developed to provide podcast subscribers an easy way to keep up on new programs. The functionality of the podcatcher is now built into a wide range of applications. By the middle of 2007, it will be a feature of several operating systems.

- The podcatcher you choose should be compatible with the media player you use to listen to music and to synch to a portable device, such as an iPod, because it simplifies your self-scheduled listening.

- Don't make your podcatcher the default application for all RSS feeds, unless you never intend to subscribe to text-based feeds. By leaving podcast feeds to manual subscription processes, you make your text subscriptions easier, and this changes as applications and operating systems become more aware of the distinctions between file types in RSS feeds.

- When installing a podcatcher on a Windows system, be sure you associate it with the media player you use for other purposes. For example, if you use Real Media Player or Winamp, third-party media players, the podcatcher may not be able to recognize that is the default application you want, so tell it during installation.

- Consider using the custom labeling capability in your podcatcher to create special categories of audio in your audio library, such as "News" or "Business Training." It makes browsing for news or work-related audio easier on a portable player.

- Set your podcatcher's preferences for retaining copies of files on a per-show basis, so you can assemble libraries of shows you'd like to keep or enjoy listening to several episodes at a time.

- With iTunes on Macintosh, you don't need a separate podcatcher application, but you can use another podcatcher to segregate feeds into special categories.

- Don't assume that a podcast needs an iPod or other portable player, because you can burn them to a CD and listen on legacy audio equipment, like the CD player in your car.

- The number of podcast directories grows every month, so start with our list and look around for sites that does a good job of discovering what you like. It's your schedule, so listen to people who like what you do to discover hidden podcast gems.

- Audio and video search is still a very rudimentary technology, but some sites do a good job of finding nuggets of information that are not described in show notes. Keep an eye on this category of directory, because soon you will be able to find programs based on ad hoc and scheduled searches by keyword.

Part II

Podcasting Production

Chapter 4

Defining Your Podcast

The reason you podcast and the audience you podcast to are the factors that determine the answers to a number of questions about how to configure your production and distribution systems. Because podcasting can be an intensely personal medium, podcasts can be developed to serve one person or one million people. The choice is yours, and your decisions will set some boundaries around your efforts, because some formats don't stretch easily to accommodate different audiences.

The size of your audience and your reasons for wanting to reach them raise incontrovertible questions of economics. We take a look at the various approaches to hosting a podcast from the economic perspective — in later chapters you learn about the *how* of those hosting strategies — so that you can decide if the effort will be worthwhile.

Finally, we turn to the question of format. Do you want to be Oprah, hosting a conversation that engages the audience, or are you more in the story-telling mold of *This American Life*? Maybe you want to unleash your inner disc jockey? The format you choose creates expectations in the audience, so you need to think carefully about the approach you take to the beginning, middle, and end, and all the talk or music in between.

The basic message: Think before you jump.

It's All About Your Passion — No, It's Not

"Passion" is overrated because it is hard to sustain. Producing a program daily, weekly, or monthly takes discipline too. But if you don't care deeply about what you're doing, it dulls the sound of the podcast. If you clearly labor to get excited about your topic, your audience hears it and turns away. No one wants to listen to or watch someone struggling to care about what they are saying. That's why passion is the first criterion to look for in your choice of a topic.

So start by asking what you care about. What comes to mind every day? Does something wake you up at night? When reading the news, do you make sure you visit a certain topic first? If you didn't start with an idea that was self-evident, you can ask these questions to narrow the potential list of podcast topics to the things to which you can bring real passion on an ongoing basis. If you can't keep up the passion, there's nothing to subscribe to, and hence no podcast.

If you're thinking of producing a podcast as a business, you may want to begin with something that you can share with a few people with whom you want to keep in touch, whether family, friends, or colleagues. Perhaps you have been recording interviews with your grandparents, parents, aunts, or uncles about family history; taking that raw material and turning it into a subscription program for your family would be excellent practice and a starting point for learning the ins and outs of producing a podcast from raw recording through distribution. Already a production pro? Then, we're back to the same question: What do you care about? Let's walk through an exercise in choosing your podcast topic.

Making your choices

Get out a piece of paper. You need about 10 minutes today and 15 minutes tomorrow to complete this exercise. Really, if you just wait a day or two between the phases of this exercise, you'll get a much better program by following this process:

1. Make three columns on the page. Place a heading for the left column, "Topics," and call the middle column "What I can add."

2. Under "Topics," write down five things you think about every day, whether it's a hobby, your business, sports, politics, or something you argue with friends about frequently and energetically — things people enjoy talking with you about. Don't take too long, just a couple minutes. What wakes you up? Are you worried about finances, the state of your relationships? What gets you going?

3. Now, under "What I can add," write the ideas you've had about each of your topics in the past couple of days. These could be your "original notions" about the topic, such as a theory that the Red Sox consistently under-invest in third basemen, that there are three regions of the world or industries that are ripe for investment by people like you seeking improved returns, or maybe your ideas about how to resolve the political problems in the Middle East. You get the idea; write down what, if you were to do a podcast on that topic today, you would talk about. Got it all on paper? Now, stop. Let it percolate.

4. On day 2, return to your worksheet. Add a title to the third column, "Sound." Have you thought of additional topics? Add them to the Topics column. More importantly, as you went about the intervening day, did you find yourself identifying stories in the news, ideas in your head, or things people said to you in conversation that you'd like to have recorded for a podcast? Write these under "Sound" for each of the topics. Seriously, are you already looking for audio as a natural part of your day? That's the producer's habit that we're looking to cultivate, starting with this list. Finally, write down the ideas you'd add about each of the topics or the sound you'd record; that's the raw material of your own comments.

After the second visit, your list probably looks somewhat lopsided. Some of the ideas you had yesterday yielded little or nothing, because they aren't sustainable topics. This is the problem with picking a topic: Unless you genuinely engage with the subject, you'll quickly find yourself experiencing burn-out. Don't be one of the people who launch two or three podcasts on a whim and then fade away. You may want to repeat the exercise for a few days; this is an approach we've used with programs created for a news network staffed by young journalists who needed to work through the difference between what they could talk about and what they really wanted to talk about day-in and day-out on a regular program.

Of the topics you've identified, which produced the most notes? Take a look at the environment for that topic. Begin by doing searches on news and search sites for articles that relate to the topic. You're looking here for how much material you can expect to draw from. Whether you're doing topical political humor or investing ideas, you need fresh material to write about. If the topic doesn't present you with enough subjects to talk about as frequently as you hope to produce, then you need to look again at the list and combine topics or find another more fruitful one.

This exercise also forces you to begin the process of producing the show on paper, making you test your resolve about the topic and the frequency with which you can expect to deliver programs. Even if there is lots of material, you may not find all of it particularly interesting to talk about, so you must start to think through what you're going to do with outside information, especially how you're going to link it to the ideas you want to add — after all, it's your head that people will want to tune into. Make sure you're offering a podcast that accesses the busier parts of your brain. You can discuss your ideas about phenomenology, a branch of philosophy, or global warming, as long as you know you'll be productive and engaging.

Look, if you're contemplating a show for your family, they'll probably want to listen just to hear you. Your family loves you, or at least we hope they do. But if you want to earn the attention of an audience — whether they're your customers or complete strangers — for a long time to come, these are serious questions to ask yourself. Some labor now will save you from totally retooling the show after launch.

Finally, how often should one produce? That answer depends very much on the format and topic you choose. For example, doing news commentary once a week will not keep up with the pace of events, so you'll have difficulty convincing listeners you are timely. Daily may be your only option, unless you decide to focus on some aspect of the news that can be wrapped and summarized less often, such as *The Week in Advertising* or *This Week's Seattle Mariners Moves*. A show about history or math, however, that goes into detail about events or concepts can be a weekly or monthly program that is listened to repeatedly in order to get the most out of it.

Frequency is up to you, although you should avoid the temptation to over-deliver. People may not be able to keep up with your production schedule and feel they are falling behind if, at first, you offer a program a day (music programming, where there is no narrative to lose track of, can be daily from the get-go). It's probably best to start with a less frequent production, gather feedback from your listeners, and then decide about increasing how often you deliver new shows. That way, you will not find yourself backing off an original and overly ambitious promise to offer a daily show when it's not what is needed. Or, think of it this way: It is better to add shows — it's like increasing the value — than justify producing less.

CROSS-REF If you're considering using music in your podcast, see Chapter 23. It's less expensive than you may think to do a music podcast "legally," replicating the format of a radio station, but with the freedom to play music that's not on the current Top 40 lists.

Why, why, why?

Agent Smith, the viral program who battles the heroic Neo in *The Matrix* trilogy, asked over and over near the end of the last film, "Why? Why, why, why?" Without purpose, what was the point of fighting back, prolonging the pain of life, which Smith believed had no purpose other than to end. We want to create a podcast that isn't going to end any time soon. Neo responded that he fought because he chose to, and you've got to make your choice and stick with it — that's the promise you make to your audience, even if it is your grandmother: "I'll be podcasting every week (or day or month)," so be sure you know why you're doing it.

Now, for lots of people, it's going to be enough that five, ten, or a hundred people start listening to them. They enjoy a huge advantage, because any additional success they may have — bigger audiences, networks calling to offer advertising or a salary, subscribers paying for a show — anything is gravy. That's the spirit that animates much of the podcasting movement. Even a star like Ricky Gervais, who has a hit BBC television series, enjoys the sheer vastness of his podcast audience. It reconfirms his celebrity. But he also had someone paying for the delivery of those shows from the very beginning, so he got to focus only on the positives.

We presume that, if you are reading this book, audio isn't necessarily your first love. Instead, you're probably looking at podcasting as an outlet for your talent or expertise, and you likely have a pretty specific audience in mind. The listeners you're aiming to serve may be customers of your private practice, your company, or a large number of folks out there with whom you believe you can connect, building a loyal audience for your own gratification or profit.

Whatever your motivation, you must set some goals so that, by meeting them, you can keep your enthusiasm up to the challenge of producing regularly. Sure, you could have lots to say, and you'll need to, as we explained a few pages back. But if you can't say to yourself at the end of the first month or first year that you've met the goals you set, your podcast is likely to wither on the vine. That means you have to be fairly mercenary in examining your reasons for starting a podcast. Here are just a few of the reasons you may want to consider, should you ever be confronted by your own Agent Smith, demanding in the middle of the night or as you reach to turn on your microphone, Why? Why, why, why:

- **Gratification:** Okay, you really just want to express yourself, no matter what. You've got something to say. Plenty of people have begun careers as writers, producers, performers, or speakers simply because they felt that if they didn't say it, it would not be said at all. This sense of mission can be incredibly powerful, but even great talents have moments when, after lots of hard work that earned them nothing but rejection or a devoted audience of a few dozen people, they have to justify the effort to themselves. The great ones are the talents who don't give up; thousands of people who do give up go back to their day jobs with renewed vigor instead of giving their talent a full-time shot. We know the great talents because they didn't give up. They found some measure of their progress to satisfy them. In podcasting, those small steps, such as having reached 100, 1,000, or 10,000 subscribers are critical to keeping your creative juices flowing. Getting a podcaster you admire to listen to you and provide feedback may be another option, or finding your first sponsor. It can be small or large, but you need something to keep you going, because the going will not always be easy.

> **NOTE** Seriously, you need motivation to tap now and again. We're going to take lots of time to look at the costs of podcasting. The costs are not just economic. Pouring even a little of yourself into a production that people will listen to and sometimes criticize is hard work. It may be a hobby, but when was the last time your hobby sent a note because you didn't get around to it? The first thing you're going to do is promise an audience you'll deliver something good, something engaging, thought-provoking, or entertaining, and you need to engineer your effort to keep you going first and foremost, because everything else hangs on your ability to produce.

- **Marketing:** A podcast may be the most effective way to engage your customers on a regular basis in your authentic voice. Unlike a blog, which requires very frequent updating — as often as several times a day — to make it a destination, either by browser or RSS reader, podcasts are far more flexible with regard to delivery schedules. And, because it is your voice, the audience is getting something that they cannot find in text, the familiar tones that they came to trust when doing business with you. If you are a doctor, think about offering some updates on medicines each month and put the address of your RSS feed on appointment cards so that people can find out about the program at their convenience. Small businesses that thrive on personal touches can find all sorts of ways to engage, from thoughts on seasonal products and decorating to audio promotions aimed at people who bought the 2005 Camry during a program that discusses next year's models or the cost savings with a hybrid vehicle. With these concrete goals in mind, that is the simple fact that you need and want to engage with an identifiable group of people, you can make tremendous headway while keeping your own energy level high, because you know how many people you want to reach and can count each month to see your progress. Done right, your podcast will be recommended by your customers or patients to their friends, who become highly qualified potential customers. Imagine the day when your customer podcast gets more listeners than you needed to justify the time, and then shoot for having more listeners than you have customers and start looking for a partner to support the new business.

- **Evangelizing:** Marketing leads to sales, evangelism leads to devoted members of the cult of you or your product or service. The evangelical podcast can include insider tips and hints about getting the most out of what you make or sell. It can also become a venue for discussions with customers who are making the most of their purchase. Evangelizing makes fans, so here you want to start looking for evidence that your message is moving beyond the limits of your market, either geographically or in terms of the type of customers who are getting excited about what you do. If you're actually a religious evangelist, you'll know the podcast works when you start receiving notes from listeners in another state, people you'd never have reached before without a massive investment in radio or advertising. With a podcast, your cause can spread through listeners' actions, when they e-mail a friend to tell them to check out what you have to say. So the goal to set — and the action to ask your listeners to take — is to get pass-along or word-of-mouth adoption working to spread your message. This is also the reason a political group or campaign will want to podcast, though the goal in that world is to raise campaign money and, most importantly, to get people to actually vote for the candidate or initiative.

- **Ad/Sponsor Revenue:** If you want to "go pro," beginning to earn part of your living from a podcast, the goals you set must be similar to any entrepreneurial undertaking. You need to get increased exposure and convert listeners into fans so that you can show advertisers that you have not just a passive audience but an engaged and supportive community. Advertisers today don't just want to put a message in front of a group of people and hope that some of them will react. That model went out the window with the World Wide Web and notions of interactive television, where ads are the first step in a sales process that can be tracked and analyzed. For the journeyman podcaster, the simplest actions can be tracked, such as offering a discount on an advertiser's products if the listener visits a specific Web page. These pages, known as "landing pages" in direct marketing lingo, can be associated with your podcast, so that when someone clicks through, the advertiser can associate it with you and count your successful effort to call the listener to action. Even better, if the landing page has an additional call to action, such as a Buy or Learn More button, the advertiser can count how often your listeners take the next step. These metrics allow you to set higher prices, because you can make specific statements about how frequently your promotional audio turns into a lead or sale. Think in terms of goals that can be set based on getting some revenue through the door, such as "Win three sponsors in the first year," and then begin to focus on improving the performance of your ads and promotional messages so that, instead of having to sell more ads, you get more per ad and keep most of the program for what you want to say.

- **Love:** In addition to anything else you may do to justify the time you put into podcasting, the show itself is a kind of gift, something you made with your own voice and hands. Dedicated amateurs may make a program just for their family or a workgroup or division of their company. They add value when they make their show one that has high-quality information and production values; it can become an invaluable resource that, if missed, subtracts from the audience's life. It is like a relationship. It is a relationship, so that's why we call this goal "love." You may not want anything back, but you still want to know how it is working for the audience, so you keep finding the energy and enthusiasm to produce what you do 364, 52, 26, or 12 times a year, which takes some creative juice that has to come from somewhere. There is no easy way to measure this, but you do know you can pick up the phone and hear the fact of your podcast influencing people's lives. Setting up a blog or wiki where listeners can provide their own contributions to the discussion, even hosting an audio feedback line where listeners can record their comments for future shows, are other viable ways to catalyze your continued efforts. No person is an island, so find a way to get sustenance.

The next question follows directly from this one. Now that you have an idea why you want to produce a podcast, can you actually find an audience out there for it?

Is there anybody out there?

You have already done some searching for news and other information about your topic, so you know people are talking about it. That doesn't necessarily mean that enough people are interested in it to justify your expenses and time to produce a show trying to capture their attention. If you want to do something for a small circle of friends, that's another issue, and the only question is whether they'd be interested in getting the program from you. But don't ask them; just send them a link to a sample show, because no one can answer the question "Do you want to hear my show?" honestly. A sample show lets them decide whether to subscribe. If they do, you've got the audience you wanted, and you're on your way. For any commercial venture and many gratification-oriented productions, you need to ask some hard questions of the marketplace to determine if you're setting yourself up for the opportunity to succeed or inevitable failure because the audience will never be large enough to pay back your effort.

Remember that you should know your goals for the show when beginning this process. Now we're talking about economics. We explore how much it actually costs to podcast in Chapter 19; for now, though, take our word for it that if you are paying for your program to be distributed, it will cost about $0.02 per show downloaded just to get the program out the door. Add on top of that any expenditures you need to make to attract the audience you want, and you've only begun to cover your expenses. You still need figure out how to make some money from the resulting program, if that's your goal, or whether you believe the expense will be returned in other forms by the improved communication you have with customers and potential customers.

Let's start with figuring out how big the market for your program may be, using Google AdWords prices as a proxy, because we're also going to need to use AdWords data for figuring out how much it will cost to find new listeners. What we're looking for here is evidence that an audience is out there looking for what you want to talk about. Google graciously makes this information available to advertisers, and because you're thinking of advertising your podcast to build the audience, you qualify.

Follow these steps for researching the audience interest for your podcast:

1. Open your browser, and enter http://adwords.google.com. If you don't have a user account, you need to sign up so you can come back and use the service again as you develop new ideas. It's free until you decide to buy ads, but you're only exploring, not actually buying ads. You should read the AdWords terms and conditions.

2. After you log in as a user, you are asked what kind of AdWords account you want to create. This choice configures the way Google displays data. We suggest that you choose the Standard Edition, because it gives you the ability to create several different ads and planning tools that we're going to look at now. Click Continue.

3. The next page, titled Welcome to AdWords, lets you pick the language your audience speaks and the level of targeting of countries you want to use. For purposes of this explanation, we're going to pick English and "Countries and territories," the highest-level targeting, because we're interested in audience size, not targeting. Click Continue.

4. On the next page, you can choose the countries you want to target. We're going to go with the United States and Canada, because those Canadians are such polite people. Select the countries you want to include in your analysis, click the Add button, and then click Continue.

5. Now we're going to write our ad. The text has nothing to do with the analysis, so you can put anything you want in the fields. However, Google does expect the ad to be viable, so do include a real URL, as you see in Figure 4.1. When you click Continue, Google looks at the content of the site your ad points to and makes suggestions for keywords, which we will likely ignore here.

FIGURE 4.1

Type your ad copy in the fields, and be sure to use a real URL in the Display and Destination URL fields.

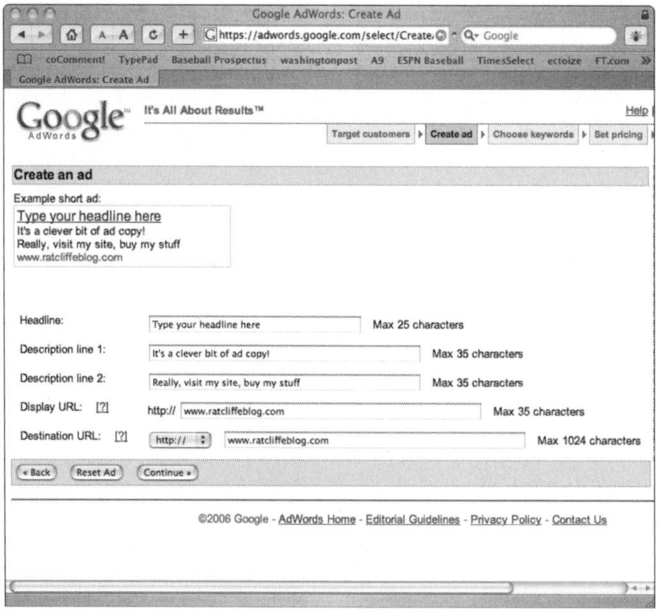

6. Here's the meat of this tool. The page that appears lets you choose your keywords. These are the words that you use to describe your podcast. In our results, Google examined the text on Mitch's personal blog and made some suggestions. If the site you pointed to is about the same topic as your podcast, some of the keywords may be appropriate and you can click the Add button next to those terms to add them to the analysis. Go to the "Want more?" field, and below the suggestions, as shown in Figure 4.2, type the keywords you want to explore. If, for example, you want to do a podcast about sunglasses, type "sunglasses" — keep the keywords general — and click Search.

FIGURE 4.2

Enter the keywords for your analysis in the "Want more?" field.

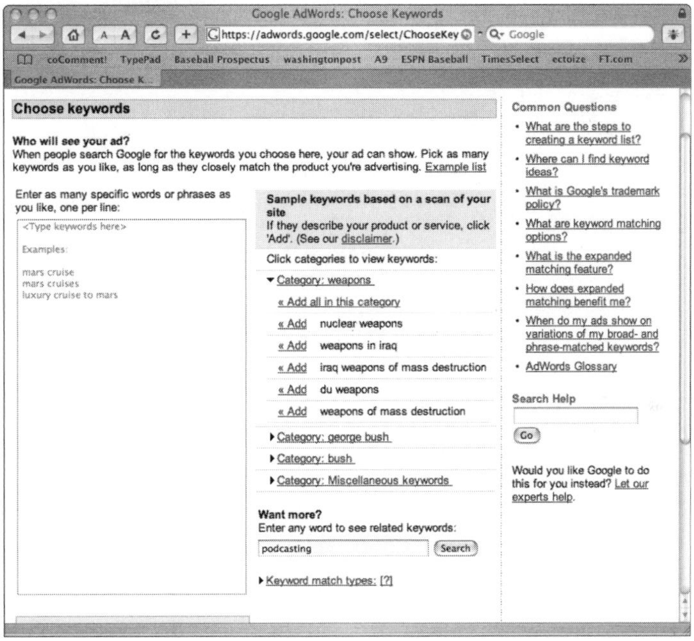

7. If you made a general query, like "sunglasses," the results that come back include broad categories, such as "sunglasses" and "eyeglasses" in addition to keywords for specific sunglass brands, like Oakley and Bollé. That's good. You can narrow the range too much and get the impression that no one is interested in your topic. For example, even when we search on a specific topic, such as "American League pitching," Google does not generate any other keywords and the results are very small. When exploring for audience size, we're interested in finding the larger population that can be mined for subscribers who respond to more specific descriptions, but that's for later.

8. When you click Continue, the next page to appear involves choosing a currency. Ignore that. Look down the page to the link called "View Traffic Estimator," which is a tool for determining how many clicks you may be able to get a day and the cost of those clicks. Click that link, and the window in Figure 4.3 opens.

Google's Traffic Estimator shows the amount of traffic and cost of clicks.

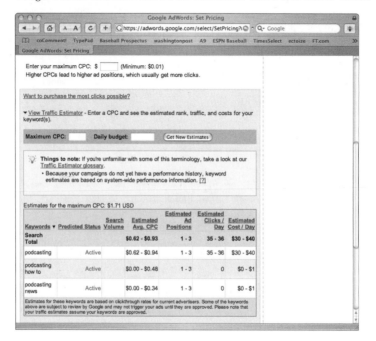

9. In Figure 4.3, you see the results for our search on the keywords "podcasting," "podcasting how to" and "podcasting news." As you can see, these terms garner very little traffic, less than 40 clicks a day, because they are too specific. Even a search for "podcast," which people would presumably enter when searching for a podcast, yields only 199 to 250 clicks a day. It is important to understand, though, that this doesn't mean that only 250 searches are conducted using the term "podcast" each day, rather it represents a percentage of the ads displayed with that term that are clicked by users. Generally, in direct marketing a conversion or click-through rate of one percent is spectacular, so we can assume that there are at least 100 times as many searches as clicks. We can guesstimate from this result that the audience searching for podcast-related information is about 25,000 a day. By contrast, there are between 2,127 and 2,660 clicks per day on ads with the search term "sunglasses," which suggests there are hundreds of thousands of such searches. There is, by the way, no podcast about sunglasses that we could find.

TIP Be very general with your search unless you are looking for a very small audience that you believe is under-served by other programs. It is always easier to reach people who have interests related to your topic than to try to find those with very specific interests. Because marketers pay only for a click on Google ads, you can use the keywords to reach the audience and the text of the ad to get people to click based on their specific interests. This research gives you an idea of the scope of the audience you may be able to attract. Nothing more.

> **10.** The Traffic Estimator has more information. As you can see in Figure 4.3, the average price range of the clicks on the term you searched is displayed in the center column. Advertisers are, at this writing, paying between 62 cents and 94 cents for clicks. At the far right of the table is the Estimated Cost/Day column, which shows you how much, if you were to buy all those clicks, you'd spend each day if you choose to start advertising your podcast. Your numbers will vary. "Sunglasses" clicks cost between $1.71 and $2.43 cents. This is interesting to you as a podcaster, because it gives you an idea of the value of the market you want to serve with your podcast. Today, there's no easy way to find out what advertisers pay for podcast placements, but if Google could set the market for text ads, we assume it could do the same thing with audio advertising.

Now you have an idea about how big an audience may be out there for a podcast about the topic you're considering. You've also got some insight into the value of the market. If you're interested in making money with a podcast, you must pick a topic where advertisers are already spending money, and the more money, the better. Financial services, for example, can generate very high click prices — $3.00 to $50.00 for some services, like mortgage leads — but the quality of your program will be judged against existing very high quality programming. Boating yields click prices of between $1.84 and $2.68, and you won't have lots of boating radio shows to compete with, will you? Remember, too, that you can go back in the Google AdWords system to pick locally targeted ads, which can produce higher prices per click because of the higher likelihood the audience will take action. If your topic is intensely local, Google AdWords has information that you can use to estimate your audience size and potential revenue.

Addressing your audience

The last thing to think about as you conceive a podcast is the approach you will take to your audience. For a personal podcast aimed at family and friends, your relationship with the listener is obvious. You are friends already. Maybe you are coworkers. In any case, you know the way you present yourself to those people with whom you choose to share the podcast. When your audience expands beyond your acquaintances, you have to make some choices about how to portray yourself. We're pretty sure that this is a social behavior that will become incredibly ornate during the next century as people adopt multiple online personae, but today it is still somewhat unnatural for most people to think about their stage presence and the message they want to send through their interaction.

Radio and television talk at their audience. The innovation of talk radio was that the audience could talk back, and as a result talk jocks acted as facilitators of discussion between members of the audience. Okay, they actually instigate arguments. Nevertheless, talk jocks started to build followings, communities that not only listened to the show (remember that less that five percent of listeners ever become callers), but they also bought books and attended conferences where they could meet the on-air personalities.

Podcasting does something different, or at least it *can*. What radio and television did was address a market, but podcasting has the capacity to build a community and to some degree get out of the way of the discussion by including features that allow listeners to call and record or upload audio to contribute their thoughts. It may be possible to do this without all the bluster we're used to in radio and television. Those media, tuned to big audiences, have to make a real stir to get the audience riled up. Podcasts could be the conduit through which a community communicates, if you, the producer, handle it right.

When you're thinking about your program, imagine what it would be like to not be the star. This may go against the grain and, from an addressing-a-market perspective, may not make sense for a commercial venture, because advertisers buy time from, and want to be associated with, stars. A community, on the other hand, decides to support itself. It could be sustained by contributions. The essential ingredient for community is contribution of more than money, and sound may be the most engaging thing for members to throw over the wall to you.

And people who give you audio also may want to ensure that audio is produced and distributed. You can meld community to commercial efforts, but it hasn't been systematized and may never be because the talent-audience relationship varies from program to program.

In any case, if you have a strong sense of how you want to talk to or with your audience, you will be in a far better position to speak with confidence the first time you turn on the microphone. Give it some thought.

Your relationship with your audience will take you a long way toward defining the format of your show.

Formats: The shape of your podcast

You should be thinking of inventing something completely new; after all, we're talking about your show, not Jay Leno's, not Anthony Robbins' infomercials, not Howard Stern's morning *schtick*. There are, however, familiar formats that you can use to give your audience a clear indication of what you intend to deliver each time they press the Play button.

Formats, like genres in literature, convey lots of information. A short story promises to provide some conflict or quandary and its resolution in a given number of pages, while a novel is more contemplative, or at least longer, and usually involves more characters. A podcast is not a radio program or a newspaper read aloud. It can draw from any of the following formats:

- **News:** The newsreader is one of the most familiar sounds and sights in our lives. They take news stories reduced for the time available and read them. If you can get a script from a local news radio or television station, you'll find they aren't written like news stories you read in the newspaper. The scripts are telegraphic. Short sentences summarize rather than explain events. Stories have "hooks," a lead sentence that catches the attention, such as "Fear strikes a local neighborhood!" Then a brief explanation of what happened follows, and if a reporter is in the field, a "throw" introduces him and segues to the reporter's air-time. The problem here is that this format has become so truncated on many networks that you never get anything but the lead; the summary is good enough to startle the audience and nothing more. You can exploit this format, providing much more than the audience expects with additional detail and information. It's also very easy to make the mistake of editorializing, or adding your own opinion, which changes your news into something else. Keep your audience's trust. If you promise them news, give them news.

> **TIP** Journalistic ethics come with the claim you're delivering news. They also buy you some of the protections of journalists, who enjoy privileges such as the ability to keep sources confidential and the right to publish (if they are taken to court). Doing the news doesn't mean that you don't have any insight into events — you can add your impression of events and what you think inspired them — but you have to constantly ask yourself if you really are getting all the information your audience needs. You are working for your audience, offering to become their eyes, ears, and other senses at important events.

- **Opinion (Open Crossfire!):** After facts, opinion took over television and radio news. Most news programs today include a heavy dose of opinion. In the worst form, it's intended to activate responses in different parts of the audience by appealing to and confirming their assumptions and prejudices, all the while offering that pandering as "opinion." Nevertheless, opinion can be offered respectfully and constructively by broadcasters and podcasters who build arguments based on solid information and make a rational case for the position they advocate. Hearing lots of people arguing intelligently and with respect for other opinions would be great, but because people tend to mimic success, you will certainly see plenty of ideological ranting that looks like "opinion" programs on CNN or Fox Network News. We hope you do the right thing.

- **Magazine:** A magazine show combines news, opinion, and "feature" reports that are like the longer stories you hear on National Public Radio or read in a national magazine. These types of shows depend on your ability to act as an editor, picking and choosing the parts that make a great listening or watching experience. Magazine shows are typically longer, presenting more opportunities for ad or sponsor messages. They are also much more expensive to produce, because having many voices requires lots of coordination. That said, this is a very attractive format for the kind of community-building show that organizes and blends the voices of members.

- **Essay/Short story:** Stories have full arcs of action, with beginnings and ends. So, too, do essays. Either format will be familiar to you, though both require some experience and training in composing the text you'll read. Reading the words of others is more straightforward, but be sure to clear the rights to the text or you may hear from lawyers. Environmental sound can play an important role in these programs, filling in audio gaps that would have to be described in text. These programs can be as short as a minute or as long as an hour, delivering a complete thought or narrative and nothing more. They can also be excellent parts of a magazine show.

- **Audioblog:** Audioblogging developed as an interim step between webcasting and podcasting. It still retains an essential element that you won't find in most professionally produced programs: an absolutely riveting immediacy. Sound can be collected by telephone or grabbed from other sources and mixed to make a brief, compelling point. The different between the audioblog and the essay is similar to what distinguishes the blog from a news story; it takes a compelling slice and puts it out there for the audience to judge itself. Again, this format is a good component of the magazine format.

■ **Roundtable:** Conversations can be interesting. Realistically, not all conversations are compelling. Your job as the producer is to pick the participants and moderate the discussion to get the best from all involved. That doesn't mean you're trying to let everyone win the argument, but that you make sure the discussion is complete and everybody gets their say. Now, in some situations, not giving someone a fair say will work with your audience, who may enjoy, say, hearing a neo-Nazi shut down. Setup for these recordings can be complicated, because you'll need multiple mics and a multi-channel mixer to do the conversation in person or a way of taking several calls simultaneously and mixing them.

CROSS-REF See Chapter 5 for information about the mics and mixers needed for a roundtable event, as well as the tools for taking calls by phone or over the Internet.

■ **Event Coverage:** Plenty of live events in the world go completely uncovered. From industry events to professional training, the world is full of free information being talked through every day. Getting permission to record is your first challenge, because many conference producers are greedy enough to think that they should be paid for your coverage. In reality, being in the audience at these events is much more about the networking opportunity, and recordings can be powerful recruiting tools for future versions of the physical meeting. Besides professional events, lots of news and debate is left unreported, lots that is easily identified in advance so that you can do a recording setup and capture the sound or video. Editing these events can be difficult if you don't have control of the audio setup, because sound can be garbled or fail completely. Getting the sound is only the first step, because you can use your coverage to win listeners. Amazingly, many people will listen to an event just because they were there.

■ **Serialized Programs (Back to the cliffhanger):** We haven't seen much drama in podcast programming, but the format is ripe for this medium. People *subscribe*, so you need to catch their attention only with a single episode to get them to subscribe. If you can write a script and capture performances that convince listeners that Indy and Marion are about to take the wheels off their airplane as the episode concludes, they are likely to subscribe to hear the rest of the story. Episodic drama is actually a proven format for young media; it worked for radio, film, and television, so there's every reason to suspect it will work for podcasting.

■ **Readings and Theatrical Performance:** You may have a favorite poet or author. Have you ever considered calling him to see if he has some work he'd like to record? How about local theater groups whose work you appreciate? Besides dealing with egos, you have to be attentive to the challenge of capturing sound performed by someone who doesn't understand how a microphone works, but with a little patience you can get something really special. The program can be serialized and be part of a magazine program, as well. For theatrical work, be ready with multi-microphone recording and the ability to mix creatively. Consider supplementing spoken performances with environmental sound. Get creative.

■ **SoundSeeing Guides:** Museums, historical sites, and many other significant locations are "unrecorded" events. The SoundSeeing guide is a spoken tour of a place or event that requires explanation. An excellent professional services business for a budding podcaster could be providing walk-through tours of a trade show; all you need to know is the location of booths and descriptions of the products the companies are spotlighting. You can charge the conference producer, but it would be much better to charge the companies themselves, who are already paying for their appearance at the event. Museums have permanent and temporary collections that can be the subject of an audio tour. In the future, we may experience guidance as a constant service; this is a significant opportunity for a producer.

- **DJ Reborn:** This book's authors have been involved in music, as a producer and as a DJ. It's fun, and you can add your creativity with simple things like the juxtaposition of songs to emphasize a unique beat or the irony of one song following another. Once, during college, Mitch fell down on the ground from the shock of mixing the end of Pink Floyd's Comfortably Numb with Alice Cooper's Clones. It required slowing one down and speeding the other up slightly to generate a resonant tone that melded the songs. He never forgot it. Picking the music people hear is gratifying and a kind of art. To do it legally, that is to avoid lawyers, you need to visit Chapter 23, but the cost of "being legal" is less than you think, and many people are looking for interesting mixes.

- **Short Form or Bites:** Many of today's existing formats were born out of broadcast time slots. Don't limit your thinking to that clock-based top- and bottom-of-the-hour schedule that makes all news shows or sitcoms 20 or 22 minutes long. Podcasting enables short form content that doesn't necessarily fit the previous categories. Think differently: Joke a Day, Daily Haiku, Trivia Question of the Day, Horoscope, or Top 10 lists. In addition to listeners subscribing to the short form feed, other podcasters can use them in their programs.

- **Video:** Podcasting isn't just about audio. Moving pictures, or "talkies," took hold of the podcast world within months of its invention. Every format we have described in this section can be translated to video, though you need to address another dimension of perception (reading poetry in video can be artful if you focus on the poet's face or by juxtaposing images with the words, for example).

Growing a Long, Long Tail

With a firm sense of what you want your podcast to accomplish, you need to turn to the economics for a few minutes. You need to consider many details, including hosting and distribution, revenue strategies (or the lack of one), and production process management, which we cover elsewhere. For now, let's look at the most important idea to keep in mind as you begin to produce: Your shows need to be accessible for a long time in order to earn the most that you can from your efforts. Even if you aren't in podcasting for money, you want people to hear your work — all of it, if they want — so that you get every opportunity to win a listener.

Podcast hosting services generally involve limits on storage capacity on a server or bandwidth available for downloads, possibly both, that encourage producers to start taking down their older programs. As we pointed out in Chapter 1, a large part of the history of podcasting is lost or misplaced because producers can't afford to keep all their shows on the network. This violates the most basic tenet of digital distribution, the fact that it is virtually free compared to any analog medium to make a copy of a digital file, which drastically reduces the cost of delivering a given show to a given listener at any time. *Wired* magazine editor Chris Anderson has developed a comprehensive economic analysis of how digital distribution and search-based shopping changes markets, showing that many micro-audiences can appear based on easy and cheap access to digital files or catalog backlogs that have never been available at retail. Because customers can find — and know that they can actively seek — more obscure programs and music or books, they buy many different titles in a year than ever before. This was because retail generally restricted inventory to a small selection, usually the "hits" that dominated mass markets.

In what Anderson calls "the long tail," titles that haven't sold at retail for years will sell many times a year, simply because they are accessible. For example, Urge Overkill's 1992 cover of Neil Diamond's "Girl, You'll Be a Woman Soon," would have sold only to fanatics as part of a rare EP before it became available on Apple's iTunes Music Store, even though it was repopularized by the films of Quentin Tarantino. Retail outlets weren't likely to carry Urge Overkill's Stull EP, and except for appearances in compilations, notably the *Pulp Fiction* soundtrack, the song languished. Now that it is available through iTunes as a single, it can be cheaply and conveniently purchased by anyone who yearns for odd reinterpretations of 1960s pop songs.

The phrase, "the long tail," comes from the graph drawn to show the distribution of sales in a market (see Figure 4.4). It's also known as a power law, because it shows how those titles or products that are at the top of the sales charts enjoy a geometric increase in sales over those below. The portion of the curve in Figure 4.4 in black is where the mass market was able to concentrate its marketing efforts — a few big current hits, while the rest of the market had very little access to customers because of limited distribution networks. In the networked market, however, all the titles along the curve have essentially equal access to buyers because they can find it by searching Google, Amazon, or other sites that provide access to back-catalog material. Yes, there still will be big stars at the top of the curve, but the possibility exists, indeed the likelihood, that lots of smaller hits can emerge from the tail, some that could sweep the world.

FIGURE 4.4

The long tail of the networked market: Whereas mass markets concentrated all marketing and sales in the top of the curve, depicted in black, today's networked market allows hits to emerge at any point out in the trailing tail of distribution represented in gray.

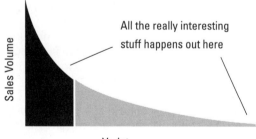

NOTE Chris Anderson's Long Tail Blog is an interesting resource for anyone contemplating digital distribution. It includes postings about many of the ideas covered in his upcoming book. From understanding Legos as a long-tail company (people order individual Lego blocks these days to complete custom projects) to actuarial analysis of record album sales, something here will get you thinking at `http://www.thelongtail.com`.

Sampling is critical to long-tail success. FeedBurner, which hosts RSS feeds for podcasts, reported in April 2006 that its customers see one download of a non-subscriber standalone program for every RSS subscriber download. You want to have all your programs available for sampling with extensive metadata, the information that describes what each show is about, so that when someone searches for a podcast or about a topic on any search engine, he will encounter your program about what he is interested in; if you can't get his attention and introduce him to your program with a topic he cares about, you'll never win the listener as a subscriber. In an era of information overload, then, most people are actually looking for ways to avoid what they think won't directly address their interests.

CROSS-REF Metadata is critically important to having your podcast found. See Part IV, which focuses on distribution, for more information.

After you have a potential customer's attention, you can more easily get her to try another show, and another, until she makes the decision to subscribe. The long tail suggests that even large audience relationships can begin with lots of small audiences that gather around specific ideas, and then find more in common with the talent they enjoy. It is the reverse perspective on what we pointed out previously: Large audiences appear only when you seek broad topics; with a podcast you are starting small, and the ease of distribution, as long as your program can be found by lots of different audiences, provides the possibility to build huge audiences.

The OPs: Stars of the Future

In 1995, Mitch Ratcliffe envisioned the career path of a new kind of personality in his newsletter, **Digital Media: A Seybold Report***:*

People talking to machines. That's the economic model of the information age breaking out everywhere. People ask machines for a news story, a movie, or the sports scores, and the machines charge them for it. People go away happy. Mostly, they just go away. For example, I read in the *European Wall Street Journal* recently that airlines see more than just added revenues from in-flight interactive entertainment: "Passengers busy playing computer games or watching movies will be less likely to harass flight attendants with endless requests." I can't wait to be lulled into that cooperative, complacent state. Peace, at last. But come to think of it, that's the condition we retreat to after voting every two years; and we always emerge in the next election more angry than before.

While the development of technology that can spit a video stream down a cable to a home, or an airplane seat, is really quite remarkable in this Paleolithic information epoch — we're really nowhere near the time when the whole world will be living together among easily accessible digital connections — video on demand is not the face of Helen that will launch a new economy.

continued

continued

Of course, that's not the way Time Warner sees it. Listening in Orlando last month to Time Warner CEO Gerald Levin gleefully anticipating his grab for a part of the $105 billion telephone market, it was clear that he doesn't want people to earn money in the information age; he just wants them to spend it.

I think we can do better by the people. You're probably thinking what my father would say: "Put up or shut up, Ratcliffe. What's this new economy supposed to look like?" Well. . . .

It's nine o'clock in the morning, sometime in 2017. Davis Allen, a 39-year-old man living in Nantucket, pulls himself up to the keyboard in his den. He's at work. He's an online star. As his computers boot up, the screens around him flicker to life; some contain text messages, others are video feeds from the places he'll be performing today. The screen directly in front of him, labeled "LIVE," is blank. This will let him see whom he's talking to when he actually taps into the lives of his audience. There are approximately 75,000 online personalities (OPs) in the United States. Folks come into contact with five to ten OPs a day. Each OP has a micro audience of 3,500 or so people who would identify with that personality. The superstars, like Davis, are very influential, because they "personally" advise half a million or more people.

The new broadband lines are standard fare in Davis's community. Everyone has vast amounts of capacity available dynamically. There's no more making appointments for T1 bandwidth: it's there instantly. Davis gobbles bandwidth keeping connected to his audience. About 420,000 people in the region — and a few who have moved across country or to Europe and Asia — count on Davis's endorsement of products when shopping, as well as his wit and eye for the ironic to provide entertainment.

The broadband lines in the house are from one of the local phone companies. They are the second set laid in. The first, installed by the now-defunct cable system, were paid for by Davis's old employer, Paracom, the entertainment conglomerate. In those days, he was doing banter in the interface of the local interactive television system, hawking new programs, connecting gamers in huge virtual Zork tournaments, and giving folks the sense that they weren't alone in the digiscape.

Paracom Online spent heavily on developing online personalities in the late 1990s. These next-generation disc jockeys followed the lead of the MTV VJ and talk-radio hosts like Rush Limbaugh, who were the first to turn participation (no matter how inconsequential) into a mass medium. Davis Allen was one of the first, joining the Paracom network as a 19-year-old to cruise the youth-oriented newsgroups on the Internet, making friends, getting those friends to bring others into the conversation; soon he was a literal Pied Piper at the vanguard of the march into interactivity.

His own experience taught him to pick out the most interesting people he met in cyberspace. As more people took up the video camera and desktop video editing systems, or turned their keyboards into expressive outlets for their ideas, Davis became a valued source of contacts — a kind of virtual editor who connected his audience with others' creative work.

Late in the first decade of the new century, Davis left Paracom's employ and set up his own company. For almost a decade, he's been contracting with media companies, advertisers, and service organizations, including Paracom, to provide the online personality for content, products, and services throughout the Northeast. The average OP, working for a production company that taps many networks to distribute its content, has hundreds of these endorsement contracts.

Davis's latest venture is the virtual shelf-talker. Whether shopping at home or in a store, a consumer plugs a PCM-CIA card into her PDA that tracks her proximity to Davis-endorsed products. When she passes one on the store shelf, for instance, a Davis video pops up and explains the comparative benefits of the product. The video is manipulated by the computers on Davis' desktop to insert the customer's name in the rap. But if she has more questions, a light flashes on Davis' monitor and he can go live to assist her. Because he covers only a part of the country and his video talkers are recorded to answer most consumer concerns in the first minute, he doesn't spend much time in live conversations. When he's not at work, an assistant takes care of people.

The rest of the day, Davis spends time in forums, producing introductions to new films and shows on the interactive networks and out in the field shooting tape for segments.

Davis found out early that the biggest challenge for the online personality was the shut-in. These people want to go live and just talk for hours, killing the time they fear, but also Davis's own production time. Two strategies paid off. First, he introduced the shut-ins to one another; but he also found out what kinds of activities were going on in their communities and got them to go out and try to join in society.

Davis, because he works at home, has considerably more time than his own father for involvement in the community and his family's life. He's on the school board and regularly meets a group of concerned parents for discussion at a local coffee shop. He eats breakfast, lunch, and dinner with his family (finally, intelligent agents and PDAs are providing flexible access to the networks that facilitate working less, but working better) and knows his children's friends by name. Involvement keeps families growing stronger. No kids in the region have been murdered by other children for almost five years.

That's a brief portrait of the world we could make. No one expects that an economy can be born in a single moment of transformation, but I think the OP is an example of a recognizable job description undergoing a transformation in the information economy. These people will require a complex assortment of support staff and technology. Literally hundreds of new job descriptions might erupt in a world where the home is a permeable membrane that collects the power of human intelligence to serve the family living in it. Imagine, for example, that the power systems in a house — heat, air conditioning, lighting — are controllable from a remote location; there's a new industry in maintenance and consulting services that help consumers get the most out of their electrical consumption.

I'm afraid, though, seeing how little incentive people have for acting as creative beings in the so-called information age of video on demand, that we're building a dystopian society in which people will be treated as mere consumers. Like Robert Louis Stevenson's perfect child, there will be the expectation that people will speak only when spoken to — and then in a voice that says "Yes, I'll take two" through the mechanics of a handheld interactive TV control. We'll pay a terrible price for such mechanistic social perfection.

If you want your company to win a place in a robust economy, in a society where you will enjoy living, think beyond the media to the people using it. And think beyond their use of media, to their lives. What are we complaining about as a nation? I see many phenomena that orbit the issue of a growing sense that there is no humanity in the world. Keep in mind what Fred Rogers wrote in the Freedom Forum's *Media Studies Journal* recently: "Television may be the only electrical appliance that's more useful after it's turned off."

Summary

You must make your podcast your own, so treat the advice in this chapter as guidelines and rules that can and should be broken. Just be sure to learn from your mistakes along the way and lest us know what you find works so we can share it in the next edition. Keep these points in mind when putting together your first podcast:

- Podcasting requires a combination of passion and discipline. You can take a number of steps in your podcast design to preserve that passion and reinforce it through simple and achievable goals.

- By spending the time to examine your own interests, you can discover topics that may make a successful podcast that is totally out of the ordinary; that's the recipe for a hit. Picking your topics carefully instead of rushing into a series of podcasts that you can't sustain is the fast path to burn-out. Take some time with this. Any undertaking that will take up a significant portion of your life, even a few weeks a month, is worth making a thoughtful plan.

- After you have picked some topics, examine your motivations so that you can set goals — achievable goals — that will reinforce your enthusiasm for the production. It will help you sustain the production.

- People will podcast for a variety of reasons, and podcasters use many formats that may work for you.

- Using Google AdWords, you can explore the size of the audience you may be able to reach with a particular topic and the potential value of that audience.

- Your expectations of the audience are as important as their expectations of you. Again, take the time to consider how you are going to interact with your audience, because it will tell you something about the format you should choose.

- After you decide on your format, plan to get every show you produce into permanent distribution in order to maximize the opportunity to win subscribers. Use metadata, the information that describes your podcast, to get your first listen from every possible person you can. It's not desperation; it's practical marketing.

- Are you the first OP? Be the trusted companion of your audience, and you will prosper. Mr. Spock didn't say exactly that, but he would have if he had been a podcaster. What does a 1960s Vulcan know about new media? Nothing. You have to go to at least *The Next Generation* to find a savvy marketer among the Vulcans.

Chapter 5

Audio Production Tools

If you're a gear hound, you're really going to enjoy this chapter. Audio gear looks really cool and has lots of flashing lights and plenty of meters; the current trend of making audio gear look slightly retro adds to the effect. Audio gear is also relatively cheap. Although you can easily spend thousands of dollars on audio gear, you can get great audio quality out of budget home recording equipment, which has vastly improved in the last ten years. And most importantly, quality audio gear immediately improves the quality of your podcast.

Most podcasts are produced from the podcaster's home or office, so the first part of this chapter talks about the tools required for a basic podcasting studio. Some folks grab interviews on the go, so a section of this chapter is dedicated to portable recording. Many podcasts include remote guests who call in on either a traditional phone line or an online phone service such as Skype, so telephone tools are covered in detail.

In any recording situation, the environment is important to the final quality, so this chapter covers things you can do to improve your recording environment. Finally, some suggested combinations of equipment are listed, so that you can make a shopping list for your audio gear.

Using Basic Production Tools

Many multimedia computers ship with microphones, speakers, and soundcards, but in general the quality of these bundled tools is not very high. That doesn't mean that you can't produce a podcast with whatever tools you have on hand. But if you want to produce to a high standard, you should invest accordingly. Your podcast quality is limited by the quality of your audio signal chain, and that starts with your microphone.

Microphones

The quality of your podcast, to a large extent, is dependent on the quality of your microphone. If you use a cheap plastic mic, your podcast sounds cheap and, well, plastic. Spend a hundred bucks, and you can compete with the best of them. But before you pull out your credit card, learn a little bit about how microphones work and which type of microphone is best for you.

Pickup patterns

Microphones have different pickup patterns, or *directional response*. Omnidirectional mics pick up sound from all directions equally. Directional mics pick up sound predominantly from a particular direction, and reject sound from other directions. Most mics are directional, with a particular pickup pattern. These are the most common pickup patterns, shown in Figure 5.1:

- **Cardioid:** Cardioid mics pick up predominantly what is in front of them, less of what is to the sides, and very little of what is behind them. The name derives from the heart-shaped pickup pattern.

- **Supercardioid (or hypercardioid):** These microphones exhibit an exaggerated cardioid pattern, with more rejection of sound from the sides and rear. Hypercardioid mics are commonly referred to as shotgun mics.

- **Figure 8 (bi-directional):** Figure 8 mics pick up sound from the front and rear, but not from the sides.

FIGURE 5.1
_____

Common microphone pickup patterns. Cardioid mics (left) are mostly sensitive to the front, with some sensitivity on the sides and very little to the rear. Supercardioid mics (center) are less sensitive to the sides than standard cardioid mics, but also have some sensitivity to the rear. Figure-8 microphones (right) are sensitive along a given axis and much less sensitive off-axis.

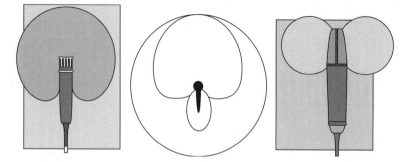

As you can see in Figure 5.1, mics have different pickup patterns, and more importantly, have a front and a back! It's pretty obvious which end you speak into with handheld mics, but it may not be so obvious with some higher-quality mics. For example, some mics have a switch to determine the pickup pattern. If you switch from a figure-8 to a cardioid, which side is the correct side to speak into? In most cases, the manufacturers put their logo on the "front" of the mic. If you're not sure, you can always try speaking into both sides of the mic. When it's set to cardioid, one side sounds much louder and brighter than the other side.

In most cases, a directional mic with some type of cardioid pickup pattern is the best choice. These mics can easily be pointed at the talent, and by design won't pick up much else. The one exception is with clip-on (or lavalier) mics. If you decide that clip-on mics are going to work best for your needs, you should buy omni versions. Even though they're omnidirectional, they really don't pick up anything other than who they're attached to. The advantage of the omnidirectinal pickup pattern is apparent when the person turns his head from side to side. With directional mics, this leads to a dramatic drop off in signal level. With an omnidirectional mic, the drop off is far less apparent.

Dynamic versus condenser mics

Most microphones fall into two basic categories, *dynamic microphones* and *condenser microphones*. Dynamic microphones have a diaphragm that is attached to a coil of wire, known as the *voice coil*. The voice coil is suspended between magnets. When the diaphragm vibrates in response to incoming sound, the magnets create a very small oscillating current in the voice coil by a process known as electromagnetic induction. This current is an electrical representation of the sound wave.

The diaphragms in condenser microphones consist of two plates coated with a conductive material such as gold. A voltage, known as *phantom power,* is placed across the plates to form a capacitor. (Historically, capacitors were called condensers, hence the name condenser mic.) When incoming sound causes the plates to vibrate, the distance between them varies, which varies the capacitance. This variation in capacitance is converted into an oscillating current, which is an electrical representation of the sound wave.

Condenser mics are much more sensitive than dynamic mics. This translates to higher frequency response and lower noise. However, the sensitivity comes at a price: Condenser mics are very sensitive to handling noise, and therefore cannot be held in your hand. They're always placed in microphone stands and sometimes in special suspension mounts. If you're in a controlled situation, you may want to take advantage of the higher quality that condenser mics offer. Some reasonably priced condenser mics are shown in Figure 5.2.

FIGURE 5.2

Condenser mics: Neumann TLM49, AKG C3000B, Audio Technica AT4033

Dynamic mics may not have quite the frequency response and dynamic range that condenser mics have, but that doesn't mean there aren't some fabulous dynamic mics. In fact, two dynamic mics are broadcast industry standards, the ElectroVoice RE20 and the Shure SM7B, shown in Figure 5.3. These mics are prized for their tone, and both are incredibly resistant to the proximity effect. Either of these would be ideal for your podcasting studio.

FIGURE 5.3

Studio dynamic mics: ElectroVoice RE20, Shure SM7B

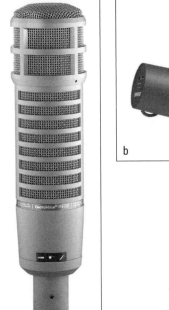

a

b

CROSS-REF The proximity effect is discussed in Chapter 6, "Basic Audio Production."

If you're going to be working on location or outdoors, or you just don't want to be tied down to a chair in front of an expensive mic, you can buy a nice handheld mic. Handheld mics are dynamic mics by definition, because they must be resistant to handling noise. They're usually sturdy enough to survive being dropped, which, as any reporter can tell you, is important. You should always have a handheld mic or two, because they're very reasonably priced and can serve as backups in case of equipment troubles. Some great handheld mics are shown in Figure 5.4.

FIGURE 5.4

Handheld mics: Electrovoice 635A, the venerable Shure SM58

Other types of microphones

All the microphones described previously will serve you well, but they're not the only mics suitable for podcasting. A number of specialized mics might be better suited for your podcast, depending on your situation.

Clip-on (Lavalier) mics

Clip-on mics are common in television news broadcast, because they're small and unobtrusive. This also can be an advantage in podcasting, particularly if your guest has little or no experience talking into a mic. Many folks can be intimidated by large broadcast mics. Clip-on mics are great because the guest can forget about the mic, relax, and give a good interview. Two great lavalier mics are shown in Figure 5.5.

FIGURE 5.5

Clip-on (lavalier) mics: ElectroVoice RE90L, Audio Technica AT803B

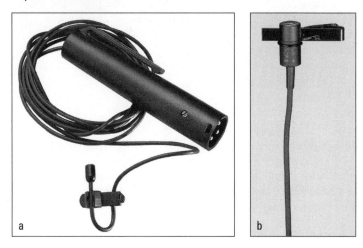

Headset mics

Headset mics can be ideal for some applications. You often see them on tradeshow floors so that the speakers can use their hands and not worry about holding a microphone. The other reason they're useful is that the microphone is very close to the speaker's mouth, so very little background noise is picked up. Some headphones include a built-in microphone, which is handy in situations where you need to wear headphones and want the convenience of a headset mic.

Many, many headsets today are sold by numerous companies to work with your cell phone, your laptop, your PDA, and who knows what else. Many of these headsets are very cheaply made. If you want to go the headset route, stick to the professional models. Most microphone manufacturers make a headset model. Two good headset mics are shown in Figure 5.6.

FIGURE 5.6

Headset mics: Audio Technica ATM75CW, Shure WBH53B

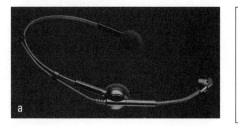 

Wireless mics

Wireless microphone technology has been around much longer than wireless connectivity has. A number of different standards and transmission methods exist. Wireless mic setups involve one or more wireless mics and receiver units that convert the wireless signal back into analog audio. Wireless can be pretty slick, but it can be pricey. Setups start at around $500 per single mic and go up from there. The other problem is that wireless systems are prone to interference. Also, wireless microphones run on batteries, and as we all know, batteries always run out right in the middle of the most important part of the interview, right?

PZM / boundary mics

Pressure zone microphones (PZM mics) are designed to be placed on a large flat surface. They're ideal for conference room tables or podiums. They're kind of cool because they don't look like mics, so folks tend to ignore them. An example of a PZM mic is shown in Figure 5.7. They're not going to give you the same performance as a quality handheld or clip-on mic, simply because they tend to be further from the people speaking. However, they can be useful in situations where it's not practical to put a microphone in front of every single speaker.

FIGURE 5.7

PZM mic: Crown PZM 185

USB mics

One of the most interesting recent developments has been the arrival of the USB microphone. USB mics have built-in digital audio conversion, so instead of connecting them to a mixing desk, you plug them directly into your workstation. All mixing and signal processing of your podcast must be done in your audio-editing software, because you aren't using external hardware. You also are limited by the number of USB ports your workstation has. However, if you're looking for the ultimate in portability, a USB mic may be ideal. A number of USB mics are available, including the ones shown in Figure 5.8.

If you're looking for the ultimate in portability, Sound Professionals makes a USB mic the size and shape of a small flash drive, which offers amazing quality for the money. While it doesn't offer the quality of a dedicated microphone placed in front of each person talking, it's an indispensable tool for the laptop warrior. This little workhorse is shown in Figure 5.8c.

FIGURE 5.8

USB mics: Samson CO1U, Blue Microphones Snowball, Sound Professionals USB Mic-1

Mics with 1/8″ (3.5mm) Connectors

The discussion of microphones in this chapter assumes that you're going to be plugging the mics into a mixing desk with professional XLR inputs or into the USB port of your computer. Sometimes, the reality is that you're going to want to plug into a MiniDisc recorder or, heaven forbid, the microphone input on your soundcard. In this case, you're going to need a microphone with a 1/8″ plug at the end. We've avoided talking about these mics up to this point, because by definition they're generally not of very high quality. The 1/8″ plug is a bit of a giveaway; it's not broadcast standard, and they're not very sturdy. But hey, sometimes you've gotta do what you've gotta do.

Some readers may be wondering whether a good quality microphone can be plugged into an 1/8″ input with some sort of adapter or custom cable. The answer is a resounding "maybe." First of all, most of these 1/8″ inputs are designed to be stereo inputs, while most microphones are mono. In theory you can use a stereo-to-mono adapter, but you should avoid using adapters because they're prone to failure and often lead to inputs being damaged because the adapters are heavy and place extra stress on the input. That leaves the possibility of using a custom cable.

A custom cable is a possibility, but your chances of success are still slim. You can't use a condenser mic because they require phantom power, and 1/8″ inputs do not provide phantom power. If you're using a dynamic mic and can find someone to make you a custom XLR to 1/8″ cable, it *may* work. In most cases you're better off using a mic that is designed to use a 1/8″ cable.

Many portable recording devices come with a small stereo mic. Sometimes, they come with a short cable so they can be clipped to a lapel; other times, they're meant to plug in to the top of your recording device. These are usually *electret* mics. Electret mics are actually a special type of condenser mic. They operate on the same principle, but don't require phantom power. While they're not theoretically inferior, they're generally mass produced to a very low standard and, therefore, noisy. They're usually omnidirectional, so they can do a decent job of picking up everything in a room. So if you're in a very quiet location, an electret mic can be a decent option.

Don't let this chapter discourage you; it is possible to find decent microphones with 1/8″ connectors. In fact, some specialty manufacturers cater to people looking for these types of microphones and headsets. One site in particular, www.soundprofessionals.com, specializes in all kinds of equipment with 1/8″ connectors and has a whole new line of USB recording tools. They even have a podcasting gear section with suggested combinations of their equipment.

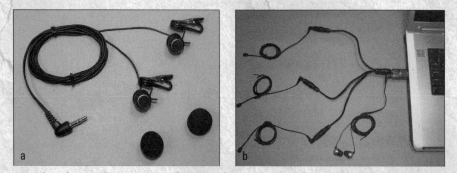

Sound Professionals CMC-20 and USB Multi-mic, both with 1/8″ connectors

If you have to buy equipment with 1/8″ connectors for one reason or another, just be sure to buy the good stuff. It's possible to find all kinds of equipment at your local computer store, but you'll be much better off if you stick to reputable audio manufacturers such as the examples in this chapter.

Mixing Desks

Mixing desks, or mixers, provide centralized control of all your audio sources. Mixing desks combine multiple audio sources into a single master mix. Each source is plugged into a separate *channel* that offers individualized control. All adjustments can be done in real time; for example, you can play music during the intro to your podcast, bring the level of the music down, and then turn your microphone up. If a guest is speaking too loudly, you can turn his microphone down. (Or, if you're a domineering type like some television talk show hosts, you can "cut it"—turn it off completely.)

Another feature of most mixing desks is multiple outputs. Most have a headphones output, as well as a master output, a control room or monitoring output, and possibly others. This flexibility allows you to do a number of things. You can listen to, or *monitor,* your audio in a number of ways. You can connect a pair of speakers to your mixing desk or use headphones. You can connect a recording device to your mixing desk if you want to record your podcast on a device other than your workstation. Mixing desks provide you with the flexibility to do just about anything you want with your audio.

Mixing desks offer these features as well:

- **Phantom power:** Condenser mics require phantom power to operate.
- **Level adjustment:** You can adjust the level of each source.
- **Equalization (EQ):** You can adjust the *tone* of each input to optimize the sound.
- **Stereo panning:** You can move inputs from side to side in your stereo mix.
- **Effects sends:** You can add special effects to your mix such as echo and reverb.

If you're going to be doing any sort of live recording, you should buy a mixing desk. The flexibility it provides is invaluable. Another reason to consider buying a mixing desk is the microphone inputs (also known as *mic pre's*, short for microphone pre-amplifiers). Microphones produce a low-level signal that must be amplified considerably. Cheap mic inputs (like the ones included on most soundcards) add a significant amount of noise during the amplification process. Mixing desks have much higher quality mic inputs, so they produce much higher quality signals. In fact, mic input quality is usually the distinguishing factor of a mixing desk.

Mixing desks come in all shapes and sizes, from portable models that offer a few input channels, to broadcast consoles that require special stands. A desktop mixing desk is probably most appropriate for podcasting. Be sure to buy a mixing desk that has more inputs than you need; people tend to "grow into" their mixing desks. After you realize that you can leave everything connected, you'll find yourself connecting everything to your mixer.

One of the latest developments in mixing desk technology has been the addition of USB and FireWire outputs. These new outputs enable you to connect the mixing desk directly to your workstation, without having to use an external audio interface or a soundcard. These are incredibly handy, because you'll have one less piece of equipment to buy (or worry about). Many mixing desk manufacturers are coming out with USB and FireWire models. In general, the FireWire models are slightly more expensive, because they enable higher sampling rates and bit depths. A couple of models are illustrated in Figure 5.9.

FIGURE 5.9

Mixing desks: Mackie Onyx 1220 (FireWire), Yamaha MW10 (USB)

Monitoring (headphones and speakers)

When producing high-quality audio, you should know that what you're hearing is accurate. It's worth investing in a good pair of speakers, which are called *monitors* in the broadcast world. You'll also need a good set of headphones to be able to monitor while you're recording to avoid *feedback* (which is explained in the "Feedback: What It Is and How to Avoid It" sidebar).

Headphones can be either *closed back* or *open back*. Open back headphones tend to be lighter and more comfortable, but the design has a couple of potential shortcomings. First, outside noise can come in via the open back, so they're not good for noisy environments. Second, if the headphone volume is turned up too loud, the sound coming out of the back may be picked up by nearby microphones. This is known as *bleed*. It's usually not too much of a problem with spoken presentations, because headphone volume tends to be low and the bleed minimal. It can be a factor when recording live music, however, which tends to be monitored at much greater levels. Closed back headphones are best for noisy environments, because they allow less outside noise to reach your ear, and less headphone noise leaks out.

A number of specialized headphones are available. Most portable players come with *in-ear* headphones. In-ear headphones offer excellent isolation because they're so close to the ear drum; some are even custom molded to the ear canal. This is a double edged-sword, though. Anything that close to your ear drum has the potential to do lots of damage. *Noise-canceling* headphones use sophisticated circuitry to minimize ambient noise such as the whine of an airplane engine. *Wireless* headphones send the audio signal via a wireless technology such as Bluetooth or UHF. For critical listening, use a good pair of wired headphones. They're less susceptible to interference, and they don't have any fancy circuitry messing up your audio. A couple of standard broadcast headphone models are shown in Figure 5.10.

FIGURE 5.10

Broadcast headphones: Sony MDR-7506, AKG K240S

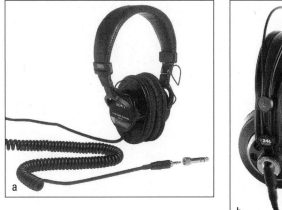

Although you can do all your podcast production with a good set of headphones, you'll also probably want to invest in a good set of monitors. Headphones can be fatiguing, and they have an exaggerated sense of stereo separation. You should always check your mixes on a set of monitors. Remember that a good portion of your audience will be listening at their desktop computers, so you should make sure their experience is going to be good. Granted, your audience may be listening on cheap plastic speakers that came with their "multimedia-enabled" computers. That's no excuse for you to produce using the same equipment. Producing your audio to the highest possible quality requires accurate monitoring.

Monitors are probably the most contentious piece of audio equipment you'll buy, because judging the quality of a pair of monitors is very subjective. You'll see all sorts of jargon tossed around on manufacturers' Web sites, along with frequency response diagrams and rave reviews from audio engineers. Generally, the more you spend, the more accurate the monitor. Also, because low frequencies are particularly difficult to reproduce accurately, more expensive monitors have better low frequency reproduction. Many desktop multimedia speaker systems use subwoofers to reproduce the low frequencies. These are fine, provided the subwoofer doesn't color the sound too much.

Feedback: What It Is and How to Avoid It

We've all heard feedback, whether at a rock concert or at a tech conference: Someone with a microphone wanders in front of the PA system, and suddenly a high-frequency shrieks out of the PA, forcing the audience to clap their hands over their ears. Ouch! That's feedback.

Here's what happens: When the person steps in front of the PA system, the microphone picks up the sound of the person's amplified voice, which is sent back to the PA system, which amplifies it again, and sends it back to the speakers. It is picked up by the microphone again, and amplified.... See what's happening? This is called a *feedback loop.* Depending on the size and shape of the room, a particular frequency (usually a high frequency) is most prominent and builds up more quickly than other frequencies. Before you know it, the PA is squealing like a stuck pig.

To avoid feedback in live situations, the simple answer is to keep microphones out of the direct line of the PA system. The other thing to do is to "tune" the PA system to compensate for the frequencies that a particular room is sensitive to. This can be done using equalization (EQ) on the PA system.

Tuning a PA system is a tricky endeavor. A microphone is placed in front of the PA system, and the volume slowly brought up to the threshold of feedback. The audio engineer identifies the frequency and reduces that frequency using a very specialized graphic equalizer. Then the volume is raised a little more until another feedback frequency appears. This is repeated until the room has been relatively "flattened." This doesn't stop feedback, but it makes the system resistant to feedback. Digital feedback suppression systems can help here as well.

Though it usually isn't quite as problematic, feedback can occur in studio situations. If your headphones are too loud and you're very close to the microphone, you may hear feedback as you remove your headphones. It's the same principle; the mic picks up the sound coming out of the headphones, the mixing desk amplifies it and sends it back to the headphones, and you've got a feedback loop. Feedback also happens if you leave your microphone on while you're editing, and it picks up the sound coming from your desktop monitors.

To avoid feedback in your studio, follow a few simple steps:

- Monitor at a sensible level in your headphones.

- Mute the microphone channel, or turn the level down before taking off your headphones.

- If you're using a handheld mic, don't ever point it at the monitors.

One thing you should definitely consider is whether the monitors are *shielded*. Shielded monitors are built so that they don't pick up interference from video monitors, which can be a problem. You also may want to buy *active* speakers, which have amplification built in, so they don't require a separate amplifier. Many professional monitor manufacturers exist, and each has a wide selection of monitors. A few examples are shown in Figure 5.11. Choose monitors that fit your budget and sound good to you.

FIGURE 5.11

Monitors: M-Audio StudioPro 3, Tapco S-5

Signal processors

In later chapters, you learn about audio production techniques that you can use to optimize your podcast. These can be done using either hardware or software. Software is convenient because you can use presets or create customized settings for your podcast that you can use every week. Even more useful is the ability to "undo." However, sometimes hardware processing is handy. You can't beat the feel of real knobs, and who wouldn't like more flashing lights in his studio? A couple of hardware processors are shown in Figure 5.12.

FIGURE 5.12

Signal processing units: Presonus Comp16, EQ3B

Equalization (EQ) units

Equalization is a process whereby tone is altered by boosting (turning up) or attenuating (turning down) certain frequencies. The bass and treble knobs on your car stereo apply EQ. Most mixing desks include simple EQ, but you may want finer control of your tone at times. In this case, you'd buy an external EQ unit. You also can use EQ units to fight feedback problems (refer to the "Feedback: What It Is and How to Avoid It" sidebar).

Compressor

Audio compressors help control your audio levels. Compressors turn audio levels down when they cross a certain threshold. They're incredibly useful because they protect your equipment from distortion due to abrupt level changes — for example, if one of your guests suddenly starts yelling. You can place a compressor between your mixing desk and your audio interface as a protective measure or compress your input channels individually.

Effects units

Effects units enable you to add special effects to your podcast, like echo and reverb. Effects are often used in music production to make the band sound like they're playing in a large hall or club. For most podcast material, this simply isn't appropriate. If you listen to the radio carefully, you'll notice that special effects are used sparingly, and even then only on the "bumpers" (the show announcements) or on advertisements.

Audio interfaces

At some point, your analog audio signal must make the transition between the analog and digital worlds. This can be done at various points in your signal chain. Once upon a time, the only way to get sound into your computer was via a soundcard, but that is no longer the case. Audio interfaces can connect via USB and FireWire, mixing desks come with built-in audio interfaces, and you can even buy USB mics.

Soundcards

Virtually every computer sold these days comes with some sort of audio interface. Usually, there's a headphone and/or speaker output, a microphone input, and a line level input if you're lucky. The problem is that these soundcards are usually built with really cheap components and are low quality. Also, as mentioned earlier in this chapter, microphone inputs on soundcards tend to be very noisy. They're very vulnerable to electrical interference (of which there's plenty inside a computer). In general, you should avoid using the mic input on a soundcard.

This doesn't mean that you can't produce a podcast using whatever soundcard you're stuck with. Hey, the idea is to get podcasting as quickly as possible, right? If you must use the soundcard that came with your hand-me-down computer, and if you must use the microphone input, go right ahead. Just remember that when you decide it's time to improve the audio quality, the soundcard is probably the place to start.

Plenty of good soundcards are available today. You should look for a soundcard that uses professional 1/4" or XLR connectors, because they're far more reliable and resistant to noise. Many soundcards these days come with a breakout box that you can place on your desk or a shelf, so you don't have to crawl behind your computer every time you want to plug something in. Check out the example in Figure 5.13.

FIGURE 5.13

Soundcard with breakout box: M-Audio Delta 44

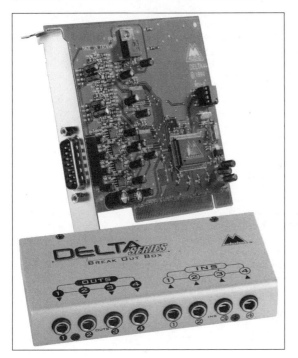

External audio interfaces

Another way to get digital audio into your computer is to use an external audio interface. This type of stand-alone unit connects to your computer via USB or FireWire. Until recently, only a few of these were available, but now you have lots to choose from. One nice thing is that most of these units come bundled with tons of great recording tools, so if you don't have an audio editor, you might consider picking up an external audio interface just to get the software!

Like soundcards, external audio interfaces come in many shapes and sizes and have different features, such as number of inputs and so on, like the ones shown in Figure 5.14. One thing to consider is power; most of these units run off the power supplied by the USB or FireWire bus, but to get power on a FireWire cable, you need the larger six-pin cable. Some laptops come equipped only with the smaller four-pin FireWire input, so you'll have to supply external power if you're using a FireWire interface. For the ultimate in portability, you may want to go with a USB version.

FIGURE 5.14

External audio interface: M-Audio Mobile Pre (USB), PreSonus Firebox (FireWire).

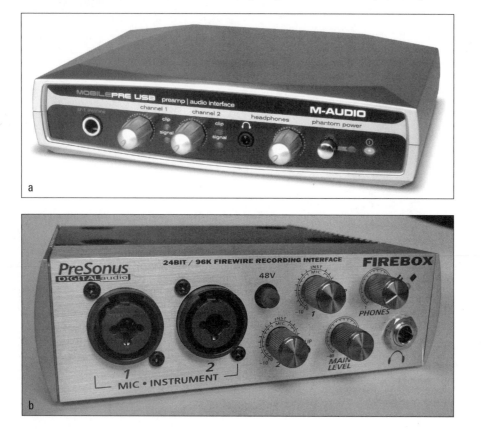

Recording devices

You have a number of options for recording. The most obvious is to record directly to your hard drive. However, this may not be an option if you're recording on location, or if you don't want to lug your computer around with you everywhere you go. Of course, these days, people bring their laptops with them everywhere, but if you don't want to do that, this section discusses other options for recording your podcast.

You can record in many different formats. Some, like the cassette, have been around for ages, but are still entirely useful. Others, like tapeless recording, are relatively new. Tapeless recording is of particular interest to podcasters, because you can transfer the files from your recorder to the computer digitally and much faster than real-time transfers.

Cassette

Cassettes were initially developed as a dictation format and never designed to be high quality. But they caught on like wildfire, so manufacturers improved the tape quality and the electronics, and they even added noise reduction systems like Dolby. If you have a decent cassette deck lying around, you can use it, but be sure to buy high-quality chrome cassette tapes and set your record levels high so you don't hear tape hiss. Of course, you can always use studio trickery later on to get rid of (or at least reduce) tape hiss.

CROSS-REF Setting record levels is covered in Chapter 6, "Basic Audio Production." Noise reduction and EQ are discussed in more detail in Chapter 7, "Advanced Audio Production."

DAT

Digital Audio Tape, or DAT, appeared in the mid-1980s as a high-quality studio format, but found its way into the consumer market. Although it has largely disappeared in the past ten years, plenty of serviceable DAT machines are still out there, and they're very high quality.

MiniDisc

Sony has been trying to convince the world that MiniDisc is a great format, but few people have listened. MiniDisc just never seems to go away, no matter how poorly it sells. This is partly due to the fact that MiniDisc units use ATRAC compression on the audio signal, which is acceptable for spoken word content, but not really acceptable for recording music masters. As a portable podcast recorder, a MiniDisc unit can be quite useful, especially because you can find them on craigslist for under $50 and MiniDisc blank discs are cheap.

MP3 recorders

A handful of MP3 players include record functionality. Most of these units do not have external mic inputs. A few have a line input that you can record from, but this means having some sort of mixing desk for the mic pre-amps and feeding the line level output into your portable MP3 player — not exactly a compact setup. Of course, you can use the built-in mic these units tend to include. If you're in a quiet location, it's probably fine. But don't expect broadcast quality.

New tapeless options

If you want the latest and greatest, look no further. Several manufacturers have released high-quality tapeless recording options in the last year. You can see some examples in Figure 5.15. These units record to compact Flash memory cards, which you can pop out and put into a USB card reader connected to your computer, or you can connect the unit to your computer using a USB cable. This allows you to transfer files much faster than real-time transfers; the transfer time depends on the type of file you recorded.

These tapeless units generally offer uncompressed recording in the WAV format, as well as MP3 recording at a variety of bit rates. Most come with built-in microphones, but for highest quality you'll want to use your own mics, of course. Some units offer XLR connectors, some 1/4" or 1/8". As of the writing of this book, models are available from four manufacturers, but we're sure you'll have many more choices by the time you read this.

FIGURE 5.15

The M-Audio MicroTrack 24/96, a portable recorder that records to Flash cards or microdrives

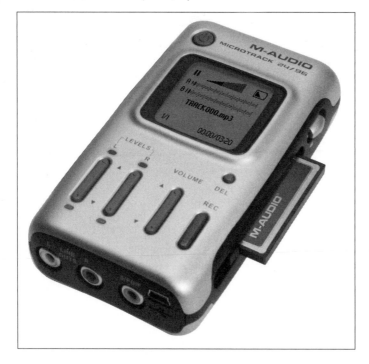

Audio-editing software

To get the most out of your podcast, you're going to need audio-editing software. Audio-editing software gives you the power to turn your raw podcast shows into things of beauty. Plenty of audio editors exist, from freeware all the way to specialized recording platforms for recording music. All are capable of basic editing operations such as cut and paste, as well as more advanced forms of signal optimization.

CROSS-REF   Signal optimization is discussed in Chapter 7, "Advanced Audio Production."

This list of some of the most common full-featured stereo audio-editing programs is by no means meant to be a definitive list:

- **Audacity** (Windows, Mac, Linux): Audacity is a free, open-source audio editor that runs on just about every platform. What's not to love?

- **Peak** (Mac): Berkeley Integrated Audio Software's flagship stereo audio editor comes in a number of versions at different price points.

- **Sound Forge** (Windows): Now a part of the Sony family, Sound Forge comes in a number of different versions at different price points.

- **Audition** (Windows): Formerly CoolEdit, Audition is now Adobe's flagship audio editor, offering all the quality you'd expect from an Adobe product.

As you'll find out throughout this book, creating a podcast involves more than just audio editing. Some audio-editing programs include additional podcast production tools, such as built-in file transfer (FTP) and Real Simple Syndication (RSS) support. Not all of the programs listed here include sophisticated audio processing. They're meant to be simple, easy-to-use tools that get the job done as quickly as possible.

- **GarageBand** (Mac): Originally intended as a very simple multi-track audio-editing program, GarageBand now includes just about everything you need to make a podcast. One problem, though, is that it does not export MP3 files; it only exports AAC encoded files, which is fine for podcasts targeted at iPods, but not for other portable music players.

- **ePodcast Producer** (Windows): This editor includes many handy podcast production features, including a teleprompter, sound effects management, and a built-in facility for recording Voice-over IP (VoIP) phone conversations such as Skype.

- **Propaganda** (Windows): This editor uses an interesting model where multiple clips are cued up to produce your podcast, much like a digital cartridge system used at radio stations.

- **Podcast Station** (Windows): This editor is similar to Propaganda in that you assemble your podcasts from lists of clips. Simple insert editing and unlimited undo make this a great platform for the podcaster who enjoys winging it. The Web site includes lots of tutorial videos to get you up and running quickly.

If you're planning on creating video podcasts, you should be aware that many video-editing software platforms also include audio editing and processing. Your decision on which audio-editing platform to buy will be based on the operating system you're working on, your familiarity with audio-editing software, and how much functionality you want in a single tool. You may want to create a few podcasts on a shoestring budget using open-source tools and see what works best for you before investing your hard-earned cash.

Additional tools

If you think your shopping list is getting a little too long, take a deep breath. You're going to need these odds and ends to produce your podcast.

Cables

Believe it or not, it's actually important to buy good-quality cables. Good cables are more noise resistant and last longer. In particular, if you're going to be doing lots of location work, you'll find that the constant plugging and unplugging of cables, as well as packing and unpacking them, can take a toll. Make sure to pay a little bit extra to buy good cables.

You should be using shielded, balanced cables wherever possible. Shielded cables include a wrapping of foil or wire mesh built in to the cable to reject outside magnetic interference. Balanced cables use an ingenious phase-cancellation method to make them even more noise resistant. Balanced cables are easy to recognize because they use three conductors in the cable: a positive, a negative, and a ground. The plugs on the end are either XLR or TRS, as shown in Figure 5.16.

Balanced plugs: Male XLR, female XLR, TRS

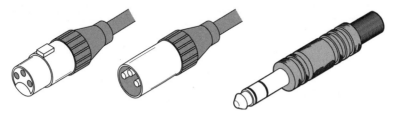

If your cable runs are very short, you don't *have* to use balanced cables. It's just a good idea, and believe me, you'll be glad you did.

Recording on an iPod?

Yes, in fact you can record on your iPod. However, there are a few drawbacks. If you're using an older iPod model (non-video model), they can record only 16-bit, 8 KHz files, which is basically telephone quality. This is fine for memos to yourself, but it's not broadcast quality. The newer models can record broadcast quality, but be careful because these high quality files are uncompressed .WAV files. WAV files require a lot of hard drive space and consequently burn through battery power because the hard drive constantly spins during the recording.

To use your iPod for recording, you need to purchase either Griffin's iTalk or the Belkin Universal Mic Adapter. (Note that these devices are not compatible with all iPods.) They're cheap, and they're ultra-portable, so it's not the worst idea to carry one around so that you can grab an unexpected interview when you're traveling.

Of course, if you're feeling brave, some very clever people have figured a way around the crippled recording capabilities of the older iPods. However, this isn't just a special sequence of keys you have to press. If you want to record pristine 16-bit, 44.1 KHz audio, you have to install Linux on your iPod.

Yes, you read that right. Some very clever people have figured out how to run Linux on an iPod, and it includes the ability to record. Needless to say, this is not something your authors can heartily recommend. In fact, forget you even read it here. We don't want any e-mails from people who break their iPods.

Pop screens

Certain letters, known as *plosives*, involve a large burst of air when they are pronounced, in particular the letters "p" and "b." This burst of air can result in a loud pop in your recording, which is very hard to remove, even with sophisticated signal processing. The simplest way to avoid pops is to use a pop screen. Pop screens come in two basic versions: a foam covering for your microphone or a disc that you place in front of your microphone that has sheer material stretched across it. Either one works, so figure out which works best with your mic and buy it.

Mic stands, clips, suspension mounts

Mic stands are important if you don't want to spend the entire podcast holding a microphone. You'll definitely need a mic stand if you're using a condenser mic, because they're far too sensitive to be handheld. Mic stands come in floor standing models, tabletop models, and spring-loaded desk-mount models. The spring-loaded models are particularly useful because they let you swing the mic out of the way after you're done recording.

Of course, you'll need a clip to hold your microphone to the mic stand. Most mics come with mic clips that are made specifically to hold them. For condenser mics, you should consider buying a suspension mount. Suspension mounts support the mic in a web of elastic bands or springs so they are floating independently of the mic stand, which makes them even more noise resistant.

Using Telephone Tools

Many podcasts include call-in guests. To get the audio from the phone into your computer, you need a telephone hybrid. Hybrids are specially designed to accomplish this with the least amount of noise possible. This is a little harder than it seems, because telephone lines are often very noisy. Telephone hybrids cost anywhere from $10 to $1,000. The $10 versions available at your local electronics store sound horrible and should be avoided.

Hybrids fall into two basic categories: analog and digital. The analog versions use basic circuitry to extract the audio from the phone line. The digital versions use sophisticated signal processing to clean up the audio signal and separate the caller from the interviewer. If you plan on doing lots of interviews over the phone, you should seriously consider buying a high-quality digital phone hybrid, as expensive as they may be. If phone calls are not a regular feature of your podcast, you can spend a little less, but you should still buy a good-quality hybrid, like the ones shown in Figure 5.17. If you make your phone calls on a mobile phone, you can buy hybrids that can be inserted between the cell phone and the earpiece.

FIGURE 5.17

Telephone hybrids: The JK Audio Inline Patch, Telos One digital hybrid

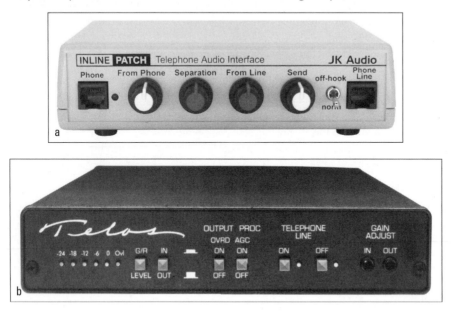

Skype

A number of technologies have been developed in the last few years that allow telephone calls to be made over the Internet instead of via a Plain Old Telephone System (POTS) line. One of the most popular is Skype. Skype is a P2P telephony system, which means there isn't a huge centralized server that's managing all the resources. It's all decentralized and distributed, and even better, it's free. Many people are taking advantage of this new service to make long-distance calls to friends in foreign countries.

Of course, this is all fine and good, but how can you record your Skype conversation? You can't use the fancy telephone hybrids discussed in the preceding section, because you're not using a phone! Instead, you use specialized software designed to record audio directly from your software audio mixer. A number of applications are designed to do this, with more appearing all the time. Here are a few examples:

- **Hot Recorder** (Windows): This application works with a number of different Internet telephony applications and even includes voicemail for Google Talk and Skype. It records into a proprietary .ELP format but converts this file to .WAV, .OGG, or .MP3.

- **Pamela Professional** (Windows): This application includes a number of features including voicemail and support for "pamcasting" (podcasting).

- **Audio Hijack** (Mac): This application records virtually any sound off your computer. It includes built-in timers for scheduled recording.

We're Serious about the Equipment We Use

You may be thinking, after reading through this chapter, that your authors have put together a wish list, talking about audio gear that we want but don't use. That is definitely not the case. To prove it, here's an *abridged* list of the audio gear we use. This isn't meant to be an endorsement of any particular brand; you'll see that between the two of us we're using equipment from a wide range of manufacturers.

- **Microphones:** Samson CO1-U, Shure SM58, Shure SM-7B, AT 4033, AKG 414, Sound Professionals CMC-20
- **Mixing desks:** Mackie 1202VLZ, Soundcraft Spirit, Mackie 1620 Onyx with FireWire option, Behringer Eurorack MX 602A
- **Signal processing:** Bellari MP 105 pre-amp, PreSonus Blue Max compressor, RNC 1773 compressor, BSS DPR 402 compressor, Alesis NanoCompressor
- **Audio interfaces/soundcards:** M-Audio Mobile Pre, PreSonus FireBox, M-Audio Delta 44, Echo Audio Gina
- **Monitors/headphones:** Genelec 1030s, Cambridge Soundworks, Tannoy Eclipse, Sennheiser HD 280, Sennheiser HD 414
- **Recording devices:** Sony TCD-7 DAT, iPod, Alesis ADAT
- **Audio-editing software:** Sound Forge, Audacity
- **Telephone hybrids:** Telos ONE

There you have it. We're serious about our audio quality, and you should be too.

Gizmo

Gizmo is another Internet telephony program. It works pretty much the same as Skype, but it has a couple of cool added features. First, it is SIP enabled, which means that you can talk to people on other VoIP networks, not just Gizmo users. It also is integrated with Google Talk, which is another up and coming Internet telephony application. Best of all, Gizmo includes recording functionality. Just push the record button, and presto — instant podcast.

Understanding the Recording Environment

So far we've spent the entirety of this chapter ogling all kinds of cool audio equipment that will produce higher-quality podcasts. However, there's a very important element that we haven't even touched on: your recording environment. Any audio engineer will tell you that the environment is a huge contributing factor to the quality of your production. All recording studios are specially built to provide an environment where things sound good.

Building recording studios is very skilled work, because recording studios must be capable of recording anything that walks through the door, from audio books to rock bands. For podcasting, we're trying to create a neutral environment, so that the sound of the guest's voices cut through. The last thing you want to hear is the sound of the room you're recording in.

A classic example is the sound of bathroom tile. We all sing in the shower because the highly reflective tile surfaces around us reflect our voices back to us, bathing us in a sea of reverb. Everyone knows *exactly* what a bathroom sounds like. You can't record in there, because folks will know you're recording in the bathroom!

The same goes for small closets or even small offices. Our ears detect the size of rooms by the reflections we hear. Think about that the next time you're stuck on a boring conference call. You can tell in a split second how big the room is on the other side of the call, and the sound quality is almost always horrible. That's because offices with whiteboards, windows, and big wooden tables have lots of reflective surfaces that fill the room with reflected sound, which is what makes it hard to listen to for long periods of time.

What you really want is a room that is nice and quiet, one that doesn't have too many reflective surfaces. If your room doesn't sound good to start off with, it's not too hard to make it sound much better with some sound treatment.

Sound treatment

If you've ever been inside a radio station, you know that the studios are nice and quiet. If you look around, you'll notice that the walls are treated so that they absorb sound. They have to be built this way, because there are microphones all over the place and all they want to broadcast is people's voices — not the sound of the room. Because you probably don't have the money to build a studio from scratch, you can do the next best thing: Use acoustic panels to treat your walls.

Acoustic panels are large pieces of foam or some other sound-absorbing material (see Figure 5.18). These panels are attached to walls and ceilings to reduce the amount of sound that is reflected. This makes the room sound *neutral*, because no sounds are reflected to give our ears a sense of space. Consequently, the sound going into your microphone is just your pristine voice, and nothing else.

You can do other things to improve your environment, some of which are just common sense. For example, if you're recording a conversation around a large table, place a tablecloth on the table. Not only does the tablecloth damp down any reflections from the tabletop, but it also absorbs noises like people putting coffee mugs down, tapping pens, and doing lots of other distracting things. If your space has windows, consider buying curtains and closing them when you're record-ing. Anything you can do to minimize large reflective surfaces will help.

FIGURE 5.18

Acoustic tiles can turn a terrible sounding room into a great recording environment.

Studio layouts

If you're going to create a dedicated space for your podcast production, take some time to think about how you're going to use it. You should consider different studio configurations, depending on how you're going to produce your programming. The simplest is a single operator studio.

Single operator

If you're going to be the producer, engineer, and star of your own podcast (of course), then you're probably going to do everything in the same room. You need enough space to accommodate all the equipment you've accumulated after reading this chapter and enough space to accommodate however many guests you plan on having. Remember that your guests probably will want some table space of their own to put their coffee, their laptop, and whatever else they've brought along. Make sure they have access to power, because they'll want to recharge all their gadgets during the podcast. (Make sure they turn off their cell phones.)

Be sure to have your equipment mounted in a special rack, or on a separate table, to protect it from spilled drinks. Equipment racks often have the added benefit of being on wheels, so when your production is finished, you can roll the equipment out of the way until the next time.

Another thing to consider is the noise generated by your computer. If you're using a modern desktop machine with a high-powered processor, the noise made by the cooling fans may be picked up by your mics, particularly if you're using condenser mics. It's best to minimize this as much as you can. One good approach is to replace the standard fans and power supplies with low-noise versions available from vendors such as PC Power & Cooling (`www.pcpowercooling.com`). If you don" feel like shelling out the extra money for quiet fans, you can reduce the amount of noise picked up by your mics by moving the offending machine as far away as possible. You also can attenuate the noise with acoustic foam or small baffles.

CAUTION If you use baffles to muffle the sound of your computer fans, be sure not to restrict the airflow too much. Computers that run too hot are highly prone to failure.

Talent + engineer

If you're fortunate enough to have some help producing your podcast, you may want to consider setting up a studio where the *talent* (meaning your guests and you, the interviewer) is in a separate room from the equipment. This accomplishes a few things. First, the audio engineer works without worrying about keeping absolutely quiet. Second, audio equipment can be somewhat intimidating to some people, so doing the interview in another room can sometimes make for a more relaxed, natural interview.

Equipping a Studio on Any Budget

Okay, we've talked about equipment until we're blue in the face. It's time for you to go out and spend some money. We know you want to. We also know you probably want recommendations. We're not going to tell you exactly what to buy, but we'll make some general recommendations, based on a total estimated budget. Remember that audio equipment doesn't go out of style as quickly as cell phones do; if you buy the good stuff, chances are it will last you a lifetime.

The following suggestions below don't include some of the extras that you're going to need with every setup, such as microphone cables, stands, acoustic treatment for your recording environment, and so on. The amount of extra equipment you need is dependent on the equipment you buy and the scale of your podcast. Whatever you do, be sure to buy good cables, and buy a few spares, just in case.

Cheapskate ($0)

Hey, no one is saying you have to spend money. You can do a lot with a little. In fact, you may want to do a few test runs with no investment to make sure you're going to enjoy podcasting and to see where the painful points are before you spend any money. If that's the case, you can make due with the following:

- The crappy mic you found in the empty office next door
- The built-in soundcard on your laptop
- Windows Sound Recorder or Mac Sound Edit 16

- The plastic speakers that come with most desktop computers
- Audacity audio-editing software

Just plug it all in and go. When you realize the quality could be better and it's time to spend some money, step up to the next level.

Novice (<$250)

The most important purchase you can make is a good microphone. The new USB mics offer good quality, or you can buy a standard microphone (so you can use it with portable recording units or for other applications) and an audio interface. The cheaper audio interfaces have a maximum of two mic inputs, so you'll be somewhat limited, but two mic inputs may be all that you'll ever need. You'll also need a decent set of headphones to monitor with, so your shopping list looks something like this:

- A USB mic (Samson CO1U, Blue Snowball), or a decent dynamic mic (Shure SM58, EV 635) and a USB or FireWire audio interface (M-Audio Mobile Pre, PreSonus FireBox)
- A decent set of headphones (Sony, AKG, Sennheiser)
- Audacity audio-editing software

With this modest investment, you can create a great-quality podcast easily. The microphone is going to increase your quality exponentially, and Audacity should take care of most of your editing and processing needs.

Enthusiast (~$600)

After you've got the bug, you'll probably want to buy some more equipment to make your life a little easier and to broaden the possibilities for your podcast. A small mixing desk is a must, and a telephone hybrid probably will come in handy. You also should buy a good set of monitors so you can hear the improved quality you'll be producing. You also may consider upgrading your audio-editing software.

- A Shure SM58 or EV 635 mic
- A USB mixing desk (Yamaha, Alesis, Mackie)
- A telephone hybrid (JK Audio)
- A decent set of monitors (Tapco, M-Audio)
- Sound Forge LE, Peak editing software

Professional ($1,000 +)

After the sponsorship money starts rolling in, you can really get serious. It's time to spring for a true broadcast-quality microphone and a top-notch digital telephone hybrid. While you're at it, you may want to upgrade your mixing desk, and heck, you may as well grab the flagship audio-editing software.

All-in-one Podcasting Kits

Podcasting is so popular at the moment that many audio equipment manufacturers and suppliers are putting together special bundles that include everything you need to create a podcast. Some feature a mixture of hardware from different manufacturers, and most come bundled with the nearly ubiquitous Audacity. One good place to shop is Broadcast Supply Worldwide (www.bswusa.com), which offers a starter, a veteran, and a pro package. Many other audio equipment suppliers offer similar package deals. These are a great way to get started and to establish a relationship with a reputable equipment dealer.

The M-Audio Podcast Factory bundle

- A top-notch mic (Shure SM7, EV RE20, Neumann TLM49)
- A Telos One digital telephone hybrid
- A Mackie Onyx FireWire mixing desk
- High-quality monitors (Mackie, Genelec, JBL)
- Sound Forge, Audition, or Peak Pro editing software

At this point, you should be in audio nirvana. You've got a fabulous mic, a telephone hybrid, a great desk to mix it all with, and fabulous audio-editing software. There is nothing you can't do. The world awaits the glorious quality of your podcast.

Summary

No doubt about it: To produce a high-quality podcast, you're going to have to invest in some audio equipment. This chapter covered the following topics:

- Because the microphone is the first piece of equipment in your signal chain, it's the most important. Buy a good mic, and your podcast quality will improve. You may need to invest in plenty of other equipment, depending on your budget and the type of podcast programming you're trying to produce.

- Don't be afraid to spend a little money. In general, audio equipment doesn't wear out: A good mic will be a good mic for as long as you own it. The same goes for good headphones, monitors, cables — you name it. If you buy the good stuff, you'll have to buy it only once.

The next chapter teaches you how to hook up all your brand new, shiny equipment so you can get cracking with your podcast.

Chapter 6

Basic Audio Production

Now that you've spent time drooling over the latest and greatest audio gear, and invested some of your hard-earned cash in decent equipment, you need to figure out how to hook it all up and produce professional sounding podcasts. The great thing about working with audio is that for a minimal investment, you should be able to produce your podcast to a very high standard. The powerful technological leaps we've seen in the world of computers have also brought great advances (and price drops) in the world of home recording. What once required thousands of dollars worth of equipment now costs hundreds, or less.

This chapter starts off showing you how to connect your equipment to get the best sound, and then talks about some general recording techniques. Audio production may seem daunting at first, but by setting up some simple procedures and sticking to them, you'll find it to be pretty simple, and more important, lots of fun.

After that, we cover editing, where much of the power of audio production actually lies. Good editing can transform your podcast from mundane to professional. The techniques described in this chapter are all standard operating procedure in radio, television, and recoding studios around the world. Though we can't hope to turn you into an audio engineer in a few short pages, we can at least point you in the right direction. Let's start by setting up your equipment — the right way.

Setting Up Your Equipment

The preceding chapter talked in some detail about the different kinds of equipment you need to produce your podcast to a high standard. Ideally, you took the plunge and bought some equipment to fit your budget and the scale of your production. Now it's time to unpack everything and connect everything together. This is actually a critical step in podcast production. If you set up your equipment incorrectly, you'll leave yourself vulnerable to noise, interference, and distortion, which will compromise the sound quality of the final production. If set up correctly, your hardware will have you on the road to creating broadcast-quality programming. To understand why this step is important, you have to understand the concept of *gain*.

Setting your levels

Gain, also known as *level*, is the measure of the power of your audio signal. When using analog audio equipment, such as microphones and mixing desks, the signal is a continuously varying voltage. The higher the voltage is, the higher the gain and the louder the audio. All audio equipment is designed to work within a certain known range of voltages. To obtain the best possible quality out of your audio equipment, without adding any noise or distortion, you want to work within the optimal range for that piece of equipment, known as its *dynamic range*.

Dynamic range

The dynamic range of a piece of audio equipment is the difference between the loudest sound it can handle without distortion and the internal noise floor of the equipment. For example, when you turn a portable radio up too loud, you'll hear the sound crackle and buzz; that's distortion. You've just exceeded the dynamic range of the radio. The noise floor lies at the other extreme of the spectrum.

All audio equipment produces some amount of noise; there's no such thing as a perfectly quiet piece of equipment. That's because they're imperfect by definition. Every piece of audio equipment has all kinds of electronic components, each one adding a minute amount of noise, which taken in total is the noise floor. You can hear this noise — just turn your stereo up really loud while you're not playing anything. You'll hear a hissing and possibly a buzzing noise. This is the system noise that is being amplified. If you were actually playing a CD, you wouldn't hear this noise, because the music would be much louder than the noise.

More expensive equipment uses better components, which produce less noise. Consequently better equipment has a greater dynamic range. Cheaper equipment, well, you get the idea. This is the argument for investing in decent audio production equipment. If you produce audio with no audible noise, your podcast sounds much better. Noise is a dead giveaway that an amateur is behind the controls. Another giveaway is distortion. After your signal distorts, you can't remove the distortion. It can't be edited out of the signal, and it compromises the quality of your podcast.

Dynamic range is measured in decibels (dB). The human ear is capable of perceiving up to 120-130dB of dynamic range, before the pain threshold kicks in. We can hear a faucet dripping down the hall in the middle of the night, and endure hours in front of our favorite rock band. Our ears are extremely sensitive, which is not necessarily the case with the equipment and/or transmission methods used to produce audio.

Different audio transmission methods have different dynamic ranges. For example, compact discs have about 96dB of potential dynamic range, whereas FM radio has only about 70dB of dynamic range and AM radio has only about 48dB of dynamic range. This is because of the noise inherent in each system. If you think about it for a second, the quality differences between these systems is obvious. The larger the dynamic range is, the higher the quality of the audio signal and the less apparent any noise is.

Using meters to monitor levels

To control your levels, you need to keep an eye on your meters. Virtually every piece of audio equipment comes with some type of meter to indicate the level of the signal. Meters fall into three main categories: VU meters, LED Peak meters, and software VU/Peak meters, shown in Figure 6.1.

The first is VU or Volume Unit meters, which are common on older equipment (and new equipment going for that hip retro look). The needle indicates the overall power of the signal, represented as an average. They're very good for comparing the volume or power of a signal, but not good at registering quick peaks. VU meters usually have two scales, one that runs from 0 percent to 100 percent, and another that has zero where the 100 percent mark is, with negative numbers below 100 percent and positive numbers above 100 percent.

FIGURE 6.1

A software VU/Peak meter

Courtesy Sony Sound Forge

The next type of meter is the LED (Light Emitting Diode) Peak meter. LED meters are very fast, so they are generally used to indicate the peak values of the audio signal. LED meters generally have a single scale, measured in dB, running from approximately -40dB, up through zero, and on to +10 or +20dB.

> **NOTE** Decibels are a relative measure of power. The decibels used to measure the +20dB measurement on a meter aren't the same as the 120dB pain threshold. One is a measure of sound pressure, while the other is a measure of voltage. It can get kind of confusing

Finally, we have the software meter. Software meters can operate as VU or LED meters, and sometimes as both concurrently. In the image on the right of Figure 6.1, the meter indicates both VU level (the bulk of the display) and peak level (indicated by the thin line hovering above the VU level). The critical difference between analog meters and software meters is that analog meters have *headroom*, which means that the signal is allowed to go above zero, and digital meters have no headroom: Go above 0dB, and you'll hear awful square-wave distortion, which is very unpleasant. Digital meters usually include some sort of clip or peak light that indicates when you have peaks above zero. These must be avoided at all costs.

The point of all this is that you need to be careful when setting up your equipment Set your input level too low, and you're liable to hear some of the internal noise of your equipment. Set your level too high, and you'll get distortion. What you want to do is set a level that is high enough so that you don't hear equipment noise and conservative enough that you don't ever get distortion. It's a fairly broad range, so spend the time to learn how to set levels correctly. The result will be a much higher quality podcast.

Setting levels

When setting a level with a VU meter, be careful because VU meters don't register peaks. Those peaks may be loud enough to exceed the equipment's dynamic range and therefore cause distortion. It's best to set your levels between -10dB and -6dB on a VU meter. This leaves quite a bit of headroom for transient peaks, and any unexpected jumps in level. When you're setting levels with a peak meter, you can be a bit more aggressive, because you can see pretty much exactly where your peaks are. You should set your level so that the indicated level is in the -6dB to -3dB range. These settings should get you a good, clean, loud signal, with very little perceivable noise. If your levels occasionally peak above zero, don't worry; most audio equipment has sufficient headroom to handle momentary peaks without distortion.

Setting levels in the digital domain is a whole different matter. Any signal above 0dB causes distortion, because 0dB is considered an absolute maximum. As long as the signal remains above 0dB, you keep getting the same maximum value. The result is a sound wave with the top squared off, which sounds horrible. This is known as square-wave distortion.

You must be conservative when setting levels on digital equipment. Digital meters are almost always peak meters for precisely this reason. When setting your digital levels, you should target -10dB to -6dB. This should leave you plenty of headroom. It's better to be a little conservative and maximize your level later on using signal processing rather than set it too high and end up with distortion.

CROSS-REF Different methods of signal optimization are discussed Chapter 7.

Setting up a gain structure: A step-by-step example

Bearing in mind all that has been discussed in this chapter so far, it's time to set up your gain structure to produce high quality audio. The procedure is simple, starting with the first piece of audio equipment and working your way through the signal chain until you get to the final destination, your computer.

For the purposes of this example, we'll assume that you're using a microphone and a mixing desk, a USB audio interface, and recording straight to your hard drive. Your audio setup may differ slightly, but you should be able to follow these steps regardless:

1. Connect your microphone to your mixing desk, your mixing desk to your USB interface, and your USB interface to your computer. You should be using balanced cables whenever possible, because they provide a solid connection point and are highly noise-resistant. Turn on your mixing desk. If you're using a condenser microphone, be sure to turn on phantom power on (or you won't hear a thing).

TIP Be sure to turn on phantom power after you've connected all your microphones. Some microphones may be damaged if you plug them in with the phantom power already turned on.

CROSS-REF Different types of microphones, phantom power, and balanced cables are discussed Chapter 5.

2. Make sure you're monitoring only the microphone channel. Some mixing desks have "Solo" buttons to accomplish this; if your mixing desk doesn't have a solo button, then make sure all the other channels are turned down.

3. First, set the *input level* of the microphone. Do this by adjusting the input level (or trim) knob at the top of the mixing desk channel your microphone is plugged into, as shown in Figure 6.2. Speak into your microphone, and adjust the input level. The Mackie Onyx 1220 uses a peak meter, so adjust until it is peaking at -6dB to -3dB. A few peaks over zero are okay.

FIGURE 6.2

Setting the input level on a Mackie Onyx 1220 mixing desk

Connect mic to input.

Adjust input level.

Use meter to adjust your levels.

Set pan to center.

Set channel output.

Put channel in solo.

Set master output.

Courtesy Mackie Designs, Ltd.

4. To set the output level of the mixing desk, take the channel out of solo mode if your desk has a solo button. The meters on the mixing desk will now show the level of all channels combined. Turn your microphone channel up to 0dB (on some desks this is marked "U" for unity gain).

5. Mixing desks allow you to move things from side to side in the mix. This is known as *panning*, and is controlled by the pan knob on your mixer. Each channel has a separate pan control. Make sure your microphone is in the center of your mix. Check the pan setting to make sure it's right in the middle. Sometimes conversations between two people can sound more intimate if the two speakers are panned slightly to the left and right, but most of the time — and especially when setting up your gain structure — all microphones should be right in the middle of your mix.

TIP When recording an interview between two people, it's tempting to pan one person hard left and the other hard right. That may sound cool at first, but it isn't. It ends up sounding like ping-pong, where the voices are jumping from one speaker to the other. If your listeners are using headphones, you'll drive them absolutely crazy. A little separation is fine, but don't go overboard. And remember that if you're using stereo for separation, you're going to have to encode in stereo, which requires a higher bit rate to sound good.

6. Adjust the final output of your mixing desk by adjusting the master volume. This is generally on the lower left of the mixing desk, below the meters. You should set the output meters to -6dB to -3dB, leaving a bit of headroom for the unexpected.

7. Next it's time to move on to the USB audio interface. Depending on the make and model, you'll have some sort of meters and some sort of input adjustment. On some models, the metering can be fairly rudimentary. Adjust to keep your level consistent with the output level of the mixing desk. If you don't have full meters on your USB interface, you can use your recording software to check your input level. Open your audio editing software. You may need to put it in record mode to get to the level meters. Make sure your level is in the -10dB to -6dB range, and remember that anything over zero will distort!

NOTE Some USB audio interfaces come with special software to adjust the input level. If so, use this software to set your levels. After you've set the level via the software application, the level is automatically set for your audio editing software.

Congratulations. You've just set up your gain structure. Each piece of equipment is operating in its optimal range, so you should be producing a high-quality, noise-free audio signal. The best part about setting up a gain structure is that after you've set it, you shouldn't have to worry about it anymore. You can make small adjustments if necessary using the channel adjustments or the master volume output of your mixing desk.

TIP If you're connecting a number of different audio sources to your mixing desk, label the channels so you know what is coming in on the channels. Some mixing desks have an area to do this, known as a *channel strip*. If your desk doesn't have a channel strip, you can always create one by stretching a strip of masking tape below the channel faders (or knobs). Then you can write on the masking tape. Believe me, when you're grabbing for a fader in the middle of a podcast recording, knowing which fader is the right one is critical.

If you have more microphones or more equipment that you want to use during your podcast, you should set the input level for each channel just as we did for the microphone channel in the previous example. You can adjust the relative volume for each channel as needed using the channel level adjustments, so that all your inputs are mixed together at the right levels. Now that your levels have been set, you need to learn a little about digital audio.

CAUTION Make sure you always plug microphones into mic inputs and line level equipment such as CD players and iPod headphone outputs into line level inputs. Most inputs are clearly labeled as one or the other or have a switch that determines the expected input level. If you plug a microphone into a line level input, you won't get enough gain. Conversely, a line level output distorts a microphone input. Just because a cable fits doesn't mean it's the right input!

Understanding digital audio

At some point, your audio is going to have to be *digitized* on the way to becoming a podcast. Digitizing is the process of converting an analog audio input into a digital audio file. Whether you're recording directly to your hard drive or you're using a digital recording device, you have to choose which digitization settings to use.

To fully understand what is involved in digitization, understanding how digital audio files are created is important. Figure 6.3 illustrates an audio signal. The audio signal starts off as a continuously changing voltage. This voltage is created by the vibrations of the diaphragm inside a microphone and is what eventually causes the cones inside a speaker to vibrate and reproduce the original sound.

FIGURE 6.3

A sound wave and how it is digitized using samples

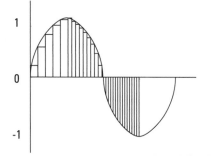

To store this as a digital audio file, we take measurements of the wave at specific intervals. These measurements are known as *samples*. In Figure 6.3, each section of the wave has different numbers of samples under it. The number and accuracy of these samples determine how accurate the digital version of our audio file is and therefore the *fidelity* of the digital version to the original.

Setting Up a Telephone Recording: Using an Aux Send

If you're including guests calling in via telephone in your podcast, you need a way to mix their voice into your podcast. The simplest way is via a telephone tap, but they're low quality. A better approach is to use a telephone hybrid, which offers much higher quality and separates the caller's voice from your voice. The output of the telephone hybrid is plugged into your mixer, enabling you to treat it as a separate input.

However, there's a small detail that is left out of this equation: sending your microphone signal *to* the hybrid, so that the person on the other end of the phone conversation can hear what *you're* saying. This is done using an *auxiliary*, or *aux send*. Each channel on a mixing desk has one or more aux sends. Just twist the knob, and you can send a signal from that channel to the aux send. The aux send output on the mixing desk can then be connected to whatever equipment you want to send a signal to.

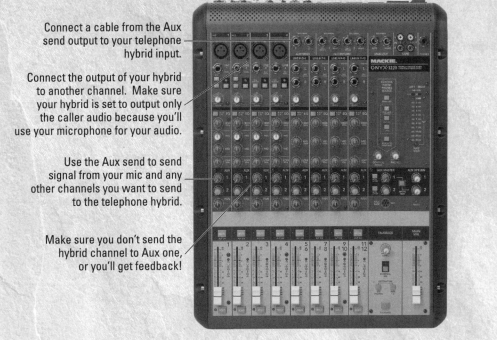

Connect a cable from the Aux send output to your telephone hybrid input.

Connect the output of your hybrid to another channel. Make sure your hybrid is set to output only the caller audio because you'll use your microphone for your audio.

Use the Aux send to send signal from your mic and any other channels you want to send to the telephone hybrid.

Make sure you don't send the hybrid channel to Aux one, or you'll get feedback!

Aux sends are used to send signals from channels to a telephone hybrid.

To set up a telephone hybrid, you have to adjust the level being sent to the hybrid via the aux send, and then the return level of the caller's voice coming from the hybrid. First, connect a cable from the aux send output to the hybrid, and adjust the level from the mixing desk to the hybrid. Your telephone hybrid may have separate input and output meters, or a switch that swaps the meters between input and output modes. Make sure you're monitoring the input, start speaking into your microphone, and turn up the aux send on that channel until you've got a good level being sent to your hybrid. This is important; if you don't have any level going to your hybrid, your caller won't hear you!

Next, connect the output of the hybrid to a channel on your mixing desk. You can set a rough level using a dial tone, but realize that a dial tone is much louder than most people's telephone voices. Set the dial tone level nice and loud, at around -3dB. You may need to adjust the level slightly when you call your guest, but that can probably be done using the fader or knob for that channel, as opposed to the gain adjustment at the top of the channel.

Make sure you don't send any of the hybrid return channel to the aux send! If you do, you'll be greeted with some feedback in your headphones, which is never pleasant.

Bit depth and sampling rates

Bit depth and sampling rate are the two things that determine the fidelity of a digital audio file. You may have seen pairs of numbers rattled off in equipment brochures such as 16/44.1, or 24/96. The first number generally refers to the *bit depth*, the second to the *sample rate*.

In the previous section, we talked about taking measurements of an analog input at specific intervals. This is the *sample rate*. As the sample rate increases, the digital representation more closely resembles the analog original. You must choose a sample rate that is high enough to give you the fidelity you require.

Bit depth is the other variable in the fidelity equation. Bit depth refers to the number of bits used to represent the measurement of the analog voltage. For example, you could represent the distance to the nearest street corner as a block, 50 yards, 143 feet, or 1,717 inches. As you increase the accuracy of your measurement, you need more digits to represent the number. The same is true for our digital samples of our audio input.

In the binary world, each bit you add doubles the range of numbers you can represent. Looked at in another way, each bit you shave off your bit depth cuts your accuracy in half. If we use eight bits, we can have up to 256 different values. With 16 bits, we get more than 65,000 possible values, and 24 bits provides more than 16 million values. So how much accuracy do we need?

Choosing your digitization settings

Ideally, you want to record using the highest sample rate possible, and use the largest bit depth you can. The problem is that using high sample rates and large bit depths creates larger files. Increasing the bit depth from 16 to 24 bits increases the file size by 50 percent, and increasing the sample rate from 44.1KHz to 96KHz more than doubles the file size. Even though storage is relatively cheap and getting cheaper all the time, there are some practical limits to how much fidelity you really need, especially given that podcasts are encoded using lossy codecs such as MP3 that compromise the fidelity. A better master provides a higher podcast quality, so how much fidelity do you really need?

Compact discs use 16 bits and a 44.1 KHz sample rate. Most people consider this sufficient to capture the full range of audio that the human ear is capable of hearing (though many audio engineers would disagree). This is probably what you should use for your master recordings. Although many recording devices and audio editing platforms now offer higher sample rates and bit depths, it's debatable whether the extra quality justifies the increase in storage requirements. You'll just end up using lots more storage space for your archived masters.

If you're producing your podcasts to an extremely high standard, consider using 24/96 (24 bits/96KHz sample rate). This "future-proofs" your masters and will impress all your audio engineering buddies. For most folks, however, the standard 16/44.1 setting will more than suffice.

> **TIP** If you're producing a video podcast, Digital Video (DV) audio is sampled at 48KHz, or sometimes even at 32KHz. These sampling rates were chosen when digital video standards were developed. They're different from the 44.1KHz audio sampling rate, because the sampling rate for audio predates them and was chosen due to technological restrictions at the time. This is fine; the key is not to resample the audio to 44.1KHz (or any other sampling rate). Re-sampling introduces artifacts and degrades the quality of the original audio.

Microphone Technique

It may seem like second nature to some to speak into a microphone. Others may look at the microphone with the same look you'd give a high-tension wire lying on the ground. The fact of the matter is that good microphone technique is important to produce a good podcast. Different mics have different pickup characteristics and different sensitivities, so you must use proper technique to get the best out of your mic.

CROSS-REF Microphones are discussed in more detail in Chapter 5.

The basic requirement is that the microphone be in front of the sound source, as close as possible, but not so close that the microphone distorts or picks up any noise, particularly from troublesome consonants such as the letters "p" and "b." These letters are known as *plosives* and can be quite problematic, because the burst of air that comes out of your mouth when you pronounce them can cause the microphone to "pop." This is audible as a loud pop or a "thunk" in your recording. You may be able to get rid of this noise later on using signal processing, but try to avoid them in the first place.

Plosives are created by letting out a big burst of air from your mouth. The pop occurs because the tiny diaphragm inside the microphone is overloaded. To avoid this, you can use a *pop screen*, which is a bit of foam or sheer material designed to break up the burst of air. Pop screens must be acoustically transparent, meaning that they should not muffle or distort the sound at all. Many handheld microphones have a pop screen built in, as shown in Figure 6.4. For other mics, you can buy foam pop screens that fit over the microphone or a pop shield that is placed in front of a microphone. All of these are very effective at reducing the incidence of microphone pops.

FIGURE 6.4

A pop screen

TIP In a pinch, you can create your own pop shield by stretching a piece of pantyhose over a coat hanger and placing it in front of your microphone.

Handheld mics

Handheld mics are generally dynamic, directional mics, which means that they are resistant to handling noise, and tend to pick up in one direction. Directional mics must be pointed at the source they're recording. That may seem obvious, but novices sometimes forget they're holding the mic. Their hand will drop to their side, completely oblivious to the microphone. For this reason, handheld mics are often better left to seasoned professionals.

Clip-on mics

Clip-on mics, also known as *lavalier* mics, are a great option for most podcasting applications. They're small and unobtrusive, so people often forget they're even wearing them. (This can be somewhat embarrassing when a guest or on-air talent attempts to walk away with the microphone still attached.) Clip-on mics come in both directional and omni pickup patterns. For interviewing applications, use omni-directional mics, because they provide better pickup when the person speaking turns his head from side to side. If you're using directional mics, the level can drop dramatically when the talent turns away from the mic. For that reason, microphone placement is important when using clip-on mics.

The placement of a clip-on mic is dependent on the pickup pattern of the microphone, the clothing the talent is wearing, and the placement of guests, as shown in Figure 6.5. If two people are facing each other, for example sitting across from one another at a table, the mics should ideally be placed centrally, about six inches below the speaker's chin. If two people are sitting side by side, the mics should be placed so that when they are talking the mics will be in the best possible position to pick up the signal.

FIGURE 6.5

Clip-on mic placement depends on the situation.

Normal placement
of a clip-on mic.

If the talent will be talking
in profile, "cheat" the mics
to the side.

The Proximity Effect

When you speak very close to a microphone, the bass frequencies are boosted, giving a warm tone to the sound. This is known as the proximity effect. It is usually quite pleasing to the ear and is one of the reasons professional DJs sound the way they do. (They are also paid for the quality of their voices.) The proximity effect is immediately apparent if you're wearing headphones. As soon as people hear their voice warm up when they get close to a mic, they stay close to the mic.

The only problem is that if you get too close, you increase the chances of popping the microphone with plosive consonants like "p" and "b." The solution, unsurprisingly, is to use a pop screen or pop shield. Not only do they force the talent back from the mic, but they also help break up any potential pops before they reach the microphone diaphragm.

Studio mics

If you have the luxury of a studio setup for your podcasts, you can use high-quality studio microphones. These mics can be used only in studio settings because they are so sensitive. They are very susceptible to handling noise and therefore impractical for handheld or non-studio applications.

Studio mics are placed on mic stands and often in special suspension mounts that make them less sensitive to vibration. The mic should be positioned so that it points at the talent's mouth. Usually, you want to have the mic a little high and pointed slightly downward towards the user's mouth, as opposed to below them and pointing up. This helps prevent pops, because the burst of air tends to be aimed downward.

Many, but not all, studio mics are condenser mics. In fact, two of the most popular radio mics, the Shure SM-7 and the Electrovoice RE-20, are dynamic mics. Both of these mics are treasured because of their lack of proximity effect and their resistance to pops.

Recording

After you've got all your gear set up and you've practiced your microphone technique, you're ready to hit the record button and go, right? Wrong. Recording is not something you should rush into. In fact, the more time you take to test, prepare, and practice beforehand, the better your podcast will be. You've seen it in the movies or on television — the rock and roll roadie going from mic to mic saying, "Check-one-two," over and over again. There's a good reason for this. He's checking to make sure:

- The mic works
- The monitoring desk at the side of the stage is receiving signal
- The mixing desk out in front of the house is receiving signal
- A person standing in front of this microphone will hear himself

Luckily, you won't have to check quite as many things, but you really do need to make sure everything is working before you start recording. It's time for your own version of a sound check.

Sound check

Sound check is what you do before you press the record button. It's the last sanity check before you commit to your podcast. Even if you've used your recording setup a hundred times before, you should always do a quick sound check to make sure everything is working as expected. Your mental check list may differ depending on your situation, but essentially you have to check the following:

- All your microphones are working and have enough gain
- Any other audio sources are working and have enough gain
- All the equipment in your audio chain is functioning properly
- Your recording device is getting a good level
- Your aux send levels (such as the send to a telephone hybrid) are good
- The level in the headphones is good (if you're using headphones)

Of course, to test whether a mic is working, someone has to be talking into it. This is where "Check-one-two" comes in. Always set and check levels with the actual talent, so you get the levels right. After all, not everyone is as much of a blowhard as you are. In fact, some of your guests may be downright wallflowers. If so, a common trick to get your talent talking before the interview is to ask them what they had for breakfast. Even if they can't remember, or if they say they don't usually have breakfast, it's usually enough to get them started and serves as an icebreaker for the actual show. Of course, you can ask your talent about anything you like — just get them talking for a few seconds so you can check your levels. After you've checked all your levels and are satisfied that they look good, you're ready to start recording.

The countdown

You need to do two things to start your recording session. First, you have to press the record button. It's actually not unheard of for complete interviews to be done before people realize that they forgot to start recording. Unfortunately, one of your authors knows from experience. Save yourself the embarrassment, and make sure to press the record button.

Next, let the talent know that the recording has actually started, and leave a good spot for you to edit later on. This is where the countdown comes in. After you've pressed the record button, put a little identifier at the start of your file, including the name of your interviewee, and a quick countdown, something like, "Interview with Charles Peterson, talking about Leica cameras, in five... four... three... two... one." Take a deep breath. Introduce your show, your guest, the topic, and you're off and running.

The countdown is important for a couple of reasons. First, leaving a small, silent gap at the beginning of your podcast makes it much easier to edit. A common mistake novices make is to go from the sound check straight into the interview, without even so much as a breath in between. It may feel natural at the time, but you'll find when you're trying to edit to clean up the start of the podcast that it doesn't sound natural when you cut out the sound check chatter. Second, the countdown is a focusing mechanism, both for you as an interviewer and for the talent. It doesn't matter how off-the-cuff you want your podcast to sound; you still want it to sound professional, and giving yourself and your talent that extra few seconds to mentally prepare works wonders.

> **TIP** A great way to test your talent's levels is to have them say their name and then spell it. This way you know how to pronounce their name, and how to spell it!

Intros and outros

Every radio and television interview program with a host has an intro and an outro. They're important, because they tell the audience what they can expect during the program, and they provide an overview of the topic. The intro to your podcast should have a "hook" in it, meaning a sneak peek or hint about the subject matter that makes the show irresistible to your audience. Not everyone in your audience is going to be riveted by every single guest and topic you decide to cover. We live in a busy world, and you've got lots of competition for your audience's time. Use the intro to tell your audience why you're excited about the program, particularly if you're covering a slightly obscure topic or you have a guest without marquee name recognition. If you do a good job of getting your audience excited, they'll stick around for the entire podcast.

Similarly, be sure to wrap up every program with a good outro. Obviously, you need to thank your guest(s) and your audience. You should also summarize the program, highlighting the subjects you covered. Then use this time to talk about your next podcast. If folks have made it this far, chances are good that they'll come back for your next podcast, perhaps even subscribe to your RSS feed. You can help ensure that they do so by letting them know what to expect next time around. This may be the first program that some listeners have tuned in to. Even if you don't know exactly who your guests will be or what topics will be discussed during the next program, you can at least give them an idea of what to expect.

Doing "drop-ins" and "pick-ups"

No matter how prepared you are, you may forget to cover something that you absolutely must have in your program. You may realize it at the end of your recording session when glancing at your notes, or heaven forbid you may realize it during the editing phase. Not to worry; if you were relatively careful setting up your levels, you should be able to do it as a "drop-in" or "pick-up."

A drop-in is when you record over an existing recorded piece and replace a section with a newly recorded version. For example, when movies are sanitized for viewing on airplanes and television, the actors have to drop-in over all the blue language and replace it with "drat!" or some other acceptable utterance. A pick-up is when you add to the end of the recording, knowing that you'll later edit the piece and insert the pick-up section where it belongs in the interview.

Drop-ins are more common in multi-track music recording, where an otherwise perfect performance may be marred by a single bad note. In cases like this, the musician or singer will sing along with the recorded version, and the engineer will "drop in" and record over the offending section. This requires quite a bit of skill and is not for the faint-hearted.

Pick-ups, however, will probably become part and parcel of your podcasting routine. For example, you may want to redo your introduction to reflect something that came up during the interview. Or you may want to rephrase some of the questions you asked, or perhaps even ask a question that you forgot earlier in the interview. In this case, you can simply do a pick-up, where you record what you need after the initial interview. Then, during the editing phase, you can move the sections around at will. Editing is covered in the next section.

Recording Skype Conversations

If you're going to use Skype to call your podcast guests, you have to figure out how you're going to record the conversation. Depending on what equipment and software you have, this can either be tricky or really simple. If you're using stereo audio editing software to record, like Audacity, it's tricky. If you're using multi-track recording software, it's a piece of cake.

The problem with stereo audio editing software is that you can choose only a single source for your stereo recording — you can't choose two separate sources, say one for the left channel and one for the right. In the case of a Skype conversation, your voice will be coming in either on a mic channel, the line in on your soundcard, or a channel on your audio interface. Your guest's voice will be played back by Skype via your main sound output. See? These are two separate signals. Plus, it doesn't help that one is an input, and the other technically is an output.

A number of applications enable you to hack your way around this conundrum. Soundflower (OSX) and Virtual Audio Cables (Windows) are two examples. These applications allow you to route audio in ways that the default audio drivers won't allow. For good tutorials on how other podcasters have solved this problem, check out the following links:

- **Windows:** `http://www.henshall.com/blog/archives/001056.html`

- **Mac:** `http://www.macdevcenter.com/pub/a/mac/2005/01/25/podcast.html`

However, it's probably easier to use one of the software packages mentioned in the preceding chapter such as Hot Recorder or Pamela. The latest versions are pretty stable and offer far more control than they did when first released. One shortcoming with these programs is that you may be forced to record in MP3, which may not be as high quality as if you were recording an uncompressed audio file from your nice microphone. It's a tradeoff between quality and convenience.

Of course, if you're using multi-track audio recording software it is much easier to record multiple sources. Multi-track recording software allows you to choose a different source for each track you're recording. Record on two separate tracks, and specify your microphone or audio interface for the first track and the stereo output for the second track. You'll end up with pristine audio from your mic on track one and your caller's voice recorded on track two. This has the added benefit that you can then process the two tracks separately, using different signal optimization techniques.

Editing

Chances are good that no matter how good you get at producing your podcast, you're still going to want to do some editing. You'll want to remove the countdown from the beginning of your recording, for one thing. And you may have plenty of other reasons to edit. Many podcasters do a quick "top and tail" edit, where they make sure the beginning and end of their podcast sounds right. This is the minimum you should do.

You can completely change the feel of a program by editing the flow of the material. You can make your guests sound better (or worse) with editing. As mentioned in the preceding section, you can also edit the program to include any pick-ups you did. Editing is a very powerful tool in your production arsenal. The following few sections are intended to give you an idea of how editing can be used to improve your podcast.

Editing for convenience

In the recording section earlier in this chapter, we covered the concept of pick-ups, where you record the intro and outro for the podcast after the actual interview, or perhaps re-record yourself asking questions to your guests, or even cover a topic that you forgot to cover in the body of the program. These pick-ups must be placed into the body of the podcast, where they belong. It's a simple copy-and-paste operation that saves you the hassle of having to do the entire show over again.

Editing for flow

Unless you (and your guests) have a significant amount of broadcast experience, chances are good that sections of your podcast may drag a little. Perhaps the answer to a question got a little long-winded, or it took you three or four attempts to frame a question the way you wanted to ask it. While a certain amount of this keeps the podcast sounding natural, too much of it can make your podcast sound unprofessional and frustrate your audience. If you find a natural place to edit, try taking out some of the extraneous material. For example, consider the following:

"I've been wondering, because you've been doing this for so many years, and, well, we've known each other for what, ten years now? Anyhow, as an observer of Internet trends and how they adapt, where do you see podcasting in five years' time?"

This could probably be cut to, "I've been wondering, where do you see podcasting in five years' time?" or even "Where do you see podcasting in five years' time?" Some of the removed content may have added color, but you really have to ask yourself whether the information is necessary, and whether your audience will be interested in it. In general, less is more, and it's best to edit when things start to wander off course.

Editing for content

Another thing to ask yourself is whether everything you recorded is necessary. You may have asked a few questions that really didn't go anywhere or didn't really yield any significant insights. Remember that your audience is tuning in for a reason, and if you're not staying on topic, you run the risk of losing them. Another thing to consider is how the topics covered in the podcast are related.

For example, you may start off talking about topic A and then realize that folks need to know about topic B to understand topic A. So you talk about topic B for awhile and then go back to topic A. You may consider moving the discussion of topic B before topic A. Of course, this depends on whether the edits are even possible and whether they feel natural. Editing is incredibly powerful, but it can be a double-edged sword. If an edit is noticeable, you're doing more damage than good. You can't always edit things the way you want.

> **TIP** Another reason to do pick-ups is to cover edits. If you need to remove a large section of content, you can hide the edit by asking a question that seemingly joins the two edited sections.

Editing for quality

Most people, particularly if they don't have lots of broadcast experience, tend to insert lots of "ums" and "ahs" in their conversation, often without even realizing it. In fact, you may be surprised to discover your own verbal "tics" the first time you listen to your podcast recording. This is where editing can be incredibly effective, and it can make you and your guests sound much better. Edit out the offending tics, and presto, you'll sound like a professional.

> **TIP** You may want to edit out breaths taken in the middle of sentences. Breath noise can be particularly problematic if you're using compression, because breaths sound louder. The simple solution is to remove the offending breaths. However, sometimes when you remove breath noise, the resulting sentence doesn't quite "flow" right. The solution is to add a small amount of silence where the breath was, so the sentence doesn't sound rushed.

Editing how-to's

Editing is a really simple operation on most audio editing platforms. All you really have to do is highlight the section you want to work on, and then either delete it or copy it so you can paste it somewhere else in your program. One thing that is really important, particularly if you're going to be doing extensive editing, is to save a "raw" version of the original interview. That way, if you somehow mess up the edited version, you always can go back to the original and start from scratch.

In fact, if you're going to be doing lots of editing, you may want to save intermediate versions. For example, the first thing you may do is tidy up the start and end, and remove all the ums and ahs to clean up the podcast. You should save this version, with something in the file name to indicate what stage of the edit you're at. After you've saved this version, you can then do further editing, removing or rearranging sections of your program. Save this as a third and final master of your program. If you decide that you don't like some of the edits, you won't have to start from scratch.

Archiving Your Masters

As you produce more and more podcasts, you'll notice your hard drive slowly filling up, particularly if you're saving numerous versions of your podcasts (which is highly recommended). At some point, you'll want to archive your files so you can clear out some space on your hard drive. A number of formats are available for your archives:

- **CD-ROM, DVD-R:** CD-ROM or DVD discs are cheap and reliable. However, they are somewhat limited in capacity, and they start to take up lots of space on your shelves as your archives grow.

- **External Drives:** External hard drives have much greater capacities than CD-ROM and DVD. They also have the advantage of speed, because you don't have to burn the disc. However, there is some question as to how long hard drives last — and if you try to prolong their life by not using them, some hard drives can freeze, taking all your data with them.

- **Tape-based Backup:** Several tape-based archival formats are available. These are extremely reliable, but tape-based systems are expensive and often very slow.

As you can see, there is no perfect archival system. Each has its advantages and disadvantages. You'll probably want to start off burning your files to CD-ROM or DVD-R, and then move up to an external drive or tape-based system when the amount of files (and the success of your podcast) justifies it. Just be sure to archive everything, because you never know what uses you'll have for your programming. When the next media distribution mechanism appears, you'll be ready to take advantage of it.

Finally, it's worth mentioning that no archival storage method is immune to fires, floods, or theft. Consider storing copies of your masters in multiple locations. Storing a portable hard drive at work or in a storage space is simple enough. Online storage solutions also are available for that extra bit of security.

TIP Ironically enough, putting your hard drive in the freezer can "unfreeze" it. The theory is that the lowered temperature shrinks the components and the fluids in the sealed bearings inside the hard drive, thereby unlocking the frozen hard drive. This is intended as a last ditch solution, and if it works for you, get your data off as soon as possible and replace the drive. (Please note that the authors haven't tried this, and we can't be held responsible if something goes horribly wrong, okay?)

Summary

Setting up your audio equipment is critical to the quality of your podcast. It's not difficult, but it's worth taking the time to do it right, particularly making sure your gain structure is correct:

- Make sure each piece of audio equipment is working within its optimal range.
- Use the right microphone for your application.
- For most podcasters, a good quality dynamic mic is a great choice.
- If you're producing your podcast in a controlled environment, you may want to step up to a condenser mic.
- Be sure to edit your podcast for content, quality, and flow.
- Always do a sound check before you begin your podcast.
- Archive master versions of your podcasts in the highest possible quality.

In the next chapter, advanced audio production techniques are covered, enabling you to match the quality of broadcast radio and television.

Chapter 7

Advanced Audio Production

T he preceding couple of chapters talked about the basic tools and techniques of audio production. Now it's time to explore the techniques that broadcast audio engineers use to make their productions sound professional. The techniques in this chapter can lift your podcast out of a sea of mediocrity and make it stand out. We can't tell you what to talk about or who to invite onto your show, but we can sure pass along a few tips and tricks that the pros have in their audio toolkit.

Keep in mind that, like any tool, audio processing can be dangerous when in the wrong hands. There's a big difference between audio that sounds great because of processing and audio that has the fingerprints of an untrained audio engineer all over it. As with most things, moderation is key.

We can't hope to turn you into fully qualified audio engineers in the course of a few pages. We can, however, point you in the right direction. The biggest assets you have at your disposal are your ears. Provided you have a good pair of headphones or monitors, you should listen critically to every bit of processing you attempt. If you're absolutely positive it adds something, stick with it. If you're not sure, don't do it. We're getting slightly ahead of ourselves, though. Before we talk any more about the philosophy of audio production, let's take a step back and talk about what it is we're going to do.

What Signal Processing Is

When we talk about audio signal processing, we are manipulating *level* one way or another. For example, when we're equalizing (EQing) a file, we're manipulating the level of particular frequencies to change the tonal quality of the audio. When we use compression, we're turning entire sections of the audio signal up or down, depending on the input level. This may not make complete sense until you've heard these two techniques in action, but it's worth remembering that all we're doing is turning things up and down. It really is that simple. The tricky part is knowing *what* to turn up or down, and *when*.

One of the great things about working with audio is that we have such amazingly powerful tools. In the next few pages, you'll see just how malleable audio is. You can make things sound better in many ways and without making things sound unnatural. In fact, we're used to hearing processed audio; virtually all broadcast audio, be it radio or television, is fairly heavily processed.

This is why signal processing is important. We expect a certain level of quality from our audio, particularly in the post-CD world. Gone are the days when people walked around with transistor AM radios with cheap mono earpieces. We're used to high-quality, full-spectrum audio. If your podcast doesn't provide this kind of experience, it sends a none-too-subtle cue: amateur. Think about the difference between a big FM radio station sound and the local community college radio. Some of the difference is the type of programming and the on-air talent, but much of it is just plain inferior processing.

Don't let your podcast fall into that category. You absolutely should be producing a program that sounds at least as good as your local radio station. Anything less is just lazy, and your listeners will know it. So pay attention to this chapter! Let's start with something we've all probably done unwittingly — equalization.

EQ (Equalization)

Equalization, or EQ as it is commonly known, is adjusting the tonal quality of audio by turning up or down certain frequencies. Audio engineers use the terms *boost* for turning up and *cut* for turning down. Many of you are probably familiar with EQ via the bass and treble controls on your home or car stereos. In fact, you may have already fiddled with these knobs to adjust the sound; congratulations, you're an audio engineer. Using your ears as a guide, you adjusted the EQ until it sounded right to you. That's exactly what EQing is.

EQ is used for a number of reasons. Sometimes you may need to enhance the tone of your audio by boosting frequencies that make your audio sound more pleasant. You may need to boost these frequencies to make up for a deficiency in your mic or because your voice sounded different one day due to a cold or a late night. On the other hand, you may want to cut frequencies that aren't helping the sound of your audio. This can also be due to a deficiency in your signal chain or to get rid of something unpleasant, like an excessively nasal sound or too much bottom end.

How to use EQ

At the end of the day, it's all about making your audio sound better. You want your podcasts to sound bright and full, not dull and thin. You may notice that the terms used to describe the effects of EQ are very subjective. Audio engineers regularly use terms like "presence," "sparkle," "warmth," and "air." Believe it or not, these terms aren't *that* subjective; they're actually ways of referring to certain parts of the frequency spectrum — where exactly in the spectrum is subject to debate, but in the next section we provide you with a table of frequency ranges, along with common terms used to describe the frequencies in each range. The first thing to do, however, is to listen to your audio critically and ask yourself a few questions. The following questions start at the bottom of the frequency range, and work up from there, but you can think about them in any order you like:

- Is it "warm" enough? Is there enough low frequency information? Be careful here, because even good studio monitors have a hard time reproducing the lowest audible frequencies.

- What about the midrange? Are the voices clear and understandable? Or is the sound too harsh?

- How about the high frequencies? Does the audio sound dull? Or do you have the opposite problem—too much high frequency information?

If you're unsure about the answer to any of these questions, do what other audio engineers do—use something else as a reference. For example, you could listen to a radio program that is similar to yours, and do what we call an A/B comparison. Listen to the radio program for ten seconds, listening in particular to the low frequencies. Then flip back your podcast, and compare. Does yours have less? More? Flip back and listen to the middle frequencies, and compare. Finally, listen to the high frequencies. This should give you an indication of whether your podcast is up to scratch, and if it isn't, what you may need to add (or cut) to make your podcast sound better. The trick is to find the right frequencies.

Finding the right frequencies

After you've done some critical listening and have an idea of what your podcast may need, the next step is to figure out what frequencies you want to manipulate. Human hearing spans a wide range of frequencies, from 20Hz up to 20,000Hz. Audio engineers divide this range into different slices when they're talking about it. In general audio engineers talk about the low frequencies, the *mids* or middle frequencies, and the high frequencies. The mids are often divided into the low mids and the high mids.

The midrange is the most important area for podcasters, because this is where human speech lies. It's no coincidence that our ears are most sensitive in this range. Small adjustments to the midrange can make your podcast easier to listen to. For example, boosting the high mids on your voice tracks can "lift" them out of the mix. Cutting the low mids on vocal tracks can help if your audio sounds cluttered or hard to understand.

Even though EQ generally operates on a fairly narrow range of frequencies, the overall effect is much broader. For example, you may want to warm up your podcast by adding a little bottom end. However, when you do this, other frequencies may not be as audible, because now all the low frequencies are louder. Similarly, if you cut the low mids, you'll probably find that your audio is a little easier to understand, because by reducing these frequencies, all other frequencies become a little more prominent and therefore more audible. Also, applying EQ at one frequency actually has an affect on other frequencies (see the "Harmonics" sidebar nearby). Maintaining the right relationship between all your frequencies is a delicate balance.

Though you may be tempted to grab a knob and twist it as far as it will go (if a little is good, more is better, right?), always be conservative with your EQ settings. If you add too much EQ, your audio will start to sound artificial. The idea is to gently polish your sound, not try to change it. If your audio sounds so bad that you feel like you need to use radical EQ, you should probably look at your signal chain (in particular your microphones).

TIP Audio engineers have a mantra for EQ: "Boost wide, cut narrow." This means that if you're going to boost frequencies, you should boost frequencies to either side of the target frequency. If you're going to cut a particular frequency, try to cut a very small area around that frequency. This makes EQ sound more natural.

Table 7.1 lists some good starting points for figuring out approximately where in the frequency range you want to work. After you have a rough idea of where you want to work, you can then try to narrow your frequency search. This depends on what type of EQ you have available. You may only have limited EQ available on your mixing desk, though chances are good that you'll have rich EQ options available in your audio editing software. The most common types of EQ are *graphic* and *parametric*, which are covered in the following sections.

TABLE 7.1

Useful EQ Ranges

EQ Range	Contents
20Hz – 60Hz	Extreme low bass. Most multimedia speakers and, in fact, home speakers cannot reproduce this. Boosting frequencies in this area can make your audio sound muddy and lead to distortion. Your best bet is to simply roll off these frequencies.
60Hz – 250Hz	This is where the audible low-end lives. Files with the right amount of low end sound *warm* and *fat*. Files without enough low end sound *thin*. Files with too much in this range sound *boomy*.
250Hz – 2kHz	The low midrange. Files with too much in the low mids are hard to listen to and sound telephone-like. Cutting in the 250 – 350Hz range can clarify your mix.
2kHz – 4kHz	The high midrange. Lots of speech information resides here, consonants in particular, so you don't want to push this range in your background music. In fact, cutting here in the music and boosting around 3kHz in your narration will make your podcast more intelligible.
4kHz – 6kHz	The presence range. These frequencies provide the clarity in both voice and musical instruments. In particular, boosting 5kHz can make your music or voiceover (not both!) seem closer to the listener.
6kHz – 20kHz	The very high frequencies. Boosting here adds "air" but can also cause sibilance problems.

Harmonics

When you EQ a particular frequency, you're actually affecting much more than just a single frequency. This is because all frequencies are interrelated. This gets pretty esoteric, but when you EQ a particular frequency, you also affect the *harmonic series* related to that frequency, Every *fundamental* tone has *overtones*, which are even mathematical multiples of the fundamental. So a 60Hz tone will have overtones at 120Hz, 180Hz, 240Hz, and so on. These overtones are much quieter than the fundamental, but they are there nonetheless. If you turn down the fundamental, the overtones also get quieter. This very subtle effect is why sometimes a very small amount of EQ can have a fairly dramatic effect.

Using a graphic equalizer

Graphic equalizers divide the frequency spectrum into a specific number of bands and assign a fader to each band, as shown in Figure 7.1. The number of bands varies, depending on the hardware or software. The more bands you have, the narrower the range of frequencies you're affecting when you move a fader up or down.

FIGURE 7.1

A typical graphic equalizer (Sony Sound Forge)

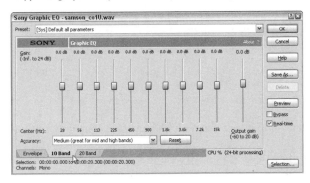

Using a graphic equalizer couldn't be easier; you just grab a fader and push it up or down. If you're not sure exactly which frequency you want to work on, don't be afraid to experiment. Grab a fader, push it up, and preview the result. You should be able to hear that frequency being boosted in your file. If you can't hear it, push the fader up even more. Push it up until the frequency is horribly exaggerated. Don't worry; this is how audio engineers do it. Exaggerate to find the frequency, and then scale back the EQ until you've achieved the effect you're after.

This also works when you're looking for a frequency that you want to get rid of. If you can hear a nasty frequency, for example a noisy hiss or even a honking quality to a vocal, hunt for the frequency by *boosting* until you find the frequency that you're after. Sure, it will make your file sound even worse, but after you find the offensive frequency, you can cut it knowing you're cutting in the right place.

Remember that you want to boost wide and cut narrow. If you're boosting a particular frequency, you should also boost the frequencies on either side — about half the amount you're boosting the target frequency, so you get a nice EQ curve. If you're cutting, cut only the offensive frequency. Don't cut *too* much; it will make your audio sound hollow and unnatural. If you've ever seen an audio engineer use a graphic EQ, you'll see them adjust their settings to get a nice smooth looking curve, perhaps with one or two nasty frequencies cut.

Using a parametric equalizer

Parametric EQ is slightly different from graphic EQ, because you don't have faders for specific frequencies. Instead, you choose a frequency, how much around your target frequency you want to affect and how much you want to boost or cut. Parametric EQ is usually implemented using knobs, with a separate knob for the frequency, the Q (which is the term used for the width of the effect), and the amount of boost or cut. Some parametric EQ systems don't provide control of the Q; this is known as semi-parametric EQ.

Some parametric EQ also have a little switch that changes the EQ from standard parametric to *shelving* EQ. Shelving EQ affects all frequencies above or below the frequency setting. Shelving EQ that affects all frequencies below the target frequency is known as *high pass*, because all frequencies above the target frequency are passed through untouched. Similarly, shelving EQ that affects frequencies about the target frequency is called a *low pass* shelf, because all the low frequencies are passed.

> **TIP** The EQ knobs on cheaper mixing desks are often fixed-frequency. They're also often shelving, so they're really not precision instruments. If you're going to use the EQ on your mixing desk, use it sparingly. After you've recorded EQ to "tape," it's hard to remove.

Figure 7.2 shows a software parametric EQ. You can see that it offers four fully parametric controls, along with both high and low pass EQ. Using a parametric EQ is very much like a graphic EQ, with the added ability to adjust the Q. To find the frequency you want, choose a very narrow Q and boost that frequency. Preview your audio, and move the frequency setting back and forth until you hit your target. Next, set your Q (remember: boost wide, cut narrow). Then adjust the boost or cut until your audio sounds the way you want it. If you want to work on another frequency, just use the same approach: Find, set your Q, and apply the right amount of boost or cut.

FIGURE 7.2

A software parametric equalizer (Sony Sound Forge)

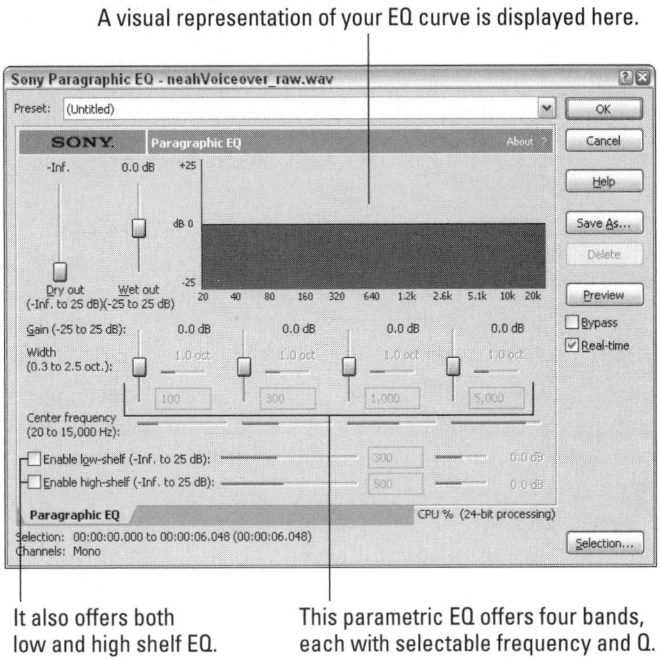
A visual representation of your EQ curve is displayed here.
Sony Paragraphic EQ - neahVoiceover_raw.wav
Preset: (Untitled)
OK
Cancel
Help
Save As...
Delete
Preview
Bypass
Real-time
Selection...
Paragraphic EQ
It also offers both low and high shelf EQ.
This parametric EQ offers four bands, each with selectable frequency and Q.

EQ: A step-by-step example

This section steps you through the EQ process, with both graphic and parametric EQ. We'll assume that this is a male voice track that needs a little bit of sparkle. We're trying to do the following:

- Add a bit of warmth to the bottom end.
- Add a little clarity to the midrange.
- Give the vocal a bit of *air*, a little extra shimmer.

Glancing back at Table 7.1, we can get starting points for each of these objectives. We're going to assume that you're using a software equalizer, though there's no reason that this couldn't be done using a hardware EQ. Also, the frequencies we're choosing in this example may not be the best frequencies for your audio, although they're probably a good place to start. Remember: Use your ears:

1. First, roll off the extreme low end. Chances are good (unless you have an extremely deep voice) that there is no information down here, except for possibly some room noise. Let's roll off everything below 60Hz.

On a graphic EQ, push down the faders below 60Hz. If you have more than one, start off gradually, rolling off about 3dB at 60Hz and then increasing the roll-off with each lower frequency.

On a parametric EQ, choose a high-pass filter at 60Hz and roll it all off. Shelving EQ has gradual roll-off built in.

2. Listen to your audio. You shouldn't hear much of a difference, if any. That's fine. You may hear a slight clearing up of the sound, and if so, that's even better.

3. Next, work on the midrange, because it's the most important. To give a voiceover a slight lift, you can boost the upper mids in the 2 – 4KHz range.

On a graphic EQ, pick a frequency in this range and boost it significantly, say 6-10dB. Preview your audio. Return that frequency to no gain, and try boosting the frequencies on either side, previewing each time. When you find the frequency that sounds best for your content, boost it 3dB and then boost the frequencies on either side 1.5dB, so there's a nice gentle lift. Preview the audio, and make sure it sounds good.

On a parametric EQ, choose a narrow Q and boost a frequency in the 2 – 4KHz range. Preview your audio. Try moving the frequency setting up and down, until you find the right frequency. Preview the audio each time you change the frequency. After you settle on a frequency, widen your Q to approximately 1.5. Boost 3dB, and give your audio one last preview to make sure you're doing the right thing.

4. Now listen to the low mids. The low mids are roughly where the sounds "er" and "uh" live. (If you've ever seen a sound check before a live gig, you'll hear the audio engineer making these sounds in the mics to check the EQ.) These frequencies give our ears infor-mation about the size of a room. You can often clear up a mix by cutting here, but be careful: You can make your audio sound too thin if you cut too much.

On a graphic EQ, you can experiment with cutting around 300Hz. You can do the same on a parametric EQ, with the added benefit that you can make the Q very narrow, to avoid thinning out your mix too much. Be sure to preview your audio to make sure you're making it sound better and not too thin.

5. If you're worried about the bottom end of your audio, particularly after cutting a little at 300Hz, you can add some warmth by boosting the bottom end. We rolled off the extreme low end earlier, but those frequencies are generally inaudible on most systems. To add audible bottom end, you need to boost in the 80 – 200Hz region. Where you boost depends on what (or who) you're EQing. The bottom end of male voices is usually around 100Hz; female voices are closer to 200Hz.

On a graphic EQ, you can find and push the frequency you're looking for. You may want to push the frequencies on either side slightly, as well. And the same goes for parametric; find the frequency, choose a fairly wide Q, and boost a bit. Preview your audio.

6. Finally, you need to decide if your audio needs any final sparkle. You can add this by boosting your high frequencies ever so slightly.

On a graphic EQ, start lifting at around 5KHz and boost the frequencies above 3dB. On a parametric EQ, select 5KHz for your shelving frequency and boost 3dB. Preview your audio. If you're happy with the sound, apply it! You may want to save this as a preset if this is a setting you think you'll be able to reuse.

Figures 7.3a and 7.3b show the results of all the preceding steps using graphic and parametric EQ. Your results may be slightly different; in fact, they should be, because you're listening to something different!

The results of the step-by-step example, illustrated on a) a graphic EQ and b) a parametric EQ.

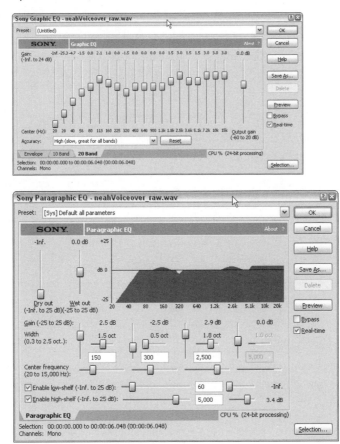

Advanced EQ techniques

EQ also can be used as a corrective measure. The techniques described in the preceding sections aimed to improve the overall sonic quality of your audio by focusing on what you wanted to be heard. You also can use EQ to remove extraneous noise that you *don't* want in the file.

Using Audacity EQ

Many of you will be using Audacity as your audio editing software, because it's powerful and — best of all — free. However, Audacity doesn't always have the best user interface. It's a great program if you know what to do, but it may not be immediately apparent what you have to do.

You must highlight some of your audio before any of the options are active on the Effects menu. Assuming that you're working on the entire file, you can place the cursor at the beginning of the file, hold the mouse button down, and drag the cursor across the entire file, or you can just press Ctrl+A (Opt+A on a Mac). Next, choose Equalization from the Effects menu.

The Audacity EQ window is by default ridiculously small. To make EQ adjustments with any sort of subtlety, you must stretch the window both vertically and horizontally. When you do this, more frequencies appear on the horizontal axis, and the dB scale on the vertical axis adds more detail.

The Audacity EQ window, resized for more detail

The way Audacity EQ works is that you draw the EQ curve you want. Clicking on the EQ curve gives you a point that you can push up or down. To limit the effect (to set a Q), you have to put points on either side of your target frequency. You can grab existing points and move them up and down, or slide them back and forth on the frequency scale.

For example, to roll off the low frequencies below 60Hz, start by clicking the curve at 60Hz. Next, click the curve below 60Hz, and drag this point to the bottom-left corner of the interface. It's a little crude and a little tricky to place points where you want them, but you'll get used to it. The results sound good, provided you choose your points correctly. Recreating the preceding step-by-step example in Audacity yields the following curve.

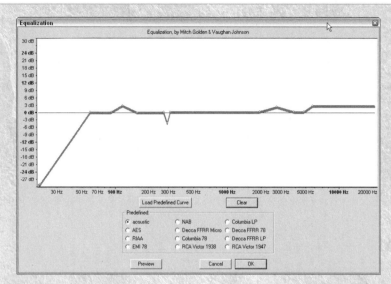

The preceding step-by-step example recreated using Audacity EQ

Another frustrating thing about Audacity is the inability to store presets, so after all the painstaking clicking and dragging, you can't save your work for next time. A handful of "predefined curves" are provided, but none is even remotely useful. In fact, we're scratching our heads wondering what the authors were thinking by providing these presets. Columbia 78? Gentlemen, it's the year 2007.

Alternatively, if you want to venture into the land of *plug-ins*, you can find EQ alternatives that "plug in" to Audacity. In fact, many of the effects that come with the default Audacity install already use the plug-in architecture. Audacity also has support for VST plug-ins, of which hundreds and hundreds are available. Some are free; for example, you could install the Voxengo EssEQ, which is a seven-band graphic EQ.

NOTE VST is an acronym for Virtual Studio Technology, a standard that enables audio software programs to exchange data. A VST EQ plug-in can be used in any audio (or video) editing program that supports the VST standard.

If you want to look around for free VST effects, you can explore a number of sites, including KVR Audio, which includes a good forum. In fact, here's a link to a discussion of this very topic:

```
http://www.kvraudio.com/forum/viewtopic.php?t=9780
```

Clearing up noise

If you recorded your audio in a noisy environment, you can use EQ to get rid of some of the worst noise. First, roll off all the low frequencies. You should do this regularly to all frequencies below 60Hz, because they're generally not reproduced by most systems. You can roll off more if you're dealing with serious noise. For example, traffic outside a busy city window will be audible as a steady low rumble, with the occasional siren or horn. If you roll off more of the bottom end, the sound of the traffic will be less audible.

Similarly, you can roll off high frequencies if you have noise problems such as air conditioning or tape hiss. In the preceding example, we boosted all frequencies above 5KHz to give the file some air; clearly, this is not something we'd want to do if we were in a noisy environment. Of course, we could have used the shelf to roll off all high frequencies above 8KHz or so and added a slight lift around 4–5KHz. Very little important voice information is in the range above 10KHz, so if you have noise problems, you can safely roll this off without any damage to the intelligibility of the audio.

Of course, in extreme situations, you can get pretty savage with EQ if necessary. For example, sometimes news reporters outside during a storm sound like they're talking through a telephone line. This is because the audio engineer at the station has rolled off all low frequencies and high frequencies, leaving just the mids.

Pops

Sometimes, a pop sneaks into your audio file, even if you're using a pop screen. If you zoom in to your audio file and look at the offending pop, you'll see that it's a very brief, very loud low frequency burst. You can highlight the offending word (or even syllable) and roll off the offending bass frequencies, as shown in Figure 7.4.

FIGURE 7.4

A pop is visible as a short, loud low-frequency burst, which can be fixed with EQ.

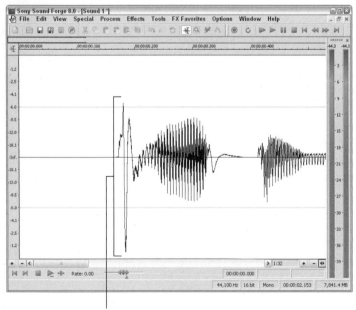

Pop!

Experiment with different amounts of roll-off at different frequencies. You'll find that if you roll off too much, you get rid of the pop, but the result may sound unnatural. Find a good balance between removing as much of the offending pop as possible, while retaining the natural feel of the original.

Dealing with sibilants

Some people have a problem with *sibilants*, which are consonants like the letter "s" ("d" and "t" can also be a problem but usually nowhere near as much) that contain a burst of high-frequency information. This is audible as a whistling or, well, an "ess" sound. A little of this is natural, but too much is annoying. Some people actually whistle when they pronounce these consonants, which is an extreme version of the same problem. Because this is usually a very localized problem, it can be dealt with using EQ.

Sibilants usually are most prominent around 5KHz. Just like the preceding example where a word was highlighted and bass frequencies were rolled off to get rid of a pop, you can highlight a word and try to cut the offending frequency. Dealing with sibilants is more troublesome than popping, because our ears are very sensitive to high frequencies, and even if it's only a momentary change, our ears may notice that the sound has changed. Not only that, but if someone has trouble with sibilants, it usually manifests itself throughout the entire interview — and the letter "s" is very popular in the English language. In general, if you want to deal with sibilants, you should use a *de-esser*. That's a fancy term we audio engineers made up to describe a "frequency dependent, side chain controlled compressor." De-essers are explained in the compression section, which comes next.

Compression

Compression is a form of *dynamics processing*, meaning that it deals with the overall levels in a file. Compression automatically turns down sections of your audio file, based on settings you specify. Think of it as an automatic volume control. In fact, you may have run into *Automatic Gain Control* (AGC) on a piece of hardware you own. Many portable tape recorders have an AGC circuit built in to the microphone. This is a fancy marketing term for a compressor. The AGC circuit ensures that all sounds are picked up and that sounds don't get so loud that they distort the microphone input.

Most compressors offer a number of controls that enable you to set where the compression effect kicks in and how drastic it is. But before we get into the details of how compression works, let's talk a little bit about why compression is useful.

Why use compression?

At its most basic, compression is useful as a safeguard against distortion. A compressor automatically adjusts the signal level when it exceeds a certain threshold, so that a guest who suddenly gets excited won't send your levels into the red. For this simple reason, compressors are very useful in live situations, when you may not be able to control situations as tightly as you'd like to.

Compression also is useful when working in lower fidelity environments, because it allows you to match the dynamic range of your production to the available dynamic range of the equipment on which it is played back. CD-quality audio has a very large dynamic range, and provided you're listening in a quiet environment, you can hear very quiet sounds as well as very loud sounds coming off a well-produced CD. This simply isn't the case for most podcasts.

First, most podcasts are played back on desktop systems, very often in slightly noisy environments. So if your podcast has very quiet sections, people will have a hard time listening, because they'll either have to turn the volume up temporarily or shush the people around them. And if you're encoding at a lower bit rate (96Kbps, 64Kbps, or even 32Kbps), the dynamic range simply isn't that great. The encoding software uses volume as a determinant of importance, so quieter sections won't sound as good as the louder sections.

CROSS-REF For a more detailed discussion of encoding software and the shortcoming of encoded audio, please see Chapter 12.

If the quieter sections of your podcast are going to be difficult to hear, then you want to turn those sections up, right? Sure you do. You want the overall level of your file evened out, so you don't have large differences between the loud sections and the quiet sections. You want the dynamic range *compressed*. This is precisely what a compressor does.

Figure 7.5 illustrates the dynamic range and headroom of a file. We'd like to turn up the quiet sections of this file, but at a certain point, the louder sections will go into distortion. Using a compressor, we can turn the file up and ensure that the loud sections don't go into distortion, because the compressor turns those sections down automatically.

The final reason to use compression is because we're used to hearing compressed audio on all the traditional broadcast mediums. Radio and television use compression liberally. This is partially for the protective reasons discussed previously, but also because of a particular side effect of compression. Compression tends to make things sound fuller, because it brings up the bottom end of the audio signal. Between the protective qualities of compression and the added warmth, this combination is hard to beat.

How compression works

Most compressors offer the same basic controls, which allow you to set the following:

- **Threshold:** Where the compression effect kicks in
- **Ratio:** The amount of compression applied above the threshold
- **Attack and Release times:** The length of time after the threshold is crossed that the effect is applied and removed

Figure 7.6 illustrates what different compression curves look like. Looking at the curve, you'll see that signal levels below the threshold are unaffected, and signal levels above the threshold are attenuated. The higher the compression ratio is, the more attenuation. When the compression ratio is high, it is known as limiting, because it more or less prevents the audio from exceeding the threshold.

FIGURE 7.5

The dynamic range and headroom of an audio file

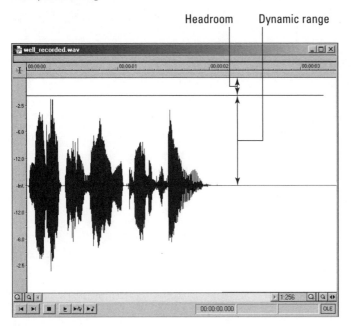

FIGURE 7.6

Compression curves with different compression ratios

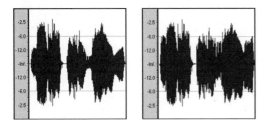

Setting a threshold

To illustrate how different threshold settings affect the output, let's assume that we're working with the audio file illustrated in Figure 7.7. We can see that this file has peaks as high as -2dB, but the bulk of the file is below the -10dB mark. If we want to compress this file lightly, we should set a threshold in the -6dB to -10dB range. Figure 7.8 illustrates compression applied to this file using two different thresholds, -6 and -20dB.

FIGURE 7.7

The audio file from Figure 7.5 after compression using a threshold of a) -6dB and b) -20dB

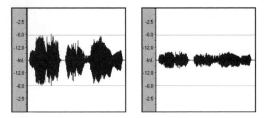

What is immediately apparent is that the file in Figure 7.7b has been compressed far more heavily than Figure 7.7a. We need to apply some gain to restore these files to their former levels. Figure 7.7b has far more headroom, so we can apply much more gain. After applying gain, we end up with the files illustrated in Figure 7.8.

FIGURE 7.8

The audio files from Figure 7.7 after applying compensating gain

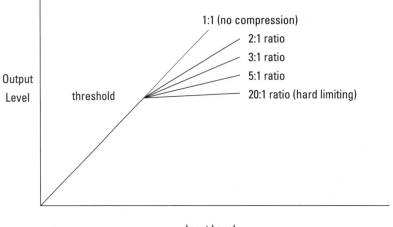

These files are both much louder than the original, but if you look closely at the figure on the right, the entire file is loud. It doesn't have any dynamics left, because the dynamic range has been *compressed*. To be honest, this file might be a little *too* compressed. Files that have been over-compressed are fatiguing to listen to, because EVERY SINGLE SYLLABLE IS LOUD. Think of drive-time radio programs; they're highly compressed, because the DJs are going absolutely nuts in the studio. The idea is to compete with all the noise of traffic and to keep you awake on your drive to and from work. But this is not the type of programming you really want to listen to all day long (see the "Compression: How Much Is Enough?" sidebar).

If your original audio file is well recorded, you should have peaks in the -3dB to -6dB range. Choosing a threshold in the -6dB to -10dB range is a safe starting point. This way, you're only compressing the loudest sections of your file, leaving most of your file untouched. If you find yourself dropping your threshold much below that, you may consider revisiting your signal chain to figure out why your recording is so quiet in the first place.

CROSS-REF Setting up a signal chain is covered in Chapter 6.

Setting a ratio

The ratio setting determines how much compression is applied over the threshold. For example, a 2:1 compression ratio means that for every 2dB by which the incoming signal exceeds the threshold, only 1dB of gain is applied. Ratios up to around 4:1 are mild and can be used safely, provided you set a sensible threshold. Ratios in the 4:1 to 10:1 range are fairly heavy and should be used with caution. Any ratio over 10:1 falls into a special category known as *limiting*.

Compression: How Much Is Enough? (by Steve Mack)

Okay, I admit it. I love compression. I love it so much that I collect hardware compressors. They come in all shapes and sizes, and I just can't seem to get enough of them. I'm not alone; audio engineers lust after compressors, especially those who record music, because compressors sound different and can be used on musical instruments to great effect. But I'm the first to admit there's such a thing as too much compression.

The most common example is the late-night commercial that jolts you out of bed. Your first instinct is to curse the television station for playing the commercial too loud, but in all fairness they have very little to do with it. Television stations broadcast to very strict standards, and their levels are set. Here's the thing: Television programming such as late-night movies may have fairly large dynamic ranges, because a movie will contain love scenes and crowd scenes. The problem occurs when a commercial follows a quiet scene.

The television station switches to a commercial, and the advertiser has compressed the living daylights out of the commercial, so it sounds extremely loud, particularly in contrast to the movie scene that preceded it. Advertisers know this, and ads are *deliberately produced this way*. Their job is to get your attention any way they can. So the next time this happens, don't blame the television station — blame the advertiser.

The larger lesson here is that short form content can be highly compressed, particularly if you're looking for a jarring effect. But if you're producing longer form content, as most podcasts are, you shouldn't go overboard with compression. Use compression to even out your levels and to get that wonderfully fat broadcast sound, but make sure your program still has some dynamics left.

Limiting can be useful as a preventative measure, but it isn't appropriate as your main form of compression. For most applications, start off with a ratio of 4:1 and experiment with using slightly more or less until you achieve the effect you're after. In particular, voices are particularly compression tolerant, so if you don't have any music in your podcast, you may be able to use more compression (see the "Compression: Voice versus Music" sidebar).

Setting attack and release times

The attack and release times control how quickly the compression effect is applied to signals that exceed the threshold you set, and how quickly the signal level is returned to the original input. For most content, you want a quick attack time, so signals that exceed the threshold are immediately attenuated. For the release time, you want something a bit longer, so the sound doesn't abruptly get returned to the original level.

This is fairly self-evident from the attack and release controls. The scale on the attack control knob generally is in milliseconds, and the scale on the release knob is in seconds. Start with a quick attack, say 10-20 milliseconds, and a gradual release around 500 milliseconds. These settings should work for most podcasting content, but don't be afraid to play around with your compressor to see how these settings affect the compression.

Compression: A step-by-step example

Now that you know a little bit about how compression works, it's time to play around with it to see how it affects the sound of your podcast. For this example, we'll be using the compressor that comes with Audacity.

1. Open Audacity, and open your podcast file.

2. Select the entire file by pressing Ctrl-A (Opt-A on a Mac). Remember that Audacity doesn't expose the effects until you highlight a section of your audio.

3. Select Compressor from the Effect menu. This brings up the Dynamic Range Compressor window, as shown in Figure 7.9.

4. You can see in Figure 7.9 that the default settings for the Audacity Compressor is a 2:1 compression ratio, a -12dB threshold, and a .2 second attack time. (This plug-in doesn't have a release time setting.) In fact, this is a nice moderate setting that may work just fine for your content. However, you may want to experiment with the settings to see what changing the threshold, ratio, and attack times do to the sound of your file.

   Audacity's Dynamic Range Compressor settings are adjustable in increments. For example, the ratios are variable in .5 increments (1.5:1, 2:1, 2.5:1, and so forth), and the attack times in tenths of seconds. Try changing the compression settings to a 4:1 ratio and a .1 second attack time. Preview the audio. Hear a difference?

   In fact, 100 milliseconds is really too slow of an attack time. To hear why, try changing the threshold to something really low, say -30dB. Preview the audio. Hear that? The audio starts off loud, and 100 milliseconds later the compressor kicks in. The compression effect is audible, because the attack time is too slow. However, if you raise the threshold up to say -15dB, the effect may not be as audible. You should be able to find a threshold that works in conjunction with the sluggish attack time.

FIGURE 7.9

The Dynamic Range Compressor in Audacity

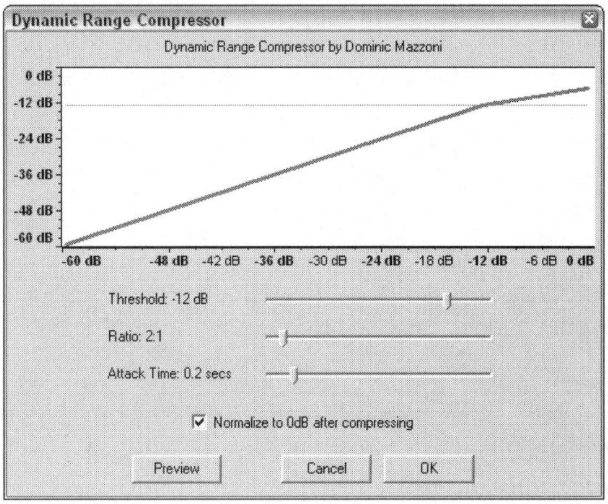

TIP   If your audio is recorded at a low level, the threshold settings discussed in this example may not work. This example assumes the audio has been well recorded with peaks in the -3dB to -6dB range. If your peaks are substantially lower, you may want to raise the overall level of your file (also known as Normalization, discussed later in this chapter).

Stacking compression

You may have noticed when you were playing around with compression in the last setting that a little bit of compression sounds good, but too much starts to sound noticeable. Sometimes, however, you may need a little more than light compression. The problem is that if you use a heavier setting, the effect starts to become too noticeable. One way around this is to *stack* your compression effects.

It's a really simple concept; apply a light compression across your entire file, and then apply another light compression. Lightly compressing the material twice is a much subtler effect than heavily compressing once. In fact, this approach is very common in recording applications. Audio engineers lightly compress material that is being recorded, to provide a little control over levels. Then, after the material has been edited, they apply additional compression to give the program that extra bit of presence.

Another approach, used in multi-track recording situations, is to use different compression effects on different tracks, and then to have a limiter placed across the master mix, to make sure the final mix never goes into distortion.

Compression: Voice versus Music

When you're using compression, you should consider what kind of content you're working on. Voice content is very compression tolerant. We're used to hearing news broadcasts and radio shows with a fairly significant amount of compression. Advertisements are even worse (see the "Compression: How Much Is Enough" sidebar). Music, however, is a different case.

When we apply compression, we're narrowing the dynamic range of the audio, and the side effect is to bring up the bottom end of the content. Obviously, this changes the sound. If you're using music in your podcast, you really have to ask yourself whether this is what the artist would want. Chances are good that the artist spent hours, if not days, getting the sound of the CD just right, and here you are changing it by applying additional compression. Because you're reducing the dynamic range, the instruments and voices will be squished together. The tonal character will change. It will sound different.

This may not be a problem, and in fact, you shouldn't worry about it too much, because all radio stations compress their broadcast signal as a matter of course. This is why songs sound different when you're playing them at home on your stereo compared to how they sound on the radio. They're not compressed at home!

Applying a bit of compression to your music is okay, but don't go overboard. As an exercise, you really should open your favorite song in your audio editing software and play around with different amounts of compression. Sure, it's fun, but it's not something you'd want to do to all your music. Stick to very light ratios (1.5:1 to 3:1 at most) and high thresholds, so the effect is minimal.

Multi-band compression

All the compression we've been talking about up to this point has been compression that analyzes the entire frequency range when determining what has exceeded the threshold. There are specialized compressors that break the frequency range into a number of different bands and then compress them all individually. Radio stations use ridiculously expensive multi-band compressors and set them up to try to get a unique, signature sound. (All they're really doing is competing to see who sounds loudest.)

One area where multi-band compression can be incredibly useful is as a corrective measure, in particular to deal with microphone pops and sibilants problems. In the EQ section, we discussed how you could deal with pops and "ess" sounds by turning down certain frequencies at the instant the problem syllable appears. A multi-band compressor does this for you automatically.

Figure 7.10 shows Sony Sound Forge's multi-band compressor, using a preset called "Reduce plosives and sibilants." It's using two bands, both of which have very fast attack and release times, because we want the compressor to react immediately. Band #1 is set to low shelf mode, meaning it monitors all frequencies below the shelf frequency, which in this case is 600Hz. Band #2 is set to notch mode, with a moderate Q of one octave, centered on 5KHz. When I preview audio, I can see the second band being compressed when the narrator pronounces "ess" sounds. Because my narrator hasn't popped the mic, the top band doesn't do much of anything. If you have a guest who has a problem with sibilants, you can use the de-ess preset (yes, that's the *technical* term for this) to get rid of the problem. Fabulous.

FIGURE 7.10

Using Sony Sound Forge's multi-band compressor to fight pops and sibilants

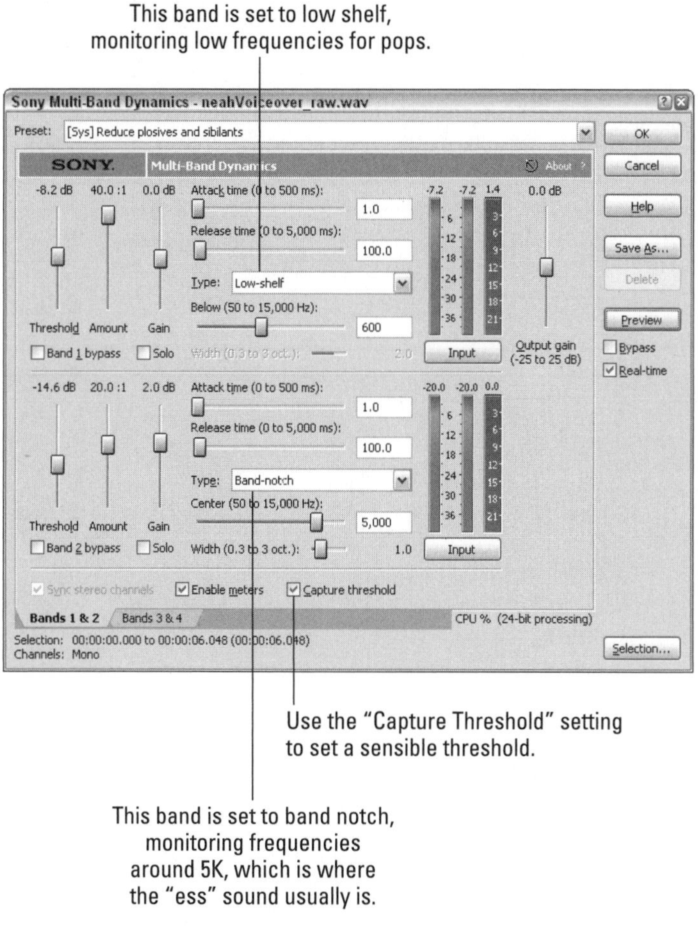

This band is set to low shelf,
monitoring low frequencies for pops.

Use the "Capture Threshold" setting
to set a sensible threshold.

This band is set to band notch,
monitoring frequencies
around 5K, which is where
the "ess" sound usually is.

TIP The Sound Forge preset can be a little aggressive at times, particularly if you're using the default threshold settings. One big tip is to check the "Capture Threshold" feature, which you can do by checking the check box at the bottom of band #2. You may also want to reduce the plosive frequency shelf setting to 100Hz.

Other Audio Processing Tricks

EQ and compression are the most common tools that audio engineers use to process their audio. But they're not the only tools, by any means. Here are a few more that you may find handy in your day-to-day podcast production.

Normalization

Normalization means turning the audio up until the peaks are at a given level. This can be very handy, for example, if your record level is a bit low and you want to turn it up but not so much that it distorts. The simplest way to do this is to use Normalization.

Figure 7.11 shows the Sound Forge Normalization window. It's very straightforward; you can choose what level you want the file normalized to using the slider at the left. In this illustration, you'll see that we're normalizing to -0.5dB, not 0dB. You can simply normalize to 0dB, but if you do, you have no headroom. If you're doing normalization as your very last step, you don't need headroom. If you're planning on adding EQ, you should probably normalize to -3dB or even -6dB to leave headroom for later EQing.

FIGURE 7.11

The Sound Forge Normalization window

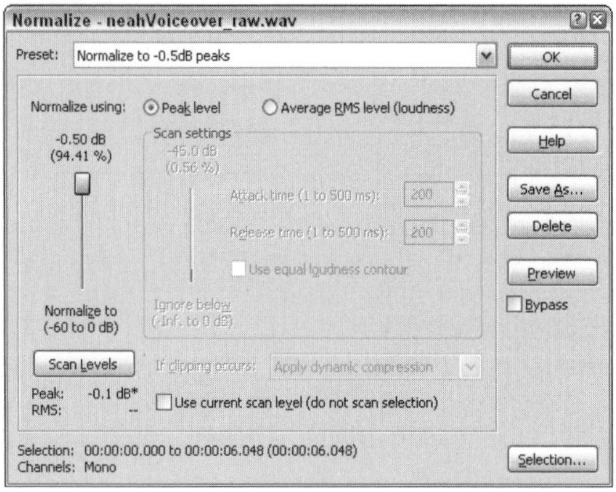

Of course, this is assuming you're using Peak Level normalization, which analyzes the entire file and raises the volume until the very highest peak is at the required normalization value. If you have one small section of the file that is loud, and the rest is very quiet, normalization is going to get you only so far. You'll have to use some compression to even out the levels throughout the file.

Another kind of normalization that's very handy if you plan on playing music is RMS normalization, shown in Figure 7.12. RMS normalization measures the overall *power* of a file, as opposed to just looking at peaks. If you combine this with an equal loudness contour, RMS normalization gives all your audio files the same apparent level.

> **NOTE** RMS stands for root mean square, which is a mathematical measure of the magnitude of a varying quantity. RMS is calculated by finding the square root of the mean of the squares of a set of values.

FIGURE 7.12

Use RMS normalization with an equal loudness contour to make all your music files sound as loud as each other.

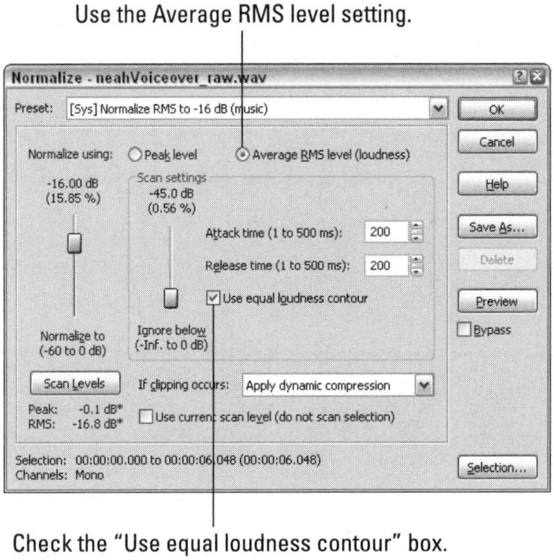

Use the Average RMS level setting.

Check the "Use equal loudness contour" box.

Audio with lots of low frequency content sounds louder to us, so even though two files may "look" the same in an audio editor (both have peaks at -3dB), one may sound much louder due to its tonal character. RMS normalization using an equal loudness contour takes into account how sensitive our ears are to particular frequencies and sets levels accordingly.

Gating to remove background noise

A noise gate mutes the audio signal when the level falls below a certain level. For example, if you're doing an interview in a room with a noisy ventilation system, you could try using a gate to get rid of the noise when you're not talking. Setting up a noise gate involves setting a threshold and attack and release times, similar to a compressor, as shown in Figure 7.13.

FIGURE 7.13

Using a noise gate to remove unwanted background noise

Set your threshold low enough so
that it doesn't cut off the beginnings or ends
of words, but high enough so that it
cuts out the objectionable background noise.

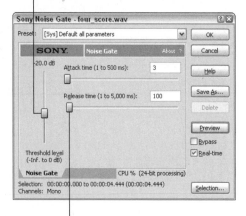

You can experiment with slower
attack and release times to make
the gating effect less noticeable.

Gating is best used when the background noise is very low; otherwise, the gating effect will be noticeable, because oddly enough our ears will notice the noise disappearing, and this can be more annoying than a constant background noise. If you have a serious noise problem, you may be better off using noise reduction.

Noise Reduction

Noise reduction is a sophisticated process that attempts to remove noise from your audio without affecting the rest of the content. As you might imagine, this is a very difficult undertaking. Noise reduction algorithms usually work by taking a "noise profile" or "noise print," which is used to determine the frequency content and level of the noise. Taking a noise print involves identifying a section of the audio file that contains only noise. The algorithm can then use this information to analyze the file and remove what it thinks is noise. Figure 7.14 shows the noise reduction windows for Audacity and Sound Forge.

You can see that both involve a two-step process — first getting a noise print, and then running the resulting filter across the entire file. Noise reduction can be incredibly effective for steady background noise. However, be aware that the urge to remove background noise can sometimes lead to audio that sounds too thin. The key is to use it sparingly, so that your audio sounds cleaner but not antiseptic and hollowed out.

FIGURE 7.14

Noise reduction, using Audacity and Sound Forge

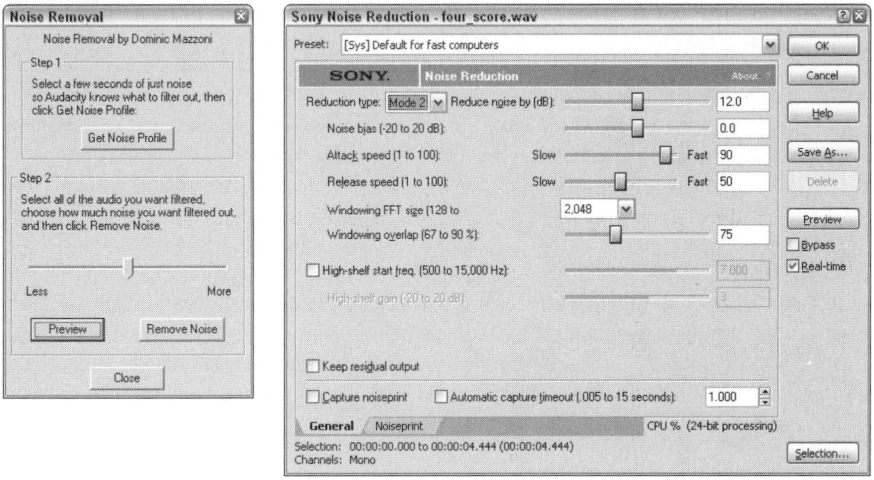

Noise Removal

Noise Removal by Dominic Mazzoni

Step 1

Select a few seconds of just noise
so Audacity knows what to filter out, then
click Get Noise Profile:

[Get Noise Profile]

Step 2

Select all of the audio you want filtered,
choose how much noise you want filtered out,
and then click Remove Noise.

Less   More

[Preview]   [Remove Noise]

[Close]

Sony Noise Reduction - four_score.wav

Preset: [Sys] Default for fast computers   [OK]

SONY   Noise Reduction   About   [Cancel]

Reduction type: Mode 2 Reduce noise by (dB):   12.0   [Help]

Noise bias (-20 to 20 dB):   0.0

Attack speed (1 to 100):   Slow ——— Fast   90   [Save As...]

Release speed (1 to 100):   Slow ——— Fast   50   [Delete]

Windowing FFT size (128 to   2,048

Windowing overlap (67 to 90 %):   75   [Preview]

☐ High-shelf start freq. (500 to 15,000 Hz):   7,000   ☐ Bypass

High-shelf gain (-20 to 20 dB):   3   ☑ Real-time

☐ Keep residual output

☐ Capture noiseprint   ☐ Automatic capture timeout (.005 to 15 seconds):   1.000

General Noiseprint   CPU % (24-bit processing)

Selection: 00:00:00.000 to 00:00:04.444 (00:00:04.444)
Channels: Mono   [Selection...]

 TIP Recording a bit of room noise at the beginning or end of your audio file is always a good idea. It can be used later as a noise print. As we find out later in the video chapter, it also comes in handy if you have to overdub audio.

When to Do Signal Processing

Given all the signal processing options at our disposal, you may very well ask when they should be done and in what order. There really are no hard and fast rules, though we can provide some guidelines. The thing to remember is that the cumulative effect of all your signal processing is going to depend on how each step in your signal processing affects the next step.

For example, if you recorded your original audio at a low level, you may be tempted to normalize it to start. However, if you're planning to add some EQ, be sure to leave headroom, because you may add to the overall level. If you're going to use compression and EQ, remember that the compression is going to warm up your bottom end and make your audio sound fuller, so you may not need to add too much bottom end. Conversely, because compression is going to fatten your sound, you may be tempted to add a touch of high end to compensate for any lost sparkle.

Multi-track Audio Production

When you begin to create podcasts, you'll probably use a simple stereo audio editing program. As your productions become more professional, you may be tempted to move up to a multi-track audio program. Multi-track systems offer a number of benefits, the most important one being the ability to

165

separate the elements of your podcast onto separate tracks. This, in turn, enables you to work on the tracks individually, applying tailored effects such as EQ and compression to each track on an individual basis.

Things to consider

Now that you're graduating to the world of multi-track recording, the first thing to do is label them appropriately so you know what is on which track. Sure, you say, I'm always going to put my mic on track #1, the guest on #2, and the music on track #3. Well, what happens when you add a telephone hybrid? What happens if you're sick and your buddy agrees to finish off one of your podcast productions for you? Believe me, it may seem pedantic, but labeling your tracks will save you lots of headaches in the long run.

Next, to take full advantage of a multi-track recording setup, you'll need an audio interface capable of multiple outputs and a mixing desk with multiple outputs. Each track can be assigned to a particular input, as shown in Figure 7.15. If you have only a stereo audio interface, you can still record to separate tracks, provided that you pan the two separate channels hard left and hard right on the mixing desk, and then record the left channel on one track and the right channel on another.

FIGURE 7.15

Sony Vegas multi-track software

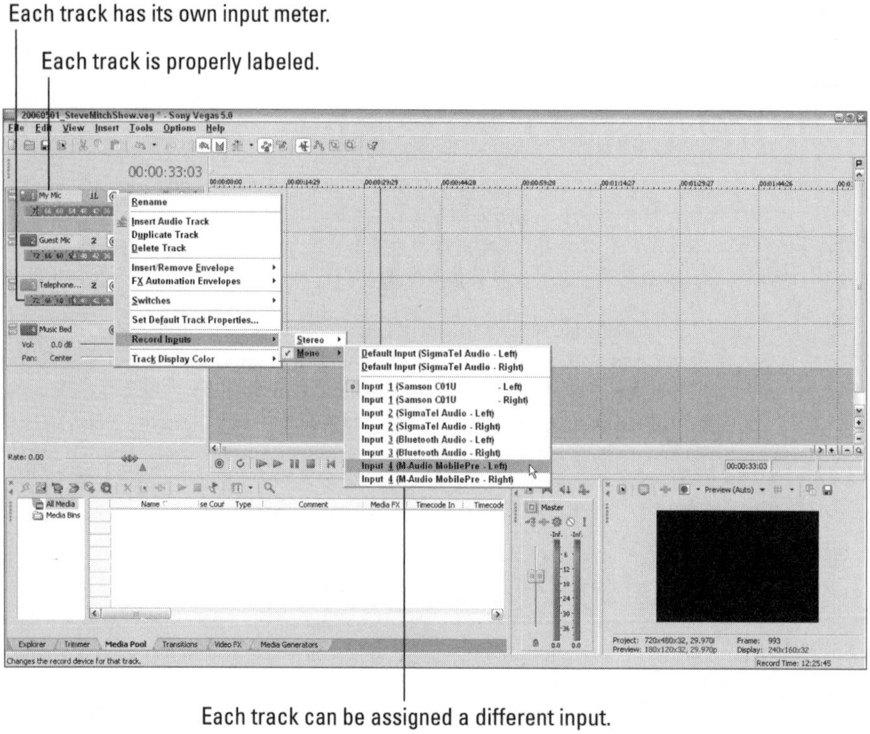

Each track has its own input meter.

Each track is properly labeled.

Each track can be assigned a different input.

After you have your audio recorded, bear in mind that the overall level will be cumulative. You have to be careful when you mix all your tracks together so that you don't end up with too much level. This can often happen if everyone talks or laughs at once. Suddenly, you have not one track but two or three, all feeding your master mix. This is why you'll want to think about using a compressor on each track or across your master mix if your software allows it.

Multi-track audio software is different in this manner, in that the effects you apply are not performed on the file. Instead, they are applied in real time as you play back the audio. In addition to being able to apply effects to each track, you can also apply effects to the master mix. In this situation, you could apply light compression to each of the input tracks and then a limiting compression to the master mix to make sure you never go into distortion.

Multi-track templates

If your podcast follows a particular format, for example if you use the same intro and outro music for each show, you can save time by creating a multi-track template that you can drop (or record) your audio into each week. Instead of having to worry about finding your theme music and worrying about levels, you just place the theme music on a separate track and then record the rest of your podcast on separate tracks. When you record using multi-track software, tracks that are not in record mode simply play back, so you'll hear the theme music in your headphones, and as it fades out, you jump in with your introduction.

Using Podcast-specific Software

All the techniques discussed in this chapter assume you're using a standard audio-editing program to record and edit your podcast. However, a number of podcast-specific software packages include audio-processing capabilities, along with other capabilities that may be of use to you. This section discusses a few of these solutions. By the time this book comes out, even more will be available.

Podcast Station

Podcast station, from Audion Laboratories, is based on its VoxPro software, which is a professional broadcasting package designed for recording and editing radio programs. Although it's priced at a fraction of the cost of VoxPro, it still offers a host of features that podcasters will find valuable. The Podcast Station interface is simple and intuitive. A sample screen from Podcast Station is shown in Figure 7.16.

All your recording and editing takes place on the main screen. A large "button block" contains one-click buttons for just about every operation you'll need. You can record from any soundcard input directly to the video time line and then insert songs, sound effects, or any pre-recorded files using the cart and deck buttons. After your program is on the time line, you can apply audio effects like EQ and compression.

FIGURE 7.16

Podcast Station offers radio station functionality in a single screen.

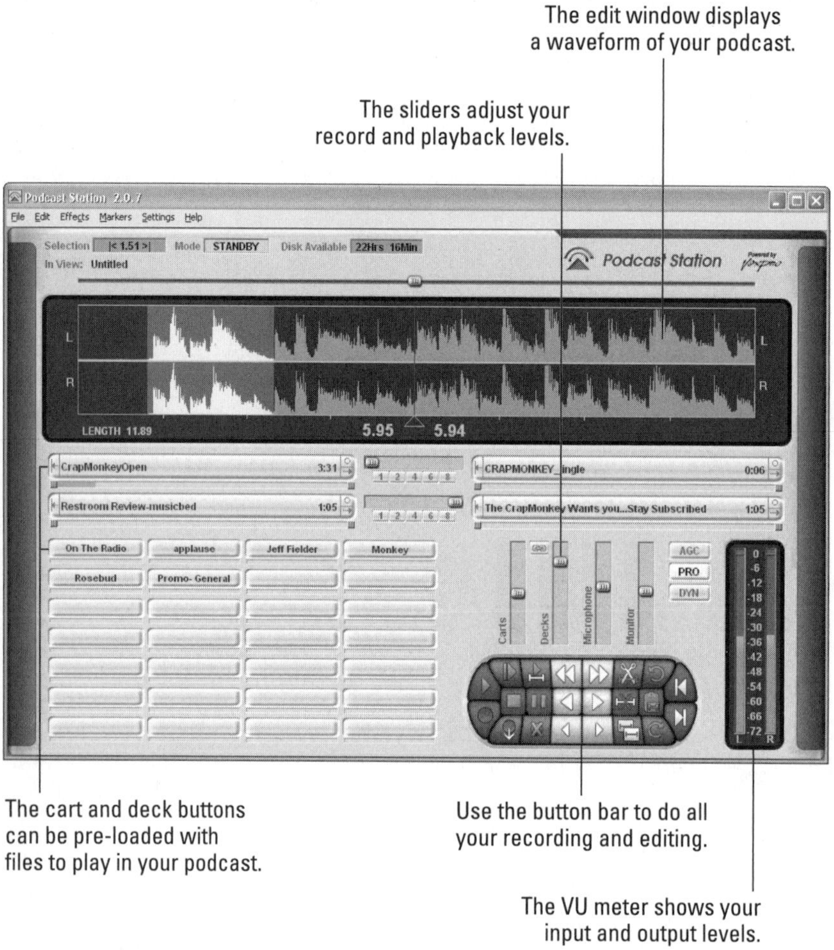
The edit window displays a waveform of your podcast.
The sliders adjust your record and playback levels.
Podcast Station 2.0.7
Podcast Station
CrapMonkeyOpen
Restroom Review-musicbed
CRAPMONKEY_Jingle
The CrapMonkey Wants you...Stay Subscribed
On The Radio
applause
Jeff Fielder
Monkey
Rosebud
Promo- General
Carts
Decks
Microphone
Monitor
AGC
PRO
DYN
The cart and deck buttons can be pre-loaded with files to play in your podcast.
Use the button bar to do all your recording and editing.
The VU meter shows your input and output levels.

Podcast Station is a well thought-out product with lots of nice touches. For example, if you right-click any of the faders (Podcast Station calls them *sliders*), the fader does a nice quick fade out, for example if you need to cough or you want to quickly fade out from an interview. Right-click the fader again, and it is restored to its previous level.

Another great feature is the ability to undo. This is similar to the undo abilities of other audio-editing programs, but Podcast Station goes one better — you can undo days or weeks later. Podcast Station keeps track of everything you do and stores it in the file along with your audio, so you can undo all the way back to your original if you need to.

Podcast Station also has a nice wizard-driven publishing feature, shown in Figure 7.17. It automatically generates your XML file, compresses your program to MP3 format, and sends your files up to your Web site. On top of all this, the folks at Audion Labs have a good sense of fun that is reflected in the documentation and tutorials that are provided. This is hard to beat for only $59.

FIGURE 7.17

Podcast Station also offers encoding, RSS authoring, and FTP through its wizard-driven publishing interface.

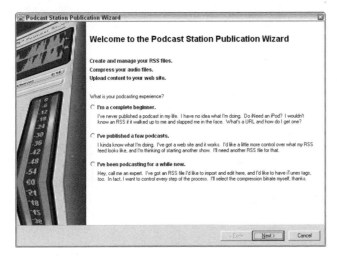

Castblaster

Castblaster is similar to Podcast Station in that it provides a simple user interface for you to create and publish your podcasts. A sample screen is shown in Figure 7.18. It also offers cart and deck functionality, enabling you to easily insert short audio pieces like sound effects or promotional pieces, as well as longer pre-recorded pieces such as songs or interviews. It has faders to control the volume of your microphone and your headphones, as well as the volume of the pre-recorded pieces.

Castblaster offers rudimentary editing, but does not offer any signal processing. Castblaster offers a publishing interface that automatically creates your RSS file, encodes your audio into MP3 format, and places the files on your server. It has tight integration with PodShow.com, because Castblaster is distributed by the good folks there, for $50.

FIGURE 7.18

Castblaster is a simple, no-nonsense way to create and publish podcasts.

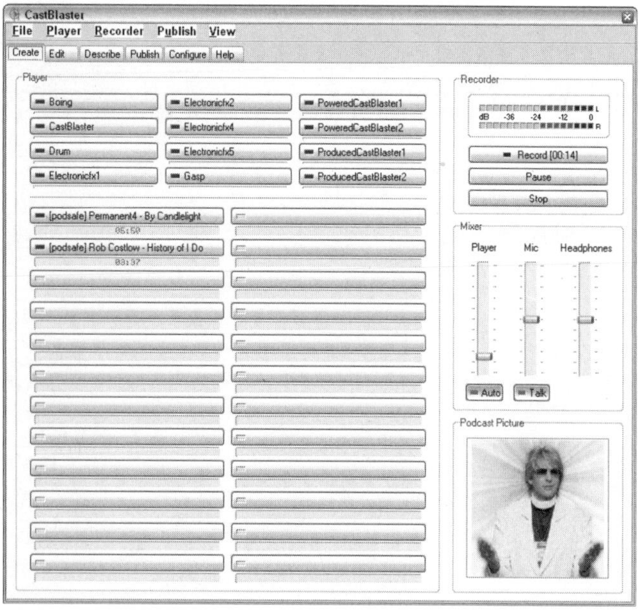

WebPod Studio

WebPod studio offers audio and video podcast production capabilities. It's available in three different versions ranging in price form $89.95 for the basic edition to $189.50 for the Enterprise edition. The main screen displays a number of icons along the top showing all the different things you can do, along with text links in the main part of the interface with links to wizards that walk you through each process. A sample screen is shown in Figure 7.19.

WebPod Studio offers no advanced editing or signal processing tools, but it does offer a few features that set it apart. First, it offers teleprompting, so you can enter a script for your podcast. It also imports PowerPoint slides and converts them to slides you can use in a video podcast. It also creates RSS feeds and automatically sends your files to your server.

FIGURE 7.19

WebPod Studio helps you create audio and video podcasts.

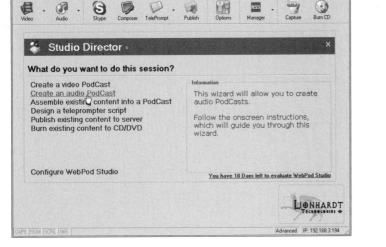

 You can buy WebPod Studio preloaded on a USB key. This enables you to carry a pod-casting studio around with you everywhere. That's pretty cool.

Summary

Audio engineers have many tools at their disposal, all of which manipulate signal level in one way or another. You can make your podcast sound more professional if you take advantage of the tools available to you in your audio editing program. Be sure to use enough to make your podcast sound professional, but not so much that it starts to sound artificial.

- Equalization, or EQ, adjusts the tonal quality of your audio by turning up or down particular frequencies in your programming.

- Compression evens out the levels of your programming by turning down sections that exceed a certain threshold.

- Compression has a wonderful side effect of making your audio sound fuller and warmer.

- EQ and compression also can be used for corrective measures, such as getting rid of pops or excessive sibilants.

- Multi-track audio software enables you to record, edit, and process all the parts of your podcast separately.

- Several podcast-specific software packages are available to help you produce your podcast.

Chapter 8

Video Production Tools

Although podcasting was originally conceived as an audio-only medium, this is no longer the case. Video blogging, or *vlogging,* is currently all the rage and is bound to get more popular. With the ever-expanding deployment of broadband connectivity and the plunging costs of digital video cameras, video broadcasting is within reach of just about anyone.

Sort of. As powerful as modern digital video cameras are, the affordable "prosumer" versions can't create a broadcast quality video, at least not without a little help. When the digital video format first appeared in the 1990s, it was laughed out of newsrooms across the country because the quality was thought to be too crude for broadcast. Within a few years, the convenience and immediacy of the format has made believers out of even the most demanding television producers. These days, a good portion of reality television programming is shot using the digital video format.

Of course, it doesn't hurt that the quality of digital video equipment has improved since the first few cameras appeared. You can now find cameras that offer fine-grained control of the image, as well as cameras that accept different lenses. Even more exciting, with the advent of HDV (High Definition Digital Video), you can shoot true widescreen video on a budget that doesn't require venture capital. To begin, however, you're probably going to be looking at an inexpensive camera and some support equipment. This chapter surveys what's available at the moment and discusses what features you should look for when you go shopping.

Choosing the Appropriate Equipment

Video production has some basic requirements. Obviously, you're going to need a camera and something to mount it on (we explain later why handheld video is a no-no). Because video is all about light, your video quality depends on the amount of control you exercise over your light. This means you should have some lights at your disposal, along with bounce cards and *flags* to stop light going where you don't want it to go. You also need plenty of spare cables and some other auxiliary video equipment. Good video production starts with your camera.

Cameras

A good camera is the single most important piece of equipment in your video signal chain. The camera records the incoming light, digitizing it and storing it as a digital video signal. The camera is therefore of paramount importance, much like a microphone is to audio. If your camera does a poor job of converting the incoming light into digital video information, you start off with low-quality video. Correcting digital video imperfections is very difficult. There are various methods of video processing available, but video is nowhere near as forgiving as audio. It's better to start off with high-quality video than to plan on fixing it later.

Video formats

The number of video formats available at the moment can be confusing to the neophyte. This is due partially to rapidly evolving digital video technology, and also due to manufacturers looking for an edge over their competition. Table 8.1 lists the most common video formats used in budget-conscious applications.

TABLE 8.1

Video Format Comparison

Format	Data Format	Quality/Resolution	Price (Cameras Unless Otherwise Noted)
HDV (widescreen) ($1,500–$10,000)	Digital	Excellent	Reasonable to expensive
DV formats: DVCPro, DVCAM, Mini DV	Digital	Very good/near-broadcast; approximately 500 lines of resolution	Reasonable to expensive ($400–$10,000)
Digital 8	Digital	Good; approximately 500 lines of resolution	Cheap ($250)
S-VHS/Hi-8mm	Analog	Barely acceptable; approximately 400 lines of resolution	Cheap if you can still find them (~$250)
VHS/8mm	Analog	Unacceptable; very noisy, poor resolution (approximately 250-270 lines)	Don't even think about it

If you're just starting out, you probably want to start off with whatever camera is lying around or whatever you can borrow. If you're the slightest bit serious about a video podcast, you should consider investing in a decent-quality DV (digital video) camera. They're ubiquitous and have a number of features that are perfectly suited to digital video production. (These are discussed in the next section.) DV cameras are available at numerous price points, with higher-priced models offering higher image quality and better build quality.

What to look for in a camera

Digital cameras come with a bewildering array of features these days. Some of these are just marketing hype and of little use to anyone, never mind an aspiring video podcaster. Essentially, two main things determine the quality of your video:

- **Lens quality:** Higher-priced cameras have better lenses, and better lenses provide better image quality.

- **Image capture mechanism:** DV cameras use charge-coupled devices (CCDs) to convert the incoming light into a digital signal. The size and number of CCDs the camera uses determine image quality.

Cheaper DV cameras use a single CCD to capture the video, whereas more expensive versions use three separate CCDs and divide the incoming light into red, blue, and green components for a higher-quality image. You should look for a camera with three CCDs if you can afford it; the higher-quality video image is worth the investment.

When it comes to the lens, each manufacturer sings the praises of their lens for "superior color and image quality." Lens quality can be very subjective — it's usually a good idea to hit a few camera ratings sites to see what people have to say about the latest and greatest models. You can find a number of these sites: The granddaddy is camcorderinfo.com.

Other features you should be concerned about are listed here. The advantages of some of the features discussed here may not be very apparent when you first start out, but become important as you become more familiar with your camera and want to get the most out of its capabilities:

- **Manual adjustments:** Many DV cameras hide functionality deep in an on-screen menu that may or may not be accessible after you're recording. Having buttons and switches easily accessible is a big plus.

- **XLR inputs for audio:** You never want to use the microphone on the camera, because they're low quality and designed to pick up everything in the room. Instead, use a professional mic or two; these generally require an XLR input. Otherwise, you'll have to invest in an external add-on box to make the XLR cable compatible with the awful ⅛ mic inputs that some cameras have.

- **IEEE 1394 (FireWire) output:** A FireWire output allows you to transfer the video from the camera directly to your computer without requiring a video capture card. If a camera doesn't have one of these, don't even think about buying it.

There are so many cameras to choose from and so many mew models coming out every year that it's virtually impossible to recommend any particular models, for fear that they will be outdated by the time you read this chapter! However, a number of cameras at the slightly more expensive end of the DV range are perennials. Even though Sony, Canon, and Panasonic keep bringing out new models, the cameras pictured in Figure 8.1 seem to stick around. They're all well proven by years of streaming video production.

FIGURE 8.1

DV camera workhorses: Sony PD-150, Canon XL-2, Panasonic HVX200

Tripods

A good tripod is far more important than you think. In fact, you should probably consider spending about one-fourth of your total camera budget on a tripod. Although it may seem hard to believe that a $500 tripod is that much better than a $50 tripod, the difference is immediately noticeable to a professional videographer. We learn more about the importance of a tripod in Chapter 9. For now, just put it on your shopping list.

Lights

When we're talking about video, we're talking about light. When you're shopping for a camera, you'll probably see all kinds of facts and figures about various models' performance under low-light conditions. Don't believe them for a second. Manufacturers make all sorts of wild claims about low-light performance. The truth is that cameras don't work well in low-light conditions. The cheaper the camera is, the worse the performance.

Luckily, lighting kits are available for precisely this reason. Using a lighting kit gives you control over the light, which in turn gives you control over the quality of your video image. A decent lighting kit runs about $800 and comes in a snazzy flight case so you can lug it with you wherever you need it (see Figure 8.2).

FIGURE 8.2

A portable lighting kit (Lowel)

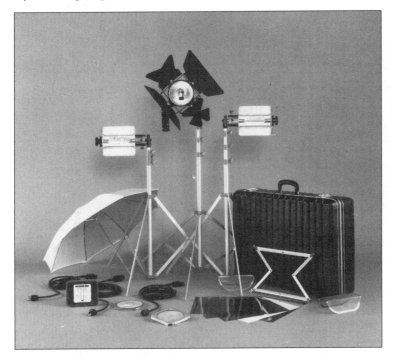

If you're on a really tight budget, you don't have to shell out for professional lighting. Shop lights purchased from your local hardware store can be used, though they don't have anywhere near the control that professional lights do. Typically, they produce a fairly harsh, unforgiving light but with creative use of diffusion and positioning, you can get lots out of a very small investment.

CROSS-REF Lighting is discussed in more detail in Chapter 9, "Basic Video Production Techniques."

Video mixers

If you're going to get fancy with your podcast and shoot with multiple cameras, you'll probably want to buy a video mixer. Video mixers, like audio mixing desks, take multiple video inputs and allow you to switch between them. They also offer special effects like picture in picture and cross fading between sources (see Figure 8.3).

FIGURE 8.3

Focus Enhancements MX-4 video mixer

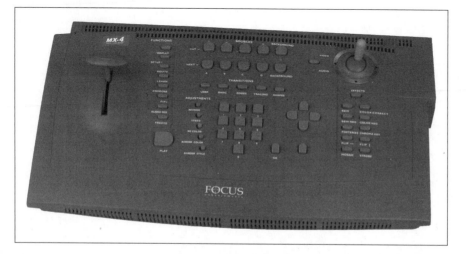

TIP Of course, you can get the effect of a multiple-camera shoot by being clever with your editing. This common technique is used in news gathering, where the interviewer asks questions off camera while the interviewee is taped answering the questions. Then, when the interview is finished, the interviewer is taped asking the questions, and the result is edited to look as if two cameras were used during the interview.

Most cameras used for podcasting applications are camcorders, so they record the signal to tape. The video signal can also be recorded directly onto your computer via the FireWire output. It's always a good idea to record to tape as backup even if you're recording directly to your computer. If you're using multiple cameras and a video mixer, you also may want to consider recording the output of the mixer to a video tape recorder (VTR). Otherwise, you must digitize the tapes from all your cameras to recreate the live edit if something goes wrong.

Of course, you can purchase a stand-alone video deck, or more interestingly, you can now record straight to an external drive such as Focus Enhancements' FireStore (see Figure 8.4). These units record digital video from a FireWire cable so you don't have to digitize later. You just attach the FireStore to your video editing station, and it appears as an external drive.

FIGURE 8.4

Focus Enhancements FireStore FS-4

Monitoring

Even though many cameras come with flip-out LCD screens that allow you to monitor your video, these screens really aren't good enough for quality control. You should buy a small monitor (which in the video sense is a small video display) so you can check the lighting of your subjects. If you aren't shooting on location, you can use a television with an auxiliary input, but be careful: Televisions are built to flatter the video image and often are far out of alignment from the broadcast standard. If you go this route, buy one of the kits that help you calibrate your television display.

Video interfaces/capture cards

At some point, you have to get the video signal out of the camera and into your video-editing workstation. If your camera and workstation both have FireWire, you're in luck: All you need to do is connect them with a FireWire cable, and you can import the video data directly. If your workstation doesn't have a FireWire card, you can pick one up for less than $50 these days.

If your camera doesn't have a FireWire output, you can get a digital video converter box that takes an analog video signal as input and outputs a DV signal via FireWire (see Figure 8.5). The nice thing about having a digital video converter is that you can plug any video signal into it, such as a DVD player or old VHS player. Alternatively, you can buy a video capture card. Video capture cards take analog video as input and digitize it to your hard drive. Video capture cards range in price from under $100 to many thousands of dollars. For the most part, however, the convenience of DV cameras with FireWire outputs is hard to beat.

FIGURE 8.5

The Canopus ADVC-300 Digital Video Converter

Video-editing software

You definitely need some video-editing software to create your video podcast. Video-editing software allows you to edit your video, adjust the video quality, and do rudimentary audio editing (on some platforms). A number of editing platforms are available; these are some of the most popular:

- **Final Cut Pro (Mac):** This is the flagship of Apple's video-editing suite.

- **iMovie (Mac):** It's no Final Cut Pro, but for podcasts, it's probably all the video editor you need. And because it's from Apple, you can bet that there's tight integration with the iPod.

- **Adobe Premiere (PC):** Adobe Premiere has been around since video editing on desktops began. It has very tight integration with Adobe Audition.

- **Sony Vegas (PC):** Vegas is tightly integrated with Sony Sound Forge. In fact, Vegas has much of the audio-processing capability of Sound Forge built in.

- **Ulead Video Studio (PC):** This software has a great price and includes output templates for iPods and SmartPhones.

- **Cinelerra (Linux):** That's right, now you can do video editing on your favorite free operating system.

Accessories

Along with all the goodies discussed previously, you need a good selection of cables to connect all your equipment. As with audio, don't skimp on cable quality. You're better off buying an expensive cable that lasts longer. Depending on the scale of your production, you also may want to consider a number of other accessories. Many of these are used either to improve your video quality or to compensate for a troublesome video issue.

CROSS-REF Video quality and troubleshooting are dealt with in Chapter 9, "Basic Video Production Techniques" and Chapter 10, "Advanced Video Production Techniques."

- **Processing amplifier (proc amp):** Proc amps allow you to tweak the video signal in real time, saving you the hassle of having to do it later.

- **Camera filters:** Filters can compensate for your lighting situation and thereby enhance your video quality.

- **Gels and diffusion materials:** If you're using a lighting kit, gels and diffusion materials help you control your light.

- **Flags:** Flags are used to direct light so it doesn't go where you don't want it.

- **Bounce boards:** Bounce boards are used to reflect light where you need it. They can be as simple as a large piece of light-colored cardboard or custom-made versions that have different colors on either side to be used in different situations.

- **Video "humbucker":** Video cables are susceptible to noise, particularly from nearby power cables. This noise shows up in the picture and degrades the quality. Humbuckers filter out this noise.

- **"Green screen" facilities:** Using a technique known as "green screen," you can film your subject against a green wall or background, and then during the edit phase a different background can be substituted for the green background.

- **Gaffer's tape, clothes pins, cable adapters, etc.:** Every videographer has a kit bag full of adapters, tape, and lots of other things that are useful during a shoot.

Most of the items in this list can safely be skipped for your first few video productions. Most videographers' kit bags are the result of years of accumulation, having had to deal with a number of issues over the years. You should definitely make sure you have plenty of spare cables and a roll of gaffer's tape, because as the saying goes, anything can be fixed with enough gaffer's tape.

TIP Duct tape (or "duck tape" as some folks mistakenly call it) is not the same as gaffer's tape. Duct tape leaves a sticky residue all over your cables, your floor, and anything else you use it on. Gaffer's tape does not. It's expensive, but do yourself a favor and get some decent tape.

Thinking about Your Video Environment

The requirements of a video studio are very similar to an audio studio. You want a nice quiet location, with plenty of power. Video studios also require good ventilation, because lights generate lots of heat. You also should find a space with a high ceiling, both for the ventilation and for the lights. Surprisingly, it's best to find a space without windows.

Power

The big power draw in video production is the lighting. Most lighting kits have three lights, with bulbs that are in the 500 to 1,000 watt range. For every thousand watts, you're pulling about an amp of current out of the wall. A three-point lighting kit can easily be pulling over three amps. So you need to make sure that you've got at least a 10-amp circuit going to your studio, because the audio, video, and computer gear also are going to need power. The last thing you need during your podcast recording is for the power to go out.

Ventilation

The bulbs used in lighting kits are fairly inefficient. Much of the energy they're burning up is given off in the form of heat. Point three lights at someone, and you're basically slow cooking them. Your video studio must have adequate ventilation, or you'll end up having to take breaks every 15 minutes to cool off.

One problematic side effect of ventilation is noise. Commercial HVAC (heating, ventilation, and air conditioning) systems are not installed with noise in mind. They hiss, rumble, and rattle all day long, which obviously is a big problem for the audio production. If you're lucky enough to be able to custom-build a space for your needs, be sure to let the contractor know that you need sound attenuation built in to the systems. HVAC noise can be reduced in many ways. It isn't cheap, but if you're building a studio from scratch, you may as well do it the right way.

Light

Because video production is all about light, gaining control over your lighting is paramount for high-quality video production. Controlling the light involves not only where the light is directed, but also the color and quality of the light. For example, you don't want to mix different types of light sources, such as fluorescent and incandescent light. You also don't want to mix sunlight with artificial light. For this reason, it's best to have a video studio with no windows so you don't have to worry about sunlight. Windows also are a notorious source of noise, which is another reason to avoid them.

Shooting Video Outdoors

Shooting outdoors is a challenge, because so many things can't be controlled. First and foremost, controlling the light is difficult. The quality of light provided by the sun changes during the course of the day, and you never know when a stray cloud will wander in front of your main light source. If the sun is bright, it casts strong shadows and forces people to squint, neither of which you want in your video.

Power can be very hard to come by when shooting outdoors. You can rent a generator or battery-powered lights, but this scale of production tends to be out of the range of most podcasts. You're probably going to have to make due with what you can carry and the light that is available. Bounce boards are invaluable when shooting outdoors, because you can use them to reflect the light from the sun and use it as a secondary light source.

Noise also is a big problem. You can't tell the world to be quiet, unfortunately, and you can't tell the wind to stop blowing. Fortunately, *windsocks* have been developed that you place over microphones to minimize wind noise. They look like big pieces of wooly foam and do a fantastic job. If you're going to do lots of outdoors work, windsocks are a necessity.

Summary

Video blogging requires a fair amount of equipment, but you don't have to break the bank to produce a decent-quality video podcast. These are your three primary expenses:

- For most applications, a DV camera makes the most sense, because of the cost and the FireWire output. When shopping for a camera, don't be fooled by silly features that you'll never use. Look for the best lens quality, the largest CCDs, and as much manual control over the image quality as you can afford.
- Plan on buying a good tripod and, if your budget stretches far enough, a small lighting kit.
- And finally, be sure you've got a decent video monitor so you can check your video quality.

We find out how to use all this equipment in the next chapter.

Chapter 9

Basic Video Production Techniques

L ights . . . camera . . . action!

You've seen and heard it in the movies — now you get to find out how it all works and why they actually still say that. Of particular importance is the first word: lights. When we're talking about video, we're talking about light. The quality of your video is going to be dependent on the quality of light when it was shot, and the ability of your equipment to capture the light information faithfully.

Capturing the light is obviously where your camera comes in. Cameras are available at a number of price points these days, with image quality corresponding fairly closely with price. Spending more gets you better optics, bigger CCDs, and more manual control over the image. The camera is as critical to video production as a microphone is to audio production. If you're not starting off with high-quality video, the quality of your video podcast will be limited.

After you've got your lighting and camera set, it's time for action. The action doesn't stop on the set, though. You're going to have to do a few things with your video before you can publish your video podcast. You need to *capture* or *digitize* the video (get it into your computer) so you can do some editing. And before you *encode* your production into a format suitable for podcasting, you should archive a master version, preserving all your edits in the highest quality possible.

Let's start with the basis of all video: light.

Light

Describing light is pretty hard—after all, physicists have been wrestling with this question for years. Talking in terms of how we perceive light is much easier, and that perception is determined by our eyes. Our eyes have two sets of receptor cells at the back of the eyeball that send information to the brain. *Rods* are sensitive to motion and light, but not sensitive to detail or color. *Cones* are more sensitive to color and detail.

Rods can operate at widely varying light levels, but cones require more light, which is why we can see at twilight, but things don't look as colorful. So if we want to record the highest possible video quality, with all the color information, we need enough light so that our cones will respond and relay the information to our brains. This is a fairly long-winded way of saying "use lights." The more light that's present, the more color information and detail we'll be able to perceive.

The amount of light in a video signal is referred to als *luminance*. The amount of color in a video signal is referred to as *chrominance*. So when we're working with light, whether we're recording it or manipulating it, we are working with luminance and chrominance. The tricky thing is that luminance and chrominance are intricately intertwined. If you add more luminance, the chrominance is affected. Think about adjusting your television set or your computer monitor. When you turn up the brightness control, colors appear brighter, which may or may not be what you want.

Color

Color is very subjective. We can never truly know how someone else perceives color, but our eyes are constantly adjusting to colors depending on the amount of light available. For example, if someone is wearing a red shirt, his shirt looks red whether he's outdoors in the sunlight or indoors under fluorescent lights. The quality of light that is being reflected off his shirt is completely different in these two situations, but our eyes adjust, and we see the shirt as red.

In a following section, you learn that cameras attempt to do the same thing, but they often need a little help. Making sure your camera is recording color information correctly is known as *white balancing* your camera. You must white balance your camera, preferably before every shoot, and every time your lighting situation changes.

CROSS-REF   White balancing your camera is discussed in more detail later in this chapter.

Using lights

Many cameras are sold on their ability to shoot in low-level lighting situations. Although this may be okay for a home movie, if you're trying to create a broadcast-quality podcast, you need some lights. Shooting with the proper amount of light adds color and detail to your presentation, making it look higher quality. Also, when you encode your video into a podcasting format, you'll find that the higher quality your original is, the higher quality the resultant podcast is.

Discussing the finer points of lighting video is far beyond the scope of this book. Many good books are available on the subject, as well as plenty of lighting professionals who are looking for work. But in the interest of giving you a firm understanding of lighting basics, we discuss the basis for virtually all lighting schemes, which is known as *three-point lighting*.

Three-point lighting

Three-point lighting is a simple technique that uses three lights to achieve a satisfactory lighting effect. These lights are known as the key, fill, and back lights. Each fulfills a specific purpose:

- The *key light* is the main light source for the scene.
- The *fill light* is the secondary light source and fills in the harsh shadows created by the key light.
- The *back light* is used to separate the subject from the background, by highlighting the shoulder and hair line.

For a simple illustration of three-point lighting, take a look at the three photos in Figure 9.1.

FIGURE 9.1

Three-point lighting in action: a) key light only; b) key light and fill light; c) key, fill, and back light.

a   b   c

In Figure 9.1a, we see the subject as lit by a single light. We can see the subject, but the left side of the subject is almost completely in shadow. To remedy this, we add the fill light, to fill in the shadows created by the key light (as shown in Figure 9.1b). The fill light remedies the problem with the shadows we had with a single light source, but the image is very flat. The subject blends into the background, creating a two-dimensional, lifeless image. To remedy this, we add the back light (as shown in Figure 9.1c). With the back light added, we now see the subject's hair line, as well as highlights on both shoulders. This helps separate the subject from the background and gives us a much more three-dimensional image.

Placement of the three lights is fairly straight forward, as illustrated in Figure 9.2. The key and fill lights are placed in front of the subject, on either side of the camera. They are usually slightly above the subject, pointing down slightly. The back light is obviously behind the subject, to one side, and usually placed fairly high, aiming downward.

FIGURE 9.2

Positioning of lights using three-point lighting

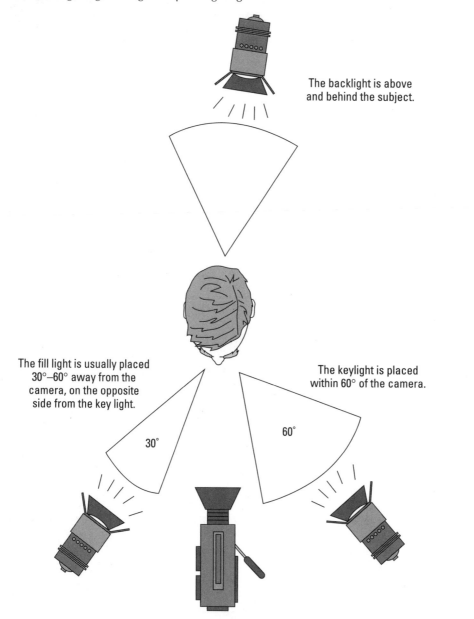

The backlight is above and behind the subject.

The fill light is usually placed 30°–60° away from the camera, on the opposite side from the key light.

The keylight is placed within 60° of the camera.

30°

60°

One thing to bear in mind when setting up your lights is the quality of the light. Light sources can be *hard* or *soft*. Hard sources cast very strong shadows. For example, if you shine a flashlight against a wall in a dark room, the resultant beam has a defined round shape, with a very distinct edge. Anything in the path of this light creates a very distinct shadow. Soft light sources are more diffuse and cast softer shadows. For example, a lamp in your living room with a lampshade casts a very soft, diffuse light. The shadows cast by this kind of light are very soft and undefined.

In general, you want a relatively hard light source for your key light, a soft source for your fill light, and a very hard source for your back light. The shadows cast by the key light let people know what direction the light is coming from (which is important to our sense of depth) and are softened somewhat by the fill light. We don't want shadows from the fill light to be noticeable. We want the back light to be hard so we can pinpoint it where we need it. We don't want back light spilling all over the place.

Professional lights usually include a lever or dial that allows you to choose between hard or soft light. If you want to soften a hard light source, you can either put a diffusing material in front of it or bounce the light off something reflective. You can purchase attachments for your lights that change a light source from hard to soft.

Another thing to consider is how bright each light should be. The key light should be the brightest, because it's the main light source. The fill light should be lower wattage, so that it doesn't overpower the key light. The backlight should also be lower wattage than the key light. If your lights are all the same wattage, you can compensate by moving lights closer to or further away from your subject. A little adjustment can go a long way. For those of you who remember your physics classes, light falls off using the inverse square law, so double the distance equals one quarter the light.

TIP   Be very careful when working with lights, whether you're moving them or attaching diffusing material or gels. Lights get extremely hot and the bulbs are very fragile — and expensive. Turn lights off and let them sit for a while before moving them. Also, never touch the bulbs with your bare fingers. The oil from your hands dramatically shortens their life.

Of course, in a situation where you have more than one subject, your lighting can be much more complex. You'll very likely need more than three lights. However, three-point lighting is still the basis of most lighting situations. You're always going to need a main (key) light source, fill lights to fill in shadows, and back lights to separate your subjects from the background.

Using reflectors (bounce boards)

One way to economize if you're stuck without enough lights is to reflect light from your key off what are commonly called *bounce boards*. Bounce boards can be as simple as a piece of light-colored cardboard to purpose-made reflectors that fold up into small, portable packages. Videographers usually travel with a couple of these in their arsenal because they're light and useful in lots of different situations.

This works quite simply. Instead of focusing the key light directly on the subject, you direct it slightly across the subject. Then you can reflect some of this light from a bounce board back toward the subject, as shown in Figure 9.3. Because the light is being reflected, it's automatically a diffuse source. It's also much lower intensity after being reflected, so it won't compete with the key light.

189

FIGURE 9.3

Using a bounce board to reflect key light back as a fill

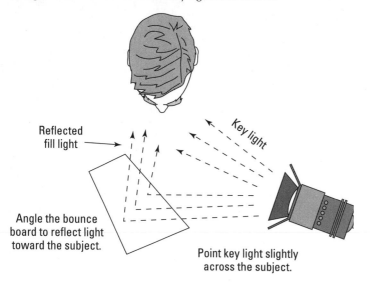

Reflected fill light →

Key light

Angle the bounce board to reflect light toward the subject.

Point key light slightly across the subject.

This setup is commonly used in video news reel (VNR) situations. Interview teams often consist of a single reporter and a cameraperson, so traveling with a full three-point lighting kit is impractical. Instead, the cameraperson brings a single light on a stand and a bounce board, which may even be held by the interviewer while he's asking questions! It's cheap and portable, and quite possibly ideal for video podcasts.

Shooting outdoors

If you're shooting outdoors, the main problem is that you have no control over your key light, which by definition is the sun. You can't control how bright it will be, or how hard or soft. On a sunny day, it will be a very hard source. On an overcast day, sunlight is very diffuse. It's ironic, because everyone wants to take photographs on sunny days, but sunny days can be the most challenging situations in which to work.

Another problem with working outdoors is power. It's not like you can bring a lighting kit and plug it in wherever you want. You may have the option of battery-powered lights or a generator, but this starts to go beyond the scope of most video podcasts. What you'll most likely want to do is make judicious use of bounce boards to try to even out the lighting available to you. It also can be quite a bit easier to work out of the direct sunlight, and shoot your video in a shady area. You still get the warm quality of the sunlight, but without the harsh shadows that can be hard to overcome.

Camera Techniques

After you've taken some time to consider and light your subject, you're ready for the "camera" part of the "lights . . . camera . . . action" cliché. As mentioned earlier, your camera is probably the most important part of your video production chain, because if your camera doesn't faithfully render your perfectly lit scene, you're starting off with compromised quality, which propagates quality issues throughout your entire video podcast.

In many ways, shooting a video podcast should be no different than shooting for broadcast. You're trying to get the best shot, with plenty of light and color information and lots of detail. Not only does this look best when you're shooting, but it also makes for a better-looking podcast. However, you should take into account a number of things, because the Internet isn't quite ready for prime-time, and podcasts are watched on computer screens and portable media players. Bearing this in mind, you should consider things like shot composition and what camera moves you have planned, because they have a direct affect on the quality of your podcast.

Shot composition

The most obvious thing to think about is shot composition. In most cases, your podcast will end up as a relatively small screen resolution, probably 320×240. An iPod screen measures about 2 inches wide by 1.5 inches tall. On a computer monitor, depending on how your resolution is set, this same resolution can be up to roughly 4 inches wide by 3 inches tall. Either way you look at it, it's not the largest screen in the world. Therefore, you probably want to do away with your long shots and concentrate on medium shots and close-ups.

Because podcasting tends to be a very personal medium, the most common video podcasts tend to concentrate on "head and shoulders" framing, where subjects' eyes are located about 1/3 of the way from the top of the screen. One common mistake that amateurs make is to frame the video subject in the center of the video. This makes the subject look short, with too much space above his head. The rule of thirds, shown in Figure 9.4, will suit you well.

To use the rule of thirds, divide your video image into thirds, both horizontally and vertically. You should try to place things of interest on the lines dividing the picture into thirds. Where the lines intersect are particularly good places. If you have a single subject, and you're shooting straight on, try to put the subject's eyes on the top 1/3 line. This makes for a well-balanced image that's pleasing to the eye. It doesn't matter how close or far away you are, the subject's eyes should remain on this line. If you get really close, you'll find that your shot crops off the top of his head (or maybe just his spiky hair). That's okay; if you place your subject at the center of the screen to try and keep his hair in the shot, it will look odd. Use the rule of thirds! It has been serving artists, photographers, and videographers for many years.

FIGURE 9.4

Basic composition using the rule of thirds

Another thing to consider is where the subject is looking. For a single talking head subject, it's best if they face directly towards the camera. In an interview situation, it's better if they are slightly to one side, looking toward where the other person is. In addition, it's most pleasing to the eye for the person to be angled toward the key light so that the part of the face getting the harsh light has the least exposure to the camera.

This may sound a bit complicated, but when you have your equipment set up it's easy to turn people one way or the other to see what effect it has on the shot. This is common practice in studios and is referred to as *cheating*. Sure, the subject may not be facing directly toward the interviewer, but if the shot looks better on camera, go with it.

Use a tripod

It is absolutely imperative to use a tripod when filming for the Web. Quite simply, using a tripod improves your video quality. Sure, most cameras come with built in handles that make them very portable, and carrying a tripod around is awkward and cumbersome. But the simple fact is that when you encode your podcast later, unnecessary motion will compromise your video quality, and hand-held content has lots of unnecessary motion.

CROSS-REF   Encoding, codecs, and the limitations of Internet video formats are discussed in Chapter 11, "Encoding: An Overview."

Focus

It may seem obvious, particularly now that so many cameras have automatic focusing mechanisms built in, but it's critical that your subject remains in focus. Properly focused frames have more detail and consequently look better, even after encoding. Ironically, the auto-focus mechanisms of modern digital cameras can cause problems with your focus.

Auto-focus mechanisms work by making assumptions about what is most important in your frame. Things that are bright or moving tend to be interpreted as important. In many cases, this is fine, but if your subject is standing in front of a lake with boats sailing by, for example, the camera has a hard time deciding whether you're trying to shoot the static subject or the moving sailboats. Often the camera becomes confused and continually refocuses on different objects. In most situations, you're better off using the manual focus option if your camera offers one.

Focusing your camera manually is easy if you follow this simple procedure:

1. Zoom all the way in to your subject, and look at something with a lot of detail, such as the eyebrows or hairline.

2. Adjust the focus until it's as sharp as possible.

3. Zoom back out to your original shot composition.

That's it. Provided your subjects don't move too much, they'll stay in focus. If they do move, or if you decide to change the camera position, remember to re-focus each time.

White balancing and exposure

Earlier in this chapter, we discussed color, in particular how our brains compensate for the differences in colors under different kinds of light. Cameras attempt to do this, but it's usually a better idea to manually white balance your camera to make sure your color representation is accurate. Manually white balancing a camera is a simple procedure. The idea is to "show" the camera what the color white looks like under the existing light. Given this information, the camera can then adjust its internal circuitry to compensate for the light, and the resulting video image will have faithful color representation.

White balancing: A step-by-step example

You need a decent-sized piece of white cardboard to perform white balancing. Follow these steps:

1. Have your talent hold the white cardboard directly in front of her, where all the lights are focused. If it's a tight shot, she may have to hold it in front of her face.

2. Zoom in until the white card fills the entire shot.

3. Find your camera's white balance control, set it to manual, and then set the white balance. Most cameras have a button to push or a menu option to select.

4. Zoom back out, and behold your wonderfully balanced picture.

When your lighting situation changes, you should rebalance the camera. This is particularly important if you're combining footage shot outdoors with footage shot indoors. If your white balance is off, people's flesh tones shift slightly, as do the colors of their clothing (if they're wearing the same color). If you're unsure whether you should white balance, do it just to be sure.

White-balancing tricks

You can use non-white cards when white balancing your camera for a special effect. Non-white balancing cards come in two flavors: *warm cards* and *cool cards*. The process is exactly the same as detailed previously, but by using a non-white card to white balance, you can trick the camera into thinking white is something different, and the result is slightly skewed colors in your video.

Why would you want to do this? Well, warm cards have a slightly blue tint, and when the camera compensates for this, the result is a slightly warmer image. This may be appropriate for a very intimate podcast shot indoors, if you want to make the viewer feel cozy. Cool cards have a slightly orange tint, so the resulting image is slightly blue. You've seen the effect in car commercials or computer commercials, where you get a very cool, impersonal look. This may be appropriate for a technology video podcast.

The best way to find out what warm and cool cards do is to play around with them. If you don't want to shell out the money for the professional versions, you can try white balancing with different shades of cardboard purchased at a local art supply store. But be careful; if you want a subtle effect, you want cards that are every so slightly off-white.

Exposure

After you set the white balance, you have to set the exposure. Many cameras have automatic exposure circuitry. However, much like the auto-focus mechanisms discussed in the preceding section, this feature often can be more trouble than it's worth.

Automatic exposure, sometimes called *auto-iris*, determines the exposure by the amount of light coming into the lens. The problem is that the amount of light, particularly outdoors, is continually changing. While it may seem like a good idea to adjust the exposure, it's distracting when the exposure changes in the middle of a scene.

Going back to the sailboat example in the preceding section, a sailboat with a big white sail coming into a scene dramatically changes the amount of light coming into the lens. To compensate, the camera changes the exposure by closing the iris slightly, and the exposure on your subject is compromised. It looks like a cloud has passed in front of the sun, when all that has happened is that the camera has changed the exposure.

Manual exposure is always a better choice if your camera offers it. Setting exposure properly should be done with an exposure meter. Setting exposure can be highly subjective, as videographers regularly overexpose or underexpose for dramatic effect. The procedure for setting exposure manually depends on your camera, the shutter speed, whether you're using filters or not, and a number of other things. A full discussion about exposure is beyond the scope of this book. You should, however, be able to set your exposure manually by "feel."

Look at your subject, particularly flesh tones if you're filming a person. Do they look right? Try opening your iris to increase your exposure, or closing it a bit to reduce the exposure. Look critically, and make sure you have what you need. If you're unsure, it's better to underexpose than overexpose. You can always add a bit of brightness during editing.

Easy on the pans, tilts, and zooming

Similarly, you should try to avoid panning (moving the camera from side to side), tilting (tilting the camera up or down), and zooming in on or out from your subject. First, these camera techniques are used sparingly by the pros, so if you use them too often or inappropriately, they're a dead giveaway that an amateur is behind the camera. Second, they place lots of motion in the video frame and consequently degrade the quality of your final product.

Recording

If you've gotten this far, we hope you've invested some time and effort in lighting and composing your subject properly, and have your camera on a tripod, white-balanced and ready to go. Action! At long last, the camera is rolling. Or is it? Much like audio-only podcasts, you need to make sure everything is ready to go before you start recording.

What you never hear in the movies is the responses to the director as she yells out "Lights . . . camera . . ." When the director yells "lights," the director waits until she hears "lights ready" from the lighting director. After "camera," the director waits to hear "speed," which means that the camera is running. ("Speed" is a throwback to the days when it took a second or two for the camera to get up to speed.) If any extras or special effects need to be cranked up, they'll be cued before the director finally yells "and . . . action!"

You don't have to yell out loud, but you should develop a mental checklist that you run through every time you're about to start shooting video. Check to make sure all that your lights are on and that they haven't been bumped. Check all your audio equipment to make sure it's ready to go. Finally, press the record button on your camera, and give it a few seconds before you start your podcast production.

After the tape is running, take a deep breath, smile at the camera, and off you go. When you're finished taping, you may want to take a moment to make sure you've got enough footage for your podcast. You may want to shoot some extra footage, such as a special intro or outro, or some b-roll for safety's sake.

Intros and Outros

If you're having guests on your podcast, you may want to consider doing the intro and outro separately. In fact, you may have to record these separately if you've only got one camera and are recording the podcast interview-style (see the "Filming an Interview with a Single Camera" sidebar). It all depends on the type of podcast you're trying to put together and the level of professionalism you want to achieve.

Asking the Right Questions

If you're going to be interviewing guests on your podcast, be sure to have a list of questions to ask them — that much is probably obvious to even the most inexperienced of podcasters. What may not be so obvious is that you need to ask the questions the right way.

Don't ask questions in such a way that they can be answered with a yes or a no. Make sure you ask what are called *leading questions*, questions that invite your guest to explain why he feels one way or another, or to tell a story about something. Most guests are eager to talk. Why else would they have agreed to be on your show? But people are also human, so if you ask a long rambling question, and end it with " . . . right?," then most people will simply agree with you to be polite.

For example, if you're interviewing someone who just made something amazing, don't ask if he thinks it's his best work. He'll be modest and start to mumble and probably defend the things he's done in the past. A much better approach would be to ask him to talk about the thought process that went into the creation or to describe what it felt like to finish it. That'll get him talking.

One final point about questions — if you have them prepared in advance, you don't have to panic about what you're going to ask next, and therefore you can do what most amateurs fail to do: Listen. It's critical that you listen to your subject, because people don't respond if they know they're not being listened to. In addition, a response might generate a question that you hadn't thought of, taking the interview to another level. The beauty of podcasting is its authenticity. Don't get so worried about your professionalism that it detracts from the human quality.

B-roll

It's always a good idea when you're filming to film some extra content to use as *b-roll*. B-roll is footage that isn't part of the main story but can be inserted into your production from time to time for color or to cover tricky edits. For example, if you're doing a podcast on the latest gadgets at a conference, you should film plenty of b-roll of people demonstrating their gadgets, people milling around popular booths, people laughing, and anything else that helps convey the vibe of the event. You never know when this kind of material will come in handy.

Room tone

Video professionals always record some *room tone* either just before or after the taping session begins (usually at the end). They do this because sometimes a line or question has to be re-recorded, or *overdubbed*. For example, a question from the interviewer might be unintelligible or night need to be rephrased. It may be impossible, or too expensive, to re-tape the interview. Instead, you can cheat by overdubbing the question.

The overdubbing session generally takes place at a recording studio, not where the original footage was taped. When the overdubbed question replaces the original question, it is immediately noticeable because you can't hear the room tone of the original interview space. To compensate for this,

Filming an Interview with a Single Camera

You commonly see a television news reporter doing an interview that appears to be a two-camera shoot, with each person framed with a medium shot, perhaps over the other person's shoulder. When the reporter asks a question, you see the reporter from the interviewee's point of view, and vice versa. What you probably don't know is that these are generally shot with a single camera.

It's simply too expensive to send out enough equipment and personnel to film every single interview as a two-camera shoot. Instead, a single cameraperson is sent out with the reporter, and he gets a little creative. To start off with, the camera faces the interviewee, and the reporter does the interview. When the interview is over, the cameraperson points the camera toward the reporter, who then is filmed asking the questions again and nodding, as if listening to the interviewee's responses. In the editing stage, the footage of the reporter asking the questions is interspersed with the original interview, and no one is the wiser!

Except you, now that you know how it's done.

you can mix in a little room tone, and your overdubbed question will sound as if it was asked during the original taping session.

Taping room tone is easy. Someone, usually the audio engineer, tells everyone to be quiet, and the cameras (and/or audio recording devices) record about 30 seconds of room tone. That's usually more than enough for later use. Be sure everyone who was in the room during the interview stays where they are, because if there are fewer (or more) people in the room when you record your room tone, it will sound slightly different from the room tone during the taping.

Digitizing

After you've shot your raw video footage, you need to load it into your computer so you can open it in your editing software and eventually encode it to a podcasting format. This is known as digitizing or capturing, and it's done in one of two ways, either via FireWire or via a video capture card. However, before we get into the specifics of video capture, you should know a little bit about how video works and how it is digitized.

How video works

Many years ago, some clever folks discovered that they could exploit something known as *persistence of vision* to create the illusion of moving pictures ("movies"). When a series of still images is projected at a fast-enough rate, the human brain "fills in the blanks" and perceives the result as continuous motion. The threshold is approximately 20 frames per second. Anything faster appears to be continuous, and anything slower is perceived as discrete frames (or at least jerky motion).

Fast forward a few decades, and along comes television, which used the same theory, but instead of projecting light through film, television frames were electronic signals that could be broadcast long distances. To create a frame of video, the image is divided into horizontal lines, and each line is scanned inside a video camera and converted into an electronic signal. This electronic signal is broadcast and received by a television, which takes the electronic signal and shoots it at the television screen, line by line.

Of course, all this scanning and projecting happens very quickly. We need to view at least 20 frames per second to see continuous motion. With television, they had to choose a higher frame rate because the frames were drawn line by line, which took some time. Thirty frames per second was chosen as the standard, which was exactly half 60 cycles per second, the oscillating frequency of AC current in the United States.

But there was a problem. Early television technology was limited, and it was discovered that 30 frames per second appeared to flicker every so slightly. The obvious solution was to increase the frame rate, but technology at the time just couldn't handle a higher frame (and hence data) rate. Some sort of compromise had to be reached. The solution was *interlacing*.

Instead of sending 30 discrete frames per second, each frame of video is divided into two *fields*, one consisting of the odd numbered lines, the other of the even numbered lines. The fields are scanned alternately, odds and then evens, broadcast, and then projected onto the television screen (see Figure 9.5).

Each frame of video contains two fields, which are broadcast at 60 fields per second. Because each field contains exactly half the data of the original frame, the data rate or bandwidth of the signal was the same as the original 30 frames per second non-interlaced signal. Interlacing solved the flicker problem, and thus a standard was born. The National Television Standards Committee (NTSC) standard was for 30 frames of interlaced video per second, divided into 525 lines of resolution, of which approximately 480 lines of resolution are visible. The remaining lines are known as the *vertical blanking interval* (VBI) and are used for synchronization (and later closed captions).

We'll see later that interlacing is no longer necessary using modern display technology. Computer monitors are not interlaced; they're known as *progressive scan* devices. For those of you interested in high definition television, this is why there are a plethora of standards in the HD world, both interlaced and progressive. Converting between the two display methods can create problems that we'll have to deal with later.

CROSS-REF For more on interlacing and the problems it creates, see Chapter 14, "Advanced Encoding and Authoring Techniques."

Digital video

To convert analog video into a digital format, the process is similar to digitizing audio. The incoming analog signal is sampled at discrete intervals, and the values are stored. Each sample is called a picture element, or *pixel*. To faithfully represent all the information in the video signal, it was determined that each line would be sampled 720 times. Combine this with the 480 visible lines, and you end up with a screen resolution of 720×480.

FIGURE 9.5

This figure shows how interlacing works.

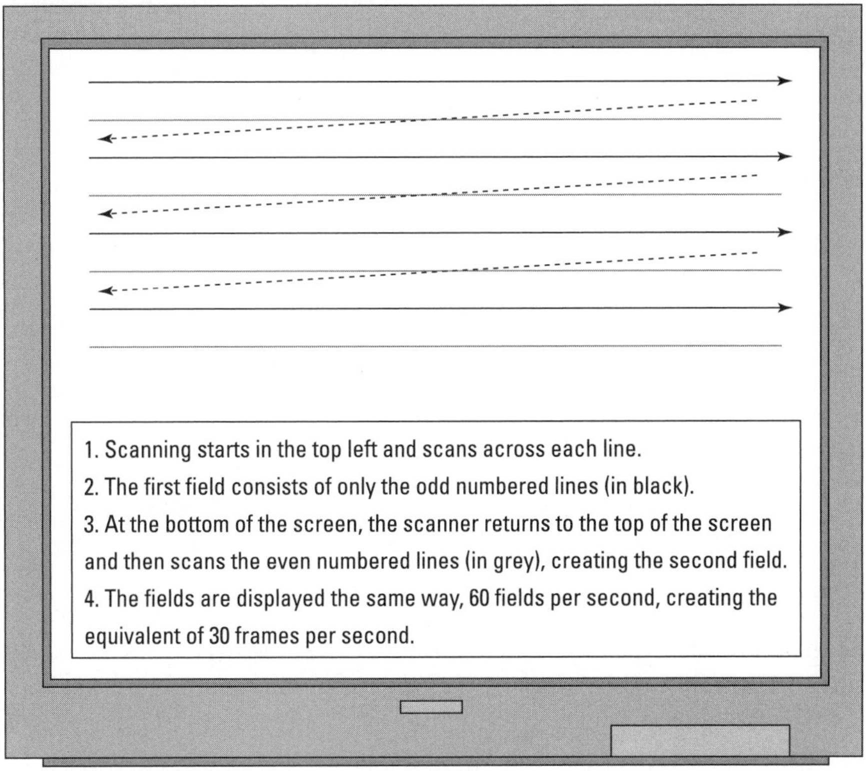

1. Scanning starts in the top left and scans across each line.
2. The first field consists of only the odd numbered lines (in black).
3. At the bottom of the screen, the scanner returns to the top of the screen and then scans the even numbered lines (in grey), creating the second field.
4. The fields are displayed the same way, 60 fields per second, creating the equivalent of 30 frames per second.

When we're digitizing video, we're storing values for each and every one of the pixels, of which there are quite a few:

```
720 * 480 = 345,600 pixels
```

Multiply that by 30 frames per second, and we're looking at over ten million values that have to be stored every second. For each one of these values, we have to allot a certain number of bits to store the value. Even if we try to limit the number of bits we use to store each value, we'll still end up with a very large file. We'll find later that this becomes even more of an issue when we're encoding for a podcast. In order to send files over the Internet, we must reduce them to a manageable size, and doing so with video requires some compromises.

CROSS-REF Encoding, codecs, and the limitations of Internet video formats are discussed in Chapter 11, "Encoding: An Overview."

One of the main compromises that can be made is the encoding scheme used to assign values to each pixel. You can assign this value in a number of different ways. Because all colors can be made out of red, green, and blue, one approach measures how much of each color is present in a pixel and then assigns a value accordingly. This is known as RGB encoding, which is the default method used on computer monitors. Different types of RGB encoding are named according to how many bits are used for the value, such as RGB 24 and RGB 32. RGB encoding can be very high quality, but it isn't the most efficient way to encode video information.

Back at the beginning of the chapter, we learned that our eyes perceive light as being composed of luminance (brightness) and chrominance (color content). Our eyes are very sensitive to brightness and not so sensitive to color. Encoding luminance and chrominance information is a much more efficient way of encoding, because the color information can be compressed, and we won't notice the difference. We can get the same video quality, but with a lower data rate. Table 9.1 illustrates the bit rates and files sizes of some common video encoding schemes.

TABLE 9.1

Data Rates and File Sizes for Common Video Encoding Schemes

Encoding Scheme	Data Rate	File Size for One Minute of Captured Video
RGB 24	~30 MB/sec	1.8 GB
YUV 4:2:2 (Digital Betacam, DVC PRO 50)	~20 MB/sec	1.2 GB
YUV 4:1:1 (DV, DVCAM, DVC PRO)	~4 MB/sec	240 MB

When digitizing, the best approach is to capture at the highest possibly quality. Starting with the highest possible quality gives you more flexibility during the editing phase and provides better raw material for your video podcast. However, the quality of your video capture may be limited by your equipment. If you're working with the DV format, it is encoded using the YUV encoding scheme and compressed at a 5:1 ratio. If you're trying to capture uncompressed video at full resolution (640×480 or above) you must have very fast hard drives and plenty of storage. Aim for the highest possible quality, and settle for whatever works within your limitations.

FireWire

By far the easiest method of capturing video is via FireWire. FireWire (officially known as IEEE 1394, and also known as iLink) is a standard by which data can be exchanged at very high speeds using a special cable and a FireWire port. Most digital video (DV) format cameras include a FireWire port. In addition to data transfer, the FireWire standard includes the ability to control remote devices (such as a camera). This makes capturing video from your DV camera a snap.

Simply connect the camera to your FireWire port, and open your video-editing platform. Most video-editing platforms include some sort of built-in "import" or "capture" functionality. You can generally control the camera from within the application and specify what part of the tape you want to capture. If you want to capture the whole tape, just rewind and hit the capture button.

If your computer doesn't have a FireWire port built in, you can buy a FireWire card for less than $50. If your camera doesn't have FireWire built in, you can buy a digital video converter (see Chapter 8, "Video Production Tools"). Digital video converters take analog audio and video inputs, for example from your camera, and create a DV signal that is available on the FireWire port. An added benefit of digital video converters is that they work both ways, meaning you can send the output of your video editor to the FireWire port, and the digital video converter converts it back to an analog signal that can be displayed on a monitor for quality-assurance purposes.

NOTE   If you use a digital video converter, you won't be able to control your device from your editing software. Only devices with built-in FireWire support have device control.

FireWire settings

One of the advantages (some might say disadvantages) of digitizing via FireWire is that there really are no settings for you to adjust. The DV standard is hard-coded into the entire process. You'll always be capturing full screen, full frame rate, using the DV codec.

The DV codec is another advantage to capturing via FireWire. Digital Video (DV) is compressed as it is recorded, making DV files about 1/5 the size of uncompressed video files. This makes them easier to store and move around. The compression affects image quality, however, and is one of the reasons that DV isn't considered true broadcast quality. However, the ease of use and the price points of DV cameras are virtually impossible to argue with.

Capturing via FireWire isn't really capturing in the truest sense; it's really just transferring the file from your camera (or tape deck) to your computer, just like you'd transfer a file from one computer to another. Because it's just a file transfer process, the video on your computer is an exact copy of the information on your camera.

Transferring files via FireWire using iMovie: A step-by-step example

Like so many things in the MacOS world, transferring DV from your camera to your Mac is a snap. Follow these steps:

1. First, connect your camera to your Mac's FireWire port, and turn your camera on to the playback or VCR position.

2. Open iMovie.

3. iMovie automatically detects that you have a camera connected and opens in "camera mode" (see Figure 9.6).

FIGURE 9.6

iMovie automatically detects a camera connected to your Mac and opens in camera mode.

Use the Import button (or the space bar)
to start the capture process.

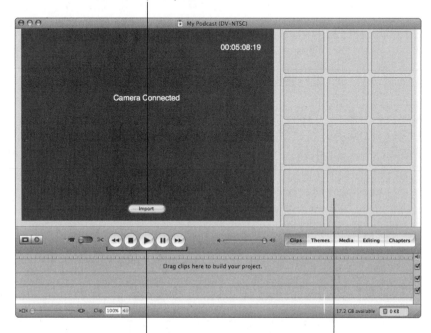

Use the control buttons to
find the video you want to capture.

Your video is automatically divided
into clips and placed in the clip area.

> **TIP**
> In camera mode, the stop, play, fast forward, and rewind buttons control your camera. You can use these controls to find the portion of your tape that you want to import.

4. To begin the import process, click the Import button (or hit the spacebar). If the tape is already playing, iMovie starts importing video from that point. If the tape is stopped, iMovie starts tape playback and begins importing.

5. iMovie automatically breaks up the imported video into clips each time it senses a new scene. This can be very handy, but it also can be a problem if you're trying to import a pre-edited piece of video with multiple scenes. You can disable this feature. From the iMovie menu, select Preferences (or just hold down the Apple button and push the comma key). Select the Import tab, and then deselect the "Start a new clip at each scene break" option.

That's it! You can now drag your clips to your iMovie timeline and edit away.

Video capture cards

If you have no way to utilize FireWire, you have to use a video capture card to convert the analog video signal into digital information. Video capture cards, like cameras, are available at a wide range of price points. The more you spend, the higher quality your video capture will be.

Video capture card settings

Using a video capture card involves connecting your camera to the capture card and then specifying the settings for your capture. Where and what settings you can specify depends on your capture card and your video-editing platform. Essentially, you specify the following:

- **Resolution:** The dimensions of your screen capture
- **Frame rate:** How many frames per second to capture
- **Data rate (or compression):** Whether to capture the video uncompressed or use a codec during capture

You also may be able to adjust the video settings for your capture, such as brightness, contrast, and saturation. However, the adjustments offered by most budget capture cards tend to be fairly coarse. A better approach is to digitize your video as purely as possible and to do your adjustments using video-editing software, which enables a much finer degree of control—and the ability to "undo."

To capture the highest quality video possible, try to capture full screen, full frame rate, and uncompressed. You may have to scale back, however, depending on your hardware situation. Full-screen uncompressed capture is a very data intensive process, requiring a fast machine and lots of storage. If you have to scale back, start by trying to use a different encoding scheme such as YUV. If your machine still can't capture full frames reliably, you'll have to reduce your resolution, possibly to 1/2 size (320×240). This is a perfectly acceptable starting point for a video podcast, provided you can capture at full frame rate.

Digitizing via a capture card using SwiftCap: A step-by-step example

If you are capturing video via a capture card, you can choose some settings. Most video-editing platforms come with a video capture application that allows you to access your video capture card and adjust your settings. In this example, we'll use SwiftCap, which is the video capture application that comes with all cards sold by Viewcast, one of the more popular video capture card manufacturers. It has some nifty features that you'll find handy for successful video captures.

Follow these steps to digitize video with SwiftCap:

1. Make sure that your capture card is installed correctly and that your camera or videotape deck is connected to your capture card.

2. Open SwiftCap. Provided your camera is running, you should see a preview of your video (see Figure 9.7). If you don't see a video preview, make sure "Preview Video" is checked on the View menu.

   If you're still not seeing video, make sure your video source is correct. Many video capture cards have multiple inputs, for example, a composite input and an S-Video input. To check your source setting, choose "Capture Settings" from the Settings menu or click the capture settings icon (see Figure 9.7).

FIGURE 9.7

The ViewCast SwiftCap application

3. Select the appropriate source from the drop-down Source menu on the left side of the Capture Settings window (see Figure 9.8).

FIGURE 9.8

Select the appropriate source in the Capture Settings window to make the preview active.

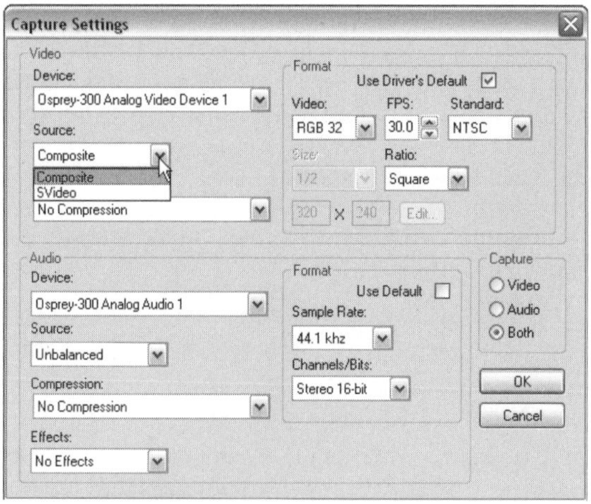

4. Before you do any capturing, make sure your system is capable of capturing the screen resolution and encoding scheme you want to use. Ideally, you want to capture full screen (720×486, or 640×480 if your capture card automatically scales the input), but this requires a fast computer and plenty of storage. SwiftCap includes a handy disk performance analyzer that can save you lots of woe. From the Tools menu, choose "Disk Performance." This brings up the Disk Analyzer shown in Figure 9.9.

FIGURE 9.9

Click "Profile Drive" in the Disk Analyzer window to analyze your hard drive performance.

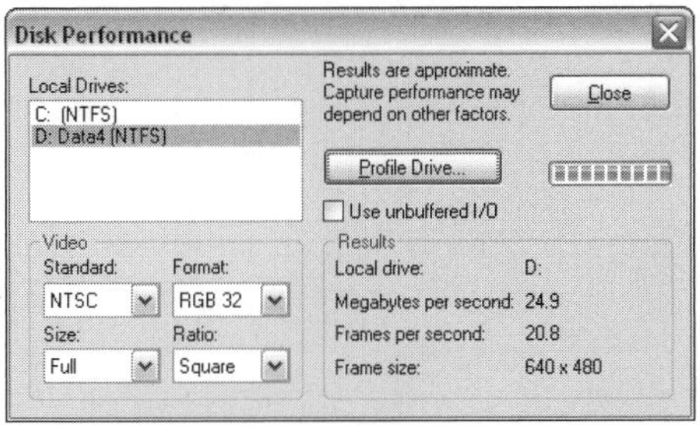

5. Select the drive you intend to capture to in the Local Drives pane, and click the "Profile Drive" button. The analyzer then determines the speed at which you can capture video and displays the results in the lower right. You can see in Figure 9.9 that this drive is capable of capturing only 20.8 frames per second using RGB 32 encoding. We'll have to choose a different encoding scheme to get the full frame rate.

TIP You should always capture video to a drive other than the system drive if possible.

6. The idea is that you have to get your frame rate comfortably over 30 frames per second. YUV encoding is more efficient, so you can usually get your frame rate up considerably by switching to a YUV encoding scheme. In Figure 9.10, you can see that switching to YUY2 puts our potential frame rate over 40, which is far more than we need.

FIGURE 9.10

Using a YUV encoding scheme is more efficient and allows higher frame rate captures.

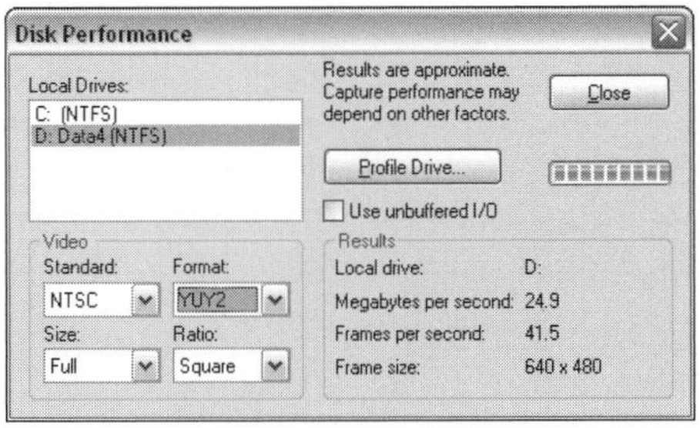

7. After you've found settings that work with your system, go back to the Capture Settings window and enter those settings (see Figure 9.11).

FIGURE 9.11

Be sure to choose the right settings in the Capture Settings window.

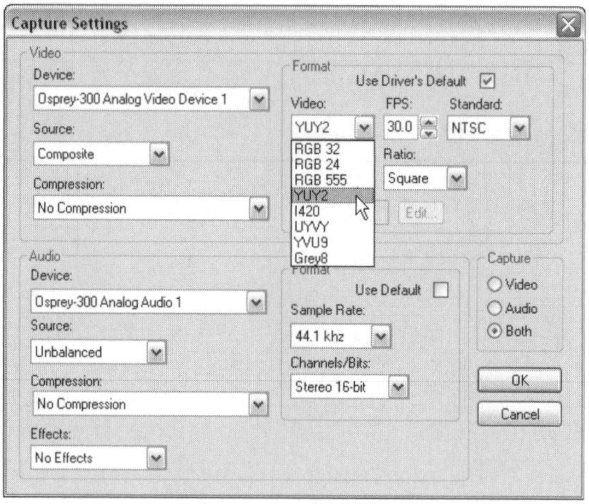

8. Next, specify which drive you want the captured file saved to. Select "Capture Destination" from the Settings menu, or click the capture settings icon to bring up the Capture Destination window (see Figure 9.12). Clicking the double arrow button at the top right opens a browse window where you can specify a location and a filename. Be sure to use the same drive that you tested in Step 5.

FIGURE 9.12

Specify where to put your captured video file.

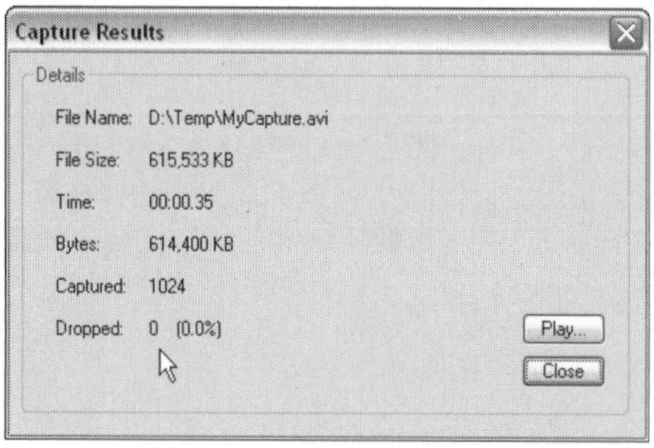

9. You should now be ready to capture video. Rewind the tape to just before where you want to start capturing, start tape playback, and then start the capture process by selecting "Start" from the Capture menu or by clicking the start capture icon.

   SwiftCap disables the video preview during capture, so you have to either monitor via your camera's monitor or an external monitor. When you've captured what you needed, choose "Stop" from the capture menu or click the stop capture icon.

10. After you stop your capture, SwiftCap displays a capture results window. It is critical that your capture have zero dropped frames. If your capture dropped frames, you should recapture your video using a different encoding scheme or a smaller capture resolution.

That should be it. Using a capture card requires a few more steps than using a FireWire setup, but you should be able to get equally good quality, provided you're using a good quality capture card.

> **TIP** Video capture is a resource-intensive process. It's best to shut down all other programs when capturing video to avoid dropped frames.

Editing

After you've transferred your video to your computer, you need to tidy up the rough edges of your video production and turn your podcast into a masterpiece. Well, we can hope, can't we? As discussed in the audio chapter, you should edit with an eye on three things: content, quality, and convenience.

First and foremost, you want your podcast to have good content from start to finish. If you are interviewing a guest for your podcast, you probably had a long list of questions to ask. When you're reviewing your footage, try to keep your distance from the material, and only keep what works best. Of course, some guests may be fantastic, and you'll want to keep every syllable they utter. Often, however, you'll find that a few questions just didn't go anywhere or didn't reveal anything new (see the "Ask the Right Questions" side bar). If so, edit it out. With a few nimble edits, the pacing of a show can change dramatically, turning a mediocre show into a great show.

Keep edits short and sharp

When you're editing, most edit platforms offer a number of transition options for you to choose from. In general, anything other than a quick cross fade (also known as a dissolve) should be avoided, for a couple of key reasons. First, if you watch closely, crazy transitions are almost never used on television or in film. Over-the-top transitions detract from the story line and call way too much attention to themselves. For this reason, they're a dead giveaway that an amateur is at the controls. Second, there's a technological reason why you shouldn't use complicated transitions. They are incredibly difficult to encode. If you're encoding for a broadband audience, the bit rates you use simply aren't capable of encoding that much motion efficiently. You'll either end up with a transition that looks like mud, or you'll be forced to encode your podcast at a higher bit rate, which means a larger file, a longer download for your audience, and a bigger bandwidth bill at the end of the month.

Cutaways

Cutaways are small pieces of film that you can use when editing video, often used to cover up an edit. Editing video can be tricky because people can see when and where you edit your video. You can't just cut out the middle of an interview without some clever editing, or people will notice that there's something missing. This is where cutaways can really help.

Imagine an interview on a conference floor, where someone rudely interrupts your guest while she's answering a question. Unless the interruption was by someone important (or it was really funny), you probably want to edit it out of the podcast. If you just cut it out, there will be a sudden jump in the video (known as a "jump cut" in the industry). You have to disguise your cut using a cutaway.

Here's how it works: When the interruption occurs, cut to some b-roll, like a shot of you nodding in agreement or a shot of the conference room floor. Let the audio of your guest's response continue to play underneath the b-roll. Then, you can cut from the b-roll with the guest audio underneath it to an appropriate location after the interruption occurred. The jump cut will be hidden by the b-roll, and your secret will be safe. This editing approach is illustrated in Figure 9.13.

FIGURE 9.13

Use cutaways to disguise your edits.

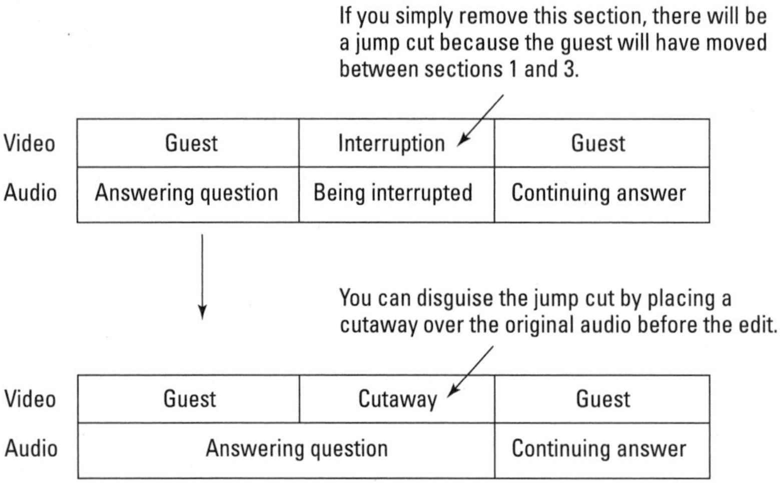

If you simply remove this section, there will be a jump cut because the guest will have moved between sections 1 and 3.

Video	Guest	Interruption	Guest
Audio	Answering question	Being interrupted	Continuing answer

You can disguise the jump cut by placing a cutaway over the original audio before the edit.

Video	Guest	Cutaway	Guest
Audio	Answering question		Continuing answer

> **TIP** Provided you have plenty of cutaway material, it's often easiest to edit your story together by editing to your audio and then covering any awkward transitions with cutaway or B-roll material.

Archiving

As you probably are beginning to realize, quite a bit of work goes into creating a video podcast. If you've got a FireWire setup, it can be pretty simple, but if you're using a video capture card and an analog camera, you may have to fiddle with your settings. Depending on how much editing you do (and how many cutaways you have to use), your final master may be quite a bit different from what you originally started off with. It's very important, therefore, that you archive your work so that you don't have to start from scratch if you decide to re-edit your podcast, perhaps for a "best-of" end-of-year show.

For that matter, your podcast may not be the only outlet for your programming. You may decide you want to put out a DVD or license your programming to a cable channel. The possibilities are all out there, but if all you keep lying around are the low-bit-rate podcast versions, you'd have to do lots of work to recreate your masters.

Save your work in as high a quality as you can. If you're working with a FireWire system, you can usually print your master right back to a DV tape. You can obviously keep a DV version on your hard drive if you've got space, but video files can fill up a hard drive quickly. DV tapes are compact and a fairly reliable backup method.

If you're not working with a FireWire system, or if you just want to keep pure digital copies lying around, consider buying an external hard drive (or two). You can use one to do all your capturing and editing and keep the other for archival purposes. Without the luxury of FireWire, you won't be able to save to DV, because video capture cards don't work in reverse; you can't print your edited master back to tape. You have to rely on digital storage.

One thing that hasn't been thoroughly established is how long hard drives will last. It's fairly common knowledge that hard drives in servers that are working 24 hours in a day have an average life expectancy of about three years. However, they're usually higher quality drives than most people have in their laptops or home desktop systems. Much like light bulbs, it's the turning on and turning off that are hardest on the drive.

If you're using external drives, you may not be using them every day, which in theory extends their life cycle, but if you put them on a shelf and forget about them, had drives have been known to "freeze." The data on the disc platters is intact, but the hard drive is unable to spin the platters to access the data. You can send drives in this condition to companies that specialize in data rescue, but the process is very expensive.

Unfortunately, we have no good answer as to how long hard drives are going to last. Institutions such as banks that rely on data use tape backup systems to maintain their data integrity. A number of pro-sumer tape backup formats are available nowadays. They're not cheap, but if you want a guarantee that your programs will be available 5, 10, or 25 years from now, you should consider investing in a good tape backup system, or open up an account with a backup company.

Summary

If all this has dampened your enthusiasm for a video podcast, please reconsider. We feel video podcasting is going to explode in the next few years. It may seem like lots to learn and keep track of, but after you get the hang of it, it really isn't that difficult, and it's one heck of a lot of fun. Just remember:

- Video is all about light, so good video production is all about controlling your light.
- A small lighting kit can dramatically improve your video quality, even if it's just a single light and some reflectors to use as fill light.
- When shooting video for a podcast, remember to frame your shots appropriately, because people will most likely be watching on a smaller screen.
- Try not to move the camera too much.
- Be sure to white balance before you start rolling.
- FireWire is by far the simplest way to transfer video.
- Use cutaways to disguise awkward edits.
- Always archive your masters in the highest quality you can afford.

Chapter 10

Advanced Video Production Techniques

So you've figured out how to shoot some video and managed to load it into your computer. It looks good, but something's not quite right. The video just isn't quite as bright and colorful as you remember. That's because there are fundamental differences between televisions and computer monitors. We talk about these differences and ways to compensate for them in this chapter.

Before we dive into the technical minutiae of display technologies, let's talk briefly about some simple tools you can use to improve your video image before it hits tape. Lens filters can be a very cost-effective way of improving your video quality.

Understanding Lens Filters

Many of you may have at one time or another played around with photography. If you ever progressed beyond "point-and-shoot" cameras, one of the first accessories you probably purchased was an ultraviolet (UV) filter for your lens. UV filters are useful because they prevent UV light from entering your lens, which can make your pictures look slightly blurry, and because they protect your lens. Mistakenly scratching a $25 filter is far preferable to scratching a fancy zoom lens that cost you hundreds of dollars.

The same applies for your DV camera. Protecting your investment by buying a cheap and replaceable filter is a good idea, and as with photography, filtering out UV light gives you a cleaner video image. If you're wondering how a UV filter works, chances are good that you've experienced it many times. Every time you put on a pair of sunglasses, you're filtering out UV light (among other things). The immediate effect is a clearer, crisper image. Even though we can't see UV light, it interferes with our ability to perceive visible light. DV cameras have the same problem, so a UV filter is always a good idea.

A number of other lens filters can be used to improve the quality of your podcast. The next few sections discuss them generally. To learn more about exactly which filter you should use with your model of camera, you should consult online discussion boards and digital video camera review sites.

Diffusion

Diffusion filters soften your video image. We've all seen diffusion at work in the movies, particularly in the film noir genre. The camera cuts to a shot of the gorgeous female actress, and she's practically luminous. This is achieved using a fairly heavy diffusion filter. Although this would be overkill for most podcasting applications, using a light diffusion filter gives your podcast a distinctive look. It also can help your encoding quality.

Many DV cameras default to shooting a very high contrast image, and some even use special processing to exaggerate the edges between objects. This can be okay in situations where there isn't much contrast to begin with, but if your scene is lit properly, you should have plenty of contrast. Video that has too much contrast looks amateurish. Using a diffusion filter can mitigate this by softening the entire image ever so slightly. Diffusion filters can make your podcast look more "film-like," which is generally desirable.

Video with too much contrast also is more difficult to encode, because it has lots of extra detail in the frame. This makes the encoder's job harder, because it tries to maintain as much detail as possible. Using a diffusion filter helps soften the image slightly, which reduces the amount of detail, thereby making the image easier to encode.

Color correction

The UV filter described at the beginning of this section is essentially a color filter, designed to filter out colors beyond our range of vision. There are many more color filters that you can buy for other situations. One of the most useful for many podcasters is the fluorescent light filter. Fluorescent lights emit a very particular type of light, with a lot of extra green in it. Because of the large amount of green content, fluorescent lights tend to make people look slightly ill. Using a fluorescent filter when filming in offices or other fluorescent lighting situations can make your podcasts look warmer and more natural.

You also can buy filters that are designed to enhance certain parts of the color spectrum. These are fairly specialized and not for the average podcast producer. If you're looking for a special effect, you're probably better off trying things out in your video-editing platform, where you can safely undo those mistakes.

Polarization

Polarization filters are used to filter out reflected light. For example, filming through a window can be very difficult because of the reflections. Using a polarization filter removes this reflected light and allows you to film what's on the other side of the glass. Similarly, if you're trying to film under water, for example fish in a pond, you need a polarization filter. Polarization is often used in sunglasses for this reason.

Display Technology Differences

Television screens display images using a completely different technology than computer monitors. This is unfortunate because it leads to problems when trying to display video on a computer screen. However, it also can be a blessing, because television technology is nearly 100 years old, and much better technology is now available. The problem is that for the foreseeable future, we're caught between the two, shooting with cameras that are designed to record video in the NTSC/PAL (television) standard, and distributing our video on the Internet to be viewed on modern displays.

This section talks about some of the differences in display technologies, in anticipation of the signal processing techniques we learn about in the next section.

Interlaced versus progressive displays

In the preceding chapter, we learned that standard television uses an interlaced display. Each frame of video is divided into two fields, one consisting of the odd lines of the image and the other the even lines. These two fields are scanned and displayed in series. So television actually is 60 fields per second, which we see as continual motion.

Computer monitors, whether they're cathode ray tube (CRT) or liquid crystal display (LCD), are progressive monitors. Each frame of video is drawn from left to right, top to bottom. There are no fields. The problems appear when we try to create a single frame of progressive video from two fields of interlaced video (see Figure 10.1).

In Figure 10.1, a minivan is driving past the camera. During the split second between the first and second field scans, the minivan has moved across the frame. When this video is displayed on an interlaced display, it appears normal, because the second field is displayed a split second after the first. However, if we try to combine these two fields of interlaced video into a single progressive frame, interlacing artifacts appear because of the horizontal motion. The front edge of the minivan is "feathered," and both tires are a blur. At either the editing or the encoding phase, something must be done to deal with this problem.

FIGURE 10.1

Converting two fields of interlaced video with significant horizontal motion to a single frame of progressive video can be problematic.

The minivan has moved between the first and second field scans.
When the fields are combined into a single frame, interlacing
artifacts are plainly visible.

Color spaces

Television and computer monitors encode color information differently. Television signals are encoded in terms of luminance and chrominance (YUV encoding); computer monitor signals are encoded in terms of the amount of red, blue, and green in each pixel (RGB encoding). We also watch them in different environments. Televisions are generally viewed in somewhat dim surroundings, whereas computer monitors are generally in bright areas. The combination of these factors means that content created for one environment doesn't look right when displayed on the other.

Digitized NTSC video looks dull and washed out when displayed on a computer monitor. Video that has been processed to look right on a computer monitor looks too bright and saturated (colorful) when displayed on an NTSC monitor. The non-compatibility between the two display technologies makes it problematic to create high-quality video, particularly if you want to display your content on both. If you're producing content for both broadcast and the Internet, at some point your project must split into two separate projects. After you start processing a video signal for display on a computer monitor, you won't be able to display it on a TV monitor.

TIP The best way to manage this issue is to work exclusively in the broadcast space during your digitizing and editing phases. Archive your masters in a broadcast format. Don't do your post-processing for Internet viewing until the encoding phase, or at least after all your editing has been done and you have a broadcast-quality master. That way, you always have a version of your video that can be broadcast or burned to DVD. Create a special version that is intended for Internet-only consumption. As new formats evolve, you can always re-encode from your broadcast-quality master.

Video Signal Processing

By this point in the chapter, you should have an understanding about why you'd want to do some video signal processing. Even if you've done a great job producing and capturing your video, there are still fundamental differences between television and computer monitor displays that should be compensated for. To do this, you need to de-interlace your video and adjust your color for RGB monitors.

Using de-interlacing filters

Most editing platforms have de-interlacing filters built into them. As we saw in Figure 10.1, the problem is dealing with the artifacts that arise when two fields of interlaced video are combined to make a single frame of progressive video. Three methods are commonly used to deal with interlaced video:

- **Blending:** This approach combines the two fields, but it's vulnerable to interlacing artifacts, as shown in Figure 10.1.

- **Interpolation:** This approach attempts to shift parts of one field left or right to compensate for the artifacts. This is very computationally complex, because only parts of the field should be interpolated. For example, in Figure 10.1, we want to interpolate the parts of the frame that include the moving minivan, but not those that contain static elements such as the trees in the background.

- **Discarding:** This approach discards one field and uses a single field twice in a single frame of progressive video. The resulting frame therefore has half the vertical resolution of the original frame, but without the interlacing artifacts.

Editing and encoding platforms distinguish themselves by how they deal with interlacing artifacts. De-interlacing video on two different platforms generally yields different quality results. Where you choose to do your de-interlacing depends on where you can get the best quality. If you're staying in the broadcast world for your editing phase, it makes more sense to de-interlace during the encoding phase. This is demonstrated for you in the next section.

However, we have to come clean about de-interlacing. For the most part, it isn't necessary for most podcasts. If you're encoding your podcasts for viewing on a video iPod (or other portable media device), chances are good that you're targeting a resolution of 320×240. At this resolution, most encoding software *drops the second field by default!* If you've got only 320 lines of resolution, it doesn't make sense to process the second field, so you don't have any interlacing artifacts to deal with. This is a very good reason to target 320×240 for your podcasts: The de-interlacing problem goes away.

If, however, you're targeting browser-based playback for your podcast and decide to use a resolution larger than 320×240 — such as 400×300, 480×360, or 640×480 — you need to de-interlace your video during the encoding phase. So, for you mavericks, the next section shows where to find the de-interlacing filter in a number of software applications.

Where to find de-interlacing filters

If you're hoping to de-interlace your video (assuming that your final video podcast resolution is larger than 320×240), you need to make sure your encoding application has de-interlacing filters. Most, but not all, do. If you're targeting the QuickTime format, use an encoding application such as Sorenson Squeeze, because QuickTime Pro doesn't include a de-interlacing filter.

Sorenson Squeeze includes a de-interlacing filter in the filter settings window, shown in Figure 10.2. Double-click any filter to open the filter settings window. The de-interlacing filter is on by default in the preset filters.

FIGURE 10.2

Sorenson Squeeze offers de-interlacing in the filter settings window.

Double-click any filter preset to open the filter settings window.

Or, if you are going to modify the settings, click the plus sign to make a copy so you can save it as a separate preset.

Make sure the Deinterlace checkbox is checked.

When you are finished, click the Apply button to see the effect previewed.

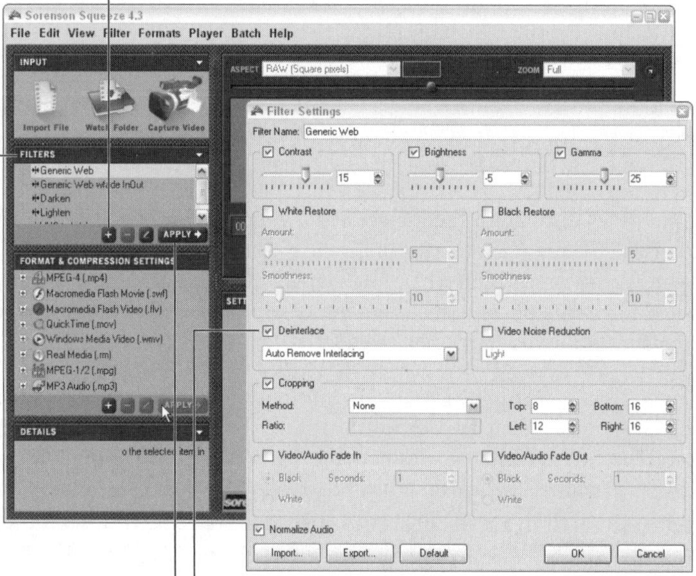

If you're targeting the Windows Media Format, you can use the de-interlacing filter included in the Windows Media Encoder. The de-interlacing filter is on the Processing tab of the Session Properties window, shown in Figure 10.3.

If your encoding application doesn't have a de-interlacing filter, chances are good that your editing platform will. Vegas includes the de-interlace setting in the Project Properties window, shown in Figure 10.4. Select Project Properties from the File menu or type Alt+Enter, and then select the de-interlacing method you want from the drop-down menu.

FIGURE 10.3

The Windows Media Encoder offers a de-interlacing filter in the processing settings.

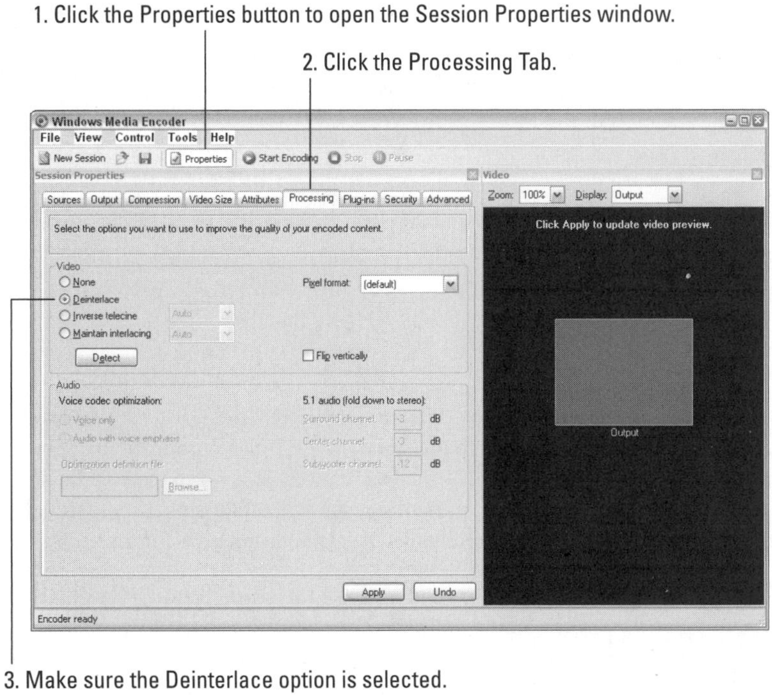

1. Click the Properties button to open the Session Properties window.

2. Click the Processing Tab.

3. Make sure the Deinterlace option is selected.

Vegas offers a de-interlacing filter in the project properties window.

Use "none" if you're targeting 320x240 or smaller.
Experiment with "blend" and "interpolate" if
you're targeting larger resolutions.

Color correction

Color correction is necessary for two reasons: (1) the different display technologies that television and computer monitors use, and (2) the difference in the standard viewing environments. We're used to looking at spreadsheets and documents on computer monitors, and we sit close to them. So we're accustomed to more brightness and contrast than is generally included on a standard television screen. If you digitize standard video footage, it looks lifeless and dull on a computer screen.

We can deal with this issue in a number of ways. We want to make the video look a bit brighter and more colorful. Depending on what video editing or encoding software you're using, you may be offered a number of different controls. The simplest tools offered are brightness, color, and contrast controls. If this is what you've got, you can try adding a touch of contrast and a bit of color, and backing off the brightness a bit. It may sound strange to turn down the brightness when we're after more vivid video, but you'll soon find that these controls all affect one another. When we're adding more color, we're essentially adding more light, which increases the overall brightness of the image. Backing off the overall brightness just a bit stops the image from getting too washed out.

One of the problems of adjusting color, contrast, and brightness is that you can do as much harm as good. If you add too much color or brightness, the black areas of your image will no longer be black, but rather a charcoal gray. Whites will be "too white." What you really want to do is make the colors more vivid, but without affecting the black levels or the white levels. The best way to do this is to adjust the *gamma*, which does precisely what we want. The actual definition of gamma is very complex and involves lots of advanced mathematics. For now, just remember that adjusting gamma is *good* and makes your video look more vivid.

NOTE Color correction can be only as good as the monitor you're using. Be sure to use a calibrated monitor when doing serious color correction. Hardware tools are available to calibrate your monitor, and also software tools such as the highly recommended QuickGamma:

        http://www.normankoren.com/makingfineprints1A.html#QuickGamma

In fact, that's one of the tricky things about doing color correction. Depending on your editing platform, you may be presented with tools to adjust brightness, color, contrast, *saturation,* gamma, *gain, hue* — the list of terms used seems endless. To make things more complicated, there is some disagreement and more commonly misunderstanding about what each of these terms actually represents. In the interest of giving you an idea of what these terms means, here are some rough definitions (which are by no means authoritative):

- **Brightness:** The amount of light a source emits, i.e. the luminance
- **Color:** The amount of color a source emits, i.e. the chrominance
- **Contrast:** The difference in luminance between objects in a field of vision, so frames with bright whites and dark blacks have lots of contrast
- **Gamma:** A way of correcting color displays in a non-linear fashion, such that black and white are unaffected, but colors are more intense
- **Saturation:** The intensity of a particular color
- **Gain:** The overall power of a video signal; analogous to brightness
- **Hue:** Refers to a pure color, such that adjusting hue adds more of a particular color to your image

Color correcting

Not all encoding or video-editing platforms offer gamma adjustment, so you may be stuck with a more generic "color" adjustment, which may or may not be a gamma adjustment. If this is the case, see if you have a preset for "NTSC color to RGB color" or "Studio RGB to Computer RGB." If you don't have a preset to work with, use the following guide as a starting point:

- **Contrast:** Try adding a small amount of contrast.
- **Color/Gamma/Saturation:** Try adding a fair amount of color.
- **Brightness:** To compensate for the boost in color, you may want to back off the brightness a bit. If your color adjustment is a true gamma control, you won't need to do this.

In general, you should do color correction at the encoding phase, because after you've color corrected for computer monitors, you won't be able to display the video on a regular television. The video will look too bright and gaudy. Unfortunately, though, only advanced encoding software offers color correction, so you may be forced to do color correction at the editing phase.

> **TIP** If you have to do color correction in your video editor, save two copies of your project, one with no color correction (for future broadcast possibilities) and one for the Internet. Be sure to put some sort of indication in your project name, such as "_NTSC" for your broadcast version and "_WEB" for your video podcast.

Color correction in iMovie

iMovie offers a number of options for video processing in the Video Effects pane. Among them is gamma correction under the Quartz Composer tools, shown in Figure 10.5. However, the drawback to using iMovie video processing is that the adjustment is somewhat crude, offering only a slider control, with no numerical values. Plus, you can't save your settings. If you have a number of different clips you want to adjust, there's no real way (other than using your eyes) to know if you're adding the same amount of gamma.

FIGURE 10.5

Color correction is available in iMovie.

1. Make sure you're in editing mode.

2. Click the Video FX tab.

4. Adjust Gamma using the slider.

3. Choose Gamma Adjust from the effects.

One thing that might help is turning off the option to turn your video into clips, and instead digitize your video as one large clip. Then you can do your color correction on the clip *before* you do your editing. This may seem a little backward, but at least you'll know your video processing is consistent across your entire video podcast.

Color correction in Sorenson Squeeze

Sorenson Squeeze offers color correction via the filters window. In fact, the Generic Web preset offers a great place to start with your color correction (refer to Figure 10.2). You can see that they add contrast and gamma, and back off the brightness just a bit. These settings should immediately improve the quality of your video, but you should fiddle around with them a bit to make sure you're getting the best quality you can. If you find a new setting that works for your contrast, be sure to save it as a new preset so you can use it over and over.

> **TIP** If you're going to tinker with a preset, make a copy first and then play around with that. Highlight the preset that you want to use as a starting point, and click the plus sign at the bottom of the filter window. A copy is created that you can rename to your liking.

Color correction in Vegas

The big advantage to Vegas is that you can apply video processing to an entire video track, which may consist of multiple clips. You don't have to apply the effect to each and every clip individually; rather the effect is applied to all clips on the track. Vegas offers a "Studio RGB to Computer RGB" preset in the Color Correction video processing plug-in, as shown in Figure 10.6.

The preset is a good place to start if you're working with well-produced video. If you need to do a little more work on your image, you can use the saturation, gamma, and gain controls to tweak to your heart's content.

VirtualDub: The Incredible Free Video Processing Tool

VirtualDub is a video capture and processing utility for the Windows Platform. It isn't a video editing application, like Final Cut or Premiere, but it offers lots of cool processing tools that can come in handy, particularly if you want to batch process a large number of video clips. For example, if you have a number of clips already edited for broadcast, you can create a batch process that adjusts your gamma and resizes your images to 320×240.

The user interface is a bit Spartan, and it isn't really a tool for beginners, but VirtualDub is a video processing powerhouse. You can find a copy of it lying around on most Internet media mavens' desktops because of its "Swiss army knife" set of functions.

FIGURE 10.6

Sony Vegas has a color correction preset suitable for podcasts.

1. Click the green plug-in icon on your video track to bring up the plug-in chain window.

2. Click the green "Add a plug-in" icon and select color corrector, and then press the "Add" button.

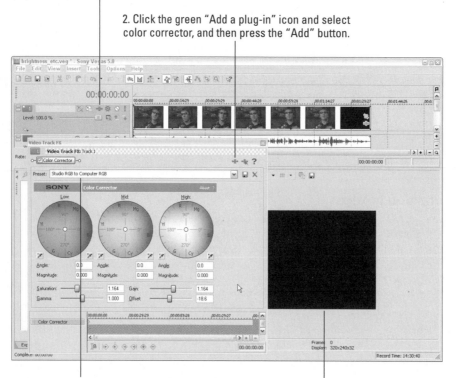

3. Choose the "Studio RGB to Computer RGB" preset.

4. The effect is previewed in the video window.

Cropping and Resizing

At some point, you may want to cut out part of your video image. For example, the original video may not have been framed well, and you may want a tighter shot. Or there may be something objectionable in the shot that you want to remove. Cutting out this unwanted video is called *cropping*. If you're targeting video iPods, you also have to resize your video to 320×240, which is the resolution of the iPod video screen. Video-editing platforms allow you to do this, but in order to do it correctly without introducing any visual distortion, you must understand what an *aspect ratio* is.

Aspect ratios

The aspect ratio is the ratio of the width to the height of a video image. Standard definition television has an aspect ratio of 4:3 (or 1.33:1). High definition TV has an aspect ratio of 16:9 (1.78:1). You've no doubt noticed that all the new HDTV-compatible screens are wider than standard TVs. When you're cropping and resizing video, it's critical to maintain your aspect ratio; otherwise, you'll stretch the video in one direction or another.

To better understand this, let's look at how NTSC video is digitized. The original signal is displayed on 486 lines. Each one of these lines, or *rasters*, is a "stripe" of continuous video information. When it is digitized, it is divided up into 720 discrete slices, each one of these slices is assigned a value, and the values are stored digitally.

However, when you display the digitized 720×486 video on a computer monitor, the video appears slightly wider than on a television, or looked at another way, the video seems a bit squished. People look a little shorter and stickier than usual, which in general is not a good thing. Why is this?

If you do the math, 720×486 is not a 4:3 aspect ratio. If you could zoom in and look really closely at the tiny slices of NTSC video that were digitized, they would be slightly taller than they are wide. But computer monitor pixels are square. So when 720×486 video is displayed on a computer monitor, it appears stretched horizontally. To make the video look right, you must resize the video to a 4:3 aspect ratio such as 640×480 or 320×240. This restores the original aspect ratio, and the image looks right.

NOTE Those of you paying attention may be wondering about standard definition television displayed on the new widescreen models. The simple answer is that most widescreen TVs stretch standard television out to fill the entire 16:9 screen, introducing ridiculous amounts of distortion. Why that is considered an improvement is anyone's guess.

With the availability of HDV cameras, some of you may be fortunate enough to be working in HDV, which offers a native widescreen format. If so, you'll be working with a 16:9 aspect ratio such as 1080×720 or 1920×1080. Regardless of the format you're working in, the key is to maintain your aspect ratio.

Cropping

If you decide you need to do some cropping, the key is to crop a little off each side to maintain your aspect ratio (see Figure 10.7). Some video-editing platforms offer to maintain the aspect ratio automatically when you're performing a crop, which is very handy. However, many of the encoding tools require that you manually specify the number of pixels you want shaved from the top, bottom, right, and left of your screen. If that's the case, then you have to do the math yourself and be sure to crop the right amounts from each side.

FIGURE 10.7

Be careful with your aspect ratio when you crop.

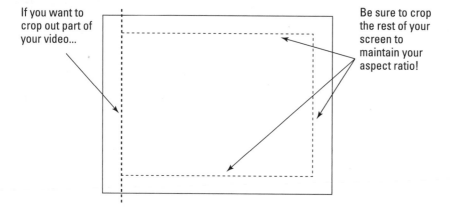

If you want to crop out part of your video...

Be sure to crop the rest of your screen to maintain your aspect ratio!

As an example, let's say that you needed to shave off the bottom edge of your video. You could estimate that you wanted to crop off the bottom 5 percent of your screen, which would mean 24 lines of video. Assuming you were working with broadcast video, to maintain your aspect ratio, you'd need to crop a total of:

```
24 * 720 / 486 = 35.5 or 36 pixels
```

So you'd need to cut 36 pixels off the width to maintain your aspect ratio. You could do this by taking 18 pixels off either side, or 36 pixels off one side. It doesn't matter; where you crop is dependent on what is in your video frame. Of course, this is assuming that you're working with NTSC video. The math varies slightly if you've already resized the video to a 4:3 aspect ratio such as 640×480.

One thing to bear in mind is that some codecs have limitations on the dimensions they can encode. Codecs divide the video frame into small boxes known as *macroblocks*. In some cases, the smallest macroblock allowed is 16×16 pixels, which means that your video dimensions must be divisible by 16. Most modern codecs allow macroblocks to be 8×8 pixels, or even 4×4 pixels. The great thing about 320×240 is that it works for even the largest macroblocks.

TIP If you're having trouble calculating your video dimensions, a number of aspect ratio calculators are available online. A god one that lets you know if your dimensions are divisible by 16 (or 8 or 4) is here:

```
http://aspect.fre3.com/
```

Resizing

Resizing is pretty easy; just make sure you're resizing to the correct aspect ratio. Table 10.1 lists a few common sizes for standard and widescreen aspect ratios.

TABLE 10.1	
Common Screen Resolutions for Standard Aspect Ratios	
Aspect ratio	Screen Resolution
Standard TV (4:3)	640×480, 320×240, 160×120
Widescreen (16:9)	1920×1080, 1080×720, 640×360, 320×180, 160×90

Inserting Virtual Backgrounds Using Chroma Key

If you've ever wondered how your local weatherman manages to stand in front of huge swirling weather maps, the answer is using a technology known as chroma key (also called green screen or blue screen). The weatherman isn't actually standing in front of those pictures. He's standing in front of a blank wall painted a very bright, unnatural green. Then, using what until recently was incredibly expensive technology, the green background is removed from the video image and replaced with the graphics that you see on television. When the weatherman is looking off to the side, he's actually looking at a small television monitor to figure out where to point.

Nowadays, chroma key is built into many video-editing platforms. Some require an additional plug-in, but others include it as part of the basic functionality. To use this feature, however, you have to film yourself (or whoever your subject is) in front of a green (or bright blue) wall. The trick is to make sure the wall color is very uniform and is lit in such a way that there are no shadows on the wall. You can buy custom paint that the professionals use to paint their chroma key walls, or if you're budget constrained, you can buy a roll of bright green butcher paper at your local art supply store.

You need a large area to film against, because you have to stand far enough away from the green screen so that you don't cast any shadows on it. Lighting for a green screen shoot is an art form in itself. This is a good example of where calling in a professional to help you out is a great idea. After you've got a lighting setup established, you can reuse it for future shoots.

After you've shot your video against the green screen, the process for substituting the background depends on your video-editing software. Figure 10.8 illustrates the chroma key effect from Vegas. After you've specified what color to use as the *key* for the chroma key effect, that color is removed from the frame and another image or video is substituted where the key was.

> **TIP** One good reason to use chroma key is that the backgrounds are generally static, and as we'll find out later, static backgrounds encode best. Conversely, don't use backgrounds with motion in them if they can be avoided.

Most video-editing programs deal with video in terms of tracks, so when the chroma key effect is used, the video track beneath the main track is revealed. This is how the weatherman appears to be standing in front of the weather maps. In actuality, the weather maps are just showing through where the original chroma key color was.

FIGURE 10.8

Vegas chroma key effect

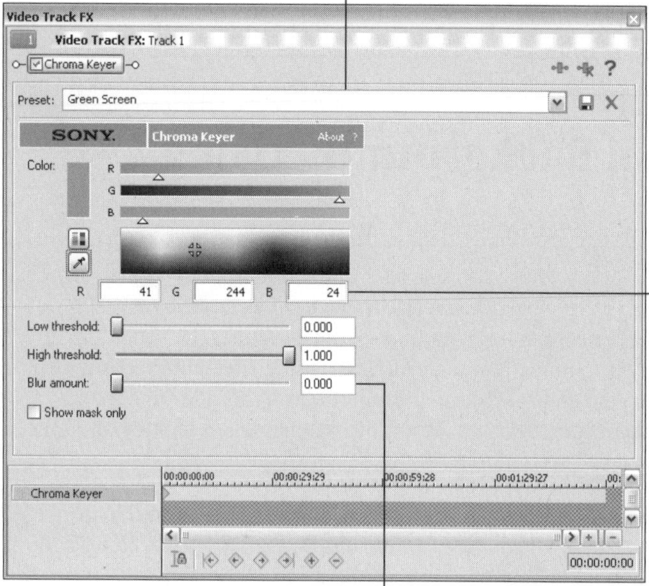
Vegas has presets for green screen and blue screen if you're using a professional green screen set.
Video Track FX
Video Track FX: Track 1
Chroma Keyer
Preset: Green Screen
SONY.
Chroma Keyer
Color:
R 41 G 244 B 24
Low threshold: 0.000
High threshold: 1.000
Blur amount: 0.000
Show mask only
Chroma Keyer
00:00:00:00
You also can type in an RGB value if you know it, or use the dropper tool to select your chroma key color.
Use these sliders to fine-tune the effect.

Adding Titles

Most professional video programming has some sort of opening sequence that usually includes lots of candid footage mixed with shots of the star(s) and some sort of graphic rendition of the title of the program. You should take the same approach. If your show has a name, let folks know about it! If they download it to their iPod and forget about it until it magically appears on their screen one day when they're browsing through their clips library, you want them to know the name of the program and who you are. So you'll probably want to use titles.

However, the problem is that what looks good (and is legible) on a television screen in general ends up way too small to be read on a small 320×240 screen. Titles at the bottom of the screen (called *lower thirds*) can be very hard to read if they're not done with large enough fonts. PowerPoint slides are particularly tough, because most people try to pack far too much information into a single slide, which makes it difficult for people to absorb, and the small fonts become very hard to read when reduced. To top it all off, video codecs have a tough time with text, because they don't treat it as being distinct from the video. So when your podcast is encoded, you're going to lose even more quality, as depicted in Figure 10.9.

The PowerPoint slide in Figure 10.9 isn't too bad to start off with; it has only five main points on the slide. By the time the slide is reduced to 320×240, the sub-points are too hard to read, and after the encoding process, even the main points are starting to look a little ragged.

FIGURE 10.9

PowerPoint slides are a good example of why text is tough: (a) Scaled to 320×240 and (b) after encoding at 300 Kbps.

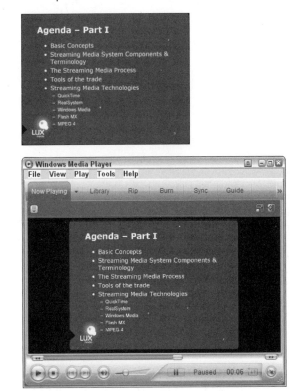

If you're going to use text in your podcast, think big. Try not to have more than three or four points per slide if you're using PowerPoint, and if you're adding titles to your show and/or your guests, make sure to use a font large enough so that it is legible after the encoding process.

Summary

Making high-quality video for the Internet is challenging. If you can't afford broadcast-quality equipment, your video may be slightly compromised to start with. Also, television displays are totally different than computer monitors, so video looks different when you display it on a computer monitor.

This chapter covered a number of ways you can fine-tune your video quality so that it's up there with the best of them, including these:

- Lens filters can be used for better image quality and for special effects.

- Standard television monitors are interlaced displays, while computer monitors are progressive displays. When interlaced video is displayed on a progressive display, feathering artifacts may appear.

- De-interlacing filters should be used if you're using a screen resolution larger than 320×240.

- You should use color correction to match the quality of the image on the computer screen with the quality of the original image you shot.

- Always maintain your aspect ratio when cropping or resizing. If you're shooting standard DV, then you'll be targeting a 4:3 aspect ratio, so you should use screen sizes of 640×480 or 320×240.

- Many video-editing platforms include chroma key effects if you want to pretend you're the local weatherman.

- When using text in your podcast, make sure that the fonts are extra large so they're still legible when the video is scaled down and encoded.

Part III

Encoding

Chapter 11

Encoding: An Overview

This chapter marks the beginning of Part III of this book, which is dedicated to *encoding*. Encoding is a process whereby your pristine, broadcast-quality audio and/or video is converted to a format that is suitable for Web distribution.

This step is necessary because audio and video files are huge. Actually, in these days of laptops with 100-gigabyte hard drives, huge files are not as daunting as they once were, but they still are too big to send across the Internet. If you've ever been frustrated waiting for an e-mail to download because someone foolishly embedded high-resolution photos inside it, you can imagine how long it takes to download broadcast-quality video, which is essentially a sequence of high-quality images.

In addition to the frustration an end-user experiences downloading broadcast-quality audio or video, you must consider the bandwidth bill. If you can distribute something that provides nearly the same experience but costs only a fraction as much, wouldn't you choose the cheaper option? Of course you would. Your podcast is just getting off the ground, and you need to keep costs under control.

This chapter covers the issues surrounding the encoding process. We start off with a summary of what we're trying to do and why, and then delve into the details of how the encoding process works and how encoding formats differ.

Why Encoding Is Necessary

You've spent countless hours and quite possibly a sizeable sum of money to produce a broadcast-quality podcast. Now you're being asked to take the polished result and convert it to a different format, which may compromise the quality of the original. Why?

The simple answer is because the raw audio and video files are too large to deliver practically via the Internet. There's no technical reason you can't deliver the original files — but it would take an incredibly long time for the files to download, and your monthly delivery bill would be sky high. To better understand the practical limitations involved, you must understand the concepts of *bandwidth* and *throughput*.

Bandwidth

Bandwidth, in the networking sense of the word, is a measurement of the amount of data that is being transmitted at any given point. Throughput is the aggregate amount of bandwidth that has been used over a given time period. Think about water coming out of a faucet: The water can come out slowly or quickly depending on how much you open the tap. A gallon jug fills slowly or quickly depending on how fast the water is coming out. The "bandwidth" of the faucet is the speed of the water coming out; the "throughput" is the total amount of water that comes out.

In podcasting, we come across bandwidth and throughput in a number of different areas. First, each of your potential audience members is connected to the Internet in some way, and that connection has an advertised bandwidth. If they're on DSL or cable modem, they may have a download bandwidth somewhere between 256 kilobits per second (kbps) to several megabits per second (mbps). Similarly, when you upload your podcast to a server or distribution service, you're using bandwidth, but you're *uploading*, not downloading. The upload or upstream speed of DSL and cable modems is usually far less than the download speed. Regardless of which direction the data is traveling, the bandwidth available determines the speed at which the transfer takes place.

Let's say you've recorded a 20-minute audio podcast. If you've recorded at CD quality, you recorded in stereo, sampling at 44.1kHz, using 16 bits per sample. We can determine how large this file is using some simple math:

```
44,100 samples/sec * 16 bits/sample * 2 channels = 1,411,200
bits/second
1,411,200 bits/sec / 8 bits/byte = 176,400 bytes/second
176,400 bytes/second / 1024 = 172.3 kilobytes per second (KBps)
172.3 KB/sec * 60 secs/min * 20 min = 206,718.75 KB
206,718.75 / 1024 = Approximately 202 megabytes (MB)
```

So the raw file is over 200 megabytes. (In fact, you can do this math much more quickly: One minute of stereo CD audio is approximately 10 MB, so 20 * 10 = ~200 MB.) Let's assume one of your audience members is on a fairly standard DSL line, with a download speed of approximately 500 Kbps. You can calculate the download time with a bit of math. All you have to do is convert the file size from megabytes into kilobits, and then divide by the download speed:

```
200MB * 8 bits/byte = 1600 megabits
1,600 megabits * 1024 = 1,638,400 kilobits
1,638,400 kilobits / 500 kbps = 3,266 seconds
3,266 seconds / 60 seconds/minute = 54.6 minutes
```

Why Does My Broadband Connection Seem Slow?

Just because you're paying for a certain Internet connection speed doesn't mean you're going to get it. Internet Service Providers (ISPs) often over-sell their capacity, because they assume their customers will use their Internet connections at different times. Consequently, they oversell their bandwidth a bit to maximize their usage (and revenue). This usually isn't a problem, but at certain times, such as early evenings, most people go online to check their personal e-mail and do a bit of surfing. When too many people get online at the same time, the capacity of the system is taxed, and the bandwidth to each individual user is constricted.

In the pre-millennial days of the Internet, this was a big problem. People were paying top dollar for a broadband connection only to find that their e-mail was downloading at a snail's pace, only marginally faster than a dial-up modem. The problem isn't as bad nowadays, because ISPs have realized that frustrating their early adopters is a recipe for disaster, particularly when sites rate ISP performance. Still, it isn't uncommon for broadband lines to deliver less than they're supposed to.

A number of sites let you measure the upload and download speeds of your broadband connection. These sites also usually include ratings for ISPs that are updated regularly, as well as forums where users swap stories, good and bad, about their experiences with ISPs. The granddaddy of them all is DSL reports:

```
http://www.dslreports.com/stest
```

So your podcast would take just under an hour to download. If the person is downloading in the background, this might not be too much of a problem, but chances are he's checking e-mail, surfing the Web, and doing other things on his computer that might further constrict the available bandwidth, which in turn makes the download take even longer. Additionally, he may not be getting the full bandwidth that he's paying for (see the "Why Does My Broadband Connection Seem Slow?" sidebar). Overall, this is not an optimal experience.

What we want to do is deliver a high-quality podcast that doesn't take hours to download. Encoding software enables us to do precisely this. For example, if we encode the file using an MP3 codec, we can achieve CD quality using only 128 kbps. In this case, our file would be:

```
128 kbits/sec * 60 seconds/minute * 20 minutes = 153,600 kilobits
153,600 kbits / 8 bits/byte = 19,200 kbytes
19,200 kbytes / 1024 = 18.75 MB
```

Our file size is less than ten percent of what it was before, and the download time is therefore reduced to about five minutes, which is much more like it. And because each of your listeners is downloading a smaller file, you use much less throughput.

Measuring Bandwidth and Throughput

Throughout this chapter, we calculate bandwidth and throughput. Lots of terms are thrown around: mega, kilo, bits, bytes, Kbps, MB. If you're a stickler for detail, you may notice that sometimes they're capitalized, sometimes not. Believe it or not, there's a method to the madness.

Traditionally, kilo and mega are used as abbreviations for one thousand and one million. A kilo, or kilogram, is one thousand grams. They're simple shortcuts that make doing math a bit easier. However, things get a little screwy in the digital world. Digital calculations are done in the binary world, where digits represent *powers of two.* Two raised to the tenth power is 1024, not one thousand. Engineers still used the kilo and mega abbreviations, and just fudged the fact that they're not *exactly* the same. As long as you were doing all your calculations in the digital domain, it didn't really matter.

However, things get messy when the two standards start to get mixed together. When measuring bandwidth, the traditional method is used, so a kilobit is one thousand bits, and a megabit is one million bits. Measuring storage or throughput is done in the binary world, so we're talking about 1024 and 1,048,576. Also, storage is measured in bytes, whereas bandwidth is measured in bits. Confused yet?

In an attempt to add some clarity to the situation, it was decided that capital letters would be used for the binary Kilo and Mega, and small letters would be used for the traditional kilo and mega. Bits are represented with a small "b," whereas bytes use a capital "B." So if you see a file size listed as 10 MB, it's 10 megabytes, meaning 10 * 1024 bytes. If you see a DSL speed listed as 768 Kbps, it means 768 *1000 bits per second.

The only problem is that this isn't a standard. You'll see "K" and "M" listed in bandwidth measurements, even though they may be referring to the traditional sense of kilo and mega. And it gets complicated when you're converting from one standard to the other, for example, trying to calculate how much throughput you'll use (measured with traditional megabits) if a whole bunch of people download your podcast (measured in Megabytes).

There's only a two-percent difference between 1000 and 1024, so you can use 1000 for estimates because it's much easier to just move a decimal point. But if you're pinching pennies, you had better make sure you understand *exactly* how your bandwidth provider is charging you, and be very careful with your calculations.

Throughput

As mentioned in the previous section, throughput is the measure of the amount of bandwidth you use over time. You'll encounter throughput when you use a service to distribute your podcast, because most offer a certain amount of throughput for free and bill you for any used in excess of that. Obviously, you want to keep your monthly bill as low as possible, so you want to try to limit the amount of throughput you use.

When you encode your podcast, you want to balance the desire to provide the highest quality possible with the reality of your throughput bill at the end of the month. Many podcast distribution services offer generous amounts of free throughput each month, so this may not be an issue when you first start out. If your podcast becomes wildly popular, though, you may be faced with a need to cut your operating costs (until that first sponsor or advertiser comes around, of course). If so, you may want to consider reducing the bit rate of your podcast, which reduces the quality of your podcast, but that may not be noticeable to your audience. Remember, most people listen to podcasts while sitting in front of their computers, and multimedia speakers aren't renowned for their quality. What you want to deliver is a podcast quality that is *equivalent* to other broadcast media, which in the case of AM and FM radio isn't that high to begin with.

Quality equivalents

Throughout this book, we've used the concept of *broadcast quality* to mean *really, really good*. However, anyone who has listened to AM radio knows that it doesn't sound anywhere near as good as FM, and for that matter FM radio doesn't sound as good as CDs. Yet they're both broadcast standards, and we still listen to radio, even AM. Different types of programming do not need as much fidelity as others.

The idea, then, is to figure out how much fidelity your programming requires and produce content to that standard. When recording the content, you should always record at a very high standard, because that gives you the most flexibility later on. But when it comes time to encode your content for Internet distribution, you may want to sacrifice a bit of quality for the cost savings it provides.

Table 11.1 lists some common bit rates offered by encoding software and brief descriptions of what quality you can expect using different encoding technologies.

TABLE 11.1

Audio and Video Quality at Different Bit Rates, Using Different Encoding Technologies

Bit Rate	Audio Quality	Video Quality
20 Kbps	MP3: unacceptable Windows Media/Real/QuickTime AAC: AM radio quality, slightly better for speech-only content.	Don't even think about it.
32 Kbps	MP3: Barely acceptable. Windows Media/Real/QuickTime AAC: FM quality if encoded in mono. Speech-only content: good quality.	Barely acceptable. Requires a very small screen resolution (160×120) with very little motion in the frame.

continued

TABLE 11.1	(continued)	
Bit Rate	**Audio Quality**	**Video Quality**
64 Kbps	MP3: Approaching FM quality Windows Media/Real/QuickTime AAC: Claim CD quality, but this is stretching it a bit.	Acceptable. Screen resolution should still be kept quite small (160×120, 176×132), unless there is very little motion, in which case slightly larger resolutions such as 240×180 may provide an acceptable image.
128 Kbps	MP3: Claims CD quality, though some might argue. Windows Media/Real/QuickTime AAC: CD quality.	Getting better. 240×180 should provide decent quality.
256 Kbps	Unless you're a stickler for quality, there is really no reason to exceed 128 Kbps for audio podcasts. MP3 starts to sound really good at around 192 Kbps; Windows Media, Real, and QuickTime AAC sound even better.	The low end of broadband quality. Screen resolution should be 320×240, and provide a good experience, depending on the amount of motion in the frame. Around 300 Kbps, the quality should be approaching VHS.
512 Kbps	n/a	Mid-level broadband quality. Screen resolutions of 320×240 provide excellent quality; larger resolutions such as 640×480 are acceptable.
1 Mbps+	n/a	Full-screen resolution at very good quality.

NOTE In Table 11.1, you should notice that MP3 audio quality is always slightly worse than Windows Media, Real, and QuickTime AAC, particularly at low bit rates. This is because the MP3 codec is older and wasn't really designed for low bit rate encoding. At higher bit rates (128 Kbps and above), the quality differential is less apparent.

Codecs Overview

By now, you should know that you need to encode your raw audio and video podcasts for bandwidth and throughput reasons. You should also know that most portable media players won't play back raw audio and video files. We know that encoded files are much smaller than raw media files; the question is how do encoders achieve this file size reduction, and why does the quality suffer?

At the heart of all encoding software lies the *codec*. Codec is a contraction of coder-decoder (or compressor-decompressor), and is the software algorithm that determines how to shrink a file to a usable size. You're probably already familiar with a number of codecs, though you may not be aware of it. For example, most digital cameras take pictures that are compressed with the JPEG codec. If you've ever used a photo-editing program to reduce the size or quality of your photos before you put them online, you've been adjusting the parameters of the JPEG codec. StuffIt and WinZip use codecs to compress files before they're sent across the Internet or put on installation CDs.

There's a key difference, however, between the JPEG codec used to compress photos and the codecs used to compress documents. Codecs used to compress documents must be *lossless*. If someone sends you a spreadsheet that has been compressed, when it de-compresses the data must be exactly the same as it was before the compression. Codecs such as JPEG, however, are known as *lossy* codecs, because some of the original information is lost during the compression. The original cannot be recreated from the compressed version of the file. Lossy codecs operate under the assumption that the quality lost either is not noticed by the end user or is an acceptable compromise required for the situation.

Web sites are a perfect example. Having lots of imagery on a Web site is great, but if the images were all 5 MB originals, each page would take forever to load. Because browsing the Internet should be a rapid, seamless experience, and because we sit so close to our monitors, the amount of detail required in a Web site image is much less than what is required for a printed page, so the image can be compressed heavily using the JPEG codec, and our experience isn't overly compromised.

The same holds true for podcasts. While it might be nice to have 256 kbps CD-quality podcasts, the reality is 128 kbps offers more than enough quality, and in fact 64 kbps might be plenty, particularly if you're not using the MP3 codec. As you reduce the bit rate of your podcast, the quality is also reduced, because the codec must delete lots more information.

Codecs try to maintain as much fidelity as possible during the encoding process, but at low bit rates something has to give. There simply isn't enough data to reproduce the original high fidelity. Given the complexity of the task, they actually do an amazing job. They're able to do as well as they do because they make use of *perceptual models* that help them determine what we *perceive* as opposed to what we hear. The difference is subtle, but key to modern codec efficiency. Before we talk about perceptual encoding techniques, let's talk a bit about basic codec technologies.

How codecs work

Codecs reduce file sizes by taking advantage of the repeated information in digital files. Lots of information is repeated. For example, a video that has been letterboxed (black stripes on the top and bottom) has lots and lots of black pixels. This results in lots and lots of zeros, all in a row. Instead of storing thousands of zeros, you could store "1000 x 0," which is only six characters. That's a significant savings. Also, you can reconstruct an exact copy of the original based on the information that you have stored.

Another way of encoding is to substitute for commonly occurring combinations of characters. For example, you could make this book smaller by replacing every instance of the word "podcasting" with "p." This wouldn't save that much space, though, and that's the problem with lossless encoding. You can achieve some file size reduction, but typically not enough for our needs. For this, you need perceptual encoding.

How perceptual codecs work

Perceptual codecs take advantage of how we actually perceive audio and video, and use this information to make intelligent decisions about what information can safely be discarded. Perceptual codecs are by definition lossy because of this. The original cannot be recreated from the encoded file. Instead, an approximation that attempts to retain as much fidelity as possible is constructed. The idea is that we won't notice what has been discarded.

Our ears are extremely sensitive. We can hear from 20Hz to 20,000Hz and sounds over a wide dynamic range, from a whisper to a scream. We can pick out a conversation at the next table in a crowded restaurant if the topic happens to catch our ear. We can do this because our brains filter out the information that is not of interest and focus on the rest. Our brains effectively prioritize incoming sound information.

For example, even a quiet classroom has plenty of sounds, such as the hum of air conditioning, people shuffling papers, and the teacher lecturing at the front. If someone sneezes in the room, for that split second, everyone notices the sneeze and nothing else. The sneeze is the loudest thing in the room and takes precedence over everything else.

Similarly, our eyes can take in a wide range of visual information, the entire color spectrum from red all the way through purple, and from very dim environments to very bright environments. Our field of vision is approximately 180 degrees from left to right. What we actually pay attention to, though, is much more focused. In general, we pay more attention to things that are brightly colored and things that are moving.

Perceptual codecs use this information to make better decisions about what information in audio and video files can be discarded or encoded with less detail. Perceptual codecs prioritize the loudest frequencies in an audio file, knowing that's what our ears pay most attention to. When encoding video, perceptual codecs prioritize bright colors and any motion in the frame.

At higher bit rates, perceptual codecs are extremely effective. A 128 kbps MP3 file is considered to be the same apparent quality as a CD and is only one-tenth the size of the original, which is pretty incredible if you think about it. Some of the savings is encoding efficiency, but the majority of it is perceptual encoding. As the bit rate is lowered and the codec is forced to discard more and more of the original information, the fidelity is reduced and the effects of perceptual encoding are more audible. Still, you should always balance the required fidelity of your podcast with the realities of bandwidth and throughput.

How audio codecs work

Audio codec technology has made spectacular advances in the last few years. It's now possible for FM quality to be encoded in as little as 32 kbps (in mono, that is). Modern codecs such as Windows Media, Real, and QuickTime AAC can achieve CD quality in approximately 64 Kbps. How do they do it?

The idea is to capture as much of the frequency and dynamic range as possible and to capture the entire stereo image. However, given the target bit rate, the codec usually determines what a reasonable frequency range is. Files that are encoded in mono are always slightly higher fidelity, because the encoder worries about only one channel, not two.

Another economy can be made if the codec knows that it will be encoding speech. Speech tends to stay in a very limited frequency and dynamic range. If someone is talking, it's unlikely that her voice will suddenly drop down an octave, or that she'll start screaming for no reason. Knowing this, a codec can take shortcuts when encoding the frequency and dynamics information.

> **CAUTION** Don't try to encode music using a speech codec. The shortcuts a speech codec uses are totally unsuitable for music, because music uses a very wide frequency range and is generally very dynamic. If you encode using a speech codec, it sounds awful. So don't do it.

After the frequency range has been determined, the codec must somehow squeeze as much information as possible into the encoded file and decide what can be discarded. Perceptual audio codecs use the concept of *masking* to help make that decision. If one frequency is very loud, it *masks* other frequencies, so the codec can safely discard them because we wouldn't perceive them.

This is why all background noise must be minimized in your original recordings and your programming must be nice and loud. This ensures that the codec doesn't discard any of the programming information.

How video codecs work

Video codecs also have improved dramatically. The challenge of encoding video, however, is orders of magnitude more difficult than encoding audio. Earlier in the chapter, we found that a minute of CD-quality audio is about 10 MB before it is encoded. That's nothing compared to video. If the video is being digitized in the RGB color space, each pixel uses 24 bits (8 for red, 8 for green, and 8 for blue). So that means a frame of video uses:

```
720 lines * 486 pixels * 24 bits/pixel = 8,398,080 bits =
1,049,760 bytes
= 1MB per frame of video
```

To get the file size for a 20-minute podcast, we remember that there are 30 frames per second, so:

```
1MB * 30 frames * 60 seconds * 20 minutes = 36000MB = 35.15 GB
```

Yes, you read that right. A 20-minute podcast can chew up an entire hard drive, or at least a good chunk of one. Of course, the preceding calculations assumed uncompressed RGB video, and most podcasts are done using a DV camera. Because DV video is compressed at a 5:1 ratio, you're only looking at around 7 GB for your 20-minute podcast. But imagine downloading a 7 GB file! That's not going to happen in a flash. It's going to take a good long time.

So the first thing we have to consider is reducing the resolution of the video so there are fewer pixels to encode in each frame. If you resize down to 320×240, you've reduced the file size by 75 percent. You also can cut the frame rate in half for further data reduction. But it turns out that this is still nowhere near the amount of reduction required to be able to deliver this video reliably and in an acceptable amount of time (and without breaking your bandwidth budget). To do this, video codecs rely on perceptual coding, using *inter-frame* and *intra-frame* encoding.

Intra-frame encoding is encoding each frame individually, just as you would when you shrink an image using a JPEG codec. Inter-frame encoding is a more sophisticated approach that looks at the difference between frames and encodes only what has changed from one frame to the next. This is illustrated in Figure 11.1.

FIGURE 11.1

Inter-frame compression encodes only the differences between frames.

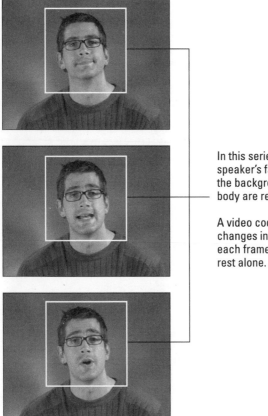

In this series of video stills, the speaker's face is changing, but the background and the rest of his body are relatively unchanged.

A video codec encodes the changes inside the central area of each frame and leaves the rest alone.

To be able to encode the difference between frames, the codec starts off by encoding a full frame of video. This full frame is known as a *key frame*. After the key frame, a number of *difference frames* are encoded. Difference frames, unsurprisingly, encode only what has changed from the previous frame to the current frame. The codec encodes a number of difference frames either until a scene change or when the amount of change in the frame crosses a predetermined threshold. The sequence of key frames and difference frames is illustrated in Figure 11.2.

The combination of reduced screen resolutions, frame rates, intra-frame compression, and inter-frame compression is sufficient to create satisfactory video experiences at amazingly low bit rates. Although no one would want to pay to watch it, you can create video files at bit rates as low as 32 Kbps. Of course, we recommend using ten times that much for your video podcast. At 300 Kbps and above, you can deliver an entirely satisfactory video experience. It won't be perfect, but it should be more than adequate.

FIGURE 11.2

Inter-frame compression uses a sequence of key frames and difference frames.

Key frames encode the entire frame–for example
at the beginning of a new scene, or when there has
been a significant amount of change in the frame.

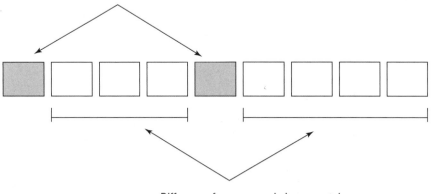

Difference frames encode incremental
changes between frames.

Codec side effects

No codecs are perfect. Even when codecs claim to be transparent, an expert somewhere can tell the difference. At higher bit rates, the differences between the original and the encoded version are minimal. As the bit rate decreases, however, the differences become easy to spot. Perceptual codecs attempt to remove things that we won't notice, but unfortunately they're not always successful.

Because so much information must be removed from files, you get less of everything in the encoded version of your file. The frequency range is reduced, as well as the dynamic range. If you're encoding video, you have a smaller screen resolution and possibly a decreased frame rate. If that's not enough, you also see or hear *artifacts* in your podcast.

Artifacts are things that weren't in the original file. In encoded audio files, artifacts can be heard as low rumbling noises, pops, clicks, and what is known as "pre-echo," which gives speech content a lisping quality. For video files, you may notice blocking artifacts, where the video is broken up into blocks that move around the screen. You also may see *smearing*, where the video image looks muddy and lacks detail.

If your podcast has audible or visible artifacts, you should check your encoding settings. Audio podcasts in particular should not have artifacts; you should be more than capable of producing a high quality audio podcast if you've followed the procedures in this book. Video, however, is a different matter. If you're delivering a 320×240 video podcast encoded at 300 Kbps, chances are good that you'll encounter a few artifacts. They shouldn't interfere with the ability to enjoy your podcast. If they do, you'll need to revisit your equipment or your shooting and editing style, or simply encode your video podcast at a higher bit rate.

Audio Codecs

Now that you know how codecs work, it's time to see what codecs are available to podcasters, how they differ, and why you might want to use them. The first thing to consider is whether you're planning on using music in your podcast. If you are, then you definitely want to use a codec that is suited for music. If your podcast is just speech, then you may want to consider using a speech codec, because you'll be able to get very good quality at ridiculously low bit rates, thereby saving you money on bandwidth.

Choosing a codec is a tricky business. Newer codecs offer better quality, and some offer advanced functionality such as book marking and embedding images. However, many of the newer codecs play back only on a limited number of portable devices. If you want the latest and greatest features, but also want to cater to the widest possible audience, you may want to consider encoding to multiple formats.

Music-optimized codecs

As mentioned previously, if you're going to include any music at all in your podcast, you must use a music codec. Luckily, you're spoiled for choice. Here's a list of possible candidates:

- **MP3:** The granddaddy of them all. MP3 wasn't initially designed as a low bit rate codec, so other codecs sound much better at low bit rates. It also does not support book marking. But just about every computer and portable media device in the world will play back an MP3 file.

- **Advanced Audio Coding (AAC):** The new and improved MPEG audio codec, meant to replace MP3. The only problem is that it isn't supported on some portable players. AAC enables advanced features such as book marking and embedded images.

- **Windows Media Audio (WMA):** The standard on Microsoft PCs. It has many advanced features such as markers, script commands, and embedded links. WMA is not supported on iPods, though it is supported on the "Plays for Sure" family of portable media devices.

- **RealAudio (RA):** The default audio codec of the RealPlayer, which offers embedded links and script commands. It is supported on a number of cell phones.

- **OGG Vorbis:** An open source audio codec offering excellent quality. Unfortunately, Vorbis isn't supported by many of the proprietary players, nor by the iPod.

Speech-optimized codecs

If your podcast doesn't include music, you should consider using a speech codec. They provide better quality at the same bit rate as a music codec, or the same quality at a reduced bit rate.

- **Audible Audio (AA):** Developed for the first portable digital media player, which was released by Audible and designed to play back audio books. AA supports a number of advanced features such as book marking. Unfortunately, Audible doesn't make an AA encoder publicly available.

- **ACELP.net:** The granddaddy of voice codecs. In fact, the AA format is based on the ACELP.net codec. ACELP.net is supported by both the Windows Media and Real players.

- **OGG Speex:** Another branch of the OGG open source project, specializing in low bit rate speech compression.

- **Windows Media Audio Voice Codec:** During Windows Media encoding you can specify that you're encoding voice content, and the Windows Media encoder will use a voice-optimized codec.

Video Codecs

Video codecs are much easier to distinguish from each other than audio codecs. Video quality is still on the rise, with each new codec release improving quality. However, most video codecs are proprietary, meaning they won't play back on other players. If you're embedding your podcast in a Web page, then you can do all sorts of checking via JavaScript to see whether people have a certain plug-in installed. If you're targeting portable media players, then you'll have to be careful about which video codec you choose.

- **H.264:** Part of the MPEG4 standard, H.264 is quite an improvement and, what's more important, is the video standard supported by the iPod.

- **Windows Media Video (WMV):** Currently at version 11, the WMV codec provides outstanding quality, along with lots of advanced functionality. It is also supported by the "Plays for Sure" family of portable media players.

- **RealVideo (RV):** Recently voted the best video codec by StreamingMedia.com author Jan Ozer. RV provides lots of advanced functionality, but is not supported on the iPod or the "Plays for Sure" devices. However, RV is supported on a number of cell phones.

- **OGG Theora:** The sister project to the Ogg Vorbis audio codec project. Theora videos play back in a number of open source players, as well as the RealPlayer and QuickTime, though they require the installation of an additional component.

File Formats

Knowing about codecs is important, because the codec determines the final quality of the podcast. However, you also have the problem of *file formats*. The file format dictates how the audio and video information is packaged. Some codecs can fit into a number of different file formats. The problem is that most proprietary systems such as QuickTime, Windows Media, and Real use proprietary file formats to hold the encoded audio and/or video information. File formats are highly guarded trade secrets and the main cause why files are not interoperable between players. However, the file formats also enable the proprietary systems to offer additional functionality. These are the most common file formats you'll encounter:

- **MP3:** MP3 is actually a codec, not a file format. The file format is actually MPEG. (MP3 stands for MPEG II, Layer 3.) MPEG files are almost universally playable and the reason most folks use MP3 to encode and distribute their podcasts.

- **QuickTime:** The QuickTime file format is the earliest multimedia file format and the basis of the MPEG 4 file format. QuickTime files also are almost universally playable, though the codecs inside may not be.

- **Windows Media:** The Microsoft standard, Windows Media obviously plays back on any PC and a large number of portable media devices, but not the iPod.

- **RealMedia:** RealNetworks' file format, this requires the RealPlayer. It is supported on many cell phones.

- **Audible:** The Audible file format was designed specifically for audio books, and consequently supports saved playback position, chapter marks, book marks, and other desirable features. Because it has been around for quite some time, it has lots of support in proprietary players and portable media players.

As mentioned earlier, your choice of codec and file format depend on what audience you're trying to reach and what features you want to use. For most folks, MP3 works well for audio because it plays on virtually every computer system and portable audio player. It doesn't support book marks or chapters, but most podcasts are short enough that they don't require that functionality.

For video, most folks are using QuickTime, again because of the near-universal support and because of the iPod, of course. However, some people are starting to experiment with other formats to see what they can do with the advanced functionalities they offer. Always offer the MP3 and QuickTime versions. If you want to play around with the advanced formats, offer them in addition to your standard podcast versions.

Summary

In this chapter, we covered the basics of encoding. All podcasts must be encoded so that they can be distributed on the Internet. The encoding reduces the file size, but sometimes also compromises the quality, depending on the bit rate being used. Your encoding choices may depend on your budget and your distribution agreements.

This chapter covered these topics:

- Good quality audio can be encoded as low as 32 Kbps; 128 Kbps should give you "CD-quality" audio.
- Encoding video is much harder due to the amount of data.
- Codecs rely on perceptual encoding to get the required amount of data reduction.
- Audio codecs favor the loudest frequencies of your file.
- Video codecs use color and motion to determine what is important.
- Artifacts appear when the bit rate is too low.

Chapter 12

Encoding Tools

You should understand clearly by now that your podcast must be encoded in a format that is suitable for Web distribution. To do this, either you must use a standalone encoding application or export directly from your audio-editing or video-editing software. If you want to be a real podcasting hot shot, you may want to encode an enhanced podcast or offer video podcasts for various portable media players. If so, you'll probably want to invest in a multi-format encoding solution. In addition to enabling you to encode a single file into a number of different formats, they let you tweak all the encoding settings so you can get the highest possible quality encoding.

Your decision about which encoding software to use will be based on a number of factors:

- Are you encoding audio or video podcasts (or both)?

- If you're producing audio podcasts, do you want maximum compatibility across media players, or would you rather produce a cutting edge podcast with features that may not work on all players?

- If you're producing video podcasts, how many formats do you want to produce?

Podcasting purists consider podcasts to be MP3 files. But video podcasts are becoming increasingly popular, and there are serious cross-compatibility issues with video podcasts. Portable media players support different codecs, and some people may not have the required player software installed to watch your video podcast on their computer.

We'll talk about these issues a little later in the chapter. To begin with, let's start with the simplest case. We'll assume that you're producing an audio podcast, and for maximum compatibility you're using the granddaddy of all podcast formats, the MP3 file.

MP3 Encoding Tools

If you're producing an audio podcast, you're probably best producing it in the MP3 format. Although it isn't the best audio codec available, it is by far the most compatible and plays on virtually any computer or portable media device. It may not have all the bells and whistles of other formats, but your audience is far less likely to have technical issues, which means you'll get fewer negative comments on your blog.

Virtually any editing platform you're working on should have built-in MP3 encoding capabilities, but on the off chance that it doesn't, a number of standalone MP3 encoding applications can get the job done; one such application is shown in Figure 12.1.

- **iTunes:** iTunes isn't really an encoding application, but it converts audio files to mp3 on import if you choose to do so in your preferences.

- **LAME-based encoders:** Despite the ironic origin of the name (**L**ame **A**in't an **M**P3 **E**ncoder), LAME is an open source MP3 encoding library that is used in almost all free MP3 encoding applications. There are probably hundreds of these available; google "MP3 encoder" and see for yourself.

FIGURE 12.1

WinLAME is one of many free MP3 encoders available.

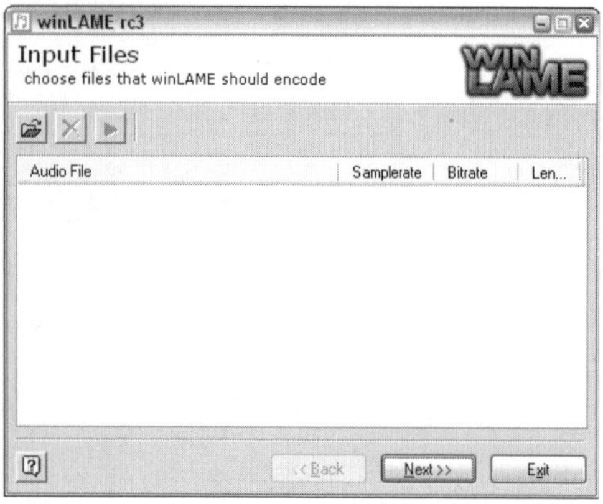

Other Encoding Formats

MP3 is perfect for audio podcasts, but you may want to work in other formats for a number of reasons. Many portable media players now include color displays. Enhanced podcasts are appearing to take advantage of these color displays that include graphics along with the audio. Enhanced podcasts can also include links for people who are watching the podcast on a browser. Enhanced podcasts also feature chapters, so people can quickly skip to the next or previous section of your podcast.

You can create enhanced podcasts using the QuickTime and Windows Media formats. Of course, enhanced QuickTime podcasts play back only on iPods or in iTunes, and enhanced Windows Media podcasts play back only in Windows Media player and Windows Media compatible portable media players. Another enhanced podcast format is the Audible format, which was developed for audio books. The Audible format includes the chapters feature, as well as the ability to store a bookmark, so that if you stop listening in the middle of a podcast, the next time you listen the podcast starts where you left off. Because the Audible format has been around for so long, it is widely supported by almost every portable media player, as well as in iTunes, Windows Media Player, and RealPlayer.

If you're creating a video podcast, a number of different formats are available, including QuickTime, Windows Media, Real, and Flash. Video podcasts have the same compatibility issues as enhanced podcasts, which means limited compatibility across portable players, and they require that the appropriate player software is installed on the audience's computer.

CAUTION **People are weird. Talk to one person and he'll tell you why he would never install media player A on his machine, while the next person swears by player A and is convinced media player B is the devil's spawn. To some extent, these people split across platform lines (Mac users swear by QuickTime, Windows users Windows Media, and Flash users hate everything else), but not always. Each media format has its strengths and weaknesses. If you're planning on a video podcast, you should support at least two formats. Regardless of which formats you choose, plan on getting disgruntled e-mails and blog comments from crazed audience members. You can't please everyone.**

Another reason to consider alternative formats is if you want to protect your podcast files using Digital Rights Management (DRM). DRM lets you place restrictions on your podcast, for example letting only paid subscribers listen to it. Not all formats support DRM. Because most podcasts are free and most podcasters want as many listeners as they can get, very few podcasts use DRM. This may change as people begin charging for their podcasts.

If you're going to offer your podcast in an alternative format, you may need to download and install encoding software (see Figure 12.2). Many of these formats will be included in your audio or video editing platforms, but if not, the software is generally available for free from the manufacturers.

- **QuickTime:** iTunes will encode in the AAC and MP3 formats and exports videos to an iPod compatible format, but if you want to tinker with the encoding settings, get QuickTime Pro. You can upgrade any copy of QuickTime to the Pro version for a mere $29.

  `http://www.apple.com/quicktime`

- **Windows Media:** The Windows Media Encoder is available as a free download from the Microsoft site.

  `http://www.microsoft.com/windowsmedia`

NOTE **Microsoft has recently dropped support for Windows Media encoding on the Mac. However, Mac users can encode in Windows Media using products from Flip4Mac:**

`http://www.flip4mac.com/wmv.htm`

- **Helix RealProducer:** If you're considering the Real format, you need the RealProducer.

  `http://www.realnetworks.com/products/producer/`

  Unfortunately, if you're targeting mobile phones (where the Real format is strongest), you need Helix Producer Mobile, which is incredibly expensive. If it's any consolation, you can download a trial version that's good for 30 days.

- **Flash:** To encode into Shockwave Flash (.swf) or streaming flash (.flv), purchase the Flash authoring tool. Several multi-format encoders also offer Flash support.

  `http://www.adobe.com/ flashpro/`

- **Audible:** Audible doesn't make their encoding software publicly available. Instead, you have to upload your original MP3 file to their Wordcast service, and they do the encoding for you.

  `http://wordcast.audible.com/`

FIGURE 12.2

The Windows Media Encoder is available for free from Microsoft for the PC platform (Mac users must use Flip4mac).

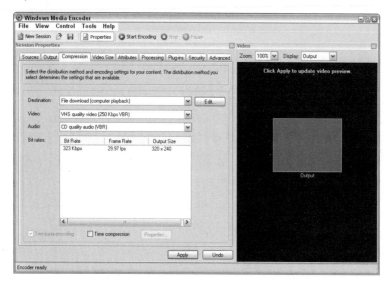

Making Format Choices

Because this is a technical manual that includes business advice concerning podcasting, you might expect that we would tell you which format is best for your podcast. Unfortunately, that's not something we can do. Things were much simpler when a podcast meant an MP3 file that was automatically downloaded to a desktop and transferred to an iPod. Now that the term podcasting has expanded to include a variety of portable media players and video, the podcasting format wars have begun.

The territory that is being fought over is very valuable. As podcasting continues to grow in popularity and people continue to time-shift their media consumption habits, the large media conglomerates are scrambling to catch up to the thousands of already-successful podcast *brands* that have been established. Similarly, the portable media player manufacturers are fighting tooth and nail for control of the player market. Control the player, and you control access to the millions of people who are discovering podcasting.

To some extent, we can learn from streaming media. The industry that RealNetworks pioneered quickly became a three-horse race when QuickTime and Windows Media entered the field. Flash was a late entry to the field and is making a dent in everyone's market share numbers. Experts have talked about the imminent demise of MPEG4 or RealNetworks, but the reality is that there seems to be room for all the streaming formats, and none of them is going away anytime soon.

The same probably holds true for podcasting. The iPod has a massive share of the portable media player market, but with Microsoft coming out with a portable media player as this book is being written, that is sure to change. As the term podcasting has broadened, so has the way people listen to and watch podcasts. Studies have shown that half of all podcasts are actually watched on a desktop or laptop computer, not a portable media player.

Because the podcasting industry is still in its infancy, the situation is likely to continue to change. There is no easy answer to the format question, nor one likely in the short term. However, in the interest of helping you make a decision, we can point out a few things to help you cut through the media hype:

- If you're producing an audio podcast, MP3 gets you the widest compatibility.
- If you're producing a video podcast, QuickTime is a good choice because it's compatible with the iPod and anyone who has iTunes installed.
- If you don't care about portable media players and are offering video playback via your site, Flash is a good option because it has good cross-platform support.
- Windows Media has better video quality than QuickTime and Flash, and there are a heck of a lot of PCs out there.
- RealNetworks are making huge inroads into the mobile market, particularly in Europe.

The best way to figure out what format is best for your podcast is to start off simple, possibly offering only a single stream option. Monitor your e-mail and your blog comments. After you've developed a bit of an audience, ask them what they prefer. Podcasting is still a relatively intimate broadcast medium, and the way to make loyal audience members is to give them what they want.

Encoding Via Your Editing Platform

If you've invested in a decent audio-editing or video-editing platform, chances are good that you'll use your editing platform to do your encoding. Most include a variety of export options. (You'll also want to export a broadcast-quality master for archival purposes, of course.) If your master includes lots of processing and complicated editing, you may want to render the broadcast-quality master and then encode using an encoding application or multi-format encoder, instead of doing all the processing twice. For most podcasts, exporting an encoded master directly from your time-line is probably easiest.

Audio

Most audio-editing platforms offer MP3 encoding. Many also offer encoding in a number of other formats:

- **Audacity (Windows, Mac, Linux):** Offers MP3 and Ogg Vorbis export
- **Peak (Mac):** Offers MP3 and AAC export
- **Garage Band (Mac):** Offers AAC export, which is fine for iPods, but does not support MP3 export
- **Sound Forge (Windows):** Offers a number of export options, including MP3, Ogg Vorbis, Windows Media, and RealAudio (see Figure 12.3)
- **Audition (Windows):** Also offers a wide variety of support, including MP3, Windows Media, and RealAudio

Video

Video-editing platforms also offer fairly rich export options:

- **Final Cut Pro (Mac):** Offers QuickTime H.264 support
- **iMovie (Mac):** Offers QuickTime H.264 support, including a preset for iPods
- **Adobe Premiere (PC):** Offers Flash, QuickTime, Windows Media, and RealVideo support
- **Sony Vegas (PC):** Offers QuickTime, Windows Media, and RealVideo support
- **Ulead Video Studio (PC):** Offers QuickTime, Windows Media, and RealVideo support, and includes output templates for iPods and SmartPhones (see Chapter 8)

FIGURE 12.3

Sound Forge offers a large number of export options.

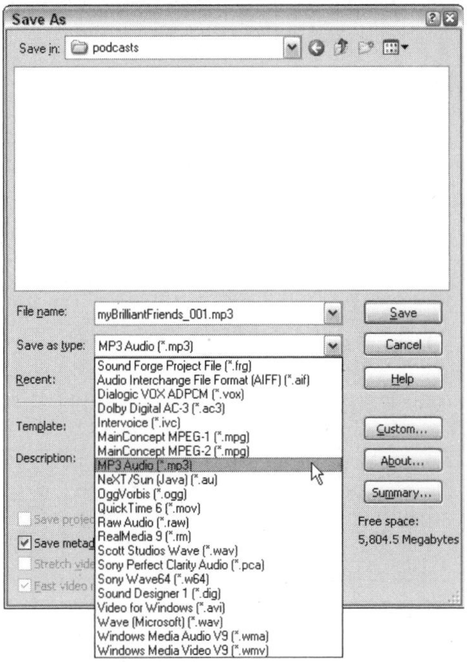

Multi-format encoding

In the beginning, podcasts were audio only and always encoded using the MP3 codec. But as people have started to realize the potential for video podcasting and portable media player displays have improved, the possibilities for podcasting have multiplied. The problem is that most of these enhanced opportunities come at a price, and that price is compatibility. Enhanced podcasts designed for the iPod do not play on other portable media players. Podcasts encoded using the Windows Media format for compatibility with the "Plays For Sure" portable players do not play on the iPod. And if you want to offer a video image larger than 320×240, it may or may not play back on portable media players.

So what can a podcaster who wants to push the envelope do? The best approach is to offer a number of formats and let your audience choose which version they'd like to subscribe to. Of course, if you're offering multiple formats, you're no longer encoding a single version of your podcast; you may be encoding three or four. For example, if you really want to offer every possible choice, you might offer the following:

- An MP3 version for older media players
- An enhanced iPod version with images
- A 320×240 video version encoded in Windows Media
- A 320×240 video version encoded in QuickTime H.264
- A 640×480 video version encoded in Flash format for Web viewing

Granted, this example may seem excessive, and the chances that someone would encode into so many different formats are pretty slim. However, it's not out of the realms of possibility. Rocketboom, one of the most popular video podcasts, is encoded into four different formats. If you want the largest possible audience and want to stay at the cutting edge of podcasting technology, you're going to have to encode multiple versions. This is where a multi-format encoder comes in handy.

> **TIP** If you're offering more than one format, offer separate RSS feeds for each so people can subscribe to their favorite format.

Multi-format encoders enable you to choose a single source file and output to multiple formats. These encoders usually allow you to set up encoding presets, so you don't have to re-enter the encoding settings every time you encode. Many multi-format encoders also allow you to pre-process your original master, so if you want to do color correction or resizing, it can be done at the encoding stage.

> **CROSS-REF** Color correction, resizing, and other forms of video signal processing are discussed in Chapter 10, "Advanced Video Production Techniques."

Some multi-format encoders offer automatic batch processing, where files placed into a specific directory are automatically processed and encoded. You can streamline your production chain if you're using a multi-format encoder with batch processing. This allows you to concentrate on your programming and let the batch processing take care of the rest.

A number of multi-format encoding solutions are available, including these popular ones:

- **Sorenson Squeeze:** The Sorenson Squeeze Compression Suite offers MP3, AAC, QuickTime, Windows Media, and Real formats (Mac users must have the Flip4Mac plugin installed to get Windows Media capabilities). You can add Flash encoding with an additional plug-in (see Figure 12.4), or by purchasing the Squeeze Power Pack.
- **Canopus Procoder:** The Express version offers QuickTime, Windows Media, and Real support. The full 2.0 version also offers MP3 encoding, and Flash encoding if you have Flash MX installed.
- **Telestream FlipFactory:** This offers MP3, QuickTime, Windows Media, Real, and Flash support. It also supports 3GPP (mobile phone format) with an additional plug-in.
- **Digital Rapids Stream:** The basic version offers QuickTime, Windows Media, and Real support. The Pro version adds MP3 and Flash support. All Digital Rapids software requires Digital Rapids capture cards.

FIGURE 12.4

Sorenson Squeeze

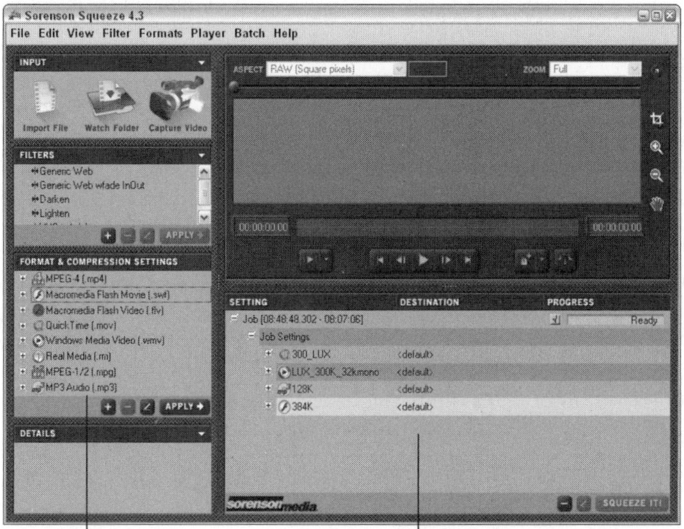

The full version of
Sorenson Squeeze
includes QuickTime, Flash,
Windows Media, Real
Media, and MPEG encoding.

Each encoding process
can include presets for
multiple formats.

Summary

This chapter covered the following topics:

- All podcasts must be encoded for Web distribution.

- MP3 is the most common (and compatible) audio format.

- Other audio formats offer enhanced functionality, but are not compatible with all portable media players, and may require your audience to install software on their computer.

- Video podcasts are tricky because portable media players support different codecs, and some people may not have the appropriate player installed on their computer.

- If you're creating a video podcast, be sure to offer a few different formats so you don't frustrate any of your audience.

- Encoding is done using the standalone software from each manufacturer. Most audio-editing and video-editing platforms also offer export to a number of different formats.

- If you're offering multiple versions of your podcast, consider using multi-format encoding software to automate your production chain.

Chapter 13

Basic Encoding Techniques

Whether you encode your podcast by exporting directly from your editing platform or by using a stand-alone encoder, you can specify a number of parameters. You may have only a few choices if you're using encoding presets, or you may have the opportunity to specify exactly how you want your podcast encoded. This chapter explains the choices you have and how to get the best encoding quality.

In the early days of low bit-rate encoding, back when people were connected to the Internet via slow modems, encoding technology was limited and required lots of tweaking to extract the best quality. Now, ten years later, codec technology and Internet connection speeds have improved so much that encoding high-quality podcasts should be within everyone's reach.

This is particularly true of audio podcasts. Modern codecs such as RealAudio and Windows Media Audio are capable of attaining FM-mono quality at a mere 32 kbps. The MP3 codec lags behind in quality, but because you can safely encode your podcast at 128 kbps, you should not have any quality issues.

Video is a little trickier. Assuming the majority of your audience is on a broadband connection, your video quality is limited by available bandwidth. Although you can't expect DVD quality at these bit rates, there's no reason why you can't create a perfectly acceptable video experience. This chapter helps you choose settings that should do the job. Let's start off with the easy stuff — audio encoding.

Audio Encoding

Audio encoding is easy, for a number of reasons. Raw audio files are large, but nowhere near as huge as video files. Therefore, the amount of compression that is needed to reduce them to a size that is suitable for Internet distribution is not excessive. Audio codec technology has progressed to a point where low bit rate encoding produces very good results. Podcasting reaps the benefits of ten years of cutthroat competition between RealNetworks and Microsoft, and the progress made by the MPEG organization with AAC encoding.

Because modern codecs sound so good, you really don't need to do much tweaking when you're encoding audio. You really have to decide only three things: whether to encode in stereo or mono, whether to use a speech or a music codec, and what bit rate to use.

Mono versus stereo

The first thing to decide is whether to encode your podcast in stereo or mono. If your program is predominantly interviews or spoken word, encode in mono. Mono encodings are always higher fidelity at a given bit rate, because only a single channel is encoded instead of two. If you're encoding in mono, you can use a lower bit rate and get the same quality or you can get better quality than a stereo encoding at the same bit rate.

If your content is predominantly music, you should encode in stereo, although it isn't strictly necessary. Even though music is recorded in stereo, most of the content is right in the center of the mix. The lead vocal, the snare drum, the bass drum, all will be right in the center of the speakers. And watch where you place your speakers. If you aren't sitting directly between the speakers, you aren't experiencing the full stereo effect anyway. However, one good reason to target stereo if you're playing music is that half your audience may be listening on headphones, which exaggerates the stereo effect.

Speech versus music

The next thing to decide is whether to use a speech codec or a music codec. If you're encoding an MP3 file, you don't have a choice. MP3 is a music codec. The good news is that MP3 is perfectly suitable as a speech codec as well, provided the bit rate is high enough.

Speech codecs can take special shortcuts during the encoding process due to the nature of speech content. With speech, the dynamic range tends to be very limited, as is the frequency range. After you start talking, the chances are good that you'll continue to speak at roughly the same volume and in the same register. Knowing this, a speech codec can make intelligent decisions about how to encode the audio.

Music content, on the other hand, has a wide dynamic and frequency range. There are bass drums and bass guitars, as well as crashing cymbals and violins. The shortcuts that a speech codec takes are completely unsuitable for encoding music content.

So the choice is fairly obvious: If you're encoding content that is speech only, you can encode at very low bit rates and still achieve high quality using a speech codec. However, for most applications, a music codec is perfectly appropriate.

Bit rates, sample rates, and quality equivalents

The most important decision to make about your audio podcast encoding is what bit rate to use. The bit rate determines the eventual file size of your podcast, which in turn determines how long it takes to download. The bit rate also determines the fidelity of your podcast. The higher the bit rate, the higher fidelity your podcast is.

Table 11-1 in Chapter 11 lists some common bit rates and the quality you can expect from each. The listed audio bit rates range from 20 kbps to 256 kbps. If you're producing audio-only podcasts, you should target somewhere between 64 kbps and 128 kbps. If you're encoding predominantly speech, you can safely stay at the low end of that; if you're encoding music, you may want to stick to the higher end of the spectrum.

> **NOTE** At the end of the day, you know best how you want the podcast to sound. Try encoding at a couple of different bit rates, and see which one sounds best to you.

The other thing you may be able to set is the sampling rate. The sampling rate determines how much high-frequency information is encoded. For example, CD-quality audio uses a sample rate of 44.1 KHz, to capture the full 20–20,000 Hz frequency range. The sampling rate has to be at least double the highest frequency you're trying to capture. Depending on what bit rate you're targeting, you may be offered a few different sampling rates.

The interesting thing about sampling rates is that a higher sampling rate isn't necessarily better. The sampling rate determines how often the incoming audio signal is sampled, so it determines how much audio the encoder has to try to encode. If you set a higher sampling rate, you're telling the encoder to try to encode more high-frequency information, but the encoder may have to sacrifice the overall quality of the encoding. Essentially, the sampling rate determines the trade-off between the frequency range and the fidelity of the encoding. At a given bit rate, an encoder can offer higher fidelity with a reduced frequency range or reduced fidelity with a higher frequency range.

We suggest that you choose a lower sampling rate, thereby allowing the encoder to create a higher fidelity version of your podcast. There is very little information above 16 KHz in most audio programming, and most people don't have speakers that reproduce it faithfully anyway. Therefore, choosing a 32 KHz or 22 KHz sampling rate should provide more than enough high-frequency information.

Video Encoding

Video encoding is more involved than audio encoding. Raw video files are much larger than raw audio, so a much greater degree of compression is required. Modern video codecs also have benefited from fierce competition between the leading streaming media platforms, as well as the MPEG organization. Most encoding software packages include a number of presets that produce acceptable video quality. If you want to try to improve your quality by tweaking the encoding parameters, this section explains the basic options available to you and how they affect video quality.

Screen resolution

The most important decision you're going to make about your video podcast is what resolution (or screen size) you're targeting. This is largely determined by the bit rates you're targeting, which in turn are determined by your audience. The higher the bit rate, the larger your resolution can be.

Most encoding software programs let you specify any screen resolution you want. You can specify that you want the full 640×480 frame encoded at 100 kbps, and the encoder does the best job it can. What you end up with is a large screen full of blurry blocks moving around, because 100 kbps simply isn't enough to encode a resolution that large.

Table 13.1 lists some common video bit rates and suggested screen resolutions. Note that the resolution is largely dependent on the content of your video. If you have lots of motion in your podcast, you have to use either a higher bit rate or a smaller resolution to achieve acceptable video quality. If your podcast is relatively static and you filmed using a tripod, you may be able to try slightly larger screen sizes.

TABLE 13.1

Suggested Video Resolutions

Bit Rate	Resolution
80 Kbps and under	High action programming: 160×120 Low action programming: 176×132, possibly 240×180
80 – 225 Kbps	High action programming: 176×132, possibly 240×180 Low action programming: 240×180, possibly 320×240
225 – 500 Kbps	High action programming: 240×180 or 320×240 Low action programming: 320×240
500 Kbps +	Either very high quality at 320×240 or good quality at 640×480. Quality is dependent on the amount of motion in the programming.

Frame rate

Another parameter you can adjust is the frame rate. NTSC video is shot at 30 frames (actually 60 fields) per second. However, for low action content, you may be able to get away with a lower frame rate. For example, interview footage often looks just fine at 15 frames per second. Higher action content requires the full frame rate for smooth motion.

Adjusting the frame rate affects the overall clarity of the video, because no matter how many frames per second you're encoding, you always have a fixed bit rate at which to encode. If you're encoding at 300 kbps, you can spread those 300 kilobits over 30 frames or 15 frames. Obviously, if you're only encoding 15 frames instead of 30, you can dedicate more bits per frame, and the result is a higher-quality frame. However, this may be a false economy for high action content.

Remember how video encoding is done. First, a key frame is encoded, which is followed by a number of difference frames. High action content has lots of motion and, therefore, lots of difference from frame to frame. If you drop the frame rate to try to economize, the encoder drops frames and doesn't encode them. There are certainly fewer frames to encode, *but the differences between them are greater!* This is illustrated in Figure 13.1.

FIGURE 13.1

When encoding at a reduced frame rate, the increased differences between frames may negate the gains of encoding fewer frames.

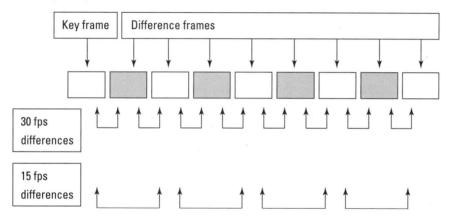

If your programming has very little motion in it, such as talking head content, you may see an improvement in quality by dropping the frame rate. However, if you have lots of action in your podcast, leave the frame rate as is. To get higher video quality, you'll have to either encode at a higher bit rate or reduce your screen resolution.

> **NOTE** The frame rate of NTSC video is actually 29.97 frames per second, although 30fps is often used as shorthand.

Bit rate

Along with the screen resolution, the other important choice you have to make is the bit rate of your podcast. The bit rate determines the quality and the file size, and it's the gating factor for the resolution. The bit rate you choose is determined to some extent by your audience, and the length of your podcast. The idea is that you don't want your audience to have to wait forever to watch your podcast. If the podcast is being downloaded in the background by an aggregator, then this isn't an issue. But many video podcasts are watched on Web pages. The user clicks a link and expects to see something in a reasonable amount of time.

Because most podcasters host their podcasts on a Web server, most video podcasts are progressively downloaded. Progressively downloaded videos have to preload a bit before they start playing back. The amount of preload is determined by the embedded player. The player knows how big the video file is and calculates how long the video will take to download. The player also knows how long the video is and tries to figure out how soon it can start playing the video so that by the time the playback reaches the end, all the video will have downloaded.

Let's say you've encoded your video at 300 kbps, which is a pretty standard bit rate. Most broadband connections can sustain this bit rate consistently, so as the video starts downloading, the player realizes in a few seconds that the data is being downloaded fast enough to begin playback. The total wait time for your audience is minimal.

Now let's take the same podcast and encode it at 500 kbps. Let's say it's a 1-minute podcast. The total file size is going to be approximately 30,000 kilobits (we'll stay in the world of bits because the math is easier). If the user's connection can sustain 300 kbps, it takes 100 seconds to download the entire file. If the file is 60 seconds long, that means the user has to wait 40 seconds before playback can begin. This is probably a little excessive, unless your audience is very dedicated. And this is if your podcast is only a minute long. For each additional minute, the audience is forced to wait an additional 40 seconds. This can get out of hand quickly.

If you're doing longer form content, longer than 5 minutes, then you should choose a bit rate that your users can receive in more or less real time. We can take a hint from streaming media sites here, who commonly target 300 to 450 kbps. If you're worried about bandwidth costs, you can choose a lower bit rate. Your video quality might suffer a bit, but if you can't afford your bandwidth bill, you won't be able to continue podcasting!

Audio bit rate

Of course, the bit rate we have been talking about up to this point has been the total bit rate of your podcast. After you choose your target bit rate, you have to decide how much of that bit rate you're going to allot to the audio stream. There are audio codecs at bit rates from 5 kbps up to hundreds of kilobits per second. How much should you give your audio stream?

One thing to remember is that audio tells the story. Audio is what draws the audience in and keeps them attentive. Think about it: When you're watching television at night with friends and a commercial comes on, what happens? If you're like most people these days, someone punches the mute button on the remote, the room immediately comes to life with conversation, and people take the opportunity to grab something from the refrigerator. When the commercial break is over, the audio is un-muted, and everyone pays attention to the program again.

The same holds true for your podcast. It's worth making sure that your audio quality is good, because people will watch low quality video if the audio sounds good. They won't watch good quality video if the audio sounds bad.

A fairly safe rule is to use about 10 to 20 percent of your total bit rate for audio. At higher bit rates, you can stay toward the bottom of that scale; at lower bit rates, stay toward the top. Another suggestion is to avoid the lowest audio bit rate settings. The difference between a 5 kbps audio feed and an 8 kbps audio feed is huge; those extra 3 kbps won't add much to your video quality.

Step-by-Step Encoding Examples

Now it's time to actually encode some files. This section demonstrates audio and video encoding using stand-alone encoders, editing platforms, and even iTunes. If your editing application isn't demonstrated, don't worry: It probably works much the same way. Let's start with iTunes, which really isn't an encoder, but it can do the job.

TIP   You should always archive the high-quality version of your file so that you can re-edit or re-encode it later.

Encoding MP3 audio using iTunes

iTunes automatically encodes all imported audio. When you insert a CD and iTunes offers to import it, the audio bits are pulled straight off the CD and encoded into whatever format has been specified. The default setting is to encode using AAC. However, iTunes will also convert music in MP3 if you prefer, and will convert any file into an MP3 file. All you have to do is import the file into iTunes, and then convert it to MP3.

Setting MP3 encoding defaults

To use iTunes as an MP3 encoder, you have to set the default encoding to MP3. Follow these steps to set iTunes to import using the MP3 codec:

1. Open iTunes, and open the Preferences window by choosing Preferences from the iTunes menu (the Edit menu on a PC). You also can open this window using the keyboard short-cut Command+, (Ctrl+, on a PC).

2. Click the Advanced icon/tab, and select the Importing tab.

3. Select MP3 encoder from the Import Using drop-down menu.

4. Select your bit rate from the Setting menu. By default, the lowest setting offered is 128 kbps stereo. For most podcasts, this is a perfectly fine setting. If, however, you want to economize on your bit rate, you can adjust the settings by selecting Custom from the Setting drop-down menu.

5. Select a bit rate from the Stereo Bit Rate drop-down menu.

6. You can select a sample rate or leave this set to Auto. If your podcast ends up sounding a little crunchy or distorted, you can try lowering the sample rate to get better fidelity.

7. If you want a mono podcast, select Mono from the Channels drop-down menu.

NOTE   If you select Mono encoding, the bit rate will be half of what you specified in the Stereo Bit Rate drop-down menu.

8. Click OK to close the Custom Settings menu, and then click OK to close the Preferences window. iTunes will now import files using the MP3 settings specified.

Importing and Encoding

To encode using iTunes, you must first import the file, and then convert the imported file. Importing couldn't be simpler:

1. From the File menu, choose Import.

2. Browse to find the file you want to encode, and click Choose (Open on PCs). The file is imported and is listed in your music library.

3. Find the file in your music library. Click it to select it, and then from the Advanced menu, choose Convert to MP3.

That's all there is to it! iTunes encodes it using the settings specified on the Importing tab of the Advanced menu. The iTunes music folder is easy enough to find, but if you want to encode to a specific location, you can change this setting in the General tab of the Advanced settings window.

CAUTION Be careful when you change your iTunes music folder; otherwise, you'll end up with your music library in two different folders. It's probably a good idea to change the music folder back to the default after you've finished your encoding.

Exporting MP3 audio from Audacity

Exporting MP3 files from Audacity is simple, if somewhat limited. You have to set your desired bit rate in the Preferences window before you export, because you aren't given an option to adjust settings when you export. Here's how to set your preferred bit rate:

1. Open Audacity, and open your podcast audio file.

2. From the Edit menu, choose Preferences, as shown in Figure 13.2. This opens the Audacity Preferences window.

3. Click the File Formats tab.

4. Select your desired bit rate from the bit rate drop-down menu in the MP3 Export Setup section.

5. Click OK.

After you set your bit rate in the Preferences window, choose the Export as MP3 option from the File menu. That's all there is to it. Audacity doesn't offer the ability to do mono MP3 encoding or VBR-based encoding. As long as you don't want to do anything fancy, Audacity is a perfectly good encoding option.

FIGURE 13.2

Use this dialog box to configure Audacity's MP3 export settings.

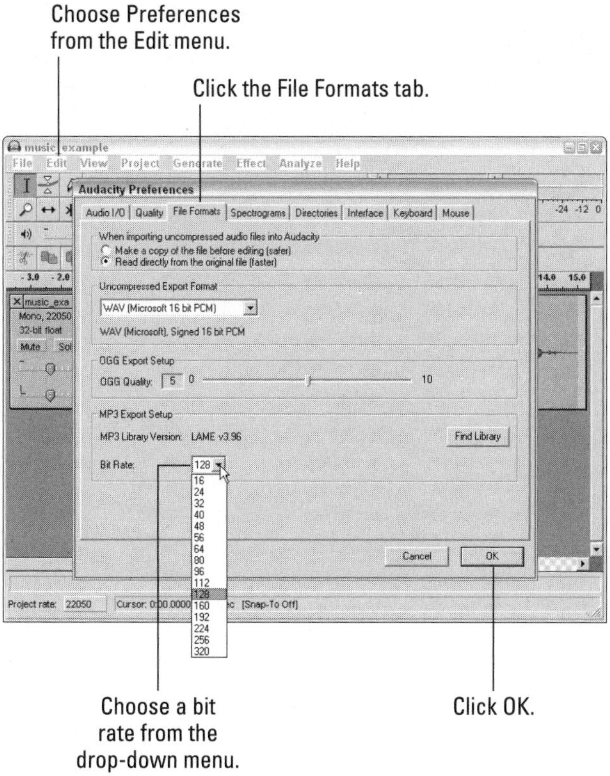

Choose Preferences
from the Edit menu.

Click the File Formats tab.

Choose a bit
rate from the
drop-down menu.

Click OK.

Encoding H.264 video using QuickTime Pro

You can export H.264 vide from QuickTime Pro in a number of ways. The simplest way is to use the iPod preset. This is perfect for creating iPod compatible files, but it gives you no control over any of the settings. You may want to tweak the settings a bit to suit your podcast, in which case you'll have to create your own encoding setting.

Using the iPod preset

Using the iPod preset is simple:

1. Open QuickTime Pro, and open the video to be encoded.

2. Choose Export from the File menu. This opens the Export window, shown in Figure 13.3.

3. From the drop-down menu, choose Movie to iPod (320×240).

4. Click Save. QuickTime Pro exports an iPod compatible H.264 video.

FIGURE 13.3

Export an iPod compatible video from QuickTime Pro using this preset.

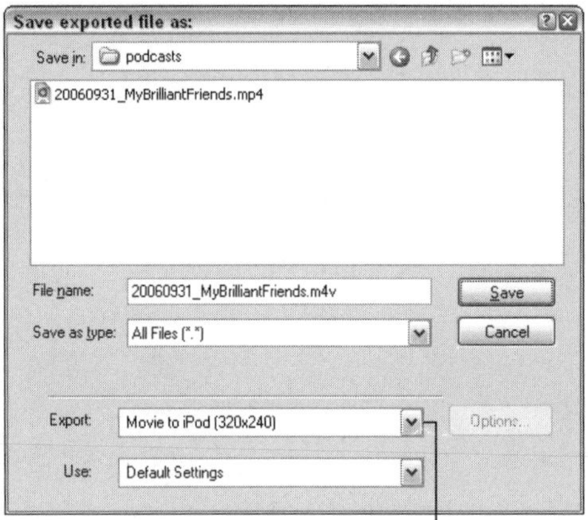

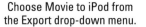

Choose Movie to iPod from
the Export drop-down menu.

The only problem with using this preset is that it doesn't give you any control over any of the encoding options. You can't select a bit rate, a resolution, or anything else. Of course, it's guaranteed to work on an iPod, which is pretty handy. But the default bit rate is rather high, clocking in at over 800 kbps. This is fine for a short podcast, but if your podcast is longer than, say, 5 minutes, you're looking at a pretty serious download. You may want to dial the bit rate down to reduce the file size. To do this, you have to set your encoding settings by hand.

Encoding using custom H.264 settings

QuickTime also makes it easy to customize the encoding settings. There are a few more steps than using the iPod preset, but you have far more control over the output. Follow these steps:

1. Open QuickTime Pro, and open the video to be encoded.

2. Choose Export from the File menu. Again, this opens the Export window, as shown in Figure 13.4.

FIGURE 13.4

Here's how to get to the MPEG-4 video export settings.

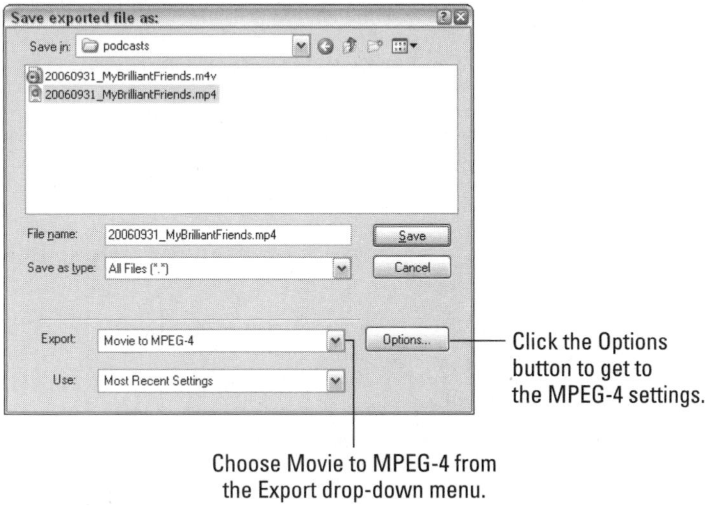

Click the Options button to get to the MPEG-4 settings.

Choose Movie to MPEG-4 from the Export drop-down menu.

3. Choose Movie to MPEG-4 from the Export drop-down menu.

4. Click the Options button to get to the video export settings. To begin with, this opens the MPEG-4 video settings, as shown in Figure 13.5.

5. Select MP4 from the File Format drop-down menu.

NOTE QuickTime Pro defaults to MP4 (ISMA) for MPEG-4 output. ISMA stands for the Internet Streaming Media Alliance. Unfortunately the H.264 codec is not yet considered ISMA compliant (as of Fall 2006). This really doesn't mean anything. The H.264 codec is part of the MPEG-4 standard and will play back in any modern QuickTime player or iPod. For best quality, you should choose the MP4 option, not MP4(ISMA), so you can use the H.264 codec.

6. Choose H.264 from the Video Format drop-down menu.

7. Enter a bit rate for your file. Remember that the total bit rate is the video bit rate plus the audio bit rate.

8. Enter your screen resolution in the Image Size field. If you want iPod compatible files, choose 320×240.

9. Click the Video Options button to access the advanced encoding options. This opens the Advanced Video Settings window, shown in Figure 13.6.

FIGURE 13.5

Configure QuickTime MPEG-4 export video settings with this dialog box.

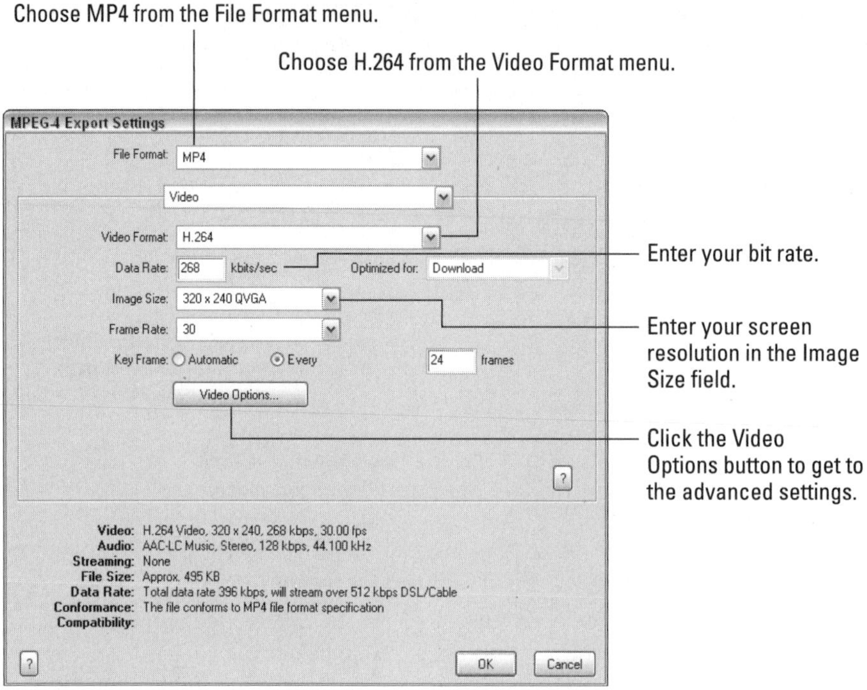

Choose MP4 from the File Format menu.

Choose H.264 from the Video Format menu.

MPEG-4 Export Settings

File Format: MP4

Video

Video Format: H.264 — Enter your bit rate.

Data Rate: 268   kbits/sec   Optimized for: Download

Image Size: 320 x 240 QVGA

Frame Rate: 30

Key Frame: ○ Automatic   ⊙ Every   24   frames

Enter your screen resolution in the Image Size field.

Video Options...

Click the Video Options button to get to the advanced settings.

Video: H.264 Video, 320 x 240, 268 kbps, 30.00 fps
Audio: AAC-LC Music, Stereo, 128 kbps, 44.100 kHz
Streaming: None
File Size: Approx. 495 KB
Data Rate: Total data rate 396 kbps, will stream over 512 kbps DSL/Cable
Conformance: The file conforms to MP4 file format specification
Compatibility:

OK   Cancel

FIGURE 13.6

Be sure to select Multi-pass encoding for the highest-quality results.

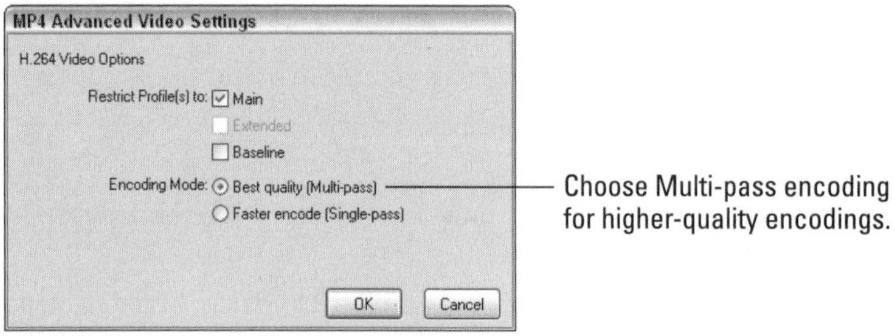

MP4 Advanced Video Settings

H.264 Video Options

Restrict Profile(s) to: ☑ Main
   ☐ Extended
   ☐ Baseline

Encoding Mode: ⊙ Best quality (Multi-pass) — Choose Multi-pass encoding for higher-quality encodings.
   ○ Faster encode (Single-pass)

OK   Cancel

10. Choose Best Quality (Multi-pass) encoding mode, and click OK.

CROSS-REF Two-pass (or multi-pass) encoding is explained in more detail in Chapter 14, "Advanced Encoding and Authoring Techniques."

NOTE You may be wondering about the profiles restriction (Main versus Baseline) on this screen. In MPEG-4 encoding profiles define the "tools" that can be used to encode the video. Consequently these profiles also define the tools required to play back the encoded video. In this example, the Main profile provides more encoding tools than the Base profile. Since our goal is the highest quality video, we chose the Main profile.

The MPEG-4 standard is incredibly broad and frankly, not written in a way that a layman can understand. For a fantastic, concise, and fun-to-read explanation of the MPEG-4 standard, we recommend Damian Stolarz' *Mastering Internet Video*.

11. Now it's time to configure the settings for your audio. Select Audio from the second drop-down menu in the MPEG-4 Export Settings window. This changes the information displayed in the bottom half of the window from video settings to audio settings, as shown in Figure 13.7.

FIGURE 13.7

Configuring QuickTime MPEG-4 export audio settings

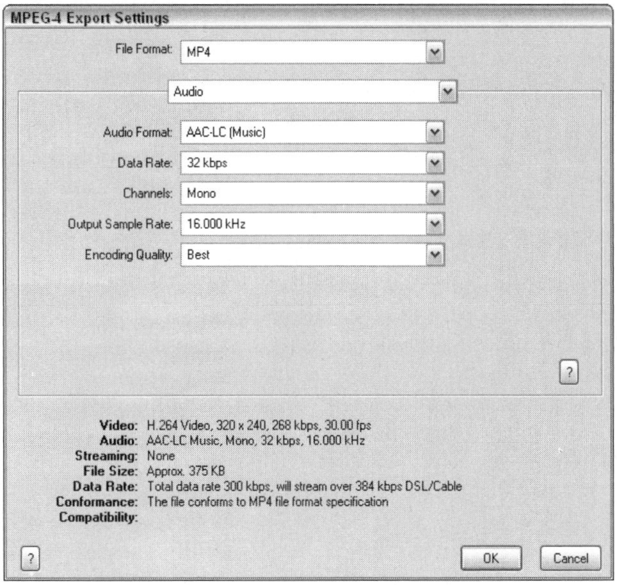

12. The first thing to choose is the audio codec you want to use from the Audio Format drop-down menu. In fact, the only codec offered for MPEG-4 encoding is AAC, which is just fine, because it offers great quality.

13. Next, select the desired bit rate from the Data Rate drop-down menu. A rate of 32 kbps should provide good quality.

14. If you're encoding spoken word content or want slightly higher fidelity, choose mono from the Channels drop-down menu.

15. The next available setting is the Output Sample Rate. This determines how much high-frequency information is contained in the final encoding. In general, the default setting works just fine. However, you can experiment with lowering the setting to get increased fidelity.

16. Finally, set your Encoding Quality to Best. This makes the encoding process take a little longer, but hey, your podcast is worth it.

17. Click OK to return to the Export menu, and then click Save to start the export/encoding process. You'll see the QuickTime Export progress window, shown in Figure 13.8, which gives you an idea how long the process will take. Depending on the length of your podcast, you may have time to grab a cup of coffee.

FIGURE 13.8

The QuickTime export progress window lets you know how long it's going to take.

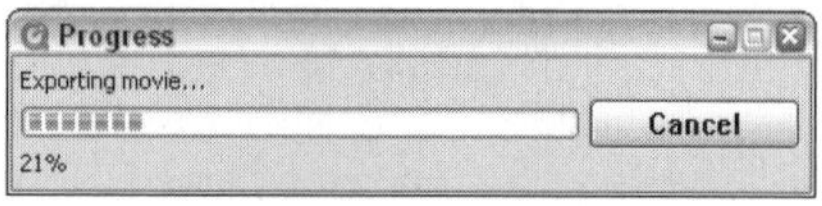

Using Windows Media Encoder

Another popular video format on the Web is Windows Media. Obviously, Windows Media video is going to play on any computer running Windows, and you'll have compatibility with a number of portable media players that support the Windows Media format.

The Windows Media Encoder is available as a free download from the Microsoft Web site. The Windows Media Encoder offers a simple wizard-driven interface to help you encode video. The wizard appears by default when you start the application. Alternatively, you can bypass the wizard and access the encoding settings via the Properties tab, shown in Figure 13.9. For the first example, we demonstrate the encoding wizard.

FIGURE 13.9

The Windows Media Encoder New Session window is where you begin encoding your podcast for Windows Media.

If it doesn't appear by default, you can start the New Session wizard by clicking the New Session icon.

You can always access the encoding parameters directly via the Properties window.

Choose Convert a File.   Click OK.

Using the encoding wizard

1. Open Windows Media Encoder. If the encoding wizard doesn't open, click New Session in the top-left corner.

2. Click the Convert a File icon, and then click OK.

3. The next screen of the wizard is where you select your input file and name your output file, as shown in Figure 13.10. Click the Browse button, and find your input file. The output file defaults to the same directory with the same name, with either a .wma or .wmv extension, depending on whether you're encoding audio or video. After you've specified the input and output files, click Next.

FIGURE 13.10

Specify the input and output files.

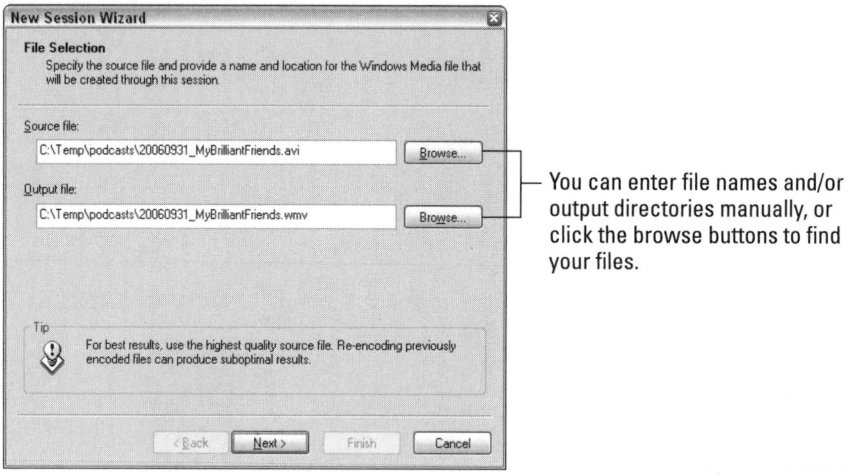

New Session Wizard

File Selection
Specify the source file and provide a name and location for the Windows Media file that will be created through this session.

Source file:

C:\Temp\podcasts\20060931_MyBrilliantFriends.avi   Browse...

Output file:

C:\Temp\podcasts\20060931_MyBrilliantFriends.wmv   Browse...

You can enter file names and/or output directories manually, or click the browse buttons to find your files.

Tip
For best results, use the highest quality source file. Re-encoding previously encoded files can produce suboptimal results.

< Back   Next >   Finish   Cancel

4. Next is the Content Distribution screen, as shown in Figure 13.11. The choice you make here determines what encoding options the wizard displays in the following screens. Choose Web server (progressive download), and click Next.

FIGURE 13.11

Choose Web server (progressive download) for your distribution option.

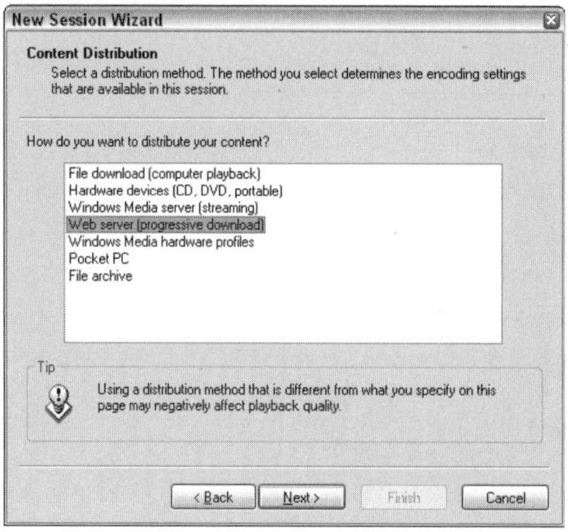

New Session Wizard

Content Distribution
Select a distribution method. The method you select determines the encoding settings that are available in this session.

How do you want to distribute your content?

File download (computer playback)
Hardware devices (CD, DVD, portable)
Windows Media server (streaming)
Web server (progressive download)
Windows Media hardware profiles
Pocket PC
File archive

Tip
Using a distribution method that is different from what you specify on this page may negatively affect playback quality.

< Back   Next >   Finish   Cancel

5. Now it's time to choose the Encoding Options. Your choices here are determined by how long your podcasts are and what sort of quality you want to offer. Another thing to consider is how much you want to spend on bandwidth.

   For this example, choose VHS Quality for the video and FM quality for the audio, as shown in Figure 13.12. You'll see two potential total bit rates listed: Choose the higher bit rate for better quality. Click Next.

FIGURE 13.12

Choose your encoding quality settings on the Encoding Options screen.

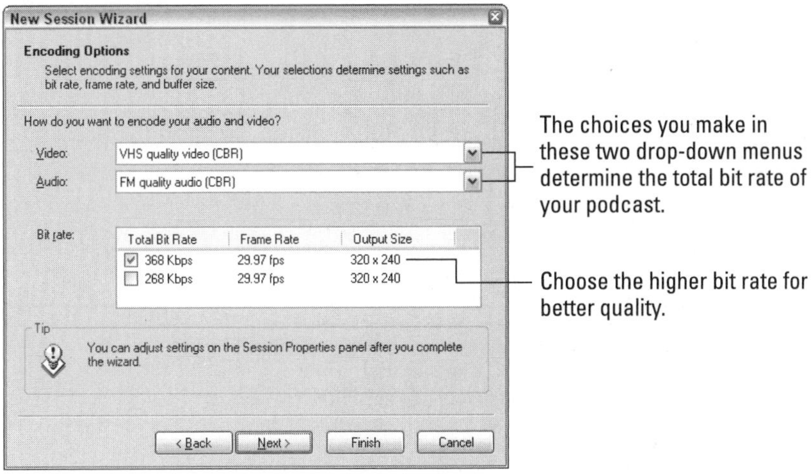

The choices you make in these two drop-down menus determine the total bit rate of your podcast.

Choose the higher bit rate for better quality.

6. The next screen is where you can enter information about your podcast, such as title, author, copyright, and description, as shown in Figure 13.13. Click Next.

NOTE It's always a good idea to enter all this information, which is known as metadata. You can read more about why we think metadata is important in the "Why Metadata Is Important" sidebar.

7. The final screen of the encoding wizard offers a summary of the encoding settings, as shown in Figure 13.14. Check to make sure the settings are correct. Provided the check box in the lower-left corner is checked, encoding begins as soon as you click the Finish button.

FIGURE 13.13

Enter information about your podcast on the Display Information screen.

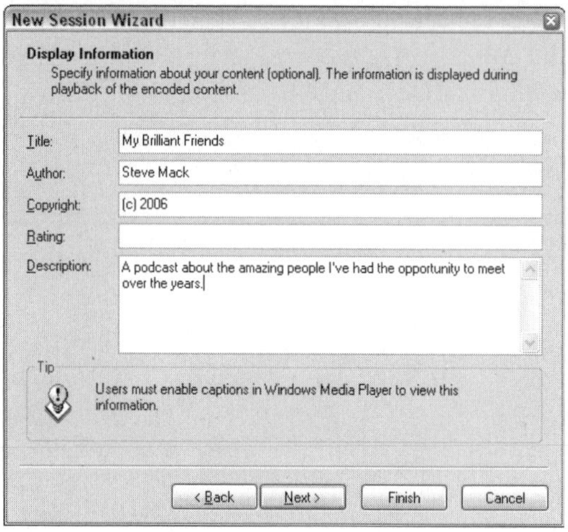

FIGURE 13.14

Check your encoding settings before clicking Finish.

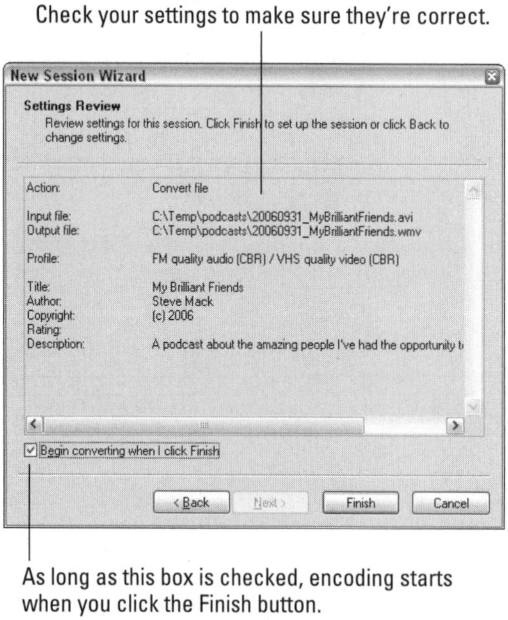

Check your settings to make sure they're correct.

As long as this box is checked, encoding starts when you click the Finish button.

The Windows Media encoder should start encoding when you get to the end of the encoding wizard. If not, you may have to click the Start Encoding button at the top of the Windows Media Encoder. When the encoding is done, the Windows Media Encoder displays an Encoding Results window, as shown in Figure 13.15. This screen can be handy, because you can play the encoded version of the file to check the quality or start a new encoding session.

FIGURE 13.15

The Encoding Results screen provides information about your encoding session.

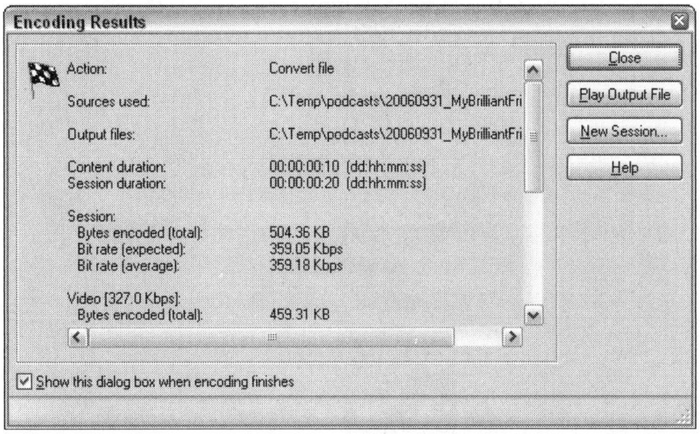

Using the properties window

Encoding via the wizard is straightforward, but much like QuickTime Pro's presets, it doesn't expose all the functionality of the Windows Media Encoder. If you want to get access to all the encoding options, you have to use the Properties tab on the main Windows Media Encoder screen, as shown in Figure 13.16.

FIGURE 13.16

Use the Properties tab on the main Windows Media Encoder screen to access all the encoding settings.

Click the Properties tab to open the Properties window. You can step through the encoding settings by clicking the various tabs.

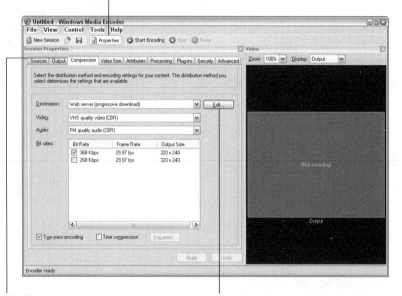

The Compression tab is where you can select different bit rates, codecs, and so on.

Click the Edit button to access the Advanced Compression settings.

You can see in Figure 13.16 that the Compression tab of the Properties window corresponds to Step 5 where we chose the encoding quality. In Step 5, we chose what quality we wanted, but we couldn't specify bit rate or audio codec. To do that, click the Edit button, and you'll be presented with the Custom Encoding Settings window, as shown in Figure 13.17.

FIGURE 13.17

The General tab of the Custom Encoding Settings window

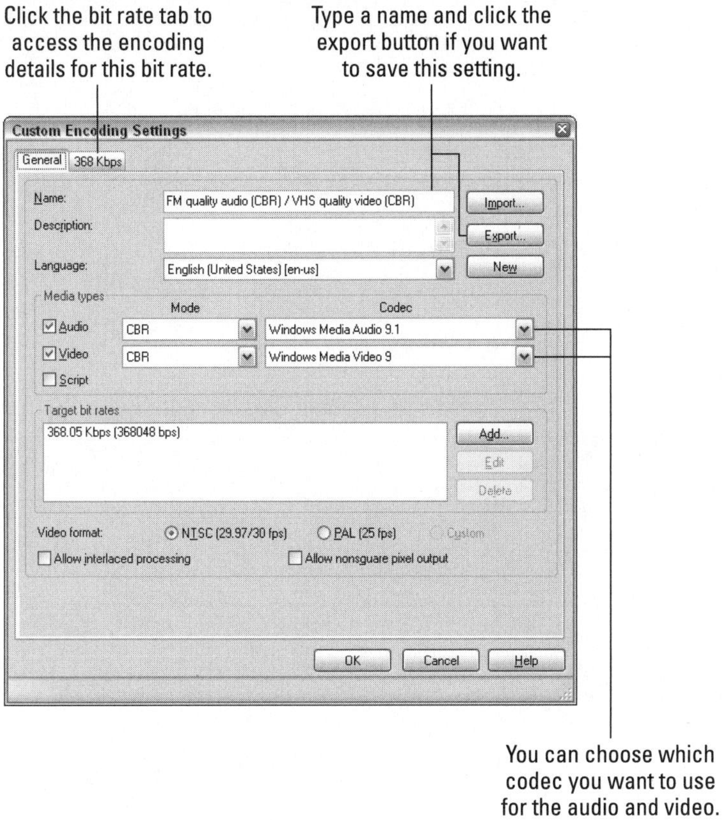

Click the bit rate tab to access the encoding details for this bit rate.

Type a name and click the export button if you want to save this setting.

You can choose which codec you want to use for the audio and video.

The Custom Encoding Settings window defaults to the General tab, which presents some basic information about the encoding and allows you to choose which codecs to use for the audio and video. The real action is on the second tab, which is labeled with the total bit rate of the preset. In Figure 13.17, it's labeled 368 Kbps. Click that tab to get to the detailed encoding settings, as shown in Figure 13.18.

FIGURE 13.18

The encoding details are displayed on the second tab.

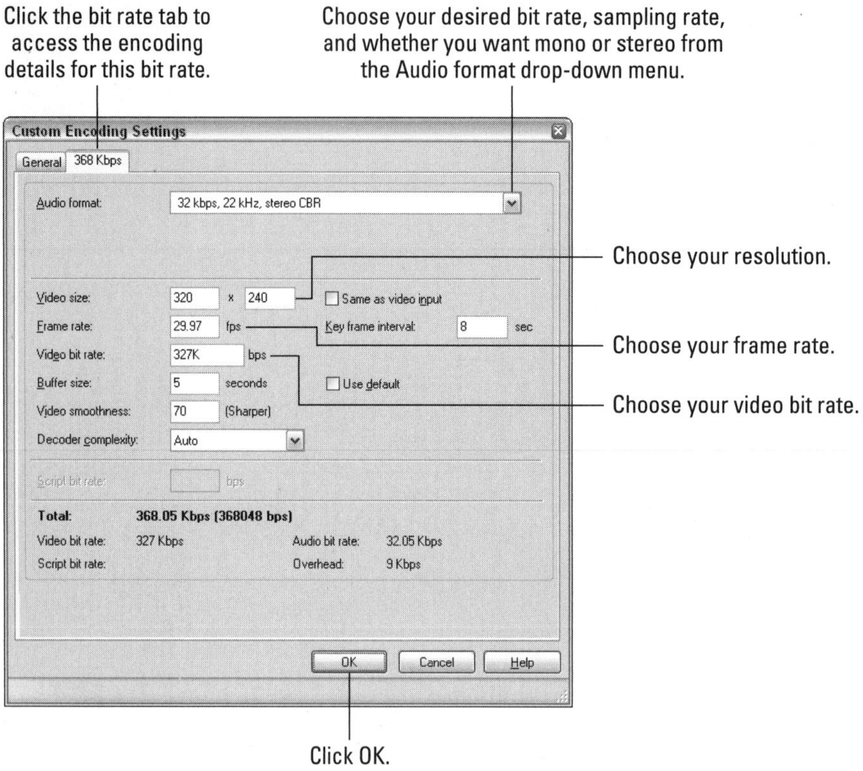

Click the bit rate tab to
access the encoding
details for this bit rate.

Choose your desired bit rate, sampling rate,
and whether you want mono or stereo from
the Audio format drop-down menu.

Custom Encoding Settings

General | 368 Kbps

Audio format: 32 kbps, 22 kHz, stereo CBR ▾

Video size: 320 x 240   ☐ Same as video input   —— Choose your resolution.
Frame rate: 29.97 fps   Key frame interval: 8   sec
Video bit rate: 327K bps   —— Choose your frame rate.
Buffer size: 5 seconds   ☐ Use default
Video smoothness: 70 (Sharper)   —— Choose your video bit rate.
Decoder complexity: Auto ▾

Script bit rate: bps

Total: 368.05 Kbps (368048 bps)
Video bit rate: 327 Kbps   Audio bit rate: 32.05 Kbps
Script bit rate: Overhead: 9 Kbps

OK   Cancel   Help

Click OK.

At the top of the window you can choose the audio format from the drop-down menu. A wide variety of bit rates are available, each at a number of different bit rates, and both mono and stereo formats. Working your way down, the next field is where you specify the resolution of your video. You can also specify the frame rate and the desired video bit rate. After you've specified the video specs you want, click the OK button.

If you're going to reuse these settings, be sure to save them as a preset so you don't have to re-enter them every time. To do this, simply type a name and description into the appropriate fields on the General tab and click the Export tab to save them to a file.

Why Metadata Is Important

Just what the heck is metadata, and why should you care?

Metadata is data about other data. For example, your podcast has a name or title, an author (you), and possibly a description. Depending on the format you're using to encode, you may have many other metadata fields available to you, including these:

- copyright
- year
- URL
- cover art
- lyrics

Some of these fields may not be appropriate for your podcast, because they were designed with music in mind. Nevertheless, you should fill in as much metadata as possible when encoding your podcast, because this information is read by media players. When your podcast is playing, some of the metadata is displayed, and some is available in an information panel. Players use this information to sort and organize a user's content. Metadata is also readable by search engines. The more metadata you provide, the better chance you have of being found.

Of course, this brings up some issues. You want to provide as much information as possible, but remember that portable devices have limited display areas. In general, any information that is too long to display is truncated. So you want to be concise with the fields that are displayed, such as the title. If your title includes an episode number, you should put that after the title of the podcast, which should always come first.

For example, if your podcast is called Big Fish, and the latest episode is about catching pike, you should call it:

```
Big Fish #12: Catching Pike
```

as opposed to

```
Catching Pike on the Big Fish podcast, episode #12
```

There are a couple of reasons for this. First, some media player displays cut off after 10 or 12 characters, so using the first naming convention, at least the name of the podcast would be displayed. Second, if the person organizes his library according to title (or album), all your podcasts are displayed in a nice group, as they should be.

Similarly, you should be consistent with your name in the artist/author field. If you're "Big Al" in your first podcast, then you should be Big Al in all your podcasts. Again, this allows folks to look for you by artist name, and they won't miss any episodes if you decided to call yourself "Sleepy Al" for a day.

Staying consistent with your metadata keeps your podcasts organized on a person's device and makes it easier for them to find you. If your podcasts are easy to find, there's a better chance they'll be listened to, which is what it's all about.

Exporting video from Sony Vegas

Sony Vegas offers a number of export options. You can export into MP3, QuickTime, Real, and Windows Media formats. Vegas uses the term *rendering* for its export/encoding. This is fairly standard for a video-editing program. In our case, we're simply going to render to an encoded format.

If you've got Vegas, chances are good that you're relatively familiar with video editing, or at least with how Vegas works. To render your encoded podcast, simply choose Render As from the File menu, as shown in Figure 13.19.

FIGURE 13.19

Rendering in Sony Vegas

Choose "Render As" from the File menu to export encoded video.

By default, Vegas renders the entire time line. You can select a smaller section to encode by dragging the region markers at either end of the time line.

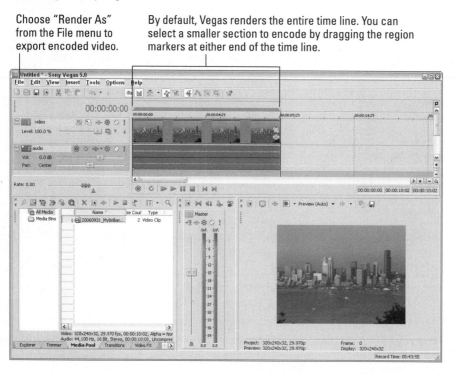

As an exercise, we'll encode a video in the Real format. Let's assume we're targeting 300 Kbps, with 32 Kbps mono audio.

1. Open Sony Vegas, and place your edited podcast on the time line.

2. From the File menu, choose Render As. This pops up the Render As window, shown in Figure 13.20.

FIGURE 13.20

The Vegas Render As window

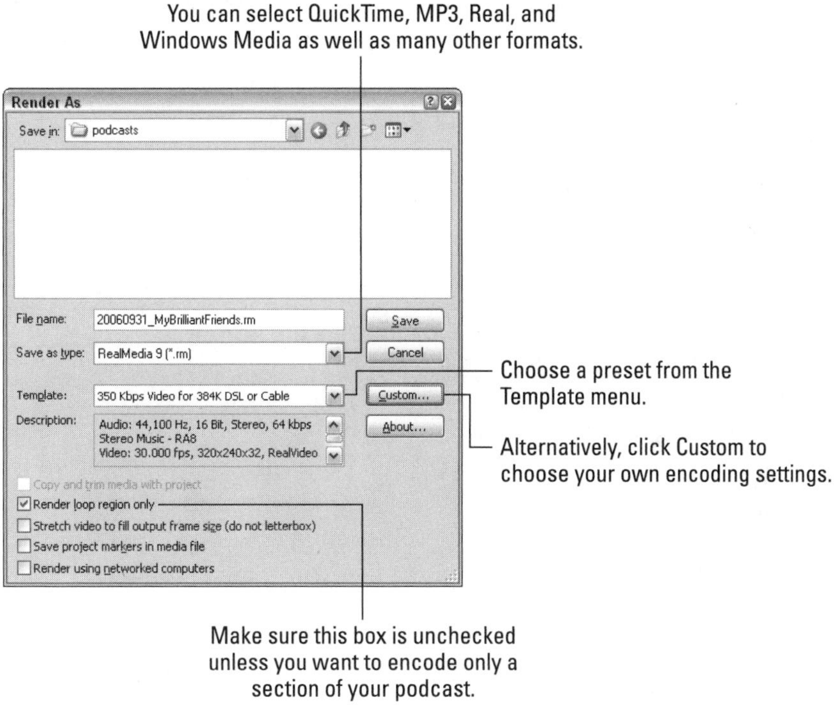

You can select QuickTime, MP3, Real, and Windows Media as well as many other formats.

Choose a preset from the Template menu.

Alternatively, click Custom to choose your own encoding settings.

Make sure this box is unchecked unless you want to encode only a section of your podcast.

3. Enter a file name for your rendered podcast.

4. Select RealMedia 9 from the Save as type drop-down menu.

5. A template that's very close to what we want is available, so select 350 Kbps video from the Template drop-down. However, we want to tweak the settings a bit, so click the Custom button next to the Template field. This opens the Custom Template window, shown in Figure 13.21. The only adjustment to do on this page is to select Best from the Video rendering quality drop-down list. This makes your encoding take a bit longer, but provides higher quality.

FIGURE 13.21

Be sure to select Best in the Video quality drop-down list.

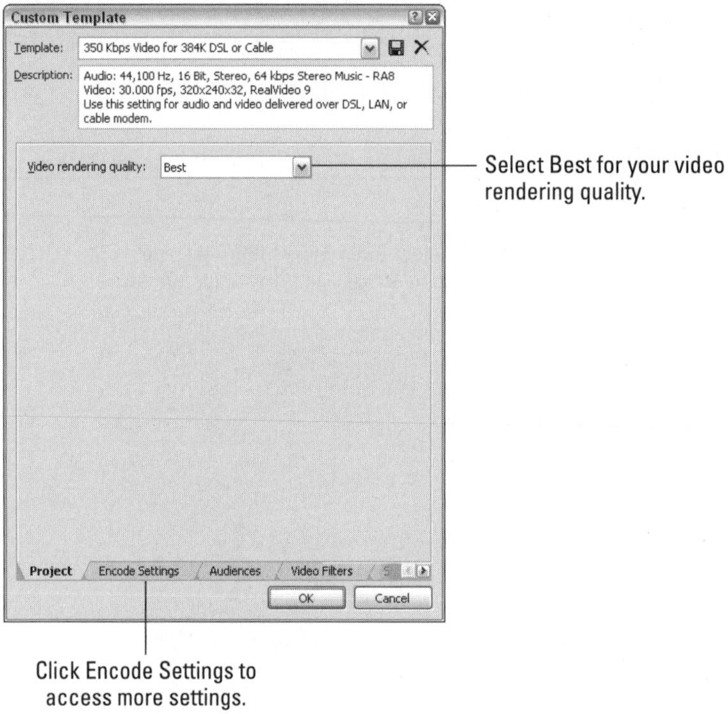

Select Best for your video rendering quality.

Click Encode Settings to access more settings.

6. Click the Encoding Settings tab at the bottom of the window to access more settings, as shown in Figure 13.22.

NOTE RealNetworks uses the concept of "audiences" to determine bit rates, so the Vegas export reflects this. The QuickTime and Windows Media exports operate much the same way as the QuickTime and Windows Media Encoders do.

7. On this screen, select the type of audio content in your podcast. This determines whether a voice or music codec is used.

FIGURE 13.22

The first screen of encoding settings for RealMedia encoding

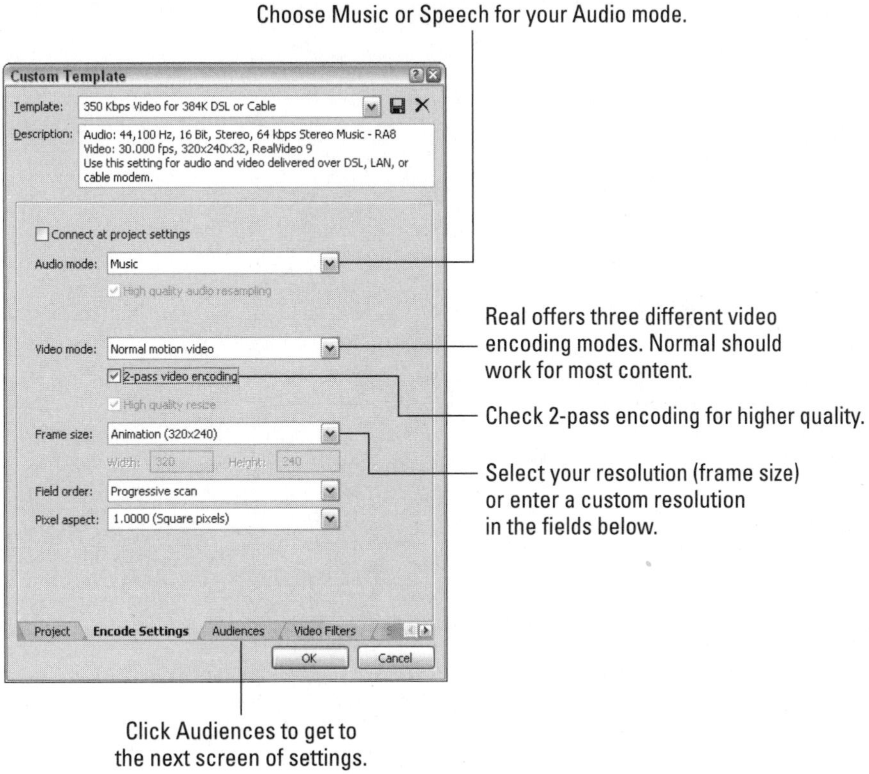

Choose Music or Speech for your Audio mode.

Real offers three different video encoding modes. Normal should work for most content.

Check 2-pass encoding for higher quality.

Select your resolution (frame size) or enter a custom resolution in the fields below.

Click Audiences to get to the next screen of settings.

8. The next field selects the Video mode. You can choose whether you prefer sharper images or smoother motion. Your choice here is determined by the content of your podcast. For most podcasts, Normal mode should be just fine.

9. Be sure to check the 2-pass video encoding. This makes your render take twice as long, but provides much higher video quality.

10. Select your resolution from the Frame size drop-down menu, or choose Custom and enter a custom frame size in the Width and Height fields.

11. Leave Field order and Pixel aspect fields alone, and click Audiences to get to the next screen of settings, as shown in Figure 13.23.

FIGURE 13.23

The Audiences screen of encoding settings for RealMedia encoding

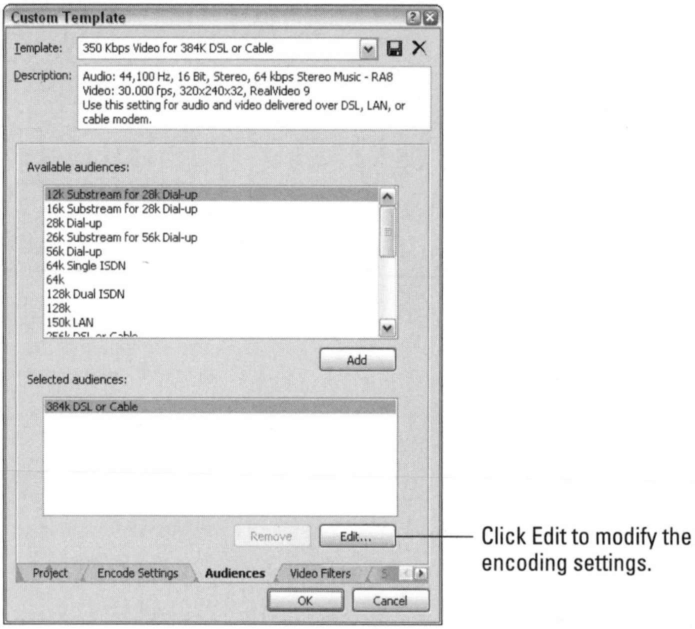

Click Edit to modify the encoding settings.

12. The Real format calls its presets Audiences. Because we chose the 350 Kbps template, the 384 Kbps DSL or Cable Audience is displayed. To modify this preset, click the Edit button. This opens the Audience editing window, as shown in Figure 13.24.

13. Enter 300 for the bit rate. When you're working with the Real format, the bit rate refers to the total bit rate. (The audio bit rate is subtracted from the total bit rate to get the video bit rate.)

14. Because we want a 32 Kbps mono codec, choose 32 Kbps Music from the Music codec drop-down menu.

FIGURE 13.24

The Audiences editing window

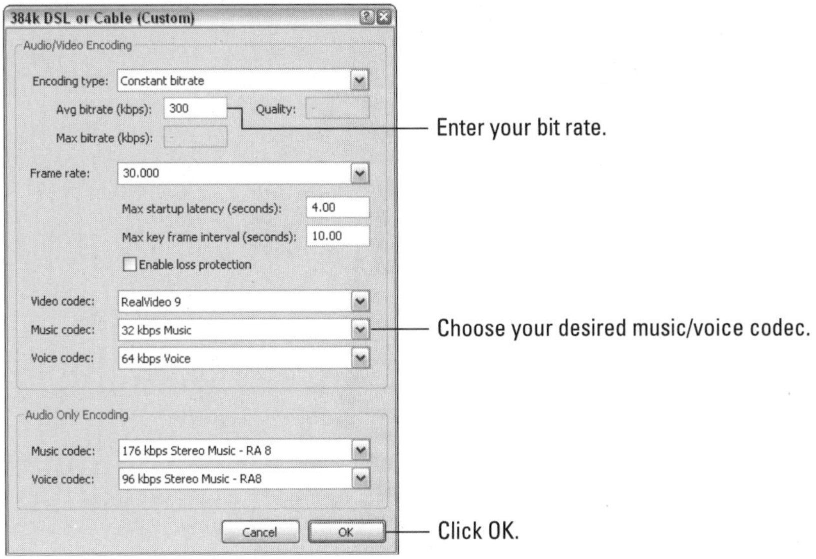

Enter your bit rate.

Choose your desired music/voice codec.

Click OK.

15. You can ignore all the other settings for now. Click OK to return to the Custom Template screen.

16. At this point, you may want to save your preset. If so, enter a new name for the Template, and click the small disc icon at the top of the screen.

17. The next tab is the Video Filters tab, but that has advanced settings that are covered in the next chapter. For now, click the last tab, Summary, shown in Figure 13.25, to bring up the summary settings.

18. Enter information about your podcast. When you're finished, click OK. If you saved your preset, you should see it selected in the Template field, along with your description of the template, if you entered one. Click Save, and the rendering/encoding process begins.

FIGURE 13.25

Enter your podcast information.

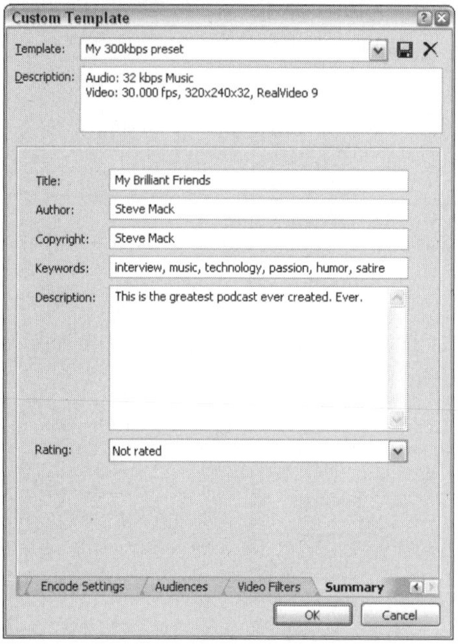

The process described is somewhat specific to the Real format. If you're using Vegas to encode into the QuickTime or Windows Media formats, the process is very similar to using their stand-alone encoding software. You'll step through the tabs in the Custom Template screen, but they'll be named to correspond with steps in the native encoding software. The fields may have slightly different names, but essentially you'll be doing the same thing.

Encoding multiple versions using Sorenson Squeeze

Sorenson Squeeze enables you to encode to a number of different formats in a single encoding job. Sorenson Squeeze also offers video processing, so if you need to do any processing such as cropping or color correction, you can do it during the encoding phase instead of during your editing phase. To get all this functionality, you have to do a bit of setup, but after you have chosen your presets, you can encode with a few clicks.

The process is very simple. Import your raw podcast file, select filters for preprocessing, select the formats you want to encode into, and then press the Squeeze It! button in the bottom right, as shown in Figure 13.26.

Encoding using Sorenson Squeeze

Click here to import
your podcast file.

When you import a video you'll see
a video preview, as well as an entry
in the job list.

Choose a format preset (or presets)
and click Apply.

Click Squeeze It!, and
you're off!

Choose processing filter(s)
and click Apply.

If you want to create your own custom preset, you copy an existing preset, modify the settings, and save it as a new preset. Because modifying a video processing filter is covered in Chapter 10, this example uses a factory preset for preprocessing, but shows you how to modify an encoding preset. As per preceding examples, we'll encode a 300 kbps file, with 32 kbps audio. We'll target MPEG-4 this time:

1. Open Sorenson Squeeze, and click the Import File icon at the top left to import your podcast.

2. Use the browse interface to find your raw podcast file, and click the Open button. You should see a video preview of your file, as well as a job entry under the video preview.

3. Use the Generic Web video filter to preprocess your video. In the filters section of the left column, click the Generic Web filter, and then click the Apply button at the bottom of the filters section. The Generic Web filter does some cropping, so you should see a dotted red outline of what Squeeze is going to encode in the preview window.

4. Now it's time to create a custom encoding preset. The best way to do this is to find a preset that is close to what you want and make a copy of it. Because we're targeting 300 Kbps MPEG-4, find the 384K_Stream preset under the MPEG-4 compression settings. Click it to highlight the preset, and then click the small plus sign at the bottom of the Format & Compression Settings section. This opens the Audio/Video Compression Settings window, shown in Figure 13.27.

FIGURE 13.27

Editing an encoding preset in Sorenson Squeeze

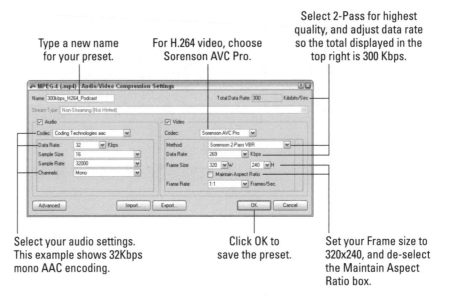

Type a new name for your preset.

For H.264 video, choose Sorenson AVC Pro.

Select 2-Pass for highest quality, and adjust data rate so the total displayed in the top right is 300 Kbps.

Select your audio settings. This example shows 32Kbps mono AAC encoding.

Click OK to save the preset.

Set your Frame size to 320x240, and de-select the Maintain Aspect Ratio box.

5. The Audio/Video Compression Settings window enables full access to all your encoding parameters. Be sure to type a new name for your preset, as opposed to 384K_Stream_copy.

TIP Sorenson Squeeze is very particular about preset names. You cannot use spaces or periods.

6. Next, it's time to set your audio encoding parameters. We want to use the AAC codec, a 32 kbps bit rate, and mono. (Obviously, you can encode in stereo if you like, though you may want to bump up the bit rate slightly.)

7. After the audio parameters are set, adjust the video settings. First, choose Sorenson AVC Pro for the Codec. This is Sorenson's version of H.264.

> **NOTE** AVC stands for Advanced Video Coding, which is the latest and greatest MPEG-4 technology. It's also referred to as H.264.

8. Select 2-Pass VBR for highest quality, and adjust the bit rate so the display at the top-right corner says 300 kbps. If you're using a 32 kbps, enter 269. Yes, 269 plus 32 is 301, but who's counting?

9. Enter 320×240 for your frame size, and deselect the Maintain Aspect Ratio check box.

> **NOTE** This may seem confusing. Preceding chapters have stressed the need to maintain your aspect ratio, but here we are deselecting this option. The reasoning behind this decision is that when this box is checked, it overrides your frame size specifications and maintains the aspect ratio of the original file, without taking into account pixel aspect ratios. Confusing? You bet. Just make sure you use frame size settings that maintain your desired aspect ratio (4:3 or 16:9) and deselect this option.

10. Click OK to save your new encoding preset.

11. You should now see your preset in the Format & Compression Settings column, and it should be highlighted. To use your preset, click the Apply button at the bottom of the section.

12. You should now see your compression settings below your source settings in the job window. You're ready to go.

13. Click Squeeze It!, and Squeeze begins the encoding process.

Of course, if you want to add more encoding options, you can select additional encoding presets (or create more custom presets) and add them to the job. The nice thing about using software like Squeeze is that you can do multiple encodes without having to adjust settings or press buttons for each one. Go ahead and try offering more versions of your podcast. Your workload won't get any heavier.

Summary

This chapter covered lots of encoding techniques, including these specific topics:

- Most audio content is mono, and mono encodings are higher fidelity than stereo. Unless you have lots of high quality audio in your podcast, you should consider encoding in mono.

- Speech codecs do a wonderful job on speech at incredibly low bit rates. However, they destroy music. Use a speech codec if your podcast doesn't contain any music.

- Choose a bit rate for your podcast that gets you the quality you need and meets your budgetary restrictions. For most audio podcasts, 128 kbps MP3 is more than enough.

■ The most important decision you'll make about a video podcast is how large you want the frame to be. Higher resolutions require much higher bit rates to achieve the same quality. Any bigger than 320×240 and your podcast can't play back on an iPod (though iTunes converts it for you).

■ Don't reduce the frame rate unless you have a very low motion podcast.

■ Choose a bit rate for your video podcast based on your screen resolution. You need about 300 kbps for 320×240.

■ Allot 10 to 20 percent of your total bit rate to audio.

Chapter 14

Advanced Encoding and Authoring Techniques

Maybe you're the kind of person who just can't help but fiddle with things. Or maybe your podcast has so much crazy motion in it that you're looking for a way, any possible way, to get higher quality out of your encoded files without doubling your bit rate. You're in luck; we still have a few tricks up our sleeve that we can reveal.

On the other hand, maybe you're the kind of person who lives on the edge, and you want your podcast there, too. You want every bell and whistle that's available to you. We have a few things for you here, too. The addition of color screens to portable media players has opened up a whole realm of possibilities when it comes to podcast production. These possibilities, called enhanced podcasts, add pictures, chapter markers, and links to audio podcasts. This is new, bleeding edge territory, but the results can be pretty slick.

Before we jump into the wonderful world of enhanced podcasts, let's talk for a bit about techniques you can use to squeeze every ounce of performance out of your encoding software.

IN THIS CHAPTER

Advanced encoding techniques

Adding a logo to an MP3 podcast

Authoring enhanced podcasts

Advanced Encoding Techniques

Chapter 13 explained the basics of encoding and walked you through the encoding process using a number of different tools. Those examples focused on the main encoding parameters: the bit rate, the codec, and the screen resolution if you're encoding video. You may have noticed that additional settings are available in some of the encoding tools. Let's talk about some of the most useful, which are video filters, two-pass encoding, and Variable Bit Rate (VBR) encoding.

Using video filters

Depending on the source and target resolution of your video, you may be able to apply a filter to get a higher-quality encoding. The three most commonly available video filters are de-interlacing, inverse telecine, and noise reduction.

De-interlacing

A de-interlacing filter is designed to remove interlacing artifacts from an encoded video. Interlacing artifacts appear when the two fields of an interlaced frame of video are combined to create a single frame of progressive video. It's most noticeable when there is horizontal motion in the frame. What happens is that the edges of the moving objects appear "feathered;" this is also referred to as field ripping. Whatever you want to call it, it doesn't look right.

CROSS-REF Interlacing is discussed in more depth in Chapter 10, "Advanced Video Production Techniques." There are also screen shots of where to find the de-interlacing filters in Sorenson Squeeze, Windows Media Encoder, and Sony Vegas.

In most encoding situations, de-interlacing is necessary only if your resolution is larger than 320×240. At 320×240 or less, only one of the fields is used during the encoding process. If you're encoding at larger resolutions, you should always de-interlace your content. In Chapter 10, de-interlacing is discussed as part of the video production process. It's actually a better idea to do your de-interlacing at the encoding phase, because you probably want to leave your master interlaced.

NOTE HD and now HDV cameras often offer the ability to shoot in progressive scan mode. If you're lucky enough to be working with progressive scan video, you can skip this section because your content isn't interlaced!

Using the de-interlacing filter is usually just a matter of clicking a check box in your encoding application. Some applications automatically de-interlace based on the incoming content. Chapter 10 includes screen shots of where to find the de-interlacing filters in Sorenson Squeeze and Windows Media Encoder. QuickTime Pro doesn't offer a de-interlacing filter. For the sake of completeness, Figure 14.1 shows where to find the de-interlacing filter in RealProducer.

Inverse telecine

Film is shot at 24 frames per second, and video is shot at 30 frames per second. When film content is transferred to video, extra frames must be inserted to compensate for the different frame rates. This process, known as telecine, inserts an extra frame every four frames. This adds a total of six frames every second, for a total of 30 frames. The inserted frames are created by taking the even field from one frame and combining it with the odd frame of the next frame.

When the video is played back, we don't notice that there are extra frames, because they're beyond our persistence of vision threshold. We see the video as continuous motion. However, the original film looked just fine at 24 frames per second, so why should we spend precious bits encoding the extra six frames of video each second? The answer is that we shouldn't. An inverse telecine filter automatically detects and removes extra frames, thereby reducing the amount of information to encode.

FIGURE 14.1

The video filters available in RealProducer

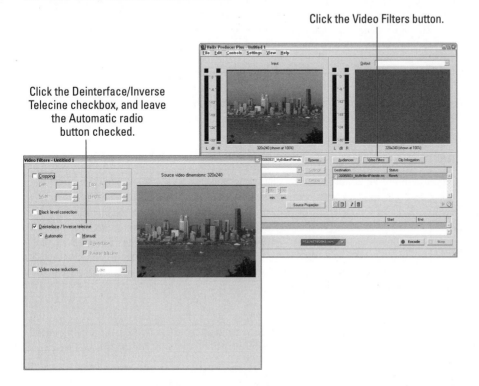

Click the Video Filters button.

Click the Deinterface/Inverse
Telecine checkbox, and leave
the Automatic radio
button checked.

However, we must reveal the ugly truth. Chances are good that you'll never need to use an inverse telecine filter. It's necessary only if the original content was shot on film, and chances are pretty slim that you're filming on Super 8 film and then converting that into video. But at least you know what the filter does and why you won't need to use it.

Noise reduction

Noise reduction filters can be useful, particularly if you're starting with low-quality video. Noise in a video frame is often visible as excessive grain. You'll notice this particularly if you're taping without enough light. In an effort to boost the image to an acceptable light level, the camera amplifies the video signal and, in the process, adds noise that we'd rather not have in the signal.

Some noise is invisible to the naked eye, but it is visible to a codec. This is a worst-case scenario, because the codec spends precious encoding resources trying to encode something we can't even see. A noise filter attempts to reduce the amount of noise, so the codec concentrates on what is important in the frame.

Noise filters blur each frame of video ever so slightly, thereby reducing the amount of detail. Depending on the level of the noise, this may be just enough to hide the noise from the codec. Some noise filters offer settings such as low, medium, and high. Avoid using the high setting. In fact, you should never have to use anything more than low noise reduction. If you're having quality issues with your video, you should try to fix it by adding more light when you shoot, as opposed to using noise reduction filters.

If you absolutely must use noise reduction, you need an encoding application that supports it. QuickTime Pro and Windows Media Encoder do not; RealProducer, Sorenson Squeeze, and Procoder do, and there are certainly others. Figure 14.2 shows how to turn on the noise reduction filter in Sorenson Squeeze. You can see the noise reduction filter in RealProducer in Figure 14.1.

Two-pass encoding

Any file, whether audio or video, has sections that are far more complex to encode than others. In audio files, some sections are loud with wide frequency ranges, and others are silent. In video files, some sections have lots of motion, and others have very little motion. Ideally, the encoder should reserve bits for the complex sections, and economize on the low-complexity sections. Also, the encoder should be sure to encode a key frame every time there's a scene change. This is possible only if the encoding application knows in advance what the material is like. To do this, the encoder must make a pass through the material so that it can figure out where the complex sections are. Then, on a second pass, the actual encoding is done.

Two-pass encoding always provides better quality. The only drawback is that it takes twice as long to encode a file. Unless you're creating multiple podcasts on a daily basis, you can probably afford the extra time to encode a higher-quality version. Always use two-pass encoding if possible.

Constant versus variable bit rate encoding

Most encoding is done using a constant bit rate. If you're encoding at 300 Kbps, 300 kilobits are used every second to encode the data. However, the complexity of a file isn't constant. Ideally, a codec should be able to use fewer bits during the low-complexity sections and more bits during the complex sections.

This is what variable bit rate (VBR) encoding does. VBR comes in a number of different variations. Peak limited VBR lets the codec use as many bits as necessary to achieve a specific quality level, with peaks limited to a specific bit rate. Bit-rate-constrained VBR targets an average bit rate for the entire file and lets the bit rate vary between specific values or as a percentage of the target bit rate. Finally, quality-based VBR is similar to peak-limited VBR, but without the peak limits.

Most encoders default to constant-bit-rate (CBR) encoding, because it's more suitable for streaming and progressively downloaded files. VBR files provide higher quality, but can be problematic to deliver across the Internet. For example, consider a podcast that has a very complex section in the middle. A peak-limited or quality-based VBR encoding might burst up to 1 Mbps or more for the complex section. If someone tries to watch this in an embedded player on your Web site, the player buffers up the first section, begins playback, and then chokes when it hits the complex section. The player would be forced to re-buffer, which is hardly a good experience for your audience.

FIGURE 14.2

The noise reduction filter in Sorenson Squeeze

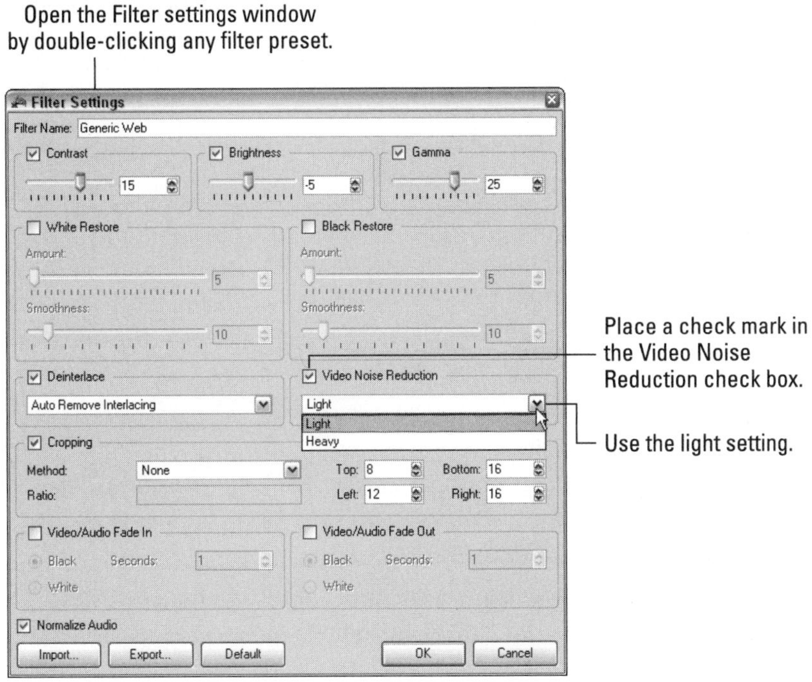

Open the Filter settings window
by double-clicking any filter preset.

Place a check mark in
the Video Noise
Reduction check box.

Use the light setting.

Constrained VBR files, however, can work well. In fact, even CBR files aren't 100 percent constant. The bit rate probably varies 5 to 10 percent over the course of the file. In fact, you can probably safely let your bit rate vary 20 percent over the course of the file without too much adverse effect. This amount of variation lets the codec dedicate more bits to the complex sections, but doesn't vary so much as to interfere with timely delivery.

VBR can definitely get you better quality, so it's worth playing around with. Different encoders implement VBR in different ways. The best approach is to play around with the settings, place your files on your Web site, and test playing them back. Most portable media players play back VBR files just fine, but there is a chance that some older players may not support VBR mode. If you decide to offer VBR encoded files, you should make sure you don't start getting complaints from your audience.

Adding a Logo to an MP3 Podcast

If you're at all serious about podcasting, you're going to want a logo. Adding a logo gives your podcast that extra bit of polish and recognition. And after you have a logo, you should embed it in every podcast you produce. However, it takes a few additional steps. Embedding images in MP3 files is a relatively recent phenomenon.

The original MP3 file specification did not include a way to attach metadata, such as the title, author, or copyright information. It wasn't until 1996 and the introduction of ID3 tags that metadata could be included in MP3 files. The original ID3 specification was fairly simple, including fields for title, album, year, genre, and comment. Over the years, the ID3 specification has grown to include much more, such as the track number on a CD, the composer, lyrics, and most important to this discussion, an embedded image, designed to contain album cover art. You can use this ability to embed a logo into your podcasts.

To add a logo to your podcast, you have to use an ID3 tag editor. Many are available, as a quick Internet search will reveal. As luck would have it, you probably already have one installed: iTunes. All you have to do is import your MP3-encoded podcast into iTunes and edit the ID3 tags via the Info window:

1. Open iTunes, and import your podcast by choosing Import from the File menu.

2. Find your podcast. If you're in library mode, you can sort by Date Added. This brings your podcast to the top of the list if you're in descending order.

3. Highlight your podcast, and choose Get Info from the File menu. This opens the Info window.

NOTE If you're not seeing the Artwork tab, then your podcast isn't yet in a format that supports embedded artwork, for example an unencoded WAV file. This is why it's a two-step process: First encode your file to MP3, and then open it and add your logo.

4. Click the Artwork tab, and then click the Add button to browse for your logo graphic.

5. Select your logo graphic, and click the Open button. You should see your graphic displayed in the Info window. Your graphic can be in BMP, GIF, JPG, or PNG format and any size up to 300×300 pixels. You should make sure that it looks good at different resolutions, because it will be displayed at different sizes on different players. iTunes provides a handy slider bar that lets you preview what your logo looks like at various resolutions. If it doesn't look good when it is scaled, you should consider revising it until it does.

CAUTION The 300×300 image size is not a strict limitation. However, using a larger resolution is not recommended because it may not be supported on portable media players, and it adds unnecessary payload to your podcast file.

6. Click the OK button to save your changes.

Your logo is now embedded in your MP3 file and will be displayed in iTunes, Windows Media Player, and on portable media player screens that display graphics.

Enhanced Podcasts

Enhanced podcasts are podcasts that include chapter markers, which provide an easy way for listeners to navigate quickly through the podcast. Enhanced podcasts can also contain embedded images and links. So you can create podcasts that offer slide show-like presentations and have links to your site, your guest's site, or anything else you'd like to link to. The only problem is that you can't create an enhanced podcast using the MP3 file format. You have to either use QuickTime AAC or Windows Media, and of course that means that you're going to have cross-platform compatibility issues.

QuickTime AAC enhanced podcasts won't play back on Windows Media portable players, and Windows Media files won't play back on iPods. So if you're going to create enhanced podcasts, you may want to offer a plain MP3 version for full compatibility, or you may want to offer multiple enhanced versions.

Enhanced QuickTime podcasts

Apple added enhanced functionality to podcast playback beginning with iTunes 4.9, which was the iTunes release that included the ability to subscribe to podcasts. It also corresponded to the release of iPods with color displays. Enhanced podcast images are displayed in the album cover art window in iTunes and on iPods with color displays. The links are displayed only in iTunes, in a small button along the bottom of the cover art window.

To see what an enhanced podcast looks like, you may want to check one out. Here are links to a few of the early adopters:

- K9Cast (`www.k9cast.com/`)
- iTunes New Music Tuesday (`www.apple.com/itunes/subscribe/`)
- MAKE Blog (`www.makezine.com/blog/archive/make_podcast/index.html`)
- Evil Primate Unchained (`evilprimate.com/podcast/`)

Creating an enhanced QuickTime podcast is a three-step process. First, you have to encode your file using the AAC format. Next, you have to create a small file that lists when you want the chapter markers, links, and images to appear. Finally, you have to combine the AAC file and the text file using Chapter Tool, which is available from the Apple Web site:

```
homepage.mac.com/applepodcast/podcasts/Resources/static/podcast_
chapter_tool_beta.dmg
```

CAUTION Chapter Tool requires Mac OS X version 10.3.8 or later, QuickTime version 6.5.2 or later, and iTunes 4.9 or later. Unfortunately, Chapter Tool is not available for the Windows platform. Also, note that the full name is "Chapter Tool Beta." Although the term beta has become relatively elastic in the last few years, it still means "you can't complain if it doesn't work." You have been warned.

There are now a few tools available on the Mac platform that allow you to create enhanced podcasts without having to create the text file by hand or having to run the Chapter Tool command in a terminal window. However, in the interest of showing you what goes on under the hood, we're going to show you how to do it by hand. For those of you who are scared of using the command line or scared of angle brackets, you should skip to the section below titled "Enhanced podcast authoring tools."

Encoding is covered in depth in Chapter 13, using MP3 encoding examples. To create an AAC file, make sure you choose the AAC codec in whatever encoding application you use. The rest of your settings, such as bit rate, sample rate, and mono or stereo, are exactly the same. The first new thing we have to do is create the text file that determines where the chapters are.

Creating the chapters text file

The text file that determines where the chapters are is written in a language called XML (eXtensible Markup Language). For those of you who have looked at HTML code, the format won't look very daunting. Essentially, it's just a bunch of text, surrounded by tags in angle brackets. Here's a very simple chapters XML file:

```
<?xml version="1.0" encoding="utf-8"?>
<chapters version="1">
  <chapter starttime="00:00">
    <title>Chapter 1</title>
    <picture>MyLogo.jpg</picture>
    <link href="http://www.mywebsite.com">More about my
show</link>
  </chapter>
</chapters>
```

Let's look at it line by line:

```
<?xml version="1.0" encoding="utf-8"?>
```

The first line is the XML name space definition. This must be the first line of your chapters text file.

```
<chapters version="1">
```

The second line, paired with the </chapters> tag at the end of the file, is used to enclose the individual chapter definitions.

```
<chapter starttime="00:00">
```

The third line, combined with the </chapters> tag on line 7, is used to enclose the information for an individual chapter. The <chapter> tag also includes the starttime parameter, which indicates where this chapter begins. The starttime parameter uses the HH:MM:SS.FF syntax, so you can specify an exact frame reference if you need a high degree of accuracy. If you don't need to be that exact, you can just use minutes and seconds, or even just seconds.

```
<title>Chapter 1</title>
```

The text for your chapter title is enclosed in <title></title> tags.

```
<picture>MyLogo.jpg</picture>
```

The location of the image for this chapter is enclosed in <picture></picture> tags.

> **TIP**
>
> **Chapter Tool doesn't play well with spaces in file names. You have to either make sure your image file names don't include spaces or replace the spaces with "%20" (without the quotes). So instead of My Logo.jpg, you'd reference My%20Logo.jpg.**

```
<link href="http://www.mywebsite.com">More about my show</link>
```

Finally, the link tag appears. The link tags enclose the text to display as a link. The URL for the link is included in the href parameter. These are the only tags used in a chapters text file. For each chapter, a new set of <chapter></chapter> tags are used, which enclose new title, picture, and link tags. Chapters don't necessarily have to include pictures or links; in fact, you don't even have to include a title! There are a few rules that dictate how iTunes and iPods interpret the chapter information:

- You must include a chapter title if you want the audience to be able to navigate to it.

- Picture and link information is *inherited*. If you don't specify a new picture or link for a chapter, the picture and link from the previous chapter remain on screen.

- To remove a link or a picture from the screen, insert empty link or picture tags like this:
  ```
  <link></link>
  <picture></picture>
  ```

- If you're just changing or removing a picture or link and don't want to insert a chapter point for people to navigate to, leave out the title tag.

That's really all you have to know to create your chapters text file. You can create it in any plain text editor. It's a good idea to save your chapters text file in the same directory as your podcast, because it makes the last step of the process easier. The last step of the process uses Chapter Tool to combine the text information with your encoded file to create the enhanced podcast.

Creating the enhanced podcast using Chapter Tool

The last step of the enhanced podcast creation process uses Chapter Tool to combine the encoded file with the chapters text file. As mentioned previously, Chapter Tool is available only on Macs. There's another bit of bad news for those of you who aren't experienced computer users: Chapter Tool is a command line tool, which means you have to manually type the command in a terminal window.

If you've never heard of a terminal window, don't worry. It's really not that difficult. First, we'll step you through the Chapter Tool syntax and then show you a step-by-step example in the next section. The syntax of Chapter Tool is simple. Here's what a Chapter Tool command looks like:

```
ChapterTool -x chaptertext.xml -a audiofile.m4a -o
enhancedfile.m4a
```

Chapter Tool takes three arguments:

- **-x:** Specifies the name of the chapters text file.
- **-a:** Specifies the name of the source audio file.
- **-o:** Specifies the name of the enhanced podcast file that will be created.

This example assumes that the chapters text file and source audio file are in the same directory as Chapter Tool. The enhanced audio file also must be written to the same directory. If necessary, you can specify directories for these files if they're not in the same directory.

Creating an enhanced QuickTime podcast by hand

Now it's time to combine the three basic steps into a simple example. Some of these steps are covered in more detail in other sections, so this example skips some of the detail:

1. Download and install Chapter Tool Beta from the Apple site. The Apple site recommends that you move Chapter Tool into the Music directory of your hard drive. It's easiest if you create a working directory in the Chapter Tool directory and place your work files there.

2. Encode your edited audio podcast in the AAC format. Make sure you place it in your working directory.

3. Create the chapters text file. Remember to start the file with the name space declaration and then the <chapters> tag.

4. For each chapter, include a title, link, and picture, if required, and enclose them in <chapter></chapter> tags.

5. When you're finished adding chapter information, add a </chapters> tag to close the <chapters> tag at the beginning of the file. Save the text file in your working directory. Although it's not necessary, it's good practice to use the .xml file extension.

6. Combine these files using Chapter Tool. If you're an experienced terminal user, run the Chapter Tool command, being careful with your paths. If you've never used terminal before, move to Step 7.

7. First, open a terminal window. To find the terminal application, open the finder. You'll find Terminal in the Utilities folder, which is in your Applications folder, as shown in Figure 14.3. Double-click Terminal to open the application.

FIGURE 14.3

Terminal is in the Utilities folder in the Applications directory.

8. The first thing you'll see is a window that lists the last time you logged in, a short welcome message, and a command prompt that looks something like this:

```
Last login: Thu Aug 17 22:24:12 on ttyp1
Welcome to Darwin!
smack-g5:~ smack$
```

The last line is called the prompt. The tilde symbol (~) indicates the home directory, and the name after the tilde indicates who is logged in. So "~ smack" means "smack is in smack's home directory."

9. Now you have to navigate to the directory that contains Chapter Tool. If you followed Apple's recommendation, navigate to the Music directory. Because the terminal window is a Unix shell, you have to know a few Unix commands:

   ▪ **cd:** is used to change directories.

   ▪ **ls:** is used to list the contents of a directory.

   By default, terminal starts you off in your home directory. To see the contents of your home directory, use the ls command:

   ```
   $ ls
   ```

10. You'll see a number of default directories, possibly along with directories that you have created. To navigate to the Music directory, use the cd command:

    ```
    $ cd Music
    ```

11. As you navigate to different directories, the command prompt changes to indicate the directory you're in. Inside the Music directory, if you use the ls command, you should see a ChapterTool directory. Navigate into the ChapterTool directory:

    ```
    $ cd ChapterTool
    ```

12. If you created a working directory in the ChapterTool directory, navigate into that directory:

    ```
    $ cd work
    ```

13. Use the ls command to make sure the audio and XML files are in the directory. Provided they are, you're ready to use Chapter Tool. But there's one thing to note: Chapter Tool is in the directory *above* this directory. That's okay; you can use the "dot-dot" syntax to call a program in the directory above the current directory:

    ```
    ../ChapterTool -x chaptertext.xml -a audiofile.m4a -o
    enhancedfile.m4a
    ```

    Of course, you have to make sure to use the correct names for your XML file, your audio file, and your output. Another way to do this would be to stay in the ChapterTool directory and execute the ChapterTool command using directory references to the files:

```
./ChapterTool -x work/chaptertext.xml -a work/audiofile.m4a -o
work/enhancedfile.m4a
```

In this case there is only a single dot and a slash before the ChapterTool command. The single dot means "this directory."

That's all there is to it. Chapter Tool creates the new output file that includes all the chapter information. You should test it in iTunes to make sure all your chapters, images, and links work as expected.

NOTE One thing you may want to consider is coming up with a naming standard to distinguish your enhanced podcasts from your standard podcasts. For example, you may want to append an "_e" to the file name to give a visual indication that it is the enhanced version.

Enhanced podcast authoring tools

The process described in the preceding steps is the not the only way to create an enhanced podcast. A number of tools with graphic user interfaces are available for those of you who fear the command line. We can't go into them all here, and more may be available by the time you read this:

- RBSoftware's ChapterToolMe: www.rbsoftware.net/?page=ctm
- Brad Wright's VizaCast: www.dvdxdv.com/VizaCast.try.htm
- Podcast AV by Old Jewel Software: www.oldjewelsoftware.com/products/podcastav/
- Podcast Maker by Potion Factory: www.potionfactory.com/podcastmaker
- Podcaster: www.kudlian.com/products/podcaster

Enhanced Windows Media podcasts

Enhanced QuickTime podcasts are great for folks who use iTunes and iPods, but they don't do much for the people who don't. Many Windows Media compatible devices are available, and any minute now Microsoft will be announcing their own portable player, the Zune. You can create a similar experience for these people by creating an enhanced Windows Media podcast.

Enhanced Windows Media podcasts are slightly different from enhanced QuickTime podcasts. You can add chapters to your file, which Windows Media refers to as markers. You can't, however, embed images in a Windows Media podcast. Instead, you embed a URL (called a *script command*), which the Windows Media player sends to a browser. The browser loads the URL, which can display a Web page, an image, or anything else a browser can display.

There is, however, a slight complication with script commands embedded in the Windows Media Player. The default install of the Windows Media player does not execute script commands. This is done as a security measure. So, if you want to create an enhanced Windows Media podcast that includes script commands, you'll have to convince people to enable script commands in Windows Media Player.

Enabling script commands isn't difficult, per se. All you have to do is choose Options from the Tools menu, click the Security tab, and make sure the "Run Script Commands when present" check box is checked, as shown in Figure 14.4. However, convincing your audience to do this may be another matter.

FIGURE 14.4

Enabling script commands in the Windows Media Player

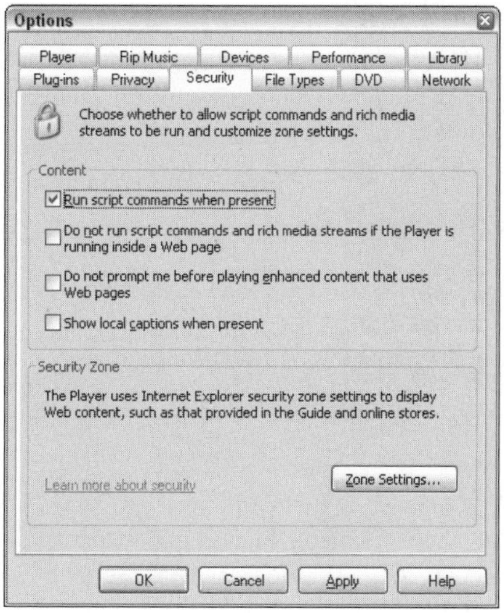

Enhanced Windows Media podcasts display differently depending on how they're viewed. In the Windows Media player, an enhanced podcast makes chapters available via the File Markers option on the View menu, as shown in Figure 14.5. If the player is embedded in a Web page, you can use JavaScript or VBScript code to expose the markers and offer the viewer navigation.

NOTE Enhanced Windows Media podcasts can be played back on portable media players that support the Windows Media format, but the script commands and markers are ignored.

FIGURE 14.5

Where chapters (markers) are displayed in the Windows Media Player

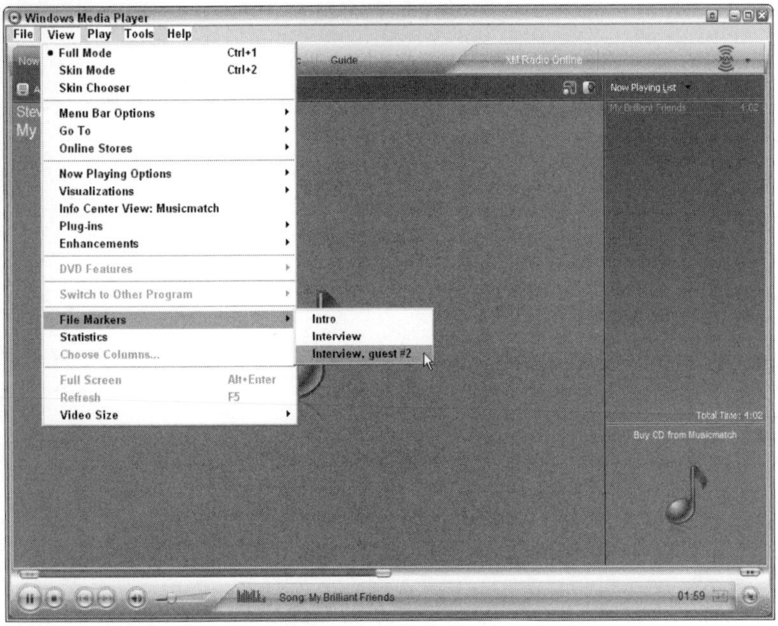

Using Windows Media File Editor

Enhanced Windows Media podcasts are created using the Windows Media File Editor, which is a free application available from the Microsoft Web site as part of the Windows Media 9 Series encoder. It's a simple tool that allows you to add script commands and markers to your Windows Media files. Just open your Windows Media podcast, and add markers or scripts where you want them:

1. Download the Windows Media File Editor from the Microsoft Web site, and install it.

   www.microsoft.com/windows/windowsmedia/download/

2. Open the Windows Media File Editor, and open your podcast by choosing Open from the File Menu, as shown in Figure 14.6.

FIGURE 14.6

The Windows Media File Editor

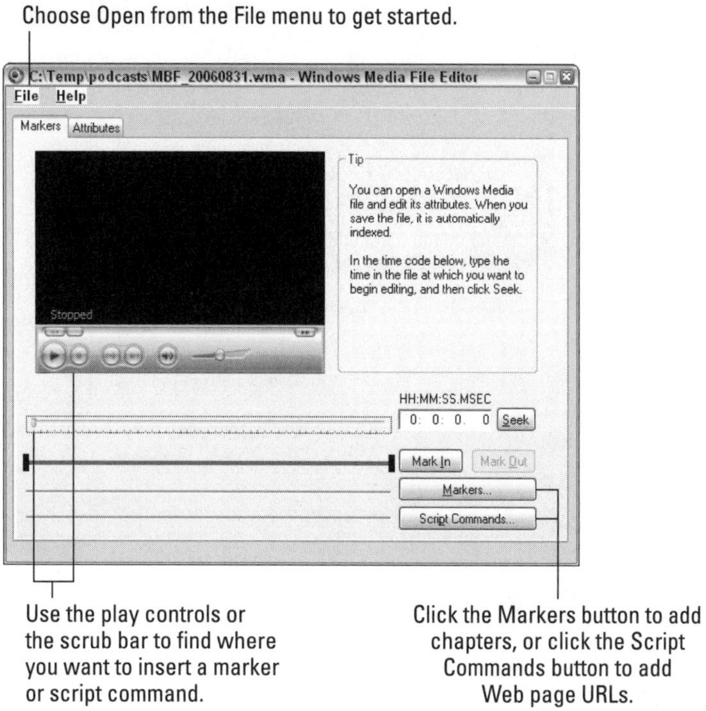

Choose Open from the File menu to get started.

Use the play controls or the scrub bar to find where you want to insert a marker or script command.

Click the Markers button to add chapters, or click the Script Commands button to add Web page URLs.

3. Use the player controls or the scrub bar to find the position in your podcast where you want to add a chapter marker or where you want a script command to send a URL to the browser.

4. When you've found the spot in the podcast where you want to add a marker, click the Markers button. This pops up the Markers window. Click the Add button to enter the information for this marker, as shown in Figure 14.7.

5. Enter text for the chapter marker. You'll notice that the time for the marker automatically corresponds to the location of the scrub bar. You can type over the time value if you want to change it.

FIGURE 14.7

Adding a chapter marker

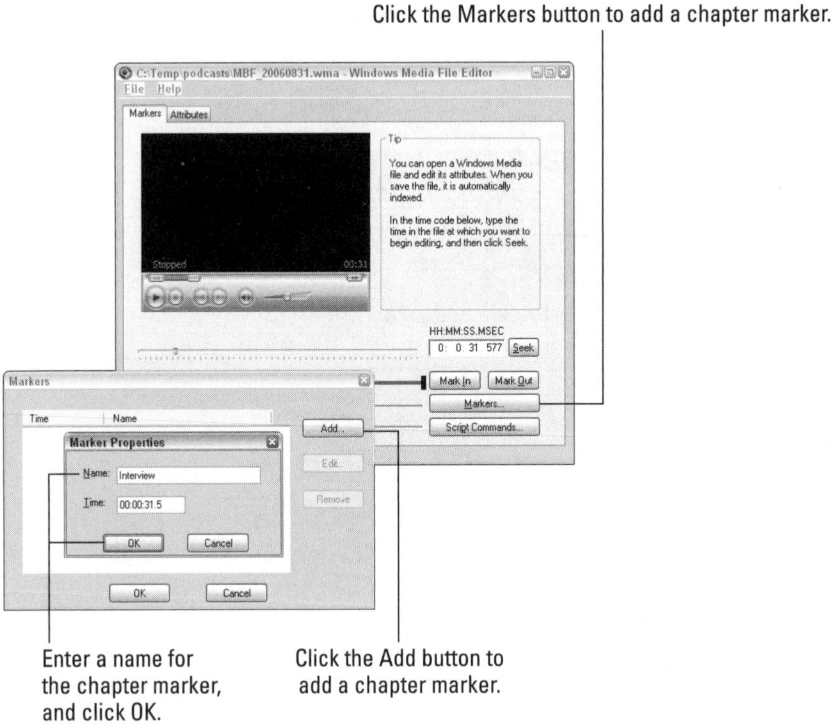

Click the Markers button to add a chapter marker.

Enter a name for
the chapter marker,
and click OK.

Click the Add button to
add a chapter marker.

6. Enter as many chapter markers as you like. The Markers window also lets you edit or remove markers. You'll notice that as you add markers, they're listed sequentially in the markers window, as well as represented as marks on the time lines next to the Markers and Script Commands buttons, as shown in Figure 14.8. These markers can be dragged back and forth if you want to adjust their position.

7. If you want to add script commands, the process is basically the same, though the pop-up window offers a drop-down menu where you can select URL or TEXT. Leave this set at URL, and type the URL where you want to direct people, as shown in Figure 14.9.

NOTE Script commands are of dubious value in podcasts, particularly because you have to convince your audience to disable a security setting to make them work. However, if they don't have script commands enabled, the Windows Media Player simply ignores them. So it doesn't cost you anything to put them in there.

FIGURE 14.8

FIGURE 14.8

The chapter markers on the time line

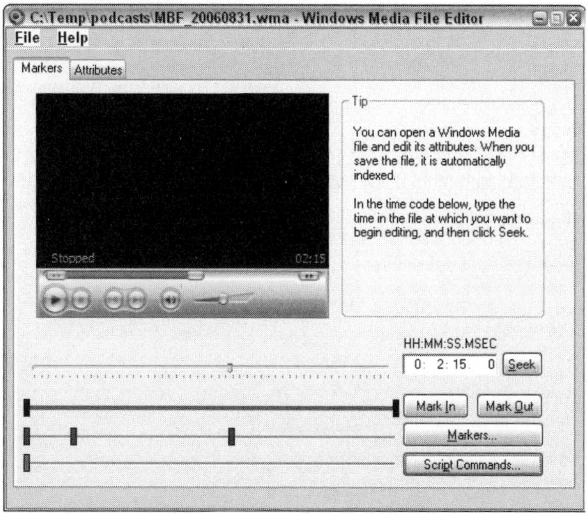

FIGURE 14.9

Adding a script command

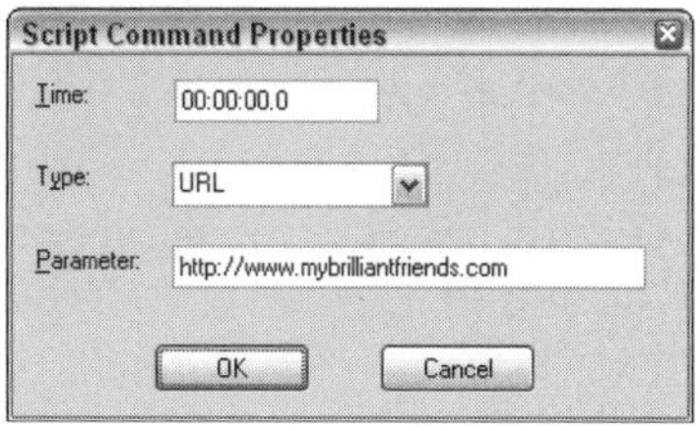

8. When you're finished adding your markers (and script commands), save your file. You can save it over the original version if you want, because any players that don't understand markers or script commands simply ignore them.

NOTE Some editing platforms support markers and can automatically export the markers to the Windows Media format. Check your audio-editing or video-editing program for details.

Chaptering in MP3 Files? Why not!

The preceding section in this chapter talked about enhanced podcasts and categorically stated that you have to create podcasts in either the QuickTime or Windows Media formats to create enhanced podcasts, because there is no way to include chapter information in an MP3 file.

This is not strictly true. In fact, the ID3 standard has already been extended to include the ability to have a table of contents and chapters. This extension of the ID3 standard was done in great part by the engineers at the BBC, who are looking to extend the open-source standard. In fact, you can already download a tool to create MP3 files with chapters at Source Forge, the open-source development site:

```
id3v2-chap-tool.sourceforge.net/
```

There's just one minor problem: lack of support. There are currently no MP3 players that support this extension to the standard. However, given the interest in podcasting, and in particular the interest in keeping it open and cross-platform, it's only a matter of time before someone adds support for this.

However, given that Apple already has an enhanced format that works on Macs and iPods, it's doubtful that this will work on iPods any time soon.

Summary

This chapter covered ways to improve your podcasts and some bells and whistles that you can add to your podcasts. Specifically, we discussed the following topics:

- If your target resolution is larger than 320×240 and your source video is interlaced, you should use a de-interlacing filter for best quality.

- Noise filters are good for cleaning up slightly noisy video, but can be rather heavy-handed. If you're having problems with noise in your video, you should check your production chain.

- You should always use two-pass encoding because it provides higher quality.

- Variable-bit-rate (VBR) encoding also provides better quality, but can be difficult to download. If you use VBR, you should use the bit-rate-constrained VBR.

- You should always embed a logo graphic into your podcast. This can be done using iTunes or any decent ID3 tag editor.

- Enhanced QuickTime podcasts offer embedded images, links, and chapter markers, but require AAC encoded podcasts; therefore, they'll play back only in iTunes and iPods.

- Enhanced Windows Media podcasts offer chapter markers and script commands that can steer people to Web pages. However, script commands are disabled by default in the Windows Media Player for security reasons.

Part IV

Distribution—Making Your Podcast Available to Your Audience

Chapter 15

Distribution: An Overview

This chapter marks the beginning of Part IV of this book, which is dedicated to distribution. Distribution is the process by which the podcast you have produced and encoded ends up in the hands of your listeners.

This chapter gives an overview of the distribution process including the basics of how distribution works, RSS, podcast aggregators (sometimes called pod-catchers), and the many ways to host and distribute your media files.

How Podcast Distribution Works

If you've made it this far through the book, you've produced a high-quality podcast and encoded it into a high-quality encoded format suitable for distri-bution. The next step is to get it in the hands of your audience. This involves three steps:

1. Creating a Web site where your podcast content is published

2. Adding your podcast to one or more of the podcasting directories so your listeners can find and subscribe to your podcast

3. Posting each episode of your podcast to your Web site

First, you must create a Web site where your podcast is published. At this stage, you also want to register a domain name to give your podcast a unique and easy-to-find home on the Web. For example, if your podcast is all about pike fishing, you may want to register www.thepikepodcast.com. Then you must decide what kind of information you want to put on the site. The simplest and most common type of site for podcasters is a blog.

IN THIS CHAPTER

Understanding podcasting distribution

RSS: Podcasting's big secret

Podcast aggregators and podcatchers

Podcast media file distributors

Blog is short for "Web log." Blogging technology was developed to give people a simple way to create and update an online journal. Blogs also include syndication using RSS (Really Simple Syndication) so that folks who want to keep in touch can subscribe to your blog and get notified when you update your blog.

Podcasting and blogging share a common heritage. The technology underlying podcast distribution is the same technology that lets people know when you update your blog. The only difference with podcasting is that the update notification includes the address to a media file, which is your podcast. The added media file is known as an enclosure. Many blogging systems now support podcasting, automatically adding enclosures to blog posts.

After you create the Web site to host your podcast, make sure new listeners can find you. If you want to build an audience, you have to make sure you're as easy to find as possible. Many podcasts are discovered when people do Web searches for content they're interested in and are directed to the site that hosts your podcast. Therefore, you should make sure that your Web site includes plenty of information about your podcast and that your search keywords and description make it easy for search engines to find you.

Another way people discover podcasts is by browsing one of the many directories that list podcasts such as Apple's iTunes, Podcasting News, and Odeo. You should get your podcast listed in as many podcast directories as possible. (See Appendix A for a list of such directories.)

CROSS-REF More information about registering your podcast in many of the popular podcasting directories is found in Chapter 25, "Promoting Your Podcast."

After your site is up and running and you're ready to start publishing, you have to post your podcast. Each time you record a new episode of your podcast, you need to do a number of things before it is available to the general public (see Figure 15.1):

1. Update the Web page content where your podcast is hosted. Put a description of the new show, and list any keywords or guest names that may attract people to your podcast.

2. Upload the actual podcast media file. Your Web site software or podcast host may have an automated way of doing this, or you may have to use FTP (file transfer protocol) software.

3. Create or update a small text, known as an RSS feed, that lets people know when you have posted a new podcast episode.

Some blogging and podcast creation software packages offer automated creation and editing of RSS feeds. The RSS feed is the critical part of your podcast, because it enables people to subscribe to your podcast and allows news aggregators and podcatchers to automatically download your podcast episodes.

CROSS-REF Creating Web pages and RSS feeds is discussed in more detail in Chapter 16, "RSS (Really Simple Syndication)."

FIGURE 15.1

The steps involved with posting a new episode of your podcast

1. Upload your media to the designated media server or podcast distribution network.

2. Update your RSS file to include information about the new episode and the enclosure URL (which indicates the location of the new episode on your media server).

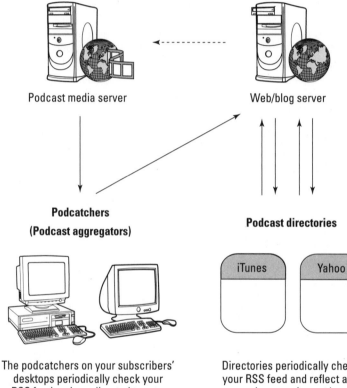

Podcast media server

Web/blog server

Podcatchers
(Podcast aggregators)

Podcast directories

iTunes   Yahoo

The podcatchers on your subscribers' desktops periodically check your RSS feed and are directed to your media server to download the noted episodes.

Directories periodically check your RSS feed and reflect any updates you've made.

This diagram shows separate servers to meet the RSS and media hosting needs. These may be on the same server or may be combined into one integrated service by a podcast hosting provider.

RSS: Podcasting's Secret Sauce

The RSS file really is the secret behind podcasting. RSS is an acronym for Really Simple Syndication.

In the late 1990s, during the first Internet "boom," companies such as Marimba, PointCast, and DataChannel offered news distribution based on a technology known as "push." Push technology delivered information to client PCs when the server was ready to push the content. This turned out to be technologically impractical because the server tried to push the information out all at once, which consumed huge amounts of bandwidth and clogged personal and corporate networks.

A new model called "poll then pull" evolved. In this model, the server did not send out updated information until it was asked for by individual clients. RSS, inspired by the various content syndication formats used in push technology, was originally proposed by Dave Winer in 1997 while he was running a company called Userland. RSS was designed to enable a particular form of news syndication known today as blogging. Other companies such as Netscape and Microsoft developed versions of their own known as RDF and CDF.

Winer attempted to work with Netscape and Microsoft until Netscape abandoned the effort in 1999, and in late 2000 Userland released version 0.92 of the standard. Optional elements including the crucial <enclosure> tag were added in 2002, and RSS was eventually standardized in its current form in July 2003. Several versions of the RSS story exist; you can read them at these sites:

```
http://blogs.law.harvard.edu/tech/rssVersionHistory
http://goatee.net/2003/rss-history.html
http://www.rss-specifications.com/history-rss.htm
```

As interesting as the RSS story is, all you really need to know at this point is that your RSS feed is a critical ingredient in the success of your podcast. It's the mechanism by which folks subscribe to and automatically receive your new episodes. RSS is covered in more detail in Chapter 16. The next section provides an overview of how RSS works and what an RSS file looks like.

How RSS Works

When you are ready to publish a podcast episode, you need to follow these two steps to make it available to your listeners:

1. Upload your media file from your computer to the server from which your listeners will download it. They can either do this directly from your Web page or by using a podcatcher.

2. Add your newly uploaded episode to your RSS feed so that when podcatchers check your RSS feed, they'll see that it has changed and automatically begin downloading the new podcast.

Podcatchers "check your feed" periodically by reading the RSS feed for your podcast and examining the results. If the podcatcher sees an episode that is dated later than the last episode it downloaded, it downloads it.

Some media distribution services/blogging services update your RSS automatically. If you want to do it manually, it is as simple as adding a new episode to your RSS feed. Adding a new episode to an RSS feed requires adding information to the existing feed using XML tags. This sounds more complicated than it actually is. The simplest way to explain this is to show an example.

Here are two instances of the same RSS feed. The first is the simplest example of an RSS feed that represents a podcast with only one episode. The details about the episode are contained within the <item></item> tags.

```
<?xml version="1.0" encoding="windows-1252"?>
<rss version="2.0">
 <channel>
  <title>Podcasting Bible Podcast</title>
  <description>Main feed Podcasting Bible Podcast</description>
  <link>http://www.podcastingbible.com/rss.xml</link>

  <item>
   <title>Episode 1</title>
   <description>My first podcast episode</description>
   <enclosure
     url="http://www.podcastingbible.com/episode1.mp3"
     length="210692"
     type="audio/mpeg"/>
  </item>

 </channel>
</rss>
```

Now let's look at the same RSS feed after a second episode has been added.

```
<?xml version="1.0" encoding="windows-1252"?>
<rss version="2.0">
 <channel>
  <title>Podcasting Pro Bible Podcast</title>
  <description>Main feed Podcasting Pro Bible
Podcast</description>
  <link>http://www.podcastingbible.com/rss.xml</link>

  <item>
   <title>Episode 2</title>
   <description>My second podcast episode</description>
   <enclosure
     url="http://www.podcastingbible.com/episode2.mp3"
     length="342112"
```

```
      type="audio/mpeg"/>
   </item>

  <item>
   <title>Episode 1</title>
   <description>My first podcast episode</description>
   <enclosure
     url="http://www.podcastingbible.com/episode1.mp3"
     length="210692"
     type="audio/mpeg"/>
  </item>

 </channel>
</rss>
```

Look closely, and you'll see that the files really aren't very different. The beginning and end of the files are exactly the same. All that has changed is that information about another episode has been added. The added information includes the title, and description of the new episode, as well as the location of the new podcast file. You can put additional information in your RSS feed, which is covered in the next chapter. This example shows how simple an RSS feed can be and how simple adding a new episode is.

Podcast Aggregators and Podcatchers

Although some users will come to your Web site, click the link to an individual podcast, and listen to a specific episode, most podcast listeners use a dedicated program called an aggregator that periodically checks your RSS feed and downloads new episodes as you post them. Aggregators that are specifically designed for podcast subscriptions are often called podcatchers.

There are nearly 100 different podcatchers that run on every conceivable platform, including mobile phones. These are some of the most popular podcatchers:

- Apple's iTunes (Mac, Windows)
- Juice (formerly called iPodder) (Mac, Windows, Linux)
- Doppler Radio (Windows)
- jPodder (Mac, Windows)
- Winamp (Windows)

You can find a list of podcatchers here:

```
http://www.podcastingnews.com/topics/Podcast_Software.html
```

We recommend using a podcatcher even if you do not plan to put your podcast content onto a portable music device because it enables the automatic downloading process and provides an easy way to navigate your ever-growing library of content.

Podcast Media File Distributors

For people to be able to download your podcast, you have to put your podcast files on a server that can be reached via HTTP (hypertext transfer protocol). Because HTTP is the protocol used to deliver Web pages, you can place your podcasts on your Web server if you already have a Web site or a Web site host. Alternatively, if you've signed up for a podcast hosting account, it inevitably includes access to a server where you can place your podcasts.

In the RSS section of this chapter, you may have noticed in the XML code that the enclosure tag, which links to the podcast media file, includes a link that uses the HTTP protocol:

```
<enclosure
    url="http://www.podcastingbible.com/episode2.mp3"
    length="342112"
    type="audio/mpeg"/>
```

Each time a podcatcher sees a new episode, it uses the URL in the enclosure tag to initiate a download from whichever server you're using to host your podcast.

Whether you're hosting your own server, using a Web site hosting service, or a podcast hosting service, you should be aware of the storage and bandwidth issues surrounding podcasting. You may be familiar with Web hosting accounts, where you are allotted a certain amount of storage and throughput for your Web site. If you decide to host your podcast on your Web site, be careful because podcast files are significantly larger than Web pages and images. Consequently, podcast files have a large impact on your storage and throughput. For example, the average Web page is less than 100 KB, including all the images. If 100 people look at your Web page, that's only 10,000 KB or roughly 10 megabytes. That's not a significant amount of storage or throughput. Let's say those same 100 people are subscribed to your podcast, which is a 20-minute audio podcast, encoded in MP3 format at 128 Kbps. First, let's calculate the size of the podcast file:

```
128Kbps * 60 secs/min * 20 mins = 153,600 Kilobits
153,600 / 8 bits/byte = 19,200 Kbytes (KB)
19,200 KB / 1024 = 18.75 MB
```

So your podcast file is nearly 20 MB. When those 100 people download your podcast, it uses 1,875 MB, which is nearly 2 GB worth of throughput. Depending on your Web site or podcast hosting deal, this may end up costing money. If you're hosting your Web site off a small server sitting at the end of your home broadband connection, you may run into speed issues, or your broadband provider may call you asking why you're using so much bandwidth.

At some point, you may want to consider working with one of the numerous services that can host your podcast files. There are plenty of them, with lots of different service offerings and pricing schemes. Do plenty of research, and choose a podcast host that offers the service that's best for you.

CROSS-REF Podcast hosting services are covered in Chapter 17, "Findind a Home for Your Podcast." For a list of podcast hosting providers, please see Appendix A, "Podcasting Resources."

Summary

This chapter covered the basic information you need to know in order to get your podcast in the hands of your listeners:

- Integrating your podcast into your Web site
- How podcasting and RSS work together
- Where to host your podcast file

In the next three chapters, we describe RSS, Web site hosting, and podcast hosting in more detail.

Chapter 16

RSS (Really Simple Syndication)

Chapter 15 gave an overview of how podcasting distribution works. At the heart of podcasting distribution is a technology called RSS (Really Simple Syndication). More and more blogging solutions and podcast hosting services offer automated solutions to take care of your RSS feed, so you don't have to worry about it. But to understand how podcasting works, it's helpful to understand the nuts and bolts of RSS.

In this chapter, we look at where RSS came from and at the contents of an RSS feed line by line. Then we create an RSS feed using special RSS creation software. By the end of the chapter, you should have a good feeling for what goes into an RSS feed and why it is necessary.

RSS = Really Simple Syndication

RSS originally was designed to enable automated distribution of news and other textual information. RSS offered a framework where client applications could determine whether new information was available on news sites. These applications, usually called *aggregators*, displayed the news headlines and made it simpler for people to keep track of news from a number of disparate sources. It wasn't long before folks figured out that the RSS standard could be used to fuel a distribution revolution.

NOTE Technically, when we talk about "Really Simple Syndication," we're talking about RSS 2.0. This is assumed throughout this chapter, although in the examples later in the chapter we have to specifically declare the RSS version we're using in our RSS files.

The short history of RSS

RSS has been around for years in many different formats. The blogging explosion catalyzed the RSS community as people demanded a way to keep track of a large number of their favorite bloggers. RSS capabilities began to be built in to blogging applications. In 2000, the RSS standard was extended to include files associated with the RSS feed. These associated files were called *enclosures*.

> **NOTE** The history of RSS is colorful and fraught with political in-fighting, accusations, innuendo, and plenty of name-calling (much like the early podcasting community). In some ways, it's hard to believe that RSS caught on at all, given the environment in which it was bred. If you're interested in the complete history of RSS, start with the Wikipedia article and browse through some of the links offered there:
>
> ```
> http://en.wikipedia.org/wiki/RSS_%28file_format%29
> ```

Enclosures were what made podcasting possible. People were already subscribing to each other's blogs, and many bloggers were experimenting with audio. Adding audio to an existing feed suddenly became as simple as adding a line of code to the existing RSS feed. Within a year, an audio experiment turned into a content explosion.

How RSS works

The beauty of RSS lies in its simplicity. An RSS feed contains information about your podcast and about individual episodes of your podcast. Each time you create a new episode of your podcast, you add information to your feed about the new episode. That's all you have to worry about on your side of the equation.

On the other side are your listeners. They'll be using a podcast aggregator, such as iTunes or FireAnt. When they subscribe to your podcast, what they're actually doing is telling their podcast software to periodically check your RSS feed to see if anything has been added. If and when something is added, the software lets the listener know that a new episode is available, and it automatically downloads the episode (if that is how they have their software configured).

That's basically it. To add a little more detail, we'll break the process into six distinct steps:

1. You create your podcast media file and upload it to a server. Sometimes, this is the same server that hosts your blog and RSS feed; sometimes, they are hosted on different servers.

2. You modify your RSS feed, to indicate that you've posted a new episode of your podcast. You can do this in one of two ways:

   a. You write a blog entry, often containing show notes, and post it to your Web site using Web-based blogging tools or using a program that talks to your blogging software. When you post your blog entry, you specify that there is an associated file and enter the link in the <enclosure> tag.

   b. You manually create your RSS feed using either a text editor or a tool (such as FeedForAll, Feeder, Podifer, WebPod) and upload the updated RSS file to your Web server.

3. Listeners who are interested in your podcast subscribe either by clicking your RSS link or by entering the URL for your feed into a podcast aggregator such as iTunes, Juice, or Doppler.

4. The podcast aggregator periodically checks your RSS feed to see if anything new has been added.

5. When the podcast aggregator finds new items with enclosures, it downloads the media files using the URL specified in the <enclosure> tags.

6. After the download has completed, the podcasts are automatically transferred to a portable media player (if that's what the listener specified).

Essentially, all you have to do is update your RSS feed, and remember to upload the updated feed to your site. The rest happens automatically. So how do you update your RSS feed? For the most part, you'll probably be using a simple tool, but before we show you the tools, you should understand what is inside the RSS feed and why.

The contents of an RSS file

An RSS feed is simply a text file that contains information about your podcast. RSS feeds are written in Extensible Markup Language (XML), which means all the information is contained within or surrounded by *tags*. If you've ever looked at HTML code, the language used to author Web pages, you won't be too frightened by an RSS feed. Here's a simple example of information contained within tags:

```
<title>Episode 1</title>
```

This is obviously the title of something; that much is evident by the fact that "Episode 1" is surrounded by the <title> and </title> tags. This tag is known as a *binary* tag, meaning that it takes an opening tag and a closing tag. The closing tag is like the opening tag, but has a slash before the tag name. Everything between the tags, including the spaces, is considered the value of the tag. RSS feeds contain many different tags that describe your podcast.

The official RSS standard specifies a single XML document that describes a *channel*, which contains one or more *items*, which in turn contain individual *content blocks*. The content blocks contain the actual information in the feed, such as title and description of the content. In the case of podcasting, the items, at minimum, contain a link to the media file using an optional element called an *enclosure* and usually contain a *description* element that describes the media.

> **NOTE** The current version of the RSS 2.0 standard is documented here:
>
> `blogs.law.harvard.edu/tech/rss`

If this is starting to sound like gibberish, don't worry. RSS feeds are actually very simple. In fact, the simplest way to learn about them is to look at one. If you can get past all the angle brackets, you can see that they're just a highly structured way of organizing information. Let's look at a simple RSS feed and then explain each of the components. First, the simple RSS feed:

NOTE   The following example has line numbers for reference only; XML files do not have line numbers. Also, the example is indented for clarity. XML files do not require this, but it sure makes your files much easier to read, especially if there's an error in your file.

```
1 <?xml version="1.0" encoding="utf-8"?>
2 <rss version="2.0">
3   <channel>
4     <title>Podcasting Bible Podcast</title>
5     <link>http://www.podcastingbible.com/rss.xml</link>
6     <description>Main feed Podcasting Bible
Podcast</description>
7     <item>
8       <title>Episode 1</title>
9       <description>My first podcast episode</description>
10      <enclosure
11           url="http://www.podcastingbible.com/episode1.mp3"
12           length="210692"
13           type="audio/mpeg"/>
14    </item>
15  </channel>
16 </rss>
```

Now we'll look at this line by line and explain what each tag is for:

1. **<?xml>:** This is the XML declaration, which lets applications know what XML version is being used.

2. **<rss>:** Along with the </rss> tag on line 16, this tag marks the beginning (and end) of the RSS feed. The version="2.0" attribute must be specified.

3. **<channel>:** Along with the </channel> tag on line 15, these tags mark the beginning and end of a particular channel. Channels have three required elements (detailed next) and zero or more items.

4. **<title>:** This is the name of the channel.

5. **<link>:** The URL of the Web site corresponding to the channel is entered here.

6. **<description>:** A sentence or phrase describing the content of the channel is entered here.

7. **<item>:** The item tags are used to encapsulate all the information about a particular blog entry and/or podcast. All tags under **item** are optional, but at least one of **title** or **description** must be present. Listed next are the tags usually used with podcasting.

8. **<title>:** Another title tag, this refers to the name of the podcast episode.

9. **<description>:** This is the plain text or HTML text of the "blog" post. Normally, podcasts have associated blog posts with show notes or links to other Web sites mentioned in the podcast.

10. **<enclosure>**: This is the key tag for podcasting, because it is the tag that describes where the actual podcast file can be downloaded. This tag has three required attributes,

NOTE The <enclosure> tag is known as a *unary* tag, in that all the values are contained within the single tag. Unary tags require a closing slash "/" before the final angle bracket.

11. **url**: This is where your media file is located (for example, http://myserver.com/podcast3.mp3).

12. **length**: The size in bytes of your media file goes in this tag.

13. **type**: This is the MIME type of your podcast file. For .MP3 files this is "audio/mpeg."

NOTE The url, length, and type attributes are all required in the enclosure tag, and all the values must be surrounded by double quotes.

14. **</item>**: This tag marks the end of this item.

15. **</channel>**: This tag marks the end of this particular channel.

16. **</rss>**: This tag marks the end of the RSS feed.

Each of the tags in this example is required. You can use many other optional tags in your RSS feed. In addition, Apple has created its own set of tags that are required for your feed to be listed on iTunes. Because iTunes is such an important place to have your podcast listed, we talk about these in the next section.

Optional RSS tags

In addition to the tags listed in the preceding example, a number of other tags can be used in your RSS feed. They're not required, but they provide more information about your podcast, which is always a good thing. The following tags are optional sub-elements of the item tag, which means they must be enclosed by the <item></item> tags:

- **<author>**: Contains the e-mail address of the author of the item
- **<category>**: Can be a list of keywords, so that the item is included in one or more categories
- **<comments>**: Allows you to provide a page for comments and encloses the URL in the comments tags
- **<guid>**: Contains a unique string that identifies the item
- **<pubDate>**: Indicates when the item was published
- **<source>**: Contains the RSS channel from which the item came

Apple RSS tags

In order to get more information about podcasts that they include on the iTunes store, Apple has created a number of tags that can be added to an RSS feed. They are required to get featured placement on the iTunes podcast page. Of course, there's no guarantee that you'll get featured placement, but it's a good idea not to disqualify your podcast from consideration by leaving them out.

The first thing you have to do if you're using the Apple RSS tags is to declare the namespace at the top of your RSS feed, right after the initial XML declaration. The namespace declaration is inserted into the <rss> tag, like this:

```
<rss xmlns:itunes="http://www.itunes.com/dtds/podcast-1.0.dtd" version="2.0">
```

This namespace declaration lets the application know where to find out what the special tags that are used in this XML file mean. The namespace parameter breaks down as follows:

- xmlns: This indicates that the parameter is an XML namespace.
- itunes: This is the name of the namespace.
- "http://www.itunes.com/dtds/podcast-1.0.dtd": This is the URL to a document that the application can download if it doesn't already understand the tags in this namespace.

After you've defined the iTunes namespace, you can use any of the iTunes tags in your RSS feed. Table 16.1 lists the iTunes tags, whether they apply to the podcast or individual episodes, and where the contained information is displayed in iTunes. These are not required, but the more you use, the better experience your audience will have if they're using the iTunes store or iTunes to listen to your podcast.

TABLE 16.1

iTunes RSS tags

Tag	Refers to Podcast or Single Episode	Where Contents Appear in iTunes
<itunes:author>	Both	In the Artist column
<itunes:block>	Both	Prevents an episode or entire podcast from appearing
<itunes:category>	Podcast	In the Category column in the iTunes Music Store
<itunes:image>	Podcast	Where the album/podcast art is displayed
<Itunes:duration>	Episode	In the Time column
<itunes:explicit>	Both	Displays a parental advisory graphic in the Name column
<itunes:keywords>	Both	Not displayed, but included in iTunes searches
<itunes:new-feed-url>	Podcast	Not displayed; used to inform iTunes that the URL for the podcast RSS fed has changed
<itunes:owner>	Podcast	Not displayed; used for contacting producer of the podcast
<itunes:subtitle>	Both	Displayed in the iTunes description column
<itunes:summary>	Both	Displayed when the information icon is clicked

NOTE iTunes categories are pre-defined — you have to select one of the existing categories. These categories have changed recently and may do so again. You can see the most recent list of categories here:

```
http://www.apple.com/itunes/store/podcaststechspecs.html
```

Creating RSS Feeds

An RSS feed is simply a text file that contains specific tags that define the name of your podcast, called the <channel> in RSS, and each of your podcast episodes, called an <item> in RSS. RSS feeds can be created using a text or XML editor or specialized tools. RSS feed creation tools allow you to enter your information into various fields and automatically produce a properly formatted RSS XML file. In addition, some podcast hosting services include Web-based tools that automatically update your RSS feed.

In the preceding section, we looked at a simple RSS feed. RSS feeds can be considerably more complex, especially if you include all the tags and namespace extensions supported by Apple's iTunes.

Let's look a fully tricked-out RSS feed. This one is from The Dawn and Drew Show. This is the real deal except that we've included only one episode:

```
<rss version="2.0">
<channel>
    <title>The Dawn and Drew Show!</title>
    <itunes:author>Dawn Miceli and Drew Domkus</itunes:author>
    <link>http://www.podshow.com/shows/?show=dawnanddrew</link>
    <description>two ex gutter punks fall in love, buy a retired farm in
wisconsin and tell the world their dirty secrets... always profane, rarely
profound.</description>
    <itunes:subtitle>listen up bitches!</itunes:subtitle>
    <itunes:summary>two ex gutter punks fall in love, buy a retired farm in
wisconsin and tell the world their dirty secrets... always profane, rarely
profound.</itunes:summary>
    <language>en</language>
    <copyright>(c) 2006 podshow.com</copyright>
    <itunes:owner>
        <itunes:name>Dawn Miceli and Drew Domkus</itunes:name>
        <itunes:email>dawnanddrewshow@gmail.com</itunes:email>
    </itunes:owner>
    <image>

<url>http://www.podshow.com/images/shows/240/shows/small/dawnndrewshow.jpg</url>
    <title>The Dawn and Drew Show!</title>
    <link>http://www.podshow.com/shows/?show=dawnanddrew</link>
    </image>
    <itunes:image
href="http://www.podshow.com/images/shows/240/shows/med/dawnndrewshow.jpg"/>
```

```
<category>Podcast</category>
<itunes:explicit>yes</itunes:explicit>
<itunes:keywords>dawn and drew, married couple, wisconsin</itunes:keywords>
<lastBuildDate>Mon, 18 Sep 2006 02:40:40 -0500</lastBuildDate>
<docs>http://blogs.law.harvard.edu/tech/rss</docs>
<generator>PodShow PDN</generator>
<managingEditor>dawnanddrewshow@gmail.com</managingEditor>
<webMaster>webmaster@podshow.com</webMaster>
<itunes:category text="Comedy"/>

<item>
    <title>DNDS-408</title>
    <itunes:author>Dawn Miceli and Drew Domkus</itunes:author>
    <link>http://m.podshow.com/media/240/episodes/26549/dawnanddrew-
26549-09-18-2006.mp3</link>
    <description>DNDS-408 - dawn talks about fishing off the pier in
california for the first time and catching a skate before we play a few choice
audio clips that i\'d been saving up, then we\'re off to dallas in the morning
for the NAB and our first ever live audience D&amp;D show this wednesday.<hr />
<ul> <li> iTunes: <a
href="http://phobos.apple.com/WebObjects/MZStore.woa/wa/viewPodcast?id=73331700"
> subscribe</a> or <a
href="https://phobos.apple.com/WebObjects/MZFinance.woa/wa/addUserReview?type=Po
dcast&amp;id=73331700"> write a review</a> </li> <li> <a
href="http://dawnanddrew.podshow.com/feed/"> subscribe via RSS</a> </li> <li>
audio comments: <strong> 206-666-3825</strong> or <a
href="http://www.dawnanddrew.com/dnds_bb/viewtopic.php?t=495"> submit an
intro</a> </li> </ul> </description>
    <itunes:subtitle>DNDS-408 - dawn talks about fishing off the pier in
california for the first time and catching a skate before we play a few choice
audio clips that i'd been saving up, then we're off to dallas in
the</itunes:subtitle>
    <itunes:summary>DNDS-408 - dawn talks about fishing off the pier in
california for the first time and catching a skate before we play a few choice
audio clips that i\'d been saving up, then we\'re off to dallas in the morning
for the NAB and our first ever live audience D&amp;D show this wednesday.<hr />
<ul> <li> iTunes: <a
href="http://phobos.apple.com/WebObjects/MZStore.woa/wa/viewPodcast?id=73331700"
> subscribe</a> or <a
href="https://phobos.apple.com/WebObjects/MZFinance.woa/wa/addUserReview?type=Po
dcast&amp;id=73331700"> write a review</a> </li> <li> <a
href="http://dawnanddrew.podshow.com/feed/"> subscribe via RSS</a> </li> <li>
audio comments: <strong> 206-666-3825</strong> or <a
href="http://www.dawnanddrew.com/dnds_bb/viewtopic.php?t=495"> submit an
intro</a> </li> </ul>
    </itunes:summary>
    <pubDate>Mon, 18 Sep 2006 02:31:58 -0500</pubDate>
    <category>Podcast</category>
    <itunes:explicit>yes</itunes:explicit>
```

```
        <itunes:keywords>dawn and drew, married couple,
wisconsin</itunes:keywords>
        <enclosure
url="http://m.podshow.com/media/240/episodes/26549/dawnanddrew-
26549-09-18-2006.mp3" length="25100364" type="audio/mpeg"/>
        </item>
    </channel>
</rss>
```

As you can see, this feed is a little longer and more complicated than the simple feed we looked at previously. It's not actually that daunting. There's just lots of information, including HTML in some of the tags. The thing to bear in mind is that with a file this long, there is plenty of room for error. If you're planning on creating or editing your file by hand using a text or XML editor, be careful and make sure your file ends up as a valid XML file. Be sure to use one of the XML validator tools discussed later in the chapter.

Text and XML editors

The simplest, although not the easiest, way to create an RSS feed is to use a text or XML editor. To use this approach, you need to have good attention to detail, be comfortable with XML syntax, and have the full details of your podcast media files. In particular you need to know the URL, size, and MIME type of your media file.

There are lots of text editors available. If you're going this route, be sure that you're using a simple text editor, not an application like WordPad or Microsoft Word. While these are excellent programs for doing word processing, they're not appropriate for creating XML files. The reason is that word processors don't show you everything that they put in a file. In fact they include lots of formatting data that is hidden from you. However, this formatting information is not valid in an XML file.

These are examples of text editors you can use:

■ Notepad (Windows)

■ BBEdit (Mac)

■ VI (Linux)

Editing in a simple text editor is pretty basic, as shown in Figure 16.1. You don't get any special tools; you just type in raw XML. One thing you can do is download an existing RSS feed from another podcast and replace the text with text appropriate to your podcast. If you're doing this, be careful not to leave text from the feed you're copying.

Another thing to remember is that you have to file size and MIME types in the length and type parameters of the <enclosure> tag. You must use the correct values for these, or your RSS feed will not work. The length parameter is the size of your file in bytes. You can get this by clicking on the properties of the file in Finder or Explorer, depending on your operating system. The MIME type will be one of the values listed in Table 16.2.

FIGURE 16.1

Editing in Notepad is rudimentary at best.

```
PodcastingBibleRSS.xml - Notepad
File   Edit   Format   View   Help
<?xml version="1.0" encoding="windows-1252"?>
<rss version="2.0">
        <channel>
                <title>Podcasting Bible Podcast</title>
                <description>Main feed Podcasting Bible Podcast</description>
                <link>http://www.podcastingbible.com/rss.xml</link>
                <item>
                        <title>Episode 1</title>
                        <description>My first podcast episode</description>
                        <enclosure
                                url="http://www.podcastingbible.com/episode1.mp3"
                                length="210692"
                                type="audio/mpeg"/>
                </item>
        </channel>
</rss>
```

TABLE 16.2

MIME Types for Common File Types

File	Type
.mp3	audio/mpeg
.m4a	audio/x-m4a
.mp4	video/mp4
.m4v	video/x-m4v
.mov	video/quicktime
.wma	audio/x-ms-wma
.wmv	video/x-ms-wmv
.ra, .rm	audio/x-pn-realaudio

General-purpose XML editors give you more features than simple text editors, including automatic reformatting, syntax checking, and highlighting. Reformatting is handy because it automatically makes your RSS feeds easier to read. The syntax checking makes sure that your file is indeed a valid XML file. The highlighting feature makes valid XML tags "light up" in a particular color. This is a great feature because if you mistakenly type a tag incorrectly, you get a visual indication, because it remains in black and white. Figure 16.2 shows an example of an XML editor, though you won't see the colorful syntax highlighting.

Some examples of XML editors are:

- Altova XMLSpy (Windows)
- Cooktop (Windows)
- XML Mind (Windows, Mac, Linux)
- jEdit (Windows, Mac, Linux)

FIGURE 16.2

XML editors offer more features than simple text editors.

Valid tags, elements, and attributes are highlighted in different colors.

These windows provide lists of valid elements and attributes you can use.

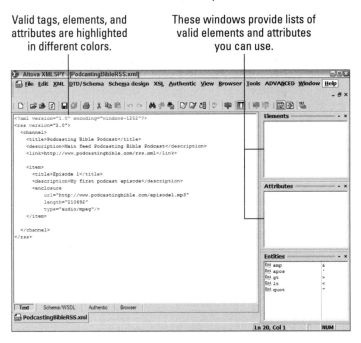

Dedicated RSS feed authoring tools

If your podcast hosting solution doesn't offer some sort of automated RSS feed creation tool, you're probably best using a dedicated RSS tool. These tools are designed to do one thing well — author RSS feeds. Sometimes, they're crude and don't offer many features, but they'll definitely create valid RSS feeds, which is what you're after.

There are a number of different RSS feed authoring tools (and may be even more by the time you read this). Additionally, many podcast recording tools include a publishing wizard to help you create your RSS feed. These are some dedicated RSS feed authoring tools:

- FeedForAll (Windows, Mac)
- Feeder (Mac)
- Podifier (Windows, Mac)

These tools all look and work pretty much the same. You are asked to enter information into a number of fields, in a step-by-step fashion, and at the end of the process, the application generates an RSS feed. This feed should then be placed on your Web server where you host your podcast.

Generating an RSS feed with FeedForAll

FeedForAll is an RSS feed creation tool available for both Windows and Macintosh. It's a form-based fill-in-the-blanks tool that makes creating RSS simple. In fact, using the wizard to create your RSS feed couldn't be easier. FeedForAll is offered as a 30-day trial, after which you must purchase a license. The FeedForAll interface has three tabs that allow you to edit information about Feeds, Items, and Images. The Feeds tab displays a list of RSS feeds and enables entry of both the required and optional data that is part of the RSS <channel> tag. Features for creating, downloading, uploading, and previewing are also available from the menus and toolbar icons. The first time you run FeedForAll, it asks if you want to use the wizard to create your RSS feed. An example of FeedForAll is shown in Figure 16.3.

> **NOTE** FeedForAll is adding iTunes namespace support, but as of the writing of this book this feature was available only in the beta version.

FIGURE 16.3

FeedForAll has a simple wizard-based interface for novices.

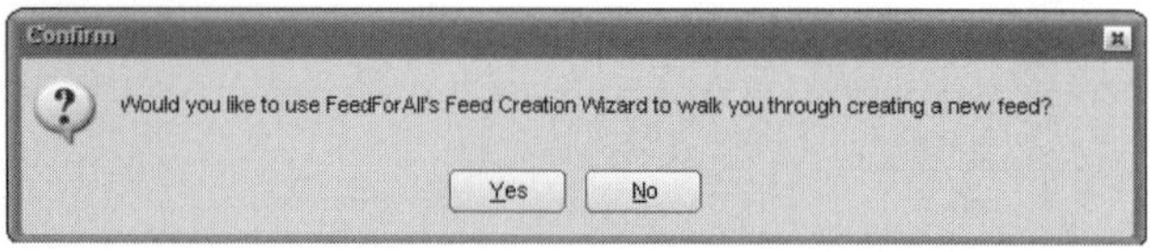

Following this procedure, you can set up the basics about your RSS feed:

1. When the Wizard window pops up, click Yes. If the Wizard window doesn't pop up, choose Wizard from the Feed menu.
2. The first window is just an introduction to the wizard, as shown in Figure 16.4. Click Next.

The opening screen of the Feed Creation Wizard

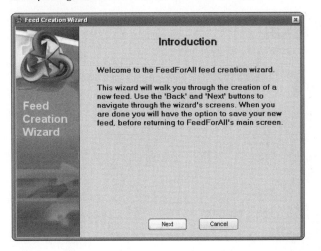

3. The next screen asks you to enter a title for your podcast, as shown in Figure 16.5. Enter your title, and click Next.

Enter a title for your podcast.

4. Next, enter a description for your podcast, as shown in Figure 16.6. Remember that this is a description for the entire podcast, not a particular episode. Click Next.

FIGURE 16.6

Enter a description for your podcast.

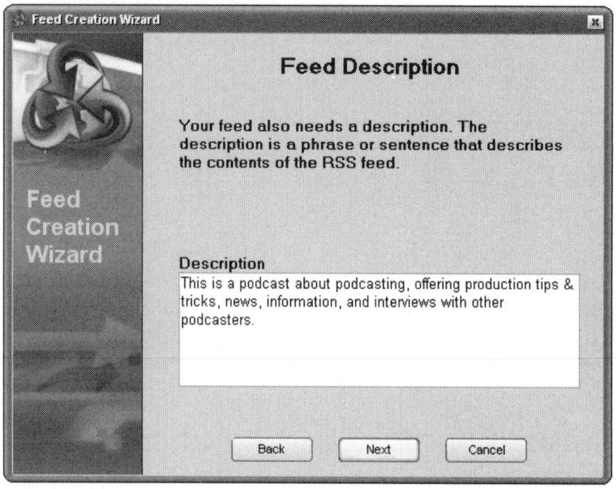

5. Now, it's time to enter a link for your podcast, as shown in Figure 16.7. This should be the link to the Web page where your podcast is hosted. Click Next.

FIGURE 16.7

Enter a link to your podcast's home page.

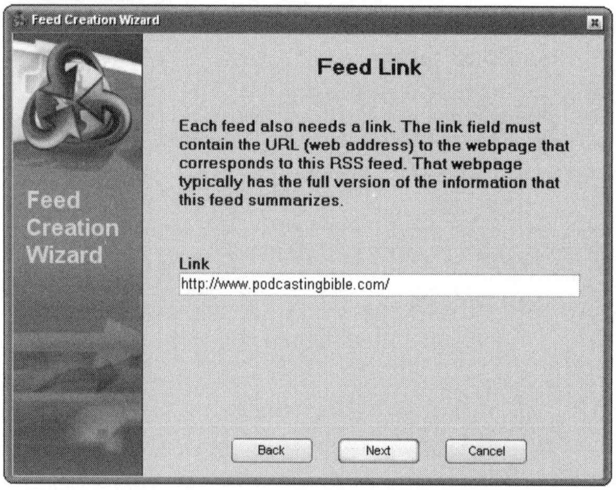

6. At this point, you can either exit the wizard or carry on and enter required information about your fist item, as shown in Figure 16.8. We'll enter the information here. Click Next.

FIGURE 16.8

Click Next to enter information about your first item via the wizard.

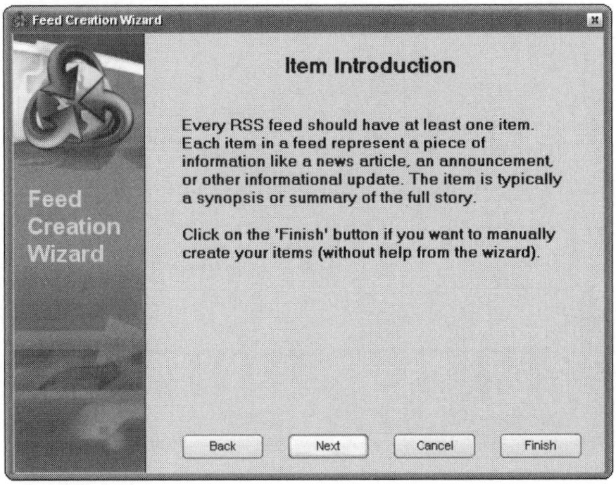

7. Enter a title for this episode of your podcast, as shown in Figure 16.9. Click Next.

FIGURE 16.9

Enter a title for this episode of your podcast.

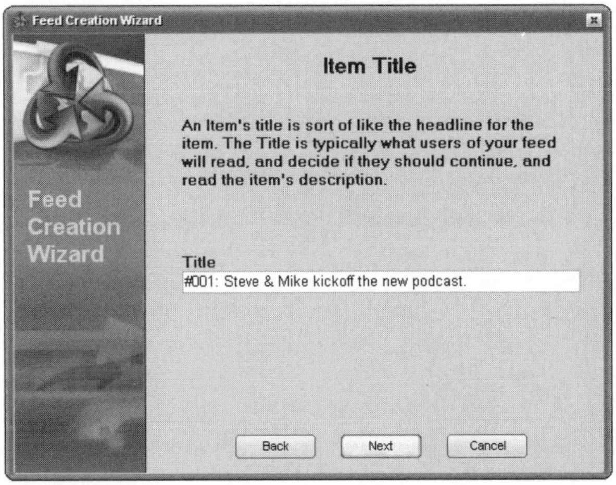

8. Now, enter a description for this episode, as shown in Figure 16.10. Click Next.

FIGURE 16.10

Enter a description for this episode.

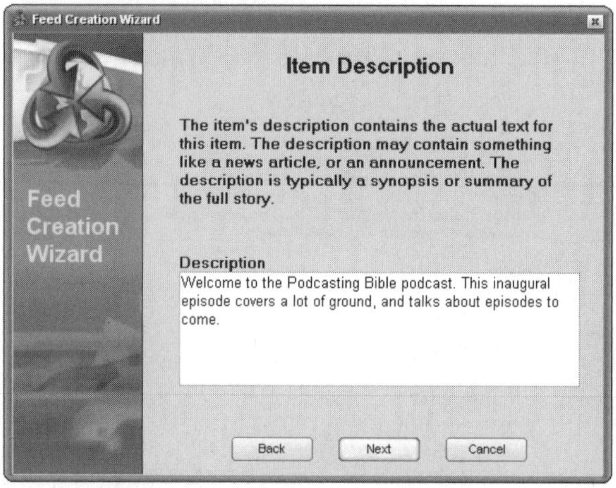

9. Now, enter a link for this episode, shown in Figure 16.11. Again, this should link to the Web page, not the media file. That also goes in the enclosure tag, later.

FIGURE 16.11

Enter a link to the page on which this episode is hosted.

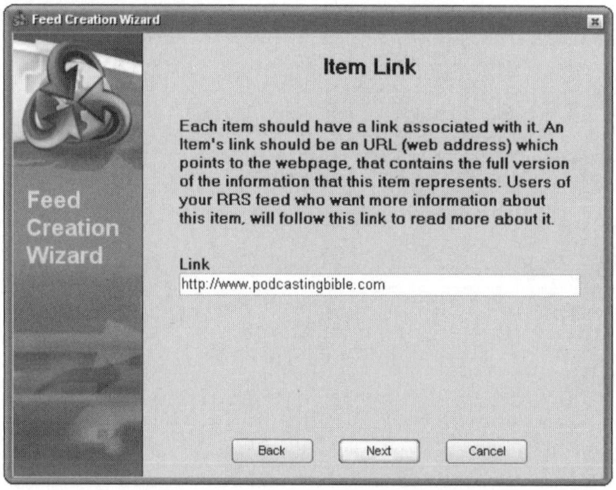

10. At this point, you've entered all the required fields for your RSS feed. You can either add more items to your feed or click Finalize to edit the optional tags, as shown in Figure 16.12. Click Finalize.

FIGURE 16.12

Click Finalize to edit the optional tags.

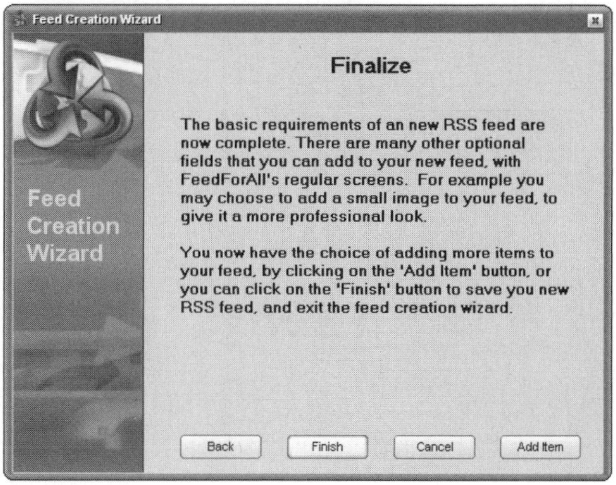

11. FeedForAll now offers to save your RSS feed, like any good program should, as shown in Figure 16.13. Save it, of course. It doesn't matter what you name it, but make sure you maintain the .xml file extension.

FIGURE 16.13

Be sure to save your RSS feed.

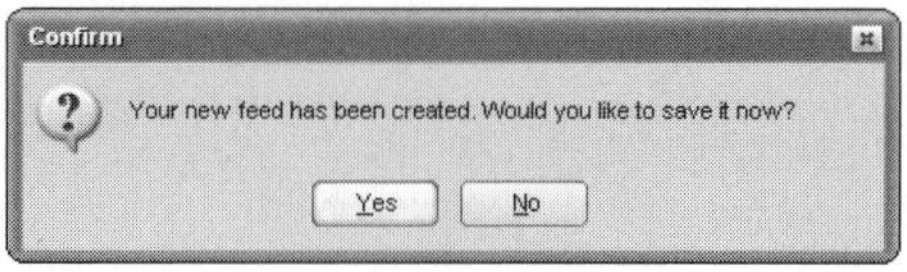

At this point, you should see your XML file listed in the feeds window, on the left side of the interface. On the right side, you should see all the information you entered for your podcast. To enter optional information for your podcast, click the Optional tab, as shown in Figure 16.14.

FIGURE 16.14

Click the Optional tab to enter optional information about your podcast.

Click the Optional tab
to enter optional
information about
your podcast.

You should see your RSS
feed listed here.

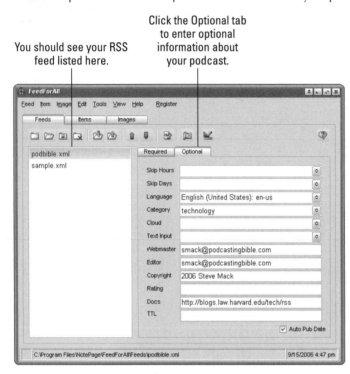

Of course, because all the information on this tab is optional, you don't have to enter it. It's always a good idea to enter the language, as well as a contact e-mail address in either the webmaster or editor field. You may also want to enter copyright information. If you want to find out what all the optional fields are for, you should consult the RSS specification on the Harvard Web site:

    blogs.law.harvard.edu/tech/rss

To enter information about your podcast episode, click the Items tab, as shown in Figure 16.15. You'll see the information you entered in the wizard displayed on the right side. To enter optional information, click the Optional tab.

FIGURE 16.15

The Item tab allows you to edit information about individual episodes.

Click the Items tab
to edit information
about individual episodes.

Click the Optional tab
to enter optional
information.

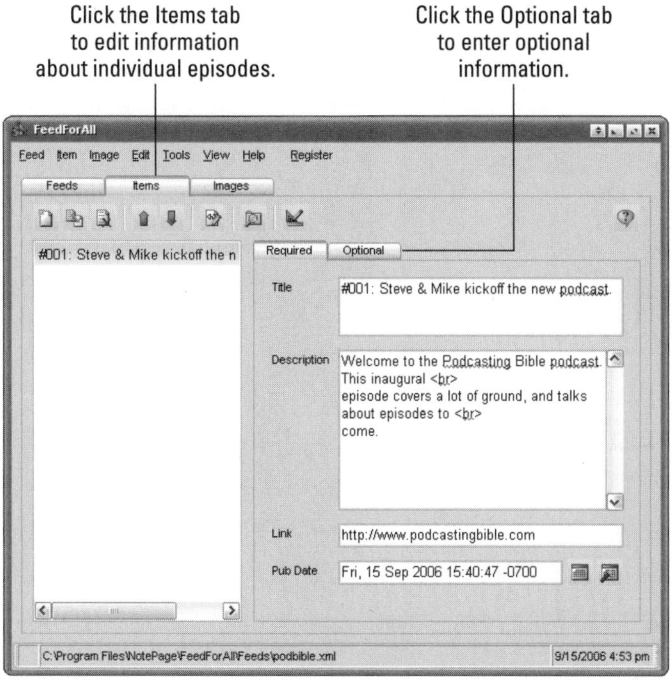

There's one piece of information that you have to enter on the Optional tab that is critical: the enclosure tag information. Without it, your media file won't be distributed. To enter the enclosure tag information, click the button at the right side of the enclosure field. This opens a small window where you enter the URL, the length, and the MIME type of your media file, as shown in Figure 16.16. You also may want to enter a category for this episode, as well as author information.

FIGURE 16.16

Even though it's optional, your RSS feed won't distribute your media file without the enclosure tag information filled out.

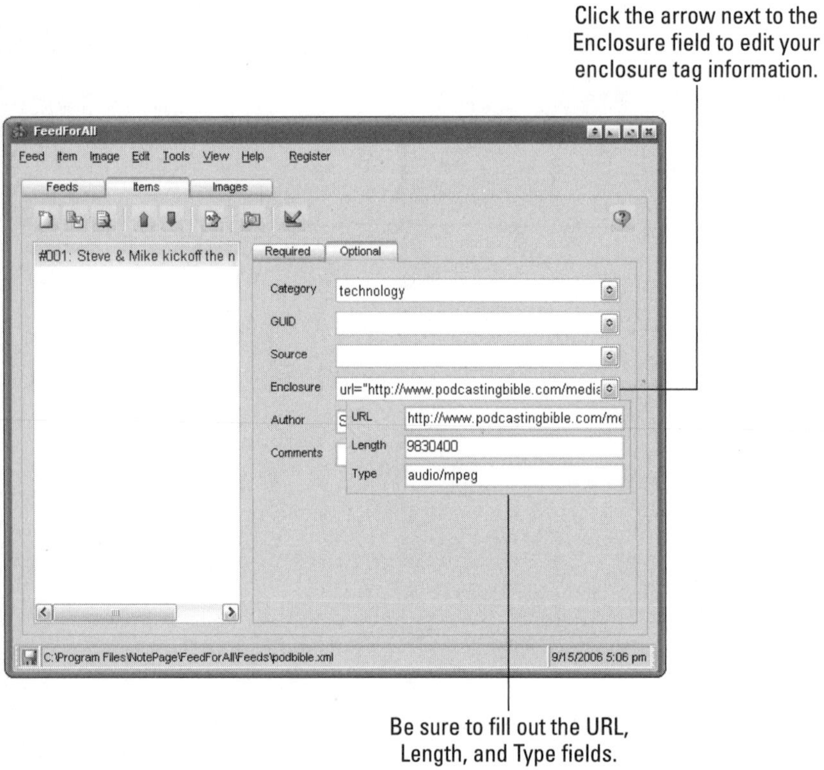

Click the arrow next to the
Enclosure field to edit your
enclosure tag information.

Be sure to fill out the URL,
Length, and Type fields.

FeedForAll makes adding additional items to your RSS feed really easy. The icons on the toolbar, shown in Figure 16.17, allow you to add, clone, delete, and move items around in your feed. They're also handy for enabling HTML editing of your description text and viewing of the final XML code.

If that isn't enough, FeedForAll also lets you add an image to your RSS feed. This isn't the same as the image you can embed in your MP3 file. This is an image that is associated with your RSS feed. Also image-editing capabilities are included, so you can crop, rotate, and resize your image if you'd like. An example of the image-editing screen is shown in Figure 16.18.

FIGURE 16.17

The FeedForAll icons make it easy to manage items in your feed.

Add an item.

Delete an item.

Edit description.

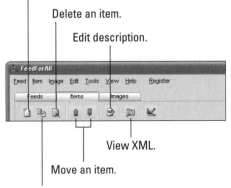

View XML.

Move an item.

Clone an item.

FIGURE 16.18

FeedForAll even includes image editing.

The icons let you load an image
and then upload it to your site.

Click the Editor tab to
edit your image.

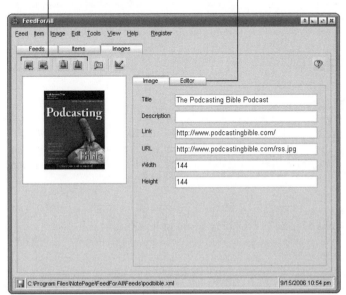

Finally, FeedForAll uploads your RSS feed to your server via FTP. Choose Upload from the Feed menu, and you're presented with a simple FTP dialog box, shown in Figure 16.19. Fill out the FTP information, and you can upload your RSS feed with a single click.

FIGURE 16.19

FeedForAll also includes FTP upload.

FeedForAll has more features, but this example should give you an idea of the things it can do. There are other RSS feed editors available, and they all work more or less the same, with slight differences between their feature sets. Obviously, if you're going to be posting podcast episodes often, you need a solution to make updating your RSS feed easy. If your hosting solution or Web site does not include a tool for updating your RSS feed, you should look into one of the tools mentioned previously.

Handy RSS Tools

Regardless of how you create your RSS feed, other handy RSS tools can make your life a little easier. Feed validators are used to make sure your RSS file uses correct syntax. Feedburner also offers validation, but adds statistical monitoring of your feed so you can track how well your podcast is doing.

Feed validators

Feed validators analyze the contents of your RSS file and tell you whether or not the syntax is valid. These tools are valuable, especially if you create your RSS feed manually. Feed validators are helpful even if you use an XML editor, because in addition to checking XML syntax, they also check to make sure your media file exists at the URL you specified in your feed. Here are three Web-based RSS feed validators:

- `validator.w3.org/feed/`: This validator, pictured in Figure 16.20, is provided by the World Wide Web Consortium (also known as the W3C), the inventors of the World Wide Web. You can either type in the URL of your feed or copy and paste it into a text box, and have it validated. Errors are highlighted in yellow, and it usually tells you how to fix it.

- `feedvalidator.org/`: Provided by the inventors of an alternate feed standard known as ATOM, this one works similarly to the W3C validator, highlighting the errors and providing helpful feedback on how to fix what's wrong.

- `rss.scripting.com/`: Provided by Userland, the company that invented RSS, this programs lets you enter in the URL for your RSS feed and gives you back specific error messages if there any problems with your feed. The error messages, however, aren't always incredibly helpful. For example, it may tell you the number of the character where the error was detected, instead of highlighting the offending line.

FIGURE 16.20

The W3C feed validator

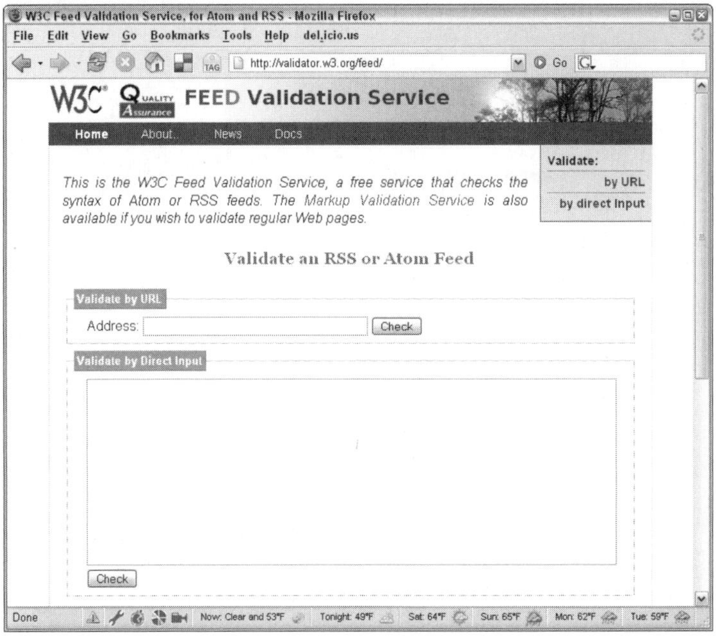

Feedburner

All podcasters want to know how many people are listening to their podcast. Most podcast hosting services feature relatively easy access to that information. However, if you're hosting your own Web site and podcast or if your host doesn't provide statistics, you can use Feedburner to get statistics about your audience.

When you use Feedburner, you author your RSS feed and then type the URL to your feed into a page on Feedburner, shown in Figure 16.21. Feedburner analyzes your RSS feed and lets you know if there is anything wrong with it. You can specify a custom URL that you want for your RSS file. This redirects your RSS traffic through the Feedburner servers so they can provide both statistics and an optional advertising-based monetization opportunity.

Feedburner also offers a service called SmartCast that reads your existing RSS feed and automatically creates a new RSS feed containing enclosure tags, based on links to MP3 files in your blog posts. This is particularly useful for those using blogging systems that don't provide native podcasting support such as Blogger and MSN Spaces.

FIGURE 16.21

"Burning" your RSS feed at Feedburner.com

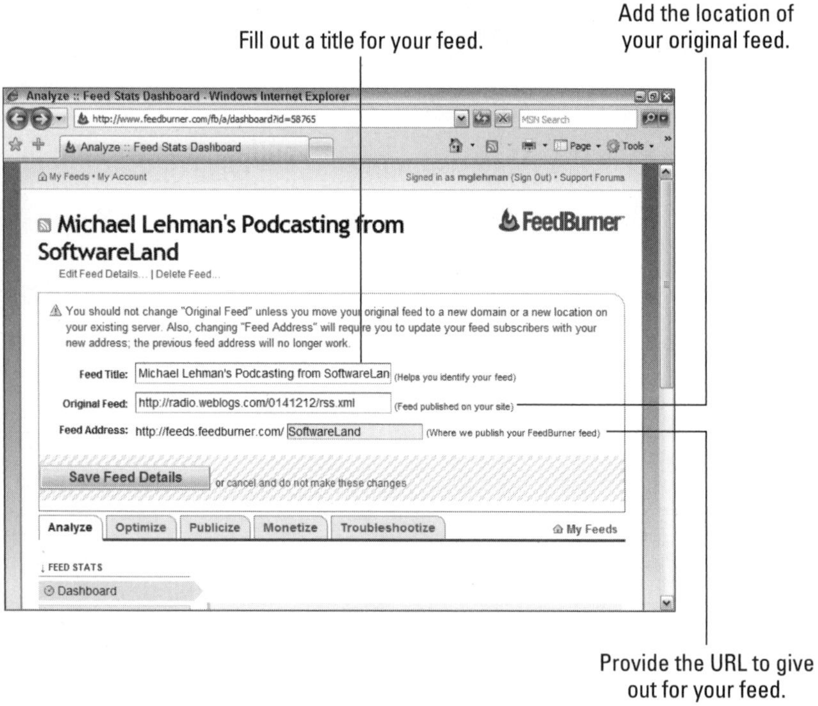

Fill out a title for your feed.

Add the location of your original feed.

Provide the URL to give out for your feed.

Feedburner also has a number of other features that may be of interest to podcasters. For example, it offers a "widget" you can include on your blog that provides a real-time readout of the number of subscribers to your podcast. You may not want to include this when you start off, but it can look pretty impressive if you've got thousands of registered subscribers.

There is one potential downside to using Feedburner. Routing all your RSS traffic through Feedburner gives Feedburner a certain amount of control over your feed. Anyone who subscribes to your podcast using the Feedburner URL will expect to find your podcast there. If you ever decide to stop using Feedburner, migrating people to your new RSS feed may be difficult.

Summary

In this chapter, we talked about RSS in detail, including the following topics:

- RSS feeds are what make subscribing to a podcast possible.
- RSS feeds are simple XML files that include information about your podcast and a link to the actual media file.
- RSS feeds can be authored manually in simple text or XML editors.
- Dedicated RSS authoring tools offer better functionality than text editors.
- It's important to "validate" your RSS feed to make sure it works.

In the next chapter, we talk about how to integrate your podcast into your Web site.

Chapter 17

Finding a Home for Your Podcast

Now that you have an understanding of what RSS is and how to create an RSS file, it's time to figure out how the RSS feed fits into your Web site, where to put it so that people can find it, and how to keep it current. It's not that difficult, but there are a number of different ways to do it, so you should do some long-term thinking about how you want to manage your podcast and your Web site.

You have to make a number of decisions revolving around the two main aspects of your podcast, your Web site and your media. The decisions you make now have a direct effect on your production chain and also affect your long-term planning. After you launch your podcast and crank up your Web site, it can be difficult to change your approach mid-stream. We hope that after you've read this chapter, you'll have a better idea of what the issues are and how you're going to deal with them.

Let's start with an overview of the different ways that you can bring your Web site and podcast to market, along with some of the basic benefits and drawbacks of each option.

What Are the Options?

Up to now, all we've really discussed is how to create your podcast media file, and we talked a little bit about authoring your RSS feed. There's another aspect that can be just as critical to your success: your Web site. Podcasting began as a way to add audio to blogs, and to have this audio automatically transferred to an iPod. However, the concept of podcasting has grown since then. Informal studies have shown that up to 50 percent of all podcasts are watched while sitting in front of a computer. Many of these may be played on iTunes running in the background, but a significant number are also watched on Web sites as embedded presentations.

Podcasting purists are quick to say that these aren't really podcasts. (Some, in fact, say that anything other than an MP3 file is not a podcast.) Call it what you want: A ton of programming is being produced and distributed on the Internet using RSS feeds. This programming can be experienced in many different ways. The question is what sort of experience do you want your audience to have?

In an effort to try to impose some sort of order on this chaos, we can divide the different options into three main categories of ways to host your podcast:

- On a Web site or blog that you manage and maintain yourself
- On a managed Web site or blogging service
- On a dedicated podcast hosting service

Each of these has advantages and disadvantages. In a nutshell, if you're willing to take on the burden of managing and maintaining your site, you'll have the most flexibility and freedom. This flexibility comes at a price, though. If you're managing your own site, you have to worry about lots of things, such as software updates, hackers, spammers, and hardware problems. If you use managed or dedicated systems, you have much less to worry about, but this ease of use comes at the price of flexibility. You may not be able to install some new gadget on your site that you found on an open-source forum, or you may not be able to embed the latest video technology due to support issues. Let's talk about the options in a little more detail.

Managing your own Web site

Managing your own Web site can be lots of fun, but it can also be lots of work. First, you have to either build a server or buy space on a shared server from a Web hosting provider. Some Web hosting providers allow full access to the operating system so that you can tinker to your heart's desire, while others place fairly serious restrictions on what you can and cannot do.

The nice thing about managing your own site is the complete freedom to do what you want, when you want. Assuming that you're running on your own server and have full access to the operating system, you can add forums, install a *wiki* (a shared space where people can add and edit content at will), change the look of your home page, or do anything else that strikes your fancy. You don't have to wait until a host adds new features; you just add them yourself.

Of course, this assumes that you're very comfortable running a server and installing software. Many blog and content management system (CMS) software packages install fairly painlessly these days. At the end of the day, however, if something breaks, you have no one to call. Everything is just fine until something breaks, at which point running your own server can become a nightmare, particularly if your podcast becomes popular and your audience is baying for more.

Scalability is another issue. If your podcast becomes wildly popular or if for some reason iTunes decides to put you on the podcast directory home page, the traffic to your Web site will spike. Web servers are not that complicated, but they can break down, and if they do, it's almost invariably due to a large increase in traffic — precisely the most inconvenient time for them to do so.

As the saying goes in the world of start-ups, having capacity issues is "a good problem to have." If your podcast is so popular that you're frying the small server at the end of your home DSL line, chances are good that you'll be able to afford a new server or afford to move to a managed hosting service. You should try to run your own server only if you're a seasoned Internet veteran with access to some reasonable server hardware and some free time. If you're just starting out, you should consider a managed hosting service or a dedicated podcasting hosting service.

Using a managed hosting service

The next step up in the hosting world is to use a managed hosting service. There are literally hundreds of different hosting options out there. When you register the URL for your podcast, chances are good that the company you use to register your URL will offer some sort of hosting package for your site. Hosting packages generally offer a certain amount of free storage and throughput each month, and you pay overage charges when you exceed either of these.

Some hosting packages come with pre-packaged software that allows you to create a Web site from pre-existing templates or a content management system that allows you to easily manage your Web site. If you're thinking about including e-commerce on your site, you'll need e-commerce capabilities. Many hosting service providers offer "shopping cart" functionality and may even be able to process credit card transactions for you.

One thing you'll want to make sure the service offers is statistics about your Web site traffic. If you're serious about turning your podcast into a business, you'll need accurate traffic statistics to gauge the success of your programming and to lure potential sponsors and advertisers. You should look for as much statistical information as you can find. A number of standardized Web stats packages are satisfactory, but the best hosting companies will offer incredibly detailed stats.

Perhaps the greatest thing about using a managed hosting service is that a significant amount of responsibility is taken off your plate. You no longer have to worry about hardware, and spammers and hackers are the hosting partner's problem. Also, if your statistics are showing a strong upward trend, you should be able to predict when you're going to run out of capacity and work with the hosting partner to add more capacity.

The only drawback to using a managed hosting service is that you may be limited in the software you can install. It depends on the type of service you purchase. You can purchase a shared server, in which case you're usually fairly limited, because the server must be a reliable hosting environment not just for you, but the other clients on the same server. There may be hundreds of other Web sites running off the same shared server.

Hosting services generally also offer dedicated servers, where you essentially lease hardware from them and they keep it up and running. Different hosting services allow different levels of access. Some let you do anything you want to do, while others limit what you can do so that the machine conforms to their standard, which makes it easier for them to maintain. The service you choose depends largely on how much freedom you want to install and modify software.

Using a dedicated podcast hosting service

Dedicated podcast hosting services are managed hosting services that are highly customized for a podcaster's needs. For example, these services usually offer tools to create and update your RSS feed. They may even be automated through some sort of wizard so that when you upload a new media file, your RSS feed is automatically updated. Many dedicated podcast hosting services also offer some sort of Web site for their clients, typically in the form of a blog. The blogs often come with their own URL, so that you can have a somewhat custom Web address. For example, let's pretend that you've decided to host your podcast about pike fishing with a company called Podcast Poodle. You'd probably be given the option to register your own URL like this:

```
mypikepodcast.podcastpoodle.com
```

As good as this may seem, it's not as good as having your own URL, such as:

```
www.mypikepodcast.com
```

In the first example, your Web site is what's known as a *subdomain* of the master domain, which in this case is podcastpoodle.com (please don't register this and sue us). Essentially, you're piggybacking on the master domain. This isn't much of an issue if you're a tiny podcaster, but if you make it big, you really want everyone coming to your Web site, not a page on someone else's site. When you use one of these services to host your site, you are giving up a degree of control, which you may not be happy about later.

That being said, it's hard to argue with the convenience these services offer. They make it extremely easy to get a simple Web site up and running, to keep your RSS feed updated, and to monitor how popular your site and podcast are, because they usually run top ten lists and feature different podcasts from time to time. Many also offer automated tools to list your podcast in a number of other directories, which is especially important when you're first starting out.

Some podcasting hosting services have become destinations themselves, either because they host other popular podcasts or have been around long enough that folks know it's a good place to find podcasts. This can be another compelling reason to go with a dedicated podcast hosting service. They already have an audience looking for podcasts, and there's a good chance that they'll check out your podcast if you're the new kid on the block.

You probably won't have lots of freedom to modify your Web site on these services, because they're so highly specialized to begin with. You also may not own all the real estate on your Web page. For example, the hosting service may reserve the right to advertise on your Web page in order to recoup some of their costs. They may also want to put an ad in your podcast. Seeing as how many of these podcast hosting services give away a serious amount of bandwidth and storage, it's not surprising that they want to try to earn a bit of money from your podcast. It comes with the territory.

CAUTION   Be very careful when signing up for a podcasting hosting service. Some incredibly bad contracts have been floating around that would make any respectable lawyer blush. One host in particular had language in its contract that specified that any podcast placed on its service immediately became the property of the host. In another case, a host was found to be modifying all the RSS feeds hosted on its service, crediting the podcasts to, you guessed it, the hosting service. It may seem like common-sense advice, but read everything put in front of you, preferably with a lawyer present.

What solution is best for you?

With all these options available, how do you choose what is going to work best for you? We can try to summarize your options here:

- **Managing and hosting your own Web site is really only an option if you're very savvy or if you already have an existing site to which you're adding a podcast.** You may run into scaling issues, but because you're savvy, you'll be able to solve them, right?

- **Using a managed Web hosting solution is a great option for your Web site if you're experienced.** The more Web savvy you are, the more you can get out of a managed solution. You'll have your own URL and the freedom to do what you like to your site.

- **Using a dedicated podcast hosting service is a great idea if you're just starting out and don't know much about Web sites.** You can't beat the convenience, and they allow you to focus on the programming, which is what you should be doing anyway. If you outgrow the service, you can cross that bridge when you come to it.

One thing to mention is that this doesn't have to be an either/or situation. For example, you could host your Web site with a managed hosting solution and then use the dedicated podcast hosting service *just to host the podcast file!* Just because a podcast hosting solution offers you a simple Web site doesn't mean that you have to use it. In fact, this is probably the best option for the savvier user. Use a podcasting hosting service to host your podcast media files, and you'll be able to take advantage of its RSS tools, its statistics, and any other special tools it may offer. Then, host your site, complete with your personalized URL, with a Web hosting service, so you can have more flexibility with your site.

Registering Your Domain

It's important to register a domain for your site, because that's your address on the Web. Sure, you can get a sub-domain on another site, which is fine for amateurs, but if you're serious, you really want your own URL. Registering a domain is simple, after you find a URL that you like that hasn't already been registered. The last part is key: While the number of combinations of letters to make up a URL is virtually infinite, the number of good URLs certainly is not. This is why so many Internet start-ups have such curious names; they have to invent something that hasn't been registered yet!

Any registrar can tell you if a URL is available. Just type the URL into the form, and check to see if it has already been registered. There are tons of registrars out there, and any one will do. After you find a URL that hasn't been registered, just break out the credit card and register it. The cost depends on how many years you register it for.

"Squatted" Domains

Lots of domains out there are being "squatted." This means that someone has registered the domain in the hopes that they can sell the URL to someone else. If you find the perfect URL for your site, but it's registered, type it into a browser and see if it's actually a site. Even if there is a site, take a closer look. It may just be a placeholder page. Some folks openly advertise that the URL is for sale; others need to be convinced.

You can usually get contact info from a squatted domain fairly easily. If it's not on the site, you can use the WHOIS command on a registrar's site to get contact information. Some folks hide this information so it isn't picked up by spammers. If that's the case, the registrar can send the owner a message for you.

Most squatters can be talked out of a URL for a reasonable price, say between $500 and $1,500. Some folks are convinced that they're sitting on "six-figure URLs." Don't believe them for a moment. Nobody shells out six figures for a URL anymore.

NOTE Registration fees have dropped significantly in the last few years, to as low as $2.95 a year for a multi-year commitment. If your registrar seems too expensive, it probably is.

After you've registered your domain, you can then set up a Web site and e-mail accounts. Your registrar may offer these as part of a package deal. The Web hosting business is extremely competitive these days. Beware, though, because the margins are getting so thin that the only way these companies can possibly make money is to have thousands and thousands of clients. Be sure to check out the forums of your potential host to see how they respond to client problems. Check ratings sites to see who is getting the highest ratings for service and reliability. Many hosts also allow you to "test drive" their service, to see what their tools can do. Finding a good Web host is just like buying a car; take a bunch out for a spin, and buy the best one you can afford with the features you need.

Is It a Blog or . . .?

Figuring out what features to look for in a hosting service is critical, and to do so you have to decide what kind of a Web site you want. Most podcasts are connected to a blog, because of the shared heritage. They're both episodic and use RSS for distribution purposes. And some blogs include built-in podcasting support. There's no reason, however, that your Web site needs to be limited to a blog.

Blogs are not necessarily limiting, but they are designed for a specific purpose. There's a simple interface that allows the site owner to post regularly and readers to post comments. Blogs automatically take care of archiving old posts, and you can use tags or categories to further organize the posts. Blogs also often allow you to create *static* pages—for example, a page that talks about the author and the podcast. All in all, they're a fairly perfect home for a podcast.

However, you may want even more functionality on your site. For example, you may want a wiki, where you can define terms used in your podcast and your audience can contribute. You may want to include a forum so people can discuss topics that are related to but not necessarily included in a particular podcast episode. You may want to include slide shows, Flash animations, a shop to sell t-shirts and mugs, or any number of other gadgets available on the Web. In this case, you may want to have a more traditional Web site, perhaps with the podcast and the blog as a section of the site.

Blogs don't necessarily preclude any of this functionality, but it's certainly not built in to the software. And because blog software is designed to do one thing well, adding these additional functionalities may not be trivial. It's certainly not impossible, but it takes a bit of know-how. So before you jump in feet first and install any software, it's a good idea to think about what you need from your Web site now, and what you envision needing six months or a year from now. Planning ahead will save you lots of woe later.

Retaining Ownership

Ownership is another thing to bear in mind when you're making the decision about where to host your podcast and what software you're going to use. Another way to think about this is using the concept of *brand*. If you're spending lots of time and effort to create a successful podcast, your podcast, Web site, URL, and everything to do with your production are part of your brand. Building a successful podcast goes hand in hand with building a successful brand.

Successful companies have what's known as *brand equity*. That's why soft drink companies are extremely protective of their brands. They know their brands have intrinsic value, and they don't want anyone else to be profiting from them. You should be thinking the same way as you build your podcasting empire. If your podcast becomes wildly successful, you want the rewards from that success to come back to you — not your podcast hosting partner or your Web hosting partner. These people may play an important part in your success, but without your success, they're just hosting companies. You're the one bringing the programming to the table.

For this reason, it's important that you seriously consider retaining ownership of everything related to your podcast. Earlier in this chapter, we mentioned that you should register a URL for your podcast, and this is a prime reason why. If you're hosting your site on someone else's service, you're surrendering some of your brand equity. As your brand builds, you're also building someone else's brand, because everyone coming to your site sees your hosting partner's branding. This isn't necessarily a bad thing; you may, in fact, be building your brand on the strength of an existing podcast directory's brand. In the long term, however, you want to be able to focus on building your own brand, not someone else's.

Similar to registering your own URL, you should also retain ownership of your RSS feed. It's great that many podcast hosting solutions offer tools that automatically generate valid RSS feeds. However, these feeds live on their servers, so the URL to your feed ends up being:

```
www.podcastpoodle.com/feeds/mypikepodcast.xml
```

Part of that URL has your branding, but the other part has your podcasting host's branding. The problem here is deeper than just the URL. After all, the URL may be hidden beneath a large "Subscribe to my podcast!" button that you put on your home page, so folks may not even notice the branding attribution. The problem is what do you do when you decide to part ways with Podcast Poodle? Everyone who has subscribed to your podcast has done so via the hosting service URL. You have to wean your audience off the old URL of your RSS feed to the new URL, which may not be a simple task, particularly if you have thousands of listeners.

A better approach is to keep control of your RSS feed, so that all your subscribers are coming in through your Web site, subscribing via your RSS feed. That way, you can change hosts at will, Web or podcast, and your audience won't notice a thing. If you change Web hosting partners, people will still find your Web site through the magic of the Internet's Domain Name System (DNS). They just type mypikepodcast.com, and presto, your site pops up. Similarly, if you change hosts for your media files, you just have to change the contents of your enclosure tags in your RSS feed, and no one will ever notice.

Granted, managing your own Web site and maintaining your own RSS feeds may not be for everyone. It requires a significant amount of responsibility and technical know-how. There's a reason that podcast hosting companies are popular: The convenience is hard to pass up. If you decide to go the hosted route, just remember that you may be faced with a difficult decision later if your podcast is as successful as you hope it will be.

Dedicated Podcast Hosting Services

Dedicated podcast services host your podcast files, provide statistics, and automatically generate your RSS. Some also include a Web site, which is usually a blog. Quite a few of these services are available at various price points and offering different services. For example, most offer some sort of Web site with your account. Some offer a free service, but place ads before your podcast. Many offer a trial period, which is a great way to see how well their tools work. Following are a few examples of podcast hosting services.

CROSS-REF For a more complete list of podcasting hosting services, please see Appendix A.

PodOMatic

PodOMatic (www.podomatic.com), shown in Figure 17.1, is a complete podcast hosting solution, complete with a Web site for each member. PodOMatic offers both free and paid accounts. The free service gives you up to 15 GB of data transfer and 500 MB of storage per month. They also have two levels of paid service called Pro and Pro+. The Pro service upgrades your storage to

2 GB and upgrades the bandwidth to 100 GB per month, which they say is equivalent to 4,000 downloads per month for a 15-minute show. The Pro+ service upgrades the transfer to 200 GB per month or 8,000 downloads. PodOMatic Pro is $9.99 per month; PodOMatic Pro+ is $14.99 per month. The Pro services also offer enhanced statistics including what they call geo-ip maps showing where your listeners are on a map of the world.

Liberated Syndication (Libsyn)

Liberated Syndication, or as it's commonly called, Libsyn (`www.libsyn.com`), is another complete podcast hosting service, offering service at rates based on the amount of storage you use, with no limit on the number of downloads. Libsyn, shown in Figure 17.2, charges by the month for its services, which come in $5, $10, $20, and $30 levels with 100MB, 250MB, 525MB, and 800MB storage capacities respectively.

FIGURE 17.1

PodOMatic is a dedicated podcast hosting solution.

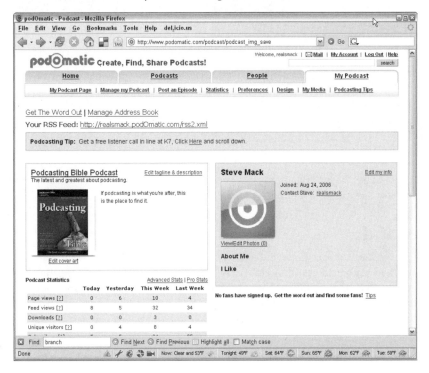

FIGURE 17.2

LibSyn charges only for storage, not for bandwidth used.

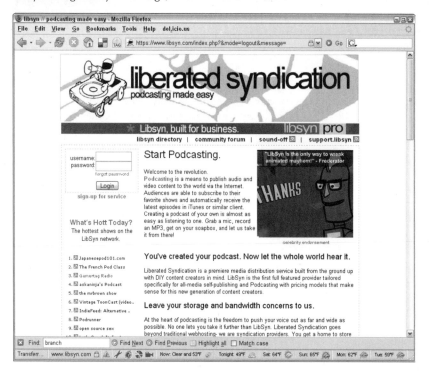

One of the nice things about Libsyn is that it gives you advanced statistics, shown in Figure 17.3, even with the lowest cost service.

Radio Userland

Userland (`radio.userland.com`), shown in Figure 17.4, was founded by Dave Winer, the inventor of RSS and co-inventor, along with Adam Curry, of podcasting. Radio Userland is the oldest blogging service and has had podcasting support built in since the very beginning. Radio Userland has both a Web and a desktop-based component to its service. A basic subscription is $40 per year. Radio Userland does not provide hosting support for your podcast files, but it does have one of the all-time best set of blogging features.

FIGURE 17.3

LibSyn offers detailed statistics to all members.

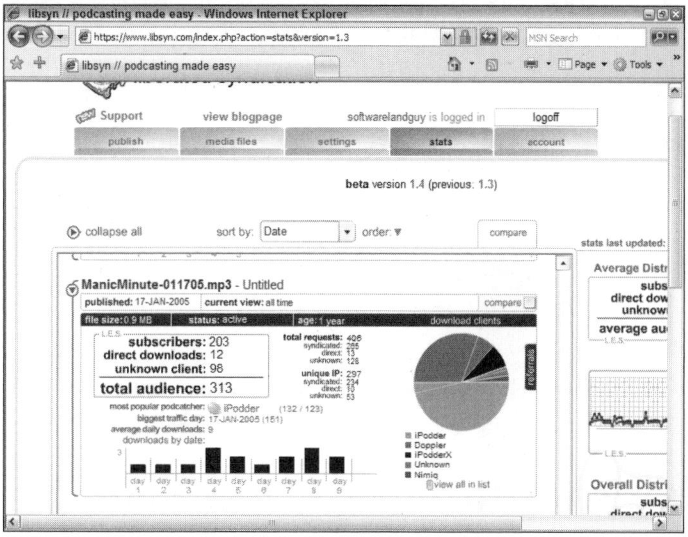

FIGURE 17.4

Radio Userland is the granddaddy of all podcast hosting services.

Blogging services with podcasting support

Many blogging services are starting to offer podcasting support. Some have integrated podcasting support, some have add-ins you can use to enable podcasting support, and some require the use of services such as Feedburner or can be used with a manually created RSS feed.

Here is a short list of some blogging services with different degrees of podcast support:

- **WordPress + PodPress:** Wordpress (`www.wordpress.com`) is a popular blogging service, and PodPress (`www.mightyseek.com/podpress/`) offers a Wordpress plug-in that supports podcasting.

- **Moveable Type:** Moveable Type (`www.sixapart.com/movabletype/`) is a free blogging service that can be used with Feedburner.

- **MSN Spaces:** MSN Spaces (`spaces.live.com`) is the largest free blogging service and can support podcasting by using Feedburner's SmartCast feature.

- **TypePad:** TypePad (`www.typepad.com`) offers built-in podcasting support.

Using Feed Icons to Publicize Your Feed

Chances are good that you'll get most of your subscribers from the larger directory services if you're diligent about listing your podcast. However, that's not the only way to get subscribers. Quite a few may find your Web page via a search engine, particularly if your topic is unique. In this case, it's important to showcase your podcast on your Web page. You want visitors to know in a split second that your Web page is more than just a blog. You want them to see that you have a podcast and that they can subscribe with a single, easy-to-find button.

Until recently, the problem was that there was no single universally accepted icon to indicate that a podcast was available. Different sites used different icons and different colors. Some folks took the original RSS icon, which was a small orange box with the letters "RSS" in white, and substituted the letters "POD." The good people at the Mozilla Foundation decided it would be best if a standardized icon were developed. The logic behind the development was that the icon should not include any abbreviations or acronyms, because people wouldn't necessarily understand what XML or RSS stood for, nor should they have to. They came up with the orange icon shown in Figure 17.5 (shown here in grayscale, obviously).

FIGURE 17.5

The "standardized" RSS icon

As with most things in the world of podcasting, the icon was loved by some and hated by others. There was plenty of lively discussion, which was pretty much brought to a halt when Microsoft decided to use the same icon for its upcoming Internet Explorer 7.0 release. Although you'll probably still see mavericks out there using their own iconography, most people will gravitate toward the Firefox/IE icon, and it will become the de facto standard.

> **NOTE** The Mozilla Foundation has publicized usage guidelines for feed icons here:
>
> `www.mozilla.org/foundation/feed-icon-guidelines/`

In most cases, you'll want the RSS icon to link to your RSS feed. However, for those folks who subscribe to podcasts using iTunes, you can make their subscription easier by posting a link to your feed via the iTunes store. For example, the link to subscribe to the Dawn and Drew Show on iTunes looks like this:

> `phobos.apple.com/WebObjects/MZStore.woa/wa/viewPodcast?id=73331700`

When you click this link, it automatically opens iTunes and subscribes you to the Dawn and Drew show, with just one click. To find out what the direct link to your podcast in iTunes is, just Ctrl+click (right-click in Windows) the image you uploaded for your show. This opens a little window that lets you copy the URL for your show for linking purposes.

Now that you have the iTunes direct link, the question is what icon should you use to link to it? You don't want to use the standard RSS icon, because it doesn't work for folks who don't use iTunes to listen to podcasts. You want some way of letting people know that the link is *specifically* for iTunes users. Unfortunately, there's no right answer here. Folks have designed their own icons for this purpose, and there is no Apple-approved version.

Of course, if you're offering a special button for iTunes listeners, you may also want to offer a button for folks who use Yahoo! Podcasts, Odeo, Google, or any other number of podcast subscription services. And if you're offering your podcast in a number of different formats, you need to have an RSS feed for each format and ideally some sort of icon for each one. Again, there are no standards here. Peter Forret has created a nice set of icons that use a miniaturized version of the RSS feed icon along with wording indicating what the buttons specifically do. You can see his icons here:

> `web.forret.com/tools/podicons.asp`

> **NOTE** If you want to tweak what Peter has done, he's kind and modest enough to admit that he used a cool online tool to create his buttons, and you can too — the Brilliant Button Maker:
>
> `www.lucazappa.com/brilliantMaker/buttonImage.php`

Providing Playback Capability on Your Site

Even though the term podcasting implies that people are listening to your programming on an iPod (or some other portable media device), the reality is that at least half of all podcasts are watched or listened to via a browser on a laptop or desktop computer. While it's nice to provide buttons so that people can automatically subscribe to your podcast, more and more sites are now offering immediate playback of podcast episodes via the Web site.

In some ways, this is counter to the podcasting ethic, because it's not automatic and it doesn't involve a subscription. But podcasting is evolving and growing, and if it's something that the audience wants, then it's something that you should give them.

There are two basic ways to offer immediate playback via your Web site. You can place a link on your site that pops up a stand-alone media player, or you can embed a player into your Web page. There are advantages and disadvantages to both approaches, which we'll discuss in the next couple of sections.

Linking to a pop-up player

Linking to a pop-up player is the easiest method of linking. You simply place the link to your media file inside a small file called a *metafile*. When the user clicks the link, the metafile is sent from your server to his browser. The listener's browser receives the metafile and opens the media player associated with the metafile.

You use a metafile instead of linking directly to your media file because of how browsers download files. If you link directly to your media file, your browser must download the entire file before it decides what to do with it. When the download is complete, the browser looks at the MIME type of the file and then decides whether it can display it or whether it needs to be handed off to a helper application. If the file is fairly large, like a podcast, this takes time. If you use a metafile, which is a very small text file, the handoff occurs much quicker.

The advantage to providing a link to a metafile is it allows people to continue surfing Web pages while they're listening to your podcast. If, for example, you talk about other Web sites during your podcast, many folks naturally are tempted to go to that site to take a look. Of course, if your podcast is playing back in an embedded player, the moment the listener navigates away from your page, the podcast stops. Whoops.

The disadvantage is that some people don't like media players popping up, and it doesn't look as slick as an embedded player. If your podcasts are short, then an embedded player is probably the better way to go, because you're not forcing folks to stay glued to your page for too long. If you have a longer format podcast, you may want to consider offering a link to a pop-up player.

Authoring metafiles

Metafiles are simple text files that contain a link to the media file. The syntax is slightly different, depending on what format you're authoring for. Here's the simplest metafile, for RealPlayer:

```
www.mypikepodcast.com/mp3/mpp001.mp3
```

That's it — one simple line of code! Save that file with the .ram file extension, and you're finshed. Here's what a metafile for QuickTime looks like:

```
<?xml version="1.0"?>
<?quicktime type="application/x-quicktime-media-link"?>
<embed src="http://www.mypikepodcast.com/mp3/mpp001.mp3" />
```

Save this file with a .qtl extension, and it pop ups a QuickTime player. It's a little more complex than the RealPlayer metafile, but not much. The first line indicates that it's an XML file, the second file defines the MIME type, and the third and most important line contains the URL to the media file. Finally, let's look at a metafile for Windows Media Player:

```
<asx version="3.0">
 <entry>
  <ref href="http://www.mypikepodcast.com/mp3/mpp001.mp3" />
 </entry>
</asx>
```

Again, the syntax is slightly different from all the rest, but not too complicated. The file opens and closes with <asx> tags. Next comes the <entry> tag, which encloses a media file and any other tags related to this particular file. In this example, a single tag, the <ref> tag, contains the URL of the media file. Save this text with an .asx file extension, and it pops up Windows Media player.

> **NOTE** Flash player doesn't have a metafile, because there is no stand-alone Flash player. The Flash player can only be embedded in a Web page.

The preceding three examples are all the simplest possible versions of metafiles. All three metafiles are capable of including additional information, such as a title, a start or end time, whether or not to play the file as soon as it's loaded, and many other things. The available parameters vary from format to format. Some of these are useful, but many of them are only used for advanced purposes. For more on metafiles, check out the references on the manufacturers' respective Web sites:

- Windows Media Player metafile documentation:

  ```
  msdn.microsoft.com/library/default.asp?url=/library/en-us/
  wmplay10/mmp_sdk/windowsmediametafileelementsreference.asp
  ```

- QuickTime metafile documentation:

  ```
  developer.apple.com/documentation/QuickTime/REF/whatsnewqt5/
  Max.2c.htm#pgfId=93766
  ```

- RealPlayer metafile documentation:

  ```
  service.real.com/help/library/guides/realone/ProductionGuide/HT
  ML/htmfiles/ramref.htm#1077208
  ```

One thing of note is that all three of these examples referenced the same MP3 file. This is a special case, because all three players are capable of playing back MP3 files. If you're creating enhanced podcasts or podcasts in a particular format, you'll be limited to that player and to the appropriate metafile syntax.

Using an embedded player

Many blogs these days seem to be offering an embedded player for folks who visit the site. This allows folks to listen to the podcast immediately, without having to subscribe or open any other applications. As mentioned previously, there's a slight disadvantage to embedded players in that they force people to stay on your Web page, so they can't surf while they listen to your podcast in the background. Another issue with some embedded players is that the code required to implement them may not work on some listener's computers.

Embedding a player is done using special HTML code. The problem is that the code required depends on the browser being used. Luckily, there's a solution that gets you cross-browser compatibility in most cases. Let's start by looking at the code used for Internet Explorer.

Internet Explorer uses the <object> tag to embed what are known as *ActiveX* controls. The syntax for the QuickTime player looks like this:

```
<object classid="clsid:02BF25D5-8C17-4B23-BC80-D3488ABDDC6B"
  codebase="http://www.apple.com/qtactivex/qtplugin.cab"
  width="160" height="16" >
  <param name="src" value="mypikepodcast.mp3">
</object>
```

It may look complicated, but when you break it down, it's pretty simple:

- classid: A unique string used to identify the ActiveX control to use, in this case the QuickTime player

- codebase: A URL where a user can find the ActiveX control if they don't have it installed

- width & height: Determines how large to make the ActiveX control

- param: Used to identify the source for the file to be played by the ActiveX control

Add a closing object tag at the end, and you're finished. Next, we'll look at the code used in Netscape-based browsers. These include Safari, Firefox, Camino, and Opera. Netscape-based browsers use the <embed> tag to embed what they refer to as a plug-in. The code to embed a QuickTime player is as follows:

```
<embed src="mypikepodcast.mp3" width="160" height="16"
  pluginspage="http://www.apple.com/quicktime/download/">
</embed>
```

This looks a little simpler, but in reality it contains pretty much the same information:

- src: The location of the file to be played
- width & height: Determines how large to make the plug-in
- pluginspage: A URL where the user can find the plug-in if they don't have it already installed

Now that we have code that works on most browsers, the question is how can we get cross-browser compatibility? The answer is that we use both sets of code, embedding the Netscape code inside the IE code as follows:

```
<object classid="clsid:02BF25D5-8C17-4B23-BC80-D3488ABDDC6B"
   codebase="http://www.apple.com/qtactivex/qtplugin.cab"
   width="160" height="16" >
   <param name="src" value="mypikepodcast.mp3">
   <embed src="mypikepodcast.mp3" width="160" height="16"
      pluginspage="http://www.apple.com/quicktime/download/">
   </embed>
</object>
```

What happens is that Netscape-based browsers ignore the <object> and <param> tags and use the information contained in the <embed> tag. IE ignores the <embed> tag and renders the <object> and <param> tags. So using this syntax, you have code that works across both browsers.

A number of other parameters can be used in both the <object> and <embed> tags, depending on which player you're embedding. We'll look at these in the player-specific sections.

Embedding the QuickTime player

The preceding section used the QuickTime player as an example, so we already know what the code looks like. However, additional parameters can be used. Most of these are fairly advanced and of little use to podcasters. However, for those of you with an inquisitive nature, you can find out more about parameters you can use when embedding the QuickTime player on the Apple Developer's site:

```
www.apple.com/quicktime/tutorials/embed.html
```

CAUTION As of Fall 2006, Apple no longer recommends using the code mentioned here because of the way it now works in Internet Explorer. Microsoft released a security update for Internet Explorer that causes it to pop up security warnings. Instead, Apple recommends a fairly complex JavaScript solution, which is detailed on the developer's site. You may want to check the above URL for the latest Apple-recommended solution.

Embedding the Flash player

The Flash player is somewhat unique because there is no stand-alone player. It must be embedded in a Web page as an ActiveX control or plug-in. There is a catch, however: There is no default Flash player! When you author a Flash movie, you can add playback controls and export the whole thing as a Shockwave Flash movie. This requires that your podcast media file be "baked into" the resulting Shockwave Flash movie. After you've done this, you can embed the Flash player using similar syntax to the QuickTime player:

```
<object classid="clsid:d27cdb6e-ae6d-11cf-96b8-444553540000"
codebase="http://fpdownload.macromedia.com/pub/shockwave/cabs/fla
sh/swflash.cab#version=7,0,0,0"
  width="320" height="32">
  <param name="movie" value="mypikepodcast.swf" />
  <embed type="application/x-shockwave-flash"
    pluginspage="http://www.macromedia.com/go/getflashplayer"
    src="mypikepodcast.swf"
    width="320" height="32" />
</object>
```

You can see that the same parameters are used, with the exception that the Flash player uses the "movie" parameter to specify the media file instead of "src." The classid value is different, because it references the Flash player. The type parameter in the embed tag is also different. But essentially the syntax is the same.

NOTE For you more advanced developer types out there, Adobe recommends embedding the Flash player using JavaScript that detects the presence of Flash and bypasses the security issues of IE. It's fairly advanced stuff, detailed here:

www.adobe.com/devnet/flash/articles/swfobject.html

The only problem with embedding the Flash player this way is that it references a single Flash movie that has the media file hard coded in it. What we really want is a way to reuse the same code and be able to specify the MP3 file we want to play back. To do this, we need a custom Flash player to which we can pass a file name or URL. Fortunately, a number of Flash MP3 players are available:

- Flash MP3 player 2.3: www.jeroenwijering.com/?item=Flash_MP3_Player
- XSPF Web Music Player: musicplayer.sourceforge.net/
- Wimpy Player: www.wimpyplayer.com/index.html

These MP3 players are embedded using code very similar to the above, but they include the ability to reference an external file or play list, so that the code can be reused, and you don't have to own a copy of Flash to create new movies each time you want to publish a new episode.

Embedding RealPlayer

RealPlayer is embedded just like the QuickTime and Flash players, but with an interesting twist. The player is embedded in pieces. Instead of one chunk of code to embed the entire player, you specify how much of it you want to embed. If you're embedding an MP3 file and want to include just the player controls, use the following code:

```
<object classid="clsid:CFCDAA03-8BE4-11cf-B84B-0020AFBBCCFA"
  width="350" height="36">
  <param name="src" value="mypikepodcast.mp3">
  <param name="controls" value="ControlPanel">
  <embed pluginspage="http://www.real.com"
    src="mypikepodcast.mp3"
    width="350" height="36"
    controls="ControlPanel" />
</object>
```

There are a couple of notable differences here. First, RealPlayer doesn't use the codebase parameter in the object tag. Second, there's a parameter called controls that specifies which part of RealPlayer this code is referring to. In this example, it's set to "ControlPanel," which gets you all the controls necessary to play your MP3 file. If you're going to embed video, then it gets more complicated, because you're going to need to embed not only controls, but also the video pane where the video is to be displayed:

```
<object classid="clsid:CFCDAA03-8BE4-11cf-B84B-0020AFBBCCFA"
  width="320" height="36">
  <param name="src" value="mypikepodcast.rm">
  <param name="controls" value="ControlPanel">
  <param name="console" value="player1">
  <embed pluginspage="http://www.real.com"
    src="mypikepodcast.rm"
    width="320" height="36"
    controls="ControlPanel"
    console="player1" />
</object>
<object classid="clsid:CFCDAA03-8BE4-11cf-B84B-0020AFBBCCFA"
  width="320" height="240">
  <param name="src" value="mypikepodcast.rm">
  <param name="controls" value="ImageWindow">
  <param name="console" value="player1">
  <embed pluginspage="http://www.real.com"
    src="mypikepodcast.rm"
    width="320" height="240"
    controls="ImageWindow"
    console="player1" />
</object>
```

We start with the same code as before, but add a second block of code, this time with the value of the controls parameter set to "ImageWindow." This specifies that we're embedding the video pane where the video is to be displayed. Also, we want the controls specified in the first block of code to control the video in the second block. This is accomplished by the console parameter, which in both blocks of code has been set to "player1." It doesn't matter what value you set it to, as long as the values match.

Using this approach, you can embed as little or as much of RealPlayer as you'd like in your Web page. As long as you set the console parameter correctly, the pieces all work together as a whole. For full documentation on how to embed RealPlayer, including additional parameters that can be included in the embed code, please refer to the RealNetworks Web site:

```
service.real.com/help/library/
```

Embedding Windows Media Player

Embedding Windows Media Player is the most challenging, for a number of reasons. Initially, Microsoft made the decision to stop supporting the Netscape plug-in with the release of the 7.0 player. During this time, you could embed a 7.0 player on IE and a 6.4 player on Netscape-based browsers.

Then, in an odd series of events, a developer figured out how to support the Windows Media ActiveX control in Netscape-based browsers, while at the same time Microsoft quietly re-instated support for the Netscape plug-in. This led to a very short period where it seemed that all would be well in the embedded Windows Media world. You could embed Windows Media Player using the <object> tag, and it worked on both browsers, provided that people installed the code that enabled the ActiveX support. It was obviously too good to last.

Somewhere along the line, the ActiveX code stopped working in the Netscape-based browsers. Or it didn't. The story gets confusing, depending on whom you're talking to. Suffice it to say that to make an embedded player work on Netscape-based browsers required a lengthy trawl through the Mozilla (the organization that continually develops the Netscape code base) forums, which most folks are not prepared to do.

Around the same time, Microsoft announced that it was dropping support for Windows Media Player on the Mac OS and handed off development to Flip4Mac, a plug-in for QuickTime that allows it to play Windows Media content. The initial release was a little buggy, and the streaming community started screaming that Microsoft had abandoned them. In reality, handing off Windows Media support for the Mac OS to a company that focuses on the Mac OS is a much better proposition than waiting for Microsoft to add Mac support. It's just going to take awhile before the Flip4Mac product has all the features of the latest Windows Media Player.

So where does that leave us? Embedding Windows Media Player in Netscape-based browsers is always going to be a risky proposition, because the support is never going to be built in. Embedding on a Mac works, provided that you don't use some of the advanced features (such as those that enable an enhanced podcast).

Bearing this in mind, there are plenty of situations where an embedded Windows Media Player might be perfectly appropriate. For example, if you're creating a podcast for an enterprise that has standardized on the Windows operating system, you can embed Windows Media Player and everyone will be able to see it just fine. In fact, anyone on the Windows operating system will be able to see your embedded Windows Media Player. And *some* folks on Netscape-based browsers will be able to see it.

The approach is exactly the same as with all the other players. Use both the <object> and <embed> tags:

```
<object classid="CLSID:6BF52A52-394A-11d3-B153-00C04F79FAA6"
codebase="http://activex.microsoft.com/activex/controls/mplayer/
en/nsmp2inf.cab#Version=5,1,52,701"
  width="320" height="32" >
 <param name="url" value="mypikepodcast.mp3">
 <embed type="application/x-mplayer2"

pluginspage="http://microsoft.com/windows/mediaplayer/en/download
/"
   src="mypikepodcast.mp3"
   width="320" height="32">
 </embed>
</object>
```

This embeds the latest version of Windows Media Player on IE and embeds the venerable old 6.4 version on Netscape-based browsers. This code should work on most browsers, but is by no means guaranteed to work on all browsers.

> **TIP** When embedding any media player, be sure to offer a link to a stand-alone player in case the listener has any problems with the embedded player.

As with the other players, you can use a whole host of additional parameters when embedding your player that control the look, feel, and performance of Windows Media Player. For full documentation on the embedded Windows Media Player, please refer to the documentation on the Microsoft Developer's Network:

```
msdn.microsoft.com/library/default.asp?url=/library/en-
us/wmplay10/mmp_sdk/usingtheplayercontrolinawebpage.asp
```

Summary

This chapter covered the following topics:

- There are three basic options for hosting your podcast: hosting it on your own Web site, hosting it on a managed Web hosting service, or using a dedicated podcast hosting service.

- Dedicated podcast hosting services are a great way for the inexperienced podcaster to start.

- Using a managed Web host is a good idea because it allows you to have your own domain and URL.

- Managing your own Web servers is only for the experienced, tech-savvy few.

- Register a domain for your podcast, even if you don't use it at first.

- Try to retain ownership of as much of your brand as possible. This includes your URL, your RSS feed URL, and anything else related to your podcast.

- A number of great dedicated podcast hosting services are available.

- Be sure to use the correct RSS icons to advertise your feed.

- If you're providing a direct link to your podcast media file, be sure to use a metafile.

- Consider using an embedded player on your site to let folks play your podcast without having to download or subscribe.

Chapter 18

Distributing Your Media File

I n the preceding chapter, we talked about finding a home for your podcast. Although the discussion was couched in somewhat general terms and assumed that your podcast and the Web site hosting your podcast were the same thing, they don't have to be. You can host your Web site using one solution and host your podcast media files somewhere completely different.

You may want to do this for several reasons, but they all generally boil down to the fact that MP3 files are much larger than Web pages, so you're going to use lots of bandwidth and lots of storage. This places unique demands on the server infrastructure, which may be a job handled by a trusted partner.

Understanding Distribution

One of the best things about podcasting is that it doesn't require any special serving software, like streaming media does. You just place the file on your Web server and update your RSS feed, and you're done. That's all fine and good when you're starting out and have a handful of faithful subscribers. But what happens when your podcast becomes wildly popular?

Several things happen. First, instead of downloading a handful of MP3 files to your listeners, you're suddenly sending out thousands of copies of your MP3 file. If your podcast is 5 minutes long and encoded at 128 Kbps, you're looking at a 5 MB file. A thousand downloads means you're talking about 5 GB of throughput. If you have a daily show, you're talking about over 150 GB per month. That's a pretty serious amount of traffic.

At this scale, things change significantly. Instead of sending out a few files when your friends check to see if you've updated your blog, your Web server is now running all day long. That means the disc drives are spinning, and much more wear and tear is being put on the machines. Servers have a much shorter shelf life than desktop computers for this reason. Most hosting companies plan on servers lasting approximately three years before they have to be replaced.

Of course, this is assuming that your podcast becomes popular enough to attract a large audience. That may not be your case. Your podcast may be niche content that is devoutly followed by a faithful few. Disregarding the size of your audience for the time being, your choices for hosting your media files break down as follows:

- Host it on your Web server.
- Host it on a content distribution network (CDN).
- Host it on a podcast hosting service.
- Use peer-to-peer distribution.

In the following sections, we talk about each of these possibilities in a little more detail.

Using Your Web Server

The simplest case is to host your podcast media files right on your Web server. When you're starting out, this is probably the way to go. Most Web hosting agreements usually include a fair amount of bandwidth these days, which cover a fair amount of downloads. For example, here are a few of the better-known Web hosting companies and the deals they're currently offering:

- IX Web Hosting (www.ixwebhosting.com): $3.95 a month, 100 GB storage, 1,000 GB throughput
- Host Excellence (www.hostexcellence.com): $2.95 a month, 5 GB storage, 50 GB throughput
- iPower Web (www.iPowerweb.com): $7.95 a month, 50 GB storage, 750 GB throughput
- Dreamhost (www.dreamhost.com): $7.95 a month, 200GB storage, 2TB throughput
- 1 and 1 (1and1.com): $2.99 a month, 5 GB storage, 250 GB throughput

As you can see, killer deals for cheap Web hosting abound. However, as the saying goes, there's no such thing as a free lunch. The only way they can offer these kinds of prices is by putting hundreds if not thousands of Web sites on each server. You'll be sharing resources with lots of other folks. In some cases, this may not be a problem. However, sometimes it can be problematic. Your listeners may have to wait longer for your pages and your podcast files to download.

When you're first starting off, prices like these with the amount of storage and throughput they're giving away are pretty hard to pass up. Many of these services also offer fairly comprehensive tool sets that allow you to build Web sites and create e-commerce pages, blogs, and forums, and they'll even host your e-mail.

If you're thinking of going this way, it's really important to comb the comparison sites and the forums of your potential partners. See what people are saying about them and whether their existing customers are happy. Don't just go by the testimonials they put on their home page; dig into their message boards if you can, and search them to death. It's not that the couple of dollars a month is going to break your budget; it's more that after you're settled into a Web host, changing can be a painful experience.

> **TIP** A number of sites out there regularly update the ratings for Web hosting services. Just search for "best web hosting" and you'll have a number to choose from.

Using a Podcast Hosting Service

Podcast hosting services are very similar to Web hosting services, but with product offerings geared towards podcasters. You generally get a certain amount of storage space and throughput, and depending on the service, you may get a Web site or a blog, tools to author your RSS feed, and statistics regarding your podcast.

The tools that podcast hosting services offer make them a great bet for folks who are not technically savvy. Also, many of the podcast hosting services are using an interesting model where they charge for the amount of storage you use, but don't charge for throughput. This is an interesting approach and a great deal if your podcast becomes extremely popular. However, as mentioned in the preceding chapter, using a podcast hosting service means giving up some of your ownership, because you won't be able to use your own URL for the site.

However, you could use a hybrid approach where you host your Web site at a Web host and your media file at a podcast hosting service. You'd still have access to the RSS tools, and you could either host the RSS feed from your Web site or point to the RSS feed on the podcast hosting service. It's a little awkward in that you're using two separate services instead of one, but you may be able to get the best of both worlds this way.

> **TIP** Another benefit to some hosting services is that they may offer the possibility of advertising or sponsorship to help pay for your podcast. For example, Liberated Syndication is partnered with Kiptronic to offer ad placement and sponsorship opportunities. Granted, you don't have to be a LibSyn user to take advantage of Kiptronic's offering, but if you are, the integration is seamless and taken care of for you.

Distributing Your Own Podcast Using Box Populi

Box Populi offers an interesting solution for folks who plan on creating a large number of podcasts. It's a two-part solution that takes care of the production and encoding of podcasts as well as the distribution.

To start off with, they have a product called Podcast In A Box that you use to create your podcasts. Plug a microphone into the 1/8" mic input, and then plug in the USB key that comes with the system. Recording begins automatically. When you're done, remove the USB key, and your podcast is automatically encoded into MP3 format and uploaded to a Web server.

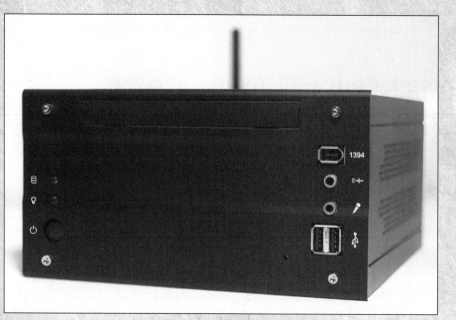

Box Populi's Podcast In A Box automates podcast production, encoding, and distribution.

Box Populi can host your podcast for you, or if you prefer they sell a rack-mountable media server that is tightly integrated with Podcast In A Box. The server auto-publishes your podcasts to a Web page and enables management through a simple browser-based interface. You can host audio or video files using the media server, and you can create multiple user accounts so many folks can contribute to your podcast. If you decide to start using a CDN, the media server can be configured to automatically upload your podcast media files to your CDN.

The entire system is built on open-source software, and Box Populi will do custom development for you if their tools don't already do exactly what you want them to do. If you're looking for an end-to-end podcasting solution, check out Box Populi.

Using a Content Distribution Network

Content distribution networks (CDNs) are designed to deliver large volumes of traffic quickly and efficiently. Whereas a Web host may have hundreds of servers in a single location, a CDN has multiple data centers, and generally the data is replicated across each data center. This is done both for data integrity, so that if there's a power failure somewhere your files are still available, and also for speed. Most CDNs also rely on *caching* to make downloads happen faster.

Caching is a technique where the most popular files are stored at multiple locations so that when they are requested, the request doesn't have to go all the way back to the *origin server*. For example, let's say CNN.com has an extremely popular story on its home page. The origin servers are most likely in Atlanta, where CNN is based. The first time someone in Los Angeles requests the CNN home page, a copy, along with all the images, is sent from Atlanta to Los Angeles. Then a copy is stored in a cache somewhere on the west coast, so that the next time someone requests that page, it can be served directly from the local cache and not re-requested from the origin server in Atlanta.

CDNs offer premium delivery services, so you won't find pricing like you can with the Web hosting services. CDNs also like to deal in very large numbers, so if you're not expecting to spend hundreds of dollars a month, you shouldn't waste your time calling CDNs. However, when your podcast is at a stage where you have a large audience that demands quality service, a CDN is your best bet.

The CDN marketplace

The CDN market is often divided into the "tier 1" providers, who have the largest and fastest networks, and the "tier 2" providers, who may have slightly more aggressive pricing but may not offer the same service. CDNs are often graded in terms of their availability, which some brag about in terms of "five nines." This means that their network is available 99.999 percent of the time. Another metric used to grade CDNs is the response time, which is the average amount of time it takes for a CDN to respond to a request. A number of services grade CDNs from time to time on their performance. The CDN market has seen lots of consolidation in the last few years, and prices have dropped considerably. The performance of the tier 2 CDNs has come so close the tier 1 providers that the tier 1 providers have had to drop their prices to remain competitive. Some even question whether there is enough distinction between providers to classify them into separate tiers anymore. Be that as it may, these are some of the better-known CDNs:

- Akamai (www.akamai.com)
- Mirror Image (www.mirror-image.com)
- Limelight (www.limelightnetworks.com)
- Savvis (www.savvis.net)

CDN pricing

CDNs use two basic models for pricing. Traditionally, they have billed using what is known as the *95th percentile* model; recently many are moving to a *per megabyte/gigabyte* model. One of the frustrating things about CDNs is that it is almost impossible to translate between these two pricing models, making it difficult for CDN customers to figure out their cost of delivery.

Using the 95th percentile model, your price is quoted as a dollar amount per megabit of concurrent throughput. For example, a CDN may offer you a price of $50 per megabit. The tricky part is how your concurrent traffic figure is arrived at over the course of a month. The CDN measures exactly how much throughput you are using many times over the course of each day. At the end of the month, the CDN tabulates all the measurements, discards the top 5 percent of the measurements, and uses the 95th percentile measurement as your billable amount.

> **NOTE**   Billing at the 95th percentile is measured in terms of megabits, not Megabytes. Be careful when you're doing your calculations!

Here's another way of looking at it. There are 720 hours in a 30-day month, so 5 percent of a month translates to 36 hours. So when you're billed at the 95th percentile, the busiest 36 hours of the month are discarded, and you're billed for the throughput your site used during the 37th busiest hour. Still confused? Don't worry, you're not alone. This model is frustrating to customers, because it is hard to understand and hard to budget for. In some ways, it's good because you don't pay for momentary spikes in your traffic. On the other hand, it's very hard to calculate your cost of delivery on a per-file basis because that varies depending on your traffic patterns.

For example, let's say you've got 1,000 subscribers, and you put up a new podcast each day. Over the course of that day, all 1,000 of them check the RSS feed and download the podcast. Assuming the same 5-minute, 5-MB file we talked about earlier in the chapter, and assuming folks are on an average broadband connection of about 300 Kbps, it's going to take the average listener about 2 minutes to download your file:

```
5 MB * 1024 MB/KB * 8 bits/byte = 40,960 Kbits
40,960 Kbits / 300 Kbps = roughly 136 seconds (fudging the
difference between K and k)
```

Given an ideal distribution, over the course of a day, just over 700 people could download your file, one at a time, and you'd never have more than one person at a time downloading. But given that most of your listeners probably will be from a limited number of time zones, and most folks will check their favorite feeds either at lunch time or early in the evening, you'll probably get the bulk of your downloads during three or four hours a day. That means you'll have around 5 to 10 people downloading at any given time. Let's say 10 for a liberal estimate. This means your concurrent throughput during these hours will be:

```
10 * 300 Kbps = 3 Mbps
```

This should end up being your 95th percentile number, because you're hitting this peak for 3 to 4 hours each day. If you're paying $50 per megabit, you can then do some math to figure out what your cost per delivery is per file:

```
3 Mbps * $50 = $150
1,000 subscribers * 20 podcasts/month = 20,000 podcasts
$150 / 20,000 podcasts = under a penny a podcast
```

So it's not impossible to get your cost of delivery, but it involves some calculation. And the calculations are highly dependent on your traffic patterns. Your bill depends on *when* people download the file, not *how many*. So it's very hard to figure out what your incremental cost per subscriber is, because it depends on when they download the file!

For this reason, some CDNs are now offering pricing on a per gigabyte basis. Using this model, customers are billed for the total amount of throughput they use. It doesn't matter when the throughput is used. This model is much simpler for customers to understand, because the math is straightforward. Using the previous example, let's calculate what the cost would be, assuming a cost of $1 a gigabyte:

```
20,000 podcasts * 5 MB/podcast = 100,000 MB = 100 GB
100 GB * $1 = $100
$100 / 20,000 podcasts = half a penny a podcast
```

Using this model, it appears that it's cheaper, and we know it's a hard cost that we can use in our calculations. Each podcast costs a half a penny to deliver. Contrast this with the 95th percentile where we know the cost is under a penny, but that could change depending on traffic patterns. However, don't let these numbers fool you. It's not quite this simple.

Let's say your podcast audience doubles in size. Using the cost-per-gig model, we know our costs would double. However, with the 95th percentile model, they may not. An audience that's twice as large quite probably would come from a much more dispersed geographical area and may distribute the load over more hours in the day. It's quite possible that you could double your audience size and not pay any more at all! That's the tricky part. If you make efficient use of your bandwidth, the 95th percentile model can be substantially cheaper.

Some companies put caps on bandwidth usage, so for example they're never using more than one megabit per second. This slows down file delivery for people if they're all trying to download at the same time, but keeps costs low. In fact, this is a tool that some hosting companies use to make sure they keep their costs low. (How else do you think they can offer so much bandwidth for free?) You may be able to do the same if you work with your CDN. This compromises performance for your listeners, but it can be a good cost-savings mechanism.

Using Peer-to-Peer Distribution

The last method of distribution you may want to consider is peer-to-peer. Peer-to-peer (P2P) distribution uses other people on the network to distribute files, instead of sending everything from a single centralized server. P2P distribution came to notoriety with the arrival of Napster, which was originally used to share music files across the Internet. Since then, it has gone mainstream, with many different types of data distributed in this fashion. Skype, the Internet telephony start-up, is actually a P2P application.

There are a number of different P2P approaches, but basically the way it works is that if you request a file and the P2P network knows that someone near you already has a copy of the file, you are directed to that person's computer to get a copy, instead of sending another copy all the way across the network. Sometimes, downloads are distributed across multiple computers, so you're download-ing parts of a file from many different participants on the P2P network.

The advantage of P2P distribution is that is uses the audience's bandwidth, so you don't have to pay for the throughput. Instead, people are being directed to other people on the network, and they're using their bandwidth, not yours. However, P2P distribution really works only if your content is very popular. To understand why this is, we'll look a little more closely at how P2P distribution works in the next section.

How P2P works

To explore how peer-to-peer distribution works, we'll look at BitTorrent. BitTorrent is perhaps the best-known P2P system. There is a vast amount of BitTorrent traffic on the Internet, by some esti-mates as much as 35 percent of the traffic at any given time. It's anyone's guess what all this traffic is and whether or not it's legal. Regardless, it's a proven system that works well.

BitTorrent is a protocol that defines how files can be shared between two or more hosts. It's also the name of one of the programs that distributes files using the BitTorrent protocol. Essentially, BitTorrent works by breaking large files into many small pieces. BitTorrent downloads are not done sequentially, like regular FTP or HTTP downloads. Instead, BitTorrent clients download files in pieces, from as many different clients as possible. BitTorrent clients find out about the different locations they can download files from by checking in with a BitTorrent *tracker*, which keeps track of everyone who is participating in the distribution of a particular file. It may seem a bit confusing, but it's actually pretty simple. Here's an example of how it works:

1. You create a "torrent" for the file you want to distribute. This is a small file that contains all the information people need to know about the file to download it. The torrent is cre-ated in your BitTorrent application.

2. After the torrent is created, it is placed on a Web server and registered with what is known as a *tracker*. The tracker keeps track of everyone who is participating in the distribution of the file.

3. Next, you have to *seed* the file. This means getting the initial copy of the file into distribu-tion. Usually this is done from the user's desktop. You click the link to the torrent on the Web site and indicate in your BitTorrent client that you're seeding for this file.

4. When the first audience member clicks the torrent link, the torrent file opens by their BitTorrent client. The BitTorrent client finds out from the tracker who is participating in the distribution. Because no one else is, the BitTorrent client begins downloading the file from the original seed file, which in this case is your computer.

5. When the next person clicks the torrent link and then checks in with the tracker, he finds that there are now two machines participating in the distribution: the original and the first audience member. Their BitTorrent client requests pieces of the file from both clients.

6. As more clients joint the torrent, the distribution becomes more and more distributed, allowing clients to download the file from many different clients. Files that are very popular have many people participating in the torrent, so the distribution process scales accordingly.

7. BitTorrent "etiquette" dictates that it's nice to leave your BitTorrent client on for a while after you've downloaded the file, so that you can help distribute the file to other people.

This is a simplified picture of how P2P distribution occurs, but essentially it's correct. For P2P distribution to be efficient, it requires lots of clients participating in the distribution. So when you're first starting out, P2P distribution offers very little benefit, because your audience most likely will be downloading at different times and won't be able to take advantage of the distributed download. When your podcast audience is in the thousands, then you can make an argument for P2P distribution.

Is P2P for you?

One thing that we've conveniently ignored up to this point is that P2P software is not built in to any podcatching software. Podcatchers can download MP3 files using HTTP, but they cannot participate in a P2P distribution scheme. So if you want to use P2P as a distribution scheme, your audience has to download and install P2P distribution software. Considering the antipathy some folks have to installing software, this may not be the easiest sell.

P2P distribution is used widely by the gaming community to distribute new releases and software fixes. It's a proven distribution technology that can potentially save you lots of money in bandwidth costs. The problem, however, is that it isn't yet integrated into podcasting in any meaningful way. Although P2P may be an effective way to scale podcasting distribution in the near future, for the time being you're probably better off sticking to other methods of distribution.

Summary

In this chapter, you learned about ways to distribute your podcasts. Specifically, this chapter covered the following topics:

■ Many Web hosting companies have crazy deals for storage and bandwidth, but remember that you'll be sharing the service with lots of other people. This may lead to longer waits and download times.

■ Podcast hosting services usually offer unlimited throughput and charge by the amount of storage you use.

■ Podcast hosting services usually come with lots of tools that make them a great choice for the less technically savvy podcaster or for folks who are just starting out.

- Content delivery networks (CDNs) offer premium delivery services, but at a premium price.

- Peer-to-peer (P2P) distribution allows the distribution of files from a number of disparate sources instead of a single centralized server.

- P2P distribution may be an effective way of scaling podcasting distribution in the future, but until it's integrated into existing podcasting software, it's probably better to use other distribution methods.

Part V

The Business of Podcasting

Chapter 19

The Basics of Podcasting Business

Making a business of podcasting may follow several different paths, from providing services to actually developing and producing shows and serving as the on-air talent, too. This is the basic primer about the costs of podcasting—there are real costs involved—and how you can plan the growth of the business you intend to launch.

Like any business, podcasting must start lean unless you are very well funded. It takes a while, possibly a long while, to reach break-even if you intend to make really big money, because you have to grow your audience through marketing efforts as well as pay to produce and distribute your audio or video programming. If your intention is to start and stay small, you still should have a solid idea about how you will minimize your costs so that the podcast doesn't drain your bank account or your time away from what pays the bills.

Growing a big hit, a show with tens or hundreds of thousands of listeners, involves planning for bandwidth, storage costs, marketing, and the rising cost of production that comes with listeners' and advertisers' expectations of high-quality programming. You're going to start small, yet the right combination of information and personality can make your podcast the platform for stardom.

Understanding Costs Before Profits

If you were starting a flower shop, you'd know that the business would have to survive on a tight budget for rent, utilities, the décor and equipment at the retail location you choose, as well as for your time or that of employees.

You'll have marketing and advertising costs, as well. Did we mention insurance? Accounting? As we begin to envision a podcasting business, these same realities, despite the different physical and distribution variables in podcasting, are important to laying the foundation for success.

If you buy the hype that podcasting costs little or nothing, you'll learn a hard lesson. Even the "cheap" hosting deals advertised to podcasters come with increasing costs as your show gains popularity or simply as your archives expand. Small audiences and advertisers can live with slower downloads and occasional interruptions of service, but as you grow and, particularly, as you charge advertisers or subscribers for your programming, quality of service issues will drive your hosting and distribution costs higher. Likewise, in order to take advantage of the digital distribution environment, you need to make as much of your catalog available as possible, as individual shows that appeal to narrowly focused audience interests are the doorways to wider subscriber relationships.

As explained in Chapter 4, the "long tail" approach to marketing virtually requires that you maintain your archives. The idea that you can save money by taking older podcasts offline may sound reasonable, but it is like discarding all your hard work before its full value has been realized. In the "long-tail" marketplace, you have the opportunity to reap value from older productions virtually forever, and those shows were too much hard work to throw them away! You can be certain that something you recorded two years ago will be of interest to some people who, by sampling those old programs, will become loyal listeners today.

CROSS-REF   For a complete discussion of the long-tail concept, see Chapter 4.

In this section, we walk through the various costs you need to account for as you plan your podcast business. Let's start, though, with a simple set of key principles:

- **Every cost must be justified.** An extraordinary microphone that costs $1,400 may make you feel good, but is it worth the money? Audiophiles will argue "Yes!" But the audience may never hear the difference. Equipment costs, especially early on, should be kept to a minimum, so that you have more money and time (that is, time you don't have to work at something else to pay for your podcasting habit) to put into growing the show. Likewise, getting all your old shows onto the Net is a great way to have new listeners discover your work, but if you're considering putting up shows that are unrelated to what you do today — if you are podcasting about sports today, your old cooking audio may not get you any new subscribers — you may want to think twice about the expense. Spend money on good ideas that are cost-justified, that will actually produce a return greater than the money you sink into them.

- **Profit grows, and losses pile up.** Don't be dissuaded by spending that seems to be loss-making if you can explain to your satisfaction how that spending will lead to increased revenue. For example, lots of people get caught up in the idea that they need the fastest possible connection to the Internet to ensure their podcasts download lickety-split. That may be important at the point where some advertisers or paying subscribers start to complain that the connection is too slow, but early in the life of a podcasting business, having more archival content available at slower speeds may be more important to success, because that's the formula for growing the subscriber base. Likewise, you may create much less value by purchasing that expensive microphone while forgoing a telephone recording interface, because it will limit your ability to talk with in-studio guests. We can't tell you all the ways you might spend money, but we can tell you to look carefully at your costs from the very beginning. And, should an expense start to prove itself unprofitable, such as having paid for too much bandwidth early on, don't be afraid to cut your losses by changing, even if there are costs to ending a hosting relationship or returning leased equipment that it turns out you don't really need.

- **Service providers exist to make money.** "Outsourcing" is all the rage in information technology today. Companies outsource hosting of their Web sites, accounting systems and services, virtually everything. That's good, but it can also be bad for you. In the podcasting world, the major buying decision for most producers has to do with outsource hosting and delivery of programming. Hosting providers are in the business of making money, so their costs are covered and employees' homes paid for, not to mention that investors are getting a profit back at some point. The reality of hosting is that you'll pay too much for something, whether it's bandwidth or storage. These companies profit in "breakage," the services they get customer to pay for but that don't get used. We believe that storage is where you are most often going to be gouged, because bandwith is shared and prioritized among the hosting provider's customers to maximize the host's profits. In other words, there is much more breakage available on the bandwidth side of the equation. Storage, on the other hand, is monopolized by the user — the hosting company can't store two customers' data in the same space — so that is where you will pay a premium for the space you use, even in the post-scarcity world of digital distribution. When you deal with these companies, keep an eye out for what they really charge for and what they are willing to give away to maximize *your* spending.

- **Partnering is another form of paying for services.** Instead of deciding to pay for services, such as hosting and distribution bandwidth, you may opt to partner with another company that promises to handle a major part of your business for a share of revenue. These companies, too, are looking to maximize their profits, so you need to understand their costs as well as yours in order to cut the best deal possible for yourself. Their initial offer is going to favor them, regardless of how generous it may seem, so, like anyone entering the bazaar, be prepared to haggle a bit. Read the "window sticker" like you would on a new car, in order to understand where you can make a better deal.

- **It's your baby; feed it properly.** A business is like a child. It always wants more than may be good for it or for you. This principle is usually conveyed in business tomes by the statement that one must "be ruthless" about the use of funds and performance of employees. Because many podcast businesses start from an outpouring of enthusiasm by the founder and others who may be involved with it (like the engineer you brought in that likes getting some on-air time, or your uncle who loves the show and loves you more), the rules of ruthlessness can be particularly difficult to live by. It helps to think a little more like the nurturing mother in these circumstances, at least some of the time. If you had a baby who weighed 70 pounds at 18 months of age, you'd know the kid was eating something that wasn't right for his body. You'd cut out sugar. You'd look at the fat content of the foods you were feeding baby. The baby would cry, stamp his feet, and demand sweets. You'd stand your ground or be a lousy parent. Same with a business that has family-like connections early on. As the parent, you need to make decisions about which the business may complain. Be strong.

As you launch your podcast, the first decisions you make that impact your current and future costs have to do with bandwidth and storage capacity. It may seem that unlimited bandwidth, the network capacity to deliver your show, would be the main component of your costs, but it won't always be so. We encourage you to select a provider that does offer unlimited bandwidth, because that is the factor that can affect your costs unexpectedly: You cannot plan on having an unexpected hit that is suddenly downloaded by a million people, but should it happen, unlimited bandwidth arrangements can keep your podcast hosting bills from soaring into the tens of thousands of dollars.

Your first choice should be your long-term choice, if possible, because moving a podcast from one server to another can be time-consuming, and if subscribers lose track of your feed, it can cost you listeners. Some hosting providers offer unbelievable deals that are, just as you might expect, not sustainable. This is a less significant problem today than 10 years ago, when the Web first came along and no one was aware of the criteria for selecting a reliable hosting provider. However, if someone tells you that you'll never pay more than $9.95 a month for hosting if you just sign up for a year or two of service, be very cautious. The host almost certainly won't refund your money if they go out of business.

The realities of hosting

Hosting providers provide two things: storage capacity, where you store your podcasts, and bandwidth, also referred to as "throughput," necessary to deliver your podcasts to an audience. They charge for both, though the mix of fees may emphasize one or the other. Generally speaking, if a hosting provider offers unlimited storage, they want you to get as many shows on their server as possible so that you pay for lots of downloads or, rather, for the bandwidth used by those downloads. These hosts typically sell bandwidth in blocks of megabytes or gigabytes per month. If the provider emphasizes free or unlimited bandwidth, they typically charge for storage at fairly exorbitant rates to ensure that they are profitable.

You can consider two basic types of hosting providers when looking at launching a podcast: the generic Web server host that likely charges based on a combination of storage and bandwidth used, and a podcasting host that provides podcast-specific services that are usually billed based on storage capacity. Each has strengths. The podcast-specific hosts is great if you don't want to deal with setting up and managing audio feeds; they also prevent you from shouldering huge bandwidth costs if you have a hit show that suddenly takes off. On the other hand, storing even a year's worth of podcasts with a host that gives you free bandwidth is more expensive than you may think. As we've explained, you need a large catalog to maximize the opportunity to win new subscribers.

The bottom line is that podcasting requires a significant investment compared to the legendary status of the medium as "free." Of course, podcasting is still many orders of magnitude cheaper than buying and operating a radio station.

Here, then, are some worksheets that will help you understand where your costs will rise with each type of hosting deal.

We'll start with figuring out how much storage you plan to use for a month's worth of podcasts:

1. First, let's make some decisions. We need to know the length of your shows and the bit depth at which you plan to produce them, which combine to give you an estimated file size for each program. Figure 19.1 provides a sample of program lengths, bit rates, and resulting file sizes.

FIGURE 19.1

File sizes for shows of varying lengths and bit depths

Show Length

MP3 Bit Depth	5 Min.	10 Min.	20 Min.	30 Min.	60 Min.
32 kbps mono	1.2 MB	2.4 MB	4.8 MB	7.2 MB	14.4 MB
96 kbps stereo	3.6 MB	7.2 MB	14.4 MB	21.6 MB	43.2 MB
112 kbps stereo	4.2 MB	8.4 MB	16.8 MB	25.2 MB	50.4 MB
128 kbps stereo	4.8 MB	9.6 MB	19.2 MB	28.8 MB	57.6 MB

2. In the worksheet shown in Figure 19.2, enter the file size of each show in the File Size field. Now, in Frequency, enter the number of times each month you plan to release a show. Multiply the File Size by the Frequency, and you have your monthly storage requirements. For example, if we produce the *Steve & Mitch Hour* at 96 kbps, the appropriate bit depth for a talk-centric show with some music, which doesn't require CD-quality fidelity, our weekly shows are approximately 42 MB in size. If we produce four times a month, we need about 173 MB of storage capacity for our show.

FIGURE 19.2

Calculating your monthly storage requirements

	The Steve & Mitch Hour	Your Show
File Size (see Fig. 19.1)	43.2 MB	_____
Frequency	4	_____
Monthly Storage Requirements	172.8 MB	_____

3. But that 173 MB is enough storage only for our first month. If we want to produce for the next year, making all the shows available to take full advantage of the fact that we talk about lots of different topics in order to attract and win new subscribers — that is, to take advantage of the long-tail phenomenon — we need 173 MB for every month of the program. After a year, we're going to have 2,076 MB, or 2.08 GB of files that need to be hosted. Here's where increasing costs come in, if the hosting provider charges for storage. In the worksheet, enter the number 12 in the Months field, and use that number to multiply the Monthly Storage to get your yearly requirements.

4. Now let's figure out your podcast storage costs at launch and after one year of operation. Assuming your podcast is going to gain subscribers over that year, the cost per show delivered will fall, but there is still a real cost associated with having the full year's catalog of programs online. In the next worksheet, shown in Figure 19.3, you'll find the cost for storing those files with your host for the full year. Because most hosts sell blocks of storage, some months you'll be just under the threshold for higher fees and others you may be just above the cut-off and have to pay for substantially more space than you are using. For this exercise, we'll use podcast hosting provider LibSyn's pricing schedule:

- **Podcast Basic, up to 100 MB of storage, $5.00 a month:** Our show is an hour long (43.2 MB) and comes out four times a month, so we need more than the "basic" storage for our first month of shows.

- **Podcast Standard, up to 250 MB of storage, $10.00 a month:** This plan is enough for our first month, but in the second month we're already over 250 MB. So in Month Two our hosting costs have already risen by 100 percent. It's only $10, but the cost has changed.

- **Podcast Advanced, up to 525 MB of storage, $20.00 a month:** Amazingly, we're going to hit this level in Month Four, when our storage requirements at 170 MB per month have grown to 680 MB. And the next month, we'll hit the top of LibSyn's published price list.

- **Podcast Professional, up to 800 MB of storage, $30.00 a month:** We can call LibSyn and ask what more storage costs, but for purposes of this example we're really looking for representative data. If each 250 MB increment of storage has cost approximately $9.00, by the end of the year our 2,076 MB will cost $86 a month.

Enter the storage required for each month, remembering to add each new month's production files to the previous month's total. In the Cost field, enter the amount LibSyn charges for that amount of storage. If you exceed the total storage allotted to Podcast Professional users, add $9 for each additional 250 MB of storage you need. We've entered our example figures and left a blank version for your use.

5. As you can see from the worksheet, the *Steve & Mitch Hour* is looking at storage costs of $554.00 in the first year. That's not "free." We may want to consider using our own servers and broadband connection to syndicate the program from home. After all, we're already paying for that bandwidth and hosting several blogs and sites on these servers. Or, if we have existing hosting services, can we add the podcast storage on those servers without increasing our costs? These aren't recommendations as much as the kind of questions you should ask when thinking about hosting services.

FIGURE 19.3

Storage costs over the first full year of production

	Total Storage	Steve & Mitch Monthly Hosting	Your Total Storage	Your Show's Monthly Hosting
Month 1	173 MB	$10	____ MB	$ ____
Add previous month to total monthly storage	+173 MB			
Month 2	346 MB	$20	____ MB	$ ____
Add previous month to total monthly storage				
Month 3	519 MB	$20	____ MB	$ ____
Add previous month to total monthly storage				
Month 4	692 MB	$30	____ MB	$ ____
Add previous month to total monthly storage				
Month 5	865 MB	$39	____ MB	$ ____
Add previous month to total monthly storage				
Month 6	1038 MB	$39	____ MB	$ ____
Add previous month to total monthly storage				
Month 7	1211 MB	$48	____ MB	$ ____
Add previous month to total monthly storage				
Month 8	1384 MB	$57	____ MB	$ ____
Add previous month to total monthly storage				
Month 9	1557 MB	$66	____ MB	$ ____
Add previous month to total monthly storage				
Month 10	1730 MB	$66	____ MB	$ ____
Add previous month to total monthly storage				
Month 11	1903 MB	$75	____ MB	$ ____
Add previous month to total monthly storage				
Month 12	2076 MB	$84	____ MB	$ ____
Total		$554		____

Now, you may be thinking that it would be better to go with a hosting provider that charges for bandwidth. However, if you're doing short shows every day or each week, but expect them to be downloaded by 100,000 listeners, your bandwidth costs may rise more precipitously than storage costs with a bandwidth-based billing structure.

Consider that a 20-minute show recorded at 128 kbps (nearly CD quality) is about 19 MB in size. If 100,000 people download it each weekday, you'll be using 1,855 GB of throughput a day or 36.24 terabytes of network throughput each month. If your hosting provider offers, say, 250 GB of throughput a month for $9.95 (which would be generous, based on the pricing we've seen) and additional throughput for $1 per GB, a show requiring 36.24 TB of throughput a month would cost you $36,869.95 a month. That's pricey, to say the least.

Picking your plan

Because we don't expect to start with anywhere near 100,000 listeners, let's compare the prices we can expect to pay during the first year when paying for storage or for bandwidth when serving a few thousand listeners.

Two factors should decide which is a better deal for you, paying for storage or paying for bandwidth: (1) how popular you expect your show to be and (2) the level of technical sophistication you bring to running a server. Let's stick with the *Steve & Mitch Hour* as an example of how to plan costs. If we assume we're going to grow the show from 500 listeners in the first month up to 12,000 a month after the first year, here's how to calculate the bandwidth-based costs:

1. First, we need to know the length of the shows and the bit depth at which we plan to produce them, which combine to give us an estimated file size for each program. See the file sizes described in Figure 19.1 to determine the files size of the show you intend to produce. The *Steve & Mitch Hour* is approximately 42 MB an episode and delivered weekly.

2. In the worksheet in Figure 19.4, enter the file size of each show in the File Size field. Now, in Frequency, enter the number of times each month you plan to release a show. Multiply the File Size by the Frequency to arrive at the number of megabytes of throughput you need to serve each listener.

FIGURE 19.4

Calculating how much bandwidth you need to serve each listener

	The Steve & Mitch Hour	Your Show
File Size (see Fig. 19.1)	43.2 MB	_____
Frequency	4	_____
Monthly Subscriber Bandwidth Requirements	172.8 MB	_____

3. Next, in Figure 19.5, we're going to calculate the total bandwidth you need for the number of subscribers you plan to serve each month of your first year of production. As before, the figures for the *Steve & Mitch Hour* are displayed so that you can see how we calculated our show's bandwidth requirements as we grow the audience from 500 in the first month to 12,000 in the twelfth month. For simplicity's sake, we'll assume we have the same number of subscribers, which you enter in the Subscribers field, for the entire month. In reality, you'll be adding and losing subscribers all the time, so this exercise is merely to approximate your bandwidth requirements. Take the per-listener bandwidth figure you arrived at in the previous worksheet (shown in Figure 19.4), and enter it in the Subscriber Bandwidth field of Figure 19.5. Remember that if you plan to change the length of the show later, you should change the subscriber bandwidth requirements accordingly. After you multiply the Subscriber Bandwidth by the Number of Subscribers, divide the result by 1,000 to arrive at the number of gigabytes of bandwidth you need each month. A gigabyte is 1,000 MB.

4. We are assuming that a gigabyte of throughput costs approximately $0.75, which you should multiply by your Total Bandwidth for each month to find the cost of hosting. As you can see, the *Steve & Mitch Hour* would cost about $8,400 to host if we hit our subscriber targets. Moreover, we aren't accounting for the many one-off downloads that we might have to support in order to win those 12,000 subscribers. We also have not factored in the cost of managing a server that often comes with these services, which requires you to set up your own Web services and feeds.

NOTE This exercise provides only an approximate bandwidth-per-user figure because a number of factors can drastically increase a single listener's use of network bandwidth. If, for example, the listener has more than one podcatcher application subscribed to your program, both podcatchers download the whole file. Also, because many first-time listeners download one, two, or more shows to get a sense of what you do, they may use substantially more bandwidth in their first month.

Clearly, the spiraling cost of bandwidth is a more dangerous financial risk than the cost of storage. But the cost of storage doesn't include all the costs you may incur when trying to make money from a podcast. You can start a blog and place ads there to make some extra cash on click-throughs, which can be very effective if you mention in the show that listeners can get a deal by clicking an ad on your site, but then you have the cost of storing Web content, serving ads and, most importantly, keeping logs so that you can study them to improve the show and the financial performance of the site. Even a moderately busy Web site can generate logs that contain several gigabytes of data each month, and if you're paying for that storage too, the added cost, based on the assumptions here, runs to the hundreds of dollars a year.

FIGURE 19.5

Calculating your monthly bandwidth requirements for the first year of production

	Subscriber Bandwidth	Number of Subscribers	Total Bandwidth	Monthly Bandwidth Cost
Month 1				
Steve & Mitch Hour	173 MB	500	86.5 GB	$65
Your Show			_____ x $0.75	_____
Month 2				
Steve & Mitch Hour	173 MB	1,250	216.25 GB	$162
Your Show			_____ x $0.75	_____
Month 3				
Steve & Mitch Hour	173 MB	1,750	302.75 GB	$227
Your Show			_____ x $0.75	_____
Month 4				
Steve & Mitch Hour	173 MB	2,500	432.5 GB	$324
Your Show			_____ x $0.75	_____
Month 5				
Steve & Mitch Hour	173 MB	3,400	588.2 GB	$441
Your Show			_____ x $0.75	_____
Month 6				
Steve & Mitch Hour	173 MB	4,300	743.90 GB	$558
Your Show			_____ x $0.75	_____
Month 7				
Steve & Mitch Hour	173 MB	5,400	943.2 GB	$700
Your Show			_____ x $0.75	_____
Month 8				
Steve & Mitch Hour	173 MB	6,600	1,141.2 GB	$855
Your Show			_____ x $0.75	_____
Month 9				
Steve & Mitch Hour	173 MB	7,800	1,394.4 GB	$1,046
Your Show			_____ x $0.75	_____
Month 10				
Steve & Mitch Hour	173 MB	9,000	1,557 GB	$1,168
Your Show			_____ x $0.75	_____
Month 11				
Steve & Mitch Hour	173 MB	10,000	1,730 GB	$1.298
Your Show			_____ x $0.75	_____
Month 12				
Steve & Mitch Hour	173 MB	12,000	2.076 GB	$1,557
Your Show			_____ x $0.75	_____
Total			11,202.9 GB	$8,401

One of the common solutions for podcasters is to use their existing servers, which is a capitol idea if you have access to lots of storage and bandwidth. If, however, you're going to exceed your current hosting limits, it may be just as expensive as outsourcing the hosting or more so.

Both the authors operate several Web sites of our own and, with podcasts that reach hundreds of people, are satisfied with keeping those files on the servers run out of our home or collocation facilities. Believe it or not, even if you have a DSL or cable modem connection in your home that supports fixed IP addresses (which you need to host a server that can be found by people on the Internet), you can probably host your non-profit or small for-profit podcast out of your house.

The key is to throttle the upstream bandwidth for each download session to a level that allows multiple listeners to get a file at a reasonable speed. In all likelihood, you seldom will have two or more downloads going on at the same time. Just because you have upstream speed of, say, 768 Kbps (roughly 5.4 MB per minute) doesn't mean you have that much capacity all the time or that you could move 5.4 MB per minute all month long to cover all your bandwidth needs. Just in case you wondered how many bits you could theoretically ship over a 768 Kbps upstream connection over the 2.6 million minutes of a month, the answer is 14 terabytes (14,230 GB). But it isn't going to happen. Either your system will crash under the load, the network management overhead will eat up ever growing shares of the throughput, or you will get a very angry call from your telco or cable company.

You can think small and operate a podcast business out of your home. However, if you hope to achieve any audience scale that makes it a viable living, be ready to spend heartily.

Knowing the Rest of the Essentials

Hosting and delivery costs make up most of the expenses for most podcasters, but there are other costs to take into account as you build that first profit and loss worksheet.

If you plan on starting a podcast production company offering services to corporate clients, you need to consider the cost of office space and marketing materials. Making a good impression on clients sometimes requires an office or at least a shared meeting room you can use to host customers. Marketing expenses include your demo reel, printed collateral, and a Web presence that sets the appropriate tone. Crazy, hip, or professional, your marketing has to match the client's expectations about the quality and tone of their message, as well as being appealing.

Service businesses have to be examined from project perspective as well as the overall costs of hosting. When you take on a job, such as a production for a local car dealership, your planning must take into account how much time, materials, and ongoing expense are involved in delivering the program. If a client plans to host the program himself, you should, at minimum, go over those costs to make sure his expectations are in line with what he will pay. Sometimes, just telling your client that that his expectations are in line with reality will earn his confidence and bring a more profitable and realistic budget to the project. But you *cannot* start with a guess about the project cost and try to make up unexpected losses later — clients are going to hold you to the costs you initially quote. Having a clear and detailed work plan for pricing that can change if the customer changes his orders later is critically important to success in a service business. As you begin any project, be prepared to lay out and explain all the anticipated costs, for yourself and the client, so that you aren't surprised by expenses or find yourself paying for the client's changing preferences.

You may be tempted to look at all the projects and think, "Hey, I make plenty on each project," but miss the fixed costs you have in operating your business. Office, marketing expenses, the cost of accounting, billing costs — everything has to be included in your calculations. As a service business, you can't expect to make all this on one or two customers.

Your fixed costs have to be split over the whole month, even if you think of it as being covered by one or two projects' profits. So, as you plan a project, look at the number of hours involved in fulfilling the contract, and allocate your fixed costs over the whole month, dividing them and including them in your hourly billing. If you don't take these costs into account, your profit margin can evaporate instantly. You'll only think you're making money when you're paying the cost of staying in business. Everything has to be included in these estimated costs. Really. We've known too many producers who, thinking they were making good money, never really broke even because they viewed projects as separate from their business.

Too often, production companies try to load all their costs on the first project of the month and, as a result, lose business to competitors with more competitive pricing.

If you aren't working 40 hours a week on projects, be prepared to lose money on those core costs of doing business for most of the month, or all month, in the first year or two of the business. Starting with a realistic approach to your costs will keep your pricing competitive *and* give you a picture of the business that reduces the unpleasant surprises that startups often run into as their plans encounter the realities of the market.

Advertising costs money, too

Launching a commercial podcast has costs beyond the hosting fees. The cost of reaching out to advertisers and sponsors is real. If you seek advertisers yourself, it comes out of the time you spend with family or friends. If you hire someone to sell ads, it costs you out of your pocket each month. Commission-only salespeople carry no "risk," but they also usually sell lots of different stuff and opportunistically, so if they are doing better with someone else, they may not be spending much time on your program. And you won't really know until ad revenue comes through the door that any sales work is being done.

After the cost of finding ads or sponsor revenue, there's the problem of collecting it. If you don't have a billing system in place, just the cost of issuing invoices must be counted as an expense. Early and simple sponsorships are relatively easy to bill, because they may be based on a general appreciation of your work. A business may pay you $500 a month to mention them as a sponsor. Problem is, the ad/sponsor billing relationship requires more documentation when you (a) ask for premium fees and (b) achieve higher traffic levels that can be tied to volume-based pricing.

Advertisers want the most for their money. You want the most for your work (admit it, you do). The answer to your common predicament is documentation. You need to be able to show advertisers how many people download and/or listen to your podcast. In magazine advertising, the business is audited by independent third parties that report on the circulation of magazines. Likewise in radio and television. Podcasting's early metrics, based on the number of downloads, is very similar to the early Web advertising business' measurement of audience size. But over the last decade, counting Web pages has matured beyond "hits," which could count multiple parts of a page as different pages and inflate the results, to a variety of sophisticated metrics, many that depend on converting audience into buyers. Google's AdSense program, for example, pays for actual clicks on ads, not the number of times an ad is displayed.

In podcasting, the measurement of ads will evolve dramatically over the next few years. We don't know all the ways that it may develop, but advertising certainly will be more complicated than it is now.

CROSS-REF For a complete discussion of how to use advertising in your podcast, see Chapter 21," Making Advertising Work."

One more thing to count

We mentioned insurance before. Yes, even podcasters have to think about insurance. If you invite people into your home or an office to record, there are risks that someone could be hurt. The insurance on your home may not cover business visits. You need to check.

Then you must consider the question of insuring yourself against errors and omissions, the mistakes you may make when providing services or doing a commercial podcast that offers advice or information on which listeners may act. If you talk about investing, for example, listeners may act on that information and lose money. Yes, they should know there are risks in investing, but *you* gave them advice. And you're earning money or seem to be from the advertising on your show, so you may look like a target for litigation.

Insurers offer errors and omissions policies, often referred to as *E&O insurance,* that you may want to purchase. If you write your own scripts or ads, offer services that clients may later dispute (think about what happens if your advertising reports turn out to be inaccurate, for example), or make recommendations on risky topics, such as health or investing, E&O insurance may be for you. However, a publisher's exemption protects from liabilities journalists and analysts who give advice. This, unfortunately, has been abused by, for example, stock analysts that pumped stocks they owned.

We don't take a position on whether you need insurance, whether for your home or errors and omissions. Instead, it is something that you need to take into your calculations and consult a professional — a lawyer, not an insurance salesman — in order to ensure that you don't put your personal assets or profits on the line because a listener decides to sue you.

Summary

The hype has made podcasting sound much easier and cheaper than it is when scaled up to compete for large audiences' attention. As in every other business, you need to be prepared to spend money to make money, just a lot less than in television or radio at the start. In this chapter, you've learned:

- Podcasting isn't free. Depending on the type of podcast or podcasting service you plan, you need to consider a wide range of expenses that must be covered before you can expect to profit. Begin by building your podcasting profit and loss statement, even if it's just to figure out how much an exciting hobby can cost you.

- You can cut expenses in many ways, but all ways have their own costs. Making outsourcing and partnering decisions without fully understanding your business needs can cost you far too much in fees or revenue shared with partners.

- Make your hosting and distribution decisions based on a combination of how much storage you need to keep all your archives online — remember the long tail — and the throughput necessary to deliver your program to an audience that will support your expenses.

- Start slow. No business has instant successes, especially show business.

- Take all your expenses into account, including equipment, marketing costs, and promotional costs. Figure out how long you need to recoup your investment, and allocate those expenses to each show or project in order to spread them fairly to your customers, whether clients or advertisers. Pricing must be fair and competitive.

- Sometimes, bad things happen to good podcasters. Talk to a lawyer, accountant, and other professionals that any businessperson would consult when starting a business.

In the next chapter, we look at the subscriptions that may start to fill the revenue side of your profit and loss statements.

Chapter 20

The Subscription Business

S ubscribers, whether people who take time to add your RSS feed or paid customers, are your strongest supporters. They want you to succeed. They want you to deliver great programming. They expect much of you, making them a mixed blessing that you'll sometimes curse. In this chapter, we're going to deal with subscription arrangements that create revenue from your podcast, as well as the really simple subscriptions enabled by RSS.

Winning and keeping subscribers is hard work. It involves making your program easily available for sampling and making the experience both convenient and more informative or entertaining for listeners that subscribe. Fortunately, podcasting's use of RSS makes free subscriptions very easy. Conversely, the simplicity of RSS subscriptions makes asking for payment even harder than in previous media. You need to come to terms with the idea that some people who never subscribe will hear or see everything you do for free. Some call it piracy, but it's just marketing.

Subscriptions that limit access to your podcast — or add extra features delivered with your show — can serve two purposes. They are a way of collecting money from paying customers, but free registration-based podcasts can also be the foundation for high-value sponsorships and advertising if you can collect information about your listeners when they register. Advertisers are willing to pay a premium for targeted audiences. This is known as "controlled-circulation model" because it provides sponsors and advertisers access to very specific audiences.

Begin by thinking seriously about what kinds of subscription ideas are right for your podcast.

IN THIS CHAPTER
Subscribe to your listeners
The inevitable question: Do you care about piracy?
Mechanisms for controlling subscriptions
Two kinds of subscriptions
Free trials, free trials, free trials

If They Subscribe, You Must Serve Them

Subscribers, whether for a fee or free, impose a discipline. After you've made a promise to deliver a program and someone has accepted that offer, you're going to have to deliver. If you've charged a fee quickly in a world where so much information and entertainment is vying for their attention, failure to deliver will have people asking for refunds. Being on time, delivering what you promised — whether information, laughs, or entertainment — will determine whether you'll keep the subscriber.

CROSS-REF Chapter 16 covered how Really Simple Syndication (RSS) lets anyone add your program to their listening schedule. Here, we focus on the various ways to use subscription controls to create revenue.

Podcasting has famously eschewed paid subscriptions, but that's because it's still young. Paid TV and radio, from ad-free HBO and XM Satellite Radio to the esoteric range of pay-per-view programming available by cable, demonstrate that people willingly pay for content that they can't get anywhere else. This is not necessarily what makes the subscription model attractive to many people, who believe that you have to pay for something for it to be valuable. As you'll see, subscribers can pay in money or information, making the subscription model far more flexible than many believe.

Limiting access to your podcast is no small matter. It seems to fly in the face of aspirations of growing a large fan base, and in many cases, it does. You may want to build an audience and then attempt to convert them to a paying relationship later. This will cost you some of your audience, yet it can enable you to serve the audience that really supports and cares about what you deliver without injecting distracting advertisements. Ricky Gervais, the star of the BBC's "The Office," launched his podcast as a freely accessible program through *The Guardian* newspaper's Web site and found that he had a huge audience. Instead of watering down his program to accommodate advertisers who might recoil from his salty exchanges with his co-hosts, he opted to make money by selling "seasons" of six programs for a subscription price of $6.95 (and $1.95 for individual shows) through Audible.com.

Gervais, the accepted logic goes, could make the leap to paid subscriptions because he was a star who already had a large audience. But volume isn't the only consideration if you're thinking about what you may charge to listen to your podcast. If you're an expert whose insight is valued in a small community, such as a successful investment counselor who has a strong record of providing high returns in foreign markets, yours may be a podcast that can support a fee-based relationship with listeners.

Naturally, many folks will choose to go a different route, but the subscription fee is still a very viable approach to making money on audio or video content.

Why embrace a subscription business model for your podcast? If you want to make money and don't want to deal with advertisers, subscriptions are one of the two ways to make money. The other is relying on donations or "tips" contributed by listeners.

CROSS-REF Merchandising is another important form of monetization for podcasts. We'll look at that in Chapter 22, "Alternative Business Models."

Even Decade-Old Shows Can Sell

Throughout this book, we've talked about the "long-tail" phenomenon, which predicts that in networked markets a copy of almost everything made available will sell, because there is someone interested in the subject of a program. Digital distribution makes a huge back catalog available, which means producers can take advantage of long-tail economics.

Sounds good, but is it true with podcasts? The medium has been around for a very short time, records of downloads aren't public, and only a small fraction of older programs have been kept online because of the cost of storing them, so we will point instead to the example of Mitch Ratcliffe's *Adventures In Technology* audio program, which he published through Audible between 1998 and 2000. It was a podcast before podcasting came long, in which Mitch talked about technology for 40 minutes to an hour.

Every quarter, Audible sells many of these old programs. For the most part, they are interesting only as historical views, because the subjects ranged from early e-commerce developments to the Y2K "bug" and what was Microsoft's OS at the time, Windows 97, and its delayed update, Windows XP. What's especially interesting from the perspective of the long tail is that so many different older *Adventures in Technology* programs sell each quarter.

In the first quarter of 2006, for example, of the approximately 40 separate *Adventures* programs Mitch produced in the series, 31 different episodes sold. More than 75 percent of the catalog sold at least once. Only nine programs sold more than one copy.

What's more, the subject of a program or its "star" need not be famous to play successfully in this world.

Does this mean my podcast is closed to the public?

Having a subscription control on your podcast doesn't mean that it must be closed to the public. You certainly need to make many excerpts or whole shows available to win new subscribers. Subscriptions can also come with enhanced services, such as downloadable documents or even a hat or t-shirt that is mailed out to paid subscribers, so that anyone can listen but supporters get a bonus.

Let's say, for example, that you are the financial planner we mentioned previously: You could give away your podcast for free to trial subscribers who get one or two shows, and if they convert to paying customers, you might include a set of worksheets or stock reports with each program that helps them follow your analysis or conduct their own. Another way to add value is to offer free streaming versions of all the shows you produce while making downloads available for a fee; this gives your subscribers the convenience of portability while keeping your ideas open to all.

The simple fact is if you place a value on your content or require subscriptions, it likely will be pirated. It's inevitable and perfectly okay, because it is just another way to get people to try out your program. In lots of circles, this is called "piracy," but it's also an effective form of marketing.

It's all the more reason for you to concentrate on what kind of premium experience and convenience you can offer to subscribers. The record industry, by spending massive amounts of time and energy chasing pirates, makes lots of enemies and only manages to raise the cost of commercial music. Let piracy be your marketing instead of expending effort trying to curb it. Eventually, if you become a monster star, you may think differently. By then, though, you may be feeling generous enough to forget the illegal copies, especially if they continue to drive some percentage of your paid subscribers.

How to deal with piracy, then? Don't threaten to sue people; just ask nicely that they take down your programs and direct people to your site to get the program. If they ignore you when you ask nicely, turn it back on them by thanking them by name for spreading the word about your program, encouraging listeners who got the show from a pirate site to come directly to you. Use the opportunity to sell the benefits of your subscription program, not the least of which is that it lets you put more time into the program when they subscribe.

Unauthorized copies: The sky's the limit

Keeping up with copying is the biggest challenge, because if you simply ignore it, you are missing the value created by those copies. We suggest that you set up Google search alerts, which deliver results to your e-mail inbox on the hour or daily, with the title of your podcast, so that you are alerted whenever someone refers to it on the Web. Most unauthorized copies, whether MP3 or Bittorrent, have slightly mangled titles to prevent creators from finding them easily. With a bit of practice, you easily can keep up, because, like you, the people looking for programs need some consistency in titling to find what they are like. Torrent and MP3 search sites come and go, so it pays to keep up on the latest sources. We currently rely on Bitoogle.com (though we think the name needs work) to track programs available in the Bittorrent format. In addition, we suggest that you use these popular media search services:

- `http://search.singingfish.com`. Singingfish, shown in Figure 20.1, is a comprehensive audio and video search engine. It allows you to search by media type by checking boxes for MP3 format (among others) and program subject. The service allows saved searches, so you can assemble a suite of searches that cover your program and run through them quickly on a weekly or monthly basis. The point is to keep up on where your program may be showing up, not to police the Net. Singingfish points to "legitimate" sites, but you want to keep an eye on these too in case, somehow, your work starts to show up on sites you didn't talk with first.

- `http://audio.search.yahoo.com`. Yahoo's audio search also aims at sources of audio that appear to be authorized to carry the content they feature. The results can be focused by format and type of source, including "music," "podcast" and "other audio," though we find the same program can show up in all three. Unfortunately, you can't mail yourself results automatically each day. If you're looking for video content, see Yahoo's video search engine at `http://video.search.yahoo.com`.

FIGURE 20.1

Singingfish media search

Pirates aren't your friends, but they also aren't the enemy you may think they are. If you exercise patience and think tactically in response to the fact your program is spreading outside the subscription service you planned, it can be turned into an advantage. Every time your show is played, it is a chance to thank subscribers for their support and encourage others to join in. Think of yourself as National Public Radio, which survives on the support of less than 15 percent of its listeners. If you can convert 20 percent of your pirated listenership, you're already ahead of a venerable institution in broadcasting.

Controlling Access to Your Podcast

Convenience is the key to a successful subscription business. If you make it difficult to get your podcast, people will look elsewhere for information or entertainment. When you blend ease of use and information or entertainment, a subscription fee will not stand in the way of a listener who is excited about you. The challenge, of course, is getting them excited about listening despite any hoops they might have to jump through. Subscription systems have only begun to mature, so we expect that eventually getting a paid podcast will be as easy for your customer as flipping the channel on a television. More on this shortly; first, we'll go over the various ways to set your subscription podcast apart from the rest of your site.

Secure Pages

Placing your podcast RSS feed in a secured private section of your Web site, where one must enter some information about oneself or pay a fee to gain access, is one easy way to create a subscription experience.

Many sites you frequent use such private sections to serve subscriber content. The first time you try to access the subscription-only material, the site offers the ability to sign up. It collects your name, contact information, and your credit card number (if there is a charge), and you get a username and password. The next time you login, the username and password let you into the subscription area. If you've clicked the "Remember Me" box, a cookie is set on your computer and you get in without having to enter your username/password combination again.

We are not talking at this point about protecting your podcasts from unauthorized downloads. Instead, the idea is to restrict access to information about where your podcasts are located. In other words, think about using a secure page to display the RSS feed URL for your podcast, as well as placing supporting materials, such as worksheets, for subscribers to download should they choose to.

By keeping your podcasts in a public file, you preserve your ability to send out links for promotional purposes or even from links on your blog or Web site. The podcasts will play when someone clicks a link to them, but there will be no subscription feed easily accessible to people who would listen but not pay for the convenience of RSS delivery. Your RSS feed URL in all likelihood will still be passed around by a paying customer, but you can occasionally change the URL, sending a message to subscribers that they need to change their podcast client's subscription, which also reinforces the fact that you want or need to be paid for the program.

It can be very simple to restrict access to a page or directory on your site to customers who have been given a username and password. The first option is to create a password file, where each subscriber's username and password are recorded so that the server can check to see if it should grant access.

Web servers use a .htaccess file to keep track of the access requirements for pages or sections of a server. You must have the right to set these preferences on your server, and not all hosting companies are going to let you do it, so check with your hosting provider before doing anything. Let's say you want to have a subscriber section of your site called "subscribers" with a number of pages that require a password.

1. **Create a subdirectory in your public_html directory called** subscribers. This directory would reside at /server/public_html/subscribers/ on the server.

2. **Create a password file called** .htpasswd. This file, which can be stored in a non-public directory of your server, will contain a list of usernames and passwords, for example, "stevemack: stevepassword" (be sure to use the colon to separate them), which tells the server that in order to gain access to your secure page, a subscriber must enter the

username "stevemack" and the password "stevepassword." You can keep this list up to date by hand, adding usernames and passwords manually, or you can use scripts to automate updates.

3. **Create a .htaccess file for the subscribers subdirectory.** Create a file that you place in the subscribers directory located at /server/public_html/subscribers/.htaccess. This file tells the server what access rules apply to your subscribers directory and where to look for the password list, which is stored in the /lib directory of the server. Here is what the content of the file would look like:

```
AuthUserFile
/server/lib/public_html/subscribers/.htpasswd
AuthName "Access to Subscriber Pages"
AuthType Basic

require valid-user
```

This system is very minimal. It grants the user access to any page within the subscribers section of the site — that is, any page you place in the subscribers subdirectory. However, it also is rather weak security, because if your server is insecure (which most are, to the determined cracker), the password file can be grabbed and used to get access. More importantly to your users, if they have used those passwords anywhere else and the attacker can associate their accounts with those used on other servers, you may have put personal information at risk. There is a more secure way to go about it.

The private section of a site also can be built using the Secure Sockets Layer (SSL) capabilities in any modern Web server. SSL is built on public-key cryptography, an encryption technology that can be used to protect the content of communication or to authenticate access to a site. It takes two keys: a "private" key installed on the server and a "public" key derived from that private key distributed to client computers. Every public key is unique and cannot be used to get around security on other sites. SSL also can be combined with cookies to automate login.

The procedure for setting up SSL-access controls varies from server to server. Here are the steps you should not miss, based on the instructions for adding security to an Apache Web server:

1. **Create a private key for your server.** Your SSL-enabled server has a utility for generating a private key. Place the key in a file called server.key.

2. **Get a certificate for the public key from a Certificate Authority.** A third party, known as a Certificate Authority (CA), issues a computer-readable document verifying that your server is authentic, allowing customers to check to see that they are not being scammed when they do business on the site. GoDaddy, Verisign, and GeoTrust are some well-known CAs. Certificates cost between $20 and $300 a year, depending on how many sites are covered (so, if you have a .com, .tv, and other versions of your domain, one certificate can cover all your domain names). Here are a few certificate authorities you can use:

   - **Verisign:** `http://www.verisign.com/`
   - **Entrust:** `http://www.entrust.com/`
   - **GoDaddy:** `http://www.godaddy.com/`

3. **Install the certificate on your server.** The certificate is an ugly thing, just a string of letters and numbers 1328 characters long, which you place in a .crt file (for example, podcastingbible.crt for a site associated with this book) in the /conf/ssl.crt/ directory of your Web server. In Apache servers, the file is located at apache/conf/ssl.crt/podcastingbible.crt.

4. **Modify your server's httpd.conf file.** Change httpd.conf to point to the location of the following:

   - SSLCertificateFile: /path/to/server.crt

   - SSLCertificateKeyFile: /path/to/server.key

   - SSLCertificatePath: /path/to/server/conf/ssl.crt

5. **You may need to recompile, or you may not.** Check your server manual.

6. **Go back to your server's httpd.conf file, find the text SSLEngine, and add a new line that reads "AccessFileName .sslaccess" immediately after it.** This tells the server that it should look for rules about access by your subscribers. The server recognizes different levels of access based on .sslaccess files that describe the rights of users on individual pages.

7. **Restart your server.**

8. **Create a new directory called** subscribers **in your server's public_html directory.** This file is where you store all the pages that point to podcast files.

9. **Now create a** /public_html/subscribers/.htaccess **file, and enable the "deny from all" directive.** This means that no regular access is allowed for the pages stored in this directory.

10. **Create a new file** .sslaccess**.** Now we have to grant SSL access to the subscribers directory by creating a .sslaccess file for the subscribers directory or individual pages within that secure directory. Open a new file, save it as "/public_html/subscribers/.htaccess, and insert this text:

```
SSLRequireSSL
# no non-ssl access
order allow,deny
```

Congratulations, you've secured your subscribers section. We do not cover how to use cookies in this book, because Wiley authors have covered this topic in a variety of books.

TIP   A powerful scripted .htaccess password protection installer is available for servers running Apache, the most widely used Web-hosting software. .htaccess Password Protector, from Techno Trade, is a $49 Perl CGI script that can be installed in Apache servers to secure pages and manage subscriber access. See `http://www.htaccess.biz`.

This approach to securing your RSS feeds and any enhanced content you offer with your podcast preserves easy sampling of the program, because each podcast still is available for free automated download. It places the onus on you to make subscribing worth the cost, so that your listeners see the value in preserving their "exclusive" access to automated downloads. The next step up the security ladder is locking down your podcast, so that only someone with a password can get a copy.

Password-controlled podcasting

Limiting downloads of a podcast to subscribers only is controversial among both podcasters and people who listen to podcasts. If you erect a barrier to the program itself, you're going to have to make the case that the audio itself is worthwhile, even if you offer supporting documents that add value.

Adding password protection is a relatively simple step from the security we've already set up. You simply move podcast files into the secure directory called subscribers and require a username and password to download. This forces a password challenge anytime someone tries to download a program.

The complications come when you want to distribute your podcast through third-party podcast feed aggregators. Most aggregators don't support secure downloads at all, so we suggest you submit only older programs to these sites as part of your marketing outreach efforts. Apple's iTunes supports full HTTP authentication through SSL, which we set up in the preceding section (just remember to move your podcast files into the secure directory), but some versions of Internet Explorer don't hand off requests to iTunes correctly, so that security doesn't work.

FeedBurner's password support is rather limited, allowing only one username and password that must be shared by all subscribers. The obvious problem with this is that if one subscriber tells someone the username/password combination, the secret is out.

Some newsreader and podcatcher applications, such as NetNewswire, NewsMac Pro, NewsFire, and Juice, support password protection, recognizing it and displaying the username/password challenge to people when they attempt to download a file. Online aggregators are a mixed bag, with standout services such as Newsgator, supporting HTTP authentication, but most are unable to deal with security. Several of these applications support a form of authentication that embeds the username and password in the RSS feed URL, such as `http://username:password@ www.yoursite.com/RSS.xml`. This is *an incredibly bad idea,* because it allows anyone to learn the answer to your server's security challenge by mousing over the URL.

You needn't make any changes to your RSS XML code to accommodate security, because the sites and applications that recognize the username/password challenge do it when they attempt to download new programs. At this writing, Apple iTunes' security requires subscribers to log in each time they update their subscriptions, even when the Remember Password box is checked in the username/password dialog box, as shown in Figure 20.2.

Anyone can build a subscription business with the HTTP authentication described here. You have to deal with the logistics of getting money from subscribers and adding their accounts to your password files. Otherwise, this currently is the best option for a self-administered subscription business. What you're missing is one of the great bugaboos of the contemporary computing scene — Digital Rights Management, which controls access to your files after they've left your server.

Organizational guru David Allen's fee-based podcast is password protected, accessible through iTunes.

Commercial/hosted-service option

Audible Inc.'s Wordcast service (`wordcast.audible.com`) was the first secure podcasting host-ing service. (*Disclosure:* Mitch Ratcliffe, coauthor of this book, contributed to the design and pric-ing of the service.) It provides a complete system for uploading a file in MP3 or WAV format, handling the encoding of programs into Audible's secure .AA file format, pricing and subscription controls, as well as reporting features that describe how much and what parts of the program were listened to by your audience.

Audible has been selling audio files for almost 10 years and now hosts the first paid podcast, by comedian Ricky Gervais, as well as the first paid podcast sermons and other early subscription pro-gramming. The Wordcast platform, which costs $0.02 per subscriber per month, delivers features that are important to keeping people happily engaged with your program. It keeps track of the pro-grams listeners have downloaded in a personal library and offers free re-downloads if they delete or lose a program, so that they don't need to go hunting for a title they need to replace. Apple's iTunes won't let you re-download if you fail to make your own backups of songs or books (even those sold by Audible on iTunes) and then your hard drive fails, but the Audible site is oriented to keep-ing each of your customers' full library available for re-use.

Yes, there is a Digital Rights Management (DRM) system involved in the Audible offering. It pro-vides you, the producer, the ability to set the number of copies you will allow, even the ability to make unlimited numbers of copies, as well as making pricing and subscription lists easy to man-age. Audible can handle all transactions, processing credit cards and managing password and user accounts for a 20 percent share of the sale price, or you can deal with transactions and update the subscriber list manually. If a user downloads the same title repeatedly, you don't pay extra for each download. All bandwidth costs are included in the two-cent fee podcasters pay each month for subscribers.

The Wordcast site also provides a marketing platform for your podcast, a directory of programs available through the site and around the Web. It also supports dynamic insertion of advertising in programs as they are downloaded (a $0.00333 fee for each ad is inserted), which lets new ads be

Drumming Up a Little Support for DRM

We know lots of reasons to hate Digital Rights Management (DRM), especially because the entertainment industry has abused the transformation of media to bits by trying to turn every title sold into a prison experience. It has become impossible to buy a song or movie, whether on CD, DVD, or downloaded from the Net, that can be copied even for backup purposes. Limits on the number of devices on which a purchase can play keep many people from enjoying music where and when they want. You can't even pass on a copy of a song to a friend on a mix tape without breaking a ridiculously restrictive law, the Digital Millennium Copyright Act passed by Congress in 1998.

DRM, nevertheless, is a tool that can be valuable for everyone involved when applied fairly to increase customers' convenient access to information and entertainment. We expect to hear howls of disagreement in some of the places this statement is read based on the reprehensible DRM practices of the music industry and Hollywood. When big institutions sense a threat, even imagined, they overreact.

DRM can be useful for individual artists and producers. It can be used to create convenient subscription systems, giving buyers the ability to make a reasonable number of copies of audio or video while making it sufficiently troublesome to place the file on the Web for unpaid reproduction.

Here's the catch and the debate to be had: Workarounds can always defeat DRM, so why put any restrictions on the customer's ability to make a copy at all? Doesn't that prevent people from learning about your program through unauthorized copies, as we have pointed out? The answer to the last question, about marketing-as-piracy, is "Yes." DRM does cut off that "benefit" of piracy, but if you value your program so much that you want to keep it limited to people who have paid for it, DRM is the only answer. So the answer to the former question is that if DRM is fair and doesn't interfere with their normal listening habits (such as requiring a specialized device that they can't use for other audio for listening to the program), most customers find this to be no burden at all and can validate the expense.

A pirate may put your audio or video online, grabbing the audio off his sound card or video card after it is decrypted, but that will cost you far fewer paying customers than those who find you through honest channels. The challenge always is for you to make the case to potential subscribers that your program is worth paying for, whether or not you use DRM.

added to the rotation rather than locking in the ads that you'd sold when the show was produced. This is an important feature for the ad market, because it gives you the ability to sell new ad insertions for all the episodes at prices that reflect your current listenership, even years after the first shows were produced.

Wordcast requires a one-time activation fee of $35.00. Because you pay only for the subscribers you have, it costs little to begin with and can grow with your audience. If, for example, you have 200 subscribers in the first month, your total Wordcast fee is $4.00.

If you are thinking about using a subscription system to control distribution to your customers for another business, where you really make your money, the Wordcast system is a solid foundation for happy customer relationships.

As you introduce subscription fees, Audible's 20-percent share of revenue may look fairly steep, but the integration of transaction functionality with the Audible library provides a proven customer experience that would be very expensive to build into your own site. Handling your own transactions and using Wordcast to handle delivering programs is perfectly reasonable; the process will take you some time each day or week.

Subscriptions Ins and Outs

You can look at subscriptions in two ways: One takes far less effort than the other. The non-recurring subscription is one that you ask for once and just once. Recurring subscriptions, such as when you ask for a renewal fee each year, take more effort but tend to be much more profitable.

Why use a one-time subscription model? Well, it's pretty simple to ask for a payment for access just once. It's like selling a book or a ticket to a concert. The problem is this: If your performance is going to continue, the entry price starts to look cheap . . . to you. It's a great deal for the customer if they pay once and get new programming every week or month forever. So the non-recurring subscription is best for one-time titles, like a book or a single show.

If you go with one-time fees, think of the series of programs that you produce as a catalog filled with individual products, each with a price of its own. This forces you to address each show as a marketing challenge on its own: About each one, you must ask "What makes this program unique?" In essence, you're building a little Amazon. You need to develop a solid description of each product, offer snippets of sample audio or video, and find a reasonable way to present the range of selections to the market.

Recurring subscriptions are likely to be most effective for a recurring podcast. And the work only begins after you get the first year's payment. Welcome to the world of renewal marketing. Magazines and newspapers have dealt with this for years, and we suggest you study how they approach you about renewals to get some ideas about what works and what is repulsive to you. Unfortunately, what is repulsive to you may work better than what you think is successful, so it's important to remember some basic concepts:

- Online subscriptions are easier than offline ones, because you don't need to send an invoice. But you do need to have a refund mechanism in place.

- Begin your renewal marketing early. As a rule, you should begin to communicate with the customer about renewal six months before the subscription lapses.

- Keeping a customer is important, but not at the expense of your margins. Many publishers start their renewal efforts by offering a discount (a special price for early renewals) and then increase the price from that initial discount, but always below the full price of the subscription, until the subscription period ends. Then they offer discounts to lapsed subscribers to get them back, but never as low as the early renewal price. After all, the cost of all those renewal offers has to be covered, too.

- Where's your football phone? Everyone has seen or heard offers of free stuff offered with a magazine subscription. Why not do the same with a podcast subscription? After all, your audience is attractive to someone who has a product or service, so why not offer a free trial to your best subscribers (the ones who renew, which is a demonstration that they are willing to spend money).

Here's the thing: We're talking about selling. Revenue comes from sales, so you need to be thinking constantly about how your podcast contributes to your customers' lives so that their next subscription payment is essential to them, to their continued enjoyment or success. Selling is about meeting and exceeding expectations, but you still need to be talking with customers to ensure that they re-up when their subscription expires.

Free-to-Fee, the Conversion Path

You have to be heard or seen before you can convert a listener into a customer. Unfortunately, many podcasters have adopted this truism as a sort of biblical truth, insisting that the only way to reach an audience is to be heard in full for free every time. This is because most folks starting a podcast believe that the proliferation of audio and video programming makes the podcast a commodity product. They do not. If you want to make a business of a program, you have to transcend the market in some way to create a product that is unique and valuable. No one makes a business being like everyone else.

You must find ways to offer snippets of your new programs and full versions of older programs with a direct path to your subscription page, where the listener can become a paying subscriber. To the degree that you can recognize repeat visitors and increase the value of your subscription offer. Keep in mind that, unlike previous media, podcasting is pretty malleable. Ricky Gervais, rather than selling a year's subscription, is offering "seasons" of six shows. Consider offering longer subscription periods for the same price instead of lowering the price of a fixed-time subscription.

Free previews can be excerpts of your best shows or complete older shows. If your information is timely, such as stock picks, the fact that you can give away older material is a huge benefit, because if your picks are successful, you can even drop in updates that point out your successes.

The only thing that determines your success is converting a listener into a paying customer. Don't be shy about asking for the subscription; your business is the podcast you produce.

Summary

Starting a podcasting business is tricky. This chapter covered these topics to help you navigate the treacherous waters of customer expectations and subscription management:

- Subscriptions for a fee impose a discipline on the customer that amateur podcasting may embrace, but those who seek to profit from podcasting must accept and learn to use to their advantage. Everything is about your customers' success or entertainment, so keep them in mind every time you turn on the microphone.

- The power of the "long tail" is working to your advantage. You must find the untapped customer for every show you ever produce so you can earn a fee or a subscription to newly produced programs. Even a 10-year-old podcast can find a listener every quarter.

- A subscription business is a balance between limited access and easy discoverability, so that new listeners are able to find and become involved with you and your show. Having a subscription business does not mean shutting the door to the world, even if that were possible in light of "piracy." Instead, it means that you have to treat your shows, including those unauthorized copies that exist, as part of a complete marketing effort that aims to turn any listener into a supporting listener, through fees or by collecting information you can use to boost your advertising revenue.

- Keep up on the unauthorized copying of your show, but don't be heavy-handed about shutting it down. Always start with a polite request, because some of your biggest fans may be pirating you. Turn them into your marketers.

- HTTP authentication is a simple solution to access control, allowing you to place RSS feeds or entire podcasts behind a password-controlled barrier. It doesn't provide any protection of your MP3 files after they've been downloaded, but that's okay if you use each show to reinforce the message that you want and appreciate the financial support of your audience.

- Digital Rights Management (DRM) technology has been used like a nuclear bomb by the music industry and Hollywood, but that doesn't mean you can't make a virtue of it in your small business. Be generous with the number of copies you allow, and turn registration with the DRM provider into a foundation for ongoing access to the customer's library in order to make subscribing more attractive.

- Subscription revenues are built on sustained positive communication with customers, asking for renewals with varied price and benefits offers. If you assume that talking with your subscribers is the foundation of your business, and start to do so early in the subscription period, you will get a higher renewal rate overall.

With subscriptions under our belt, it is time to look at the next approach to making money with a podcast, the wild, woolly world of advertising.

Chapter 21

Making Advertising Work

Most ideas about advertising are remnants of the industrial mass media. Ads in those media were interruptive, barging in on the story or discussion, and being counted by the thousands of people exposed, termed *impressions* in the biz, yielding a rate card for publications that emphasized their size. Advertisers and ad agencies are used to buying interactions with millions or tens of millions of audience members. Podcasting flies in the face of all that, because it thrives on small audiences today and likely will remain more a boutique medium, with small groups who have strong collective identities, often called *communities*.

Communities are very attractive to advertisers these days. Now that mass media is breaking into smaller fragments, the idea of a group of people with the demographic qualities that an advertiser may be looking for seems ideal for big brands. This was also the case at the birth of the Web, when lots of experimentation with ads and sponsorships turned into a strongly measured form of advertising. In fact, the much-improved measurement of media performance transformed advertising as just showing an ad and hoping it was remembered turned into pay-for-action advertising, payment changing hands only when someone clicked an ad or made a purchase.

Alas, podcasting was developed without the ability to count listeners. Dave Winer even stated that he designed the combination of RSS and MP3 audio format to thwart advertising. So today, there are competing forms of counting battling for advertisers' trust, and advertisers will ultimately decide the fate of this business model. If the folks who pay for ads have to accept the amorphous counting of listenership that made television, radio, and newspaper advertising successful, podcasters are not likely to claim premium or even poor compensation for their ad inventory.

What Is Advertising in Podcasting?

If all the concepts that define advertising come from the mass media, what's the advertising in podcasting going to look like? Because all other new media have had to provide better metrics to win advertiser confidence, we know that advertising in podcasting will be better counted and include ways to complete or at least to keep a potential transaction moving toward its fulfillment. Otherwise, it will probably sound and look very different from traditional advertising, because it will be much less interruptive and based on borrowing part of the podcaster's personal connection with the listener.

What do we mean by "borrowing" some of the podcaster's relationship with listeners? Simply this: Like the early days of television, another time when investments in talent were essential to brands, podcasting marks a moment when stars will define the relationship with the audience. Like Milton Berle, who was sponsored by Texaco — the show was *The Texaco Star Theater*, but people tuned into "Uncle Miltie" — podcasters stand in a unique position between the advertiser brand and the audience. Whether this lasts remains to be seen, but it is certain that for the foreseeable future the producer is in charge of this critical relationship.

So advertisers will be looking for podcasters who will endorse the advertised product or service. This format is familiar on talk radio, though in podcasting there is a more subtle way of going about it that could make the endorsement seem natural rather than a paid message. We think this is dangerous to the podcasters' reputation if they are not sincerely convinced of the value in the product or service being endorsed, because the listener will hold them accountable, even blogging or counter-podcasting when they feel burned, not just by the product but also by the person who "recommended" it.

CROSS-REF See Chapter 22, "Alternative Business Models," to see the other approaches to making money with podcasts. Advertising concepts, such as CPM and CPA, can be used to calculate how many books you might sell through Amazon or in other transaction-based scenarios to help project revenue.

More traditional ads, inserted into a program and recognizably different from the show itself, will also play a part in the ad model for podcasting. Instead of being interruptive, they may be concentrated at the beginning or end of a show, and based on feedback that podcasters have received from audience and advertiser alike, the message should in some way fit with the subject of the podcast. As media break down into more narrowly defined markets, this will be more easily achieved, because a podcast about cars is a natural place to advertise automobiles. By contrast, advertising a car in the middle of a television show about survivors of an airliner crash living on a tropical island populated by polar bears and mysterious "Others" seems quite out of place. This is why ads have pressed the edge of creativity; they need to find a way to stand out in opposition to shows. Advertising in podcasting is much more likely to have some context that relates it to the subject of the show.

Ultimately, following the trend established by the Web, advertising probably will succeed or fail on the ability to measure actual audience engagement with the show and the ads in it. Only 15 years ago, most advertising existed in a feedback void. Advertisers had no idea whether a message was really seen and, more importantly, whether anyone responded or why. With the interactivity of the

Web, where clicks on ads can begin an actual interaction, response rates became the gold standard, and as a result, Web pages charged much higher rates than most television shows did. That was because, for the first time, the ads were accountable in some way. That magic wore off, and today ads simply are measured when they are delivered over the Internet. Rates have fallen back to levels comparable across demographic markets, so that even if advertisers pay more per click they are reaching their desired audience at a rate not significantly different from what they believe they paid for television in the early 1990s.

Measurement and how people choose to interact with your podcast are going to be the keys to your advertising revenue. Though many may tell you that advertisers should feel lucky to get in on this market, the podcasters who establish profitable relationships for advertisers are most likely to be seen as the breakout successes in podcasting, just as Web sites that attended to both the advertiser and its audience have made out best of all. Your business is your audience, but you must also get along with your advertisers without compromising your ethics.

CPM versus CPA: Choosing Your Basic Unit

Regardless of how you decide to present advertising in your program, you need to make some initial decisions about how to measure what you are delivering to advertisers. They want to have a predictable cost for being associated with your show, one that relates the expense to the results they expect and get. This may sound like a call to simply go along with whatever the advertiser dictates, but it isn't. A good advertising sales unit has measurements that allow you to point out when the advertiser is beating its goals, meaning that you have some leverage to negotiate a higher rate, too. This relationship should not be one-sided in a medium that is already highly interactive.

Simple sponsorships, where someone pays you to mention that he supports the show, perhaps with a little chatter about his products, needs to be measured, too. If you sign an initial deal with the sponsor for $1,000 a month, when your regular audience is 10,000 listeners per show, you certainly want to be paid more when your audience reaches 500,000 per show.

This is where the basic unit of advertising from the pre-interactive world comes into play: Cost-per-thousand, or CPM ("M" is from the Latin for 1,000), is how newspapers, radio, and television stations have characterized the cost of advertising for years. CPM is a shorthand for exposures to the audience rather than a number of actual listeners, because there is no guaranteeing people will hear a specific part of a show, yet. It's how to describe the "reach" of a show advertisers understand. For example, if you deliver 10,000 listeners each week for four weeks — a total of 40,000 listeners — for $1,000, the cost-per-thousand-listeners is figured this way:

40,000 listeners divided by 1,000 = 40

$1,000 (the sponsor fee) divided by 40 = $25 CPM

Believe us when we say that a $25 CPM is pretty good money, better than almost any radio station has made in three decades, adjusted for inflation. Some television shows do better, but the explosion of cable channels has created so much advertising inventory that the vast majority of television is sold for less than a $5 CPM.

Now, what happens when your audience expands? If you've increased your audience to 500,000 per show four times a month, but you're still paid $1,000 per month by a sponsor or advertiser, well, let's do the math:

2,000,000 listeners divided by 1,000 = 2,000

$1,000 divided by 2,000 = $0.50

Things aren't working out in your favor. Sure, the advertiser is happy as a clam, but you've seen your earnings fall by a factor of 50.

What's more, your costs increased precipitously as your audience grew, so you are losing far more money now that you're a big hit than when you started out if you have not found a way to tie the performance of the show to something you can show to the advertiser to justify higher rates.

The deceptive thing about CPM is that $25 or even $5 per thousand downloads may sound like lots of money, but you probably need multiple advertisers in order to turn a profit at any level of listen-ership. If each download costs you $0.02, at $25 CPM you'll make just one-half cent per download after the cost of bandwidth. With all the other costs you have, including marketing the show to make the audience bigger for you and your advertisers and sponsors, you need several advertisers.

And the thing is you aren't going to get $25 per thousand listeners. It isn't going to happen in a world where most advertising on the Web is now measured not just for its effectiveness (how many people clicked on a banner ad), but also how many people became customers based on an ad. With no metrics other than the number of downloads you report each month, your CPM is going to be very low, probably less than $1 in many cases. See Figure 21.1 for an example.

FIGURE 21.1

CPM and CPA models

Moreover, because you cannot tell the advertiser much about how many people actually listen to your show or about what parts of the show are listened to, you can't command a premium for placing ads close to the most popular segments of your podcast.

In many ways, what we're describing now is starting to look like traditional TV and radio advertis-ing. If a broadcaster can't say with any confidence that people are watching ads, but can only say that they have popular segments, such as the Top Ten List on *Late Night with David Letterman*, the ads sold that run in close proximity to the Top Ten List command a premium based on the presumption that they will be seen by more people than an ad running close to the end of the show.

Add measurement to your advertising by counting actual listenership, and you increase the value of each ad insertion because you provide some accountability for the advertiser.

On the Web, in banner and other ads running on popular sites, that accountability has come in the form of cost-per-action (CPA) advertising. In other words, advertisers pay only for the ads that work, those that get a click or result in a closed sale. The Web site literally gives away its ad inventory in order to get the chance to earn a higher fee for a CPA event. So, instead of being paid $1.25 for a thousand appearances of the ad on pages at the site, the Web site producer is paid, say $4.50 for each click-through on the ad by visitors. If you get three people to click an ad per 1,000 impressions, that works out to a CPM of $13.50, far more than the $1.25 CPM for unaccountable ads. Yet sometimes you'll have no clicks in 5,000 impressions and make nothing. However, because you've been paid a premium for delivering an action, the average works out to more than the basic CPM for advertising with no metrics to justify the advertiser's cost other than sheer volume.

Some CPA advertising can produce extraordinarily high fees for actions. In markets where a sale can be worth $1,000 or $5,000, such as the mortgage industry, financial services sites, and medical sites, the fee per closed customer can run well above $50 and much more. It's something to think about when choosing your podcast topics and calculating your potential ad revenue.

CPA advertising is the wave of the future, because it makes the ads work for their money. Advertisers once had to live with the idea that half their ad spending was a waste; they just didn't know which half.

A smart podcaster, like a smart TV producer, recognizes that a mix of CPM, CPA, and other revenue streams, such as selling t-shirts and copies of old shows, maximizes the value of their work on each episode. Start by focusing on one, and plan to add to your repertoire to increase revenue.

Counting Ears

The reason you can't count the number of actual listeners with an MP3 file is straightforward: There is no reporting capability in the file format. When an MP3 file is transferred, it is cut loose from the server it came from and has no notion that it needs to report back what happened to it. In an interactive environment where virtually everything we do is monitored, that's refreshing, even if it is a lousy foundation for making money. We don't think you must make money to be a podcaster, and if there is an ethical concern that one "can't be a podcaster and make money," then let's call it something else. But we believe everything about podcasting is amenable to making a living through one's talent, so let's talk frankly about the need to count listeners in order to support the highest possible advertising rates.

NOTE We want to make a disclosure: One of the authors, Mitch Ratcliffe, designed the Wordcast podcasting platform for Audible Inc., so take these comments with that fact firmly in mind. The realities of media business, especially the growing reliance on metrics, informed that design and this argument about the value of advertising in podcasting.

MP3 files, as noted, don't have a reporting capability. So many podcasters have fallen back on the idea of counting downloads and extrapolating listenership from that figure. This is, unfortunately, the same argument that a radio station makes to advertisers, that with a certain amount of reach a given number of people must actually be listening. But downloads are easy to pile up, and listeners are under no obligation to listen to them. Because many podcatchers and RSS aggregators are set to download anything they find, giving the listener immediate access to the file when they want it, much that is downloaded is never heard.

So what you get is lots of talk about methodology for correcting the differences between what is downloaded and what is listened to. Just as companies like Nielsen have extrapolated television viewership by watching a small sample of homes' viewing habits (with declining success as more cable channels fragment audiences), these firms must justify themselves to everyone, which makes it hard to tell which ones are on your side as a podcaster when it comes to getting the best value for your ad inventory.

Consider that metrics emphasizing unique downloads, which eliminate redundant copies downloaded from what is counted against advertiser budgets, are useful only to the advertiser because the podcaster still has to pay for the downloads that are not counted. The reality is that this is still a very messy business lacking the hard numbers we associate with Web pages, which can be counted in small increments (how many clicks did an individual link get versus the page itself), meaning someone will have to make up for the sloppiness with lower compensation. That's reality.

Podtrac Inc. (`www.podtrac.com/`) relies on the accumulation of audiences and offers free measurement services to podcasters and advertising insertion in podcasts based on being able to identify demographic characteristics of an audience that will be attractive to paying advertisers. It does some work for podcasters, creating media kits with demographic profiles of audiences to attract advertisers based on a questionnaire the podcaster fills out. Its metrics ultimately have to serve both podcaster and advertiser alike, which will force compromises and faith in the company's methodology by both groups until it is possible to actually measure how much of individual programs are heard and by whom.

Podcasters sign up with the company, entering information about their podcast, the location of the RSS feed, the number of downloads for the show, and the number of page views on their site. A nice feature is the ability to opt out of certain types of advertising, such as cigarette or alcohol ads, so that the podcast does not represent products to which the podcaster objects (see Figure 21.2).

After you're in the program, podcasters do two things to enhance Podtrac reporting:

- **Place a survey link on their site.** This allows listeners to tell Podtrac something about themselves, increasing the value of the podcast to advertisers by improving the targeting of messages.
- **Insert a Podtrac Prefix into the URL of each podcast episode.** This allows Podtrac to record downloads by episode and day, as well as report what podcatchers and operating systems were used to download shows.

FIGURE 21.2

Podtrac's advertising opt-out choices let podcasters shape what products and services they will represent.

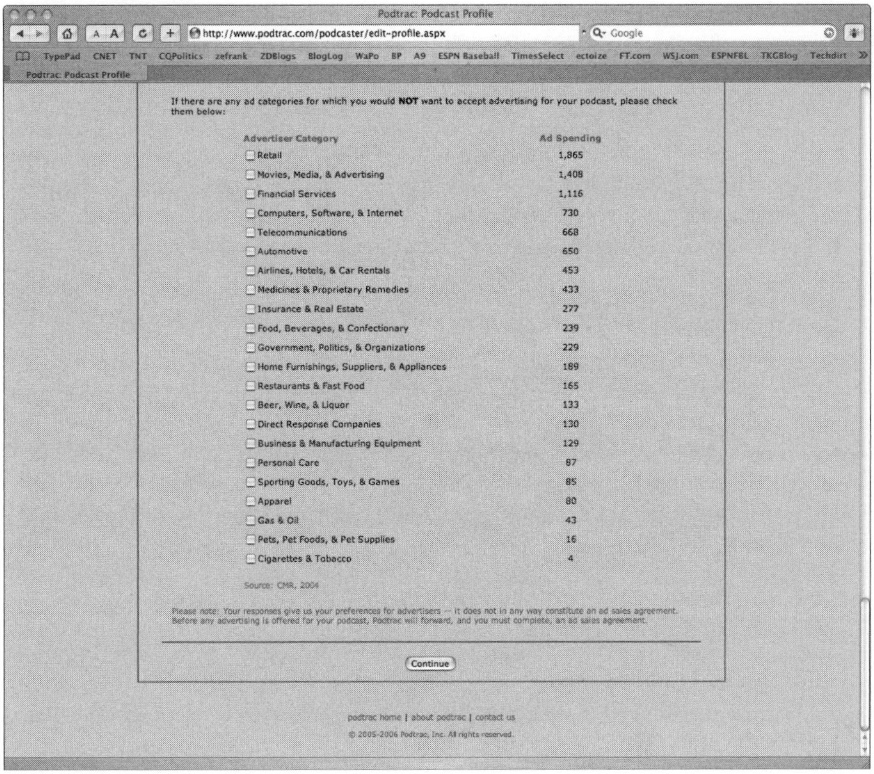

Eventually, Podtrac will have to make a choice about which constituency it really serves: advertisers or podcasters. The advertising business exists on the tension between producers and advertisers, each seeking to get the best price they can. That Podtrac and others exist as intermediary and servant of all is a feature of this market because it is so young.

PodBridge (www.podbridge.com/) takes another tack, one that attempts to add objective listening measurement that it can use to tie rates to actual listenership. But it requires listeners to download and install an application that handles the tracking, which ensures that its view of the market will be only partial because some listeners are unlikely to comply. An added barrier to adoption, in our opinion, is that part of the installation process is a short series of questions meant to improve demographic analysis, which likely will be seen as an invasion of privacy. We believe that demographic analysis should be separate from platform adoption.

PodBridge's software mends the hole in MP3 and video reporting, watching what is done with a file and sending back reports to the PodBridge server. Podcasters get reports and an automated ad insertion service that starts revenue flowing. The company has filed and/or received preliminary approval of a patent for the ability to insert an ad in programming that has already been downloaded to the listener's computer. This means that PodBridge can insert new advertising in old programming, regardless of when it is played. Of course, the listener must have PodBridge's software installed, which is the rub.

Partnerships will be the key to PodBridge's success, because PodBridge's software must be installed in hardware on the listener's desktop and set-top cable box (for the video services, mainly, but audio, too). The company has reportedly forged some key alliances, and we expect it will be a major player in the market for advertising delivered into digital video recorders and perhaps portable audio players.

This brings us to Audible Inc.'s Wordcast service (see Figure 21.3), which builds on a 10-year-old technology for distributing audio that is already built into most of the portable audio players and desktop media players on the market. Audible uses a different audio format than MP3, the .aa format that was originally designed to move parts of audio books into portable devices with very little available memory. Audible invented the portable audio player; its original player is in the Smithsonian today. Because it was developed to be delivered in small parts, the .aa file format already supports on-the-fly insertion of an advertisement in any program downloaded and reporting back to Audible what parts of each program have been played.

CROSS-REF Wordcast is discussed in Chapter 20, "The Subscription Business." Audible has not announced advertising insertion services at this writing.

Wordcast (`wordcast.audible.com/`), introduced in 2005 and released in 2006 is an end-to-end platform for measurement and ad insertion, as well as support for paid services. Audible has come down firmly on the side of partnering with the producer, even if it hasn't made clear all the ways it can help the producer. As a publisher, Audible's profit depends on the success of the person or company creating the program, so if Audible were to start selling advertising, it would aim to get the best price for inventory.

Even if Audible has not offered ad insertion as a service, you can use Wordcast to place your own ad inventory. When uploading to Wordcast, programs can be cut into segments that are assembled into a complete show at download time. You can upload your new ads, replacing the old ones, if you use a standard name for each one (see Figure 21.4). So if you want to have three ad segments in a show, upload ads as "Ad1," "Ad2," and "Ad3," replacing old ads with new ones when you have a new advertiser and are dropping an old one. This way, Wordcast builds each show with the newest ads, even though you haven't gone back and changed the insertion rules.

FIGURE 21.3

Audible's Wordcast provides simple publishing tools combined with reporting about what parts of a program have been listened to after a download.

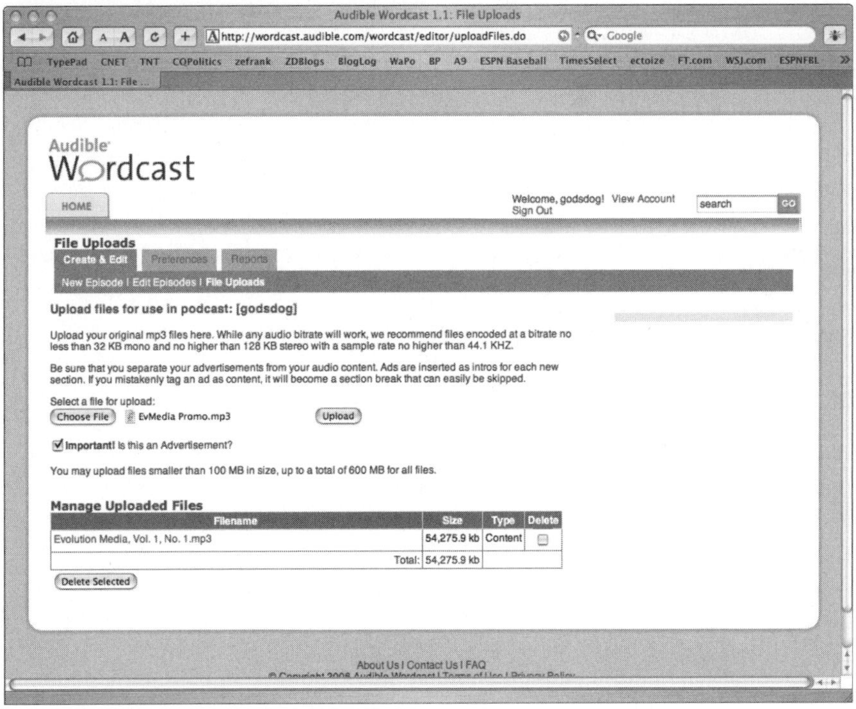

Because Audible's codec is supported in so many devices, notably Apple's iPod, which dominates the market, along with more than 145 other portable players, as well as iTunes, Windows Media Player, and mobile phone-players, reporting on listenership to .aa files is almost ubiquitous without any additional software installation. The objection, of course, is that .aa is not MP3, so it is not podcasting. By that logic, FM radio isn't radio because it is not amplitude modulated (AM).

FIGURE 21.4

Audible's Wordcast episode editing system lets you arrange segments, including ads, so that old inventory can be removed and replaced by uploading new files with the same name, for example, "Ad1."

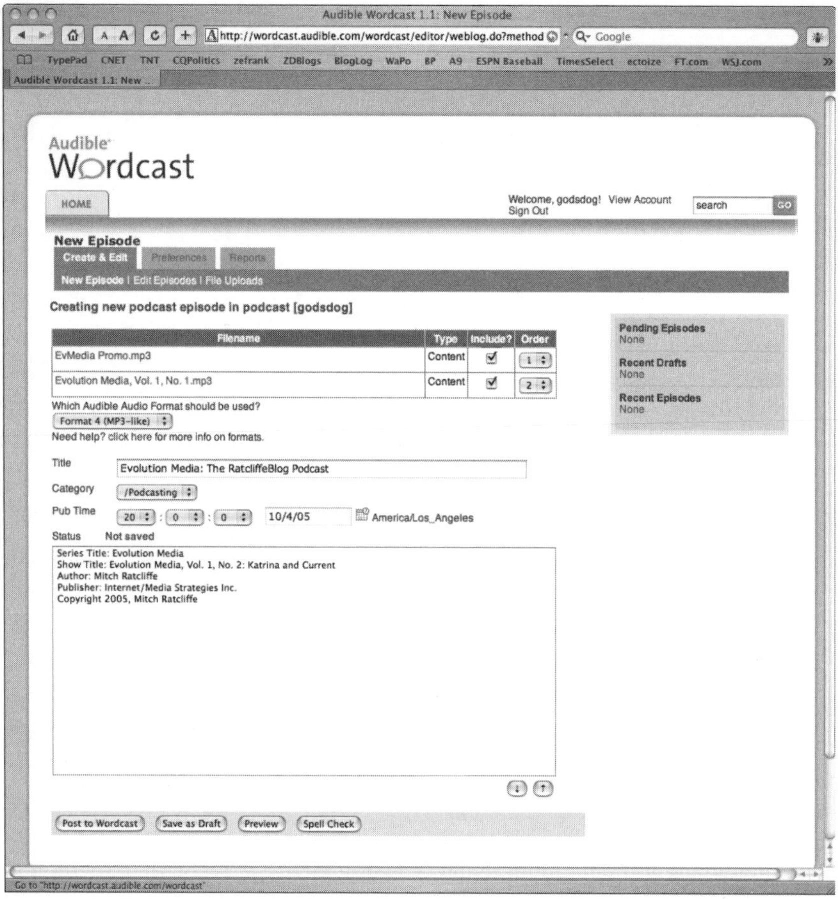

Finding Your Allies in Ad Sales

Selling advertising is time-consuming. It's something you may need to deal with early on, but it's better to find a trusted partner who specializes in selling media and leave the job to them. Salespeople are easy to come by, and getting them to work to their best with compensation based on their actual performance rather than having to pay an advance you won't earn back requires energetic management. Unless you have time to ride herd on your ad salesperson, a partner that sells ads is the way to go.

Two forms of podcast networks have started to take shape, both aiming to help producers make money. The earliest network was IT Conversations, founded by Doug Kaye, who began assembling a rich stable of programming in 2003 that has become the foundation of a company, GigaVox Media, which is emblematic of the first kind of podcast network, an alliance of producers with complementary interests.

Advertising sales is the basis of the other kind of podcast network, where podcasters join a sales organization, becoming part of their stable of inventory that is sold to advertisers.

Both types of network are worth your consideration, and you should look around for what you think is the best combination of compensation and services. Keep in mind that these companies want to appear attractive to you but are in business to make money for themselves.

New entrants join both categories of networks every month. Today, there are culinary podcast networks, sports podcasting networks, wedding podcast networks, and more than a dozen ad-sales networks that represent podcasts on various subjects. Companies like Federated Media and Gawker Media, which are building sales organizations to support for some of the leading blogs, will eventually enter this market as well. This section contains a representative sample of the two kinds of networks.

Ad sales networks

A number of startups have begun selling advertising on behalf of networks of podcasters and bloggers, hoping to fill a void in the market between the individual producer/publisher and the traditional advertising business, which is accustomed to spending hundreds of thousands of dollars at a shot. By aggregating advertising inventory, the following firms seek to make podcasting fit into older media-buying habits:

- **BackBeat Media** (www.backbeatmedia.com/): The podcasters who work with BackBeat Media report they are very happy with the experience and revenue. The company maintains "boutique networks," focused networks of podcasts into which they sell advertising, including audio and banner ads. The company hosts its clients' sites and provides billing and ad insertion so publishers can focus on their programs. BackBeat is selective about what sites and podcasts it works with, so be ready to sell your idea.

- **FeedBurner Ad Network** (www.feedburner.com/): FeedBurner pioneered RSS metrics, and although it hasn't dealt with tracking actual listenership of audio programs, it is well placed to serve ads in podcasts and video RSS feeds because of its reach and tracking reputation. At this writing, it reaches an audience of 3.5 million regularly through a network of 65,000 podcasts and offers CPM-based ad placement in podcasts. Better yet, FeedBurner has lots of features for improved promotion of your blog and podcast.

- **Fruitcast** (www.fruitcast.com/): Like Google AdSense, Fruitcast is building an ad-auctioning network, seeking to get the highest fee for available inventory that can be targeted by the description of the podcast provided by the producer. Auctions can also produce a very low fee for any unwanted inventory. At this writing, it represents 238 podcasts across 16 subject categories. Fruitcast is a project of a five-year-old Web media and branding agency, Forty Media.

- **Kiptronic** (`kiptronic.com/`): Launched in early 2006, Kiptronic had signed 450 podcasts with approximately 15 million downloads per month by Fall 2006. The company also partnered with popular podcast host, Libsyn, to offer podcasters access to a network of sponsors that can make offers to them through the Kiptronic site. Podcasters complete a survey about their audience and the topics they cover to begin the sponsorship negotiation.

- **PodBridge** (`www.podbridge.com/`): Discussed previously, PodBridge is patching untrackable MP3 and video files with an add-in application that must be adopted by the audience in order to work. Nevertheless, it's a very interesting player, because its system can place new ads in previously downloaded programs. The company has partnered with a media representative agency to sell its ad inventory, but it's still in beta so little information about the terms is available to podcasters. One of the most interesting things the company has done is to partner with Ingenio's Ether pay-per-call system to make direct connections between the audience and advertiser available from within ads.

- **Podcast Ad Network** (`www.podcastadnetwork.com/`): The site is sloppy and did not work properly in any browser we tried, even Internet Explorer, which it explicitly asked us to use. The system works as an intermediary between advertisers and podcasters, sending an audio file that the podcaster must insert in his show, so an ad insertion system is still needed on your end.

- **Podtrac** (`www.podtrac.com/`): Discussed previously, Podtrac's measurement system relies on download numbers rather than actual listenership. Using the information podcasters enter, audience surveys, and a sales campaign, the company seeks advertisers for the podcast. However, the company doesn't seem to have enabled any automated insertion of ads, meaning you still need a way to mix in ads.

- **Podvertiser** (`www.podvertiser.com/`): Another recent entrant, Podvertiser was founded in 2005 to host podcasts and insert advertising based on the topic of the podcast the advertiser would like to target and geographical location of the listener. Compensation is based on the number of downloads, not actual listenership, and the company promises 50 to 70 percent of revenue will be shared with producers. Because the system handles automated insertion of ads, it seems revenue should be easy to collect. No information is available about what podcasts it has worked with or how sales have gone.

- **RadioTail** (`www.radiotail.com/`): An end-to-end system for ad sales and insertion, RadioTail is aimed at companies that want to advertise on podcasts, providing an automated system and metrics based on the number of downloads. It's not entirely clear which side of the fence — the advertiser's or the podcaster's — the company is on, but regarding our comments about who pays for the uncertainties associated with counting downloads versus actual listening, we suspect the discount will fall harder on the podcaster here.

Content networks

In contrast to ad network providers, content network companies start from the podcast or blog and build out, bringing together related programming to create a package attractive to advertisers looking for connections to specific demographic audiences, such as people interested in cars or dieting. This is a more traditional approach to media, and one that, if the company you work with is any good, should help you improve your blog with advice and feedback from advertisers.

- **Culinary Podcast Network** (`www.gildedfork.com/culinarypodcastnetwork/`): A food channel of podcasts, this network features both well-known celebrity chefs, little-known chefs, and foodies. A part of the GildedFork network of blogs, this is a seriously interesting example of niche production.

- **My Sports Radio** (`www.mysportsradio.com/`): This network is a true upstart in sports programming assembled by the participants, many of whom have been sports fanatics and bloggers before taking up a microphone.

- **The Podcast Network** (`www.thepodcastnetwork.com/`): This eclectic network of programs spans technology, business, sports, lifestyle, and educational topics.

- **Podcast Entertainment Network** (`www.tsfpn.com/`): Listener ratings play a big part in this network, which brings together podcasts of all sorts, from gaming and sports to drama and fanzine shows.

- **PodShow** (`www.podshow.com/`): Founded by Adam Curry, this is the most polished podcast network around, with heavy emphasis on promotion and audience development with production values that are virtually indistinguishable from network television. PodShow's terms, however, have rubbed many podcasters the wrong way, because they require signing over all the ideas in a show; basically, you go to work for PodShow. When big media comes into this market, it will look like this.

- **PodTech Network** (`www.podtech.net/`): A venture-backed network founded by John Furrier, PodTech made headlines when one of the most famous bloggers, Robert Scoble, quit his job at Microsoft to join the company. It focuses on technology, the technology business, and coverage of technology events.

We have listed only a few of the content networks that are forming, because they are changing all the time. Again, we can only caution you not to sign documents making your program someone else's property if the terms are not right. Spend time being recruited; don't just try to sell yourself with these companies. When you find the right fit, it will feel right and the terms will be rewarding, both in the short term (we hope you get better support for production, some spending money for use in production, and so on) and the long term. If the network's management is going to get rich, you should get proportionately rich because you are the talent being sold.

The Short Guide to Ad Sales Kits

Whether you decide to sell your own advertising or work with a company that sells advertising for you, your podcast needs a promotional package that sells itself. This is essential to winning a relationship with ad and content networks, because it demonstrates that you are thinking about how to promote yourself—no one wants to go into business with a partner who thinks they don't need to sell successfully.

Ad sales kits need to convey the following information along with providing a sample of the flavor of the program itself:

- Length and frequency of the show
- Topics discussed, best summarized in a short statement about the show
- The available inventory of advertising and cost.

Figure 21.5 provides a hypothetical promotional sheet for The Steve & Mitch Show, which is a template you can use to begin an ad sales kit of your own.

Begin with the headline, which is the name of your podcast, a short description of the show. We reduced our pitch to a single line: "Smart talk for business podcasts." It says what we want to convey, that The Steve & Mitch Show is for people who want to think about and improve their business podcasts. At the bottom of the page is an endorsement from a listener that gives a quantifiable success (fictional, alas), that we helped her increase the response rates on the BigCo podcast by 500 percent.

Next, it's critical that you tell the advertiser or the representative selling your advertising what they get for the money. Who listens? Remember, we've talked elsewhere about the need to communicate with your audience, conduct polls, and generally get to know exactly who you are serving. Now , take that data and reduce it to a simple description of the demographic groups your podcast addresses. Do you have a young audience or an old one? Is it mostly men or women? Do they have money to spend on the product advertisers want to promote? Do you know how many of them own a particular kind of car, if yours is a automotive podcast, or game console if you talk about gaming during the show?

When it's time to talk about pricing, remember that you hope to grow your audience quickly. At the same time, the advertiser wants to know the costs in the short term, so we've gone with a flat rate for advertising insertions in the show rather than giving a cost-per-thousand figure that could dramatically change the actual cost of the show next month. In other words, we'll need to return to change these prices, redistributing them to reps at least once a month.

Updating can be a very good thing, because each time you raise your audience numbers and pricing, the salespeople have something to talk about. Be sure you place the sales sheet on your Web site for downloading and, if possible, get potential advertisers to sign up for e-mail updates of your ad rates so that they, too, get involved in the excitement of your growing audience.

You'll also notice that we included CPA-based advertising placements on our Web site so that advertisers have some idea about their ability to supplement in-show promotion with actionable advertising where people gather to talk about the show. Advertisers think in terms of packages of placements that reinforce their message, whether it's how good their product or brand is because it supports nifty podcasts or that they want your listeners to buy something, right now. Using CPA advertising here is a strategic decision, as the audio advertising is CPM-based and, therefore, not the most confidence-inspiring way for advertisers to spend money. After all, you cannot click a link in a podcast playing on an iPod to view an offer for a free car tune-up. By allowing the advertiser to pay only for clicks, you give them greater control of their costs. At minimum, CPA click fees turn the advertisers' spending into a more accountable form of ad spending.

The rest of the sales kit is about putting the face on the podcast. Who are the personalities behind the show? Pictures of people looking like they are having fun get people involved with the information. We also tagged the pictures with a blurb that conveys the tone of the show, so that we're reinforcing the image we want to create. Finally, there's the credibility-enhancing fact that we published a book on the subject we talk about. In your case, it may be that you have 23 years of dental practice or a record for building great software behind your ideas.

Don't stop with the single page, either. As your show collects reviews and other feedback, including impassioned letters and links in other people's blogs, be sure to collect them into the ad sales kit. Everything people have to say about you is a part of the story you need to tell to get advertisers.

FIGURE 21.5

Our sample ad sales kit: Convey the personality of the program and subjects covered while providing information about reach and ad costs.

Summary

Adding advertising to your podcasts can really bring in bucks for you, but you should know the pitfalls to avoid. This chapter covered many aspects of advertising, specifically the following topics:

- Advertising will change with this medium, as it has changed in previous ones. Despite the deliberate effort to prevent advertising from being part of podcasting, it looks like this medium will adopt advertising revenue as one of the ways programming gets paid for.

- Ads may not be interruptive; they could be spoken endorsements or acknowledgement of sponsors during a show. Being careful to associate your podcast with reputable products and services is as important as the revenue you will earn.

- Cost-per-thousand (or CPM) pricing is the traditional way media has been priced. It depends on the idea of reach and the number of people exposed, and no longer commands premium ad fees.

- Cost-per-action payment, such as for clicks or customer's starting some kind of transaction, is the new standard for advertising pricing, because today's media is far more measurable.

- Most podcasting advertising is sold on a CPM basis calculated by the number of downloads of a show. That's not likely to last as a basis for premium ad fees.

- Downloads do not equal listenership. Systems for "patching" MP3 files to provide actual listenership are being introduced now. Other formats, such as Audible's .aa files, have the ability to report actual listenership and may represent alternatives to MP3 for revenue-generating podcasts.

- As important as counting, ad insertion and ad sales are time-consuming tasks that you should consider partnering or farming out rather than handling yourself. Creativity should be aware of business issues, but not dominated by them.

- Advertising will likely be sold based on the aggregation of ads delivered to a network of podcasts or a network of producers with common interests (though this may be very broad) represented by sales people.

- Whatever direction you go with advertising partners, be sure the relationship is mutually beneficial from the start.

Chapter 22

Alternative Business Models

Podcasting is a young enough technology that business and distribution models to fuel the economics run neck-and-neck with the podcasters' imaginations. Little has been tried compared to what's possible, and if you'll excuse the observation of some folks who have been through a couple Net revolutions, we're still at a point where the Web was in 1995, when there was no sure path to success.

Brave originals with something to say and a new place to say it will pop on and off the public radar depending on the draw of their topic, the timing of its delivery, and the luck of striking a chord with people bobbing about on the Web looking for something current and interesting. For example, Ze Frank's "Fingers in Food" episode is decidedly brave and original (and funny). But the podcast itself has a business model very similar to early Web entrepreneurs, because Ze Frank sells t-shirts emblazoned with his catch-phrases. The podcast creates demand for the t-shirts, which is the definition of good marketing.

Apple CEO Steve Jobs once called podcasting the next generation of radio. If so, then certainly looking at working business models in radio is as good a starting point as any. Advertising, sponsorship, and the relatively low cost of distribution makes some sense. But maybe podcasting is more like ham radio, with individuals speaking out to the world through their personal communications system, hoping to reach anyone who will listen and even engage in a little conversation. So there are likely hundreds of variations on business models that will support podcast producers.

Growing Your Podcasting Business

Several podcasting models are at work today, as we explained elsewhere in this book, and a number of people are running companies tapping into the emerging medium. Not much is known yet as to whether they are sustainable, but several are experiencing at least current profitability. What exists today is only the beginning, so be sure not to assume that the market is defined. Experiment, experiment!

Which model will work for you? Broadcasting models are complex relationships between advertisers, marketers, distribution channels, audience measurement companies, content providers, syndication, and ad sales. Ze Frank and Rocketboom are doing something like a business, trying different pieces of the revenue puzzle to see what works, as shown in Figure 22.1.

FIGURE 22.1

Ze Frank's t-shirt economics

Some have said that there are few if any workable business models, that everything in podcasting should be free and ad-free, because traditional business strategies won't work. One of particular note is from a pioneer in Internet media.

An instructive debate on the topic of podcasting as a business took place over the last year on Mark Cuban's blog, "blog maverick" (www.blogmaverick.com). In July 2005, Cuban wrote, "Creating your own podcast and trying to make a business out of it is a mistake."

Those are strong words, and coming from someone who turned the advent of streaming media over the Internet into a multibillion-dollar payday when Cuban sold Broadcast.com, a business that never produced any profits, to Yahoo for more than $5 billion, you have to give his opinion some credence. Why, though, is it a mistake to make a business of a podcast? Cuban draws his conclusions from his experience in streaming and explains many of the similarities between what happened in the 1990s and what is happening in podcasting today. He notes that many jumped onto the streaming bandwagon, but virtually all original content conceived for streaming failed. "That's not to say some didn't survive," he goes on. "Those projects that are labors of love, rather than financially motivated, can do well."

The point from Cuban's perspective — and it's true of most business ventures — is that they come into being not because of calculated investment but because of a fierce determination to make something valuable and keep at it regardless of the barriers to success encountered. Making a podcast is fun. Making a business of a podcast requires you to give up something to achieve your goals, because there is a long road between the idea and a sustainable business, a "success." With so much emphasis on launching and selling companies for millions of dollars in the press, it's hard to keep this simple fact in mind.

Labors of love do have their reward, and those that are financially motivated can do well. But to make a business work demands that you combine the two. Because something is a labor of love, that helps an original thinker through the often difficult periods of a new business venture. It keeps them motivated, passionate, and excited by others' interest while revenues build enough to support them. Applying good business to a passionate pursuit worked out well for Steve Jobs and Steve Wozniak, the founders of Apple Computer, two mavericks in the technology and media world, yet Mark Cuban's right: You have to love and live the idea first.

Knowing Your Audience

During an exercise meant to demonstrate different brainstorming techniques in a project management class at the University of Washington at Tacoma, a group of students were asked to come up with a list of ideas on how to market a band online. "Build a Web site," "distribute songs," and "start a message board" were offered up pretty early in the exercise. Like microwave popcorn, the roiling pops of ideas started to slow down and looked to be coming to a rather pedestrian halt, because each was only a part of the process of distributing ideas, not promoting them. In desperation, one of the students blurted out, "Set yourself on fire," more due to frustration than participation in the lesson. It was the first original and interesting idea to come out of the discussion.

Not that setting oneself on fire is a good idea, but *finally* someone had generated an attention-getting device instead of an operational given for any business on the Web. Of course you are going to build a site, and if you are going to have a music distribution business, you are going to distribute songs. Making someone stop what he is doing and pay attention to you, though, that's marketing.

Brand is in itself an ideal. According to the American Marketing Association (AMA), a brand is defined as:

> "A name, term, design, symbol, or any other feature that identifies one seller's good or service as distinct from those of other sellers. The legal term for brand is trademark. A brand may identify one item, a family of items, or all items of that seller. If used for the firm as a whole, the preferred term is trade name."

Okay, that's a very perfunctory business-like explanation, one that misses the core experience of brand, that of the person who finds something, a product, like a car, that screams his priorities or a podcast that challenges or comforts him.

Joe LePla, author of *Brand Driven* and *Integrated Branding*, says, "by definition, values are those beliefs a company prizes above all else, beliefs to be held at any cost, even at the expense of short-term profitability. Values speak to the commitment a brand makes to society at large. Because a brand and its customers operate within society, the values a company assigns to a brand will have an impact on customer relationships. In fact, these values can strongly influence customer preference and loyalty."

One powerful way of putting this is "How to own a word or concept in the mind of the consumer." Think potato chips, and what comes to mind? Think auto safety. Think family vacation. Anything pop up? Those are the brands that have successfully engaged your experience, becoming the standards you apply to categories of products and services and your experience of them.

Most important to your thinking about a brand is the concept of "sustainable differentiation," which happens, according to LePla, when you begin living your brand values, so that those values speak to your customer through every interaction. A sustainable difference between you and your competition is what, in human interaction, we talk about when we say "integrity." A podcast, because it is a message from one person (or a group) to another person or group — every one of that group an individual with her own ideas — that cements a relationship, is a growing catalog of checkpoints that can be weighed against expectations. When you, the producer, meet the listener's expectations, she comes to trust you to do it again. Living those brand values online can "differentiate your product or service in a way that creates long-term customer loyalty."

Consider the advantages, and create strategies in order to build your brand as you see it. For more information, see a podcast called *Building Your Brand in Bits & Bytes,* at `blog.brandego.com`.

Whatever your message, the attentive listener wants to ask questions and make comments. After he does, he has placed a little piece of himself out there and has created media himself. This gives him reason to come back and feel involved, and it establishes him within the community of the discussion.

To make this possible, you need to create opportunities in and around your podcast. Integrate it with a blog or as part of a community site where your audience can talk among themselves and engage you. We are aware that there is a movement against the idea of "audience," which is portrayed as a passive player in media ("the people formerly known as the audience" are celebrated by blogger and journalism professor Jay Rosen, who rails against the passivity of consumers of previous media), but we also believe that you need to embrace the idea of audience as a way of describing your obligation to the people who download and play your podcast. You've made a kind of solemn promise, even if your show is comedic, to deliver something in particular. Don't turn away from that obligation, and don't tell your audience to be quiet and just listen, like television and radio often does.

Create polls and surveys if your audience is interested in participating. Make them simple and sincere. Beware of using a survey or poll as a sales pitch rather than a community tool. Talk about the survey in your podcast, so people want to listen to hear the results. Make participation with your show part of the show.

Know-how has always been given its due. Everyone appreciates a little know-how. But in the world of advertising and sales, know-*who* is the key.

In the *Marketing Week* article, "Getting a Piece of the Podcast Pie," Steve Cooke, marketing director at research firm BMRB, has explained why knowing your audience is vital for business. "For advertisers, this presents an opportunity for tightly targeted campaigns to niche audiences. For Internet properties, the potential is there to develop download portal sites, which in turn will attract advertising content. . . . It is crucial to understand the audience and how they interact with this fast-growing media."

Knowing your audience will be a key factor in advertisement, sales, marketing, and continual delivery of consistently interesting content. Even if your message or your music is the only thing that matters to you, if you want to build any business around its delivery, then you need to do some investigation about your audience's expectations. Remember that they are the people you've committed to serve in some way, so do anything you can to get to know them.

More practically, why would an advertiser or sponsor want to support you if they didn't know anything about the audience you were reaching? How do you determine what to sell on your site or program without knowing what your audience might be interested in buying? Talking with and becoming engaged with the audience gives you the opportunity to extrapolate out to a broad picture that you can use to make editorial and business decisions. It is a starting point.

In 1995, Free Range Media, a Web development and design company, launched two online communities. One, *hyperfuzzy*, focused on art, literature, and the uncommon voice and had content from an active and eclectic group of counter-culture artists. The other, *FreeZone*, was narrowly targeted, aimed toward parents, teachers, and kids. *FreeZone* required a high degree of maintenance and original content creation, as well as a growing number of paid staff. On the other hand, *hyperfuzzy* was an excellent early example of "consumer generated media" — almost all of its content was created by members of the community. Both had active, growing audiences, but in the end, *FreeZone* was sold for a profit to a large newspaper and media company, and *hyperfuzzy* was shut down because there was no revenue to support the business. The reason was that sponsors, advertisers, contributors, and subscribers were willing to play in the *FreeZone* pool, because they knew who they were engaging with, where as they were not interested in paying to support *hyperfuzzy* because, as the name suggested, it was a site with no center.

Now, a show about nothing can do quite well, as *Seinfeld* proved. But Seinfeld had a network defining its message as the best thing to do on a Thursday night at a particular time. In podcasting, where everything from the sources people turn to for programming to the times the audience engages are in the public's control, simply being funny at a given time of day isn't enough to make a revenue stream erupt around a show.

The more you know about the audience, the more targeted the message is and the more valuable their attention is. Google, Amazon, and countless others have realized and acted on this with their personalization engines. These work because they are able to filter through an enormous number of users. You have a much smaller eco-system, and it's about creating a relationship between you and the people who download your podcast.

Audiences for podcasts are self-filtering. Listeners and viewers identify their interests and opinions by their very actions in searching out that information and entertainment. No personalization engines are needed when the active pursuit of information and requests is driven by the content itself. Know your audience. Those audience members have their own personal space, and depending how you treat them, they will let you stay in it or will show you the proverbial door.

The Alternative Business Models

We've talked about possibilities and, of course, just about everything is possible with podcasting now, as the medium begins its life. Then again, not everything is *viable* for podcasting. Be ready to learn from your mistakes, and dive into the possibilities of the following business models.

At the root of what we are discussing is the ability for an individual to implement a method of doing business that can sustain the business monetarily. Generating enough revenue to cover expenses and create enough profit to cover more than a daily Starbucks habit may come from a single approach, but often is a combination of models that provides multiple revenue streams. Models continue to evolve, and some are very simple while others require relationships with multiple partners to be effective. Broadcasters need content providers need sponsors need distributors and so on. If your content is your value proposition, then you may leverage its value though being an intermediary, infomediary, or affiliate to create revenue without advertising or subscriptions.

While planning the operational aspects of your podcasts and actively investigating what business model would be the most successful for you, keep in mind what makes podcasting advantageous to other media delivery systems. Podcasting is still young enough to leverage early entry into the space, especially with a unique perspective or a consistently interesting voice. In business, even when there are established companies and players in a particular space, figuring out how to do something faster, cheaper, more efficiently, or with greater impact can create opportunities to make money.

So what are some of the advantages that you can leverage?

Podcasting has great advantages over traditional media sources in a number of ways, including its portability, the ability to time-shift your consumption of programs by recording and consuming when convenient (referred to often as repurposing hostage time), and the automation of the gathering of interesting programs just to begin with. Additionally, those who use podcasts display a higher degree of attention span. Podtrac's May 2006 survey reports that 88 percent of podcast audiences listen or view the entire broadcast.

Keep in mind these and any other advantages that podcasting provides as you read through some of the various business models that you can deploy.

Sponsorship

Though it took around ten years for Web text and banner ads to really get a foothold, straight up sponsorship has provided ample examples of revenue generation from a multitude of sites.

Sponsorship is often tied to content, but not always in obvious ways. *FreeZone*, the parent/teacher/child community mentioned earlier, is a prime example of how sponsorship can help fund a business. Two of its most supportive early funders helped the site build and grow through sponsorship. Spry, which was launching a product called "Internet in a Box for Kids," needed an active and appropriate home Web site for the purchasers of its software. EDS, the technology services firm founded by Ross Perot, wanted to provide funding for Web-based educational materials for kids. This was at an early stage in the Web's history, so there wasn't a great deal of online material available at the time. Between the two, *FreeZone* made up a great deal of the cost needed to build and operate the community in its first year. For Spry, the venture supported the business model of their product line, driving demand for a browser application when there weren't many browsers installed on PCs, and for EDS, it provided an opportunity to support education in an emerging technology environment as part of their community service.

Other examples of sponsorship related to podcasting are as follows.

- Dixie (Georgia-Pacific's disposable dinnerware brand) signed on as the sole sponsor of the MommyCast podcast. The show isn't about dinnerware, but it serves the primary buyers of disposable dinnerware.

- In association with the *Observer Food Monthly, The Observer,* a British publishing company, will launch its first podcast sponsored by the food brand Seeds of Change, which is seeking to reestablish natural foods as a mainstream product rather than a niche market.

- Volvo paid Weblogs Inc. $60,000 to sponsor the Autoblog.com Web log and podcast for six months. It was downloaded 20,000 times in the first four months, and although the show is about all car brands, the podcast audience is repeatedly exposed to the Volvo name. Sometimes, simply being the brand that makes a new medium happen can have huge benefits. Texaco, the petroleum company, earned customer loyalty and established its brand of full-service gas stations through its sponsorship of Milton Berle's early television shows.

- *Skeptic Magazine* recently named the independently produced podcast Skepticality, shown in Figure 22.2, its official podcast. In this case, enthusiast production is embraced by the "name brand" in a niche market (alas, yes, scientific skepticism is still a niche market), bringing benefits to both partners and letting the magazine gain a foothold in a new medium.

- About.com, a popular Internet portal, launched a health and fitness podcast, sponsored by AstraZeneca, a pharmaceutical company. In many ways, this is just like any pharmaceutical advertising, but because the podcasts are about specific health issues, it provides better targeting for AstraZeneca than television at a much lower price.

FIGURE 22.2

Skepticality, sponsored by *Skeptic Magazine*

In each of these examples, there's a selling point that supports the investment by the sponsor. They don't pay for sponsor messages simply to feel good about themselves, but to achieve a business goal. You absolutely must think about why a sponsor would want to associate itself with your podcast, your brand and what it delivers to the audience, and the people to whom you've committed yourself.

And those are just a few. This suggests, just as in the early days of radio and television, sole sponsorship or limited numbers of sponsorships are early leaders in emerging medium business models.

Work with your sponsors on a number of levels to keep the relationship fruitful. In order to get the most from the sponsorship, promote the podcast itself just as you would if it were any of their other media productions and get them to agree to provide that promotion through their channels.

Also, plan for promotion of your podcast through Web and print advertisement as "My Podcast" sponsored by Microsoft, or Home Depot, or whomever your generous sponsor may be. In this way, the sponsor not only sees the value of its support, but it helps to build your brand as well.

When working with your sponsor, discuss whether the greatest value is in the sponsorship of the podcast of a particular topic, or a one-time sponsorship, or whether the sponsor might experience greater impact by sponsoring multiple episodes. The sponsor will have a greater opportunity to gauge the impact of its sponsorship through several podcasts one after the other, and you will have the benefit of covering a longer period of production and operation.

Direct and retail sales

Are you selling a product? Should you be? It's natural to think of your product as the podcast itself, and we will look at utility models such as pay per unit or per download. But additionally there is an opportunity for sales of other products in the course of your program. You can certainly advertise products for sale in a number of ways, but with the availability of the tools and software to support direct sales, why not take the order while you are at it? This requires that you begin to view yourself as a merchant of wares as well as ideas, and if it pays the bills, why not? In many cases, this requires Web page support to complete any transactions, so your podcast may simply be a pointer to where the business is conducted.

What is sold does not have to directly relate to the podcaster either. In other words, podcasters can sell a lifestyle. An example would be 43Folders, which focuses on productivity and lets them retail productivity-related products.

What would you sell? Probably not lemonade, even if that's the only prior sales experience you have. During the gold rush, the real moneymakers sold shovels, so perhaps you can leverage what you have learned about podcasting and provide the means for others to create their own podcasts. If your concern is the means to complete any type of sales transaction, you can still completely separate yourself from having to understand the mechanics of retailing online by choosing to be an affiliate. Amazon.com is an excellent example of an affiliate program. These types of programs are usually based on performance, so even if you generate low or no sales, there should be no cost after setup.

Set up your own store if you need to. Amazon, eBay, PayPal, and other big names in the online business community offer packages to help you get started. Amazon recently introduced the aStore, a complete retail environment that can be enclosed in your Web site using frames or hosted at Amazon; see an example in Figure 22.3. The particular benefit of aStore is the ability to feature a collection of products on the front page of a store with thousands of products, which lets your visitors browse and buy not just what you suggest, as with regular Amazon Associate links, but what strikes their fancy.

FIGURE 22.3

Amazon's aStore, a retail outlet of your very own

Amazon aStore also makes fast work of choosing new featured products and adding a personal endorsement for each product, which is likely to increase conversion rates; see Figure 22.4 for a sample of searching by ISBN or ASIN, the standard product identifiers, to get a product listing to which you can add your own text. Your podcast, too, is a way of doing "hand selling," the personalized retailing you experience when someone working in a store pulls a product off the shelf and tells you why she likes it and what it's like to own it and use it. There's a limit to how much you can do this, because your listeners may object if you are ham-handed about it, but you can use it as a setting for preparing your listeners to become customers in your online store or eBay auctions.

FIGURE 22.4

Amazon aStore offers easy product endorsements.

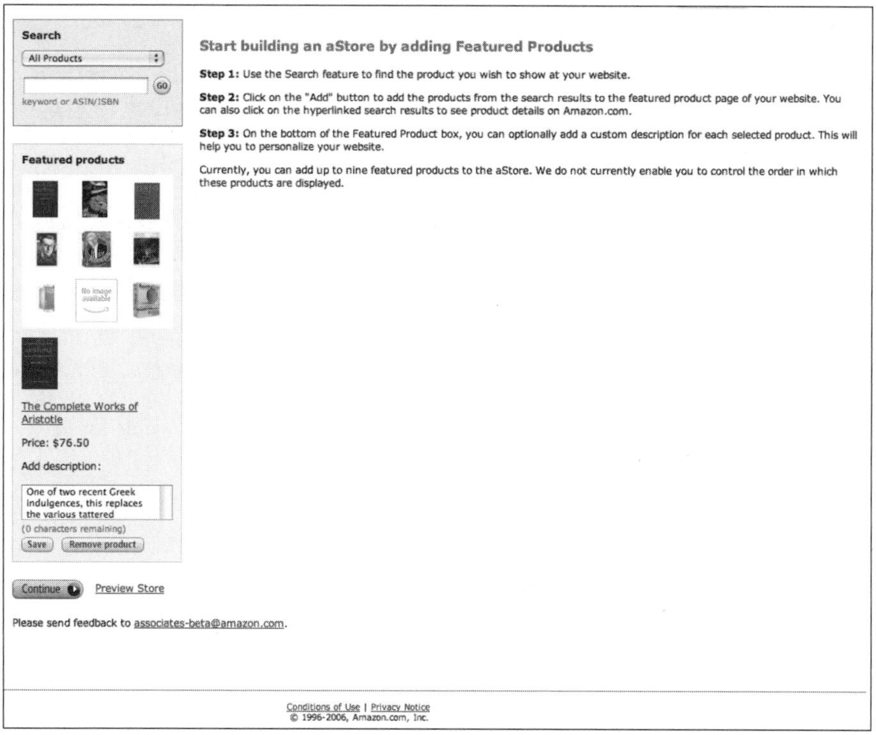

Search

All Products

keyword or ASIN/ISBN   GO

Featured products

The Complete Works of Aristotle

Price: $76.50

Add description:

One of two recent Greek indulgences, this replaces the various tattered

(0 characters remaining)

Save   Remove product

Start building an aStore by adding Featured Products

Step 1: Use the Search feature to find the product you wish to show at your website.

Step 2: Click on the "Add" button to add the products from the search results to the featured product page of your website. You can also click on the hyperlinked search results to see product details on Amazon.com.

Step 3: On the bottom of the Featured Product box, you can optionally add a custom description for each selected product. This will help you to personalize your website.

Currently, you can add up to nine featured products to the aStore. We do not currently enable you to control the order in which these products are displayed.

Continue   Preview Store

Please send feedback to associates-beta@amazon.com.

Conditions of Use | Privacy Notice
© 1996-2006, Amazon.com, Inc.

Given the portability of the environment, there is a 40+ percent chance that your audience isn't sitting at the computer but out on a bike or walking the dog. Give them easy-to-remember phone numbers and contact information. There is a good reason why some radio jingles are annoyingly successful and why many phone numbers are songs and words (call 555-podcast). These are easier to recall later when you are ready to respond to an offer. That still leaves a 55+ percent chance that your audience is listening at the computer. Keep the URLs pertinent, simple, and easy to spell.

Reselling

A reseller is a company/person authorized to sell someone else's goods and/or services. Going through a reseller is the easiest entry point into a business model for those looking to sell their podcasts via subscription or download. This doesn't mean, however, that you are best served by this model. One of the difficulties is getting noticed among the other products. You also must split the revenue with the reseller.

One example is Indiecentric, an upcoming online store and community hub for the makers and fans of independent music, shown in Figure 22.5. Fans become part of the sales process and take a share of revenue of the bands that they help succeed. It is also a good example of a community model. Indiecentric refers to itself as the "the ultimate reseller of podcasts."

Often the reseller offers multiple packages, from free services for trial purposes to monthly rates for posting and selling files. Indie911, which fashions itself as a "unique entertainment network created to serve both artists and audiences in today's ever-changing entertainment industry," is an example of a reseller that offers tiered services.

As in many of the models mentioned, creating a trusting relationship is key to success. In this case, the trust built between you and the reseller. You will be giving over to them all of the hard work you have put in to production and creation of the product, and they will be responsible for handling and selling it.

Donations

Have you ever gone to a street fair and walked passed the guy with the guitar and an open case? If he's good, have you ever dropped any coins in? In August 2006 at Showcase Tacoma, an event that spread throughout the museum district and the University of Washington at Tacoma, I witnessed a young girl about 12 years old set up a 14-piece drum set complete with cymbals, chimes, and amps and put out a donation jar. Often, podcasting is called a natural extension of blogging, even to a point of being called audio blogging. One revenue source that has helped to keep bloggers capitalized is the donation driven model.

FIGURE 22.5

Indiecentric: Fans become part of the record-selling business

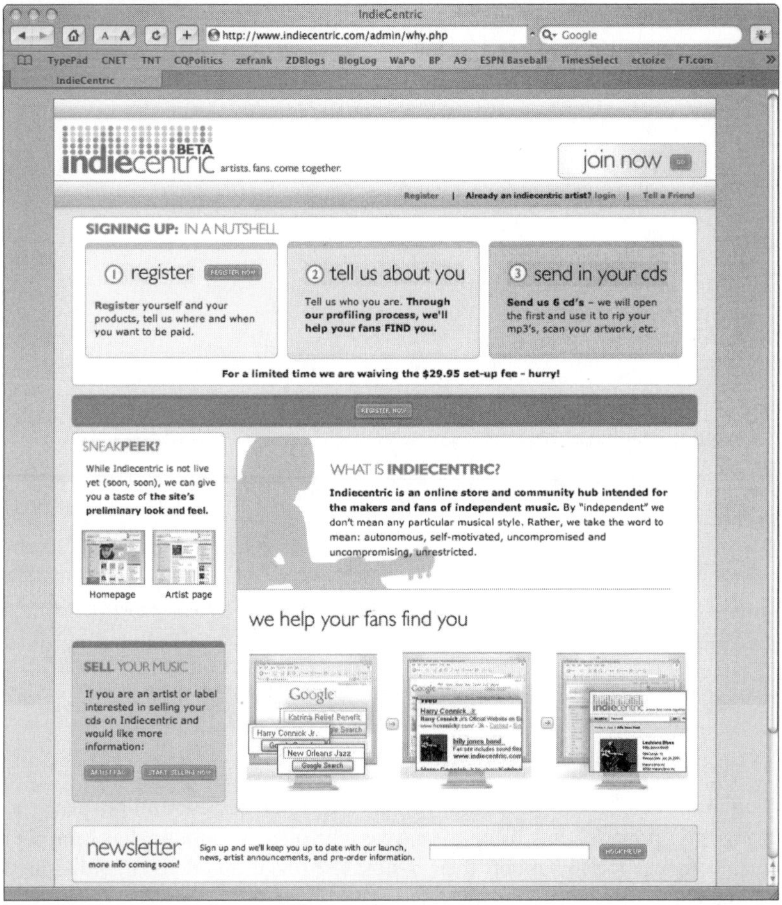

Christopher Allbritton has been referred to as "the Web's first fully reader-funded journalist-blogger" after raising $15,000 from readers of his "Back to Iraq" blog. The cash enabled him to travel to Iraq and continue to report on the war.

Another example comes from *This Week In Tech*, an indie podcast. According to a November 2005 *Business Week* report, it generated around $10,000 per month with the help of two-dollar donations from among its large listener base.

In order to initiate a donation driven podcast, or pledgecast, you may want to set up a tip jar. Tip jars allow podcast listeners to make their donations. As an example, PayPal allows for the operation of a tip jar that deducts funds from the listener's PayPal account, as shown in Figure 22.6.

FIGURE 22.6

The PayPal Tip Jar: Modern gratuity

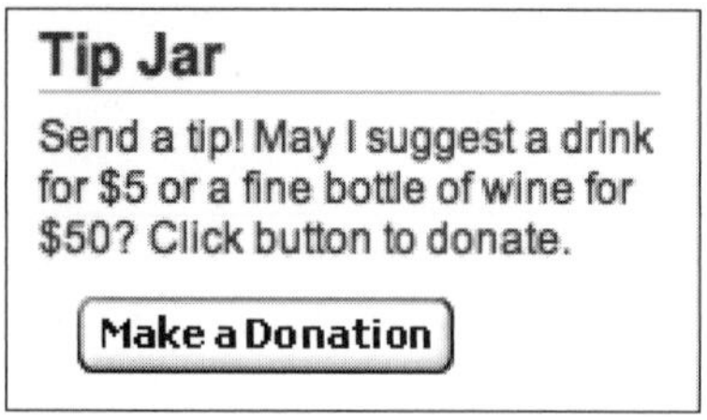

A number of plug-ins for blogs enable the tip jar:

- Movable Type Tip Jar at `http://everything.typepad.com/blog/2005/09/index.html`

- Drupal PayPal Jar at `drupal.org/project/paypal_tipjar`

- WordPress PayPal Plugin at `ejoneclicks.com/2006/06/14/paypal-donate-plugin-for-wordpress/`

Sheila Ann Manuel Coggins has a simple and well-written how-to on setting up a tip jar at About.com. You can find it at `weblogs.about.com/od/improvingweblogs/ht/donatepaypal.htm`.

How will it work for you? You can only ask and see. If you have a strong message and people respond to it and the value you provide, then by all means pass the plate. It certainly has been the mainstay of many a small congregation to support their pastor. The suggestion doesn't apply solely to religious pursuits, as many have the passion to evangelize their ideas and opinions.

PodChef provides the following example of how donations are working for him in a note he wrote on Paul Colligan's Blog, `www.paulcolligan.com`: "When I first began my show, I had no expectations. Six months into the thing I had received perhaps $100 through a donations button. After that, however, things slowly began to pick up. I offered a downloadable cookbook which generated quite a bit of cash—even though I offered it for free. And I constantly receive non-monetary gifts from listeners who know I'll appreciate the items they send—specialty pasta, cooking tools, spices, cookbooks, as well as donations. Some of the items have come from across the world."

Utility model

If you have ever been to Audible.com and paid for the download of an audio book, then you know that a pay per download or utility model can work. In 2005, the company posted $63 million in revenue with approximately 80 percent of that from the sale of monthly subscription plans to periodicals, according to AGC analyst Christopher Kinkade. This is very similar to the idea of selling podcasts.

As mentioned earlier, Stephen King gave it a shot with the episodal download of his work in progress, *The Plant*. Though his effort stalled when the good faith payment plan dropped in number below what King was willing to work with, it may be enough for you. *Forbes Magazine* states that industry watchers believe that only around the top 5 percent will be able to coax dollars from consumers this way.

With the vertical lines of interest available through an unlimited number of podcast channels possible, that 5 percent is low. If you have a hook, if you can create value with your ideas, art, or opinions, then you can reach some of the 9 million people who will listen to a podcast this year (according to research group Bridge Ratings).

Keep in mind that you have to deal with the intellectual property rights associated with what you create, and you need to respect the intellectual property rights of others. You also need to invest in the necessary sales and processing software to support the business.

Community model

The idea behind the community model is to build an infrastructure and utilize a variety of means by which to drive revenue. Think of a shopping mall. Someone owns the mall and leases out the space, provides the support systems, and drives other forms of revenue through additional services to the public who visit the companies and individuals who are leasing the space. For a mall to work, it must have a variety of stores, restaurants, and entertainment venues in easy reach of each other.

You don't necessarily have to build a community from scratch, but can build a sub-community within a larger one. Successful communities have commonality among the members, but necessarily have a variety of opinions. To build community, you need to welcome members in, allow them to claim space for themselves (in the form of posted ideas, surveys, discussion, and personal pages), and participate in the establishment of rules and accepted practices.

To harness the power of community for revenue generation, you have to allow for points of trade. Like any storefront, you need traffic to create commercial success. By building a larger community, you are building "foot traffic" around these points of trade and allowing for more opportunities for sales, advertisements, donations, and sponsorships.

Being an infomediary

Having any degree of ownership of a community allows for the business model of the infomediary. An informediary is "a Web site or service that gathers and organizes large amounts of data and acts as an intermediary between those who want the information and those who supply the information."

John Hagel coined the term "infomediary" to describe a business model for adding intelligence to existing markets in his 1996 *Harvard Business Review* article titled "The Coming Battle for Customer Information."

With enough focus on a topic or cluster of topics, you can offer a consumer a place to gather information about specific areas of interest, including products, companies, and events that will allow them to make better-informed decisions about purchasing and attendance. In turn, they provide you with valuable feedback and aggregate opinion, which become valuable to those products and companies whose information is being provided.

Calls to action within the podcasts as well as peripheral calls to action within blogs, message boards, and Web pages accumulate that information. Surveys, polls, contact information, and Web traffic patterns become revenue-generating opportunities and support other models such as advertising and sponsorship.

Of course, the best way to destroy a community is to break the members' trust, invade their privacy, or harass them with too many calls to action. Escaping from the commercials that have propagated throughout traditional free media is one of the reasons that podcasting has grown so swiftly, so a careful balance has to be struck.

Vertical podcasting

One of the great ideas behind the long tail of podcasting is that niche markets are unlimited. The balance you need to find within your podcast business model is what market your ideas serve. The broader the market is, the larger the audience, and the larger the audience is, the greater potential for your volume of sales. The greater the niche is, the smaller the audience, and the greater potential is for a targeted sale with a more specific value provided to the listener.

Wikipedia defines a vertical market as a group of businesses, organizations, or enterprises that are viewed as a classification of the larger group of all businesses, organizations, or enterprises on the basis of the unique and specific nature of the products or services that they sell to the markets of the world or of the activities in which they are engaged.

This is what publishers of magazines to the vertical markets have done well for many years. You can learn from *Heavy Machinery Manufacturer* or *Wind Energy Farmer* or others who have noticeable followings like *Filmmaker Magazine*. Small markets have taken root and grown. If you are a player in a small market that grows, you can grow and succeed with the market. *Cardplayer Magazine* was small once, as was *Videomaker Magazine*. Find your niche, and you may grow with it as well.

By establishing yourself as a service to a vertical market now, you have an inside track as the leading provider for that market even as new podcasts serving that market spring up around you.

Summary

If you want to make it big in the podcasting business, you need to follow a business model. This chapter covered the following topics related to choosing a model:

- Just like the Web, podcasting is likely to spawn many different forms of revenue. Some of the most interesting podcasters are showing that ads aren't the only way to earn money.

- Founding a business on your podcast requires thinking through your relationship with the audience and how you can ask them for support. Retailing, sponsorships, and communities that create their own revenue streams may be better routes to profit.

- Branding, the experience you leave people remembering when they finish your podcast, is critical to getting them to take the next step, whether that's subscribing or going to your online store.

- After researching your podcast topic, you also need to understand the audience that actually forms around your program. Talking with your audience, through surveys and directly through your blog or Web site, is essential.

- You are your own promotional arm.

- When you work with a sponsor, look for many ways to engage the sponsor's brand. It increases the value of the relationship for them and creates more opportunities to bill for your services.

- A podcast is a natural medium for selling what you love. That's also the basis of retailing. Consider setting up an online store or auction where listeners can buy the stuff you talk about.

- Extend the retail opportunity by becoming a reseller of products. This is an emerging channel in music, for example, where fans are becoming the sellers of their favorite music for a cut of the revenue.

- Tip jars, which can be implemented on your Web site or blog, are another way to drive revenue for your podcast. Communities where your listeners are involved with one another may be a good place for a tip jar or sales-based businesses.

- Your expertise and the ability to connect people and information — being an infomediary — is a sound basis for a show, so why not a business, too?

Chapter 23

Rights and Responsibilities: Licensing Music and Managing Your Liabilities

Starting a business is the first step toward creating value that you need to protect and grow. Your little media company has to understand the rules of music licensing if your podcast will use popular music, and you need to know how to manage the risks associated with publishing information and opinion so that you don't end up giving away more of the value you build than necessary.

Music has been a part of your recording experience for years. It's integral to commercial broadcasts, and for the audiophile, music has been a lifetime obsession. Using music for a mix tape, or if you are like us, a faux radio show made in your bedroom when you were a kid, is second nature, because it was free and fun. When you use music for non-commercial programming, you are making a copy for which the music industry wants to be paid, even though you made nothing on the transaction. Adding revenue makes your program all the more attractive a target to music executives, and podcasts will certainly be at the center of some labels' business plans as they grow in popularity. Know how to surf the limits of fair use and when you should be prepared to pay, so that you can make intelligent decisions about how much music to use and when.

Bloggers and podcasters are already winning some of the privileges that journalists have enjoyed for decades, but they still need to be aware of the laws regarding libel, slander, and defamation, all of which are facets of the same thing, abusing someone's reputation publicly. It's really a matter of staying within well-established lines, but know those lines can prevent a world of headaches.

Copyright Is Built In

Back in the 1980s, The Whole Earth 'Lectronic Link, or WELL, operated on the basic rule that "you own your own words." It served two purposes: (1) to make the rule of copyright automatic and (2) to make it clear that members had to treat one another respectfully and own up to what they said. Both features of the words produced remain incredibly important to podcasters today.

Copyright, the protection afforded to the creator of a work, such as an article, book, song, or other performance, is virtually automatic today in the United States. Authors do not need to register a work with the U.S. Copyright Office to gain protection for their work. Every show you produce is yours. After the world moved past the moment of "publication" — when you made a book or pressed a copy of an album — that characterized the analog era, the simple act of creating a work equates with copyrighting it, so filing papers to get a copyright became unnecessary. The United States joined the global intellectual property rights regime in 1989, supporting what is known as the Berne Convention.

Even though it is assumed that you own your work, you can claim a copyright by affixing a copyright symbol, the familiar "©" or the word "Copyright" or "Copr." and the year the work was created in metadata on your audio files and in the show notes and text of your Web site. For example, John Smith would include this text to copyright a file in the ID3 data: "(© 2006 John Smith" or "Copr. 2006 John Smith."

Keeping your copyright requires one more step: You must submit two copies of your podcast to the Library of Congress. The U.S. Copyright Office calls this "mandatory" within three months of publication, but the reality is, in an environment where publication is ephemeral (just a file posted to the Net rather than a book), an author can claim publication at a more leisurely pace. We suggest assembling two copies of a CD containing the programs you produced during a quarter, along with a printout of the metadata and program notes for all the shows, and sending them to:

Library of Congress
Copyright Office
Attn: 407 Deposits
101 Independence Avenue SE
Washington, DC 20559-6000

We also suggest submitting podcasts as "serial work," the form in which a magazine is submitted. Use Form SE, available at www.copyright.gov/forms/formsei.pdf. The initial registration costs $45 and each quarterly update is $25. Otherwise, you'll pay $45 per submission.

With copyright on a work, you have the power to control all reproduction and derivative works based on your work. However, copyright doesn't cover something like a slogan or phrase, so if you coin the term "pleasure weasel" and hope to sell lots of t-shirts with the phrase emblazoned on the chest, you do need to apply for a trademark, a different form of intellectual property protection. This prevents you from keeping others from discussing an idea you created . Additionally, there is a notion of "fair use" in copyright law that gives anyone the ability to quote briefly from a work so that they can respond to it in some way.

A common argument about the abuse of copyright today goes this way: "I bought a copy of the book or song or movie, so why can't I make some work using parts of it?" This is a foundational point for people claiming that today's digital rights are more restrictive than those applied during the era of analog communications. While some uses of digital rights management (DRM) technology are incredibly abusive, it has always been a basic principle of copyright that purchasing a copy of a work did not transfer rights of ownership in the ideas and arrangement of the information in it. This is why unlicensed sampling of audio from a song for use in another song is prohibited.

Taking the extra step of actually registering has another benefit: Your podcast becomes a part of the collection at the Library of Congress. Even after your server is down and you're dead and gone, the sound or video you made is preserved for posterity. Small consolation for some, but very important to others.

Copyright lasts for the whole of your life plus 70 years after you die for a total of 95 years from publication or 120 years from the creation of the work, "whichever is shorter," according to the U.S. copyright law. In other words, a work created in 2006 will be protected until 2131, unless it is published today, in which case it will be protected until 2101. That is, unless you died in 2006, in which case the copyright endures only until 2076. That's a bit much, if we may express an opinion.

Making Fair Use Feasible and Machine-Readable

Copyright has been extended to extravagant lengths in recent years, and elsewhere we've discussed the consequences for podcasters and anyone who buys digital audio, video, and other media. You can get and use copyright on your works without being a jerk about it. It can be valuable to do so, because it does allow you some control over what happens to your work while allowing others to quote you or sample audio or video within the limits you've specified.

"Fair use" is a term bandied around these days, as rights are in the midst of so much change because of the ease of copying and sampling others' works. In the simplest terms, it accords an author the right to excerpt another work without permission in order to comment on it. For example, excerpting a quote or a paragraph of a book or playing a short clip of a song or video so that you can critique the content—something that can include arguing with the work, not just doing a review—is perfectly legal under U.S. copyright law. You can even make money on the work that excerpts another work, such as when you sell the review of a movie or when a news report "quotes" from the audio recorded by a podcaster. However, there's a bright line when it comes to making money primarily from the excerpted work. It is not fair use to sell the last 20 minutes of an audio book or a movie so that people can find out how it ends. A teacher can pass out a copy of an article for discussion in class, but the limits are constricting so much in the digital era that almost any copying is treated as a violation of copyright by some industries, especially the music business and Hollywood, though the typical software company isn't going to be kind to someone who copies part of its source code, even for educational purposes. There are few saints left in this world, so try to join the team with the white hats on this topic; be very generous with your fair use thinking, but be careful and respectful of others' intellectual property because mistakes can get you sued.

Lawrence Lessig, an attorney and Stanford Law School professor, conceived of a supplement to copyright that expresses an author's intentions for her work while preserving a strong form of fair use. Called Creative Commons, the system relies on a license that allows people to make copies and redistribute all or parts of your work with or without changes as long as they give you credit. It restricts people from reselling or profiting from your work if you don't allow any commercial use.

Creative Commons licenses are designed to be embedded in works as machine-readable descriptions of the rights you grant to others. This is important to future implementations of intellectual property systems, but isn't supported in digital media players today, so it doesn't mean your Creative Commons-licensed program is protected against unauthorized copying. It's not DRM; it's just a form of metadata that travels with your podcast to streamline re-use of the sound or images.

Behind Creative Commons is the important notion that society is engaged in conversations and debates through media, so the ability to refer to and modify other works when participating in these discussions is critical to a free and informed society, one that prospers on the sharing of ideas as well as on sales. Making your intentions easily accessible allows people to use your work without having to check with you first, but it doesn't mean that you've closed all other options. So if you don't allow commercial use in your Creative Commons license, someone wanting to republish it for commercial purposes must contact you to negotiate a fee. The Creative Commons license carries your contact information so people can communicate with you about commercial uses.

You'll need to register each work you want to protect with Creative Commons, which means you can protect all your podcasts under one license. If, however, you want to create different programs or treat different programs differently, you'll need to create a license for each one.

Configuring Your Creative Commons License

Visit `creativecommons.org/license` to create a Creative Commons license for your podcast, as shown in Figure 23.1. After providing your answers to the questions, the Creative Commons site generates a license that contains all the terms you've selected. You'll find a number of options to consider:

- **Allow commercial uses of your work?** *Yes/No:* If you choose "Yes," others can copy part or all of your work and use it in commercial works with no obligation to compensate you. Selecting "No" means that if someone does want to use your work in a commercial product, he must contact you to negotiate terms.

FIGURE 23.1

The Creative Commons license configuration page. Note the "pre-fab" options at the left.

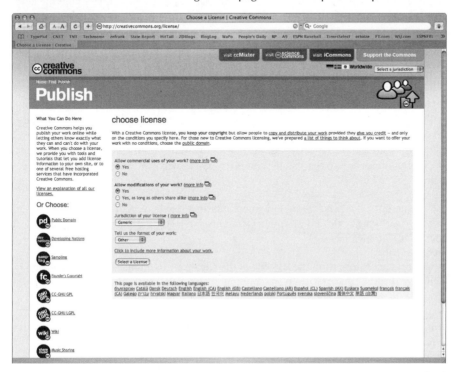

- **Allow modification of your work?** *Yes/Yes, as long as others share alike/No:* This is where "fair use" gets interesting. What do you want done with your work, if wherever it goes it reflects on you? In music, allowing sampling can get you a riff in a big hit. With spoken material or video, where a quick cut could be used to insert words or images that mock your ideas, you may not be so comfortable with being sampled. The thing is, if we podcasters are making public statements, doesn't that mean we are "public figures" who can be criticized or satirized? Even though Creative Commons makes your preferences clear, the law isn't clearly defined yet. Your options here are:

  - "Yes," which allows others to create "derivative works" using your work. If, for example, you make a show with lots of swearing, someone else could edit out your cursing and offer a "clean" version. This option allows any form of re-use.

  - "Yes, as long as others share alike" forces your choice to share on those who choose to use your work. If someone uses some of your sound, he has to make his program available for derivative works as well.

  - "No" tells the recipient that you don't want her to use all or part of your work without permission. She can still contact you to request permission to remix you.

- **Jurisdiction of your license:** Creative Commons is a legal document, a contract that relies on established law for enforcement. You can choose a generic license that can be used in any jurisdiction, or you can choose one that associates the contract with the laws of a particular country. It's best to use a generic license or one tied to your local law, because in both cases if you come into conflict with someone, you can have the hearing in your jurisdiction rather than having to travel or hire a lawyer somewhere else.

- **Tell us the format of your work:** As a podcaster, your choices are "Audio" and "Video." Pretty simple.

- **Click to include more information about your work:** Click this. It opens an important section where you can enter the title of the work, a description of the work, your name and copyright claim, the year of the copyright, and if you sampled someone else's work, links to the source material you used. We suggest including your contact information in the description section so that people can reach you to negotiate terms for rights you've retained.

We repeat: Be sure to open the "Click to include more information about your work" panel to include your name, the work's title, a description (remember to include contact information), copyright, and links to source material.

The pre-fab options, which appear on the left side of the Creative Commons licensing page, are designed to address specific concerns, such as sampling or software distribution. They have the virtue of explaining more completely the options you can choose. In Figure 23.2, the Sampling License is designed to describe your preferences for use of parts of your work in anything other than advertising or redistribution of the whole work. The license assumes that you want to be paid for advertiser's use of your work. You have these options:

- **Sampling:** This choice allows commercial use of part of your work, "sampling" of it in a nutshell. Redistribution of the whole work is not allowed, and samples may be used by others to make money without compensating you.

- **Sampling Plus:** In addition to the sampling allowed by the first option, this one allows someone to take the whole work and redistribute it for a profit. For example, your work could be included in a collection of podcasts assembled by a company or another podcaster and sold for $10.

- **Noncommercial Sampling Plus:** This option limits re-use of your work, whether in whole or in part, to non-commercial purposes. Again, your podcast could be collected into a larger work, but no one can profit from using your work.

Should you just want to put your work into the public domain, which means anyone can do anything they want with your work as long as they acknowledge you, choose the Public Domain License offered by the Creative Commons. It asks for your e-mail address and the title and the name of the copyright holder, which could be you or the name of your company or organization. It gets your name around.

FIGURE 23.2

The Creative Commons' Sampling pre-fab license offers three sampling preferences.

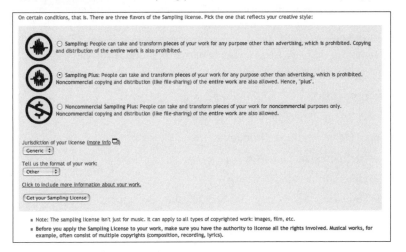

Why use more than one Creative Commons license? Let's say that you have a paid podcast that you don't want pirated and another that is the promotional version of the paid program or something totally separate that there's no need to protect. That free show may attract attention to your paid podcast, for example, so you want to see it spread around as a form of marketing. Using Creative Commons, you can configure a non-commercial license that prevents any modification of your paid program — so no one can resell even parts of your podcast — and a second license for the "free" podcast that doesn't limit commercial use or modifications by others. However, both licenses assume a broad concept of fair use, so people may still excerpt your paid program to comment on or review it.

We've covered protecting your rights. Now it's time to look at how to deal with the most licensed content in the world, music.

Licensing Music if You Must

Music adds emotional energy to any program, and a podcast without music is perceived as sparse by listeners who are accustomed to hearing music that reinforces what the host is saying. The problem is, popular music costs money when you want to redistribute it, even as background sound in a podcast.

You have a variety of free music options, including these:

- **Writing your own music:** You don't have to pay yourself, but you do need a band. This is actually easier than you may think since the advent of music mixing programs that come stocked with loops of sound for many different instruments. These loops, which include guitar riffs, rhythms, horns, and just about every other instrument, can be combined to make songs or bumpers. These are some of the applications you can use:

  - GarageBand (Macintosh), from Apple Computer
  - M-Audio Pro Tools (Macintosh and Windows), from Digidesign
  - Cakewalk Sonar Producer (Windows), from Cakewalk
  - Cakewalk Sonar Home Studio XL (Windows), from Cakewalk
  - Acid (Windows), from Sonic Foundry
  - Audition (Windows), from Adobe Systems

- **Using "PodSafe" music:** Creative Commons-licensed and other music.

- **Using public domain music:** Feel free to use music on which copyright has expired or that has been placed into the public domain for use by anyone. The place to search for U.S. public domain music is `http://pdinfo.com`. However, you still need to verify that the music you find there is cleared for commercial use, if you intend to charge for your podcast or have other revenue streams, such as advertising.

- **Understanding fair use of music:** A short excerpt of music can be used to criticize or comment on it, to report on the release of a song, and to teach. But don't get carried away. Fair use doesn't let you make The Kinks' *Lola* into your theme song. It doesn't let you play the whole song in order to discuss it, not even if you break it into segments and talk over each section in tedious detail.

Then there is all the music you have to pay for. The several types of payments you face are for performance rights and, if the label that published the music is feeling the need, fees paid to the music label. If you are going to record a song written by someone else, such as a cover of *Lola,* you need to pay for "mechanical rights" fees based on the number of copies of your rendition of the song you intend to distribute.

Making regular use excerpts of songs in your podcast, in title themes and bumpers, and as incidental music requires a license to reproduce that music, which ensures the artists are paid for their work. These rights are known as performance rights. Three organizations represent most of the recorded music companies, collecting performance licensing fees on their behalf: ASCAP (The American Society of Composers, Authors and Publishers), BMI (Broadcast Music Inc.), and SESAC (Society of European Stage Actors and Composers). To be safe, it is best to get a license from all three, because you'll save time not having to bother finding out if the music is covered by your payments. Quick, which licensing company represents Bob Dylan? Which represents The Red Hot Chili Peppers? And which rapper 50 Cent? The answers: SESAC, BMI, and ASCAP, in that order. The roughly $750 per year you'll pay to not have to answer those questions is likely worth it if you want to use commercial music in your podcast.

Choosing music licenses

ASCAP offers two kinds of licenses: one for non-interactive and one for interactive distribution. These factors help you determine which one you need:

- **ASCAP Non-Interactive 5.0:** Choose this license for use of incidental music, bumpers that include commercial music, and so forth, unless you are offering a music podcast that includes a collection of complete versions of songs in each show. "Non-interactive" means that the listener doesn't get to choose what they hear and that excerpts of songs will not be longer than 60 seconds. The minimum annual fee is $288, and the basic rate is $0.0009 per show. Download the ASCAP form for this license at `www.ascap.com/weblicense/release5.0.pdf`.

- **ASCAP Interactive 2.0:** If you do a music podcast, you're offering a library of music that the listener can play on command, giving them a choice of what to hear and when they hear it. The minimal annual fee is $340, and the basic rate per show is $0.0014. Download the ASCAP form for this license at `www.ascap.com/weblicense/release2.0.pdf`.

Note that the licensing fees are a minimum. To calculate what your rates will be, visit `www.ascap.com/weblicense/license.html`, where an interactive form asks which license you want and requires the following information:

1. **User revenue:** This may include your subscription fees and any other fees you receive for delivering your podcast, such as payments from a wireless carrier that compensates you based on how much airtime the listener consumes to download the file. If you don't have any of these fees and don't anticipate any in the coming year, leave this blank. If you expect to make money from subscriptions, you need to enter a good faith estimate of what you believe that revenue will be for the coming year.

2. **Sponsor revenue:** This includes sponsor fees and advertising revenue. Again, if you don't anticipate any fees, leave this blank. If you do plan to sell sponsorships or advertising, make a good faith estimate.

3. **Adjustment to sponsor revenue:** Here's where you subtract the cost of selling sponsorships or advertising provided by a third party that you pay to handle your advertising inventory. It can't exceed 15 percent of revenue, and you cannot count your Internal sales expenses against this, so if you have your own salesperson, that cost does not count here.

4. **Number of Internet/site/service sessions:** If you leave everything else blank, you still have to estimate how many streaming sessions or downloads of non-interactive programs (where the music used is incidental or for bumpers) expected during the year. Here, we recommend that you go back to the calculations you did in Chapter 18 in order to get the number of downloads you expect. This is as far as you need to go for a non-interactive podcast. If you will be delivering full songs as part of a music podcast, you need to fill out the following fields.

5. **Number of music sessions:** This number cannot exceed the number you entered in field 4, "Number of Internet/site/service sessions," and represents the total number of downloads expected for a year. It's the same question asking for use in a different place in the ASCAP calculation.

6. **Number of music performances:** Here, you are estimating how many times all songs delivered in their entirety via download will be downloaded during the year. If, for example, you expect to use eight songs for each show, multiply that times the number of downloads you expect for the full year. You can leave this blank if you know how many ASCAP songs you intend to deliver during the year. (Again, we recommend that you go back to the calculations you did in Chapter 17 in order to get the number of downloads you expect.)

7. **Number of ASCAP music performances:** This can be a smaller number than the one you entered in field 6, "Number of music performances," because it represents the number of copies of ASCAP-licensed songs you expect to deliver during the year. This way, you can pay ASCAP only for those songs it covers and save some money by not having to pay BMI and SESAC.

When you finish the calculation, you can click the button "Finish Agreement" using whichever schedule is appropriate and enter your address and other information to have a pre-filled PDF file downloaded for your signature and payment. If your fees are less than $1,000, you can pay for a full year up front. If you expect higher fees, you must file quarterly payments based on actual numbers of downloads.

Remember that you have paid only for rights to ASCAP-licensed music at this point. There's still BMI and SESAC to take care of.

The BMI site has a podcasting license form at `www.bmi.com/licensing/podcasting/index.asp`. BMI's payments are based on estimated revenue from all sources. The company wants 1.75 percent of your revenue (revenue times 0.0175), but if you expect to make less than $50,000, you can start by paying for a minimum fee for the full year and then pay the difference, should you exceed the minimum. If you do so, you must submit your updated revenue and payment by the end of the year. If you expect to make more than $50,000, you must submit quarterly reports and payments.

The minimum BMI licensing fee is $238. If you expect to make $49,999 on your podcast in the coming year, your annual payment will be $874.98. So, start by paying the minimum and submit the difference later.

SESAC's license is also available online, at `www.sesac.com/pdf/internet_ATH_2006_click.pdf`. It is the most complicated of the licenses, but the meat of it can be found in Schedule A and the second to last page of the agreement, the Initial License Fee Report for SESAC Internet License Agreement. Schedule A provides the "multiplier" for use in the calculation in the report form, asking you how many "components" you plan to offer on your site. If you will be offering just podcasts, you have one component. If you offer a streaming version of your program as well, then you have two components. But here's the catch: Advertising revenue is treated as a separate component.

SESAC treats revenue as a separate component of your podcast, so if you expect to make more than $3,000 on advertising or sponsor revenue during any quarter of the year, you must count an additional component when calculating your fees.

Now, continue to the Initial License Fee Report for SESAC Internet License Agreement. It asks for your name, company name, and the period for which you want the license. Enter this, remembering that if you continue to offer these programs next year, you have to license them again. Under section 3, License Fee, you'll see a field for the "Total ATH for the Initial Reporting Period." This figure, the ATH (aggregate tuning hours) is the number of podcast downloads you expect times the total length of the podcasts. If, for example, you expect 30,000 downloads of 10-minute shows, your total ATH is 5,000 hours (30,000 times 10 minutes divided by 60 minutes).

In Line B, check the components you offer. Again, if you offer just non-commercial podcasts, check the Podcasting box. If you have ads in your podcasts that will earn more than $3,000 per quarter, also check the Advertising Promotional Revenue box. And if you also offer streaming or video, check those boxes.

Refer to Schedule A for the multiplier based on the number of components you have to enter in Line C of the Initial License Fee Report.

In Line D, you enter the sum of Line A times Line C, which gives you the total expected fee for the year.

Go back to Schedule A and see if the Minimum Semi-annual Fee is less than the figure in Line D. If so, the minimum is what you owe. You'll need to file a supplemental report in six months verifying your actual listenership and pay the remainder of the year's fees.

The minimum you should expect to pay for SESAC fees during a year is $168.

Understanding mechanical rights and label fees

Finally, there is the issue of mechanical rights and label fees. We address the labels first. The ASCAP, BMI, and SESAC fees should cover almost all commercial labels; if a label comes calling on you to collect fees, simply point them to those organizations to get their money, because that's what you pay the licensing companies for in the first place. Sometimes, however, the label has no licensing representative and may ask you to pay for the music you use directly. We'd be very careful with those requests, asking for verification of the fact that the label has contracts that allow them to collect fees on behalf of the bands they publish. Then, if they've avoided the licensing systems you use, they are probably pretty small, so ask them if they would prefer you remove their music from your podcast before you agree to pay. Chances are good that they need the promotional exposure more than they need a fee for the music you used.

Mechanical rights are handled by one company: the Harry Fox Agency. Mechanical rights are for the production of covers of existing music: You would pay these fees if you are going to use the tune, lyrics, or both for a song written by someone else. You need to check whether the music is handled by the Harry Fox Agency before paying the fees, which are based on the number of copies you expect to distribute. You can search the Harry Fox database of songs here: `www.harryfox` `.com/songfile/public/publicsearch.jsp`.

Be careful with lampooning songs or otherwise rewriting them while preserving the basic melody, because you have to pay for that. For example, a parody of *Lola* by The Kinks called *Yoda* by Weird Al Yankovic is also a registered song, but if you record *Yoda*, Ray Davies of The Kinks has to split the fee with Weird Al. If you come up with your own lyrics, Ray Davies or the publisher he sold the song to gets all the fees, after the Harry Fox Agency takes its cut.

The Harry Fox Agency Web site has a simple licensing mechanism, HFA Songfile, for purchasing mechanical rights for up to 2,500 copies of a song, based on the Congressionally specified rate of $0.091 per copy for songs of up to 5 minutes in length. Long songs are more expensive.

Whether you're covering *Lola* by The Kinks or doing a takeoff on a new song by Pink or 50 Cent with lyrics of your own, you need to pay this fee. Songfile is located at www.harryfox.com/public/songfile.jsp.

How much did that music cost?

As with other elements of the podcasting business, you need to enter the cost of your music into the profit and loss statement we've encouraged you to build. At a minimum, the three licensing organizations, ASCAP, BMI, and SESAC, will cost you $684 a year, with podcasts delivering hundreds of thousands of downloads per year facing much larger bills. If you intend to produce cover versions of songs for your podcast, it's going to be much more if you have a large audience.

Don't forget to count this cost or, if it's unpalatable, to look to "PodSafe" music as an alternative.

Saving on Tunes

The idea behind PodSafe music is that bands will enjoy greater exposure if they make their music available under Creative Commons licenses that allow robust fair use of excerpts in podcasts and, in some cases, complete rights to redistribute a song or songs from an album in hopes of winning fans and selling full CDs of their music.

As a podcaster, you do need to use music to spice up each episode and to give your listeners cues that you are changing topics or coming to a regular segment. PodSafe music is ideal for this, because it allows you to integrate segments of songs as long as you give credit to the performers. There is a wide spectrum of music available under various PodSafe licenses and through aggregator sites; in some cases, you have to buy the song for a small fee, but you are then free to use the song in your show.

The one area we believe you need to be careful with in the PodSafe music world is covers of songs where the artist may not have paid the Harry Fox Agency for the right to make and distribute his own performances of others' songs.

These are the leading sites for PodSafe music:

- `music.podshow.com`: The podsafe music network is part of the PodShow network founded by Adam Curry's PodShow Inc. The music is freely usable in podcasts, but the company has alienated podcasters with an aggressive intellectual property contract for listing programs.

- `www.garageband.com`: Garageband.com, not associated with Apple Computer, which makes a music mixing application of the same name, was founded in 1999 and promotes new bands. Not all the music on the site is available under a Creative Commons license, so be sure to check before you remix.

- `www.podsafeaudio.com`: Much of the music here, which includes hundreds of artists' works, all of it PodSafe, is virtually unheard, with only hundreds or dozens of plays, so if you find something you like, you can introduce it to the world.

- `www.beatpick.com`: This site offers a large catalog of music with online licensing for podcasters. The bands here are looking to be compensated for use of their music, but the terms are reasonable, and often the terms are only that you give them credit in the show. Artists get half the fee. You'll also find links for commissioning a band to perform a song for your use.

- `www.soundclick.com`: This is another good site for music and samples that you can remix. Not all the music here is under Creative Commons licenses that allow remixing or use in podcasting, but it has an excellent selection and links to contact artists directly to work out podcast rights.

- `www.opsound.com`: At this all Creative Commons Attribution–ShareAlike licensed site, everything you find can be used in a podcast as long as you provide credit to the artist whose work you sample. It has a wide selection, and the stuff is well tagged by users to help you find inspired music.

Bands have already discovered podcasts as a promotional tool, so the PodSafe music movement is already an explosive phenomenon. More and more music will be available to choose from as time passes, but do remember that even if someone gives you rights, that's the beginning of a relationship, not just a cheap deal. Be good to podsafe musicians, and they will be good to you.

What if you change your mind about a podcast or song that has been released to PodSafe or unlimited use under Creative Commons? This is a quandary, because you cannot pull back all the unrestricted copies out on the Web. You can, however, rerelease the audio under a more restrictive license. Ultimately, you have to let the restricted version compete with the free one, but by doing marketing on behalf of the commercial version you can probably recoup more than enough to avoid regretting that PodSafe decision from the past.

Staying Out of Lawsuits: Know Your Defamation Law

You're going to talk to make money, so your words can land you in court more easily because there is the perception that you have assets someone can go after if you offend them. There is much that podcasters and bloggers can learn from journalists, who have learned how to cause the most trouble possible without landing in jail over the course of centuries. It's worth understanding this stuff even if you don't want to be journalistic, because anyone can be sued for libel, slander, or defamation.

We recommend that you pick up a copy of *The Associated Press Stylebook and Briefing on Media Law*, which is the essential text for many journalists. A solid guide for high school journalists just starting to pick up the basics of the law, and a second good source for beginners, is the *Massachusetts Bar Association's Journalists' Handbook*.

The first thing to understand about all subjects relating to journalists' privileges is that they are different everywhere; there is no international standard set of laws, though journalistic professional societies have pressed for these kinds of uniform expectations. Most of what is laid out here relates to the United States, where the press enjoys the most liberal protections available. In Canada, for example, there is no presumption that a journalist can protect her source. In much of Europe, the subjects of photographs retain far greater control of pictures through their moral rights, or *droit moral*, which provides both the photographer and the subject protection from the unauthorized reuse of the image in whole or in part—juxtaposing the image of a person into an advertisement, which is common in digital media, is prohibited without his permission.

Defamation, slander, and libel are the same thing, essentially, but each is defined based on the way a false statement about a person is conveyed. According to ExpertLaw.com, defamation, the general principal behind all three, must include the following elements:

- A false and defamatory statement concerning another;
- The unprivileged publication of the statement to a third party (that is, somebody other than the person defamed by the statement);
- If the defamatory matter is of public concern, fault amounting at least to negligence on the part of the publisher; and
- Damage to the plaintiff.

In the context of defamation law, a statement is "published" when it is made to the third party. That term does not mean that the statement has to be in print. The moment you post your podcast to the Net, the statements in it become published because they are available to a third person.

Damages claimed in libel cases are typically to the reputation of the plaintiff, but depending upon the laws of the jurisdiction, it may be enough to establish mental anguish. Most jurisdictions also recognize "per se" defamation, where the allegations are presumed to cause damage to the plaintiff. Typically, the following may constitute defamation per se:

- Attacks on a person's professional character or standing;

- Allegations that an unmarried person is unchaste;

- Allegations that a person is infected with a sexually transmitted disease; or

- Allegations that the person has committed a crime of moral turpitude.

Libel is committed when a statement that meets this standard is published in a document, whether a newspaper, magazine, book, or Web site. Podcasters and bloggers need to keep this firmly in mind when writing about someone, especially someone who is not a public figure (we'll get to that in a moment).

Podcasters are more likely to be accused of slander, a spoken defamation, whether that act of speech is public and one-time or recorded and redistributed, though it's possible that someone could sue a podcaster for libel or defamation. Slander also includes defamation by gesture, which could include making a gesture that suggests professional incompetence or mental illness. Slander carries the additional burden for a plaintiff of having to prove that he suffered actual loss due to the false statement.

If you are webcasting, podcasting, producing digital video, or otherwise using the Internet to convey information that may be construed to be slanderous, this is the branch of defamation law about which you need to be aware.

NOTE The Radio and Television News Directors Foundation offers a deep resource on the use of many different kinds of information in a broadcast that deals with a variety of liabilities and ethical questions radio and television journalists face. It is available at `www.rtnda.org/members/legalnotes/legalnotes1002.asp`.

The truth is your ally

In all cases, the truth is an absolute defense against charges of libel, slander, or defamation (except in totalitarian countries or those not under the rule of law, where a judge can rule arbitrarily in favor of a powerful person). If you are going to call someone "a crook" or "a philanderer," for example, be sure that you can prove he's a criminal or that he is stepping out on his spouse or carrying on multiple affairs simultaneously. Be ready for challenges to your proof, so don't take for granted that one item of proof is sufficient.

However, the truth is a relative thing, because public figures are the subject of varied opinions about which the writer or producer is largely convinced. Public figures have to prove that the writer or speaker willfully ignored the truth or acted with flagrant disregard to the truth. And that is hard to prove. In the case of Dan Rather's broadcast accusing President Bush of having avoided his National Guard service based on documents it failed to vet completely, the fact that it involved a source's documents insulated CBS from charges of slander and libel (because they both broadcast and published articles on the cbs.com Web site). If CBS had not relied on that source in making the statements, it would have been open to libel litigation.

Fox News has mastered the practice of deflecting an accusation by attribution, as in the phrase "people say . . ." or "according to sources" before leveling an untrue or highly opinionated statement that depends on subjective interpretation of fact. This is not a defense against libel or slander if the criteria described previously are met. The burden for a journalist would then fall to the question of whether a source really made the accusation. And this is where the issue of confidentiality comes in.

Know the rules of attribution, and keep good notes

The confidentiality of sources involves protections that are somewhat mythical. In many jurisdictions, including the United States, there is no guarantee that a journalist can protect her sources. It's not in the U.S. Constitution, but has been interpreted to be a journalist's privilege in a number of state and federal cases. Shield laws have been passed in many cities and states, but these do not protect someone publishing on the Web, who may be indicted in another jurisdiction that has no such laws.

Requests for anonymity are used by government and corporate officials, who should be on the record to launch test balloons, make attacks on opponents, and much else. It is also just plain lazy on many journalists' part, because they should use a background statement to delve into the truth in order to get the facts on the record. But in the race to make a scoop — and, unfortunately, many journalists just think being first, rather than being complete and accurate, makes a scoop — solid sourcing often goes out the window.

Sources can sue you for libel or slander, as well, if they dispute what words you put in their mouths. This is why a journalist's notes or recordings are so terribly important. In one case, a journalist whose source disputed a phrase lost the case because the words were in his notebook but not in quotes. A journalist learns to annotate carefully because of these kinds of realities.

A confidential source who has extracted a promise of anonymity is in a position to say almost anything, and in the course of reporting, you may find that some of the things said get you in more trouble than is necessary. This is not to say that you shouldn't source an accusation, but sometimes the accusation's falseness raises many more barriers to finding the truth than the confidential source claims they eliminate with their information, so judge carefully whether you are really advancing a story by offering confidentiality to a source.

In the case of Valerie Plame, the wife of former U.S. Ambassador Joseph Wilson, who was outed by someone as an active CIA agent, the journalists who looked into the story and are now facing jail for protecting sources absolutely made a good decision to use sources that led them closer to Karl Rove.

If the source has something to lose and can demonstrate that it is materially important to them, then confidentiality may be necessary. If confidentiality is a convenience for the source, you're better off doing more footwork yourself.

This brings us to the issue of attribution and knowing when and why to go from being on the record with a source. Always begin a conversation by identifying yourself as a journalist (or a blogger writing "on the record"), if you want to enjoy any of the protections normally accorded to a journalist; begin and stay on the record until it becomes necessary to go off the record.

After "on the record," which means you can write or broadcast anything said in the conversation, comes "on background" and its many hues. In a background conversation, you can write down what is being said but cannot attribute it directly to the source. The source becomes generally identifiable to the reader as "a source in the Defense Department" or "a senior manager at Example Corp." Remember that background information still needs to be confirmed elsewhere, so don't be afraid to take the conversation back on the record to try to get the information in an attributed quote; background conversations are still a matter of convenience for the source.

We're talking here about how you handle relationships with people. We all know that some circumstances demand that we protect confidentiality. Sometimes, a source is giving you information that will get the person who really needs to be on the record to speak, because you come to them with information that, after they know you have it, they have to address on the record. This has worked for me with corporations, two White House administrations, and a variety of other situations. What I want to emphasize is that a background quote or an off-the-record or confidential source does not make a publishable story in all but the most extreme cases. Can you prevent a catastrophe with an off-the-record quote? Publish! If it's a matter of getting a scoop, do more legwork.

That's it in a nutshell, the beginning of a lifetime of exploration and growing subtlety if you want to jump into the journalist's role in society.

Summary

You need to protect yourself from lawsuits stemming from what you say and do online. This chapter provided tips and info on the following topics:

- Your podcast is an asset and a potential source of liabilities. Learn a little about the law in order to avoid major headaches. Become a student of copyright law if you find it interesting or strategically useful as you balance free distribution with the ways you make money.

- Copyright is granted to a work when you create it. Registering the work with the Library of Congress gives you additional leverage if you have to enforce your copyright, but it isn't necessary.

- "Fair Use" is the most important idea in intellectual property today, because it is under attack. The principle is important to an informed society, that it is perfectly legitimate to sample some one else's work to comment on or review it, particularly in the context of covering it as news or an issue.

- Fair use doesn't extend to sampling for commercial purposes, such as taking a guitar riff from a song or including an extended excerpt from a book or podcast in a commercial collection of works without first negotiating for the rights with the creator.

- The Creative Commons has developed a machine-readable approach to expressing the property rights creative people wish to assert over their works. It simply lists those claims in metadata that can be attached to a file, but does not enforce limits on use like Digital Rights Management software does.

- There are a variety of Creative Commons licenses that can be configured for your needs.

- Using music in podcasts is tricky business. Sampling a song to talk about it comes at no cost under fair use, but using a song as your theme every week requires you pay for the rights to do so.

- As an alternative to paying for music, consider creating your own using one of the music looping applications on the market that let you build a song from a library of instrument files. The other option is PodSafe music, songs distributed with a license to use the music in podcasts in exchange for promotional mentions.

- PodSafe music can be found on dozens of sites. Be attentive to the rights the artists grant. Whether you like limits or not, it is their music, not yours.

- When licensing music, check which licensing organization the song is managed by and purchase the appropriate license.

- Licensed music may cost you more if your audience grows.

- If you are playing a performance of a song by another artist you need not pay for "mechanical rights" to use the song. But if you decide to perform a cover of another artist's work, such as The Beatles' "Lady Madonna," mechanical rights must be acquired, usually from the Harry Fox Agency.

- Podcasters need to be aware of defamation laws, particularly rules governing libel and slander, since they publish a spoken record of their ideas.

- Generally, the truth is a defense in libel litigation, but the way you make an accusation and support the claim is the key to whether you'll be sued successfully.

- Don't make the mistake of reporting someone else's libelous assertions. If you do not couch accusations by others in facts you may be accused — successfully — of propagating their libels, which is not protected.

- The rules of attribution are important to keeping your podcast out of trouble. Since most audio interviews are the record of a conversation, they will stand as evidence that the subject said what they did, but if you relate a conversation that is unrecorded, be sure you have good notes.

Chapter 24

Corporate and Institutional Podcasting

Podcasting is a tool for organizations to use to communicate within their teams and to customers. Universities and schools also can put podcasts to work to extend the reach of their teaching efforts. Neither of these applications has the same economic imperative as the entrepreneurial podcasts discussed in most chapters of this book. Rather, there are reasons to spend time and resources to develop programming for use in outreach to specific groups, such as employees who need training or access to information for use in sales and support services, or to current customers who need to be supported and marketed to with a different level of attention than potential buyers.

Many of the same practical questions need to be addressed for these uses of podcasting as with entrepreneurial podcasts:

- How can I secure the content so it reaches only those to whom I want to expose the information?

- What do I need to spend to achieve my goals, whether for outbound marketing or internal communication?

- What are the production issues associated with bringing together the talent and knowledge needed to make my show relevant and useful?

Several unique questions also must be asked:

- How will the information I expose in a podcast change my company's compliance with Securities & Exchange Commission rules?

- What is the impact of a lecture distributed via podcast on attendance at a college class?

In this area, as with all other markets where podcasting is helping to change economics, some potentially profound questions about the value of control of, and benefits of freeing, information must be asked as you plan your strategy.

Podcasting as a Customer Relationship Channel

You've sold a car or a pair of skis—whatever you sell, it's going out the door with a customer—and now you need to ask yourself "How do I stay in touch with that customer so that I get follow-on business, such as auto service or new boots when that customer is ready to spend again?" Suppose you interviewed the customer before he left, asking about his commute and what he listens to on the radio or where he likes to ski, and then told him to subscribe to your podcast to hear himself. Many people will do it just for the fun of hearing themselves, and some will tell others about it, too. You may get referral business out of the effort.

Marketing podcasts like this should emphasize getting the most out of the product or service that your customer buys. It could be something as simple as getting your massage customers to talk about their stretching routines or favorite recipes while you do your work, and then offering everyone who comes through the door the opportunity to join in on the shared conversation. A podcast can keep your customers close and get them talking about your product or work.

The question for this type of podcast is not what you will make in direct revenue, but how much you should invest in order to increase repeat business. Any organization knows it is easier to sell an existing customer than win a new one. Podcasting's low cost and the ease with which programs can be distributed make it an ideal medium for extending your engagement with customers. For a few cents per copy, including all your costs, you can continue to talk with customers long after they've left your business. Consider making a segment of service recommendations with comments by customers who've come in for follow-on purchases. We're not salespeople, but the salesperson reading this will have dozens of ideas that can be integrated into a podcast.

The expense to consider is how much to spend on the production and promotion of the podcast itself. The extra production costs of having a recording setup available to record customers in your store or at a cubicle may seem extravagant. If you can convert one-time customers into lifetime customers by making them the stars of your marketing, every one of those customers may spend two or three times as much as any first-time customer. When your podcast can also be used to promote your business to non-customers, such as when you are distributing pamphlets or on your Web site, where you can print your RSS feed URL, the investment in repeat business can pay additional dividends as well. Who better to have speaking on your behalf than your customers?

What about the ultimate lock-in, giving a customer an MP3 player on which to listen to your podcast? At this writing, a cheap MP3 player with 32 MB of storage—enough memory to pre-load several hours of audio—is about $14. Purchased in bulk, your cost would be less. Now, if you have a product or service that sells for hundreds of dollars, this could be a sound expense in order to make customers into repeat customers. If you are a dentist whose services involve, if the patient is really engaged, two $50 visits a year with the potential for hundreds or thousands of dollars in dental work, the cost of a device may be worthwhile as well. In both situations, you'd want to have a couple of hours of high-quality audio explaining how to be a power user of your product or discussing the benefits of different types of dental or orthodontic work and how to care for one's teeth — something that will be remembered, even if the customer listens just once and throws away the player.

Then make sure customers have the instructions about how to subscribe to your podcast after they get home, so that you have a direct channel to them in the future. Is there a controversy about fluoridating water in your community? Most folks will tune in to the dentist to get his opinion, and if you make your first contact with existing clients who tell their friends to check out your podcast for your views on fluoridation, you may win some new patients.

An auto dealer who sells a car with an auxiliary audio input jack and no MP3 player to plug into it is missing the opportunity to have a customer listen to the many reasons to be happy with her new car on the way home, lowering buyer's remorse and increasing the likelihood that she will make after-market purchases. Imagine, for example, that your podcast — the voice of the guy who sold the car to her — provided a guided tour of the dashboard as she drive home, touting some add-ons that you probably already mentioned in the showroom. Be sure the podcast starts with the word "Congratulations" and explains every award for safety and style the car has earned, telling her what an exceptional investment she's made. Even if the customer throws the cheap MP3 player away without subscribing to your podcast, that $20 may be the catalyst for one out of ten customers to come back to buy the sealant he originally said no to or for an upgraded stereo or window tinting.

If there is no audio jack, you can hand your customer a CD of the show. If you don't want to give someone a player, hand him a CD so he can get a taste of the podcast you offer.

In other words, unlike the entrepreneurial podcast, where you need to manage costs because of the high churn rate, a customer-relationship podcast is aimed at a pre-qualified audience that is worth spending on to win, because there are immediate and long-term benefits.

These podcasts should be posted in MP3 format so that they are easily played in any circumstances. Maintain your feed on an accessible server without security challenges: Unlike an advertising-supported podcast with measurement of listenership or one where you need to have the e-mail access or other information about the listener in order to start a transaction, these podcasts are going to existing customers, at least to people who have had some contact with you. They are qualified, so be permissive with the podcast files.

Consider placing your podcast RSS feed in these places:

- Sales receipts
- Web sites
- E-mail signatures

- Bills and invoices
- Business cards
- Pamphlets and other collateral
- The customer-facing side of your cash register
- On CDs at the counter

Anytime you hand out a CD, make sure the RSS feed is on the disc and repeated in the programs on the disc.

What we've covered in this section is information with which you want to be, indeed must be, permissive. You need to spread it around and get it heard, but another type of corporate information needs to be protected — the knowledge you share with employees that gives you a competitive advantage.

Corporate Podcasting and Training

Next quarter's sales strategy, the specifications of a new product, or the new therapeutic uses of a drug in your company's catalog — these are valuable pieces of data that need to be disseminated within a company, but would be harmful if released to the competition. At the same time, employees have to absorb more information than ever before, and they have many recreational forms of information contending for their attention. Podcasting is another way to engage employees' intelligence. It can supplement written material and make useful times that are not usually accessible to educational effort, such as during the commute, exercise, and other times when people's hands and eyes are busy.

Unlike every other form of podcasting discussed in this biblical tome, you don't want these podcasts to be freely distributed; you want to keep them strictly controlled so that the information they contain reaches only those who are authorized to have it. Some folks may argue that podcasting, like blogging, *must* support a more transparent organization, and there is much to be said for that perspective, except when spreading information around could cause economic losses or regulatory fines. Some programming, such as programming containing information that will have a material impact on a publicly traded company, does need to be secured.

Here, it's necessary to return to the security approaches discussed in Chapter 20, "The Subscription Business." Just like any other podcaster, you have to put your sound files someplace where they can be retrieved by users. It should be a secure server, and you may want to add more security by using a digital rights management system to tie the files to specific users, so that if they are redistributed to unauthorized users, you can find out who's responsible.

TIP There is no such thing as complete security in audio, video, or text files. In every case, someone can capture the sound from a DRM'd podcast from their system's soundcard; likewise, video can be copied after it is decrypted, and even if you disable copying, text can be copied by hand or reproduced by taking a screen capture. Podcasting is no more insecure than any other medium. The challenge is making sure your employees or other authorized users understand that the information contained is confidential and how it may be used.

Secure pages

Chapter 20 contains a detailed explanation of how to set up a secure page on a Web server. The secure access with an .htaccess file, however, is the minimum configuration for a corporate podcast, because many additional layers of security can be applied within the enterprise. Depending upon the network environment, you can use Windows, Macintosh, or Unix/Linux filesharing protocols and security to limit access to the server and record the fact the file has been copied.

You can use myriad approaches for securing files on a server. A variety of excellent titles on network and operating system security are available from Wiley, including these:

- *Windows Vista Ultimate Bible,* by Joel Durham, Jr.
- *Security Complete*, by Sybex Inc.
- *Windows Server 2003 Security Bible*, by Blair Rampling
- *Content Distribution Networks: An Engineering Approach*, by Dinesh C. Verma
- *Linux Administrator Street Smarts: A Real World Guide to Linux Certification Skills*, by Roderick W. Smith
- *Linux Bible 2005 Edition*, by Christopher Negus
- *Linux Network Servers*, by Craig Hunt
- *Mac OS X Bible Tiger Edition*, by Samuel A. Litt, Thomas Clancy Jr., Warran G. Gottlieb, Douglas B. Heyman, Alejandro Prado, and Craig Zimmerman
- *Managing IP Networks: Challenges and Opportunities*, by Salah Aidarous (Editor), Thomas Plevyak (Editor), Paul Levine, Joberto Martins, Burkhard Stiller, Mostafa Hashem Sherif, Andrea Fumagalli, Javier Aracil, and Luca Valcarenghi
- *Setting Up LAMP: Getting Linux, Apache, MySQL, and PHP Working Together,* by Eric Rosebrock and Eric Filson

Password-controlled podcasting

As explained in Chapter 20, podcasts can be protected with two forms of password security. You can secure the location of the podcast or the file itself so that the podcast can play only on a device belonging to a registered user.

Simply protecting the location of a file is a very limited form of protection, because a file, after it leaves the server, becomes an infinitely reproducible briefing on your business plans. Let's say, for example, that you have a podcast for a sales group and a second podcast used for training customer support staff on upcoming products. If you have protected these files with a single group password, so that every employee gaining access to the sales podcast uses the same password and support staff uses a different password to access their program, you don't have an auditable trail to any individual in either group.

Logging network file access, because of the inherent insecurity of networks, is the most important thing you can enable to backtrack to the source of leaks and misuse.

Creating a security system that assigns a unique username and password for each individual is far more effective because, if a podcast is exposed to the outside world, you can narrow down exactly who in the organization downloaded the file as a starting point to discovering how it leaked. Third-party sites and services that provide secure RSS feeds are not adequate corporate security. For example, Feedburner's secure RSS feeds assign a single password to an entire group of users. RSS hosting services that pass the username and password in the RSS URL are intrinsically insecure and should not be used by organizations concerned with confidentiality.

Audible's Wordcast service is the only hosted service that currently supports user- and file-level authentication. Because Audible is built on a DRM technology that allows programs to play only on registered devices (PCs or mobile players), it is a viable foundation for a corporate security regime. At $0.005 per download, Wordcast is an out-of-the-box solution to the problem of delivering a file that can be traced and secured to an individual listener.

A Wordcast corporate podcast account can be set up on an employee's credit card and costs $10 per month for 500 subscribers receiving four podcasts per month. When configuring the feed, as shown in Figure 24.1, be sure to check the box labeled "Hide this Wordcast from the public directory" so that it is not listed in the public Wordcast directory or Apple iTunes. If you set the yearly subscription price and price per episode to $0, the files are delivered free to your registered users. Wordcast provides an RSS feed for each podcast series you create and distributes this internally to authorized recipients with their username and password, which they must use to authorize their account. After an employee has an account, he can add other secure podcasts quickly, so that the sales team can also download support information, for example.

Be prepared, though, to educate people when you introduce podcasts to the organization. A podcast will be a new experience for most people, so whether you're distributing updates to the staff by the CEO or sales training as a downloadable audio file, explain how people should use it after it has been moved from the server to the listener's computer or portable device. A reasonable podcasting policy for confidential information should include these guidelines, along with your company-specific rules:

1. Don't share podcast passwords, whether for the server where it is stored or the file, if the podcast is a password-protected file.

2. Don't share RSS feed URLs for corporate podcasts with anyone. If you don't provide a target, intruders don't know where to start looking for confidential material.

3. After it is downloaded, the podcast becomes the employee's responsibility. He should not reproduce the file, except for his own use, such as burning a CD to listen to, and after he's finished with the file, he should destroy it by erasing it or making any readable version of it unreadable (by breaking the CD, for example).

4. Define the consequences of deliberately redistributing the podcast.

5. If a copy of the podcast or a device on which it is stored is lost, the employee must report the loss immediately.

Audible's Wordcast is the only secure hosted podcasting platform that provides user- and program-level passwording.

Supporting your corporate podcast deployment

Getting podcast-ready devices into the hands of the people who need them may not be a big challenge because so many people now have iPods and portable players or mobile phones that are MP3 and Audible-compatible. But setting policies for use of audio on devices owned by employees may be problematic, because your IT people cannot define the software on personal devices.

Begin by conducting an audit of staff devices that are owned by the company, such as wireless phones and PDAs that may play audio.

PDAs

Some of the devices that your employees may be using include the following:

- ASUS MyPal A632
- ASUS MyPal A636
- Dell Axim x51v
- Dell Axim x51
- Dell Axim X50v
- Dell Axim X50
- Dell Axim X30
- Dell Axim X5
- Fujitsu Pocket LOOX C Series
- Fujitsu Pocket LOOX T Series
- Fujitsu Pocket LOOX N Series
- Fujitsu Pocket LOOX 700 Series
- Fujitsu Pocket LOOX 600 Series
- Fujitsu Pocket LOOX 400 Series
- Dolphin 7900
- Dolphin 9500
- Dolphin 9550
- HP iPAQ Pocket PC hx2790
- HP iPAQ Pocket PC hx2490
- HP iPAQ Pocket PC hw6500 Mobile Messenger
- HP iPAQ Pocket PC hw6510 Mobile Messenger
- HP iPAQ Pocket PC rx1950
- HP iPAQ Pocket PC rx1955
- HP iPAQ Pocket PC hx2495
- HP iPAQ Pocket PC hx2190
- HP iPAQ Pocket PC hx2795
- HP iPAQ Pocket PC hx2410
- HP iPAQ Pocket PC hx2110
- HP iPAQ Pocket PC hx2755
- HP iPAQ Pocket PC hx2750
- Intermec 730 Color
- Intermec 700 Color

- Itronix GoBook Q-100
- Mitac Mio A701
- Mitac Mio P350
- Mitac Mio P550
- Mitac Mio A201
- Mitac Mio 168 GPS Pocket PC
- Mitac Mio 339
- Mitac Mio 558
- NEC MobilePro 250E
- Palm TX
- Palm Life Drive
- Palm Tungsten E2 Handheld
- Palm Tungsten T2 Handheld
- Palm Tungsten T3 Handheld
- Palm Tungsten T5 Handheld
- Palm Zire 72 Handheld
- Sony PEG-NX80V
- Sony PEG-NX73V
- Sony PEG-NZ90
- Sony PEG-TG50
- Sony PEG-TJ25
- Sony PEG-TJ27
- SpaceMachine SkyWalker GPS-500 Pocket PC
- Symbol PDT 8100
- Symbol PPT 2800
- Symbol MC50
- Toshiba e310/e335 Pocket PC
- Toshiba e350/e355 Pocket PC Toshiba
- Toshiba e400/e405 Pocket PC
- Toshiba e740/e750/e755 Pocket PC
- Toshiba e800/e805 Pocket PC
- ViewSonic Pocket PC V36
- ViewSonic Pocket PC V37
- ViewSonic Pocket PC V35

Phones

Your employees may be using one of the following popular cell phones:

- Audiovox PPC-6700 Pocket PC Phone
- Audiovox SMT5600 Pocket PC Phone
- Audiovox PPC-6600 Pocket PC Phone
- Audiovox PPC-6601 Pocket PC Phone
- Cingular 2125
- Cingular Nokia 6682
- Cingular Palm Treo 650
- Cingular HP iPaq hw6515
- HP iPAQ Pocket PC h6315 Phone
- iMate PDA-N
- iMate K-Jam
- iMate SP5
- iMate SP5m
- iMate JASJAR
- iMate PDA2k EVDO
- iMate JAMin
- Mitac Mio A701
- Motorola Q
- Palm Treo 700P
- Palm Treo 700W
- Palm Treo 650
- Palm Treo 600
- Samsung i600
- Siemens SX56
- Sony Ericsson M600i
- Sprint Palm Treo 700WX
- Spring Palm Treo 700P
- Sprint PPC-6700
- Sprint Treo 650
- Sprint Treo 600
- Sprint Audiovox PPC-6600

- Sprint Audiovox PPC-6601

- Sprint Samsung SP-i600

- T-Mobile Pocket PC Phone

- Verizon Treo 700P

- Verizon Palm Treo 650

- Verizon Palm 700w

- Verizon XV 6700

- Verizon SCH-i730

If employees have MP3 or Audible-compatible devices, you may want to simply offer them the ability to subscribe to podcasts using their current PDA or phone. However, if you want to segregate work audio from personal audio, it may be necessary to purchase portable devices or offer a full or partial subsidy for purchases. If you do pay all or part of the cost of a device that becomes the employee's device, it will be difficult to enforce company IT standards.

As you learn in the next section, keeping information on corporate devices may be necessary to maintain the audit trail in regulatory reviews of company information.

Knowing the Regulatory Issues

Podcasts are yet another form that the record of the life of a company can take, and it is only a matter of time before the Securities and Exchange Commission (SEC) or another federal agency uses the content of a podcast as a reason for levying a fine. Here, then, is where your corporate lawyers will probably tell you, when you broach the question of using podcasts internally or externally, that podcasting is a bad idea because it increases the risks faced by the company. Keep in mind, though, that they've said this about e-mail, Web pages, and even the telephone and internal memos, too.

Used judiciously, podcasts can be a vital new channel of communication among your employees and partners. We're not suggesting that you record every word spoken in meetings and distribute them to folks who missed the appointment. That would be overkill and likely, based on the incredibly stupid things people say during meetings, would be potentially dangerous — the jokes like "If we just took the safety restraints off this car, it would go 250 miles per hour on the highway. . . . Sure, some people would die, but think of the sales in the youth market!" are the raw material of lawsuits when recorded.

The main concern lies with public companies that are required by law to disclose material information in a timely manner to investors. Podcasts intended for internal distribution that are improperly secured, for example, could be interpreted to be public. So imagine, for instance, that your sales briefing podcast describes next quarter's new products and an unexpected decrease in price for the product that's responsible for 90 percent of your company's revenue. When do you tell the public?

According to Regulation FD, an SEC rule that requires that any information disclosed to someone outside the company who is not the company's investment banker, attorney, accountant, or who agrees not to disclose the information must be shared with the public "promptly," within 24 hours by filing a Form 8-K with the SEC. Not the way to spring bad news to investors, but if you made the information public by failing to protect it, you have no recourse.

Furthermore, if your company fails to live by the rules of the Sarbanes-Oxley Act of 2002, which was passed in the wake of the Enron and other corporate scandals, every document created by the company may be reviewed by the Public Company Accounting Oversight Board for irregularities. The lawyers concerned with risk may want to review what you intend to podcast, and as with other information you commit to paper and hard disc, it is probably a good idea until the lawyers are comfortable and your podcasting teams understand what they can and cannot do. This will take time, because change is hard.

Private companies, on the other hand, need to be aware of the promises made to customers in marketing podcasts, whether they relate to product capabilities, which is regulated by the Federal Trade Commission, or the terms of a loan to purchase a home discussed in a real estate podcast, which is overseen by the Federal Reserve under the Federal Truth in Lending Act and Competitive Equality Banking Act of 1987.

TIP   We cannot give you solid guidelines about what you can and can't do, because we are not lawyers. These are questions you should address to your attorneys. But there is one guideline to keep firmly in mind:

If you record it, save it. Podcasts are another form of corporate record, and like the rest of the records that bedevil you, you should store every podcast for the same length of time you do all corporate files.

Educational Podcasting: How Much Is a Lecture Worth?

Professor Robert Schrag of North Carolina State University decided to sell podcasts of his lectures for students who may want to miss his class. "If a student doesn't want to be there, I don't want him there," he told *The Chronicle of Higher Education.* "I want him to go away because he degrades the educational experience for the other students around him."

The university shut down Professor Schrag's podcast, but other schools, such as Seton Hall University, are making podcasts of study materials available to every incoming freshman through a partnership with Audible. In one case, the university was concerned with diluting the value of attending class, and in the other, the podcasts were acceptable because they augmented the classroom experience. Both point to the rising importance of audio for use in learning and the increasing marginality of the classroom as the primary setting for learning.

Schools are going to come to terms with the changing mix of classroom and digital interaction that may define a new standard of excellence in education. Podcasting, which makes the essential element of the classroom portable, will certainly play a part in redefining what is delivered by schools at every level of education, from pre-school, when listening plays a critical role in early learning, to post-graduate studies at the world's top universities. In fact, the top universities will probably be extended to every corner of the globe through networked services that include virtual classrooms and podcasts. But first some sticky issues must be addressed, such as the content of education and how to pay the people talking in the classroom.

When Professor Schrag sold his own lectures, which by tradition he is free to do with his ideas as a university professor, North Carolina State University likely saw his actions as competing with its own efforts to get paying students into the seats. Schrag reportedly made a total of $11 on $30 in sales from 12 lectures through the site where the podcasts were offered, Independent Music Online. The university's only comment was that it was "in everybody's interest" for the podcasts to come off the network, which sounds like the beginning of a negotiation to us. That's the beginning of change that will sweep the educational world.

Why, then, consider offering podcasts in schools? For the lower grades, podcasts may at first be directed at parents more than students. An elementary teacher, for example, could send parents a weekly or monthly summary of what the class is covering and how to help keep the learning going at home. Eventually, we expect that early learning materials will be offered via audio, because the cost of producing and distributing podcasts will make entrepreneurs of teachers who have unique ways of engaging kids.

At the university-level, education may explode to include the voices of many professors rather than one for each class. An Oregon State University education may be augmented with listening to scholars at Oxford and the Sorbonne. The next question, though, is how to make the economics work. We certainly don't know, but it seems likely that podcasts from distant universities will be introduced into classes by professors who want to be the point of integration between many ideas the students will encounter. If they don't, they'll be out of the loop, literally making their undoing by taking their curriculum out of the mainstream.

Aggressively entrepreneurial universities, notably Stanford University in Palo Alto, already have staked out academic, sports, and entertainment brands in audio. Stanford on iTunes features programming from the campus, including speakers about global issues, books, and authors, as well as music and sports. This kind of broad approach to taking the Stanford brand to new audiences only scratches the surface of what is possible when an institution has a huge stable of brilliant and talented people.

As with corporate podcasting, many school podcasts will need to be secured, this time because of the privacy of students. Sounds a bit paranoid, maybe, but what happens when a child molester downloads a podcast, listens to it, and uses the information he gets to pretend to be a parent in the class to lure one of the students into taking a ride home? Better to start from a secure foundation so this story doesn't come true, especially if you're the school administrator who deals with liability lawsuits.

Again, we urge you to revisit the security strategies discussed in this chapter and in Chapter 20 to consider the approach you want to take.

Summary

Along with the financial boon that can come from producing podcasts, there are educational and corporate applications that can benefit many people. But risks are associated with corporate and educational uses, and you need to be mindful of these. This chapter covered the following topics:

- Training and education podcasts demand many of the same technical and security considerations, but may be justified by a different economic rationale, such as lowering the cost of learning.

- Talking with your existing customers increases the likelihood of repeat sales. A podcast is another way to stay engaged with customers after they leave your store or complete their online purchases.

- Customer-oriented podcasts should emphasize how to get the most out of the product or service you sell. Celebrate your customers in podcasts, making them the stars of the story of your product.

- Compared to the entrepreneurial podcast, which must factor in the cost of subscriber acquisition in order to make a profit, the most influential factors in a customer relations/support podcast are the production values and costs.

- Determine the value of keeping a customer. If it is more than five times the cost of a portable media player, consider giving a device to customers pre-loaded with your current podcasts. If you want to spend less, consider handing a CD to customers.

- Be promiscuous with your RSS feed URL. Put it everywhere, including on your sales receipts, sales counter, and business cards. Podcasts are your next opportunity to speak with potential customers.

- Marketing podcasts should be freely available. Again, promiscuity pays.

- Training podcasts, because they may contain confidential information, should be stored on secure servers.

- Podcast deployment within your organization may require that you provide each employee who will get podcasts with a device to listen on, one that is controlled by corporate IT guidelines rather than personal habit.

- The information in podcasts is another form of corporate record that must be carefully planned and managed in order to avoid running afoul of federal and state regulations that govern information disclosure to investors and customers, such as lenders.

- Because podcasts are another record of your business, keep them as long as any other document your company produces.

- Educational podcasts will be an important feature in the changing the landscape of education, at every level of schooling.

- Security will be critical in K-12 applications of podcasting, because children's privacy is involved. In the university setting, the fundamental questions will revolve around the value of what is delivered in the classroom versus what may be purchased or downloaded from global universities.

Chapter 25

Promoting Your Podcast

After all the time, energy, and expense you've put into your podcast, it's time to attract some attention. Talk all you want about business models, but your audience delivers the coin; without an audience, you have no business model, regardless of the business model. You won't find a "Build it, and they will come" model. You have to actively recruit and hold the interest of people before you can make something work.

Fortunately, dozens of sites exist where podcasts are listed and discussed. Getting your podcast into those sites and enabling listeners to talk about your show with social tags and other community systems is the keystone of your marketing, because your listeners are really in charge of the outcome. You can only start the conversation, so get people talking.

Promotion as Process

The two essential pieces of the puzzle, for any type of business, are promotion and passion. Any successful business requires a passion for success and knowledge about the customer. You have that, or you would not be reading about how to make this dream into a business.

Promotion is another thing altogether. Some people are gifted with the ability to gain attention. Ivar Haglund, a Seattle legend and restaurateur, was one of those gifted individuals. When a syrup truck overturned on February 6, 1947, on the Seattle waterfront, he was one of the first on the scene, carrying with him a plate of pancakes. *The Seattle Post-Intelligencer* carried pictures of him — not just of the accident — the next day. He knew how to gain attention. Passion can exist without promotion, but without promotion, your passion cannot be effectively shared on a large scale.

NOTE   For more information on promoting your podcasts, check out www.wikihow.com/
Promote-a-Podcast?, or read *How to Promote Your Music Successfully on the
Internet* by David Nevue.

When the local newspaper profiled one of your authors after he opened a business, he jumped on
his desk and spread his arms, giving the photographer a low-angle shot with computers in the
foreground. Very dramatic, at least to a photo editor. Instead of a small photo, the story was the
whole top half of the front page of the business section. Like Ivar, whose pancakes were featured
instead of a truck accident, you must recognize your opportunities and take them, because you
cannot buy marketing like that. It comes only when you promote yourself.

Catching the attention of the audience is just the first step; holding it is another. One of the most
important things you can do is find your voice and establish your brand. Audiences and communities are not switched on; they are built over time. When you build your audience, you are building
equity in your business. The audience is your *only* asset.

CROSS-REF   See Chapter 4, "Defining Your Podcast," for a detailed discussion of how to user
Google's AdWords Traffic Estimator to test your ideas in the marketplace before actually
floating your first podcast.

You need to think about how to establish a brand for yourself for a number of reasons. Brand is the
memory, specifically the qualities remembered, such as "funny" or "honest" or "profitable," that the
listener takes away from every encounter with your podcast. It is a reflection of who you present
yourself as or who you are, and if approached as a set of values for what you are delivering, it creates consistency and legitimacy and provides for a decision-making tool when problem solving.

When you have a stated set of values to refer to and work from, you'll be able to stay close to your
message. You'll maintain legitimacy as viewers and listeners come to trust the message and respect its
consistency. The decision-making support from a brand springs from the same cloth as a mission and
vision statement. If you are true to your value, brand, mission, and vision, tough decisions are made
easier when they are measured by how they represent these ideals. For a good audiobook on the subject, you may want to download *The 22 Immutable Laws of Branding* by Al Ries and Laura Ries.

You are your promotional arm. You can plug your podcast automatically in a number of ways. Keep
your podcast address in your signature file. If you or your company has any marketing materials at
all, be certain they contain all pertinent podcast information. Mention your podcasts, when appropriate, during discussions and postings on other forums. Visit other podcasters, guest for them, host for
them, or interview with them. Invite them on your show, and create cross-promotional opportunities.

Find your audience elsewhere. Who are you trying to reach and why? This is a good exercise in
building the audience you are targeting. What product or brand would you think best exemplifies
who you would want as a sponsor or advertiser? Is it REI, Snapple, or that great tavern in old town
that features local band webcasts? Ask them if you can do a podcast for them, even if it is just once.
Many companies have determined that podcasting is a way to open dialogue with their customers,
but they have no venue or the talent to do so. You have the equipment, the interest, and the know-
how. All they can do is say no. If they say yes, you've just tapped into the audience you were looking for.

Teasers

A time-honored approach to building an audience is to utilize teasers in every podcast. Since the days of serialized adventures like Flash Gordon to today's movie trailers, teasers are used to create interest in, and anticipation of, the next installment and upcoming feature. They also help to hold attention between commercial breaks and weekly episodes. Make room and production time to talk about what's coming next and why it's essential that your listeners stand by or come back for more.

The take-away we want you to have from this discussion is that you must constantly be thinking about how to engage with your listener, to make your podcast an essential part of their day, week, or month so that they will be listening the next time, too. That's because you have to spend some money to win each new customer — even if it's just in giving your time to create shows, it is time spent — and you want to maximize the value of each relationship you start.

Cultivating Your Community

No one has a big audience right out of the gate. Think about television shows that rely on advertising dollars or driving subscriptions for premium channels. You hear about them well in advance of an audience for the show. It is necessary for them to establish a strong viewer base before the first episode is even aired. So you and I get to hear and view pitches for this "Must See TV" or any number of spins on the new Fall lineup months in advance. Television shows are able to do this in part because they belong to an establish network of shows, stations, and prearranged advertisers. Does that mean you need to join a network? Maybe.

Podcasting networks are being established all over the Web, and if they themselves are targeting, not unlike the many cable networks that exist on topics ranging from science fiction to home improvement, they may fit into your business strategy. You may share in revenue if you do, but they bring the power of aggregation to the equation. Examples include www.thepodcastnetwork.com, www.podtech.net, and www.odeo.com.

CROSS-REF See Chapter 20, "The Subscription Business," where we cover how to set up subscription systems and enable payment. Chapter 25, "Promoting Your Podcast," explains in detail how to tap into the podcast aggregators' services to get your podcast in front of potential listeners.

If you look at your audience as a customer base, you may want to get your product out there, advertise it to friends and family, and place a couple of inexpensive ads to build a small following and listen to them. Refine and repeat. Over time, if the product is good, it will find an audience and your customer base will grow. The concept of "Word of Mouth units," or WOMs, has taken root in marketing and is a likely path of growth for your podcast audience. The idea is that in order to create growth, you need to create testimonials, conversation, and buzz. It is up to you to engage and collect this dialogue at the beginning, but with time and luck, it can take on its own life.

You'll know if you have grabbed people's attention when they arrive with predetermined questions and comments.

When looking to monetize an audience, bigger is usually thought to be better. Remember that volume is good, but in the market today, targeted is better. Forrester Research saw only one percent household penetration in podcasting in April 2006, but analyst Charlene Li sees that expanding to 12.3 million households in 2010. So for now, odds are good that your podcast audience is on the smaller scale and targeting is the factor that will increase your revenues. Combine the knowing with the building to create your core, and then you may be able to execute on a profitable strategy. However, don't expect anyone to just take your word for who your audience is and how many they are. You need evidence in the form of measurement.

CROSS-REF   See Chapter 21, "Making Advertising Work," for a description of measurement systems available at this early stage of the podcasting business.

Knowing the Value of a Subscriber

Over the course of this book, we've talked about many of the costs — and the benefits — of building your podcast into a business. If you plan to spend any money at all on promotional activities, it will be worth it to know just what a subscriber may be worth once you've got their attention, After all, you don't want to spend more to acquire a subscriber than that subscriber will return in revenue. The cost of production, hosting, delivery, and so forth add up to a total expense that, for planning purposes, we can use to project how much must be made on each subscriber to make up the costs and earn a profit.

In order to do this calculation, we need to look back over the worksheets in the chapters on the business of podcasting, choosing the ones that are appropriate to your show. You've had the opportunity to calculate the cost of delivery for a target audience size for a month and year, as well as the cost of producing a show.

Because podcasting is a serial form of media that requires subscriptions, whether paid or unpaid, to make an audience, it is a hybrid of the publishing world and radio, so we can borrow some of the basic concepts and calculations from publishing to do some of this analysis. A magazine, for example, typically sells a 12-month subscription in order to (a) recoup the cost of delivering the individual issue to the subscriber and (b) calculate a total readership for use in pricing advertising inserted in each issue. That's a bit of a simplification, but for our purposes it will suffice.

What we need to figure out is how much you can make on an individual subscriber over the course of her relationship with your podcast. Figure 25.1 describes the basic calculation. First, you have projected, based on advertisements or subscription fees, how much you will earn for each episode. Revenue may come from multiple sources, so be sure to add up everything you expect to make for a typical program during the next year. Depending on how you make money, you'll need to calculate the total revenue by adding up subscription fees (multiply the number of subscribers by the fee charged for a subscription for the whole year and divide by 12 to get an average), ad revenue, or total of multiple revenue streams for each episode.

Now that you know how much you anticipate earning over the next year, divide by the average number of subscribers per month; here you must look back at the calculations you did in Figure 19-5 in Chapter 19, "The Basics of Podcasting Business," to the number of subscriptions you expect per month. You projected growth, not a fixed number of subscribers from Month 1 to Month 12, so take the total number of subscribers you projected and divide by 12 to get an average number of subscribers per month.

This calculation assumes that you produce one show per month. If you have a weekly or daily show, you may need to adjust the "per month" to "per week" or "per day" numbers that represent your plans, or you can just add the number of shows delivered to subscribers for the total month to get the revenue per month.

FIGURE 25.1
_____

Worksheet for calculating the average revenue per subscriber you can expect

Projected revenue per episode (total) x 12 months
$ _____
Divide by average # of subscribers each month

_____
Equals average revenue per subscriber/episode
$ _____
Multiply by # episodes average subscriber will play
$ _____
This is the amount a subscriber is worth.

Next, divide the average revenue projected per episode by the average number of subscribers during each month. This gives you, in the simplest terms, what you can expect to need to earn per subscriber for each episode — assuming you hit your subscription targets — of your podcast. Should you fall short of your target growth, you will need to recalculate your expected revenue as time passes based on real performance.

After you know how much you can expect to earn per subscriber per show, given these caveats, you can begin to look at how long you have to recoup your investment in the show and winning subscribers. We haven't provided you a number to work with, because we need to look at the experience of other media first.

Magazines have extraordinarily high "churn rates," the pace at which people subscribe but drop out. At first, you may have many subscribers to your magazine, but because some percentage of them never actually pay after placing the order, you actually have to discount your subscription numbers to figure out how many issues you can expect to deliver before the customer becomes unprofitable. Lots of magazines keep unprofitable subscribers so they can justify their advertising rates, which may be fine if the ad revenue makes up for the loss of delivering an issue to those subscribers. But for our analysis, let's be ruthless and assume that, if you are trying to make money, you need to cut off non-paying subscribers if they haven't paid for their order in two months.

Typically, about 15 percent of paying subscribers flake on the subscription cost. If, however, you are doing a show that makes money by playing advertising, you'll want to keep those subscribers in order to bill more for advertising. Unless, that is, you are being paid for actual listeners or on a cost-per-action (CPA) basis. If someone is downloading but not playing your show, you'll want to pare them from your subscription roles quickly because they cost you money when serving them a download of the show and may never turn that investment on your part into revenue by listening or following an advertisement link. It's impossible to tell if a downloaded MP3 file is listened to, but Audible's Wordcast provides reports on whether files are played on an anonymous basis that can be used to cull non-listeners to free ad-supported programming.

So, after that initial 15 percent non-paying subscriber hit on your circulation numbers, you need to recognize that out of every 100 new subscribers, only 85 pay you from the beginning. You're also likely to lose another 5 percent of your total audience every month, some wanting refunds or just disappearing from your ad inventory because they never download. To see the impact of that churn on your subscription numbers, see Figure 25.2. Likewise, if people subscribe but never actually play your podcast, they are not going to contribute to your earning money from advertising (after your advertisers begin to require that you prove someone listened to your podcast, which will happen sooner rather than later, if the history of the Web is any guide). Even if you expect to earn money on a CPA basis, you have to have listeners to figure out how many will be converted to action.

Say, for instance, that you earn $20 per action ("a $20 CPA") from your advertising. In order to get a $20 CPM (cost-per-thousand), you would need to have one action per thousand ads, or a one-tenth of one percent conversion rate. Typically, advertising links perform well if they convert one half of one percent to action. An excellent conversion rate of ads displayed to listeners acting would be near one percent. Amazing peaks of performance will happen, but do not expect to see consistent 2.5 percent conversion rates.

We come then to the last line of the calculation in Figure 25.1: the number of episodes the average subscribers will play. There's a simple way to figure this out, though it requires you take into account not only the initial group of subscribers who sign up but never pay or listen, but also the monthly loss of subscribers due to normal attrition — the churn rate.

You will see that we're using two churn rates to calculate the total number of subscribers at the end of each month of the year, the 15-percent rate representing the fall-off in new subscribers after the first month (we discount the total number of new subscribers by 15 percent by multiplying the total by 0.85) and a monthly churn rate of 5 percent. In other words, you'll probably lose about 5 percent of all subscribers every month. These percentages represent a kind of best-case scenario. You may have a perfectly viable business — and remember, for purposes of this discussion we are assuming you want to build a business, while many people just want to podcast for fun — with higher churn rates, but you'll need to adjust your ad or subscription rates higher to account for the extra churn. If you are looking for a very targeted audience, a high churn rate may be exactly what you want to make sure that you are arriving at the audience that is really interested in the topic of your show and what your advertisers are selling.

FIGURE 25.2

Worksheet for calculating the total number of subscribers gained each month and cumulative subscriber count after accounting for churn rate

	Number of new Subscribers	Churn Rate		Total Subscribers at month-end
Month 1 *Steve & Mitch Hour*	500	*New* x 0.85		425
			Total	425
Month 2 *Steve & Mitch Hour*	750	*New* x 0.85		637
		Existing x 0.95		404
			Total	1,041
Month 3 *Steve & Mitch Hour*	1,250	*New* x 0.85		1,062
		Existing x 0.95		989
			Total	2,051
Month 4 *Steve & Mitch Hour*	1,750	*New* x 0.85		1,487
		Existing x 0.95		1,948
			Total	3,435
Month 5 *Steve & Mitch Hour*	2,250	*New* x 0.85		1,912
		Existing x 0.95		3,263
			Total	5,174
Month 6 *Steve & Mitch Hour*	2,750	*New* x 0.85		2,337
		Existing x 0.95		4,915
			Total	7,252
Month 7 *Steve & Mitch Hour*	3,500	*New* x 0.85		2,975
		Existing x 0.95		6,890
			Total	9,865
Month 8 *Steve & Mitch Hour*	4,250	*New* x 0.85		3,612
		Existing x 0.95		9,371
			Total	12,983
Month 9 *Steve & Mitch Hour*	5,000	*New* x 0.85		4,250
		Existing x 0.95		12,334
			Total	16,584
Month 10 *Steve & Mitch Hour*	6,000	*New* x 0.85		5,100
		Existing x 0.95		15,754
			Total	20,854
Month 11 *Steve & Mitch Hour*	7,000	*New* x 0.85		5,950
		Existing x 0.95		19,811
			Total	25,761
Month 12 *Steve & Mitch Hour*	8,000	*New* x 0.85		6,800
		Existing x 0.95		24,473
			Total	31,273

Another thing to recognize is that these subscriber numbers represent the number of subscribers you have to serve for the *next* 12 months, so we need to account for that in figuring out the total number of episodes these subscribers will play *this year*. A subscriber who joins in Month 12 will hear only one show (and you still owe them 11 more, so don't write up a profit for this year based on those future obligations), while the subscriber who is with you all year, starting in Month 1, is more likely to listen to 12 shows. Both are worth the same to you over time, but the more you get current subscribers to listen, the more you can earn.

Going back to Figure 25.1, then, we need to add up the total number of episodes that the subscriber who joins in Month 1 will listen to in order to calculate the appropriate number to use to find out how much you earn per subscriber. The average subscriber joining in month 1 is not going to listen to 12 shows; rather, she will listen to approximately six and a half shows, because attrition will leave fewer than half of your listeners at the end of the year.

How do you figure out the estimated number of episodes the average subscriber will hear? Take the total listener percentage for the first month (85 percent), and multiple that by the 95 percent retention rate for the next 11 months. In other words, multiply 0.85 by 0.95 and then multiply the result by 0.95 ten more times. Add the results for each month — with the churn rates we used in this example, the results will range from 0.85 down to 0.4835 — and divide the result by 12 (the number of months in the year). The resulting percentage is 0.65. This is very close to the standard numbers in magazine publishing for successful publications. Short-lived subscription products perform worse.

Don't be discouraged by this, because it is the economics of attention in action. People seldom stay engaged with a media source. The good news is that research shows that when people listen to podcasts, they tend to listen to the entire show, ads and all, which means that you have a shot at making real money from each subscriber that comes along. If listeners pay you for a subscription and go away without getting their money back, you are still a winner, because you don't have to incur the cost of delivering the files. However, if you count on subscriptions and ad revenue, a departed listener represents lost ad revenue.

So, what does Figure 25.1 look like when we enter the numbers for *The Steve & Mitch Hour*, our hypothetical podcast? Let's see in Figure 25.3.

FIGURE 25.3

After doing the math, we discover the average user represents $1.14 in revenue. Your results will vary based on your revenue target.

Projected revenue per episode (total) x 12 months
      $ 2,000
Divide by average # of subscribers each month
      11, 391
Equals average revenue per subscriber/episode
      $ 0.176
Multiply by # episodes average subscriber will play
      $ 1.14 (our average is 6.5)
    This is the amount a subscriber is worth.

Assuming that we budget $2,000 per episode of our monthly show — that is, that we hope to make $24,000 in revenue from our show during the first year — and dividing by the average number of subscribers we'll have throughout the year, we find that *The Steve & Mitch Hour* needs to earn $0.176 per listener per episode. Because we face churn rates and can calculate that for each subscriber we win, we'll get 6.5 shows of listening, the value of every subscriber is $1.14, regardless of how we earn it, through advertising or subscription fees.

If you start with the assumption that you want to make $50,000 in revenue from a podcast during the first year, you'll get a different value per subscriber from the calculation in Figure 25.3, but you can still use our estimated number of episodes listened by each subscriber. If you use higher churn rates, you have to adjust the number of episodes.

Now, this tells you that you have to charge more than $1.14 per subscriber per year to earn this much, because not all subscribers will stick around. If you were to charge $1.14 per subscriber, and 35 of every 100 subscribers asked for their money back, you've only earned $74.10 (we're assuming you give a full refund to simplify things, however you may pro-rate the refunds, subtracting for episodes delivered) from 100 subscribers, or $0.741.

CROSS-REF You should check your estimated revenue per subscriber against the costs per subscriber that you calculated in Chapter 19, "The Basics of Podcasting Business." Of course, these are not your only costs. If you have spent money on promotions to win customers, you'll need to account for those costs, too.

How much do you really need to charge per subscriber or for advertising placed in the show? There's one more expense to look at: how much it costs to acquire your listeners. In Chapter 19, we worked out how much it costs to deliver a podcast to a user, which you'll need to add to your cost of acquiring listeners.

Let's assume that you give away three episodes to win a subscriber. These could be free shows, but it could also be three extra episodes you give as a bonus to people who sign up for a year of your podcast. Each one costs you something to deliver, and you need to count that. But what if you also spent $100 on advertising to attract 200 new listeners? Each of those customers has already cost you $0.50. And because each of those subscribers is likely to stay for only 6.5 months, you need to recoup these costs at more than 50 cents per subscriber to recover the expense.

Here, then, shown in Figure 25.4, is the basic calculation for assessing how much you need to charge for a subscription:

Items *a* and *b* explain our per-episode and per-subscriber costs and how we arrived at them based on expenses calculated here and in Chapter 19. For item *c*, the cost of acquiring a customer, let's assume we spent 50 cents to acquire the customer and another 25 cents during the year to provide support, which can be much more expensive than $0.25 per support event, but we expect to have to deliver customer support for far fewer customers than we have. This gives us a total cost per customer of $2.72.

FIGURE 25.4

Calculating the price of a subscription

a.) Total cost of production per episode

$400 (you'll need to adjust for your show)

Divide by average # of subscribers each month

(11,391) = $0.0351 per subscriber

Multiply by number of episodes/year

(12) = $0.4214 per subscriber/year

b.) Total cost of delivering podcast to one subscriber

for one year = (12 x cost of bandwidth per episode)

Our show costs $0.1298 per episode at 173

MB per show for a per-subscriber cost

of $1.55/year

c.) Cost of acquiring and serving customer for a year: $0.75

Cost per subscriber: $2.72

Multiply by 2.5 to yield a gross margin of 150 percent.

Whoa. If you look back a bit, we estimated that we are going to make $1.14 per subscriber. But as we pointed out, that's not the actual number we need to shoot for if we are going to profit from this show. At the same time, you aren't going to see those delivery expenses for every subscriber, only the ones who stay for a full year. Unfortunately, you'll still be spending to acquire subscribers who don't stick around.

Figure 25.4 demonstrates that we have to multiply that cost of serving a customer by at least two to account for the files (roughly half of your inventory) you'll deliver in the year that are not driving any revenue. We'd recommend aiming to charge 2.5 times your costs for a subscription, which would be a cost of $6.80 a year for our show. Remember to adjust your calculations based on the frequency of the program and your costs, not those in this example.

Now, what about advertising? How do you price your ads to make the same kind of profit? Well, first, remember that you don't have much control over what you will charge for your show until you have a hit on your hands. The reality is that you have to make do with what you can get for your available ad inventory, though you can budget to get started.

As with the cost of delivering subscriptions, an advertising-supported show is going to cost, in our example, $2.72 per year to deliver to your audience. The difference is that you're looking to maximize the number of actual listeners you can get, so you may be delivering far more copies of your program than in the subscription scenario. In short, you're going to spend more to take your shot at advertising success.

What we have to figure out is how many ad impressions you can expect to deliver during the year. The answer is a multiple of the total number of subscribers you have during the year. Look back at Figure 25.2, where you see the total number of subscribers for each month in the right column. We're going to add up those totals for the year, which comes out to 136,698 files delivered to subscribers.

On a CPM (cost-per-thousand) basis, you have 136.7 units to sell if you have only one advertisement per show. *The Steve & Mitch Hour*, however, is long enough that we can insert six ads in each episode, for a total ad inventory of 820.2 units. If you want to make the $24,000 goal for revenue this year, the show has to earn $29.26 per 1,000 ad impressions. This revenue can be built on a tiered rate, so one advertiser may pay a $60 CPM rate for a show sponsorship that gets them placement at the top of the hour, while others pay a $15 CPM for placement at the end of the show, when fewer people will be assumed to be listening.

Here's where actual measurement of listenership, instead of downloads, starts to show its value. If you get paid for people hearing or seeing an ad at the same rate, regardless of when it occurs during the show, you'll earn more revenue. If you can show advertisers that you create customers by providing links on your site that people can follow, becoming qualified leads for your advertisers, you can earn much more for each action that your podcast initiates.

These numbers are for illustrative purposes, but they show you how to begin to account for the cost of producing and promoting your show and what the potential results are. You probably won't make a profit in the first year, even though we aimed for that in these examples. However, if you look at the size of the audience you can achieve at the end of the year and project forward from there, the potential for profit becomes self-evident. Laying a foundation of solid metrics for understanding your business is the beginning of that process, which starts with where and how to promote your podcast.

Where to promote your podcast

Promotion need not cost you much. The examples we've used assume that you spend heavily on every subscriber acquired when you probably will find that promotional costs come in bursts. You may spend only $100 to acquire your first 5,000 subscribers, but then decide that in order to get more people paying attention, you will give a t-shirt with your logo and URL to the next 500 subscribers at a cost of $4.75 per subscriber. After that promotion, you have paid $0.45 per subscriber for your first 5,500 subscribers. If the promotion drives another 5,000 subscribers before you spend again, it will have been worthwhile; if not, you are still spending about 50 cents per subscriber.

The first item on your promotional checklist should be getting your podcast listed on the many sites that feature podcast indices and links for subscribing. These sites are generally free and easy to use, though it can be time-consuming to get to them all. Some require special XML formats and custom data fields in your feeds, but they can be worthwhile because, after your podcast is submitted, each new show is promoted through sites like iTunes, Podcastalley.com, Yahoo Podcasts, and Odeo. We recommend that you register your podcast with these sites; we also list a couple that you needn't worry about:

- **Yahoo! Podcasts** (`podcasts.yahoo.com/`): The big portals were relatively late to the podcasting game, if you were counting from the very beginning. After the phenomenon became a medium, however, Yahoo was fast and accurate in its embrace of podcasting. The sheer volume of traffic at Yahoo makes this an essential place to register your podcast. Shows are well promoted in the interface with a subscribe button, so the listener can take action right away. Better yet, Yahoo sends the subscriber directly to your feed, staying out of the way of your relationship with the listener. Robust support for social tagging and user reviews give you a great platform for promotion.

- **Odeo** (`www.odeo.com/`): One of the early sites where podcasts were aggregated, we've discussed Odeo as a podcasting production platform, but it is also a community where about a million people purportedly find new programs. Users must be registered to get all the features of the site, such as the ability to rate shows and collect a playlist that can be heard online and on a portable player after downloading, as well as a sharing system that lets your listeners recommend your show to others. The registration barrier, though, is also a drawback, because people just passing through the site cannot subscribe to your show using their own podcatcher. The feature that makes up for this, in our opinion, is the ability to embed an Odeo online player in any site, which you can use to spread word about your podcast from your own site and elsewhere.

- **Feedster** (`www.feedster.com/`): Feedster searches RSS feeds for blogs and podcasts, offering visitors the ability to search many of the feeds on the Web to find programs by keyword. Links in the search engine direct subscribers to your RSS feed, putting you in direct contact with the listener. The site generates RSS feeds for each search conducted, so many people use it to create "subscribe to" searches on topics they want to follow. If your podcast falls into that search, it appears in their feed. It's free and useful, a fine combination for a promoter seeking tools.

- **Technorati** (`www.technorati.com/`): No, Technorati is not a podcast site, but it does provide many people their first exposure to and guidance for exploring blogs and podcasts. Submit and claim your feed so that you get information about who is pointing to your podcast and site, using that knowledge to cultivate relationships with bloggers and other podcasters who are talking about your work. It's a promotional must-have tool, and it, too, is free.

- **Podcast.net** (`www.podcast.net/`): One of the most comprehensive directories of podcasts available, Podcast.net provides a sampling platform for the listener searching for new programs. The site offers an online player for individual programs in your feed, sending subscribers directly to your RSS feed so you retain the relationship after you've won a new listener. It's not the prettiest of sites, but the categorization and ratings offered are a solid basis for people new to podcasting to find something that will interest them.

The link to add your podcast and a description is at `www.podcast.net/addpodcast`. You'll enter a general description of your show, where your RSS feed is located, the categories you want applied to your show, the language you speak, and an age-appropriate rating, as well as the keywords you think best describe your podcast. After this initial registration, Podcact.net extracts show summaries from your feed and displays them for individual episodes.

- **Syndic8 Podcasts** (`www.syndic8.com/podcasts`): A community site that provides feed search for blogs and podcasts, Syndic8 lets members add and categorize RSS and Atom feeds. Its podcast directory lists subscriber statistics based on what members tell Syndic8 about their subscriptions, so get your friends and listeners to visit the site to increase your visibility. An alternative route to exposure is to pay between $25 and $650 for one week up to one year for a featured listing, but paying for promotion shouldn't be your first choice. Syndic8 directs subscribers to your feed.

- **SingingFish** (`search.singingfish.com/`): One of the leaders of the next generation of media search engines, SingingFish doesn't index feeds. Instead, it finds a variety of media files and lists them, so if you want to have your podcast discovered here, use the ID3 metadata fields in your podcast files to inform searchers what is inside, who is featured, and how long the show is. Podcasters listed here are competing with every form of media, but that's already what you are doing and it is better to get into the ring with Beyonce, *The Lord of the Rings*, and Eminem now rather than later. You'll need to tell the SingingFish crawler where to look on your site to ensure you get its attention, which you can do at `search.singingfish.com/sfw/submit.html` (see Figure 25.5). Enter the directory on your server where your podcasts are stored, *not* your RSS feed. Be sure to enter the category to help searchers discover what they want.

- **PodcastPickle.com** (`www.podcastpickle.com/`): Another community site where listeners rate and promote podcasts, Podcast Pickle was recognized by *Time Magazine* as one of the coolest sites of 2006 and has the potential to be very influential for programs that catch its members' attention. You need to become a member to submit your podcast, and in that process you're asked to enter an extensive list of instant messaging, gaming, and other user handles that offer other venues for communicating with the audience. Depending on your willingness to get an IM or voice call from a listener, we recommend that you use at least a few of these channels for becoming engaged with listeners. After you're listed, you'll want to listen to and discuss other members' podcasts, too. This is not a set-and-forget promotional tool.

- **Podcasting News** (`www.podcastingnews.com/`): One of the leading sites reporting on podcasting and podcast technology, the Podcasting News site also hosts a popular directory. This is another site where membership pays off, because joining lets you submit your podcast rather than send the small staff information about your podcast for processing, which can take a long time. Podcasts are listed by individual shows that can be downloaded or streamed (if streaming is supported by the podcaster). The RSS feed for each show is displayed in the introductory text, but it's pretty well hidden. Podcasting News uses Podcast Alley's "vote for this podcast" features to rate shows listed in the directory.

FIGURE 25.5

On the SingingFish podcast submission form, don't list your feed. Instead, use the URL of the directory where podcasts are stored on your server.

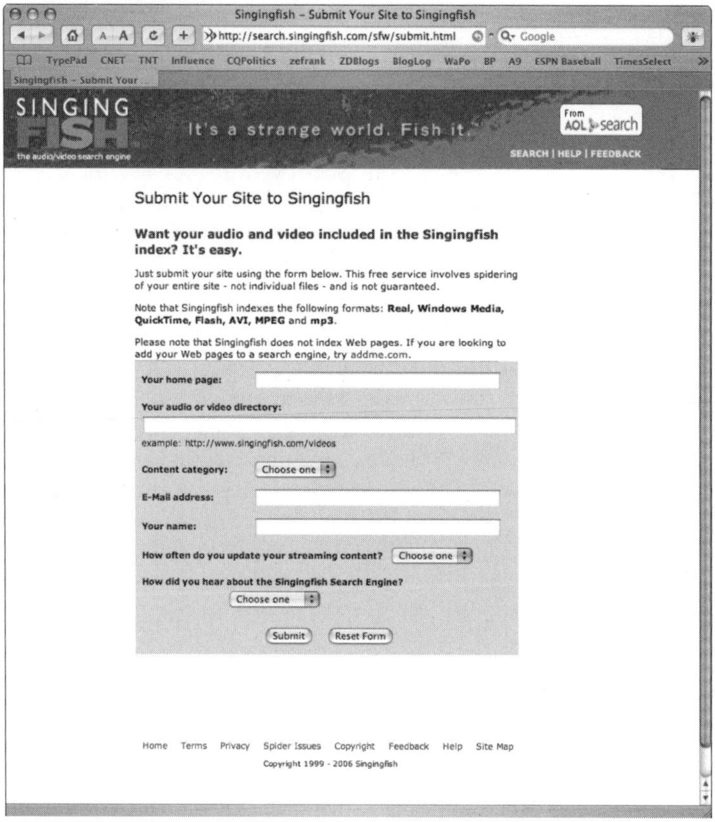

- **Ourmedia** (www.ourmedia.org/): An open media project, OurMedia was created by journalist J.D. Lasica and multimedia pioneer Marc Canter to provide perpetual free storage of shareable media of all types. Using storage provided by the Internet Archive (www.archive.org/), most of the files uploaded to the service are provided under the Creative Commons or GNU Public Licenses, which allow reuse of media. Your listings should include all the usual information, as well as credits for engineers and the equipment used, including sampling rates, because some folks are looking for material they can use in their own remixes, as well. Like SingingFish, this site puts your content into direct competition with lots of other media programs, and that's a good way to carve out some attention in an increasingly crowded business.

- **Blinkx Selfcast** (`tv.blinkx.com/`): For the vlogger and video podcaster, Blinkx Selfcast is an essential place to list programs. Your podcast will show up in the same list as NBC, Reuters, Bloomberg, and dozens of other media providers. Blinkx is not just a directory; it hosts the video featured on the site, so you'll be sacrificing a direct relationship with the audience. Membership is required, and data-describing files are limited to only a title, show notes, and tags, which are essential to being found when people search Blinkx. Getting on Blinkx.tv requires a business relationship with the company. Start with Selfcast.

- **Melodeo** (`www.melodeo.com/`): Another new entrant, Melodeo is a community-driven directory with an interesting mobile delivery option, offering streaming of podcasts over wireless networks to handheld phones. Programs listed on the site include mainstream and podcast productions. Members of the site can tag, rate, and share programs, building playlists based on their own interests or recommendations of friends. Because it's part social network, your participation certainly enhances pickup of your podcast by others. With an online player, sampling is easy, but the actual downloading to an iPod is a pain. Because of "security restrictions," the site requires you to copy the file URL into a media player on your PC. It's something that needs to be fixed, and we believe the site will be a barrier to a direct relationship with the audience, because Melodeo wants its community to be the place that relationship happens.

- **PodNova** (`www.podnova.com/`): A search engine, PodNova is a simple search interface, very much like Google, where visitors enter keywords and results are displayed. Submitting feeds, which PodNova then monitors for new programs and show notes to use in searches. The way to leverage this site is to embed its search on your own blog or site, but that's not necessarily going to increase your traffic from PodNova. Just paste your RSS feed URL into a field at `www.podnova.com/index_for_podcasters.srf`.

There are many others, so keep your eyes peeled for new indices where you can list your podcast. Again, promotion is an ongoing process, not a one-time project. If you choose to get involved in one of the community sites, stay engaged because you'll be getting messages on those sites that, if unanswered, will affect the way people see you and your brand.

Submitting your podcast to iTunes

Apple's iTunes uses standard RSS with some special tags that Apple uses to display additional information that most podcatchers would ignore. You can use a standard RSS feed for your podcast, but doing so misses some metadata that you can use to make your podcast more findable in the iTunes Music Store.

The following tags let you include data about the show that is displayed in the Get Info window displayed in iTunes when someone Ctrl+clicks or right-clicks on the title of a podcast. Some of these tags are required by Apple to keep a listing in iTunes. For example, if you use "explicit language" in your podcast and have not tagged your show as explicit, the feed will be deleted. Talking about sex or swearing makes a show explicit.

Before you test your feed, take time to review your existing RSS and add the tags, because they also provide more information that can be used to return a hit when someone searches for a show in iTunes. The tags are highlighted in bold in the example that follows:

```xml
<?xml version="1.0" encoding="UTF-8"?>
<rss xmlns:itunes="http://www.itunes.com/dtds/podcast-1.0.dtd" version="2.0">

<channel>
<title>My Amazing Podcast</title>
<link>http://www.MyAmazingPodcast.com/Amazing_Podcast/index.html</link>
<language>en-us</language>
<copyright>&#x2117; &amp; &#xA9; 2005 Super Podcaster</copyright>
<itunes:subtitle>A celebration of Me</itunes:subtitle>
<itunes:author>Super Podcaster</itunes:author>
<itunes:summary>Sometimes, one must talk and others must listen. This is the
podcast for those who want to know everything about podcasting and live by those
insights as though by rules.</itunes:summary>
<description>A brilliant person podcasts his definitive thoughts on the art of
podcasting and everything related to podcasting, which, by the way, is
everything in the world, so our host never deviates from his topic even when he
deviates completely from his subject.</description>
<itunes:owner>
<itunes:name>Super Podcaster</itunes:name>
<itunes:email>SuperPodcaster@MyAmazingPodcast.com</itunes:email>
</itunes:owner>
<itunes:image href="http://www.MyAmazingPodcast.com/art/AmazingPodcast.jpg" />
<itunes:category text="Technology">
<itunes:category text="Media"/>
</itunes:category>
<itunes:category text="News"/>

<item>
<title>I am the smartest podcaster ever</title>
<itunes:author>Super Podcaster</itunes:author>
<itunes:subtitle>Must I tell you in advance. You must trust Super
Podcaster</itunes:subtitle>
<itunes:summary>Who shot the sheriff? A conversation with Dave
Winer.</itunes:summary>
<enclosure url="http:// www.MyAmazingPodcast.com/Amazing_Podcast/Episode7-
Winer.m4a" length="8727310" type="audio/x-m4a" />
<guid>http://www.MyAmazingPodcast.com/Amazing_Podcast/archive/ Episode7-
Winer.m4a</guid>
<pubDate>Wed, 16 May 2006 21:00:00 GMT</pubDate>
<itunes:duration>17:04</itunes:duration>
<itunes:explicit>Clean</itunes:explicit>
<itunes:keywords>Winer, podcasting, podcast, how-to</itunes:keywords>
</item>

</channel>
</rss>
```

Now, to explain the custom iTunes tags:

- **<itunes:subtitle>:** This tag adds a second line to the title in either the <channel> or the individual program <item> segment of the RSS feed.

- **<itunes:author>:** This tag identifies the author of the work. Note that the feed can have a different author than the individual shows, allowing multiple and different authors to produce under a single title.

- **<itunes:summary>:** This is the description of the podcast when used in the <channel> segment of the feed and for individual shows when used in the <item> tag.

- **<itunes:owner>:** This tag describes the rights holder and includes a field for the name of the producer, **<itunes:name>,** and a contact e-mail address field, **<itunes:email>**

- **<itunes:image.../>:** A field for displaying art associated with the show, this is a <channel>-level selection used across all shows in a feed.

- **<itunes:category.../>:** Multiple instances of this tag can be used to place the podcast in different categories in the iTunes Music Store. In each instance of the tag, use the variable "Text = [Category Name]"

  The categories supported by iTunes are

  - Arts
  - Business
  - Comedy
  - Education
  - Games & Hobbies
  - Government & Organizations
  - Health
  - Kids & Family
  - Music
  - News & Politics
  - Religion & Spirituality
  - Science & Medicine
  - Society & Culture
  - Sports & Recreation
  - Technology
  - TV & Film

- **<itunes:duration>:** The time of the podcast is shown in standard hours:minutes:seconds format.

- **<itunes:explicit>:** The three options are "Yes," "No," and "Clean," which sounds slightly redundant, but we suggest using this tag in the <channel> segment of the feed. If some of your shows are explicit, using the "Yes" tag here and "Clean" in the <Item> segment will distinguish the clean show from the explicit channel.

- **<itunes:keywords>:** Making your podcast easy to find means picking descriptive keywords, which you should insert here.

After you've set up your iTunes-compatible feed, test it in your copy of iTunes by attempting to subscribe to the feed. If it works, it's time to submit the feed to the iTunes Music Store. The feed can reside anywhere; you aren't giving a copy or any right to Apple. Open the iTunes "Submit a Podcast" page.

1. Paste the URL of the iTunes-compatible RSS feed into the field for the Podcast Feed URL, and click Continue. You'll be prompted to enter your username and password for iTunes; if you don't have an account, you can't submit a feed. Apple checks the URL and extracts the fields from the feed, including graphics and description, displaying it for you to confirm. The category is displayed, based on the RSS feed we configured previously, but the Subcategory is not, and iTunes asks you to select from a pop-up menu of options.

2. If you didn't specify a language in the <itunes:language> tag, you're asked to pick an option from a pop-up menu.

3. If you did not designate an <itunes:explicit> tag, a checkbox appears at the bottom of the page that you should check if the content is mature.

4. Now, click Submit and wait.

Apple has a staff that checks submissions, and based on whether you've broken the rules against using mature language or discussing sex when you did not designate your podcast as explicit, or used copyrighted materials or offensive materials, such as hate speech or child pornography, your podcast will probably make it through the review quickly.

If at first your podcast appears only in search results but not the browsable listings, don't worry; it takes a little longer to reach the catalog.

Summary

Promoting your podcast can seem like a full-time job, but that needn't be so. Use the tools described in this chapter, and you'll be well on your way to building your subscriber list. This chapter covered these topics:

- All the creativity in the world won't help your podcast succeed if it doesn't capture the attention of a potential audience.

- Promotion is a process that takes constant attention to opportunities to gain publicity.

- Branding is simply creating an impression that stays with your audience even when they aren't listening, because it is what brings them back for more. Your brand also determines what you should deliver, so be sure not to define yourself too narrowly or too broadly. A brand can grow and change, but every time it does, you have to win your customers all over again.

■ The cost of promotion is real, even if it is just the time you spend looking for publicity opportunities. It is one more (the last) factor to include in calculating how much you may need to make in order to cover your costs and turn a profit on a podcast.

■ Ultimately, you should figure out what each subscriber is worth to you in terms of what you can earn from them so that you can decide the right amount to spend acquiring and serving them. If each subscriber can earn you $100 a year, you may want to spend $20 to win them, because spending too little may mean your competitors who shoulder higher marketing costs get the subscriber.

■ Understand how long your subscribers stay by looking at how long it takes them to leave; this is called the "churn rate." The number of episodes for which the average subscriber stays is how long you have to make your profit.

■ Knowing how long you have and how much it costs to win a subscriber and serve them for a year — including all the programming you have to give away to win subscribers — helps you calculate a subscription price or profitable amount of advertising. All business comes down to simple mathematics.

■ Promoting your podcast is easy but time-consuming because there are so many sites and directories where subscribers can look for new shows.

■ Learn not to think of promotions as a fixed cost-per-subscriber but as something you spend money on in bursty manner, with a little money winning many subscribers and large investments to start another cycle of gains.

■ When submitting to Apple's iTunes Music Store, use Apple-specific RSS tags to add information that improves your podcast's findability. Other sites using a standard RSS feed — which works in iTunes, without the extra data — and where to submit your feed is explained in our list of useful directories.

Part VI

Case Studies

Chapter 26

Podcasting from Home: The Dawn and Drew Show

The Dawn and Drew show is perhaps the greatest podcasting success story. Some may point to the success of Ricky Gervais' podcast and its transition to a subscription model. Others may point to "This Week in Tech" or the "Daily Source Code" as early success stories. But those podcasts were anchored by hosts with well-established reputations and covered topics that were tailor-made for an Internet audience. The Dawn and Drew Show was something completely different.

Here were two self-anointed "gutter punks" who moved out of the city, bought a retired dairy farm, and started to tell the world about it, before the term podcasting had even been coined. Here were two people, living ordinary lives, doing ordinary things, encountering the same frustrations that everyone else does, and talking about it. It caught on like wildfire.

Of course, it helps that Dawn and Drew are incredibly likeable, funny, irreverent, and completely addictive. The thing that is so surprising is that their subject matter rarely strays from the mundane. Somehow, they manage to take everyday life, put a unique spin on it, and leave their audience wanting more. Their podcast underscores the fact that the world of podcasting is a new frontier, unbound by the rules that constrain traditional broadcast media.

How It Started

The Dawn and Drew Show was born when Dawn and Drew made a change of life decision. They were tired of living in the city and looking for a way out. Dawn had always dreamed of owning a big barn and turning it into an art studio and gallery. When they found the perfect location, they bought it and started the Dawn and Drew farm.

Drew is a self-professed "Web-nerd" who started playing around with creating his own show online. Dawn quickly realized that what he was doing had lots of potential and promptly took over the show. When the Dawn and Drew show started off, they had no idea that it would become as popular as it has become. It was supposed to be a simple, honest dialogue between two people "who happen to love each other."

In fact, they had no idea anyone would be interested at all. They figured a few friends might listen in once or twice, but they never consciously stopped to think about who their audience would be or even if they'd have an audience at all. As Dawn says, "It's our show. We did it for ourselves and never gave it a second thought."

However, reality dictated otherwise. The show became one of the most popular podcasts, and with their success came something they hadn't expected — a huge bandwidth bill. In December 2004, they almost had to stop the show, because they could no longer afford the monthly bandwidth charges. Thankfully for Dawn and Drew and for their devoted audience, they were able to hook up with the nascent Podshow network, and the rest, as they say, is podcasting history. Figure 26.1 shows Dawn and Drew's Web site.

FIGURE 26.1

The Dawn and Drew Show Web site

Programming and Production

The Dawn and Drew Show grew out of inauspicious surroundings. In the beginning, the show was recorded using a single, cheap plastic USB mic, shown in Figure 26.2a. This got them through many of their early shows. As their popularity increased, and they realized that they could turn their hobby into a living, they upgraded their audio setup. They now have two microphones like the one shown in Figure 26.2b, which are plugged into a small mixer. They use the Eurorack UB1204 and the JVC headphones shown in Figure 26.3. Currently, they do their recording in their living room, but they are building a dedicated recording studio.

The original USB mic that got Dawn & Drew through 296 episodes, and one of the MXL 990s they now use.

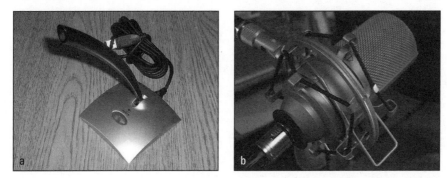

When they're on the road, they travel with a Marantz PMD660 portable Flash recorder. This records directly into MP3 format, which can be dragged and dropped directly into their audio editing software.

On the software side, they record their audio directly into GarageBand. Drew handles most of the technical duties, although Dawn does the video editing. When they do video podcasts, they use a sharp Viewcam Z VL-Z1 and a Kodak DX4530 digital camera that has video capabilities. All video editing is done using iMovie.

When it comes to editing, there is very little to be done. As Dawn says, "We leave in 99.9 percent of the warts. There may be a time or two when we've had to bleep out someone's name or something like that." Most of the post-production is adding the ads, inserting audio comments (The Dawn and Drew show has an audience call-in number where you can leave messages), and adding songs to the end of the program.

The Dawn and Drew show is somewhat unique among podcasts, because they're part of the Podshow network slot on the Sirius Satellite network. Podshow has a four-hour block, to which Dawn and Drew contribute their show. Luckily, this doesn't affect their production chain too much, because all they have to do is upload a 128 Kbps MP3 file to their contact at Sirius, and Sirius takes care of editing all the Podshow content into a four-hour block.

FIGURE 26.3

The Eurorack UB1204 and the JVC headphones used on the Dawn and Drew Show.

When it comes to pre-production, Dawn and Drew are lucky. They don't really have to prepare too much. Drew notes that, "We try to have a few things in mind, maybe a few sound clips to play, but that's about all the preparation we ever do." Yet somehow, five days a week, they still manage to keep their show fresh.

Encoding and Distribution

Dawn and Drew keep their encoding and distribution simple. They encode into MP3 format, at 96 Kbps for general distribution, and at 128 Kbps for Sirius Satellite. They encode using iTunes. They've never done any enhanced podcasts, but they have done a few video podcasts. The video podcasts take a little longer to produce, but similar to their audio podcasts, they keep the production simple and the editing to a minimum.

The Dawn and Drew show is available on the Dawn and Drew Show Web site, which is hosted by the Podshow network. They also list the show in the iTunes directory. Podshow provides all the bandwidth for their distribution. They also use the tools available on Podshow+, which includes tools to upload the shows and to maintain the RSS feed. Initially, Drew took care of listing the show in various podcast directories, but now most of the publicity is taken care of by Podshow.

The Dawn and Drew Show site is a Wordpress blog. They use the PodPress plug-in, but only for the Flash audio player it enables. Dawn notes, "We both had blogs, but we wanted the show to have its own blog that was totally separate." In addition to the main blog, the Dawn and Drew Show Web site also includes a forum. Initially installed as a way to relieve some of the e-mail traffic, it quickly grew and took on a life of its own. Drew says, "At first, we installed the forum to alleviate some of the e-mailing that we were trying to keep up with. But as it started to fill up, we realized that it's actually all for the audience. Some strong friendships have been formed on our forum. And the forum is always busy."

Turning a Hobby into a Network

Dawn and Drew are in some ways two of the least likely stars you'll meet. As Dawn said, "We had no idea anything would ever happen. It was just a hobby we were getting into." From these humble origins, the Dawn and Drew Show has grown into a podcasting powerhouse. They regularly get 850,000 downloads a month.

> **NOTE** Do the math: 850,000 downloads a month, a 30-minute show, 96 Kbps encoding rate:
>
> ```
>     850k * 96,000bps * 60secs/min * 30mins / 8bits/byte
> = over 17,500 Gigabytes a month
> ```

The Dawn and Drew Show has a tight relationship with Podshow. Dawn recalls, "Adam was there at the very beginning of podcasting. There weren't many other shows at the time, so we started communicating way back then. When Adam started putting Podshow together, he asked us if we wanted to help change the face of media with him. We met with him and his partner Ron Bloom, joined PodShow, and haven't regretted a minute since."

Joining Podshow allowed Dawn and Drew to go full-time on their show. In August 2005, one year after the start of the Dawn and Drew Show, Podshow's funding came through, and in turn they began paying Dawn and Drew. Drew was able to give notice at his day job. Since then, they've been able to focus on making the Dawn and Drew Show. It also has allowed them to think about the future and how they can expand beyond their current format.

Future Plans

The Dawn and Drew Show appears to have a recipe for success. On the surface, it appears pretty simple. As Dawn puts it, "We just try to be as honest as possible, and people appreciate it. I don't think that's really a secret, but it seems to work." They hope to take this approach and apply it to more programming that is in the works.

A couple of new podcasts are being spun off the original. Dawn elaborates, "There's an advice show and one aimed at environmental issues, plus we're launching Dawn and Drew TV, which is a video podcast station. We're going on tour to promote the show and will be traveling the world, spreading our Dawn and Drew cooties!"

See and hear for yourself at `http://www.dawnanddrew.com`.

Summary

The Dawn and Drew Show began as a hobby and turned into a podcasting sensation. They're practically the poster children for podcasting because they're the perfect example of what a podcast can become.

- The Dawn and Drew Show broke new ground in the world of podcasting because of the subject matter.
- The Dawn and Drew Show is produced with very modest equipment, yet it sounds totally professional.
- Their approach is to do very little editing, leaving it all in, "warts and all."
- Their audience appreciates their simple, honest approach.
- Distribution is done via the Podshow.com network.
- By providing their audience with a forum, they've created a space where their audience can interact with them and with each other.
- The Dawn and Drew Show proves that there is an audience out there for content that would never find a home on traditional broadcast outlets.

Chapter 27

Channel 9: Humanizing the World's Largest Software Company

Although podcasting was born as a consumer medium, it is rapidly being deployed by many companies. Companies are using podcasting as a means of communicating with their employees and also with people outside the company, such as partners and even customers. The first company to realize the potential of podcasting — Microsoft — stumbled upon it almost by accident. In fact, you could say that it was fear of an accident that got its Channel 9 podcasting effort underway.

The story of podcasting at Microsoft in many ways parallels the story of podcasting as a whole. It began innocently enough, when five guys at Microsoft decided to start walking the halls with $300 video cameras and talking to developers. The original idea was to provide outside developers and partners with a window into the development process at Microsoft. They had no idea the impact they were going to have not only on Microsoft, but also on the world of podcasting. Channel 9 was launched on March 26, 2004, and now serves nearly four million unique visitors each month delivering video podcasts, audio podcasts, and screencasts to a vibrant community of developers. The site regularly receives more than four million visitors a month, up to 40,000 of whom are regularly online simultaneously.

IN THIS CHAPTER

Channel 9: At the birth of video podcasting

Helping fly the plane

Podcast production at Channel 9

Channel 9 distribution

Getting results

The future of podcasting at Microsoft

Channel 9: At the Birth of Video Podcasting

Lenn Pryor, a director within the Developer and Platform Evangelism group at Microsoft had a serious fear of flying, until he discovered that United Airlines piped the cockpit/ground radio communications over channel 9 on the in-flight audio system. Being able to listen in on the pilot's communications helped him understand what was going on behind that locked cockpit door.

In late 2003, Lenn and his team were part of one of Microsoft's biggest developer events, the Professional Developer's Conference, known as PDC '03. Thousands of developers from all over the world came to Los Angeles to get the straight scoop on what Microsoft had planned for the next few years directly from the developers themselves. Lenn's team was responsible for making sure the attendees got to interact directly and frequently with the employees.

To realize this goal, a number of decisions were made to change the overall tone of PDC. First, the employee-only lounge and eating areas were eliminated to force Microsoft employees to mingle and interact with the conference attendees. This proved to be a genius move. Because of the increased interaction, the attendees started to see the developers, and therefore Microsoft, in a different light. Instead of the company being perceived as a monolithic "empire," the employees gave Microsoft a human face.

On the return trip from Los Angeles, Lenn and his team decided that they wanted to continue to facilitate direct developer-to-developer interaction. They decided to post short interviews with developers to the ASP.Net forums, which also allowed viewers to respond by leaving textual replies. Lenn and his team reasoned that if channel 9 on United airlines could help passengers feel like they were part of the crew flying the plane, and thus relieve their fear of flying, hearing directly from Microsoft's developers might do the same for independent software vendors who had a similarly opaque view of how Microsoft operated.

The channel 9 development team, which included Jeff Sandquist, Charles Torre, Bryn Waibel, and Robert Scoble, wanted to provide as much interaction on the new site as possible. Already savvy in the ways of blogging and RSS, the team decided to provide an RSS feed including the video links as enclosures so that developers could subscribe and download the videos for offline viewing. Thus was born `channel9.msdn.com`, one of the very first video podcasting sites, shown in Figure 27.1. This was in March 2004.

FIGURE 27.1

The original Channel 9 home page

Courtesy of the Internet Archive

Helping "Fly the Plane"

The channel 9 team reasoned that Microsoft's independent developer community could not only "listen in to the cockpit," but also help Microsoft "fly the plane" by contributing to a discussion. They set out to build a community that they as developers themselves would want to be a part of. They even put their customers on the home page.

To help communicate the spirit with which they wanted to engage their listeners, they came up with what they called the "Channel 9" manifesto:

- **Channel 9 is all about the conversation.** Channel 9 should inspire Microsoft and our customers to talk in an honest and human voice. Channel 9 is not a marketing tool, not a PR tool, not a lead generation tool.

- **Be a human being.** Channel 9 is a place for us to be ourselves, to share who we are, and for us to learn who our customers are.

- **Learn by listening.** When our customers speak, learn from them. Don't get defensive; don't argue for the sake of argument. Listen and take what benefits you to heart.

- **Be smart.** Think before you speak; there are some conversations that have no benefit other than to reinforce stereotypes or create negative situations.

- **Marketing has no place on Channel 9.** When we spend money on Channel 9, the goal is to surprise and delight, not to promote or preach.

- **Don't shock the system.** Lasting change only happens in baby steps.

- **Know when to turn the mic off.** There are some topics that will only result in problems when you discuss them. This has nothing to do with censorship, but with working within the reality of the system that exists in our world today. You will not change anything by taking on legal or financial issues; you will only shock the system, spook the passengers, and create a negative situation.

- **Don't be a jerk.** Nobody likes mean people.

- **Commit to the conversation.** Don't stop listening just because you are busy. Don't stop participating because you don't agree with someone. Relationships are not built in a day; be in it for the long haul, and we will all reap the benefits as an industry.

Podcast Production at Channel 9

You may think that delivering podcasts on such a large scale requires a large team, but in the case of Channel 9, you'd be wrong! Channel 9's infrastructure is operated by a three-person team, and most podcasts are produced by individuals operating independently, all within the Developer and Platform Evangelism group.

The production is not done by a team, but instead each producer chooses the most productive tools to use for his particular podcast. Applications used range all the way from Sound Recorder (built into Microsoft Windows) to Sonar/Cubase for audio and from Windows Movie Maker to Avid non-linear editing software for video. Screencasts are produced using either Windows Media Encoder or TechSmith's Camtasia Studio.

The production process at Channel 9 is a relatively simple one:

1. Media is captured using a variety of consumer and/or pro-sumer devices — for example, the Sony DCR-HR21 video camera or the Olympus DS-330 hand-held audio recorder.

2. Audio is imported and edited on desktop PCs with a variety of applications ranging from Sound Recorder to Cakewalk Sonar. Then the produced podcasts are saved in both MP3 and WMA format using Sony Sound Forge and Windows Media Encoder.

3. Similarly, video is imported and edited on a desktop PC using Windows Movie Maker. After trimming the start and end of the video to eliminate unwanted footage, the video is then saved, using Windows Movie Maker at a variety of bit rates, the most common being 512 K.

4. Raw screencasts from Windows Media Encoder and Camtasia are saved, as with videos, at a variety of bit rates. If textual information is included in the screencast, the video is

usually captured and encoded using a resolution of 1024×768. Otherwise, the screencast may be encoded at 320×240 at 512 Kbps to reduce file size and improve the streaming experience.

5. Finally, the completed podcast (WMV, WMA, MP3) file is uploaded to a server farm running Microsoft Windows Media Services. Video is uploaded using a custom tool written in-house that supports transcoding to H.264 and other formats designed for portable media devices. Audio podcasts are uploaded using either a Web interface or FTP software if they are larger than 10 MB. So you can see that even at the world's largest software company, podcasting is a fairly simple and self-contained process. The Channel 9 team doesn't rely on any other departments for production services. They're using tools that are either built in to the operating system or readily available to Microsoft employees.

Channel 9 Distribution

Obviously, the Channel 9 team has the advantage of being able to leverage lots of existing infrastructure at Microsoft to distribute the content that they produce. Video streaming for Channel 9 is done via a large Windows Media Services cluster. Most podcasts are also available for download via the Microsoft.com download service. Figure 27.2 shows the Channel 9 Web site today.

FIGURE 27.2

The Channel 9 Web site today

One of the prescient things that the Channel 9 team did is what they call "RSS everywhere." Not only did they support an RSS feed of the main video posts, they also created individual RSS feeds for each conversation so that listeners could follow an individual topic as it evolved. Channel 9 supports video podcasts, audio podcasts, screencasts, and even a full blown Wiki, all RSS-enabled. What this does is encourage visitors who previously participated anonymously to join the conversation by posting a profile and replying to individual videos.

Obviously, providing this level of interactivity and RSS subscription options requires a significant maintenance effort. In this regard, Channel 9 again can leverage in-house resources. In fact, all the RSS feeds exposed by the Channel 9 site are automatically generated and maintained by an SQL Server database.

A variety of in-house tools are used to monitor download and streaming statistics.

Getting Results

Before Channel 9 was launched, the public face of Microsoft was the executives. In that pre-podcasting world, everything was vetted by the public relations team, and to most developers, it came across as hype.

At a PDC, developers connect with Microsoft engineers and program managers directly without the intervening PR and marketing. With Channel 9, Microsoft is able to reach not only those few thousand developers who can afford to go to PDC, which happens only every two years or so, but to any developer who wants to participate. This has been key to Channel 9's success. As Jeff Sandquist says, "One of the reasons C9 is successful is that it was created by developers for developers."

Microsoft management has continued to invest in Channel 9 production and infrastructure precisely because the number of developers who watch, listen, and participate continues to grow consistently every month. Jeff Sandquist, the Microsoft Director who now runs the Channel 9 team, says, "You can spend a lot of time trying to analyze why are you successful, but I really think it all comes down to content and having stuff that's relevant to your audience."

According to Sandquist, "We're not trying to build a community in the traditional Web sense. We're trying to build the equivalent of a music festival, similar to Seattle's yearly Bumbershoot event, where everyone from the buskers, to the food vendors, to the crowd all join together to create the experience. I get really excited when the people who watch the videos not only talk about the content, but also start to create their own content and share it with the other visitors. When you can mash it all together like that, then you've really got something."

The Future of Podcasting at Microsoft

Channel 9 has been so successful at Microsoft that it has spawned other community Web site efforts, most notably www.on10.net, hosted by Laura Foy and Tina Wood, formerly of TechTV.

On10.net features enthusiastic users, instead of developers, who are doing creative and inspiring things using the technology that Microsoft sells.

On10 is hosted on a custom-designed Web site application, and Channel 9 will be transitioning to this new infrastructure in late 2006. This will allow Channel 9 to distribute video podcasts in additional formats compatible with portable players such as the Apple iPod, Sony PS2, and Microsoft Zune. On10 had the advantage of starting from scratch a few years after Channel 9, so it could easily build in new features that users wanted. Again, Channel 9 has the advantage of being able to leverage other corporate resources, which translates to a better experience for its audience.

Microsoft is currently beta-testing a new service called "Soapbox," which allows users to upload video and audio content, similar to sites such as YouTube.com. One of the important things that "Soapbox" does is it allows contributors to tag their content, and both Channel 9 and On10.net will be featuring, in the near future, aggregated feeds based on the tags contributors select. Find more about these sites at:

```
http://channel9.msdn.com
http://www.on10.net
http://soapbox.msn.com
```

Summary

Podcasting has had a major effect on the ability of the world's largest software company to communicate with its customers. This chapter covered these topics:

- Channel 9 puts a human face on the world's largest software company.
- Channel 9 lets developers around the world interact with the developers at Microsoft.
- Production at Channel 9 is done using a range of tools, some built in to Windows, others readily available at Microsoft.
- Distribution of Channel 9 is done on existing company resources.
- Channel 9 offers multiple RSS feeds to encourage greater interaction.
- All RSS feeds are automatically maintained.
- The Channel 9 team is small and focused, yet the return is almost incalculable.
- The richer interaction between Microsoft and the developer community results in better Microsoft products.

Chapter 28

A Museum's Experience: The Ontario Science Centre

The Ontario Science Centre opened September 27, 1969. This natural sciences museum receives over one million physical visitors each year. Attendance demographics represent a large cross section of the population: 56 percent of visitors are 18 and over, 7 percent are 12-17, 22 percent are 6-12, and 14 percent are under 6. School field trips account for approximately 25 percent of total attendance.

The Ontario Science Centre's Web sites attracted more than 2.5 million visitors in 2005. Although the online audience is impressive, this institution continues to focus on education through physical interaction. Right now, the Centre is working to complete a $47-million initiative that will transform more than 30 percent of the public spaces. This project is not just about creating exhibits; it focuses on creating experiences that will inspire and actively engage teens and young adults in new ways of seeing, understanding, and thinking about themselves and the world. Podcasting serves the Ontario Science Centre as a relatively new avenue to educate and engage audiences of all ages. Program coordinator and host Ken Dickson launched the RedShift Report in June 2005. The podcast aims to educate online audiences through episodes focusing on natural science. As of September 2006, there were 39 RedShift Report episodes on the institution's RedShift Now Web site, shown in Figure 28.1, which is available here:

```
http://www.redshiftnow.ca/report/
```

FIGURE 28.1

The RedShift Report Web site

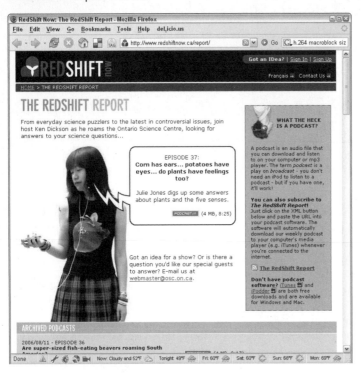

How It Started

The premise behind the RedShift Report is to answer questions from listeners using the scientists and researchers at the Centre. One of the keys to its success is that it expands the Centre's traditional educational outreach. The Centre is always looking for new ways to engage visitors with the institutional Web site. Using podcasting to not only present material but to create a dialogue with visitors was a natural fit.

The Centre has always received questions from visitors. Previously, a staff member would send out a written response. Now, instead of the response being a one-to-one dialogue between the visitor asking the question and the staff member responding, it's one-to-many. The RedShift Report enables the Ontario Science Centre to broadcast the response to their entire podcast audience.

Host and programmer Ken Dickson has not noticed a great difference in the demographic makeup between his program's audience and the Centre's onsite attendees. He knows the RedShift Report reaches a global audience based on the e-mail feedback received after each episode. The program encourages correspondence to collect topics of interest to the audience for future shows. The institution has not yet conducted a formal survey to confirm this hypothesis.

Programming and Production

The RedShift Report maintains a schedule of featured guest experts for upcoming programs. At the start of the week, Dickson meets with the guest to discuss the inventory of questions that have been received from the audience.

The guest's discipline (be it physics or biology or another scientific specialty) has much to do with the question that is selected. At the same time, Dickson is looking for a topic with enough breadth that it can be used as a catalyst to go off in different directions and keep the conversation moving quickly.

After the question has been selected, Dickson and the guest research the subject. A script is generated with notes on the subject and a few pivotal questions. The expert returns to the studio later in the week to make the recording.

The RedShift Report format is an informal interview between Dickson and one of the in-house scientists or researchers. The conversational approach replicates how a visitor to the Centre would typically engage one of the staff. Because each episode revolves around a question that has been e-mailed to the program, the host's role in the podcast is as a proxy for the visitor. The follow-up questions are ones Dickson imagines might be asked.

The program is targeted at individuals who are curious about the world around them, but may not necessarily read scientific literature or pursue schooling in the topic. The goal is to provide the listener with a lively discussion about the topic at hand. If the listener talks to a friend about the topic or perhaps decides to pursue the topic by searching for more information online, the program staff considers the podcast a success.

The podcast is generated entirely in-house by a small team. Dickson is the host and also creates and manages the final podcasts. The RedShift Report team also includes the knowledge expert from the Centre and the A/V Producer. The A/V Producer ensures good recording quality. After the recording has been approved, Dickson receives a file of the finished product. He mixes in the music and performs the conversion and compression on the final file to produce the .mp3 file for distribution. Any sound effects used on the recordings come from royalty-free compilation discs. The music that the team typically opens an episode with is acceptable "fair use." The fact that the Centre is a non-profit, educational institution helps, as does limiting any music to only a few seconds.

The RedShift Report has experimented with a variety of technical equipment. Currently, they are using a Shure wireless lavaliere microphone — one of the "tie-clip" microphones with a transmitter pack that can be placed in a pocket. Neither the host nor the guest is a professional broadcaster, and the tie-clip microphone ensures that voices are captured in spite of movement or gestures. The A/V Producer wears a pair of headphones to listen to what the microphones pick up and records directly to a .wav file.

Dickson then uses Audacity to perform the mixing and any editing required. After the mixing has been completed, iTunes is used to compress the file to the .mp3 format and to add ID3 tags.

Encoding and Distribution

Because the RedShift Report is predominantly composed of speech, the team has settled on the MP3 format, encoded in mono at 64 kbps, using a 44.1 kHz sampling rate. It results in a file of about 4MB for each episode. At that size, subscribers can easily download the file to the player. In addition to downloads, the visitor can listen to the program directly by clicking a link to the .mp3 file.

Dickson found definite benefits to enhanced podcasts, but his aim was to be as universal as possible. Due to their accountability to the public served, museums have an increasingly important role in encouraging accessibility; access is of particular concern to the RedShift Report team.

The podcast is primarily made available in two locations — either via direct download from the RedShift Report Web site or via the RSS feed. The RedShift Report team tries to list the program in as many locations as possible. These include the iTunes Music Store, Podnova.com, Zencast.com, podcasts.yahoo.com, and ipodder.org. By far, the majority of listeners to the podcast come from iTunes. The RedShift Report team talks about the podcast at any occasion they can — at conferences and meetings with other Science Centre professionals — and prints promotional posters, shown in Figure 28.2. Primarily though, the team relies on word-of-mouth.

The most popular RedShift Report episode received just over 5,000 downloads. Since launching the podcast in June 2005, the team has had more than 85,000 downloads of the various episodes.

The RedShift Report podcast is hosted on an in-house Web server, and Dickson manually updates the RSS file. He feels that there is nothing to fear from a little XML. To ensure that the feed is valid, he runs it through `www.feedvalidator.org/` when he's finished updating each file.

FIGURE 28.2

The RedShift Report is lucky enough to have a budget to print promotional posters.

Gauging Success

At the end of each episode, Dickson encourages listeners to e-mail the program with questions that may be included as topics for subsequent episodes. The size of his inbox has exploded with feedback from listeners, and the team feels that this is a very positive indicator of the show's success.

The thing that Dickson finds most fascinating is that the podcast attracts a very global audience. The team has received questions from visitors and been mentioned on blogs around the world. For example, a Chinese language blog once listed The RedShift Report as being an interesting podcast from which, "you could learn about daily phenomenon while simultaneously practicing your English listening skills!"

The museum management is very pleased with the project. Financially, it costs the institution very little to produce. The same microphones are used for other projects and presentations at the Centre. The software used is free, and the staff time involved is not that much more than previously was spent answering questions via e-mail. With practically no investment, any return is a good return. Management is very impressed with the numbers; 85,000 downloads is an impressive figure.

Dickson believes that the program is definitely creating awareness. The team has received mention on Web sites ranging from Slashdot.org to Sydney, Australia's Powerhouse Museum blog. But he is not convinced that podcasting is directly driving attendance. Certainly, the more people who know about the program, the more likely they are to come to the Centre, but he is not confident that anyone has visited the Centre directly as a result of something they heard in a podcast. Dickson is comfortable with this; while getting bodies through the front door is certainly something he would like to see happen, the museum's mission is "to delight, inform, and challenge visitors," whether that happens on site or online. He believes that the podcast does exactly that.

As a marketing vehicle, Dickson finds it difficult to compare the podcast's success to a print ad or billboard. The Ontario Science Centre has other marketing efforts, such as a monthly "Café Scientifique" discussion held at a local bar, but directly comparing the RedShift Report's success to something in a different medium is elusive.

As for the future of the RedShift Report, Dickson would like to expand the network by including non-Science Centre guests in the program. He feels that recording with a live audience would also be interesting. Beyond that, it's a bit of "wait and see." The team knows it is onto a good thing, and members can't wait to see what happens. So if you know anyone who has a love of science, or just a healthy dose of curiosity, be sure to tell them to visit RedShiftNow.ca and listen to the RedShift Report!

Summary

As this case study shows, podcasting can be used by governmental and educational facilities. Podcasts often can be produced at very little cost and using existing infrastructure. In the Ontario Science Centre's case, we've seen how a podcast can be of benefit to a museum:

- Museums can use podcasting to extend their reach and better fulfill their mission statement.

- Podcasts enable greater and more meaningful contact between museums and their visitors.

- The tools required to produce a podcast often already exist in-house.

- Podcasts give the entire museum staff the opportunity to interact with visitors.

- Although it is too early to compare podcasting to traditional marketing efforts, the cost of producing podcasts is so low that the return on investment is easy to justify.

- Even with the proliferation of niche content channels available on television today, people still can't get enough science!

Podcasting Resources

It would be wonderful if we could include every single thing you'll ever want to know about podcasting in this book. The truth is we can't. There isn't enough space (or time in the day), and the field of podcasting is changing every day. Fortunately, there are lots of places where you can keep up with the latest and greatest in the podcasting world.

This appendix includes information about sites where you can learn more about podcasting, sites where you can ogle cool podcast production gear, and other sites that may come in handy. Enjoy.

IN THIS APPENDIX

Podcasting information

Podcast hosting services

Podcasting directories

Podcasting Information

There are a number of sites where you can get updated news, technical tips, and even gossip about the world of podcasting. These are some of our favorites:

- **Jake Ludington's Media Blab** (www.mediablab.com): Jake Ludington is a digital media maven. His site has lots of great content, from helpful how-to articles to news about the podcasting world.

- **My Podcast Center** (www.mypodcastcenter.com): This directory includes helpful podcasting information.

- **The Podcasting Bible** (www.podcastingbible.com): You didn't think we'd launch this book without a companion site, did you?

- **Podcast Alley** (www.podcastalley.com): This is mostly a directory, but the forum has lively discussions about all aspects of podcasting.

- **Podcast 411** (`www.podcast411.com`): The name says it all; this site includes just about everything you need to know about podcasting.

- **Podcasting News** (`www.podcastingnews.com`): This is a great RSS feed about all things podcasting.

- **Podcasting Tools** (`www.podcasting-tools.com`): This is another great podcasting resource.

- **RSS spec** (`blogs.law.harvard.edu/tech/rss`): The full RSS 2.0 specification document can be found at this site.

- **Voxmedia.org** (`voxmedia.org`): This site includes a blog and a wiki full of valuable information.

Podcast Hosting Services

Lots of people want to help you get your podcast up and running. So many, in fact, that a good number of them are offering their services for free. The services we list here are podcasting-specific; plenty of Web hosting companies are more than capable of hosting a Web site with an accompanying podcast. A survey of those companies is beyond the scope of this chapter.

This list is accurate as of Fall 2006. Many more (or many fewer) may exist by the time you read this. Of course, we don't endorse any specific service, and you should shop very carefully:

- **BIPmedia** (`bipmedia.com`): This hosting service offers podcasting-specific packages.

- **BlastPodcast** (`blastpodcast.com`): This podcast hosting service inserts audio adds automatically into podcasts. Publishers receive free hosting and earn revenue from the ads.

- **Blip.tv** (`blip.tv`): Here you can find a free hosting service that includes a blog.

- **Blog Matrix** (`blogmatrix.com`): This site has an all-in-one podcasting service, including hosting.

- **Christian Podder** (`ChristianPodder.com`): If you're looking for a Christian podcast community and hosting service, this is it.

- **Gabcast** (`gabcast.com`): This service is based on recording phone conversations. They can be converted to podcasts or used as promotional clips, such as spoken descriptions of eBay items.

- **Genetic Hosting** (`www.genetichosting.com/podcasting.php`): This service provides a Podcast Management System named PodKive that lets users create a Web site, post MP3s, .MOV files, and other media file types. It also includes full Web site hosting.

- **Hipcast** (`www.hipcast.com`): This service offers audio recording via phone and browser. Their monthly plans offer unmetered bandwidth and the monthly fee you are charged is based on the amount of storage you're using.

- **Jellycast** (`www.jellycast.com`): This UK-based firm hosted the ground-breaking Ricky Gervais podcast. It offers free and paid plans, based on throughput used, not storage, which is free.

- **Liberated Syndication** (www.libsyn.com): This service offers plans ranging from $5 per month for 100 MB of storage space to $30 per month for 800 MB. It also has lots of additional features for podcasters.

- **MyPodcasts.Net** (www.mypodcasts.net): Another podcasting host that charges based on storage, this service offers a 30-day free trial. Each account includes a blog with a mypodcasts.net URL.

- **OurMedia.org** (www.ourmedia.org): This service offers free video, audio, text, and image hosting. It's not podcasting-specific, per se, and it requires that you make your files freely available.

- **Pcastbaby** (www.pcastbaby.com): Yet another podcasting host, this one charges according to storage used. A free account with 10 MB is available.

- **Podbus** (www.podbus.com): Five dollars gets you 300 MB of space and 10 GB of monthly bandwidth. The service offers a two-week free trial. It's affiliated with the School of Podcasting.

- **Podbazaar** (www.podbazaar.com): This podcast directory and hosting site targets the international market.

- **Podcast FM** (www.podcastfm.co.uk): Another UK-based host, this service is described as a "one-stop solution for podcast hosting and syndication." The service places limits on the amount that can be uploaded each month, the total storage, and the number of podcasting channels, depending on the service you sign up for.

- **Podlot** (www.podlot.com): "A cheap place to park your podcast" is this service's motto. It offers unlimited bandwidth, starting at $5 per month.

- **PodshowCreator** (www.podshowcreator.com): This service provides hosting service with Web-based interfaces starting at $9.95 per month. Interestingly, they offer password-protected security for an additional $4.95 per month.

- **Shockpod** (www.shockpod.com): This service offers free hosting if you're willing to accept an ad inserted into to your stream. Paying users don't get the ads, and they get a blog.

- **SwitchPod** (www.switchpod.com): You can get services from this company for anywhere from free to $30 per month. The free account doesn't get statistics.

Podcasting Directories

You can find lots of directories out there, and obviously you want to be in as many of them as possible. Some require membership, others don't. Some actually require that you route your RSS feed through them. We wouldn't recommend this, because it may be troublesome later. In the interest of completeness, these are the known podcast directories as of Fall 2006:

- **All Podcasts** (www.allpodcasts.com)
- **Amigofish** (www.amigofish.com)
- **Blinkx.tv** (www.blinkx.tv)

- Blog Explosion (www.blogexplosion.com/podcast)
- Blog Universe (www.bloguniverse.com)
- BluBrry (blubrry.com)
- Digital Podcast (www.digitalpodcast.com)
- Every Podcast (www.everypodcast.com)
- Family Friendly Podcasts (www.familyfriendlypodcasts.com)
- Feedster (podcasts.feedster.com)
- Fetching Podcasts (www.fetchingpodcasts.com)
- Fluctu8 (www.fluctu8.com)
- Fresh Podcasts (www.freshpodcasts.com)
- Get A Podcast (www.getapodcast.com)
- Gigadial (www.gigadial.net)
- IdiotVox (www.idiotvox.com)
- Meefeedia (mefeedia.com)
- Melodeo (www.melodeo.com)
- My Podcast Center (www.mypodcastcenter.com)
- Odeo (www.odeo.com)
- Open Media Network (www.omn.org)
- Penguin Radio (www.penguinradio.com/podcasting)
- Plazoo (www.plazoo.com)
- Podblaze (www.podblaze.com/podcast_directory.php)
- Podcast 411 (www.podcast411.com)
- Podcast Alley (www.podcastalley.com)
- Podcast Bunker (www.podcastbunker.com)
- Podcast Charts (www.podcastcharts.com)
- Podcast Directory (www.podcastdirectory.com)
- Podcast Empire (www.podcastempire.com)
- Podcaster World (www.podcasterworld.com)
- The Podcast Network (www.thepodcastnetwork.com)
- Podcast Shuffle (www.podcastshuffle.com)
- Podcasting Station (www.podcasting-station.com)
- Podcasting Tools (www.podcasting-tools.com)
- Podcast.net (www.podcast.net)

- **Podcasting News** (www.podcastingnews.com)
- **Podcast Pickle** (www.podcastpickle.com)
- **Podcast Pup** (www.podcastpup.com)
- **PodFeeder** (www.podfeeder.com)
- **Podfeed.net** (www.podfeed.net)
- **PodNova** (www.podnova.com)
- **PodScope** (www.podscope.com)
- **Singing Fish** (www.singingfish.com)
- **Syndic8** (www.syndic8.com)
- **Triyo** (www.triyo.com)
- **Vital Podcasts** (www.vitalpodcasts.com)
- **vlogdir.com** (www.vlogdir.com)
- **Yahoo! Podcasts** (podcasts.yahoo.com)

Not seeing a directory you like? Then build your own! There is an open-source podcast directory project on SourceForge: https://sourceforge.net/projects/opda/

Glossary

artifact Artifacts are things that weren't there before in an encoded file. For example, distortions such as jagged edges along diagonals or metallic sounds that are introduced into an audio or video file are artifacts. Many artifacts can be reduced or masked by clever production techniques.

aspect ratio The ratio of the width to the height of a video image. Standard television uses a 4:3 aspect ratio. High-definition television uses a 16:9 aspect ratio.

blog A blog (short for Web log) is a regularly updated Web site. Initially designed as a simple, automated way for people to maintain an online journal, the blog format has grown to include a variety of sites. The main characteristics of a blog are the ability to subscribe via RSS (see *RSS*) and leave comments. The RSS component of blogs was one of the key factors in the development of podcasting.

chrominance The color component of a video signal.

codec A contraction of **compressor-dec**ompressor, or **co**der-**dec**oder, a codec is a software algorithm used to reduce file sizes. Codecs use perceptual models to determine what data can be thrown out when extreme file size compression is required.

compression (audio) A processing technique whereby portions of an audio file that exceed a certain signal level are attenuated. Compression is used to protect input levels from distortion and to even out the overall levels throughout a program.

compression (file size) A technique used to reduce the size of digitized files. Many common

Internet file types such as JPEG, GIF, and PNG are compressed. They use "lossy" compression, where the resulting file is only an approximation of the original. In lossless compression, such as .zip files, the original file(s) can be recreated exactly from the compressed version.

constant bit rate (CBR) An approach to encoding data that keeps the bit rate constant.

Cost-Per-Action (CPA) A measurement of advertising revenue in which the advertiser pays for a specific action, for example, clicking a banner ad or text link.

Cost-Per-Thousand (CPM) A measurement of advertising revenue in which the advertiser pays a given rate per thousand deliveries of their ad.

Creative Commons A non-profit organization dedicated to alternative methods of copyright. Creative Commons licenses enable content creators to share their work with others while retaining some of their rights. These licenses have been developed to avoid the problems with current copyright laws.

decibel (dB) A unit of measure used in audio that measures the power of an audio signal. It is a logarithmic measure, so each increase of 3dB means a doubling of power. To complicate matters, there are various types of decibels: dBU, dBV, and so on. In this book, we are using the term in its most generic form.

de-interlacing A process that attempts to remove the artifacts from an interlaced signal that is intended to be displayed progressively (see *interlacing*).

523

difference frame In a compressed video sequence, a frame that contains only the information about the current frame that is different from the previous frame. A difference frame requires a key frame as a reference.

Digital Rights Management (DRM) Technologies designed to protect and control access and usage of digital content.

dynamic range The operational range of a piece of audio equipment, which stretches from the noise floor to the loudest signal the equipment can reproduce without adding distortion.

Enclosure A tag within an RSS 2.0 file that references an external file. In the case of podcasting, the enclosure tag references an audio or video file. The enclosure tag contains the URL, length, and content type of a file.

equalization (EQ) A processing technique that changes the tone of an audio file by boosting or attenuating certain frequency ranges in the audio signal. Desired frequencies can be turned up, or boosted, while undesired frequencies or noise can be turned down, or attenuated. A common example is the bass and treble adjustments on your home stereo.

feed (RSS Feed) Used to refer to the RSS XML file that contains the information about a podcast. Subscribing to an RSS feed automates the delivery of new podcasts.

field One-half of an interlaced video frame, consisting of either the odd- or even-numbered scan lines.

FireWire See *IEEE 1394*.

FTP (file transfer protocol) A protocol used to transfer files from one computer to another. Many podcast and Web site hosting companies provide users with an FTP account so they can upload new files.

gain In audio terms, gain refers to the amount of amplification being applied. Similarly, the *gain structure* of an audio setup refers to the amount of amplification being applied at each stage.

headroom (audio) The difference between the maximum signal a system can reproduce without distortion and the standard operating level.

hertz (Hz) A unit of measure used for audio frequency. One cycle per second is equal to one Hertz (Hz). The human hearing range extends from 20-20,000Hz, or 20-20kHz. In this case, the "k" stands for 1000 instead of 1024 as is generally assumed in computer applications.

HTTP (HyperText Transfer Protocol) The protocol used to deliver Web pages; also used to deliver podcasts.

ID3 tag Tags that allow metadata to be stored in MP3 files. Initially conceived in 1996, the name comes from "**ID**entify an MP**3**." A number of different ID3 tag standards have been developed since, with ID3v2 being the most widely adopted.

IEEE The Institute of Electrical and Electronics Engineers, Inc. (pronounced "I-triple-E"). An organization dedicated to promoting standards in computing and electrical engineering.

IEEE 1394 (also known as FireWire or iLink) An IEEE standard for exchanging digital information at rates of 100, 200, or 400 megabits per second. Originally developed by Apple and trademarked as FireWire, it was standardized by the IEEE 1394 working group. iLink is Sony's implementation of the IEEE 1394 standard.

iLink See *IEEE 1394*.

interlacing The system used by television displays and cameras whereby each frame is divided into odd and even lines. Each group of lines is referred to as a field. The combination of the two fields, displayed in rapid succession, makes up one frame of video (see *field; de-interlacing*).

Inverse Telecine The process of removing the extra fields in a video signal that result from the Telecine process. Removing these redundant fields leads to greater encoding efficiency.

iris The opening behind a camera lens that determines how much light is allowed to enter. Some cameras have an auto-iris feature that reacts automatically to changes in lighting. This feature is usually problematic and should be disabled.

key frame In a compressed video sequence, a frame that contains a compressed version of the entire frame, as opposed to a difference frame (see *difference frame*).

level See *gain*.

luminance The black and white portion of a video signal.

macroblock A square group of pixels, i.e 4×4 or 8×8, analyzed during encoding. Codecs use different macroblock sizes. The resolution of your encoded video must be divisible by the macroblock size.

metadata A neologism from the Greek *meta* (among, with) and data. Metadata is information about data. For example, the title, author, and copyright are metadata associated with a podcast. You want to provide as much metadata as possible to make your podcasts easier to find.

namespace A collection of names used in an XML document as element types and attribute names. The namespace declaration at the top of an XML file lets the application know what element types and attributes are contained within a file. For example, here is the namespace declaration of an RSS feed that uses the additional iTunes tags:

```
<rss xmlns:itunes=
"http://www.itunes.com/dtds/podcast-1.0.dtd"
version="2.0">
```

normalization An audio signal processing technique that analyzes a file to discover exactly how much the level can be turned up before distortion and then applies that level change.

NTSC (National Television Standards Committee) The broadcast standard for television signals in the United States and most of Central and South America, which specifies 29.97 interlaced frames per second. Each frame consists of 525 horizontal lines of resolution.

open source Generally refers to software that is free and developed by a community of programmers. Open-source development encourages the community at large to contribute to the project. Open-source software is free to use, but typically may not be resold.

OPML (Outline Processor Markup Language) An XML specification for organizing hierarchical information, often used for blog and podcast directories to enable easy exchange between aggregators.

PAL (Phase Alternation by Line) The broadcast standard for television signals in most European countries, which specifies 25 interlaced frames per second. Each frame consists of 625 horizontal lines of resolution. PAL color is considered superior to NTSC.

Peer-to-Peer (P2P) A file distribution method that leverages the bandwidth of participants in the network to deliver content as opposed to depending solely on a primary distribution server.

phantom power The charge placed across the diaphragm of a condenser mic. Condenser mics cannot operate without phantom power. Always make sure phantom power is turned off when connecting or disconnecting a condenser microphone.

Podcatcher Slang term used to describe an RSS aggregator with built in podcast support.

Podsafe (music) Music that is safe to use in your podcast, because the copyright owner(s) have specifically released their rights for this purpose.

proc amp Short for video processing amplifier. A proc amp is used to adjust the quality of a video signal by manipulating the brightness, contrast, and color content.

Q (in relation to audio equalization) The width of the frequency band to be affected by a parametric EQ operation. Q relates to the number of octaves — a Q of 1 means one octave is affected, centered on the chosen frequency.

render In video editing systems, the act of committing desired special effects or transitions to the hard drive. In some systems, encoding to compressed formats is done via rendering.

RSS (Really Simple Syndication) A file format used to enable subscription and syndication on the Web. Web sites post RSS files or *feeds,* which are read by aggregation software. When new content is available on a Web site, the RSS feed is updated. Aggregation software determines that the RSS feed has changed and downloads the new information. Podcasting uses RSS 2.0 feeds that have a special tag, <enclosure>, which includes the URL of the new podcast.

SECAM ("Systeme Electronique Couleur Avec Memoire" — Sequential Color and Memory) The broadcast standard for television signals in France, Australia, and a few other European countries, which specifies 25 interlaced frames per second, each frame containing 625 horizontal lines of resolution.

tag A tag is a label that is applied to help classify something online. For example, people can browse podcast directories for podcasts that have been tagged "funny." Tags often are used in addition to standard categories and subcategories so that people can more easily find content they're interested in. Also, in XML documents (such as RSS feeds), tags refer to elements enclosed in angle brackets used to delimit data, such as:

```
<title>My Podcast</title>
```

Telecine The process of transferring film content to video.

Transcode Converting digital media from one format to another.

Unicode A standardized system that assigns a unique numerical value to every letter and character used in every language. There are over 94,000 Unicode characters defined, with more being added every day.

URL (Uniform Resource Locator) The "address" of a document online that specifies where a document is located and what protocol is to be used to retrieve it. The protocol precedes the "://" and may be HTTP, FTP, RTSP, or any other valid protocol. Following the protocol is the IP address or name of the server, followed by the directory structure to follow to find the document.

Variable Bit Rate A system of encoding that allots variable amounts of bits to different sections of the file. Fewer bits are used to encode the low-motion sections, so that more bits can be used to encode the difficult, high-motion sections. Variable bit rate files in general are not suitable for streaming due to the large variation in data rate in the file.

white balance An adjustment done on a camera to make sure it is recording colors correctly. Cameras should be white balanced every time the lighting situation changes.

XML (Extensible Markup Language) A flexible markup language that is used to exchange data between applications. Data is enclosed by tags, which are enclosed in angle brackets.

Index

Index

G

N

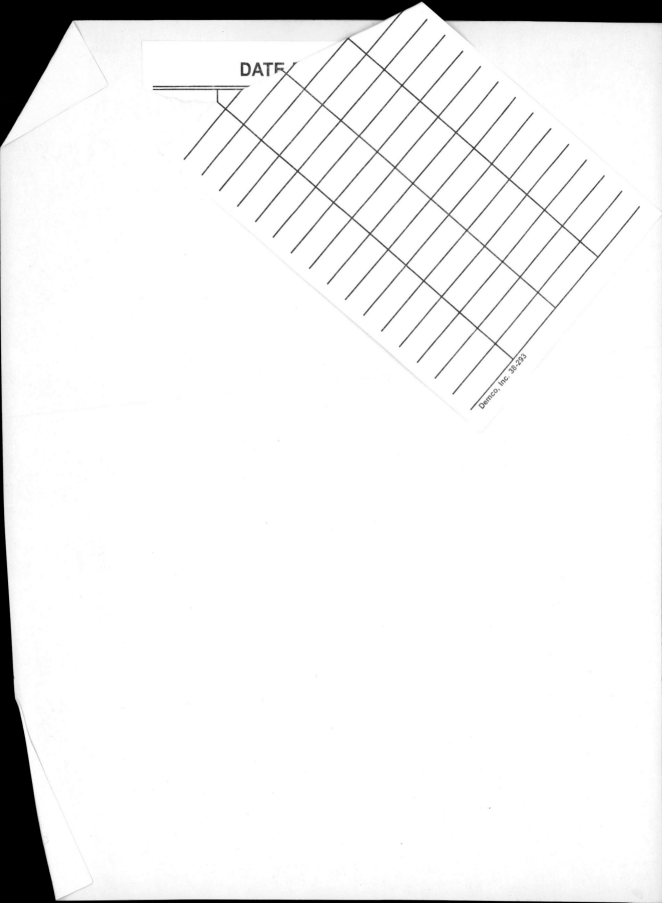

DATE

Demco, Inc. 38-293